TRANSITIONAL JUSTICE, IMPUNITY AND THE JUDICIALIZATION OF POLITICS

TRANSITIONAL JUSTICE, IMPUNITY AND THE JUDICIALIZATION OF POLITICS

Michael Humphrey
Estela Valverde

INTERSENTIA

Intersentia
Lefebvre Sarrut Belgium SA
Rue Haute, 139/6
1000 Bruxelles
Belgium
Email: contact@larcier-intersentia.com

Distribution for the UK and
Rest of the World (incl. Eastern Europe)
Ingram Publisher Services UK
1 Deltic Avenue, Rooksley
Milton Keynes MK13 8LD
United Kingdom
Tel: +44 1752 202 301 | Fax: +44 1752 202 331
Email: orders@nbninternational.com

Distribution for France and Other Countries
Interforum Editis
92 avenue de France
75013 Paris
France

Distribution for the USA and Canada
Independent Publishers Group
Order Department
814 North Franklin Street
Chicago, IL 60610
USA
Tel: +1 800 888 4741 (toll free) | Fax: +1 312 337 5985
Email: orders@ipgbook.com

Transitional Justice, Impunity and the Judicialization of Politics

ISBN 978-1-83970-553-3
D/2025/7849/104
NUR 828

GPRC
Guaranteed
Peer Reviewed
Content

British Library Cataloguing in Publication Data. A catalogue record for this book is available from the British Library.

CONTENTS

LIST OF ACRONYMS AND ABBREVIATIONS

ACHR	American Convention on Human Rights
AfriCOG	Africa Centre for Open Governance
ARMH	*Asociación para la Recuperación de la Memoria Histórica* (Association for the Recovery of Historical Memory)
ARSIWA	Articles on Responsibility of States for Internationally Wrongful Acts
AU	African Union
AUC	*Autodefensas Unidas de Colombia* (United Self-Defence Forces of Colombia)
BACRIM	*Bandas Criminales* (Criminal Bands) (Colombia)
BOE	*Boletín Oficial del Estado* (Official State Bulletin) (Spain)
CBPD	*Comisión de Búsqueda de Personas Desaparecidas* (Search Commission for Missing Persons) (Colombia)
CE	*Comisión de Estudios sobre la Violencia* (Commission of Experts) (Colombia)
CED	UN Committee on Enforced Disappearances
CEV	*La Comisión para el Esclarecimiento de la Verdad, la Convivencia y la No Repetición* (Commission for the Clarification of Truth, for Coexistance and Non-Repetition) (Colombia)
CHCV	*La Comisión Histórica del Conflicto y sus Víctimas* (Commission on the History of the Conflict and Its Victims) (Colombia)

CI	*La Comisión Nacional Investigadora de las Causas y Situaciones Presentes de la Violencia en el Territorio Nacional* (The National Commission of Investigation into the Causes and Current Situation of Violence in the National Territory) (Colombia)
CIPEV	Commission of Inquiry into Post-Election Violence (Kenya)
CKRC	Constitution of Kenya Review Commission
CNMH	*Centro nacional de Memoria Histórica* (National Centre of Historical Memory) (Colombia)
CNP	*Comisión Nacional Pro-Plebiscite* (Committee for the Plebiscite) (Uruguay)
CNRR	*La Comisión Nacional de Reparación y Reconciliación* (National Commission for Reparation and Reconciliation) (Colombia)
CNT	*Confederación Nacional del Trabajo* (National Confederation of Labour) (Spain)
CNV	*Comissão Nacional da Verdade* National Truth Commission (Brazil)
CODESA	Convention for a Democratic South Africa
COSENA	*Consejo de Seguridad Nacional* (National Security Council) (Uruguay)
COVID-19	CoronaVirus Disease of 2019
CSR	Corporate Social Responsibility
DDR	Disarmament, Demobilization and Reintegration (Colombia)
DML	Democratic Memory Law (Spain)
ECK	Electoral Commission of Kenya
ESC	Economic and Social Council
FA	*Acuerdo Final para la Terminación del Conflicto y la Construcción de una Paz Estable y Duradera* (Final Agreement) (Colombia)
FARC-EP	*Fuerzas Armadas Revolucionarias de Colombia – Ejército del Pueblo* (The Revolutionary Armed Forces of Colombia – The People's Army)
FCO	Foreign and Commonwealth Office (Great Britain)

FEDEFAM	*Federación Latinoamericana de Asociaciones de Familiares de Detenidos-Desaparecidos* (Latin American Federation of Associations of Relatives of Detainees-Disappeared)
FN	*Frente Nacional* (National Front) (Colombia)
GMH	*Grupo de Memoria Histórica* (Group of Historical Memory) (Colombia)
GNU	Government of National Unity (Kenya)
GOC	Government of Colombia
IACFDP	Inter-American Convention on Forced Disappearance of Persons
IACHR	Inter-American Commission on Human Rights
IACtHR	Inter-American Court of Human Rights
ICC	International Criminal Court
ICCAL	*Ius Constitutionale Commune en América Latina* (Common Constitutional Principles in Latin America)
ICPPED	International Convention for the Protection of All Persons from Enforced Disappearance
ICRC	International Committee of the Red Cross
ICTR	International Criminal Tribunal for Rwanda
ICTY	International Criminal Tribunal for the former Yugoslavia
IHL	International Humanitarian Law
IHRL	International Human Rights Law
ILC	International Law Commission
ILDO	International Development Law Organization
JEP	*Jurisdicción Especial para la Paz* (Special Jurisdiction for Peace) (Colombia)
JPL	*Ley de Justicia y Paz* (Justice and Peace Law 975/2005) (Colombia)
KADU	Kenyan African Democratic Union
KANU	Kenyan African National Union
KHRC	Kenyan Human Rights Commission

LFA	Land and Freedom Army (Kenya)
LHM	Law of Historical Memory (Spain)
MLN	*Movimiento de Liberación Nacional – Tupamaros* (National Liberation Movement – Tupamaros) (Uruguay)
MOJ	*El Marco Jurídico para la Paz* (Legal Framework for Peace) (Colombia)
MOVICE	*Movimiento Nacional de Víctimas de Crimines de Estado* (National Movement of the Victims of State Crimes) (Colombia)
NARC	National Alliance Rainbow Coalition (Kenya)
NCEC	National Convention Executive Council (Kenya)
NFDLA	Northern Frontier District Liberation Army (Kenya)
NGO	Non-Governmental Organization
OAS	Organization of American States
ODM	Orange Democratic Movement (Kenya)
OHCHR	Office of the United Nations High Commissioner for Human Rights
OTP	Office of the Prosecutor
PCE	*Partido Comunista de España* (The Communist Party of Spain)
PLO	Palestine Liberation Organization
PNU	Party of National Unity (Kenya)
PP	*Partido Popular* (People's Party) (Spain)
PSOE	*el Partido Socialista Obrero Español* (Spanish Socialist Workers' Party)
PT	*Partido dos Trabalhadores* (Workers' Party) (Brazil)
R2P	Responsibility to Protect
RND	*Registro Nacional de Desaparecidos* (National Registry of Missing Persons) (Colombia)
RoL	Rule of Law
RUV	*Registro Único de Víctimas* (National Register of Victims) (Colombia)

SATRC	South African Truth and Reconciliation Commission
SERPAJ	*Servicio de Paz y Justicia* (Service for Peace and Justice) (Uruguay)
SIVJRNR	*Sistema Integral de Verdad, Justicia, Reparación y no Repetición* (Comprehensive System for Truth, Justice, Reparation and Non-Repetition) (Colombia)
STL	Special Tribunal for Lebanon
TJRC	Truth, Justice and Reconciliation Commission (Kenya)
UARIV	*Unidad para la Atención y Reparación Integral a las Víctimas* (Unit for the Comprehensive Care and Reparation of Victims) (Colombia)
UBPD	*Unidad de Búsqueda de Personas dadas por Desaparecidas* (Search Unit for Missing Persons) (Colombia)
UDHR	Universal Declaration of Human Rights
UNCHR	United Nations Commission on Human Rights (replaced by the UNHCR in 2006)
UNDP	United Nations Development Programme
UNGA	The United Nations General Assembly
UNHRC	The United Nations Human Rights Council
UNIIIC	The United Nations International Independent Investigation Commission
UNSC	United Nations Security Council
UNSCR	United Nations Security Council Resolution
UN WGEID	United Nations Working Group on Enforced or Involuntary Disappearances
UP	*Unión Patriótica* (Patriotic Union) (Colombia)
URT	*Unidad de Restitución de Tierras* (Land Restitution Unit) (Colombia)
VOF	*Valle de los Caídos* (Valley of the Fallen) (Spain)
ZIDRES	*Zonas de Interés de Desarrollo Rural, Económico y Social* (The Areas of Interest for Rural, Economic and Social Development) (Colombia)

CHAPTER 1
INTRODUCTION
The Judicialization of Human Rights Politics

1.1. INTRODUCTION

1.1.1. AIMS

This book is about the increasing turn to international law to manage violent internal political conflicts and their outcomes. Historically, conflicts have been brought to an end by a variety of means:

> ... mediated agreements, withdrawals by one or both parties, compromises, surrenders, laying down of arms, peace treaties, armistices, constitutions, trials, amnesties, pardons, purges, international covenants, apologies, laws, topic changes in arguments, reparations.[1]

These paths to conflict resolution involve the participation of different actors, orientations and audiences producing different outcomes that vary in their durability. The concern of this book is with the expanded use of international law to manage violent internal political conflict in the context of legal globalization and post-Cold War international interventions. In other words, the way the increased application of international law represents an expansion of the global rule of law in the context of both diminished state sovereignty and the expansion of the protection of peoples and persons through international humanitarian and human rights law.

The contemporary expansion of the role of international law in internal conflict resolution and peacemaking has occurred in the context of legal globalization and the rapid growth of law as the framework and mechanism regulating transnational affairs.[2] The judicialization of politics has also seen

---

1 R. Wagner-Pacifici and M. Hall, 'Resolution of Social Conflict' (2012) 38 *Annual Review of Sociology* 181, at 190.

2 C. Rodríguez-Garavito, 'Toward a Sociology of the Global Rule of Law Field: Neoliberalism, Neo-Constitutionalism, and the Contest over Judicial Reform in Latin America' in Y. Dezalay and B.G. Garth (eds.), *Lawyers and the Rule of Law in an Era of Globalization*, Routledge, London/New York 2011, p. 156, at p. 177.

the 'ever-accelerating reliance on courts and judicial means for addressing core moral predicaments, public policy questions, and political controversies'.[3] National high courts are increasingly called upon to resolve issues over individual rights and public policies relating to 'criminal justice, property, trade and commerce, education, immigration, labour and environmental protection'.[4] The judicialization of politics has meant that courts and judges resort to dealing with 'mega-politics', 'core political controversies that define (and often divide) whole polities'.[5] These include the judicialization of electoral processes, economic development plans, national security but also restorative justice and constitutional questions about membership in the political community.[6] There has also been 'judicialization from below' facilitated by neo-constitutionalism and bills of rights which have provided the structure for legal mobilization and grass roots rights-claiming. Since the 1970s, the democratization of international lawmaking with the inclusion of civil society and professional organizations, and not just states, in the UN lawmaking processes has allowed human rights advocacy to rescale justice through the strategy of international legalization and universalization of human rights claims. Legal mobilization from below has been 'aided by the commonly held belief that judicially affirmed rights are self-implementing forces of social change removed from the constraints of political power'.[7] By making a political issue that is 'deeply morally contested a matter of basic rights is to make it non-negotiable, since rights … are unconditional entitlements, not susceptible to moderation'.[8]

The judicialization of politics deploys law as a technology to manage political transition with the aim of producing lasting social change. The role of law as a technology for social change can be minimalist or maximalist in scope. The minimalist vision views law as the regulation of human conduct in accordance with officially sanctioned rules, whilst the maximalist vision expands the role of law to include shaping the direction and development of society.[9] The transitional justice project has a maximalist vision of the role of law in advancing social change. The book investigates how the judicialization of political conflict has come to dominate strategies to end violence and produce lasting peace. The logic of judicialization translates political violence into matters of criminal justice with the aim of politically neutralizing them and achieving closure through judicial

---

3 R. Hirschl, 'The New Constitutionalism and the Judicialization of Pure Politics Worldwide' (2006) 75 *Fordham Law Review* 721, at 721.

4 Ibid., p. 721.

5 Ibid., p. 727.

6 Ibid., p. 727.

7 Ibid., p. 726.

8 J. Gray, *Enlightenment's Wake: Politics and Culture at the Close of the Modern Age*, Routledge, Abingdon 2007, p. 34.

9 J.L. Balint, 'The Place of Law in Addressing Internal Regime Conflicts' (1996) 59 *Law and Contemporary Problems* 103, at 105–106.

processes and determinations. The centrality of dealing with past violence during political transition is underscored in contemporary transitional justice by its emphasis on criminal accountability for gross human rights violations. The apolitical judgment of law, it was hoped, would exert a 'civilizing' effect on political behaviour.[10]

The dominant 'atrocity justice' script of transitional justice, which was established during the 1980s transitions from authoritarian (illiberal) to democratic (liberal) regimes, still prevails today.[11] This work focuses on extreme acts of physical violence largely ignoring, or only treating as context, broader questions of structural violence and quotidian insecurity. Even though transitional justice has developed into a multifaceted approach to past violence encompassing both retributive and restorative justice, the international tribunalization of justice, especially with the establishment of the International Criminal Court (ICC) and the expanded role of the UN embedding transitional justice in global governance, made retributive justice for crimes against humanity non-negotiable. The dominant criminal accountability paradigm regards impunity, especially in the form of self-amnesty laws, as a serious failure of transitional justice and a barrier to peace.[12] But impunity is not merely the failure to enforce positive law for egregious violations of International Humanitarian Law (IHL) and International Human Rights Law (IHRL). While it undermines the role of law and justice in re-establishing state legality and legitimacy, it also disables the generative potential of criminal justice in transition arising from the character of justice rituals as norm generating through blaming/scapegoating, through the community creating effects of liminality, and through closure from the verdict and legal truth. Impunity also limits the broader role of transitional justice in advancing the universalization of human rights and democracy as the basis of global governance.

The corollary of the legal critique of impunity as the failure to uphold the rule of law is the faith in the transformative potential of law to produce enduring justice and peace through democratic reform.[13] The rapid expansion of transitional justice since the 1980s has been taken as a promising sign of the potential for international legal norms to achieve justice and peace in post-conflict societies. This optimism is captured in Catherine Lutz and Kathryn Sikkink's phrase 'the justice cascade' – the idea that criminal accountability is now internationally

---

10 L. Vinjamuri and J. Snyder, 'Law and Politics in Transitional Justice' (2015) 18 *Annual Review of Political Science* 303, at 304.

11 D.N. Sharp, *Rethinking Transitional Justice for the Twenty-First Century: Beyond the End of History*, Cambridge University Press, Cambridge 2018, p. 4.

12 C. Binder, 'The Prohibition of Amnesties by the Inter-American Court of Human Rights' (2011) 12 *German Law Journal*, 1203.

13 J.E. Alvarez, 'Promoting the "rule of law" in Latin America: Problems and Prospects' (1991) 25 *The George Washington Journal of International Law and Economics* 281, at 287.

normalized as something that should happen after atrocity.[14] However, from a political bargaining perspective, the move towards international criminal justice is not just a question of criminal accountability, but of international law's impact on the internal balance of power to shape negotiated settlements and political outcomes.[15] The first two chapters outline the analytical framework used in this book to explore just what kind of justice and what kind of peace is imagined and implemented through transitional justice. Transitional justice has established itself as an academic field, a framework to produce social peace, and a legal toolkit. Without a better understanding of the legal and political context of contemporary transitional justice, its mechanisms, achievements, and shortcomings cannot be fully appreciated as legal policy, legal theory and efficacy as social engineering. There are four key themes that frame our investigation of the role of transitional justice in managing transitions to achieve justice and peace. First, transitional justice in the evolution of international law and global governance; second, contemporary transitional justice as an instance of transitional jurisprudence, the historical role played by law during moments of political transition; third, transitional justice as legal intervention in a genealogy of conflict; and fourth, the analytical fuzziness about law's generative processes and the risk of the misrecognition – or headlining – of its symbolic effects for instrumental ones. These four themes are briefly outlined below and developed further in Chapter 2.

Theme 1. Transitional justice is a post-Cold War expression of the evolution of international law and global governance in the context of globalization. The historical development of international law charts the evolution of the global imaginary of a legal and political order. The fundamental element constituting this global imaginary is the sovereign nation-state. In the late 19th century, the role of international law in global governance expanded to legitimate European colonization and protect free trade. The 1885 Berlin Conference established the legality of European colonization of Africa based on the forfeiture of sovereignty to European colonisers, justified by their claimed superior 'civilized' status as demonstrated by their capacity to govern by law and civilize the people they now ruled. After WWI, the League of Nations supported a new global imaginary based on self-determination through which former imperial subjects from the collapsed Russian, German, Austro-Hungarian and Ottoman Empires were incorporated as citizens of new nation-states or mandated territories. After WWII, a new global imaginary of co-equal states emerged through the UN-supported process

---

14 E. Lutz and K. Sikkink, 'The Justice Cascade: The Evolution and Impact of Foreign Human Rights Trials in Latin America' (2001) 2 *Chicago Journal of International Law*, 1.

15 C. Bell, 'Contending with the Past: Transitional Justice and Political Settlement Processes' in R. Duthie and P. Seils (eds.), *Justice Mosaics: How Context Shapes Transitional Justice in Fractured Societies*, International Center for Transitional Justice, New York 2017, p. 85, at p. 90.

of decolonization based on the right to self-determination as a threshold right for everything else.[16] While these new post-colonial states strongly asserted their sovereignty, they often found their sovereign rights were circumscribed by colonial era agreements over the use of economic resources. The Cold War era saw their sovereignty encroached upon by the clientelist constraints imposed by the rival superpowers, the United States and USSR, to establish spheres of regional influence. The post-Cold War era brought a new liberal international order based on legal and political universalization – human rights and democracy. However, the protection of rights under the new liberal international order reintroduced the conditionality of sovereignty in international affairs. Doctrines such as 'the responsibility to protect' saw the dominant liberal states claim the prerogative to intervene in sovereign states when they failed to protect the rights of their citizens. The denunciation by African political leaders and the African Union (AU) of the role of the International Criminal Court in Africa as a neo-imperialist institution reflects the ongoing conflict between international law, sovereignty, and human rights protection. In other words, the transitional justice project is regarded as an expression of contemporary global liberal governance which supports rules to protect and promote fundamental individual human rights on the one hand, and rules to protect the sovereignty of other liberal – but not illiberal – states, on the other.[17]

Theme 2. Transitional justice has emerged in the post-Cold War moment to shape post-conflict societies according to a liberal legal and political international agenda. Historically, transitional justice involves the use of law during moments of transition to legitimate the formation of a more liberal regime. Transitional jurisprudence refers to the phenomenology of law at times of political change through the construction of norms to develop the rule of law, criminal justice, and constitutional justice.[18] The transitional justice project is distinctive in its international intervention in internal conflicts to promote a universalizing political and legal liberal agenda. Originally, transitional justice measures were introduced after political violence had ended through negotiated agreement. Increasingly, transitional justice measures are now introduced in ongoing conflicts, with the aim of ensuring the terms of negotiated agreements meet universal legal norms and standards and support democratic agendas. As transitional justice has evolved, the issue of criminal accountability for serious human rights violations has been foregrounded to challenge impunity by strengthening victims' rights to justice and by insisting that states meet their

---

16 S. Moyn, *The Last Utopia: Human Rights in History*, Belknap Press, Cambridge, MA 2012, p. 98.

17 R. Buchan, *International Law and the Construction of the Liberal Peace*, Hart Publishing, Oxford 2013, p. 51.

18 R.G. Teitel, 'Transitional Jurisprudence: The Role of Law in Political Transformation' (1997) 106 *Yale Law Journal* 2009, at 2015.

obligations to investigate these violations under international law. However, the emphasis on dealing with historical injustice through criminal accountability overlooks the role that constitutional justice plays as a bridge to a 'future founded on the recognition of human rights'.[19] Constitutional justice refounds the state as a normative and transformative project with respect to the previous illiberal regime. The phenomenon of transitional constitutions highlights their work-in-progress character. They are constitutive and constituting, creating the political opening for transition to occur and how the pre-existing constitution is to be transformed. The new constitution embodies the political agreement, the political identity of the polis, membership, and representation. Transitional constitutions are not just forward-looking but they also seek to consciously delegitimize the predecessor regime and guard against a return to authoritarian government.[20] Jennifer Balint questions whether the state, in going beyond its role as prosecutor to include educator, truth-teller and reconciler, has over-extended the capacity of law to achieve such broad agendas.[21]

Theme 3. Transitional justice judicializes conflict, with the intention of depoliticizing it, by translating acts of egregious political violence into crimes. However, transitional justice intervenes in conflicts with their own history, cyclical crises, and elite negotiated pacts – their specific 'genealogy of conflict'. It intervenes at a particular moment in the overall history of internal conflict in which changing geo-politics can quickly alter the internal balance of power of the parties. 'Dealing with the past' is not just about criminal accountability but also what the larger conflict is about – the 'meta-conflict'.[22] Before parties can reach an agreement about how to end conflict, they first have to reach a consensus about the 'meta-conflict'. Is it about uneven ethnic/sectarian representation? Is it about national identity and minority inclusion? Is it about the centralization or decentralization of government? Is it about competition between authoritarian or democratic forms of government? At times, the meta-bargaining ends up in 'an agreement to disagree'.[23] The meta-bargaining over dealing with the past, which can include competing demands for accountability or impunity, shapes the narratives of state legitimacy and illegitimacy and which transitional justice mechanisms are included as part of an agreement. Consequently, the judicialization process itself can become politicized as courts and truth commissions are turned into arenas to continue the meta-contestation through competing interpretive frameworks. The reach of international judicialization can be circumscribed by political and military elites when they define political violence as common crime thereby avoiding its legal characterization as conflict

19 Bell 2017, o.c., p. 93.
20 Teitel 1997, o.c., p. 2078.
21 Balint 1996, o.c., p. 107.
22 Bell 2017, o.c., p. 91.
23 Bell 2017, o.c., p. 94.

to which international humanitarian law applies.[24] However, international judicialization can also help create a new victim constituency to contest the influence of elite bargaining over negotiations and the scope of transitional justice measures agreed upon.

Theme 4. The development of the transitional justice toolkit law by practitioners employs law as a technology to produce social change. But how law functions as a technology for change is less clear and not well theorized. Law is founded on abstract legal concepts; punishment serves as a deterrent, justice is seen as necessary for reconciliation, victim recognition is viewed as a mechanism for social inclusion, the rule of law is regarded as a condition for peace. But, in transitional justice, legal processes are better understood as generative processes, setting the direction and goals of justice rather than necessarily achieving justice through the enforcement of legal norms as positive law. The transitional justice project's liberal peace imaginary based on human rights, democracy, and the rule of law is not an instruction manual. It conceives of peace as the product of the universalization of human rights and democracy achieved through the vertical international integration of states in the global legal order based on their consent, as signatories to human rights treaties, and their agreement to harmonize domestic laws with international norms. Transitional justice mechanisms are 'rituals of political passage', in an anthropological sense, which enact change by employing a temporal ritual mechanism marking the rupture between before and after.[25] The 'transition' is managed by mechanisms with ritual structures, such as trials and truth commissions, to produce closure through a trial verdict about culpability or a truth commission report revealing the history of regime violations and acknowledging the victims. These judicial rituals are 'mythmaking' machines producing an official truth. These rituals of political passage are performative, seeking to enact change through legal processes as steps toward achieving certain goals: a verdict builds trust in the judicial system; a truth commission report is a step towards producing a consensus about past wrongdoing and responsibility; constitutional reform is a step in the direction of establishing enforceable positive law. Other rituals of political passage such as democratic elections function as participatory, inclusive, consensus driven mechanisms to mark a break between illiberal and liberal regimes and promise a better future.

1.1.2. COMPARATIVE CASE STUDIES

This study investigates the role of law in managing transition and producing social change. Specifically, it examines how transitional justice functions as a

---

24 Bell 2017, o.c., p. 87.

25 R.G. Teitel, *Transitional Justice*, Oxford University Press, Oxford 2000, p. 217.

legal technology – the four pillars of truth, justice, reparations and guarantees of non-repetition – to produce lasting social effects. By definition, transitional justice is an exception to normal justice but insufficient attention has been paid to the ways in which they differ.[26] While the challenges of transitional justice are distinct – how to manage the scale of criminality; how to achieve justice after moral outrage over atrocity; how to re-establish the authority of the law in a post-conflict society still divided by the impact of violent conflict; how to establish state legality based on global legal norms. Law is generated through symbolic and instrumental legal acts with the aim of establishing legal norms, self-discipling citizens in accordance with those norms, and their enforcement if transgressed. In other words, while the political circumstances in which law is produced in transition may be distinct from that of ordinary justice, the generative processes, and mechanisms producing legality are not. The question becomes 'what combination of symbolic and instrumental legal acts deployed during transition normalize the law and establish legal order'?

This study uses case studies as the key methodological framework to investigate the role of international legal interventions in internal conflicts with the aim of bringing peace.[27] Each case study contextualizes contemporary transitional justice interventions within the history of internal political conflict, cyclical crises, and political fixes. This 'within-case' method explores the determinants of a particular phenomenon for a particular case.[28] Each case study investigates transitional justice interventions as the latest iteration of transitional jurisprudence constituted by the rule of law, criminal justice, and constitutional justice and shaped by a specific political history of internal conflict and peacemaking.[29] The changing configuration of transitional jurisprudence – the particular emphasis on legality, criminal justice and constitutional justice – charts

26 E.A. Posner and A. Vermeule, 'Transitional Justice as Ordinary Justice' (2004) 117 *Harvard Law Review*, 761.

27 The study draws on both primary and secondary sources. The primary sources include data from an extensive research programme conducted by the authors investigating the impact of internal political violence on different societies and their transition towards liberal democratic states over several decades. This research has included decolonization in Kenya and South Africa, democratization after authoritarian repression in Uruguay, Argentina and Spain, civil war and state renewal in Lebanon, the Balkans and Colombia and social protest after election violence in Kenya. Primary research in the form of interviews was conducted over 10 years in Uruguay, Lebanon, Colombia and Spain. Data from these interviews contributes to our accounts of contemporary transitional justice interventions. The historical analysis of earlier transitions, peace initiatives and political agreements is based on primary and secondary sources. The primary sources include reports of commissions of inquiry, trial records and transcripts. The study also draws on the extensive secondary sources on political transitions, the development of transitional justice policy and practice, and the development of international human rights law and humanitarian law.

28 M. Lange, *Comparative-Historical Methods*, SAGE Publications, London 2013.

29 Teitel 1997, o.c., p. 2009.

the trajectory of political conflict, the role of political elites in determining outcomes and the breakdown of past political agreements and fixes. The five selected case studies reflect the evolution of transitional justice across four phases and the shifting emphasis of transitional jurisprudence towards individual protection. The case studies reveal the patterns of international legal intervention in historical transitions (Spain), in post-conflict societies after dictatorship or civil war (Uruguay, Lebanon), in societies during ongoing conflict (Colombia), and in unstable post-Cold War post-colonial democracies (Kenya). The political aim behind transitional justice is to make illiberal states more liberal through their integration into the global liberal order of states conditional on them meeting their legal obligations under international law.[30] It constitutes a top-down intervention designed to reform state political and legal institutions based on human rights and democracy as international norms.

This study examines the character and impact of transitional justice interventions in different political conflicts over the past 40 years through the comparative study of five cases – Uruguay, Spain, Lebanon, Kenya and Colombia. The study undertakes a comparative historical sociological analysis of the evolution and application of law in the management of conflict and peace in these case studies. There is an essential historical dimension to our comparative analysis in three senses. Firstly, transitional justice is the latest iteration of transitional jurisprudence directed towards managing internal political conflict, secondly, each conflict has its own genealogy shaped by internal and external shifts in the balance of power, and thirdly, transitional justice is an expression of the historical development of the role of international law in global governance. In this book, the case studies are introduced according to a four-phase periodization reflecting the evolution of transitional justice mechanisms, aims, and changing contexts of intervention. The four phases include Ruti Teitel's three-phase periodization of transitional justice and an additional fourth phase suggested by Dustin Sharp.[31] Teitel's three phases reflect the changing historical character of transitional justice intervention with the expansion of its aims, mechanisms and global reach of international human rights and humanitarian law. Phase I (post-WWII, 1945) is associated with the criminalizing of state wrongdoing based on universal rights (Nuremberg trials) and the exceptional conditions for international nation-building through the expansion of international law. Phase II (post-Cold War, 1989) is associated with the major shift in international politics and the expansion of conflict resolution and justice directed towards democratic nation-building and restorative justice.

30 Bell 2017, o.c., p. 90.

31 R.G. Teitel, 'Transitional Justice Genealogy' (2003) 16 *Harvard Human Rights Journal*, 69; D.N. Sharp, 'Interrogating the Peripheries: The Preoccupations of Fourth Generation Transitional Justice' (2013a) 26 *Harvard Human Rights Journal*, 149.

National level prosecutions were constrained by the political balancing of criminal justice and democratic peace. The lack of international tribunalization limited the opportunity for international legal remedies. In this phase, the truth commission was adopted as the vehicle to overcome the democratic deficit at transition and demands for justice were balanced by prioritizing peace. Phase III (post-2000) is associated with a return to international justice and the normalization of transitional justice through tribunalization and the prosecution of war crimes and crimes against humanity.[32] The establishment of the International Criminal Court (ICC) in 2002 consolidated the criminal accountability agenda.[33] Teitel argues this phase also saw the normalization of transition as a trope for humanitarian intervention in the name of global rule of law. Phase IV is associated with the expansion of social and economic rights protection and focus on distributive justice alongside the dominant focus on civil and political rights.[34] While Sharp does not clearly periodize what he refers to as 'fourth generation transitional justice', his emphasis is on the growing need for transitional justice measures to engage at the local level. This includes the need for international tribunals to enhance their legitimacy at the local level through community outreach programmes and the need to address the impact of economic violence by promoting economic justice through affirmative action, land redistribution and anti-corruption commissions to consolidate peace.[35] Phase IV represents a political stocktaking of transitional justice outcomes and the issues that have become apparent in the conflict between victims' rights to justice, truth, reparations and guarantees of non-recurrence and post-conflict state development priorities supporting the interest of agribusiness and resource industries.

The case studies illustrate the changing forms of international legal intervention through regional human rights courts such as the Inter-American Court of Human Rights (IACtHR), through the mobilization of victim movements in pressuring states to meet their international human rights law and humanitarian law obligations, through the growing role of ICC in enforcing accountability for crimes against humanity through prosecutions in national courts – positive complementarity – or international courts, and through the UN role in normalizing transitional justice as part of peace agreements.

---

32 R.G. Teitel, 'Global Transitions, New Perspectives on Legality, and Judicial Review' in A. Sarat (ed.), *Transitions: Legal Change, Legal Meanings*, The University of Alabama Press, Tuscaloosa, AL 2012, p. 213, at pp. 222–224.

33 Rome Statute of the International Criminal Court, done at Rome on July 17, 1998, in force on July 1, 2002, United Nations, Treaty Series, Vol. 2187, No. 38544, Depositary: Secretary-General of the United Nations, https://treaties.un.org.

34 D.N. Sharp, 'Addressing Dilemmas of the Global and the Local in Transitional Justice' (2014) 29 *Emory International Law Review* 71, at 80.

35 Sharp 2013a, o.c., p. 163.

These case studies are contextualized firstly, within the historical patterns of transitional jurisprudence used to manage earlier political transitions, and secondly, within the history of political conflict and elite negotiated agreements. They are arranged chronologically to illustrate the evolution of transitional justice from its emergence in the context of dictatorship and atrocity crimes in Latin America (the Uruguayan case study); in the post-Cold War destabilization of the terms of third wave democratic transitions (the Spanish case study); in the emergence of hybrid tribunals to strengthen the rule of law in weak/fragile states (the Lebanese case study); in the expanded role of the ICC in challenging impunity for the normalization of large-scale political violence in elections (the Kenyan case study); and the maturing role of transitional justice in shaping peace negotiations to rebuild state institutions and overcome the resistance of politically polarized societies through an emphasis on restorative justice to promote reconciliation (the Colombian case study).

The first case study examines transitional justice in Uruguay. It focuses on the amnesty law (the Expiry Law) legislated by the new democratic Uruguayan government after 12 years of military dictatorship (1973–1985) and its gradual erosion and eventual repeal after 25 years through human rights advocacy by non-governmental organizations (NGOs) and families of the disappeared before the IACtHR and the emergence of a Latin American regional transformative constitutionalism to force states to meet their obligation under the American Convention on Human Rights (ACHR).[36] The Uruguayan case represents a Phase II transitional justice example in which the recovery and consolidation of democratic government took precedence over demands for accountability for serious human rights violations. The terms of the transition were established by a negotiated pact between the military and the political elite premised on amnesia and amnesty. But uniquely, the impetus towards democratic transition was precipitated and consolidated through acts of direct democracy – referenda and plebiscites. There were three (at least) competing visions of transition and democratic restoration in Uruguay. Firstly, democratic transition as restorative; seeking to preserve the partidocratic traditions – a political party-dominated political system – guided by the 'Uruguayan Way' of elite political reconciliation, amnesty, and amnesia.[37] Secondly, democratic transition as transformative; seeking to upend the hegemony of the traditional partidocracy that had endured for 100 years and allow the emergence of full democratic pluralism incorporating the Left. Thirdly, democratic transition as the enactment of the post-Cold War project of global liberal governance; founded on the universals

36 D.W. Arguelhes, 'Transformative Constitutionalism in Latin America: The Emergence of a New *Ius Commune*' (2019) 17 *International Journal of Constitutional Law*, 368.

37 C. Demasi, 'La partidocracia uruguaya: aportes para la discusión de una hipótesis' (2013) 3 *Contemporánea: Historia y problemas del siglo XX*, 267.

of human rights and democracy. In Latin America, the vision of global liberal governance was conceived as the harmonization of domestic political and legal institutions through neo-constitutionalism, based on the ACHR under the guidance of the Inter-American Commission on Human Rights (IACHR) and IACtHR. The military and traditional parties backed the first vision, the Left backed the second vision, and the human rights groups and families of the disappeared backed the third vision. Even after the Expiry Law was repealed in 2011 by Law 18.831, the state's prosecution of dictatorship era crimes has been slow in part because of Supreme Court decisions preventing prosecutions. Moreover, the repeal of the Expiry Law did not result in the government taking the lead on transitional justice for national reconciliation and left unrevised the two demons narrative – equal blame was attributed to extremists on both sides – adopted by the Sanguinetti government at transition.

The second case is a Phase III example of transitional justice concerned with the contemporary politics of historical memory and the Spanish Civil War. The chapter focuses on the Law of Historical Memory (LHM) and the role of victims' organizations in the internationalization of human rights politics seeking to challenge an earlier post-Franco Phase II transitional justice settlement in 1977 based on amnesty and amnesia. At the time, the Spanish transition from an authoritarian to democratic regime was held up as a model which many democratizing Latin American states subsequently adopted. The chapter examines the role of the grass roots exhumation movement in challenging the 1997 transition policy of amnesty and amnesia by using exhumations of clandestine graves as a strategy to demand historical justice for the surviving family members of the disappeared. The movement was galvanized by the failed attempt in 1998 by Chilean human rights organizations to have General Pinochet, who was shielded by an amnesty law in Chile, prosecuted under universal jurisdiction in the Spanish courts. In 2007, the Spanish human rights movement succeeded in getting the support of the Zapatero Socialist government to promulgate the LHM (2007). The Law condemned the Franco regime and promised to recognize the victims of repression that occurred both during, and after, the Civil War. The Zapatero government also provided state grants to support human rights organizations to exhume and identify the missing, required the removal of Francoist symbols from public spaces and prohibited celebratory fascist events in the Valley of the Fallen. However, the failure of the state to assume responsibility for the exhumation of mass graves meant that the signification of exhumed remains produced individualized, privatized or factionalized memorializations and not the consolidation of a more inclusive national historical memory. The attempt by Judge Baltasar Garzón to use the LHM to open investigations into many mass graves was blocked by his political opponents who accused him of exceeding his judicial authority circumscribed by the amnesty law. The struggle over historical memory leads to fundamental questions about state sovereignty, the origins of democratic government in

Spain, the legitimacy of the democratic Second Republic, and the illegitimacy of Franco's military *coup d'état*.

The third case on Lebanon looks at the role the United Nations Security Council (UNSC) played in creating a special 'internationalized-national' tribunal, the Special Tribunal for Lebanon (STL), to investigate the assassination of ex-Prime Minister Rafiq Hariri (2005) as an act of international terrorism. It represents a Phase III transitional justice initiative involving international tribunalization and the support for prosecution under a domestic jurisdiction. The STL was created to strengthen the rule of law in Lebanon and recognize the right to justice for the victims of the assassination by terrorist bombing after a long history of impunity for the many political assassinations dating back to the 1950s and the largescale serious human rights violations committed during the civil war (1975–89) shielded by an amnesty law (1991). Despite the initial bipartisan political support for the UN investigation and proposal to create the STL, the Lebanese political parties quickly divided into pro- and anti-STL camps forcing the UNSC to establish the STL by itself under Ch VII. From its inception, the legitimacy of the STL was undermined by elite pactism and the sanction of veto implicit in the Lebanese confessional power-sharing political system. The political denunciation of the STL as partisan by its opponents and the political and legal crisis engendered by ongoing assassinations of pro-STL politicians, journalists and intellectuals, including the assassination of a key STL investigator, forced the relocation of the investigation to The Hague. The issue of the legitimacy of STL investigations and prosecutions dominated and paralysed government and forced PM Sa'ad Hariri, the son of the assassinated Rafik Hariri, into exile because he refused to withdraw his support for the STL to placate pro-Syrian interests in Lebanon. The refusal of Hizballah to cooperate with the STL and comply with the request to hand over its indicted members highlighted the barriers to prosecution, resulting in absentee trials in The Hague. While the STL trials continued until 2022, the hope that this internationalized national tribunal would strengthen the rule of law in Lebanon has eroded.[38] The political polarization into pro- and anti-STL camps was not merely over the question of accountability or the legitimacy of the STL, but goes back to the unresolved foundational issues of state sovereignty, national identity and confessional powersharing at independence. The subsequent impact of the Syrian civil war on Lebanon with the arrival of more than one and a half million refugees, the significant military involvement of Hizballah in support of the Asad regime, and the failure to effectively investigate the widespread war crimes in Syria have only further eroded the authority of the STL and its relevance for legal reform in Lebanon.

---

[38] N. Shehadi 'Shutting down Hariri tribunal a reckless move', *Arab News*, June 25, 2022, https://www.arabnews.com/node/2110686.

The fourth case looks at the intervention of the ICC in Kenya in 2011 after the Kenyan government failed to establish a Tribunal, as required by the Waki Commission Report on post-election violence, to prosecute those responsible for the election violence in 2008. The case represents an example of the ICC policy of positive complementarity in which states are supported to take responsibility for the prosecution of serious human rights violations, with the sanction of ICC prosecutions, if they failed to meet their responsibility. Because Kenyan human rights organizations had such little trust in Kenyan judicial institutions they opposed the creation of the national Tribunal and lobbied for direct ICC intervention. Elite pactism and ethnic clientelism were mobilized against the ICC prosecutions by the indicted political leaders who denounced ICC intervention as neo-colonialist and partisan. In the end, the ICC prosecutions either failed or had to be abandoned in large part because of government action obstructing access to evidence and witness intimidation. The 2013 election won by the pragmatic anti-ICC alliance between the indictees (and former opponents) Kenyatta and Ruto effectively refounded political power on elite pactism and ethnic clientelism and the marginalization of human rights standards. Political violence has been a chronic feature of party competition for state power since independence managed by elite pactism and ethnic clientelism.

The fifth case is the application of transitional justice measures in the Colombian peace process overseen by the IACtHR and ICC in their roles investigating human rights violations and monitoring human rights standards. The Colombian case involves the introduction of transitional justice norms into a peace process involving negotiations between the state and a guerrilla insurgency. Transitional justice has increasingly shaped the content of successive peace agreements and expanded its scope to include truth, justice, reparations, and non-recurrence measures. The transition is about the end of a civil war, not political transition involving regime change. The Colombian case highlights the embedded nature of conflict, its genealogy, and the enduring veto power of elites over decades to stall or undermine negotiations to end armed conflict. The Colombian case highlights the role of transitional justice in state-building in a state which has neither control over all its territory or a monopoly over the use of violence. The adoption of the transitional justice has been a politically constitutive act through an inclusive discourse around human rights for all Colombians underpinned by the 1991 Constitution. It also taps into a popular constitutionalization of everyday life in which Colombians had embraced the idea of rights-claiming in response to the failure of politics. The Colombian case highlights the conflicts over priorities reflected in competing rights of victims for land restitution and promotion of neoliberal development strategies focused on largescale agribusiness and mining. The Special Jurisdiction for Peace reveals the primarily symbolic role of prosecutions in situations where there are huge numbers of crimes, perpetrators and victims.

1.2. TRANSITIONAL JUSTICE AS A MODEL – THE FOUR PILLARS

1.2.1. TRANSITIONAL JUSTICE AS AN INTERNATIONAL NORM

What kind of justice is transitional justice? This section explores how transitional justice has been established as an international norm through the process of international legalization and judicialization of human rights norms. Transitional justice has evolved from an emancipatory rights discourse concerned with transformative justice to become a largely administrative justice project managed by UN human rights bodies and concerned with state conformity, with soft law policy and compliance with human rights instruments and customary international law.[39] Transitional justice has emerged as a multifaceted judicial and non-judicial approach to post-conflict justice that includes both restorative and retribution justice approaches. Yet, as transitional justice measures have broadened, the obligation of states to investigate, prosecute, and punish those individuals responsible for gross violations of international human rights law and serious violations of international humanitarian law has hardened. However, the concept of transitional justice has shifted from dealing with the past by politically balancing peace and justice, to legally vindicating the rights claims of victims based on individual criminal accountability. Nevertheless, the core accountability mechanisms in transitional justice remain the right to truth, justice and redress which are intended to have both punitive and preventive outcomes.[40] The victim has been placed at the centre of UN transitional justice policy and the justice objectives of the ICC.[41]

Historically, the term 'transitional justice' referred to the use of trials, purges, and reparations against a defeated enemy. Its contemporary meaning – the application of international legal norms to bring an end to political violence and reconcile divided societies – dates from the 1980s when it referred to the political constraints on legal responses to the criminal behaviour of repressive authoritarian regimes in Latin America. Several leading scholars have identified the Latin American context of transition from authoritarian to democratic government as the contemporary origins of transitional justice.[42] Samuel Moyn

---

39 Teitel 2003, o.c., p. 69.

40 M.C. Bassiouni, 'Searching for Peace and Achieving Justice: The Need for Accountability' (1996) 59 *Law and Contemporary Problems* 9, at 18.

41 S. Kendall and S. Nouwen, 'Representational Practices at the International Criminal Court: The Gap Between Juridified and Abstract Victimhood' (2014) 76 *Law and Contemporary Problems* 235, at 239.

42 C.S. Nino, *Radical Evil on Trial*, Yale University Press, New Haven and London 1996; D.F. Orentlicher, 'Settling Accounts: The Duty to Prosecute Human Rights Violations of a Previous Regime' (1991) 100 *Yale Law Journal*, 2537; R.G. Teitel, *Transitional Justice*, Oxford University Press, Oxford 2000; K. Sikkink, *The Justice Cascade: How Human Rights*

describes transitional justice as a 1980s 'optic based on the Latin American experience to allow human rights to be not just a moral criticism of terrible regimes but internal political resource in the erection of their successors'.[43] Transitional justice was conceived as exceptional justice in two senses. Firstly, the particular political context of the return to democracy after military dictatorship in Latin America where the military remained politically powerful and able to secure their impunity as a condition for their return to barracks; and secondly, the resort to retroactive justice for political, as well as legal, ends.[44] An important factor shaping this early period of transitional justice – Teitel's Phase II transitional justice that prioritized nation-state building – was the absence of an international criminal justice court or tribunal to enforce international criminal law, and the only recent establishment of a regional human rights body: the Inter-American Court of Human Rights (IACtHR) in 1979.[45] At that time, national courts were the only jurisdiction able to hold those responsible for serious human rights violations, criminally accountable. It was not until the late 1990s that new options for criminal accountability were created with international tribunalization through the *ad hoc* international criminal tribunals and later the International Criminal Court (1998), through the development of regional human rights courts, and through the resort to universal jurisdiction in domestic courts.[46] The legacy of its Latin American origins was that transitional justice continued to be framed as 'atrocity justice' and criminal accountability as 'synonymous with individual criminal accountability for extreme acts of physical violence' as a state policy of systematic repression.[47]

In response to the pattern of elite impunity negotiated during transitions from illiberal to liberal regimes in Latin America, the transitional justice project evolved in two directions driven by victims' demands for justice supported by the advocacy of human rights organizations. Firstly, domestically, there was a turn to restorative justice measures – truth, reparations and recognition – to acknowledge victims' rights claims and suffering as a substitute for retributive justice measures denied them by elite imposed amnesty laws. Secondly, internationally, human rights lawyers and victim organizations rescaled their demands for criminal accountability by appealing to the higher authority

Prosecutions are Changing World Politics, W.W. Norton & Co, New York 2011; A. Paige, 'How "Transitions" Reshaped Human Rights: A Conceptual History of Transitional Justice' (2009) 31 *Human Rights Quarterly*, 321.

43 Moyn 2012, o.c., p. 221.

44 Teitel 2003, o.c., p. 76.

45 The IACHR and the IACtHR were established by the American Convention on Human Rights and ratified by the Organization of American States in 1959 and 1979, respectively.

46 R. Aldana-Pindell, 'An Emerging Universality of Justiciable Victims' Rights in the Criminal Process to Curtail Impunity for State-Sponsored Crimes' (2004) 26 *Human Rights Quarterly*, 605.

47 Sharp 2018, o.c., at p. 3.

of international law. Their strategy was to rescale justice by legalizing and judicializing human rights claims to bring pressure to bear on states to meet their obligations under international law to investigate and prosecute serious human rights violations.[48] Through legalization, victims gradually gained recognition of their claims as rights in international law. It represented a moral victory for victims and reinforced their hope that those rights would be enshrined in a binding treaty – for example, the crime of 'enforced disappearance' eventually became recognized as hard law in the Convention for the Protection of All Persons from Enforced Disappearance (ICPPED).[49] In the early stages of transitional justice, victims' groups adopted human rights as an emancipatory discourse which promised transformative justice. In Argentina, the Mothers of the *Plaza de Mayo* became a symbol of human rights as an emancipatory and mobilizing discourse which succeeded in gaining the attention of the international human rights community.[50] Human rights organizations also saw transitional justice as a lawmaking vehicle to strengthen international human rights mechanisms and instruments. Transitional justice is characterized by these two impulses – on the one hand, it is a grass roots emancipatory and generative human rights project such as human rights forensics in Argentina,[51] on the other hand, it is a lawmaking project seeking to institutionalize new international human rights law.

The dual track development of transitional justice policy since the 1980s has produced a multifaceted approach to post-conflict justice combining retributive and restorative justice approaches – judicial and non-judicial – anchored in rights under IHRL and IHL but with no exceptions for criminal accountability for extreme violations – crimes against humanity, war crimes and genocide. In the process of evolution, transitional justice lost its status as 'exceptional' or 'extraordinary' justice to become the international justice norm to manage post-conflict societies.[52] Today, transitional justice normative framework has become internationally institutionalized as the four pillars – truth, justice, reparations, and guarantees of non-repetition – and formalized in the UN 'Guidance Note of the Secretary-General: United Nations Approach to Transitional Justice' (2010)

---

48 C. Turner, *Violence, Law and the Impossibility of Transitional Justice*, Routledge, Oxford 2016, p. 135.

49 C. Turner, 'Human Rights and the Empire of (International) Law' (2011) 29 *Minnesota Journal of Law & Inequality* 313, at 326.

50 M.G. Bouvard, *Revolutionizing Motherhood: The Mothers of the Plaza de Mayo*, Rowman & Littlefield Publishers, Wilmington, DE 2002.

51 L.A. Smith, 'The Missing, the Martyred and the Disappeared: Global Networks, Technical Intensification and the End of Human Rights Genetics' (2017) 47 *Social Studies of Science* 398, at 412.

52 T.O. Hansen, 'The Vertical and Horizontal Expansion of Transitional Justice: Explanations and Implications for a Contested Field' in S. Buckley-Zistel, et al. (eds.), *Transitional Justice Theories*, Routledge, Oxford 2014, p. 105.

and supported by the UN Human Rights Council resolution 18/7 (September 11, 2011), establishing a mandate to promote justice, truth, reparations, guarantees of non-recurrence carried out by a Special Rapporteur.[53]

The original conceptualization of 'transitional justice' as politically compromised justice reflected the dominant idea that criminal trials should be the primary mechanism for the enforcement of the principle of accountability because they were essential to re-establish the rule of law in transition.[54] In traditional criminological theory, trials function as a deterrence. But, from its inception, transitional justice measures were differentiated by their deviation from the ideal of full criminal accountability. Unlike the role of ordinary justice in a settled liberal democratic regime where law is supposed to be above politics, the aims of transitional justice are necessarily both legal and political. Justice policy is viewed as an instrument to bring about change in a liberal direction. From a liberal legalist perspective, 'law has, or ought to have, a generatively transformative and normative role in establishing the conditions for a virtuous politics'.[55]

Implicit in transitional justice policy is the idea of a model – the optimal set of justice measures to achieve desired legal and political goals. Since the 1980s, transitional justice models have increasingly become anchored in international human rights instruments and focused on atrocity justice. Phase II transitional justice models were descriptive and differentiated according to the intensity of criminal accountability they required. Phase III models were programmatic and adopted a holistic approach, requiring more than just criminal justice. Krotoszyński identifies three basic transitional justice models differentiated by their degree of criminal accountability: the retribution model, the historical clarification model and the thick line model.[56] The retribution model requires the new regime to impose formal sanctions on those associated with the predecessor regime. The historical clarification model exposes the nature of the predecessor regime and those individuals connected to it but does not impose sanctions. The 'thick line model' adopts amnesty and amnesia in which there are no sanctions and no public disclosure. Phase II models – the 1980s and 1990s – were historical cases which other transitioning countries selectively adopted as templates. Thus, the Spanish model – amnesty and amnesia – was widely exported to South America and the South African model (truth, reparations, conditional amnesty) established the truth commission as an important truth-seeking mechanism for national reconciliation. During Phase II, consequentialist

53 Special Rapporteur on the promotion of truth, justice, reparations and guarantees of non-recurrence, https://www.ohchr.org/en/issues/truthjusticereparation/pages/index.aspx.

54 R.G. Teitel, *Transitional Justice*, Oxford University Press, Oxford 2000, pp. 28–9.

55 D. Scott, *Omens of Adversity: Tragedy, Time, Memory, Justice*, Duke University Press, Durham, NC 2013, p. 149.

56 M. Krotoszyński, 'The Transitional Justice Models and the Justifications of Means of Dealing with the Past' (2016) 6 *Oñati Socio-Legal Series* 584, at 588–94.

moral justifications prevailed over deontological ones. For example, the Spanish transition model was justified by the consequentialist argument that criminal justice would undermine peace and democratization – the morality of action is justified by the outcome. Deontologists opposed amnesty and amnesia on the grounds that criminal accountability is required to respect the dignity of victims and their families, as well as the requirements of truth and justice.[57]

Phase III transitional justice models no longer referred to typologies but to 'programmes' combining retributive justice and restorative justice measures with the political goal of reconciliation underpinned by a shared historical truth about the past.[58] These justice measures aimed at achieving two goals: first to respond to suffering from the past, and second, to prevent similar suffering recurring in the future. One example of the development of multifaceted justice models is TARR – truth, accountability, reparations and reconciliation. This model, formulated in the early 2000s, addresses the impact of the establishment of the ICC on global justice.[59] It identifies truth, accountability, reparations, and reconciliation as the key issues governing transition from illiberal to liberal regimes. Reparations and reconciliation were the emerging issues at the time. The TARR model sought to provide a framework for understanding the evolving inter-relationship between retributive and restorative justice mechanisms and their impact at the national and international levels on post-conflict justice. Another example of transitional justice packaging is Lambourne's 'transformative justice model' which adopts a longer-term perspective beyond political transition. Its key measures are accountability, psychosocial justice, socioeconomic justice and political justice.[60] It includes distributive justice and democratization (described as political justice) measures alongside retributive and restorative justice measures designed to achieve sustainable peace.

In Phase III, transitional justice measures are increasingly normalized as 'toolkits', 'toolboxes', 'legal mosaics' or 'menus', to be used as legal technologies to implement social change.[61] Yet, the technocratic mastery conveyed by characterization of justice measures as legal tools tells us little about the inter-relationship between justice measures and whether they are complementary,

---

57 Ibid., p. 598.

58 N. Roht-Arriaza, 'The new landscape of transitional justice' in N. Roht-Arriaza and J. Mariecurrena (eds.), *Transitional Justice in the Twenty-First Century: Beyond Truth and Justice*, Cambridge University Press, Cambridge and New York 2012, p. 8.

59 S. Parmentier, 'Global Justice in the Aftermath of Mass Violence. The Role of the International Criminal Court in Dealing with Political Crimes' (2003) 41 *International Annals of Criminology*, 203.

60 W. Lambourne, 'Transformative justice, reconciliation and peacebuilding' in S. Buckley-Zistel, et al. (eds.), *Transitional Justice Theories*, Routledge, New York 2014, p. 19.

61 J.L. Balint, 'The Place of Law in Addressing Internal Regime Conflicts' (1996) 59 *Law and Contemporary Problems* 103, at 113; F. Ní Aoláin, 'After Things Fall Apart: Challenges for Transitional Justice Futures' (2017) 11 *Human Rights and International Legal Discourses* 23, at 38.

reinforcing or conflicting.[62] Moreover, individual justice measures have often been treated as options to try to see what works, or to trade off against each other, rather than as holistic justice programmes.[63] In addition, legal professionals and international human rights NGOs have come to dominate the design and implementation of tailored transitional justice packages based on international 'best practice'.[64] Their role as legal entrepreneurs has created international advocacy networks and helped diffuse human rights through their international legalization and judicialization.[65] Keck and Sikkink refer to this process as the 'boomerang pattern' in which the legal entrepreneurialism of experts and international human rights NGOs seek to force change on justice policy towards criminal accountability in national courts by rescaling justice demands to the international level.[66] The outcome is the 'four pillars' model – truth, justice, reparations and guarantees of non-recurrence – as the UN endorsed transitional justice norm.

Behind the emergence of the four pillars model as the UN transitional justice norm are important developments in international lawmaking to promote change through new human rights norms which date from the 1970s.[67] Firstly, it is important to remember that the core international human rights instruments only came into force in the 1970s. The key human rights instruments – International Covenant on Civil and Political Rights (UNGA Res 2200A (XXI) adopted December 16, 1965) and International Covenant on Economic, Social and Cultural Rights (UNGA Res 2200A (XXI), adopted December 16, 1965) – entered into force on March 23, 1976 and January 3, 1976, respectively. Treaties became the favoured method to promote human rights with the expectation that treaty committees would achieve implementation through their monitoring compliance processes – shaming over non-compliance. Secondly, the sources of

---

62 P. Gready, 'Culture, Testimony, and the Toolbox of Transitional Justice' (2008) 20 *Peace Review*, 41; Vinjamuri and Snyder, o.c., p. 303.

63 Transitional justice models have been critiqued as lacking a clear strategy and haphazardly applied. P. Gready and S. Robins, 'Transitional Justice and Theories of Change: Towards evaluation as understanding' (2020) 14 *International Journal of Transitional Justice* 280, at 289. Justice measures such as truth commissions have become a standard feature of transitional justice policy but often without clear design, goals or any understanding how they work. J. Sarkin, 'Why the Theory and Practice of Transitional Justice Needs to be Better Integrated in all Places around the World' (2021) 4 *Al Muntaqa* 39, at 40; P. De Greiff, 'Theorizing Transitional Justice' in M.S. Williams, et al. (eds.), *Transitional Justice: Nomos Li*, New York University Press, New York, NY 2012, p. 31, at p. 32.

64 R.G. Teitel, *Globalising Transitional Justice*, Oxford University Press, Oxford 2014, p. xvi.

65 M.E. Keck and K. Sikkink, *Activists beyond Borders: Advocacy Networks in International Politics*, Cornell University Press, New York, NY 1998, p. 79.

66 Ibid.

67 The newly independent states saw UN General Assembly Resolutions as a way to participate in soft lawmaking. See J. Wouters, 'International Law, Informal Law-Making, and Global Governance in Times of Anti-Globalism and Populism' in H. Krieger, et al. (eds.), *The International Rule of Law: Rise or Decline?*, Oxford University Press, Oxford 2019, p. 249.

international human rights law and the participants in international lawmaking expanded from the 1970s. The sources of international law went beyond treaty and custom to include soft law as a mechanism to promote change, which allowed non-state actors to participate in international lawmaking, by advocating for soft norms in the UN bodies such as the General Assembly and the United Nations Commission on Human Rights (UNCHR).[68] Soft laws were seen as stepping stones towards legislation and a way to create normative discourse designed to influence political action.[69] Although these UN bodies lacked legislative authority, their resolutions and decisions increasingly served as soft law supporting progressive interpretation of international law with the prospect of their crystallization into hard norms, either as a new treaty, or achieving recognition as general international law.[70] The relative decline in multilateral treaty-making since the 2000s has only reinforced the trend towards informal and non-binding agreements and norms.[71]

Human rights soft law – in the form of declarations, guidelines and principles – developed by UN and Organization of American States (OAS) bodies with international prestige and weight but without lawmaking authority, functions as a rhetorical discourse seeking to produce legal effect. Human rights soft law plays on the ambiguity in the relationship between universal moral human rights and legal human rights where the latter is assumed to mirror the former.[72] From a mirroring perspective, international human rights law gives effect to an underlying morality of human rights 'through the medium of individual legal rights ascribed to all human beings'.[73] Universal human rights norms, from an idealist perspective, are constitutive of social and political reality 'by shaping actors, power, interests, institutions, rules of conduct, and outcomes'.[74] The idea that legal human rights mirror existing moral human rights has been reinforced by the transitional justice focus on 'justice for victims' from a rights-based approach. The evolution of transitional law has proceeded through the path of soft lawmaking driven by human rights organizations and victim advocacy to expand the international legalization and judicialization of human rights. In the post-Cold War period, soft law has been in ascendancy over binding rule

68 Turner 2011, o.c., p. 330.

69 L. Grover, 'Transitional Justice, International Law and the United Nations' (2019) 88 *Nordic Journal of International Law* 359, at 359.

70 If a norm is recognized as general international law, it can transcend the limitations of the treaty regime to become an obligation *erga omnes*, binding on all states regardless of consent. See Turner 2011, o.c., p. 332.

71 Wouters 2019, o.c., pp. 251–3.

72 Vinjamuri and Snyder 2015, o.c., p. 305; J. Tasioulas, 'Saving Human Rights from Human Rights Law' (2019) 52 *Vanderbilt Journal of Transnational Law* 1167, at 1175; S. Besson, 'The Law in Human Rights Theory' (2013) 7 *Zeitschrift für Menschenrechte – Journal for Human Rights* 120, at 123.

73 Tasioulas 2019, o.c., p. 1169.

74 Vinjamuri and Snyder 2015, o.c., p. 305.

making, especially in the field of human rights.[75] The transitional justice soft laws are notable for 'their detail and the obligations they attempt to impose on States'.[76] Transitional justice can be understood as a human rights soft law generating project, whose success is reflected in its status as an international norm under UN management, based on the hegemony of international law standards.[77] The normalization of transitional justice goes hand-in-hand with the UN rule of law project to develop rights as legal tools anchored in international human rights instruments.[78] The transitional justice norm, constituted as the four pillars, represents measures 'recognized as treaty-based obligations that the state owes victims'.[79]

What distinguishes the four pillars model from earlier ones is its character as a legal framework constituted by legal concepts – truth, justice, reparations and guarantees of non-recurrence. It is important to note that these concepts are abbreviations for the 'right to truth', the 'right to justice', the 'right to reparations' and the 'right to guarantees of non-recurrence'. The 'rights-based-approach' of the four pillars is anchored in UN human rights instruments and mechanisms which reflect the dominant managerial role the UN now plays in the field of transitional justice. The four pillars also reflect the increasing hegemony of IHRL with respect to internal conflict which had historically fallen outside the jurisdiction of IHL. The transitional justice project has become, at its core, a lawmaking project through the international legalization and judicialization of human rights with the aim to strengthen legal remedies for victims by ensuring states meet their obligations under international law and incorporate human rights standards into domestic law. While each of the four pillars as justice measures have their specific aims – to establish the rule of law, promote reconciliation, support democratization – their legal core is the recognition of victims as individual bearers of rights and state obligations in international law.[80]

The four pillars framework was drawn directly from the Joinet/Orentlicher (2005) 'Principles to Combat Impunity' Report commissioned by the UNCHR which represented the culmination of earlier initiatives – Van Boven (1993),

75 J. Von Bernstorff, 'The Decay of the International Rule of Law Project (1990–2015)' in H. Krieger, et al. (eds.), *The International Rule of Law: Rise or Decline?*, Oxford University Press, Oxford 2019, p. 33.

76 Grover 2019, o.c., p. 366.

77 Grover 2019, o.c., p. 377.

78 UN OHCHR 'Rule of Law Tools for Post-Conflict States: Reparations Programmes' (Geneva OHCHR 2008); UN OHCHR, 'Rule of Law Tools for Post-Conflict States: National Consultations on Transitional Justice' (Geneva OHCHR 2009). See also P. McAuliffe, *Transitional Justice and Rule of Law Reconstruction: A Contentious Relationship*, Routledge, London 2014.

79 J.E. Méndez, 'Victims as Protagonists in Transitional Justice' (2016) 10 *International Journal of Transitional Justice*, 1.

80 P. De Greiff, 'Theorizing Transitional Justice' in M.S. Williams, et al. (eds.), *Transitional Justice: Nomos Li*, New York University Press, NY 2012, p. 44.

Joinet (1997)[81] – to investigate impunity dating from the 1980s.[82] These four pillars were subsequently strengthened by the UN General Assembly Resolution 60/147 adopting the Basic Principles and Guidelines on the Right to a Remedy and Reparation for Victims of Gross Human Rights Violations (hereafter Basic Principles) (2005) and the ICPPED (2006). In September 2011, the Human Rights Council adopted Resolution 18/7 creating the mandate of the Special Rapporteur to promote justice, truth, reparations, guarantees of non-recurrence in situations in which there have been gross violations of human rights and serious violations of international humanitarian law.[83] The mandate of the Special Rapporteur included the following objectives: end impunity; provide recognition and redress to victims; fostering trust; strengthening the rule of law; and contributing to reconciliation.[84]

The processes of legalization and judicialization of the human rights norms are constitutive of the four pillars model. A constructivist perspective is adopted to understand transitional justice as a generative process in which human rights discourse is used by international lawyers, human rights organizations, and victims to rescale justice by mirroring moral human rights as legal human rights and by using victims claims as the vehicle to advance legalization in international human rights bodies such as the UN and OAS – the United Nations Human Rights Council (UNHRC), IACHR and IACtHR. The process of legalization involves firstly, getting the claims of victims of serious human rights violations onto the international agenda; secondly, strengthening human rights standards; and thirdly, establishing new human rights instruments. Serious human rights violations are put on the international agenda by getting the UNCHR and/or the United Nations General Assembly (UNGA) or the IACHR to acknowledge claims of violations and respond with resolutions to investigate

81 T. van Boven, Special Rapporteur, 'Study concerning the right to restitution, compensation and rehabilitation for victims of gross violations of human rights and fundamental freedoms' E/CN.4/Sub.2/1993/8, July 2, 1993; L. Joinet, 'Question of the impunity of perpetrators of human rights violations (civil and political). Final report prepared by Mr. Joinet pursuant to Sub-Commission decision 1996/119', in (ESC, UNCHR, Sub-Commission on Prevention of Discrimination and Protection of Minorities, 1996); D.F. Orentlicher, 'Impunity: Report of the independent expert to update the Set of principles to combat impunity. Addendum: Updated Set of principles for the protection and promotion of human rights through action to combat impunity, UN Doc. E/CN.4/2005/102/Add.1'.

82 Updated Set of principles for the protection and promotion of human rights through action to combat impunity, UN Doc. E/CN.4/2005/102/Add.1, February 8, 2005, https://www.ohchr.org/en/special-procedures/sr-truth-justice-reparation-and-non-recurrence/international-standards.

83 Report of the Special Rapporteur on the promotion of truth, justice, reparations and guarantees of non-recurrence, https://www.ohchr.org/en/issues/truthjusticereparation/pages/index.aspx.

84 Report of the Special Rapporteur on the promotion of truth, justice, reparation and guarantees of non-recurrence, P. De Greiff, Human Rights Council August 9, 2012, A/HRC/21/46, 4.

claims through different mechanisms – e.g. appointing experts, commissioning reports, establishing mandates or creating thematic working groups. These UN and OAS resolutions – declarations, principles or guidelines – serve to gradually establish human rights standards as soft law. Overtime, the cooperation between the UN and OAS multiplied through the work of the IACHR and IACtHR and the system of periodic review of the implementation of human rights treaties.[85] The advisory opinions and court decisions of the IACtHR also contribute to strengthening human rights standards and their recognition as customary international law. These standards become hard law if they achieve the status of a human rights instrument.

1.2.2. RIGHT TO JUSTICE

The right to justice is based on a victim's right to fair legal remedy and the expectation that the state will meet its obligations to investigate, prosecute and punish those responsible for serious human rights violations. M. Cherif Bassiouni describes accountability as a 'pillar' of justice for victims and the cornerstone of prevention and deterrence.[86] Transitional justice emerged in response to the denial of the right to justice in transitions from illiberal to liberal regimes, especially in Latin America, where post-transition amnesty laws were the norm.[87] From the 1970s, the right to justice became a major focus of the human rights movement first in their international advocacy campaign to expose the serious human rights violations of the regions' dictatorships, and second, in their support of victims' right to justice blocked by amnesty laws at transition. In order to legally empower victims in the face of impunity, the human rights movement sought to rescale justice by legalizing and judicializing human rights.[88] However, effective remedy was only able to be sought 'for a very narrow – if not egregious – band of international human rights and international humanitarian violations'.[89] In other words, transitional justice from its inception was about 'atrocity justice', 'individual accountability for extreme acts of physical violence', that states were obliged in international law to prevent and, if they occurred, to investigate and prosecute.[90] The universal logic of human rights

85 A.M. Cisneros De Alencar, 'Cooperation Between the Universal and Inter-American Human Rights Systems in the Framework of the Universal Periodic Review Mechanism' (2010) 7 *SUR International Journal on Human Rights*, 171.

86 Bassiouni 1996, o.c., p. 9.

87 Paige 2009, o.c., p. 321.

88 A. Kurze, et al., 'Contested spaces of transitional justice: legal empowerment in global post-conflict contexts revisited' (2015) 19 *The International Journal of Human Rights*, 260.

89 Sharp 2018, o.c., p. 3.

90 Sharp 2018, o.c., p. 4.

makes it imperative to prosecute and punish all serious violations of IHRL and IHL. Moreover, the liberal project of the rule of law holds that there is nothing outside the law; there are no exceptions, no impunity.[91]

The issue of post-conflict impunity and the failure of states to meet their obligations towards victims of human rights violations did not become established on the international human rights agenda until 1990.[92] Bell argues that accountability for human rights standards were not significant in peace agreements, except in Central America, until the 2000 Lomé Accord dissent over amnesty provisions.[93] Largely in response to the pervasive issue of impunity in Latin America, the UN commissioned three key reports by Van Boven (1993), Joinet (1997), Orentlicher (2005) to address impunity with the of aim of strengthening the human rights standards. These UN reports drew on the developing jurisprudence of the IACtHR which held that states had the responsibility to investigate and prosecute violations of IHL and IHRL and that victims had the right to a legal remedy and reparations under the ACHR.[94] The approach of the IACHR and IACtHR reflected a policy-oriented approach to the development of human rights standards whereby international lawmaking is 'conceived as an ongoing process of authoritative decision-making, in which legal criteria serve not as mechanical limits, but as explicitly postulated public order goals reflecting values of human dignity, to guide decisionmakers'.[95] While IACtHR orders were binding on member states, they were not self-executing. States had to fulfil their obligations as 'compliance partners' for orders to be implemented.[96]

The issue of justice for the 'disappeared' in Latin America, provides a window on the process of legalization and judicialization of human rights to challenge amnesty laws in the UN and OAS, driven by human rights activists and victims' groups. Disappearance was a signature practice of military repression in Latin America during the 1970s and 1980s which they used as a tactic to terrorize the population into submission, especially in Chile and Argentina.[97] As early

---

91 Koskenniemi 2002, o.c., p. 2.

92 Paige 2009, o.c., p. 352.

93 Bell 2009, o.c., p. 120.

94 See N. Roht-Arriaza, 'State Responsibility to Investigate and Prosecute Grave Human Rights Violations in International Law' (1990) 78 *California Law Review*, 449; R.G. Teitel, 'Transitional Justice and Judicial Activism – A Right to Accountability?' (2015) 48 *Cornell International Law Journal*, 385.

95 D. Cassel, 'Lessons from the Americas: Guidelines for International Responses to Amnesties for Atrocities' (1996) 59 *Law and Contemporary Social Problems* 197, at 229.

96 R. Kunz, 'Judging International Judgments Anew? The Human Rights Courts before Domestic Courts' (2020) 30 *European Journal of International Law* 1129, at 1138.

97 The IACHR had noted the use of disappearance in Guatemala in the mid-1960s. See R. Brody and F. González, '*Nunca Más*: An Analysis of International Instruments on "Disappearances"' (1997) 19 *Human Rights Quarterly* 365, at 366.

as 1977, the IACHR in its Annual Report noted the seriousness of 'enforced disappearance' occurring in the region.[98] After the transition to democracy in Argentina the landmark report 'Never Again: Report of the Commission about the Disappeared' (*Nunca Más, informe de la Comisión sobre la Desaparición de Personas*, CONADEP), revealed the largescale and systemic use of disappearance as a key instrument of repression in the military's 'dirty war'.[99] The practice of enforced disappearance produced a double impunity. Firstly, disappearance was very difficult to investigate because it was a clandestine act that was officially deniable, and secondly, amnesty laws prevented criminal accountability for acts of enforced disappearance. In response to the impunity at the national level, human rights organizations and victims' groups rescaled justice by bringing the practice of disappearance to the attention of the UNCHR and the IACHR to try to pressure states to investigate enforced disappearances and to prevent further occurrence. Their goal was to gain recognition of enforced disappearance as a crime against humanity institutionalized as a human rights instrument on enforced disappearance which would automatically impose an obligation on a state to investigate and prosecute offenders. However, it proved difficult to get 'enforced disappearance' onto the international human rights agenda. It first came to the attention of the UNCHR and IACHR after the widespread use of enforced disappearance by the Pinochet regime after the 1973 coup in Chile. The UNCHR responded by increasing NGO participation in meetings and consultations which gave greater visibility to plight of victims and relatives, by sending a Working Group on Chile (1978) on an investigative mission to Chile to look at disappearance and by setting up the Working Group on Enforced or Involuntary Disappearances (WGEID) – Resolution 20 (XXXVI) was its first thematic human rights mechanism with a universal mandate in February 1980.[100] During the 1970s, the IACHR devoted special attention to enforced disappearance which was first mentioned in its country report on Chile (1974).[101] Despite numerous attempts by the IACHR to get the OAS General Assembly to take action, its first resolution directing states to stop passing laws preventing investigations into the disappeared was only made in 1979.[102]

98 'The Right to Truth in the Americas', Inter-American Commission on Human Rights on August 13, 2014, OEA/Ser.L/V/II.152 Doc. 2, August 13, 2014, p. 28.

99 *Nunca Más, informe de la Comisión sobre la Desaparición de Personas* (Never Again: Report of the Commission about the Disappeared, CONADEP), Universitaria De Buenos Aires, Buenos Aires 1984.

100 D. Kramer and D. Weissbrodt, 'The 1980 U.N. Commission on Human Rights and the Disappeared' (1980) 3 *Human Rights Quarterly*, 18.

101 M.C.G. Patiño, 'Rights Related to Enforced Disappearance: New Rights in the International Convention for the Protection of All Persons from Enforced Disappearance' in A. von Arnauld, et al. (eds.), *The Cambridge Handbook of New Human Rights*, Cambridge University Press, Cambridge 2020, p. 415, at p. 416.

102 Brody and González 1997, o.c., p. 368.

The IACHR conducted a fact finding mission to Argentina in 1979 and collected overwhelming evidence of the use of disappearance by the military dictatorship. In 1983 and 1984, the OAS, in response to repeated demands from human rights NGOs and relatives of the disappeared, characterized forced disappearance as a 'crime against humanity'.[103] The IACtHR cited these OAS resolutions in the first two cases about enforced disappearance – *Velásquez Rodríguez* and *Godínez Cruz* – that came before it.[104]

Another dimension of the activism of human rights organizations and victims' groups around the disappeared was their role in drafting international standards on enforced disappearance. During the 1980s, the Latin American Federation of Associations of Relatives of Detainees-Disappeared (FEDEFAM) with the Human Rights Institute of the Paris Bar Association, the Permanent Assembly for Human Rights (Argentina) and the Initiative Group for an International Convention Against Forced Disappearance (Argentina) prepared the draft 'Declarations and Conventions on Forced Disappearances' using as a template the UN Convention on the Prevention and Punishment of the Crime of Genocide. The key objectives of the draft human right instrument were the recognition of enforced disappearance as a crime against humanity and an effective mechanism to prevent disappearance happening, to investigate and punish acts of disappearance, to compensate surviving relatives and to trace children born to the disappeared in captivity.[105] Further lobbying at the UN and OAS resulted in draft Conventions which were developed in parallel in the UNCHR and IACHR in 1988. The ICPPED was adopted by the UNGA in December 1992. However, the original IACHR draft faced opposition and the OAS General Assembly did not adopt it until 1994.[106] By 2010, Sikkink argues, the individual criminal accountability model had become 'embodied in international law, international and domestic institutions, and the global consciousness'.[107] She characterizes this moment as the 'justice cascade' when individual accountability becomes a universal norm through the diffusion of human rights norms. The efforts of prosecutors, states and nonstate actors to strengthen international human rights law and international humanitarian law culminated in the Rome Statute (1998) of the ICC.

---

103 Brody and González 1997, o.c., p. 369.

104 *Velásquez Rodríguez v. Honduras*, Case 7920, Ser. C, No. 4, Inter-Am. Ct. H.R. 35, OAS OEA/Ser.L/V/III.19/Doc.13 (1988) (judgment of July 29, 1988); *Godínez-Cruz v. Honduras*, Case 8097, Ser. C, No. 5, Inter-Am. Ct. H.R. OAS Doc. OEA/Ser.L/V/III.21/Doc.14 (1989) (judgment of January 20, 1989. On the development of IACtHR jurisprudence on enforced disappearance, see Teitel 2015, o.c., p. 385.

105 Brody and González 1997, o.c., p. 376.

106 Brody and González 1997, o.c., p. 371.

107 K. Sikkink and H.J. Kim, 'The Justice Cascade: The Origins and Effectiveness of Prosecutions of Human Rights Violations' (2013) 9 *Annual Review of Law and Social Science* 269, at 274.

1.2.3. RIGHT TO TRUTH

The right to truth refers to the right of individual victims and society to know the truth about violations of IHL and IHRL and the duty of the state to preserve the memory of those events. The principle of objective truth is a fundamental concept in law independent of any overall legal right. Criminal trials establish a narrow legal truth as legal evidence which is the by-product of a dispute settlement mechanism.[108] In transitional justice policy, truth is more than merely criminal accountability, firstly because victims seek both knowledge and acknowledgement of events – why victims were targeted, what happened to them, who was responsible – not just the legal truth determining guilt or innocence; and secondly, because national/international trials prosecuting violations of IHRL and IHL seek to achieve broader political goals which include the 'restoration of peace, reconciliation, fighting impunity, deterring future violations, upholding victims' rights, removing dangerous figures from politics, re-establishing the rule of law and the principle of legality'.[109] International criminal trials for offences under IHL and IHRL move away from collective blame towards individual responsibility with the aim of unifying divided communities by producing an 'official historical record with legal imprint'.[110]

The demand for the 'right to truth' emerged in response to the use of 'enforced disappearance' as an instrument of terror by authoritarian regimes in Latin America. The relatives of the disappeared asserted their right to know the fate of their family members. As early as 1977, the IACHR noted in its Annual Report the serious levels of enforced disappearance in the region. Overtime, the right to the truth expanded to include the right of victims to information about the circumstances of serious human rights violations.[111] Although the claim that the right to truth is an autonomous right remains contentious, international courts have generally inferred the right to truth from the right to justice and the right not to be subjected to torture. Since 2006, it is a subsumed right in the ICPPED.[112] Since the *Velázquez Rodríguez* case, the jurisprudence of the IACtHR has repeatedly supported the right to the truth from articles of the ACHR ensuring the protection of human rights, the right to a fair trial,

---

108 Y. Naqvi, 'The right to truth in international law: fact or fiction?' (2006) 88 *International Review of the Red Cross* 245.

109 Ibid., p. 246.

110 Ibid.

111 P. Naftali, 'The 'Right to Truth' in International Law: The 'Last Utopia'?' in A. Gliszczyńska-Grabias and U. Belavusau (eds.), *Law and Memory: Towards Legal Governance of History*, Cambridge University Press, Cambridge 2017, p. 70, at p. 71.

112 ICPPED Article 24/2 states '[e]ach victim has the right to know the truth regarding the circumstances of the enforced disappearance, the progress and results of the investigation and the fate of the disappeared person. Each State Party shall take appropriate measures in this regard'. ICPPED A/47/133 December 23, 2010.

and right to judicial protection.[113] Nevertheless, the right to truth is ubiquitous in transitional justice soft law/policy and key UN resolutions.[114] The UNCHR 'Study on the Right to Truth' provides a legal genealogy of the evolution of the 'right to the truth' as a human rights norm.[115] The right to truth has its origins in IHL where the principle of the right to the truth for relatives of missing persons during armed conflict, including the victims of enforced disappearance, is codified in Article 32 of the Additional Protocol I to the Geneva Conventions, of August 12, 1949. In the 1970s, the adoption of the practice of enforced disappearance as a form of state terror in Latin America saw the right to truth in IHL transferred as a right to IHRL and applied to situations of internal conflict or repression. The UNCHR Study traces the role of the International Committee of the Red Cross (ICRC), the United Nations Working Group on Enforced or Involuntary Disappearances (UN WGEID) and the IACHR in developing the doctrine of 'the right to the truth' with regard to the crime of enforced disappearance.[116] In the case of the IACHR, the doctrine of the right to truth led to the judicial innovation of 'truth trials' which justified investigations of enforced disappearance irrespective of whether the state prosecuted crimes against humanity or not.[117] The right to truth was also frequently cited as the legal basis for many truth commission mandates. However, the claim by the 'Study on the Right to Truth' in its conclusion that there is an 'inalienable and autonomous right to truth' has been criticized for overreach and failing to engage 'recognized sources of public international law at all'.[118]

The right to truth has had its greatest influence as transitional justice soft law. It is widely acknowledged that criminal accountability and punishment is inadequate to redress the individual and social impact of atrocities and that truth is also a form of moral reparation which can contribute to reconciliation. Trials, truth and reconciliation commissions, public apologies, memory laws,

---

113 In the *Velázquez Rodríguez* case, the IACtHR interpreted art. 1(1) of the ACHR as entailing a duty of states to investigate violations and to identify those responsible. See K. Dykmann, 'Impunity and the Right to Truth in the Inter-American System of Human Rights' (2007) 7 *Iberoamericana* 45, at 49. Also E.F. Ferrer, 'The Right to the Truth as an Autonomous Right under the Inter-American Human Rights System' (2016) 9 *Mexican Law Review*, 121.

114 UN instruments enshrining right to the truth include International Covenant on Civil and Political Rights, art. 2; ICPPED, art. 24/2; Report of the independent expert to update the Set of principles to combat impunity, UNCHR E/CN.4/2005/102/Add.1, principles 2–5; Guidance Note, UNSG, March 2010, 1. OAS documents include *Right to the Truth in the Americas*, IACHR, OEA/Ser.L/V/II.152, Doc. 2, August 13, 2014, p. 21.

115 'Study on the right to the truth. Report of the Office of the United Nations High Commissioner for Human Rights', February 8, 2006, E/CN.4/2006/91 (UNCHR, Geneva, 2006).

116 Ibid., p. 5.

117 E.A. Romanin, 'Decir la verdad, hacer justicia: Los Juicios por la Verdad en Argentina' (2013) 94 *European Review of Latin American and Caribbean Studies / Revista Europea de Estudios Latinoamericanos y del Caribe* 5, at 10.

118 J.A. Sweeney, 'The Elusive Right to Truth in Transitional Human Rights Jurisprudence' (2018) 67 *International and Comparative Law Quarterly* 353, at 358.

memorials and museums are now all justified in the name of the 'right to the truth' which engenders the reciprocal state duty to preserve collective memory of atrocities to prevent their recurrence.[119] The expansion of the scope of the right to truth reflects an ever-increasing faith in human rights to deliver lasting effects: healing, closure, dignity, and accountability.[120] In the early phase of transitional justice, truth commissions featured as an alternative way for states to meet their international obligations to investigate serious human rights violations primarily as truth seeking exercise when states had failed to respond to the abuses. In the South African Truth and Reconciliation Commission, truth in the sense of a confession was a condition for amnesty. Both the IACHR and IACtHR have strongly supported the establishment of truth commissions as a way for the state to fulfil its obligations to guarantee the right to the truth by creating an authoritative account of the past and vindicating victims' rights and for the wider society to learn what had happened.[121] Today, truth commissions have become a standard justice measure in transition but are no longer acceptable as a substitute for criminal investigations because they are seen to diminish the authority of the legal process.[122] The success and legitimacy of truth commissions has derived from the broad participation and involvement of victims and civil society. Their limitation has been the restrictions they have faced getting access to state archives and preserving them.[123] However, as the mandate of truth commissions has expanded from their original narrow fact-finding role – as a commission of inquiry – to include broader restorative justice aims, they risk raising expectations beyond their capacity to deliver.[124] In addition, the framing of investigations by truth commissions in terms of IHL and IHRL violations to enhance their legitimacy proceeds apace but without judicial powers to create binding obligations.[125]

The grassroots – moral – claim of the right to the truth, especially in the search for the disappeared, has expanded beyond the individual's right to know the fate of their family member to become a larger struggle over collective

---

119 M.C. Bassiouni, 'Searching for Peace and Achieving Justice: The Need for Accountability' (1996) 59 *Law and Contemporary Problems*, 9.

120 Naftali 2017, o.c., p. 70.

121 'The Right to Truth in the Americas', Inter-American Commission on Human Rights, OEA/Ser.L/V/II.152 Doc. 213, August 2014, p. 62.

122 D.F. Orentlicher, 'Settling Accounts: The Duty to Prosecute Human Rights Violations of a Prior Regime' (1991) 100 *Yale Law Journal* 2537, at 2456; M.C. Bassiouni, 'Searching for Peace and Achieving Justice: The Need for Accountability' (1996) 59 *Law and Contemporary Problems* 9, at 20.

123 'The Right to Truth in the Americas', o.c., p. 98.

124 P. De Greiff, '"Truth without Facts" On the Erosion of the Fact-Finding Function of Truth Commissions' in P. Alston and S. Knuckey (eds.), *The Transformation of Human Rights Fact-Finding*, Oxford University Press, New York, NY 2016, p. 281.

125 P.L. van den Herik and C. Harwood, 'Commissions of Inquiry and the Charm of International Criminal Law: Between Transactional and Authoritative Approaches' in P. Alston and S. Knuckey (eds.), *The Transformation of Human Rights Fact-Finding*, Oxford University Press, New York, NY 2016, p. 233, at p. 240.

memory and state memorialization policy. The contest between victim and state in the memorialization process is illustrated by the political struggle to revise the preamble of the *Nunca Más* Report (1984) which documented the systematic use of disappearance by the military in Argentina.[126] The original *Nunca Más* Report (1984) attributed blame for the excesses of the 'dirty war' war to both sides – the 'two demons' thesis – but the revised preamble of the *Nunca Más* Report (2005) accused the military dictatorship of pursuing genocide.[127] In the case of the Mothers of the *Plaza de Mayo*, the leading victims organization in the search for the disappeared in Argentina, memory was a source of political identity and the right to truth a demand that the state investigate the past and fulfil its duty to remember.[128] State memorialization is now regarded as an important symbolic reparation and remembering those who died as a form of insurance against repetition. The UNHRC has reinforced the state's duty to remember by adopting memorialization standards for mass crimes set out in a report by the Special Rapporteur on truth, justice, reparations and guarantees of non-repetition in 2014.[129] In 2020, Fabian Salvioli, the Special Rapporteur on truth, justice, reparations and guarantees of non-repetition, suggested that memorialization should be included as a fifth pillar of the transitional justice model concluding that 'without memory, the rights to truth, justice and full reparation cannot be fully realized and there can be no guarantees of non-recurrence'.[130] Yet the standardization of memorialization is homogenizing and institutionalizing, marginalizing individual memories, the very source of the emancipatory moral human rights claims, for the collective goal of reconciliation. The dynamic between the creative/generative character of human rights claims as a utopian/aspirational movement and their institutionalization as soft and hard laws, highlights a dilemma for transitional justice as a project of justice renewal. The early human rights activists and victim mobilization around strengthening human rights represents the bottom-up renewal of justice which, through institutionalization of rights, becomes the top-down administration of justice.[131]

---

126 *Nunca Más* 1984, o.c.

127 M. Humphrey and E. Valverde, 'From private memory to public memory: transitional justice and the revision of official memory of the Dirty War in Argentina' in C. Andrews and M. Mcguire (eds.), *Post-Conflict Literature: Human Rights, Peace, Justice*, Routledge, London 2016, p. 130.

128 M.E. Burchianti, 'Building Bridges of Memory: The Mothers of the Plaza de Mayo and the Cultural Politics of Maternal Memories' (2004) 15 *History and Anthropology*, 133.

129 L. David, 'Against Standardization of Memory' (2017) 39 *Human Rights Quarterly* 296, at 308–9. See also Report of the Special Rapporteur in the Field of Cultural Rights. S. Farida: Memorialization Processes UN GAOR, Human Rights Council, 25th Session Agenda Item 3, at 6, UN Doc A/HRC/25/49 (January 23, 2014).

130 Report of Special Rapporteur for accountability, truth, reparations, guarantees of non-repetition: 'Memorialization processes in the context of serious violations of human rights and international humanitarian law: the fifth pillar of transitional justice' A/AHRC/45/45 (July 9, 2020), para. 100.

131 See Section 2.2.1 on generative normative orders.

Klinkner and Davis provocatively ask what legal status of the 'right to truth' best serves the victim: the right to truth as 1) an autonomous directly enforceable legal right; 2) as a subsumed right inescapably tied to rights to justice, judicial protection and reparations; and 3) a background moral right articulated as part of the 4 pillars.[132] They argue that the current status of the right to truth is a background moral right and 'an aspirational goal with increasing recognition, linked persuasively with other rights in the sense of providing jurisprudentially sound justifications for developing and refining legal rights in directions that help to satisfy victim and public interest in knowing what happened'.[133] The realization of the right to truth is ultimately a matter of the political will of the state tied up with the aims of its transitional justice policy. The investigation of individual human rights violations, either through truth commissions or trials, is shaped by the political will of state to find the truth and communicate it.[134] Its political significance is shaped by whether it is introduced as a transition or post-transition justice measure.

1.2.4. RIGHT TO REPARATIONS

Reparations have become an increasingly important measure in transitional justice to promote restorative justice. Reparations are seen as 'the embodiment of a society's recognition, remorse and atonement for harms inflicted'.[135] As a legal remedy, reparations aim to redress egregious wrongs and restore the victim to the *status quo ante*. Reparations are a justice measure conceived as redress for the infringement of a right. In transitional justice the 'right to reparations' has emerged through the convergence of the application of IHL and IHRL in internal conflict and strengthened as transitional justice soft law by the UN Basic Principles and by the Rome Statute of the ICC (1998). In Latin America, the IACtHR has played a major role in the development of the right to reparations, but has also revealed the way states have strategically manipulated reparations to limit the impact of IACtHR decisions.

The idea of a 'right to reparations' in transitional justice emerged from the convergence of IHL and IHRL in their application to situations of internal conflict. The IHRL category 'crimes against humanity', which criminalizes large-scale atrocities in both war and peacetime, has facilitated the convergence of

---

132 M. Klinkner and H. Davis, *The Right to the Truth in International Law: Victims' Rights in Human Rights and International Criminal Law*, Routledge, London 2020, p. 242.

133 Ibid., p. 241.

134 Ibid., p. 243.

135 N. Roht-Arriaza, 'Reparations Decisions and Dilemmas' (2004) 27 *Hastings International and Comparative Law Review* 157, at 158–9.

these distinct legal fields. Whereas IHRL protected and empowered individuals by conferring rights on them, IHL empowered states in their conduct of war – military necessity – and protected individuals, not by granting rights, but by imposing humanitarian obligations on states.[136] The convergence of IHL and IHRL has been driven by the ascendancy of a rights-based approach to violations of IHL through the humanization and legalization of violations of IHL making individual victims, not just states, the beneficiaries of reparations.[137] Nevertheless, legal scholars remain divided over whether IHL creates rights to protect and empower individuals.[138] From the perspective of IHL, criminalizing all suffering in war as crimes against humanity is a legal utopia ignoring the tension between humanitarianism and military necessity in the laws of war.[139] The key UN document on the right to reparations is the 'Basic Principles' commended by the UNGA to members states in 2005.[140] It founds the 'right to reparations' on binding law developed by the International Law Commission in Articles on Responsibility of States for Internationally Wrongful Acts (2001) (UNGA A/RES/56/83).[141] However, the Basic Principles do not create new law. They set out the legal contours of the 'right to reparations' in treaty law and customary international law, and develop a victim centred rights-based approach towards reparations in IHRL and IHL. The Basic Principles were developed over 15 years, initiated by the Special Rapporteur, Theo van Boven, to study the right to restitution, compensation, and rehabilitation of victims of gross violations of human rights and fundamental freedoms, with the aim of combating impunity and strengthening victims' rights to redress and reparation. Because the Basic Principles are concerned with the worst violations – those constituting international crimes under the Rome Statute of the ICC – eligibility for reparations is limited to a narrow range of human rights violations.[142]

---

136 L. Hill-Cawthorne, 'Rights under International Humanitarian Law' (2018) 28 *European Journal of International Law* 1187, at 1189.

137 Ibid., p. 1211.

138 Ibid., p. 1212.

139 P. Akhavan, 'Reconciling Crimes Against Humanity with the Laws of War: Human Rights, Armed Conflict, and the Limits of Progressive Jurisprudence' (2008) 6 *Journal of International Criminal Justice* 21, at 36.

140 Basic Principles and Guidelines on the Right to a Remedy and Reparation for Victims of Gross Violations of International Human Rights Law and Serious Violations of International Humanitarian Law, December 16, 2005, General Assembly Resolution 60/147, https://www.ohchr.org/en/instruments-mechanisms/instruments/basic-principles-and-guidelines-right-remedy-and-reparation.

141 B. Saul, 'Compensation for Unlawful Death in International Law: A Focus on the Inter-American Court of Human Rights' (2004) 19 *American University International Law Review* 523, at 536.

142 T. van Boven, 'The United Nations Basic Principles and Guidelines on the Right to a Remedy and Reparation for Victims of Gross Violations of International Human Rights Law and Serious Violations of International Humanitarian Law', *United Nations Audiovisual Library of International Law*, 2010, https://legal.un.org/avl/pdf/ha/ga_60-147/ga_60-147_e.pdf, p. 2.

The growing importance of the right to reparations as a transitional justice measure is reflected in the jurisprudence of the IACtHR dealing with the serious violations of IHRL and IHL committed by the dictatorships in Latin America. The Court developed a reputation for progressive interpretation of international law and the ACHR to expand the scope of reparations.[143] The Court's reparations orders have included symbolic memorialization – public places named after victims; official acknowledgement of victims; state acceptance of responsibility; the requirement to publicize Court findings; provide compensation; and locate the remains of the disappeared.[144] Litigation before the Court has three stages: admissibility, merits and reparations.[145] In its early years – 1980s, 1990s – the Court mainly awarded monetary compensation for survivors – the relatives of deceased or disappeared – but later reparations expanded to include measures for access to justice, restitution, rehabilitation, satisfaction and guarantees of non-repetition, and access to information.[146] The expansion of IACtHR reparations orders was driven by several factors. Firstly, reparations, delivered through administrative justice programmes, were particularly important where amnesty laws prevented prosecutions. Secondly, victims and human rights organizations lobbied the Court to expand the scope of reparations as recognition of their victimhood. Thirdly, permission for consulting lawyers and victims to participate in the Court processes – previously restricted to OAS member states and the IACHR – increased the visibility of victims and their claims. Fourthly, strong state compliance with Court orders on reparations reinforced their symbolic importance in restorative justice. For victims, appearing before the Court increased their leverage over domestic transitional justice policy.

By contrast with the uneven compliance with orders to investigate and prosecute those responsible for violations and to reform domestic laws, there has been strong compliance with IACtHR orders for reparations.[147] Truth has become linked to reparations, not justice.[148] Thus states have been increasingly willing to publicly acknowledge responsibility for violations as part of reparations orders

---

143 The legal basis for the Court's orders on reparations is art. 63(1) of the Convention which refers to state responsibility with respect to protections for violations of right or freedom. See D. Cassel, 'The Expanding Scope and Impact of Reparations Awarded by the Inter-American Court of Human Rights' (2004) 27 *Hastings International and Comparative Law Review*, 91.

144 D. Cassel 2004, o.c., pp. 98–9. See also H.S. Galván Puente, 'Legislative measures as guarantees of non-repetition: a reality in the Inter-American Court, and a possible solution for the European Court' (2009) 49 *Revista IIDH (Instituto Interamericano de derechos humanos)* 69, at 74–5.

145 J.L. Cavallaro and S.E. Brewer, 'Re-evaluating Regional Human Rights Litigation in the Twenty-First Century of the Inter-American Court' (2008) 102 *American Journal of International Law* 768, at 781.

146 Cassel 2004, o.c., p. 91.

147 Cavallaro and Brewer 2008, o.c., p. 770.

148 H. Rojas and M. Shaftoe, 'Reparations for the Victims' in H. Rojas and M. Shaftoe (eds.), *Human Rights and Transitional Justice in Chile. Memory Politics and Transitional Justice*, Springer International Publishing, Cham 2021, p. 91, at p. 103.

before the Court. These are positive signs of the Court's success in strengthening human rights and its judicial authority in the region.[149] For victims, reparations are a tangible expression that the state is serious about redress, recognition, and respect.[150] Yet state compliance with reparation orders is often a strategic move designed to limit the jurisprudential significance of individual cases and thereby speed up processing. The increase in state acknowledgement of violations is occurring in the context of increased Court caseloads and limited resources which has reduced the time of hearings.[151] Acceptance of state responsibility increases the Court's efficiency in processing cases but, by minimizing the jurisprudential significance of individual cases, it limits the potential scope of reparations for a much larger group of victims who will never appear before the Court. Reparations can also provoke division rather than support reconciliation. In Argentina, the Mothers of the *Plaza de Mayo* split over accepting reparations and the remains of the disappeared from CONADEP. The more radical group demanded justice for all the disappeared, rejected compensation as blood money and refused to accept the remains of the disappeared as a depoliticizing gesture.[152]

1.2.5. RIGHT TO GUARANTEES OF NON-REPETITION

The 'right to guarantees of non-repetition' is the fourth and the least developed pillar.[153] Nevertheless, the promise of 'Never Again' (*Nunca Más*) became a central theme in the demands of human rights movement at the transition to democracy. The expression *Nunca Más* (Never Again), which embodies the idea that truth is an antidote to impunity and a deterrence to future atrocities, became the signature title of numerous truth commission reports in Latin America.[154] In Argentina, The *Nunca Más* campaign emerged as a rejection of

149 Cavallaro and Brewer 2008, o.c., p. 810.

150 P. de Greiff, 'Justice and Reparations' in P. de Greiff (ed.), *The Handbook of Reparations*, Oxford University Press, Oxford 2006, p. 1, at p. 14.

151 Cavallaro and Brewer 2008, o.c., p. 799.

152 Roht-Arriaza 2004, o.c., p. 180.

153 P. de Greiff, 'The Future of the Past: Reflections on the Present State and Prospects of Transitional Justice' (2020) 14 *International Journal of Transitional Justice*, 251.

154 Examples include: *Nunca Más, informe de la Comisión sobre la Desaparición de Personas* (Never Again: Report of the Commission about the Disappeared, CONADEP), Universitaria De Buenos Aires, Buenos Aires, 1984; *Uruguay Nunca Más: Informe Sobre Violación a los Derechos Humanos* (*Uruguay Never Again: Report on Human Rights Violations*) Servicio Paz y Justicia, Montevideo, 1989; *Guatemala Nunca Más, Proyecto Interdiocesano de Recuperación de la Memoria Historica*, Guatemala City: Oficina de Derechos Humanos del Arzobispado de Guatemala, 1998; *Nunca Más en Chile: Síntesis Corregida y Actualizada del Informe Rettig, Comisión Chilena de Derechos Humanos*, LOM, 1999. Human rights organisations have also incorporated 'Never Again' in their titles: *Colectivo de Derechos Human Nicaragua Nunca Más* (Human Rights Collective Nicaragua Never Again) 2019.

the military's self-amnesty – The National Pacification Law (*Ley de Pacificación Nacional*), No. 22.924, 1983[155] – and a denunciation of the historical cycles of military intervention in electoral politics which had plagued Argentina since 1930.[156] José Zalaquett, a Chilean human rights defender, argues that the concern of human rights activists with preventing future human rights abuses only emerged during political transition when successor regimes had to prevent the recurrence of serious abuses and repair the damage caused.[157] One of the key objectives of truth commissions – a term that was only adopted in the mid 1990s – has been non-repetition of human rights violations.

The idea of the 'right to guarantees of non-repetition' in international human rights law has its origins in international law regulating diplomatic disputes in which states demanded assurances and guarantees of non-repetition of state behaviour. In 2001, the International Law Commission's (ILC) Draft Articles on Responsibility of States for Internationally Wrongful Acts (ARSIWA) codified state responsibility for an internationally wrongful act making states legally obligated to cease the harmful acts and to provide assurances and guarantees of non-repetition.[158] The ILC effectively transformed a tool of diplomacy into a legal instrument creating binding obligations on states against their consent.[159] It exercised its UN mandate to support the progressive development of international law to establish state responsibility to guarantee non-repetition as customary international law.[160] However, as a legal concept, the right to guarantee of non-repetition has become much more prominent in IHRL. As UN soft law, the Basic Principles conceptualized guarantees of non-repetition as a right of victims of IHL and IHRL violations.[161] The Basic Principles evolved from the UN mandates

155 *Ley de Pacificación Nacional*, No. 22.924, September 22, 1983, República Argentina, BO September 27, 1983.

156 E. Crenzel, 'Genesis, Uses, and Significations of the Nunca Más Report in Argentina' (2015) 42 *Latin American Perspectives* 20, at 23.

157 J. Zalaquett, 'Confronting Human Rights Violations Committed by Former Governments: Applicable Principles and Political Constraints' (1990) 13 *Hamline Law Review* 623, at 628.

158 Draft Articles on Responsibility of States for Internationally Wrongful Acts, in Report of the International Law Commission on the Work of Its Fifty-third Session, UN GAOR, 56th Sess., Supp.10, art. 30, UN Doc. A/56/10 (2001), https://legal.un.org/ilc/texts/instruments/english/commentaries/9_6_2001.pdf.

159 S. Sullivan, 'Changing the Premise of International Legal Remedies: the Unfounded Adoption of Assurances and Guarantees of Non-Repetition' (2002) 7 *UCLA Journal of International Law & Foreign Affairs* 265, at 273–4.

160 Ibid., p. 279. The UN allowed the ILC a role in the progressive development of international law and not just codification. The ILC could develop draft conventions on subjects not yet regulated by international law or where the law has not been sufficiently developed. Scholars question whether 'progressive' is an adequate foundation for guarantees of non-repetition.

161 Article 23. Guarantees of non-repetition should include, where applicable, any or all of the following measures, which will also contribute to prevention: (a) Ensuring effective civilian control of military and security forces; (b) Ensuring that all civilian and military proceedings abide by international standards of due process, fairness and impartiality; (c) Strengthening

of the Special Rapporteurs of Theo van Boven, and later M. Cherif Bassiouni, to study the right to remedy and identified guarantees of non-repetition as an emerging international norm.[162] The Basic Principles do not claim to introduce new norms but to reflect existing law found in different treaties and customary law.[163] In addition, Louis Joinet's draft of the principles on combating impunity (1997) and Diane Orentlicher's updated version of them included guarantees of non-repetition as a component of reparations.[164] The right to guarantees of non-repetition was finally established as a fourth pillar in the *Guidance Note of the Secretary-General: United Nations Approach to Transitional Justice* (2010). The UNHRC's appointment of the Special Rapporteur on the promotion of truth, justice, reparation and guarantees of non-repetition (2011) confirmed its status as the fourth pillar.[165] Nevertheless, the status of the right to guarantees of non-repetition as binding law has been challenged as being without legal foundation, to be recognized as customary international law and representing a shift from 'remedial norms of restitution and repair to a paradigm of prospective relief'.[166]

The right to guarantees of non-repetition refers to a range of measures concerned with the cessation of ongoing violations and prevention of future ones. Their primary focus has been on the reform of state institutions to reduce the likelihood of gross violations of IHL or IHRL in the future. The measures include strengthening the rule of law, vetting procedures, security reform, an independent judiciary, access to justice and constitutional reform. The Basic Principles in Article 23 on guarantees of non-repetition sets out measures for prevention through civilian control over military and security forces, the

the independence of the judiciary; (d) Protecting persons in the legal, medical and health-care professions, the media and other related professions, and human rights defenders; (e) Providing, on a priority and continued basis, human rights and international humanitarian law education to all sectors of society and training for law enforcement officials as well as military and security forces; (f) Promoting the observance of codes of conduct and ethical norms, in particular international standards, by public servants, including law enforcement, correctional, media, medical, psychological, social service and military personnel, as well as by economic enterprises; (g) Promoting mechanisms for preventing and monitoring social conflicts and their resolution; and (h) Reviewing and reforming laws contributing to or allowing gross violations of international human rights law and serious violations of international humanitarian law. 'Basic Principles', o.c.

162 Final report submitted by Theo van Boven, Special Rapporteur, 'Study concerning the right to restitution, compensation and rehabilitation for victims of gross violations of human right and fundamental freedoms' (E/CN.4/Sub.2/1993/8, July 2, 1993).

163 D.L. Shelton, 'Soft Law' in D. Armstrong (ed.), *Routledge Handbook of International Law*, Routledge, London 2008, p. 68, at p. 73.

164 D. Orentlicher 2005, o.c., p. 76.

165 'Guidance Note of the Secretary-General: United Nations Approach to Transitional Justice' March 2010, https://www.ohchr.org/en/documents/tools-and-resources/guidance-note-secretary-general-transitional-justice-strategic-tool; 'Special Rapporteur on the promotion of truth, justice, reparation and guarantees of non-repetition' A/HRC/RES/ 18/7 October 13, 2011.

166 Sullivan 2002, o.c., p. 265.

separation of powers, human rights education, ethical standards, and monitoring mechanisms. It conceptualizes guarantees of non-repetition as a right of the victim for reparations.[167] The jurisprudence of the IACtHR has expanded the scope of guarantees of non-repetition measures through its strong preventive approach to reparations. Under Article 63 of ACHR, the Court can remedy the violation of a right or freedom by awarding fair compensation.[168] Initially, the Court ordered only monetary compensation as reparations but later included the full range of reparations – restitution, compensation, rehabilitation, and satisfaction and guarantees of non-repetition. What distinguishes guarantees of non-repetition from other forms of reparations – although they clearly overlap – is that they are usually designed as a preventive measure to benefit the wider society – or category of victims – not just violated individuals. Court orders expanding guarantees of non-repetition have been shaped by the prominent atrocity focus of the Court, especially enforced disappearance where restitution is impossible. As a consequence, Court orders have expanded the range of remedial issues to attenuate suffering of families as much as possible.[169]

The right to guarantees of reparations has been criticized as being too broad, too ambitious, and unenforceable. Roht-Arriaza argues it has become 'something of a catch-all category.[170] Davidovic argues that 'continuous normative expansion and openness keep the norm-affirming potential of GNRs weak'.[171] Balint observes that guarantees of non-repetition may identify what is wrong and must not be repeated, but they do not provide the tools to deliver on the guarantee. As mentioned earlier, the strong compliance with IACtHR orders for individually focused monetary and symbolic reparation measures does not apply to prosecutions and domestic law reform guaranteeing rights protection.[172] Selective compliance with Court orders remains an ongoing problem. For example, the adoption of the term 'right to guarantees of reparations' in the Colombian Final Agreement (2016) to refer to a broad range issues that masks what is omitted – vetting and security sector reform. The transitional justice lexicon of the 'right to guarantees of non-repetition' is used without clear guidance based on principles of state responsibility.[173] The Court's increasing deferral of responsibility to Colombian institutions to deliver reparations as 'compliance partners' also appears to be weakening rights protection and failing

167 'Basic Principles' 2005, o.c.
168 Cassel 2004, o.c., p. 91.
169 Cassel 2004, o.c., pp. 98–100.
170 N. Roht-Arriaza, 'Measures of Non-Repetition in Transitional Justice: The Missing Link?' in P. Gready and S. Robins (eds.), *From Transitional to Transformative Justice*, Cambridge University Press, Cambridge 2019, p. 123.
171 M. Davidovic, 'The Law of 'Never Again': Transitional Justice and the Transformation of the Norm of Non-Recurrence' (2021) 15 *International Journal of Transitional Justice* 386, at 405.
172 Galván Puente 2009, o.c., p. 86.
173 Davidovic 2021, o.c., p. 405.

to bring the hoped for transformation – peace dividend.[174] The 'Never Again' promise wanted justice for the victims, punishment of those responsible and a guarantee state atrocities would not happen again. The right to guarantees of non-repetition has translated the expectation into cessation of continuing violations and future compliance with legal obligations.[175]

1.3. CONCLUSION

Transitional justice emerged in the context of the global human rights movement in the 1970s, third wave democratization and the end of the Cold War. Its utopian vision imagined that justice based on human rights norms offered a way to manage political transitions from illiberal to liberal regimes and consolidate peace. In this imaginary criminal accountability for atrocities has become pivotal, even as it has become multifaceted in its combination of retributive and restorative justice approaches. From the perspective of victims, transitional justice has provided an emancipatory discourse that promises justice and dignity and a mechanism to rescale rights claiming to international legal arenas. The ability of victims and human rights organizations to legalize human rights as soft law and hard law has allowed them to erode impunity at home by increasingly forcing states to meet their obligations under IHL and IHRL. In Chapter 2 the four themes outlined in Section 1.1.1 are developed. Its aim is to contextualize the emergence of the transitional justice by situating it in the development of modern international law, in the post-Cold War project of global liberal governance based on human rights and democracy, in its emergence as an international norm alongside UN management of lawmaking, peacemaking and statemaking. The theoretical framework developed for the analysis of transitional justice measures is also outlined drawing on anthropological and sociological theories about performative rituals and event construction.

---

174 Kunz 2020, o.c., p. 1129; G. Lessard, 'Preventive reparations at a crossroads: the Inter-American Court of Human Rights and Colombia's search for peace' (2017) 22 *The International Journal of Human Rights* 1209, at 1221.

175 Roht-Arriaza 2019, o.c., p. 114.

CHAPTER 2

TRANSITIONAL JUSTICE AS A GENERATIVE PROJECT

2.1. TRANSITIONS, INTERNATIONAL LAW AND GLOBAL GOVERNANCE

2.1.1. THE EVOLUTION OF INTERNATIONAL LAW AND GLOBAL GOVERNANCE

Theme 1: In the late 19th century, the leading European states established modern international law and used it to justify their colonization of much of Africa, Asia and the Pacific on the grounds that sovereignty was the prerogative of the European 'civilized' states, not the 'non-civilized' ones.[176] With the gradual retreat of imperial and colonial power after WWI and WWII, the number of states recognized under international law rapidly expanded as the legal basis of sovereignty evolved from control over territory, to the right of self-determination, and to state endorsement of universal principles. The global project of transitional justice represents the latest stage in the evolution of global governance of a world of states through their integration, by consent, into the liberal global order founded on the legal and political universalisms of human rights and democracy. The transitional justice project is informed by a progressive, aspirational and utopian view of history in which public international law provides a vision of a cosmopolitan future of 'a united humanity governed by law'.[177] International law exists as 'a promise of justice' in a world imagined as governed by cosmopolitan public institutions.[178] From an historical perspective, the transitional justice project embodies the paradox of contemporary international law. On the one hand, the jurisdiction of international law is seen as universal, based on legal principles, and not state sovereignty; on the other hand, the nation-state remains

176 M. Koskenniemi, *The Politics of International Law*, Hart Publishing, Oxford 2011, p. 246.

177 M. Koskenniemi, 'International Law as "Global Governance"' in C. Tomlins and J. Desautels-Stein (eds.), *Searching for Contemporary Legal Thought*, Cambridge University Press, Cambridge 2017, p. 199, at p. 199.

178 Koskenniemi 2011, o.c., p. 266.

the basic political unit upon which the international legal order is constituted. This section looks at the relationship between international law, transitional justice, and global governance. It argues that the emergence of transitional justice needs to be historically located in the role of modern international law in the evolution of liberal global governance founded on the principles of sovereignty and legal universalism.

Modern international law emerged with the formation of the European state system, dating from the Treaty of Westphalia (1648), based on the doctrine of sovereignty which came to be understood as absolute and unaccountable power. Theories of international law had to address the problem of the legal basis of relations between states and state accountability. From the 16th century, theories of natural law proposed that reason provided the basis for limiting sovereign power and for ordering legal relations between states. The non-positive obligatory character of natural law applied to all nations, irrespective of their European or non-European origin.[179] By the late 19th century, positivist international law had displaced natural law as the leading international law doctrine. It distinguished between civilized and non-civilized states and held that international law only applied to the sovereign states belonging to the civilized 'family of nations'.[180] Modern international law has evolved through four stages: pre-WWI (1885–1914); between the World Wars (1920–1939); the Cold War (1945–1989); and the post-Cold War world (1989 and onwards). Before 1914, the international political hegemony of the European powers and their extensive colonization of most of Africa and Asia saw them aggregate responsibility to themselves for international lawmaking justified by their claim to 'civilized' status. In this era, positivism replaced naturalism as the dominant theory of international law which applied only to sovereign states constituted by the civilized family of nations.[181] The binary civilized/non-civilized represented an asymmetric counter-concept in which the former was the negation (not opposite) of the latter.[182] The binary civilized/non-civilized remains inherent to the universalist concept of international law as a transnationally binding legal system in which the dominant states continue to set the terms of emancipation – i.e. self-determination and recognition of sovereignty.

The Berlin Conference on West Africa in 1885 established the prerogative of European sovereignty over non-Europeans justified on the grounds that they

---

179 P. Schröder, 'Natural Law, Sovereignty and International Law: A Comparative Perspective' in I. Hunter and D. Saunders (eds.), *Natural Law and Civil Sovereignty: Moral Right and State Authority in Early Modern Political Thought*, Palgrave Macmillan, London 2002, p. 204, at p. 210.

180 A. Anghie, *Imperialism, Sovereignty and the Making of International Law*, Cambridge University Press, Cambridge 2005, p. 36.

181 Ibid., p. 35.

182 R. Koselleck, *Futures Past: On the Semantics of Historical Time*, MIT Press, Cambridge, MA 1985, p. 161.

lacked the capacity for sovereignty and therefore legal personality. After 1918, the exclusivity of European dominance over international law was challenged by the collapse of empires (Ottoman, German, Austro-Hungarian, Romanov) and the reality that new states would emerge independent of European sovereignty. Also, the Wilsonian view that each distinctive culture was entitled to self-determination raised expectations throughout the European colonies.[183] In 1920, the League of Nations established a new global imaginary of a world of sovereign states equal in international law as the basis for the peaceful resolution of disputes. It laid down the ground rules for self-determination and became the guarantor of nation-state sovereignty. Minorities from the collapsed empires sought protection from the League of Nations but national sovereignty trumped minority rights.[184] The solution the League of Nations thought up was the Mandate system in which the League administered through trusteeships those former imperial territories/colonies that were considered ready (civilized enough) for self-determination, to ensure their protection and development. The Mandate system perpetuated the trope of the civilizer. The aim of the Mandate system, outlined in Article 22 of the League Covenant, was to 'integrate previously colonized and dependent peoples into the international system as sovereign, independent nation-states'.[185] It marked a shift in the role of international law and institutions from usurping sovereignty to creating sovereignty. The whole administration and supervision of the Mandate was based on legal norms and legal obligations and produced a whole new jurisprudence. The Mandate system established an enduring template for global governance conceived as external intervention in societies because they lacked the economic, political or legal conditions for full sovereignty. As Anghie observes, 'the new universalizing mission of international law now acquired an even more powerful character: through the interior of non-European societies and peoples, ostensibly to liberate them'.[186] The Mandate System contributed to the new sciences of social and economic development strongly focused on economic growth.[187] It foreshadowed the emergence of 'global governance' conceived as 'development' to create the necessary social, economic and political conditions for a sovereign state to emerge. Global governance translates contentious political questions into a 'policy package of best practices and comparative lessons crafted by technocrats'.[188] The terms 'modernization', 'backwardness', 'the Third World',

183 Anghie 2005, o.c., pp. 139–40.

184 D. Levy and N. Sznaider, 'Sovereignty transformed: a sociology of human rights' (2006) 57 *The British Journal of Sociology* 657, at 666.

185 Anghie 2005, o.c., p. 116.

186 Anghie 2005, o.c., p. 146.

187 Anghie 2005, o.c., p. 182.

188 V. Nesiah, 'The ambitions and traumas of transitional governance: Expelling and replicating colonialism' in E.H.D. De Groof and M. Wiebusch (eds.), *International Law and Transitional Governance: Critical Perspectives*, Routledge, Oxford 2020, p. 139, at p. 145.

'undeveloped/developing', 'Global South', 'weak states' and many more, including transitional justice (intervention because of the lack of the rule of law), indicate the need for external intervention and supervision to help developing states meet international standards, norms and practices to remedy deficiencies. In the Western Hemisphere, the asymmetrical conceptualization of Latin America justified US intervention to 'cure' Latin America's underdevelopment, to promote political stabilization against the threat of communism and most recently to promote human rights and democratization.[189]

After WWII, the UN made decolonization and self-determination and integrated new states based on their consent as signatories to UN conventions. The basis of sovereignty shifted from sovereignty as effective control over territory to the maintenance of basic standards or values which could not be abrogated.[190] Decolonization supported the idea that international law had finally become universal through the integration of colonies as equal sovereign states. For these states, self-determination was emancipatory and anti-imperialist. However, the expectation that they would be recognized as equals under international law and that the General Assembly would provide an opportunity for their participation in international lawmaking proved wrong. They were confronted by the challenge of development and regaining control over their natural resources which international law defended as rights acquired under the colonial regime.[191] The new UN system of IHRL allowed international law and institutions to regulate relations between the sovereign and citizens. It also revealed the limits of self-determination.[192] It was only in the 1960s and 1970s, after the legalization of the field of human rights with the core instruments – the ICCPR and ICECSR, that human rights began to penetrate international institutions.[193] The significance of the growth of human rights was to constrain politics. Human rights were claimed to be non-political because they were universal, ahistorical and were self-evidently fact-like.[194] They enabled the individual to represent their claims as in the interests of all rights holders, not just their personal interest. The political significance of rights is in their absoluteness – they exist outside political society and are introduced by legislation, they are individualist and do not articulate 'the value of collectives to individual lives'.[195]

---

189 J. Feres Júnior, 'The Semantics of Asymmetric Counter-concepts: The Case of "Latin America" In the US' (2005) 7/8 *Anales: Iberoamerikanska Institutet* 83, at 84.

190 D. Levy and N. Sznaider, *Human Rights and Memory*, Penn State University Press, University Park, PA 2021, p. 57.

191 Anghie 2005, o.c., p. 213.

192 Anghie 2005, o.c., p. 254.

193 International Covenant on Civil and Political Rights (ICCPR) was adopted by the UNGA Resolution 2200A (XXI) on December 16, 1966 and entered into force March 23, 1976. The International Covenant on Economic, Social and Cultural Rights (ICCPR) was adopted by UNGA Resolution 2200A (XXI) on December 16, 1966 and came in force from January 3, 1976.

194 Koskenniemi 2011, o.c., p. 136.

195 Koskenniemi 2011, o.c., p. 150.

In 1975, the radicalization of decolonization and self-determination as emancipatory movements provoked a right-wing alliance to destroy the revolutionary Left, especially in Latin America. The insurgent Left's defeat by military governments throughout the continent saw them slowly turn to human rights. As Moyn argues, 'human rights thus emerged on the ruins of one sort of hope (liberation through armed struggle) for former colonial areas and the search for some alternative'.[196] By embracing human rights, the Latin American Left strengthened its role in the fight against authoritarian regimes in the international arena – e.g. the case of Uruguayan political exiles' decision to petition the United Nations Human Rights Council (UNHRC).[197] The emergence of the international human rights movement at this time was not just because of its rights-based doctrine or global vision and its aspirational moral claim to transcend politics, but because of the crisis of other utopias.[198] The international 'vernacularization' of human rights to express demands in a language acceptable to Western audiences was reinforced by international lawyers strengthening human rights through legalization and institutionalization.[199] The transitional justice focus on atrocity justice – genocide and crimes against humanity – cemented the new importance of human rights in international law and international relations.

Transitional justice has become a lawmaking project given impetus by the rights claims of victims against states for atrocity crimes. This model emerged in Phase II transitional justice when victims (and human rights advocates), denied legal remedies under domestic law, adopted 'transnational legalization' as a strategy to strengthen human rights and force states to meet their obligations to investigate serious human right violations. In this phase, human rights discourse served as an impetus to generate legal rights by providing a language to expand entitlement and legitimate aspirations.[200] The emancipatory force of human rights discourse, and their ability to generate solidarity and identity based on shared victimhood, occurs at that moment when rights have not yet become positive rights. The emancipatory impetus of human rights is the product of its usage as 'an anti-sovereigntist cosmopolitan utopia';[201] the shift

196 Moyn 2012, o.c., p. 116.

197 For a discussion of the turn to the discourse of human rights by the militant Uruguayan left in exile see Chapter 3.4. The original Commission of Human Rights was established in 1946 as subsidiary body of the UN Economic and Social Council. It was renamed the Human Rights Council in 2006 as the key independent intergovernmental body responsible for human rights.

198 Moyn 2012, o.c., p. 213.

199 Ibid., p. 219.

200 C. Smulovitz, 'Petitioning and Creating Rights: Judicialization in Argentina' in R. Sieder, et al. (eds.), *The Judicialization of Politics in Latin America*, Palgrave, London 2005, p. 161, at p. 178.

201 F. Hoffman and B. Assy, '(De)colonizing Human Rights' in J.V. Bernstorff and P. Dann (eds.), *The Battle for International Law: South-North Perspectives on the Decolonization Era*, Oxford University Press, Oxford 2019, p. 199, at p. 202.

of international law from a state-centred to person and persons centred law – Teitel's 'humanity's law'; and the inclusion of non-state actors in international lawmaking.[202] The impact of human rights-based discourse as a political tool signalling individual and group aspirations has been strongest 'before the positive dimension of law constrains and predefines the reach of claims'.[203] The juridification of political relations is a central feature of the institutionalization of the Human Rights regime which is sustained by, among other things, self-conscious references to memories of past abuses.[204] The transitional justice discourse about 'international standard setting', 'models', 'toolkits' and 'lessons' point to the process of the consolidation of human rights in soft international law and hard international law. Self-emancipation through universal rights claiming imagines a world regulated by public institutions, yet the institutionalization of universal rights in treaty law delimits those rights to those states that become treaty signatories.

Transitional justice lawmaking focused on UN human rights processes allowing victims to petition UN bodies (UNHRC) or, in the case of citizens of Latin American states, the American system – IACHR and referral to the IACtHR. Moreover, the United Nations has increasingly assumed a leading role in the field of transitional justice by shaping the terms of negotiated transition agreements and providing a forum for the development of soft international law (in declarations, principles, guidelines) and hard international law (conventions, treaties). The UN's role changed from relying on international law to support nationally determined transitional justice efforts, to expecting states to conform to a growing body of international law standards it has set. Grover characterizes this phase as a turn to 'international legal hegemony and UN managerialism'.[205] The UN Human Rights Commission, the Human Rights Council, the General Assembly and Security Council have all become involved in setting the terms for recognition and support of states emerging from conflict. As the primary international body for global governance, the UN plays the official role of post-conflict reintegration of states as members in global legal order through treaty law. The concept of 'good governance' is closely linked to universal international human rights norms institutionalized in the ICCPR. Transitional justice, as the rule of law, forms part of the repertoire of policies, doctrines, and principles to manage societies that lack good governance.[206] The UN now asserts its authority through soft law to shape transitional justice norms.[207]

---

202 R.G. Teitel, 'Humanity's Law: Rule of Law for the New Global Politics' (2002) 35 *Cornell International Law Journal*, 356.

203 Smulovitz 2005, o.c., p. 178.

204 Levy and Sznaider 2006, o.c., p. 663.

205 Grover 2019, o.c., p. 359.

206 Anghie 2005, o.c., p. 249.

207 Grover 2019, o.c., p. 361.

But can global liberal governance be reliably built upon international law based on state obligations? Posner thinks not:

> International law is the product of agreements and practices of democratic governments that favour their own citizens over the rest of the world and authoritarian governments that favour some subset of their own citizens; of powerful governments imposing their will on others and weak governments submitting because they have no alternative; of governments pursing time-bound interests with little concern for future generations. There is little reason to believe that the resulting system as a whole is just – though particular regimes or arrangements within the international system may be – and that individuals throughout the world, or their governments, owe any duty to it.[208]

There are just too many contingencies to have any confidence in states meeting their obligations. Jouannet questions whether the global liberal order, based on the transcription of human rights into positive international law, ratification, and near universalization at the textual level, is not liberal imperialism, a new version of the civilizing mission.[209]

2.1.2. THE DEVELOPMENT OF TRANSITIONAL JURISPRUDENCE IN A LIBERALIZING DIRECTION

Theme 2: Transitional justice, in the broad sense of post-conflict justice, is not new. It has been a recurring historical practice in which a victorious successor political regime uses trials, purges, and reparations to establish their authority and legitimacy by blaming and punishing the predecessor regime.[210] In his historical review of transitional justice, Jon Elster identifies three forms of justice along a continuum of legal, administrative and political justice.[211] At one end, 'pure political justice' occurs when the successor regime unilaterally condemns those it designates as the wrongdoers and determines their punishment. Political justice is victor's justice conducted in show trials which have the appearance of legality but, in practice, have pre-determined outcomes. The successor regime uses trials to eliminate their predecessors as political rivals and engender 'public feelings of loyalty and gratitude towards those who have delivered

---

208 E.A. Posner, 'Do States Have a Moral Obligation to Obey International Law?' (2003) 55 *Stanford Law Review* 1901, at 1916.

209 E. Jouannet, 'Universalism and Imperialism: The True-False Paradox of International Law?' (2007) 18 *European Journal of International Law* 379, at 391.

210 J. Elster, *Closing the Books: Transitional Justice in Historical Perspective*, Cambridge University Press, Cambridge 2004, p. 1.

211 Ibid., p. 84.

them from evil'.[212] By contrast, administrative justice refers to lustration, the purging of the appointments and supporters of the predecessor regime from state administration. At the other end of the spectrum is 'pure legal justice' based on unambiguous law, an independent judiciary, unbiased judges and jurors and due process.[213] The mix of justice policies deployed during a transition is determined by the nature of the conflict – its duration and level of repression; how the conflict ends – by military contest or negotiated agreement; and who determines the terms of the political agreement – elites, the opposition, or foreign intervention. Characteristically, the reach of contemporary transitional justice has been determined by the ability of political elites to resist international legal intervention. What makes contemporary transitional justice policy distinct, as the four phase periodization of transitional justice illustrates, is the evolving role of international law in shaping post-conflict societies and, increasingly, the political agreements that underpin them.

In general, transitional justice scholars have not paid much attention to the political agreements underpinning transition except as obstacles to post-conflict justice, especially the inclusion of self-amnesty laws.[214] The imperative of dealing with the violent past to realize peace has been viewed through a human rights lens focused on the crimes of perpetrators and the suffering of victims rather than the history of the political conflict underlying the latest violence and previous attempts at conflict resolution – the genealogy of conflict. Mahmood Mamdani notes that the prominence and attention given to particular transitional justice measures during transition have overshadowed the political agreement that initiates them. He argues the high-profile role attributed to the South African Truth and Reconciliation Commission (SATRC) in achieving a peaceful transition to democracy in post-apartheid South Africa downplayed the key role of the Convention for a Democratic South Africa (CODESA), the political process that preceded and established it. SATRC and CODESA had distinct orientations to justice – criminal justice and political justice, respectively. While criminal justice targets individuals, is concerned with punishment, and is past-oriented, political justice affects groups, is concerned with political reform and is future-oriented.[215] The logic of political justice requires the decriminalization and legitimization of both sides of the conflict to incorporate them as members

212 O. Kirchheimer, *Political Justice: The Use of Legal Procedure for Political Ends*, Princeton University Press, Princeton, NJ 2015, p. 10.

213 Elster 2004, o.c., pp. 6–7.

214 An important exception is the work of Christine Bell. See C. Bell, 'The "New Law" of Transitional Justice' in K. Ambos, et al. (eds.), *Building a Future on Peace and Justice: Studies on Transitional Justice, Peace and Development*, Springer, Berlin, Heidelberg 2009, p. 105; Bell 2017, o.c., p. 85.

215 M. Mamdani, 'Beyond Nuremberg: The Historical Significance of the Post-Apartheid Transition in South Africa' (2015) 43 *Politics & Society* 61, at 67.

of the future political community and to make negotiations possible. The post-apartheid political community are the 'survivors', 'yesterday's victims, perpetrators, bystanders, and beneficiaries'.[216] The concern of political justice is with political inclusion, reform, and reconciliation with the aim of allowing the survivors to live together into the future. In the transition to post-apartheid South Africa, it was the CODESA process that determined transitional justice policy – the celebrated inclusive truth commission model and its provision of amnesty for full confession.

The foregrounding of criminal justice and accountability on the one hand, and the neglect of political agreements that determine justice policy on the other, reflects the way contemporary transitional justice has conceptualized politics as able to be constrained by law. Order and political stability are seen as emerging from the rule of law rather than negotiated political agreements.[217] Ruti Teitel has very usefully reviewed the scope of transitional law by examining three aspects of transitional jurisprudence – the rule of law, criminal justice and constitutional justice – which function as legal mechanisms mediating between illiberal and liberal regimes. She argues that transitional legal agendas in these areas are distinct from ordinary justice and its goals. While the ordinary function of law is to produce order and stability, after political upheaval and conflict law is used to create order and enable social transformation. In transition, 'law is caught between the past and the future, between backward-looking and forward-looking, between retrospective and prospective'.[218] By delineating these three areas of transitional law, Teitel's model draws our attention to the fact that as the criminal justice orientation has been foregrounded in contemporary transitional justice, so the role of the rule of law and constitutional justice in transition have been obscured.[219] In practice, the three transitional legal processes are interdependent. 'Adjudications of the rule of law reflect understandings of legitimacy; criminal justice establishes wrongdoing; and transitional constitutionalism defines the state's political identity – all in a liberalizing direction'.[220] These three interdependent components of transitional jurisprudence will now be briefly outlined.

The rule of law plays a key role in transition founding the successor state's sovereignty and legitimacy. In the modern state, legality is premised on the idea that nothing is outside the law and the state possesses, through the law, a

---

216 Ibid., p. 87.

217 L. Gissel, 'Contemporary Transitional Justice: Normalising a Politics of Exception' (2016) 31 *Global Society* 353, at 357.

218 Teitel 1997, o.c., p. 2014.

219 L.E. Fletcher and H.M. Weinstein, 'Writing Transitional Justice: An Empirical Evaluation of Transitional Justice Scholarship in Academic Journals' (2015) 7 *Journal of Human Rights Practice* 177, at 178.

220 Teitel 1997, o.c., p. 2015.

monopoly of symbolic power as well as force. Law functions as a universalizing state discourse and the jurists are its agents.[221] The challenge for the successor state is to recover respect for the law and justice as an essential component of state legitimacy.[222] In transition, the dilemma of the rule of law is whether there is legal discontinuity or continuity between the predecessor and successor regimes. Legal positivists argue for legal continuity with the prior regime to restore due process and adherence to settled law.[223] On the other hand, the natural law advocates claim discontinuity is justified by the predecessor state's immorality and the need to ground legality on principles other than pre-existing law. The natural law perspective sees legality as a transformative principle through normative change. It sees the rule of law as a bridge breaking with the illiberal justice of the predecessor regime. It views the role of international law as a mediating concept providing a source of legal continuity above domestic law. What is most important for the recovery of state legality and legitimacy is not merely justice based on international legal norms, but the rule of law as legal culture – what the public perceive to be justice.[224] In transition, the rule of law is not adherence to settled law so much as its transformative role in establishing liberal legal norms – the vision of the rule of law as anti-politics.[225]

In Teitel's genealogy of transitional justice, the character of the rule of law shifts between the local and the global.[226] In Phase I, the rule of law is conceived in universalizing terms concerned with accountability and humanity; in Phase II, the rule of law prioritizes the national state's legitimacy and sovereignty; in Phase III transitional justice becomes normalized making international humanitarian law the basis for global rule of law and international intervention to protect the human rights of individuals against systematic state abuse. In Phase III, international humanitarian law is used to delegitimate the illiberal predecessor regime, to support and even instigate transition and to intervene to enforce state respect for human rights.[227] The global rescaling of the rule of law in transition is a response to the limitations of legality in states where liberal judicial institutions are weak. Through this rescaling process transitional justice

---

221 As Bourdieu argues: 'As I see it, jurists are the driving force of the universal, of universalization. They have the law on their side, that is, discourse with a universal claim; their particular capacity, which is their professional capacity, is to reason, to give reasons, produce reasons, thus to bring things from the order of fact – "that's how it is", "that's not possible", "that's intolerable", etc. – to the order of reason, in two ways: by appealing to universal juridical principles – there is no state without a constitution, for example – and by recourse to history'. P. Champagne, et al. (eds.), *Pierre Bourdieu: On the State: Lectures at the Collège de France, 1989–1992*, Polity Press, Cambridge 2014, p. 270.

222 Ibid.

223 Teitel 1997, o.c., p. 2019.

224 Ibid., p. 2029.

225 Ibid., p. 2030.

226 Teitel 2003, o.c., p. 69.

227 Teitel 2003, o.c., p. 93.

has become a lawmaking project concerned with institutionalizing the protection of human rights and strengthening state obligations to uphold them through the hardening of international human rights law and international humanitarian law. The former, which emerged after WWII primarily to prevent recourse to war, establishes the right to life, while the latter balances the license to kill and destroy to achieve military objectives with the aim of avoiding excessive civilian casualties.[228]

Criminal trials are seen as playing a foundational role in transition by re-establishing a new legal order underpinning liberalization. Teitel emphasizes their transitional role marking a normative transformation and public legitimation of the new legality.[229] Trials function as a mechanism for normative transformation by publicly condemning past wrongdoing to establish a new state legality. The defining normative shift is the principle of individual responsibility through criminal trials which serve as a mechanism to recall and disown past wrongdoing while affirming norms and judicial authority.[230] Yet, the use of criminal law primarily for normative and not punitive purposes to address large-scale atrocities, can only lead to partial sanctions. The principle of individual responsibility and 'the jurisdictional principle of universality and prosecutability by all nations' for crimes against humanity greatly expands the potential number of prosecutions.[231] But the sheer scale of violations can only be managed by selective prosecutions determined by their political status (leaders) and/or the seriousness of the crimes (crimes against humanity). From the victims' perspective, the prosecution of crimes against humanity confers recognition of the moral enormity of the offence committed against them.[232] Failure to prosecute those responsible for such egregious crimes denies them this recognition.[233]

Constitutional justice is an integral part of transitional jurisprudence after periods of repression firstly, because constitutions continue to be important foundational acts in state-making and state renewal, and secondly,

---

228 E.L. Camins, 'Needs or Rights? Exploring the Limitations of Individual Reparations for Violations of International Humanitarian Law' (2016) 10 *International Journal of Transitional Justice* 126, at 136.

229 Ibid., p. 2037.

230 Teitel 1997, o.c., p. 2037.

231 Teitel 1997, o.c., p. 2046.

232 In Argentina the families of the disappeared and human rights organizations have denounced 'dirty war' crimes as genocide – the most morally repugnant crime against humanity. Although no Argentine court is yet convicted anyone for genocide, one Federal Court judgment in 2006 convicted senior police for crimes committed 'in the context of genocide' publicly acknowledging the extreme moral repugnance of their offences. See M.K. O'Donnell, 'New Dirty War Judgments in Argentina: National Courts and Domestic Prosecutions of the International Human Rights Violations' (2009) 84 *New York University Law Review* 333.

233 See Section 1.3.1 for the discussion of the logic of selective prosecutions at the national and international levels.

because contemporary liberal constitutions increasingly shape the scope and implementation of transitional justice policy. In the history of the modern state, constitutions are seen as foundational acts of nation-state making and treated as enduring documents that establish the legal order, political community, and national identity. While creating new constitutions remains a foundational act – a new beginning – transitional constitutions are now viewed as transformative and not fixed. They are viewed as treaties reflecting the political consensus at the moment of transition. They function as mechanisms to ratify political agreements and institutionalize them. In Latin America, transitional constitutions have often been regarded as peace treaties, such as the celebrated 1991 Colombian Constitution.[234] As transitional constitutions, they are shaped by political compromises and are sometimes formally acknowledged as 'provisional constitutions' – e.g. Brazil's 1988 provisional constitution ratified by referendum in 1993.[235] But they also create the conditions for the transformation of that consensus.[236] In other words, they function as a bridge between the predecessor and successor regimes. Nevertheless, the role of constitutional justice in peace agreements is understudied.[237] As Weiner notes, participation in constitution-making during transition can help create a more inclusive political community but it can also result in polarization and conflict over future visions of society.[238]

Despite the influence of political agreements on constitutional politics, transitional constitutions are now inescapably shaped by global legal processes. Firstly, the judicialization of politics through 'the global transfer of power from representative institutions to judiciaries, whether domestic or supranational' impacts on transitional constitution making.[239] Neo-constitutionalism refers to the way states are constitutionally obligated to uphold international law adjudicated by national constitutional courts. In cases where the UN has become directly involved in peacemaking and nation-building such as in Bosnia Herzegovina and Kosovo it has embedded international law in national constitutions as superior law.[240] Secondly, the international democratization of constitution-making through participatory and deliberative process has made popular sovereignty the basis of constitutional legitimacy. Constitutional politics

---

234 M.J. Cepeda Espinosa, 'Responsive Constitutionalism' (2019) 15 *Annual Review of Law and Social Science* 21, at 26.

235 K. S. Rosenn, 'Brazil's New Constitution: An Exercise in Transient Constitutionalism for a Transitional Society' (1990) 38 *The American Journal of Comparative Law*, 773.

236 Teitel 1997, o.c., p. 2076.

237 *Constitutions and Peace Processes: A Primer*, Berghof Foundation and the UN Department of Political and Peacebuilding Affairs, Berlin, 2020, https://peacemaker.un.org/sites/peacemaker.un.org/files/2021_ConstitutionsPeaceProcessesPrimer_EN.pdf.

238 A.S. Weiner, 'Constitutions as Peace Treaties: A Cautionary Tale for the Arab Spring' (2011) 64 *Stanford Law Review (Online)*, 1.

239 Hirschl 2006, o.c., p. 721.

240 E. Hay, 'International(ized) Constitutions and Peacebuilding' (2014) 27 *Leiden Journal of International Law* 141, at 146.

have been democratized by establishing 'constituent assemblies' to draft a new constitution and ratifying it by national referendum. Neo-constitutionalism has also stimulated the bottom-up judicialization of politics through rights claiming in Constitutional Courts and regional human rights ones. In Latin America, a regional transformative constitutionalism referred to as the 'Common Constitutional Principles in Latin America' (*ius constitutionale commune en América Latina* – ICCAL) has emerged from the interactions between national constitutions; the Inter-American system – IACHR and IACtHR; and the Latin American human rights community.[241] ICCAL is underpinned by neo-constitutionalism, the opening of national legal systems to international human rights law and the strategic use of litigation by civil society organizations in the Inter-American system. IACtHR decisions contribute to constitutional justice by requiring states to harmonize national laws to meet their constitutional obligations under the ACHR. Transformative constitutionalism has emerged in response to the shared regional structural challenges of violence, social exclusion, and weak state institutions and produced new constitutions in Brazil (1988); Colombia (1991); Paraguay (1992); Peru (1993); Ecuador (1998, 2008); Venezuela (1999); Bolivia (2009); and major constitutional reforms in Argentina (1994) and Mexico (2011). All these liberal-democratic constitutional charters converge in their recognition of the fundamental rights set out in the UDHR (1948) and the American Convention of Human Rights (1969). Von Bogdandy and Urueña characterize this regional constitutional approach as responsive law aimed at producing social change.[242] The key to transformative constitutionalism has been the legalization of social problems as human rights issues.[243]

The construction of transitional constitutions as progressive and transformative mechanisms anticipates their liberalizing trajectory and fulfilment of the hope for a better future. The regional emergence of an ICCAL illustrates the way a regional transnational neo-constitutionalism can reinforce legal liberalization by opening up national legal systems to international human rights law and in the process creating a transnational legal order in Latin America.[244] However, because what is at stake in transitional constitutions is the redistribution of political power, the scope of constitutional reform is often contested and limited.[245] As ratifications of negotiated political agreements, transitional constitutions contain unresolved residual issues restricting their capacity to

241 Arguelhes 2019, o.c., p. 368.

242 A. von Bogdandy and R. Urueña, 'International transformative constitutionalism in Latin America', (2020) 114 *The American Journal of International Law* 403, at 406.

243 Ibid., p. 430.

244 J. Couso, 'The Possibilities and Limits of a Constitution-Making Transnational Legal Order: The Case of Chile' in G. Shaffer, et al. (eds.), *Constitution-Making and Transnational Legal Order*, Cambridge University Press, Cambridge 2019, p. 265, at p. 267.

245 Ibid., p. 278.

act as a bridge between predecessor and successor regimes. Amnesty laws are just one example of the way transitional justice policy can be constitutionally restricted. They highlight the obstacles transitional constitutions confront in their attempt to change the distribution of state power. As Couso observes, 'while fundamental rights travel well across continents and legal cultures, the distribution of state power remains a highly localized affair'.[246] Take the case of the 1980 Constitution in Chile introduced under the Pinochet dictatorship and ratified by constitutional plebiscite which was preserved as the price paid for the negotiated transition to democracy in 1990. The unreformed 1980 Constitution entrenched many 'authoritarian enclaves' in post-dictatorship Chile which were only able to be challenged in 2021 with the creation of a Constituent Assembly Convention. A central issue for this Constituent Assembly was whether political power would be redistributed from the present strong presidency to the parliament. The task of constitutional reform remains incomplete after a radical 'ecological' constitution was heavily defeated by plebiscite in September 2022.[247] A very similar popular constitutional politics emerged in Brazil to challenge the residual parts of the Brazilian transitional constitution (1988) and revive the hope that constitutional reform would happen with a new Constituent Assembly to be convened in 2023. As in Chile, a key issue was the dominance of presidential power in the political system in the context of political polarization and threat of authoritarian rule in Brazil.[248] As Acunha observes, '[the Brazilian Constitution] is a parchment that aims to crystallize the future in the present, the promise in the law, but it is no magic'.[249]

In Latin America, the IACtHR has played an important role in challenging the political agreements that restricted transitional justice policy by making orders directing states to uphold their obligations under national constitutions and the ACHR. The Court's decisions rest upon 'the transformative mandate of domestic constitutions' for their efficacy.[250] However, the Court has been increasingly criticized by several Latin American states for encroaching on national jurisdictions and for its broad interpretation of legal norms. Because the Court's orders are not enforceable state compliance is unpredictable. But the impact of IACtHR orders cannot be measured by just the level of compliance

---

246 Ibid., p. 271.

247 J. Nicas, 'Chile Says 'No' to Left-Leaning Constitution After 3 Years Debate', *New York Times*, September 4, 2022.

248 B. Ackerman, 'Brazil's Constitutional Dilemma in Comparative Perspective: Do Chile and Spain Cast Light on the Bolsonaro Crisis' (2020) *Blog of the International Journal of Constitutional Law*, July 17, 2020, https://macmillan.yale.edu/news/brazils-constitutional-dilemma-comparative-perspective-do-chile-and-spain-cast-light-bolsonaro.

249 F.J.G. Acunha, et al., 'The Brazilian Constitution of 1988 and its ancient ghosts: comparison, history and the ever-present need to fight authoritarianism' (2018) 5 *Revista de Investigações Constitucionais* 17, at 36.

250 von Bogdandy and Urueña 2020, o.c., p. 408.

which is quite uneven. The impact of the Court's orders are best understood as contributing to a Latin American community of human rights practice and the deepening of transformative constitutionalism.[251] The community of practice is constituted by the Inter-American system, national judges, legal bureaucracies, national human rights organizations, victim organizations and legal academics. The community of practice helps drive the judicialization of diverse social conflicts as human rights issues which can then be addressed by the legal system. And the Court itself has, through its case law, the epistemic function of constructing a specific legal reality and categories – 'victim', 'femicide', 'disappeared' – which in turn shapes how the community of human rights practice frames cases brought before the Court.[252]

Constitutional justice establishes the legality and scope of transitional justice policy. If a transitional justice mandate is not explicitly included, neo-constitutionalism imposes one through international human rights obligations. States become constitutionally obligated to investigate, prosecute and punish serious human rights; states are obligated to document the past through truth-seeking but with constitutionally limited judicial functions; states have responsibility to provide reparations for victims of human rights violations; state institutional reforms such as lustration must be based on procedural fairness.[253] As the Latin American example of transnational constitutionalism reveals, constitutional justice can be reinforced by a regional community of human rights practice in which the IACtHR is able to gradually leverage compliance by generating human rights consciousness, culture, and practice.

2.2. TRANSITIONAL JUSTICE IN LAWMAKING, PEACEMAKING AND STATEMAKING

Theme 3: Transitional justice intervention in post-conflict societies has been strengthened through its gradual integration into top-down UN guided lawmaking, peacemaking, and statemaking activities managing societies in conflict. As a consequence, the role of elites in transition has been reduced and the role of international institutions and processes increased to enhance the scope of transitional justice norms to ensure criminal accountability. The following three sub-sections address (2.2.1) the issue impunity and the limits placed on the judicialization of conflict in the context of the 'genealogy of conflict' arising from unresolved meta-conflicts dating back to the foundation

251 Ibid., p. 408.
252 Ibid., p. 422.
253 J.E. Méndez, 'Constitutionalism and Transitional Justice' in M. Rosenfeld and A.S. Sajó (eds.), *The Oxford Handbook of Comparative Constitutional Law*, Oxford University Press, Oxford 2012, p. 1270.

of the state; (2.2.2) the erosion of the role of political elites at transition through the convergence of transitional justice and peacemaking, lawmaking and statemaking under UN management; (2.2.3) the central role of trials in the broader processes of lawmaking and statemaking designed to institutionalize liberalizing legal and political change.

2.2.1. IMPUNITY AND THE GENEALOGY OF CONFLICTS

Theme 3: A persistent theme in the literature on transitional justice is the 'need to deal with the past'. The premise is that if the legacies of repression – from colonization, dictatorship, or civil war – are left unaddressed the traumatic memory of historical injustice will generate further conflict. Justice is offered as a remedy to prevent revenge, restore human dignity to victims, and end conflict. Impunity prevents any criminal accountability. But impunity is not just determined by the balance of power at transition. It is shaped by historical conflicts which political elites bargain over and make pacts to stabilize unresolved/able systemic conflicts, manifested as cyclical crises, dating from the foundation of the state. At transition, transitional justice is one among several interpretive frameworks competing to frame the conflicts and offer political fixes/solutions for peace. For example, in post-dictatorship Argentina in 1983 the criminal justice narrative emphasized the importance of re-establishing the rule of law to hold perpetrators accountable for mass disappearance, the political justice narrative emphasized democratic consolidation to end the cycle of military coups (there had been six since 1930), while the Argentine military narrative depicted their *coup d'état* as an act to save the nation from leftist subversion and fulfill their role as guardians of the nation since the 19th century. These conflict narratives are anchored in foundational questions about 'mythic violence' and unresolved political conflicts dating from independence.[254] In response to the political obstacles to justice after mass violence at transition, transitional justice has converged with other international interventions concerned with lawmaking, peacemaking, and statemaking to establish global liberal governance based on human rights and democratic norms.

Transitional justice intervenes in internal violent political conflicts which have their unique historical trajectory of political crisis, cycles of violence and state renewal. Each conflict has a specific 'genealogy of conflict'. Transitional justice intervenes in political conflict by translating political violence into individual crimes under IHL and IHRL. Justice is seen as a key mechanism to re-establish

[254] Mythic violence refers to the idea there is no ontological basis for the powers of ideologies such as liberalism or capitalism which have become naturalized as the order of things. See B. Walter, 'Critique of Violence' in P. Demetz (ed.), *Reflections*, Schocken Books, New York, NY 1978.

state legality and legitimacy on terms set out under liberal global governance involving state integration based on its consent to comply with international legal and political norms. Yet behind the transitional justice legal construction of political violence as criminal acts, there is an underlying meta-conflict serving as the driver of recurrent crises and conflicts dating back to political agreements made at the foundation of the state. The meta-conflict refers to the unresolved tensions regarding political representation and the administration of power – centralized/decentralized, authoritarian/democratic, the power relations between ethnic majorities and minorities. In the case of post-colonial states of the Global South, underlying meta-conflicts have revealed themselves in cycles of political crisis and conflict usually managed by elite pactism through temporary political fixes. In other words, transitional justice, emerging at the end of the Cold War, represents the latest project contributing to external state formation in the Global South, shaped by international law and institutions of liberal global governance. Only by situating contemporary political violence in the context of a particular genealogy of conflict can the political constraints on transitional justice intervention be understood as more than just the product of the balance of power at that moment.

External intervention is not a new experience in the Global South.[255] External state formation became the dominant mode of state formation in the 20th century arising from the dismantling of empires and decolonization after both WWI and WWII. Transitional justice intervenes in the internal conflicts of postcolonial and/or dependent states, whose territorial boundaries were often the product of European colonization and whose post-colonial governing institutions were shaped by the dominant states – often the former colonial power, and/or concerts of nations such as the League of Nations under the mandate system, or the United Nations that ratified them as independent states and, in many cases, sustained their existence as independent states.[256] Even though Latin American states had gained their independence early in the 19th century, their development became increasingly dominated by the US under the Monroe Doctrine (1823) in the name of US protection against new European colonization or puppet monarchs. In the Cold War era, superpower rivalry had co-opted post-colonial states in Africa, Asia and Latin America by securing clientelist relations with elites whose authoritarian hold on power depended more on external protection and aid than on domestic democratic consent.[257] The emergence of transitional justice as an instrument for liberal global governance marked the redirection

[255] C. Tilly, 'Coercion, Capital, and European States, A.D. 990–1990' in E. Castañeda and C.L. Schneider (eds.), *Collective Violence, Contentious Politics, and Social Change: A Charles Tilly Reader*, Routledge, London 2017, p. 140.

[256] Ibid., p. 151.

[257] R. Hinnebusch, *The International Politics of the Middle East*, Manchester University Press, Manchester 2018.

of external state-making away from the Cold War pattern in which many recently independent colonies were turned into authoritarian client states, to post-colonial post-Cold War external state-making based on legal and political universalisms of human rights and democracy supervised by the United Nations and international organizations such as the WTO, the IMF and the World Bank.

Contemporary transitional justice has largely intervened in postcolonial post-Cold War states with their different histories of external state formation. At independence, the postcolonial state was shaped by their inherited coercion-intensive colonial state institutions and by the UN's requirements for their recognition as independent states. The characteristics shared by post-colonial states which have continued to be the source of ongoing conflict include the dominant role of the military in politics, a legacy of the role of the military in the governance of the colonial state, and territorial borders established by the colonial power. Post-colonial states' inherited borders that were enforced by the UN as a condition for their recognition as independent states.[258] Because many ethnic minorities experienced the post-colonial centralized national state as a continuation of the centralized colonial state, decentralization, arising from 'competition for state power by religious, linguistic, and territorial groups for autonomy or for control of an existing state', has been an ongoing demand.[259] These political legacies, unresolved at independence, remain embedded in founding constitutions as ongoing meta-conflicts. During the Cold War era, superpower clientelism tended to reinforce centralized authoritarian rule allowing nationalist elites to continue to dominate politics and resolve internal conflicts through pactism.

In each of our case studies, the genealogy of conflict has been shaped by the conjunction of the historical processes of external state formation through colonization, decolonization, Cold War superpower clientelism, and post-Cold War globalization. The genealogy of conflict is distinct for different regions. In our Latin American case studies of Uruguay and Colombia, the 19th century postcolonial state was shaped by postcolonial republican nationalism and political competition between the liberal and conservative party elites who mobilized their respective urban and rural constituencies to fight civil wars, and subsequently elections, to secure and monopolize state power. Uruguay and Colombia are distinctive in that the 19th century dominance of the Liberal and Conservative parties, a pattern found throughout Latin America, persisted into the 20th century. Eventually, leftist political movements and guerrilla insurgencies emerged to challenge the electoral monopoly of these traditional parties. In Uruguay, the radical leftist challenge emerged in the 1960s and culminated in a coup in 1973. In Colombia, the leftist challenge emerged in

---

258 G. Sørensen, 'War and State-Making' (2016) 32 *Security Dialogue* 341, at 347.
259 Tilly 2017, o.c., p. 149.

the 1950s, during the period of civil war known as *La Violencia*. Over a period of 50 years, the Colombian state became increasingly militarized to reassert its authority over territory and populations that were controlled, at different times, by leftist guerrilla forces, right wing paramilitaries, and criminal drug cartels. In both cases, these conflicts were seen through a Cold War anti-communist lens as revolutionary insurgencies and threats to the state and to US hegemony in the Western Hemisphere. In our case studies of post-colonial Lebanon and Kenya, the genealogy of conflict centres on the challenge of post-colonial nation-state building and conflicts over the distribution of power amongst ethnic/religious minorities, the centralization or decentralization of power and their geo-strategic importance in the Middle East and East Africa respectively. In both cases, external patronage played an important role in changing the internal balance of power and influencing how conflict was resolved. In our case study of Spain, the genealogy of conflict was shaped by the impact of the loss of Spain's last colonial possessions on the post-imperial Spanish state at the end of the 19th century. The central conflict that emerged was between the traditional elite who wanted to preserve the monarchy and the church as the core of a unitary centralized state and the republicans, who wanted to overthrow them by democratizing government and giving greater recognition to the provinces – *autonomías*. The defeat of the Republicans by Franco's Nationalists in the Spanish Civil War and the Franco's 40–year dictatorship suspended this contest until the transition to democracy in 1977.

Our case studies show that when transitional justice mechanisms intervene in an internal conflict, they confront a genealogy of conflict with its particular trajectory, experience of external state formation imprinted with foundational political conflicts, and a history of elite bargaining to resolve conflicts. The genealogy of a conflict is narrated as a chronology of events punctuated by axial crises and turning points largely managed by elite political fixes. The narrative form constructs conflict as a chronological and causal sequence of events.[260] The latest crisis is burdened by the past and each political fix sets the parameters of the next crisis. For example, the genealogy of conflict in Colombia consists of a series of failed peace agreements over 60 years which burdened the peace process initiated by President Santos and finalized in 2016. The Colombian peace process carried 'the weight (as well as the ghost) of the many failed peace processes that came before, a failure which often involved the tragic elimination of the rebel fighters and the political forces associated with them'.[261] Transitional justice intervenes at a particular historical point in the trajectory of a conflict and seeks to transform the meta-narrative – how a conflict is viewed – by translating it into a legal problem.

---

260 See Chapter 2.2.4 on event construction.

261 B. De Sousa Santos, 'Colombia Between Neoliberal Peace and Democratic Peace' (2017) 11 *In Factis Pax* 41, at 44.

The transitional justice model imagines external state formation as a process in which justice serves as a mechanism to re-establish state legality and legitimacy through international legal harmonization. However, the future role of this model in managing internal conflict depends on its success in delivering peace and on the continued post-Cold War dominance of the Western-led international institutions. One concern is that the peace being delivered is a limited neoliberal peace rather than a democratic peace, in other words, a peace that prioritizes corporate interests and investment as the dominant drivers of economic development rather than one in which the state addresses social inequality by strengthening social and economic rights and participatory democracy.[262] The post-Cold War assumption that the US will remain the hegemonic power shaping liberal global governance may be premature. Gray prophetically wonders whether the post-Cold War will not be more like pre-1914 – 'not the hallucinatory perspectives of Marxism or American liberalism, but the history of authoritarian regimes, great-power rivalries, secret diplomacy, irredentist claims and ethnic and religious conflicts'.[263] As early as 1989, Gray had forecast the increasing alienation of democratic electorates from established political elites in the West arising from the negative impact of neoliberal globalization.

2.2.2. HARMONIZATION OF POLITICAL AGREEMENTS WITH TRANSITIONAL JUSTICE NORMS

Theme 3: Transitions are supposed to mark the end of conflict. Simmel (1964) identified five ways in which conflicts can be terminated: '(*a*) disappearance of the object of conflict, (*b*) victory for one of the parties, (*c*) compromise, (*d*) conciliation, and (*e*) irreconcilability'.[264] Each one of these outcomes 'entails a set of assumptions about winners and losers, power dynamics, justice, identity, and the relationship between the past and the future'.[265] Mechanisms for the termination of conflict seek to fix transitions of power by ending wars (surrender); ending dictatorships (negotiated peace, return to barracks); or ending internal ethnic conflicts (negotiated power sharing, demobilization). Military defeat is associated with specific patterns terminating conflict: 'more or less humiliation for the vanquished, more or less magnanimity from the victor, more or less definitive change of identities and fealties, more or less freedom for those defeated'.[266] The way internal conflicts end is determined by the balance of power

262 Ibid., p. 42.
263 Gray 2007, o.c., p. 53.
264 Wagner-Pacifici and Hall 2012, o.c., p. 187.
265 Wagner-Pacifici and Hall 2012, o.c., p. 190.
266 Wagner-Pacifici 2010, o.c., p. 1358.

between parties, the terms of political agreements, and who participates. These terms are shaped by the character of the conflict, its duration, its intensity and its impact on society targeted at a particular group or was widespread. While an agreement might bring an end to the immediate conflict, it can leave unresolved the meta-conflict, disagreement about how the conflict is addressed and which interpretive framework should apply.[267] In other words, negotiated agreements can end up as political fixes rather than resolutions of conflict. Negotiations and political agreements between the political elites first require 'reciprocal legitimation' to make them partners in transition.[268] Transition agreements may appear to bring about a rupture with the past regime – such as a transition from dictatorship to democracy – but in practice may not be transformative, only restorative. For example, in the Chapter 3 case study on Uruguay, the Naval Club Pact (1984) between the military and political party leaders set out the process for the return to democracy. However, the restoration of democracy the military envisioned was one that would best protect their interests by ensuring their impunity. To this end they supported the rehabilitation of the pre-dictatorship clientelist partidocratic order dominated by the two main traditional parties which had historically excluded the left from power.[269]

Transitional justice was originally conceived as a post-conflict project to prevent the recurrence of political violence by holding those responsible for serious human rights violations criminally accountable. As a post-conflict project, transitional justice measures were introduced after an elite brokered political agreement, in which the balance of power of the parties, had established their scope.

As Posner and Vermeule argue, '[w]here the elites lead the transition, transitional justice is limited. Where the elite and opposition enter a bargain, transitional justice is moderate. Where the opposition or a foreign national lead the transition, transitional justice is significant. In short, transitional justice increases as the influence of elites decreases'.[270]

The very term 'transitional justice' was originally coined to acknowledge the dilemma over the competing goals of peace versus justice.[271] In the immediate post-Cold War period, the aims of political agreements and transitional justice policy were often in tension with each other. In Phase II transitional justice, amnesties were a common feature of political agreements. Today, political agreements and transitional justice policy have converged through their harmonization under international legal norms. As a consequence, blanket

---

267 Bell 2017, o.c., p. 92.

268 L. Berat and Y. Shain, 'Retribution or Truth-Telling in South Africa? Legacies of the Transitional Phase', (1995) 20 *Law and Social Inquiry* 163, at 170.

269 See Chapter 3.3.1 on the restoration of the traditional partidocratic order in Uruguay.

270 Posner and Vermeule 2004, o.c., p. 770.

271 C. Bell, *On the law of peace agreements and the lex pacificatoria*, Oxford University Press, Oxford 2008, p. 241.

amnesties are now deemed unacceptable in political agreements because they only secure temporary peace and risk embedding and recycling conflict. Yet banning amnesties for crimes against humanities in political agreements does not guarantee accountability. Often elites are still able to undermine transitional justice policy and secure impunity through domestic politics to block or delay their implementation and even sabotage trials at both national and international levels. Our case studies on (Chapter 5) Lebanon and (Chapter 6) Kenya illustrate the way politicization of judicial processes, supposedly agreed to by all sides, can be undermined by elites more interested in securing their own impunity.

As a post-conflict global human rights project, transitional justice is offered as an objective legal framework to deliver truth and justice able to transcend politics. Accountability for past crimes is headlined over the equally vital peace negotiations and agreement. But the construction of political violence as human rights violations can circumscribe the scope of accountability. In his analysis of the transition in South Africa, Mamdani argues the strong focus on the role of the SATRC in delivering a peaceful transition was the result of the human rights construction of political violence under apartheid as criminal violence between perpetrators and victims. Consequently, the political violence inflicted by the state's apartheid policy was excluded as a matter for criminal accountability. Thus, the SATRC Report compiled the record of apartheid violence as a long list of gross human rights violations inflicted on individual victims.[272] But it was CODESA, not the SATRC, that provided the foundational moment of transition through the political justice delivered by the Interim Constitution (1993) – effectively a peace agreement. Adding historical weight to the importance of CODESA in transition is the fact that constitutional reform had been the central goal of the African National Congress (ANC) from its foundation in 1912, galvanized by its original opposition to the first racialist South African constitution (1910).[273] For the ANC, the Interim Constitution was an historical foundational moment marking the end of apartheid in South Africa. Symbolically, it signified the final break with the historical injustice of the colonial state in Africa. What distinguished the SATRC and CODESA as foundational moments was the public experience of the former as constitutive of justice. The SATRC functioned as a performative ritual of national reconciliation which generated widespread public witnessing of victim testimonies and (limited) perpetrator confessions culminating in its major Report. By contrast, CODESA's performative moment was the publication of

272 *Truth and Reconciliation Commission of South Africa Report*, Macmillan Reference, London, 1999.

273 H. Ebrahim and L.E. Miller, 'Creating the Birth Certificate of a New South Africa' in L.E. Miller and L. Aucoin (eds.), *Framing the State in Times of Transition: Case Studies in Constitution Making*, United States Institute of Peace, 2010, p. 111, at p. 113.

the Interim Constitution which was not publicly endorsed through a national referendum.[274] The CODESA process was incremental, building trust amongst those willing to make a deal and gradually bringing potential spoilers onboard. Although a national referendum was canvassed to endorse the CODESA agreements, it was ultimately rejected as too politically risky.[275] It was feared that political campaigning would unravel negotiated deals and polarize the electorate, not unify them, thereby undermining the CODESA peace process.[276] A more accurate account of the relationship between the SATRC and CODESA in transition is that both were foundational but played different roles in the peace process. The SATRC functioned as an important performative public ritual, designed to provide a collective experience of transition to unify the post-apartheid political community in agreement about the historical injustices of apartheid expressed as gross human rights violations and witnessed in the testimonies of suffering victims. The SATRC's overall significance in the transition process was exaggerated by presenting its model of victims' justice as transformative. The role of the SATRC was to honour victimhood as a moral victory, insofar as victims were willing to accept victory as enough, as Meister puts it.[277] CODESA, on the other hand, produced the Interim Constitution (the 34 principles) which then had to be implemented under the legal supervision of the Constitutional Court. The SATRC's historic role was to generate a nationally shared experience of victims' justice to underwrite the fragile political agreement reached through CODESA for constitutional reform. The theory developed in this book about the generative character of hinge legal rituals concerned with truth and justice to produce lasting effects is outlined in Chapter 2, Section 2.3 (Transitional Justice and Theories of Social Change).

With the expansion of the role of international law in liberal global governance, political agreements and transitional justice have converged through the processes of judicialization and universalization. The judicialization of political agreements has made commitments more enforceable and their universalization has imposed human rights standards on them. Peace processes evolve through stages characterized by different kinds of

---

274 After the establishment of CODESA in December 1991 to deliberate on a new constitution President FW de Klerk and the National Party held a Whites-only referendum in March 1992 seeking a mandate to enter into binding agreements with the ANC and other Black leaders to end apartheid. See A. Strauss, 'The 1992 Referendum in South Africa' (2008) 31 *The Journal of Modern African Studies*, 339.

275 Report on CODESA Agreements, The Nelson Mandela Foundation, https://omalley.nelsonmandela.org/omalley/index.php/site/q/03lv02039/04lv02046/05lv02047/06lv02049/07lv02059.htm.

276 Ebrahim and Miller 2010, o.c., at p. 113. See Chapter 7.3.5 for a discussion of the failed referendum on the Final Agreement (2016) in Colombia.

277 R. Meister, 'Human Rights and the Politics of Victimhood' (2002) 16 *Ethics and International Affairs* 91, at 95.

agreements – 'pre-negotiation agreements, framework/substantive agreements, and implementation/ renegotiation agreements'.[278] They move from being documents with abstract and imprecise language to ones with more precise legal language. Pre-negotiation agreements are often secret, limited in participation, and take the form of political pacts expressed as 'declarations' or 'records of agreement'.[279] Often, pre-negotiation agreements are presented as unilateral understandings, addressing their own side only. By contrast, framework or substantive agreements aim at consolidating ceasefires and are more inclusive and formulate commitments as legally binding. They address issues such as demobilization, constitutional reform, elections, rule of law and transitional justice policy. They set out detailed programmes and/or provide guiding principles for reform but vary in the extent to how they resolve foundational conflicts over 'sovereignty, statehood and identity'.[280] But as hybrid documents they don't fit easily into legal categories such as 'treaty, international agreement or constitution'.[281] Because they often lack strong legally binding force, they are buttressed by making the terms of their agreements sound legal, by referring to international law as a basis for commitment, and delegating enforcement talks to a range of international actors.[282] The judicialization of implementation or renegotiation agreements reflects the move away from transitional measures towards the normalization of legal and political processes. At this stage, constitutionalization based on international legal norms becomes the main strategy for the consolidation of the rule of law.

The convergence of peace agreements and transitional justice policy dates from the late 1990s with the expansion of the UN's political and normative roles in managing conflict. UN scrutiny of peace agreements grew with the ascendancy of the human rights position that peace was incompatible with impunity. What Bell characterizes as 'the new law of transitional justice' was the gradual application of 'the normative constraints of human rights and humanitarian law to peace agreement amnesties'.[283] The process of universalization of transitional justice has been the product of the convergence of four legal regimes all requiring accountability for serious human rights violations committed during conflict – domestic criminal law, humanitarian law, human rights law and international criminal law.[284] Koskenniemi characterizes the dominance achieved by the UN in shaping peace agreements and transitional justice policy as a product of the

278 C. Bell, 'Peace Agreements: Their Nature and Legal Status' (2006) 100 *American Journal of International Law* 373, at 376.
279 See Chapter 3.2.3 for a discussion of the Naval Club Pact in Uruguay.
280 Bell 2006, o.c., p. 378.
281 Bell 2006, o.c., p. 378.
282 Bell 2006, o.c., p. 386.
283 Bell 2008, o.c., p. 239.
284 Bell 2008, o.c., p. 242.

hegemony of UN managerialism.[285] The trend toward prohibiting amnesties in peace treaties has occurred through UN soft lawmaking, what Bell refers to as UN 'norm-creep'.[286] In 1999, the UN Secretary-General issued guidelines about human rights standards and peace agreements. In 2004, the UNSG Report on 'The Rule of Law and Justice in Conflict and Post-conflict Societies' rejected broad amnesties and capital punishment.[287] In 2004, the UN Commission on Human Rights passed Resolution 2004/34: The right to restitution, compensation and rehabilitation for victims of gross human rights violations and fundamental freedoms. In 2010, the UNSG issued a Guidance Note declaring the UN would not endorse peace agreements that did not include accountability for genocide, war crimes, crimes against humanity, gross violations of human rights and the right of victims to reparations, to know the truth about violations and to guarantees of non-recurrence of violations in accordance with international law.[288] The Guidance Note represented a statement about the UN's assertion of authority over the whole field.[289] Moreover, after the Rome Statute (1998) universalized international criminal justice, all peace negotiations took place in the shadow of ICC jurisdiction. The impact of universalization on transitional justice has been the prioritization of accountability for crimes against humanity with the ICC as the centrepiece of enforcement.[290] UN managerialism has played the important role of asserting the hegemony of international law in transitional justice policy. However, transitional justice policy has largely been a soft law strategy which has sought to impose detailed action and obligations without much reference to international law sources but full of mandatory language about what states must do with reference to duties, rights and guarantees.[291] UN soft lawmaking serves as a path towards the generation of legal norms to shape political decision-making.

The UN's managerial approach to peace agreements and transitional justice constructs them as technologies to design social transformation according to the imaginary of global liberal peace. While transitional justice originally referred to practices determined by national actors, it has now become a field managed by the UN and its partners including donors, aid agencies and NGOs.[292] UN managerial intervention signifies a lack of confidence in the capacity of post-conflict

---

285 M. Koskenniemi, 'Hegemonic Regimes' in M.A. Young (ed.), *Regime Interaction in International Law: Facing Fragmentation*, Cambridge University Press, Cambridge 2012, p. 305.
286 Bell 2008, o.c., p. 246.
287 Bell 2008, o.c., p. 248.
288 Guidance Note of the Secretary-General, 'United Nations Approach to Transitional Justice', March 2010, UN, New York.
289 Grover 2019, o.c., p. 375.
290 Grover 2019, o.c., p. 380.
291 Grover 2019, o.c., p. 366.
292 Koskenniemi 2012, o.c., p. 376.

states to fulfill the commitments made in peace agreements.[293] Consequently, the UN assumes a mandate to manage these states through international law and UN expertise, often as a long-term project. Peace agreements become standardized blueprints for democratic state building and the rule of law in accordance with international norms. Transitional justice is seen as a 'result-oriented' concept with justice the output optimized by 'best practice and lessons learned'.[294] The 'result' imagined is liberal democracy underpinned by the rule of law and a constitution based on human rights norms. The convergence of peace agreements and transitional justice has occurred through the top-down processes of legalization and universalization of international legal norms.[295] This convergence has led to the idea that there is a single international model for peace and justice. The phenomenal aspects of peace agreement practice point to a 'univocal political meaning' on the global front, which operates to legitimate internationalized processes and blueprints. This legitimating narrative presents peace agreements as always a good thing and peace processes as always moving straightforwardly from conflict to peace, and from internationalized processes to domestic constitutionalization, in conformity with human rights standards. International actors appear as neutral and legitimate, and national actors as violent and equally at fault.[296] While peace agreements are usually presented as voluntary agreements between equal parties, the power differential underlying them is revealed in their implementation. What is in fact a fundamental shift in power between parties needs to be monitored and enforced. International brokers can no longer be neutral.[297]

The legalization and universalization of international legal norms have made accountability a non-negotiable component of transitional justice measures and made trials the key measure to determine criminal responsibility and affirm the rule of law. However, trials are not necessarily good at stabilizing and extending 'the fragile meta-bargain by providing a shared narrative of the rights and wrongs of the conflict capable of underwriting a new political and constitutional settlement'.[298] Criminal trials involve a contest in which there are winners and losers each with their respective constituencies – followers – who may see the perpetrator as a hero not a criminal, and vice versa.[299] The adversarial nature

---

293 Grover 2019, o.c., p. 377.

294 Grover 2019, o.c., p. 376.

295 D.N. Sharp, 'Beyond the Post-Conflict Checklist: Linking Peacebuilding and Transitional Justice through the Lens of Critique' (2013b) 14 *Chicago Journal of International Law*, 165.

296 Bell 2006, o.c., p. 411.

297 Bell 2006, o.c., p. 411.

298 Bell 2017, o.c., p. 108.

299 See the case of the Croatian Gen. Gotovina and Gen. Markac who were celebrated as national heroes on their acquittal on appeal by the ICTY. M. Szpala, 'The acquittal of Croatian generals is challenging the reconciliation process in the region', *Analyses*, Center for Eastern Studies, November 11, 2012, https://www.osw.waw.pl/en/publikacje/analyses/2012-11-21/acquittal-croatian-generals-challenging-reconciliation-process.

of trials works against the wider goal of producing a shared justice narrative to underwrite the political/constitutional settlement. In transitional justice, universalization produces a pendulum swing towards maximizing justice by requiring states in transition to sign onto international law treaties as a condition for international support, recognition, and development assistance. Nevertheless, the implementation of peace treaties and transitional justice measures relies on the state fulfilling its obligations under international law. But if there is a lack of political commitment to implement peace agreements and transitional justice measures it makes them vulnerable to being undermined by domestic spoilers and by the competing interests of different political constituencies.

2.2.3. TRIALS AS THE FULCRUM OF LAWMAKING AND STATEMAKING

Atrocity justice is attributed with the moral force of unifying humanity in condemnation of an extreme transgression of human rights. It makes an atrocity the fulcrum for refounding state legality through the dignification of victims and punishment of perpetrators. Nation-states invariably have founding violence stories about large-scale sacrifice, now transitional justice seeks to re-found the state on the (sacrificed citizen) victims of state violence. Thus, transitional justice's insistence on criminal accountability for atrocities is more than a question of individual criminal responsibility. Trials serve as a key mechanism for state renewal in a liberalizing direction by getting states to meet their obligations under international law. Ruti Teitel's observation that transitional justice jurisprudence has shifted from a focus on punishment to establishing normative aims makes the same point.[300] The successor state's denunciation of the predecessor's violence juxtaposes its legality and legitimacy with the illegality and illegitimacy of the latter. In transitional justice, criminal accountability for atrocity has become the most important mechanism to champion the universalism of human rights and democracy to consolidate liberal global governance. What the predecessor regime had justified as law preserving violence against the 'enemy within' to 'save the nation' is exposed as governance through terror – lawless arbitrary repression – by the successor regime. Thus, those 'disappeared' during the Argentine dictatorship (1976–83) symbolized the hidden violence of repression which dehumanized those targeted as the enemy, expelled them from the protection of the law, and extinguished any relationship they had with the living lost in their clandestine graves.

As explored earlier in Section 2.2.1, transitional justice intervenes in a 'genealogy of conflict' arising from the foundational processes of state

300 TEITEL 2002, o.c., p. 360.

formation and the history of post-crisis state renewal. Political violence can be 'law founding violence' or 'law preserving violence'.[301] Law founding violence, Walter Benjamin argues, is performative – it is lawmaking by re/creating the state through political acts. Law preserving violence defends existing state legality and authority and, at the same time, conceals the violent origins of state legitimacy. Quotidian state enforcement of the law constitutes an act of preserving violence which implicitly refers back to the founding violence that institutes law's original authority. Benjamin calls this 'mythic violence', the projection of economic and political power as legitimate authority and law.[302] The state naturalizes 'mythic violence' without any real ontological basis, which remains hidden in foundational acts such as creating borders, a constitution, and the law. 'The foundational violence of an inaugural constitutional text lives, if at all, in the dominant narrative tradition as a ruin of memory, not, as with the subaltern, as a lived and generationally embodied histories of collective hurt'.[303] In his book *Toward the Critique of Violence*, Benjamin argues that the death penalty represents the ultimate expression of the power of the law over subjects and that its purpose 'is not to punish the infringement of law but to establish new law'.[304]

When naturalized, 'mythic violence' is challenged and so too is the very legitimacy of a regime. For example, the case study of Spain explores the contemporary struggle over the historical memory of the Spanish Civil War. More than 60 years after its end, the claims of the rightists about the legitimacy of the Francoist – the winners and their heirs – victory to 'save Catholic Spain' is pitted against the leftist claims of the Republican – losers and their heirs – denounce as illegitimate Franco's 1936 military coup against the legitimate Second Republic. Moreover, from the Republican perspective, all judgments decided in Franco's Military Tribunals against Republicans during Franco's authoritarian rule are illegal and historical justice requires they be declared void. It was only in 2022, 47 years after the Spanish democratic transition, that the Socialist government of Prime Minister Pedro Sánchez passed the 'Democratic Memory Law' which promises just that.[305]

---

301 W. Benjamin, et al., *Toward the Critique of Violence: A Critical Edition*, Stanford University Press, Redwood City, CA 2021, p. 60.

302 Mythic violence refers to the idea there is no ontological basis for the powers of ideologies such as liberalism or capitalism which have become naturalized as the order of things. Ibid., p. 57.

303 U. Baxi, 'Constitutionalism as a site of state formative practices' (2000) 21 *Cardozo Law Review* 1183, at 1192.

304 Benjamin 2021, o.c., p. 47.

305 S. Jones, 'Spain passes law to bring 'justice' to Franco-era victims' *The Guardian*, October 6, 2022, https://www.theguardian.com/world/2022/oct/05/spain-passes-law-to-bring-dignity-to-franco-era-victims. See Chapter 5.4.1 for a discussion on the legal contest to overturn the legality and legitimacy by annulling the verdicts of the military tribunals.

In post-conflict societies, trials are key state-making mechanisms by exposing and sanctioning as illegal the violence of the predecessor regime. They provide a founding moment for society marking transition by producing a statement of facts, acknowledging the victims, punishing the perpetrators and giving impetus to social healing and reconciliation. They resignify, through a legal lens, the symbolic order produced by violence by translating acts of violence into individual crimes. By prosecuting those responsible for serious human rights' violations, they seek to bring everyone inside the law, to make everyone equal before the law, and to re-establish a normative legal order based on international norms. Whether trials, as 'technical, politico-juridical measures', have the capacity to refound the post-conflict state/political community in the name of justice is questionable because, while justice motivates the law, it is not internal to the law.[306] Where political agreements include amnesty provisions, the ability of the successor state to pursue accountability is constrained and the scope of transitional justice measures limited. Where trials have been substituted by truth commissions, the rights of victims to justice are diminished and, in best case scenarios, only their humanitarian needs are addressed to alleviate their suffering.[307] Drawing a line on the past through a policy of amnesty and amnesia is an illusion because it 'does not erase the memories of the victims or challenge the continuing influence of the old regime's perpetrators and supporters'.[308]

The logic of the universalization of human rights norms has resulted in the hegemony of accountability in transitional justice based on the liberal legal perspective that everyone should be accountable for their actions. The evolution of the hegemony of anti-impunity has been noted in Teitel's periodization of transitional justice, in Sikkink's 'justice cascade', and in the UN development of soft law established in the Joinet/Orentlicher Principles to Combat Impunity.[309] For the human rights movement, anti-impunity emerged as the normative ideal and mobilizational goal.[310] However, the universalization of accountability has different effects in the international and the domestic spheres. Koskenniemi points out that while selective and symbolic prosecutions at the national level still can have a community creating effect, this is not the case with international trials.[311] International criminal trials cannot affirm a moral community beyond

306 J. Hall, 'Tragedy of State: The 1991 Lebanese Amnesty Law and the Possibility of Justice' (2010), Balamand University, Beirut (unpublished) 1; Balint 1996, o.c., p. 103.

307 S. Cobb, 'The Domestication of Violence in Mediation' (1997) 31 *Law & Society Review* 397, at 398–9.

308 Posner and Vermeule 2004, o.c., p. 825.

309 See Chapter 2.1.2 'Right to justice' for a discussion of this development.

310 S. Moyn, 'Anti-Impunity as Deflection of Argument' in D.M. Davis, et al. (eds.), *Anti-Impunity and the Human Rights Agenda*, Cambridge University Press, Cambridge 2016, p. 68.

311 M. Koskenniemi, 'Between Impunity and Show Trials' (2002) 6 *Max Planck Yearbook of United Nations Law Online*, 1.

the elusive and abstract 'international community'.[312] As a consequence, at the international level the logic of the universalization of accountability requires that all serious human rights violations be prosecuted. 'Every failure to prosecute is a scandal, every judgement too little to restore dignity of victims, and no symbolism persuasive enough to justify the drawing of the thick line between the past and the future'.[313] Yet, beyond the hegemony of accountability as a principle establishing the rule of law, the aims of trials in transition are multiple. Teitel argues that criminal trials in transition pursue justice not only to punish individuals but to establish a normative order – humanity's law.[314] More than the punishment of individuals, the importance of international criminal trials, Koskenneimi argues, rests on establishing an official truth.[315] As events grow more distant, and memory is reduced to historical accounts, the pedagogic importance of the official truth has, in some cases, been protected by memory laws.[316] Bikundi argues that the importance of international criminal law in prosecuting crimes against humanity is its function as 'a political apparatus for generating humanity'.[317] International criminal law is the epicentre of the construction of the protection of humanity as the protection of life. Genocide and crimes against humanity are constructed as the worst category of inhuman crime because they threaten life itself, not just the victims of individual crimes.[318] The International Law Commission developed the Draft Articles on Prevention and Punishment of Crimes Against Humanity (Draft Articles) in 2019 with the aim of establishing a Convention.[319]

The political significance of amnesty laws is not just their exceptionalism, granting some individuals impunity, but their disabling impact on the retributive and normative functions of prosecutions in transition. By blocking trials, amnesty denies the successor regime the opportunity to use them as foundational ritual mechanisms to mark transition and a rupture with the past, and benefit from their community producing effect. Amnesty curtails the capacity of the state to produce an official account of the past through legal investigation and to generate a consensus about the past based on legal facts and rational argument. It compromises the principle that there is nothing outside the law and therefore the ability of the successor regime to make legality the foundation of state legitimacy. If criminal accountability is blocked as a mechanism to produce

312 Ibid., p. 2.
313 Ibid., p. 11.
314 Teitel 2002, o.c., p. 356.
315 Koskenniemi 2002, o.c., p. 4.
316 Ibid., p. 7.
317 E. Bikundo, *International Criminal Law: Using or Abusing Legality?*, Routledge, London 2016, p. 16.
318 Ibid., p. 120.
319 Analytical Guide to the Work of the International Law Commission, International Law Commission, updated June 9, 2022, https://legal.un.org/ilc/guide/7_7.shtml.

a consensus about the past, then mechanisms based on popular sovereignty, such as elections and referenda, become important alternatives to mobilize and generate a consensus to produce community creating effects.[320]

2.3. TRANSITIONAL JUSTICE AND THEORIES OF SOCIAL CHANGE

2.3.1. THEORIZING TRANSITIONAL JUSTICE

Theme 4: Section 2.1 explored the generative character of transitional justice by outlining the development of its international legal architecture through the legalization and judicialization of human rights as enforceable international norms.[321] These processes were characterized as international lawmaking promoted by human rights advocates and NGOs in the UN human rights bodies and regional human rights courts. Section 1.2 outlined the development of the four pillars model constructed through a project of strengthening specific rights: the victim's right to truth, justice, reparations and guarantees of non-repetition. These rights are identified as the basis for 'justice' in transition and 'embodied in mechanisms such as trials, truth commissions and reparations'.[322] These justice mechanisms, instituted by the UN Secretary General's Report 'The rule of law and transitional justice in conflict and post-conflict societies', are anchored in rights legalized in IHL and IHRL, as well as emerging rights found in proliferating transitional justice soft law.[323] The dominant narrative of transitional justice lawmaking is that of the instrumentality of law – a normative legal order generated by strengthening rights, however it is not well theorized.[324] This Section investigates the generative legal processes underpinning transition by drawing on three different areas of sociological and anthropological theory. Firstly, theory on the symbolic and instrumental efficacy of legal acts;[325] secondly, theory on ritual structure and process concerned with transition

---

320 See the case study on Uruguay Chapter 3.1 and 3.4.3 for an analysis of the use of popular sovereignty to generate a consensus about the past.

321 J. Subotić, 'The Transformation of International Transitional Justice Advocacy' (2012) 6 *International Journal of Transitional Justice*, 106, at 118.

322 C. Turner 2016, o.c., p. 51.

323 Ibid., p. 51.

324 P. Gready and S. Robins, 'Transitional Justice and Theories of Change: Towards evaluation as understanding' (2020) 14 *International Journal of Transitional Justice*, 280.

325 J.R. Gusfield, 'Moral Passage: The Symbolic Process in Public Designations of Deviance' (1967) 15 *Social Problems*, 175; M. García-Villegas, *The Powers of Law: A Comparative Analysis of Sociopolitical Legal Studies*, Cambridge University Press, Cambridge 2018; M. Freeman, 'Anthropology and the Democratisation of Human Rights' (2002a) 6 *The International Journal of Human Rights*, 37.

and rupture;[326] and thirdly, theory on event analysis concerned with narrative structure and political semiosis.[327] These theories are introduced below in Sections 2.3.2, 2.3.3 and 2.3.4. These theoretical lenses provide a way to dissect the co-constitutive judicial and non-judicial mechanisms at work during transitions. They enable us to differentiate between legal acts and their effects; to recognize the ritual structure of transitions as ruptures; to appreciate the generative core of legal rituals and their legal and social effects; and to recognize the centrality of event construction in legal and political narratives. The focus on generative legal processes in transition reveals the tensions between symbolic legal acts and instrumental legal acts and their efficacy in establishing legal norms. What is distinctive – exceptional – about the transitional justice project is not the way law seeks to normalize its authority and naturalize legal culture in society, but the role it plays in contexts where legality and legal authority have been radically undermined by political violence. In these destabilized contexts, justice measures seek to generate a public consensus about culpability and injustice for acts of extreme political violence as the basis for reconciliation in societies deeply polarized by conflict.[328] However, the uneven impact of repression on populations, fragmented by differential exposure to violence and memories of it, make any consensus about the past very difficult to achieve. Gusfield argues that it is precisely 'when consensus is least attainable that the pressure to establish legal norms appears to be greatest'.[329] Why? Because authoritative legal norms provide an alternate interpretive framework to those of the conflicting parties through which to shape and manage the impact of past conflict on society.

This section is divided into three parts: Section 2.3.2 identifies trials and truth commissions as the key justice measures of the four pillars, their importance as performative rituals of political passage, their instrumental and symbolic effects, and their distinct justice goals; Section 2.3.3 explores the ritual character of justice measures, how they are constructed as turning points, how their tripartite form – segregation, liminality, reaggregation – structured by time, space, subject and intensity, works through *communitas*, the shared experience of community unity and solidarity generated through engagement in the ritual process; Section 2.3.4 explores how the performative intent of justice measures produce lasting effects. It explores the concept of 'event analysis' and the method of political semiosis to extend the ritual analysis of justice measures.

---

326 R. Girard, *Violence and the Sacred*, John Hopkins University Press, Baltimore, MD 1977; V. Turner, *The Ritual Process: Structure and Anti-Structure*, Aldine Publishing, Chicago, IL 1969.

327 L.J. Griffin, 'Narrative, event-structure, and causal interpretation in historical sociology' (1993) 98 *American Journal of Sociology*, 1094; R. Wagner-Pacifici, 'Theorizing the Restlessness of Events' (2010) 115 *American Journal of Sociology*, 1351.

328 Posner and Vermeule 2004, o.c., p. 761.

329 J.R. Gusfield, 'Moral Passage: The Symbolic Process in Public Designations of Deviance' (1967) 15 *Social Problems* 175, at 188.

The recognition that events are restless and are never really finished drives the politics of memory and memorialization. Moreover, different temporalities correspond to different interpretive framings of events often making them irreconcilable. 'Events emerge and punctuate lived experience'.[330] Their social impact is determined by the extent to which they are experienced as shared. They are given meaning by their collective identification as turning points and their insertion in a particular sequence of historical events as a narrative. Almost inevitably there will be competing narratives shaped by different interpretive frameworks, temporalities and spatiality. A criminal prosecution constructs a momentary and singular violent act as a serious individual human rights violation. When that single serious human rights violation is constructed as an instance of a state policy of repression used as a mode of governance by an authoritarian regime, it becomes a crime against humanity.

2.3.2. JUSTICE MEASURES: INSTRUMENTAL AND SYMBOLIC EFFECTS

The key performative justice measures used to realize the rights of the four pillars model are trials and truth commissions. They function as rituals of political passage to enact turning points or ruptures between the predecessor and successor regimes. They seek to realize the four pillars – the right to justice, truth, reparations and guarantees of non-repetition (legal norms) – as authoritative and enforceable norms, not merely aspirational ones. They contribute to re-establishing the force of law as 'a cultural system of meaning as well as a system of instrumental controls'.[331] Law's instrumental efficacy lies in its power of enforcement while its symbolic efficacy is found in its capacity to communicate meaning about essential social values such as justice, equity and security.[332] Law's extraordinary power is its ability to 'transform force into a legitimate exercise of authority'.[333] From a constructivist perspective, law's generative capacity lies in its instrumentality to establish enforceable norms to regulate human behaviour and in its symbolic capacity to produce meaning in social relationships. In contexts where legal authority and the rule of law have been undermined, the primary thrust of lawmaking is symbolic.[334] For example, 'symbolic legislation' is intentionally aspirational, designed to promote norms through persuasion rather than sanctions. Such legislation emphasizes the

330 R. Wagner-Pacific, *What is an event*, University of Chicago, Chicago, IL 2017, p. 6.
331 M. García-Villegas, *The Powers of Law: A Comparative Analysis of Sociopolitical Legal Studies*, Cambridge University Press, Cambridge 2018, p. 20.
332 Ibid., p. 20.
333 Ibid., p. 23.
334 Ibid., p. 27.

symbolic generative dimension of lawmaking.[335] Transitional justice lawmaking has a strong symbolic emphasis because its first task is to generate legal norms and re-establish the rule of law. In transition, the challenge for law is not merely to administer justice with respect to past violence/atrocity but to re-establish state legality and legitimacy to recover the force of law.

Trials are the key justice measure to realize the goals of the four pillars model and to combat impunity. The legal purpose of trials is to punish those individuals responsible for violations of IHRL and IHL, to affirm the norm transgressed, to provide justice for the victim, and to deter future crime. The objectives of accountability are firstly, as a matter of morality, to hold perpetrator accountable to provide justice to victims of the predecessor regime; secondly, as a matter of law, to re-establish the authority of the law to prevent vengeance and deter new crimes; and thirdly, as a matter of politics, to adopt accountability measures to strengthen democratic institutions.[336] Trials renew justice by enforcing legal norms and communicating the authority of those norms. In ordinary – peace – times, the instrumental and symbolic aspects of criminal law operate within an anticipated range of well-established legal concepts calibrating the degree of criminality and corresponding punishment. In times of transition, the role of trials in transitional justice is more complex and burdened with large moral and political challenges. In fact, law's generative character is more apparent when trials are not just used to reaffirm legal norms and the authority of the law but to re-establish the rule of law in compliance with universal human rights norms. After periods of mass crimes, criminal justice faces multiple challenges: In which jurisdiction should offenders be prosecuted? Which laws should apply? How many offenders should be held to account? What is the appropriate punishment for atrocity crimes? How should victims be recognized? How can trials serve to deter future violations?

Even though the institutionalization of transitional justice norms has been consolidated at the international level, trials are expected to be conducted at the national level. The creation of the ICC under the Rome Statute emphasizes complementarity and its role as a court of last resort when no effective legal remedy is available in national courts. Consequently, even though human rights advocates and victim organizations rescale justice by making claims in international legal arenas to strengthen human rights through legalization, in most cases their aim is to get states to meet their obligations under international law in national courts, not international ones. Even when international tribunals or courts assume jurisdiction over prosecutions to overcome barriers to justice at

---

335 B. Van Klink, 'Symbolic Legislation: An Essentially Political Concept' in B. Van Klink and B. Van Beers (eds.), *Symbolic Legislation Theory and Developments in Biolaw*, Springer, Cham 2016, p. 19.

336 M. Freeman, 'Transitional Justice: Fundamental Goals and Unavoidable Complications' (2002b) 28 *Manitoba Law Journal* 113, at 114.

the national level, they have frequently been undermined by domestic politics – see Chapter 5 on the Special Tribunal for Lebanon and Chapter 6 on the ICC prosecutions of Kenyan political leaders. The question of which laws apply – national or international – also shapes who can or will be prosecuted and for what. Transition trials are frequently denounced as political trials because they target former adversaries on the basis of laws not in force at the time of the violations – i.e. laws not respecting the legal principle of retrospectivity.[337] Even when a state is a signatory to the relevant human rights treaty and has obligations to investigate and prosecute serious violations of IHL and IHRL, Supreme Courts can decide they don't apply. For example, the case of Uruguay where the Supreme Court rejected the classification of crimes against humanity on the grounds they were ordinary crimes and therefore subject to a statute of limitations.[338]

Trials are at the heart of criminal justice and the rule of law. According to the liberal view of the rule of law, no-one can be outside the law for everyone to be equal before the law. The universalization of the rule of law applies to both domestic and international spheres.[339] However, the pragmatic response to largescale violations committed during periods of mass violence has been to selectively prosecute either those most responsible – the leadership – and/or those who have committed the most egregious crimes. But the combined effect of the policy of selective prosecution and the principle of individual criminal responsibility – which individualizes guilt – can encourage the myth of collective innocence.[340] Selective prosecutions can serve to replicate ritual scapegoating whereby a few individuals are overburdened with guilt while benefiting society by unburdening it of any collective guilt. Ritual scapegoating remains inherent in the ritual structure of trials as a generative legal process. By meticulously following formalized legal procedures, the court legitimates the collective – in the sense that the law acts in the name of, and with the authority of, the community – punishment of the one found guilty. The generative character of legal processes are explored further in the next section. Selective prosecutions, Koskenniemi argues, can be effective if supported by a range of restorative justice measures – public witnessing of trials, truth seeking, lustration, restitutive measures, and victim compensation.[341] Just how these transitional justice measures combine to produce lasting symbolic and community creating effects is not elaborated. In practice, selective prosecutions can divide rather than unify a community. Malamud Goti, who was responsible for prosecutions policy in the post-dictatorship

337 Koskenniemi 2002, o.c., p. 1.
338 See Chapter 3.4.3.
339 Koskenniemi 2002, o.c., p. 2.
340 L.E. Fletcher and H.M. Weinstein, 'Violence and Social Repair: Rethinking the Contribution of Justice to Reconciliation' (2002) 24 *Human Rights Quarterly* 573, at 580.
341 Koskenniemi 2002, o.c., p. 10.

Alfonsín government in 1985–6, argues the selective Junta trials in Argentina were divisive because they failed to meet the high expectations people had for post-dictatorship justice. Firstly, the trials reproduced a new bipolar vision of society by replacing the previous authoritarian divide between allies and enemies with one in which society was divided between the guilty and innocent. Secondly, neither side was pleased when 'not guilty' verdicts, by default, absolved the accused of any responsibility for the repression of the 'dirty war'. The convicted generals saw themselves as scapegoats while the human rights activists were disappointed because they had expected more convictions and tougher sentences.[342] Thirdly, the restricted scope of the trails resulted in history being re-invented by putting most of the blame for violence on the military.[343] As a consequence, the selective trials did not manage to provide a unifying account of what had happened and who had caused the suffering. Moreover, the pedagogical value of the trials was limited because the verdicts failed to engender community consensus about the repression or consolidate a rights-based democracy.[344] The military approached the trials as 'trials of rupture' in which there were two incompatible frameworks of interpretation.[345] If generating a moral consensus about justice is difficult for post-conflict national trials, it is even harder for international trials.[346]

Truth commissions have become a standard justice measure in transitional justice policy. When they first emerged in the 1980s in the context of democratic transitions in Latin America, they were known as 'commissions of inquiry' and were adopted as an alternative to trials prevented by amnesty laws. They were established as either national commissions by executives or parliaments, or as international commissions by the UN or regional bodies.[347] Their original goal was to provide some measure of redress for victims through truth and reparations with the aim of preventing repetition of violations by recommending institutional reforms and prosecutions, especially of the military and police. Increasingly, truth commission mandates explicitly included the 'right to truth' as their rationale.[348] The Guidance of Note of the UNSG (2010) describes truth commissions as 'an important step in realizing the right to the truth'.[349] In the UN 'Study on the Right to Truth' (2006), truth commissions are seen as a necessary complement to trials because they can contribute a broader

342 J.M. Goti, 'Dignity, Vengeance, and Fostering Democracy' (1998) 29 *The University of Miami Inter-American Law Review* 417, at 431.
343 Ibid., p. 449.
344 Ibid., p. 445.
345 Koskenniemi 2002, o.c., p. 27.
346 Koskenniemi 2002, o.c., p. 13.
347 N. Roht-Arriaza and M. Popkin, 'Truth as Justice Investigatory Commissions in Latin America' (1995) 20 *Law & Social Inquiry*, 79.
348 Klinkner and Davis 2020, o.c., p. 160.
349 'Guidance Note' 2010, o.c., p. 8.

perspective on the past and allow a higher level of public participation than selective prosecutions.[350] Yet the discourse of the 'right to truth' over-promises because the scope of truth is circumscribed by the truth commission mandate – the time period covered; the serious human rights violation to be investigated; whether or not the commission has legal powers of subpoena; the duration of the commission's mandate; and the resources allocated. Truth commissions have usually focused on the worst human rights violations.[351] For example, in Latin America the truth commissions focused on disappearance and extrajudicial killings, deniable crimes committed secretly and anonymously, making them difficult to investigate. The Chilean Commission on Truth and Reconciliation (Rettig Commission) Report, published in 1990, focused exclusively on the disappeared and those anonymously killed by extrajudicial acts and neglected the treatment of detainees. As Lagos observes, torture remained largely a private crime and difficult to mobilize public support around.[352] It was not until 2005, with the publication of the National Commission on Political Imprisonment and Torture Report (Valech Report), and its second report in 2011, that human rights violations against political detainees came onto the official human rights and reparations agenda.[353]

What has distinguished truth commissions as a justice measure is their victim-centred focus and their policy of victim participation. The internationally high profile South African Truth and Reconciliation Commission (SATRC) historically headlined the key role of the victim testimony in gaining access to the past through their recounted experience. It was hoped that once ordinary people – the 'beneficiaries' of apartheid – learn the truth about the crimes of apartheid committed in their name, it would engender moral outrage in them against their leaders, and hopefully remorse in the leaders, and realize national reconciliation.[354] However, the main importance of victim testimonies is not usually in the information they provide, but their performative role in the dramatic staging of the experience of repression for public witnessing. As already noted above, the performative role of the SATRC in realizing reconciliation was politically foregrounded to the neglect of the foundational role of CODESA, the political negotiations which had established it.[355] More accurately, the SATRC played the distinct and vital role as a dramatic ritual

---

350 'Study on the right to truth': Report of the Office of the United Nations High Commissioner for Human Rights, Geneva: UN, 8 February, 2006 E/CN.4/2006/91, 6.

351 Roht-Arriaza and Popkin 1995, o.c., p. 81.

352 Ibid., p. 84.

353 R. Lagos, '"To Never Again Live It, To Never Again Deny It": The Valech Report on Torture' in E.Q. Hutchison, et al. (eds.), *The Chile Reader: History, Culture, Politics*, Duke University Press, Durham, NC 2013, p. 588.

354 N. Sundar, 'Toward and anthropology of culpability' (2004) 31 *American Ethnologist* 145, at 149.

355 See Chapter 1.2.1.

of political passage publicly giving momentum to the enactment of CODESA by generating *communitas* – a shared experience of transition – through national witnessing of victim testimonies as an historical 'turning point'. Truth commissions have often functioned as transitory performative mechanisms to get around the institutional barriers to justice in transition and to meet the urgent need to engender a collective experience of things changing for the better through the public recognition of past injustice in its victims. The authority of truth commissions is usually embodied in an independent ethical figure, such as Bishop Desmond Tutu, who stood in for the as-yet-to-be renewed trust in the judiciary and justice system.

The dramatic staging of past violations through victim testimony and public witnessing is designed to engender public support for the truth commission recommendations which are not legally binding: the official report on past violations, the recognition of victims and reparations, the legislative and institutional reforms and accountability for perpetrators. They have also played a pedagogical role in promoting rights consciousness in the wider population and strengthening civil society.[356] Yet truth commissions, despite their high profile and promotion as essential justice measures, have been legally and politically constrained and in many cases failed to implement their recommendations. Reports include only the names of victims, not those of the perpetrators. Due process prevents victims' accusations without the opportunity of legal defence. Blame is often shared in an attempt to neutralize further politicization of the past. Parliaments block recommended reforms, delay reparations and compensation payments, and ignore recommendations to prosecute and leave amnesty laws in place. For example, in Colombia, the lack of progress in implementing the Final Agreement (2016) was reflected in a recommendation of the Truth Commission Report (2022) – with the not so optimistic title *Hay Futuro si hay Verdad* ('There is future if there is truth')[357] – to provide protection for human rights defenders from the ongoing political violence.[358] The Democratic Centre, the party of President Duque, dismissed the Report as an 'interpretive truth'.[359] In summary, truth commissions have played an important role as hinge mechanisms to reinforce the right to justice, but their recommendations have often been cherrypicked by governments who are

356 M.D. Paolantonio, 'A Memory of Justice as a Democratic Pedagogical Force' (2006) 28 *Review of Education, Pedagogy, and Cultural Studies* 141, at 152–1.

357 *Hay futuro, si hay verdad, informe final de la Comisión de la Verdad sobre el conflicto armado*, Comisión de la Verdad, Bogotá, 2022 https://www.comisiondelaverdad.co/hay-futuro-si-hay-verdad.

358 Stopping the escalating number of murders of social leaders since the Final Agreement (2016) is a priority of the new Colombian President Petro. M.J. Pizarro, 'After 50 years, could Colombia finally have awoken from its nightmare?' *The Guardian*, August 20, 2022.

359 J. Turkewitz and G. Glatsky, 'Colombia Panel's Report Is a Step Toward Mending a Civil War's Scars' *New York Times*, June 28, 2022.

much more likely to implement recommendations concerned with reparations and memorialization than those concerned with prosecutions.[360] However, the strength of truth commissions has been as a ritual of political passage which engenders *communitas* through collective witnessing victims' testimonies and sets out an agenda for redress and reform to prevent the repetition of extreme violations. The haunting truth commission promise of 'never again' foregrounds the imperatives for peace, but its performative truth is only a first step on the way to justice, not justice itself. In the absence of truth commissions, documentary film and dramatic fictional re-enactment have provided an alternative medium through which to dramatically stage the past for wide audiences. Surely, one of the most extraordinary examples of 'acting out' past atrocity as a way to educate the public about historically silenced events, occurs in the film 'Act of Killing' in which perpetrators dramatically re-enact their memory of their actual roles in the 1965 Communist massacres in Indonesia.[361] The dramatic re-enactment formed part of a longstanding human rights campaign to expose the scale of the 1965 massacres and to contest the official Cold War version of saving the nation from Communism.

2.3.3. TURNING POINTS: RITUAL TRANSFORMATION

The key transitional justice measures, trials, and truth commissions, have generative ritual structures constituted by three phases – segregation, liminality and incorporation. Their tripartite ritual structure functions as a cultural mechanism to renew the social order undermined by violence. Teitel's expression 'rituals of political passage' suggests the idea of the collective experiencing of transition. In Victor Turner's analysis of ritual, liminality creates the experience of transition as in-betweenness and generates *communitas*, the experiencing of liminality together as equal members of a community. The experience of *communitas* generated in justice rituals reinforces the expectation of equality before the law. The concepts liminality and *communitas* represent antistructure. '*Communitas* is of the now; structure is rooted in the past and extends into the future through language, law, and custom'.[362] The nature of the ritual experience of subjects is shaped by temporality, spatiality, and intensity. Liminality can be experienced by an individual, a social group – minority, cohort – or whole society. Its temporality can be for a moment – sudden event, a period – weeks, months, years, decades, an epoch or generations; and its spatiality can be a

360 O. Bakiner, 'Conclusion' in E. Skaar, et al. (eds.), *Latin American Experiences with Truth Commission Recommendations: Beyond Words, Vol. II*, Intersentia, Cambridge 2022, p. 485, at p. 489.

361 'The Act of Killing', Director: Joshua Oppenheimer, Final Cut for Real, (film) 2012.

362 Turner, V. 1969, o.c., p. 370.

threshold – house entrance, bodily opening, lines distinguishing pure/impure, an area – borders, nations, courts, or a country or region.[363] Justice measures seek to engender the experience of *communitas* to move the community into a new social order. Justice measures are performative rituals in two senses – they produce truth and justice through court verdicts and commission reports, and they generate an experience of *communitas* during the liminality engendered by the trial or truth commission process to achieve consensus as a positive outcome to bring closure. When there is no closure or outcome, individuals experience being stuck, trapped, or stranded in a state of unresolvable liminality and left with the experience of negative *communitas* motivated by resentment, envy, and hate. An opportunistic leader, the trickster in anthropological theory, can manipulate negative *communitas* to perpetuate, rather than resolve, the uncertainty and confusion of liminality.[364] Tricksters are not charismatic leaders, not truth-telling prophets, but the opposite, the outcast who has somehow captured power during highly liminal moments.

The transitional justice focus on atrocity crimes invites a Girardian perspective to understand the equation between accountability for crimes against humanity and peace. These justice measures seek to move societies from a state of war to a state of peace, from a state of disorder to order, from a state of violence to the rule of law. Girard's theory of the ritual scapegoat resolves the threat of contagious cycles of revenge killing and chaos through sacrifice of a random innocent victim. A taboo against killing is enforced by generating community agreement, solidarity, and unity – *communitas* – about who is to be blamed and punished. The ritual sacrifice of the scapegoat conferred the benefit of peace by unifying the community in their condemnation of the scapegoat. While the random selection of the victim is antithetical to modern criminal law's requirement for proof and the presumption of innocence, at a deeper level, Girard argues, a sacrificial structure underlies both conceptual pairs of taboo/sacrifice and law/punishment. The exceptions to the principle of random selection of the scapegoat and to the requirement for proof and presumption of innocence reveal the shared sacrificial structure in both conceptual pairs. The principle of random selection of the sacrificial victim often masked the practice of targeting individuals from the margins of society – a surrogate figure from a group routinely blamed for immorality, criminality and causing social disorder.[365] What distinguished the 'marginal' scapegoat was their impotence to avenge the punishment of the collective. In the case of criminal justice, exceptions made

---

363 B. Thomassen, 'Thinking with Liminality: To the Boundaries of an Anthropological Concept' in A. Horvath, et al. (eds.), *Breaking Boundaries: Varieties of Liminality*, Berghahn Books 2015, p. 39, at p. 48.

364 Ibid., p. 53.

365 R. Van Damme, 'The Presumption of Innocence: an Antidote for Sacrificial Venom? Patterns of Girard's 'Primitive' Sacred in Late Medieval and Early Modern Criminal Law' (2016) 45 *Netherlands Journal of Legal Philosophy* 10, at 14.

to the principles of proof and presumptions of innocence through profiling and suspicion as modes of governance also expose an underlying sacrificial structure in normal justice. For example, suspicion of involvement in a terrorist plot has justified legal torture – the ticking bomb scenario – and criminal profiling – the algorithmic driven 'usual suspect' – producing the over-representation of minority populations in prison; or pre-emptive punishment of particular groups by police – the Black Lives Matter movement denounced the disproportionate killing of African Americans by police in the United States.

The rationale of transitional justice trials in punishing extreme violence – crimes against humanity signify the threat of systemic violence to the very foundation of social life – parallels sacrifice for the transgression of the taboo on killing as a threatening contagion. Both sacrifice and punishment for murder/mass murder are mechanisms to unify everyone against the individual blamed/found guilty – the community against the scapegoat in ritual sacrifice and humanity against the individual found guilty of serious violations of IHL and IHRL in trials. Crimes against humanity are framed as taboos, behaviour universally condemned as such serious violations of civilizational standards, codified in IHL and IHRL, that they generate international moral revulsion. Mark Osiel argues that 'liberal law enshrines a species of taboo on atrocity, one that may be threatened by forthright exploration of the facts surrounding administrative massacre'.[366] Criminal law, he argues, does not just prohibit these acts, 'it imposes a kind of ritual avoidance of their detailed examination'.[367] Atrocities are denounced and distanced as evil or incomprehensible acts which cannot be truly legally translated for risk of rendering them intelligible and thus normalized. Disaggregating specific acts by individuals against individuals misconceives 'the nature of the wrong in a way to diminish its full horror and heinousness'.[368] Both trials and truth commissions, by revealing the truth about the predecessor regime's repression, aim to provoke public moral outrage and thereby engender consensus and solidarity about guilt and the taboo transgressed. But they are equally likely to divide as unify. They can generate negative *communitas* – the experience of unresolvable liminality. In post-dictatorship Argentina, the facts revealed in the *Nunca Más* Report about the Junta's policy of enforced disappearance, failed to generate a new national consensus about the 'evil' of the dictatorship. In particular, the Argentine officer corps believed that the Report had made them scapegoats and the subsequent selective prosecution of senior military for their role in the 'dirty war' only reinforced their sense of victimization.[369]

366 M.J. Osiel, 'Why Prosecute – Critics of Punishment for Mass Atrocity' (2000) 22 *Human Rights Quarterly* 118, at 146.

367 Ibid., p. 146.

368 Ibid., p. 121.

369 D. Beard 'Ex-Leaders on Trial Defended for 'Trying to Save' Argentine' *Chicago Tribune*, May 26, 1985, https://www.chicagotribune.com/news/ct-xpm-1985-05-26-8502020506-story.html.

They responded to the Report by publishing their own counter-narrative of the 'dirty war' in an unofficial report.[370] From the military's perspective, the CONADEP truth commission and the subsequent trials functioned as scapegoating rituals by placing the burden of guilt on them thereby unburdening society – especially their supporters, collaborators and the bystanders – of collective guilt. Both ritual sacrifice and criminal justice distinguish between the pure and legitimate violence of sacrifice and punishment on the one hand, and the impure and illegal violence of transgression on the other.[371] Both operate on a triangle of transgression, damage, and causality articulated through their own rationality to produce truth through a carefully managed ritual process.[372]

These rituals of sacrifice and justice are performative mechanisms designed to end violence, generate community consensus about who is to blame, and affirm the taboo/norm transgressed. However, Girard argues that in the age of disenchantment, the sacrificial scapegoating mechanism has broken down and must be constantly repeated to renew its effects. As highlighted above, the performative efficacy of trials and truth commissions is uncertain. The four pillars model provides a multifaceted solution to performative uncertainty of the justice measures by reinforcing retributive justice with restorative justice measures to achieve broader transitional justice goals. But just how these measures combine to produce lasting effects is not well theorized. In fact, the emphasis on the performative character of these hinge transition rituals, masks their aspirational character and mistakes their enactment for the realization of their goals. Outcomes such as trial verdicts, truth commission reports and recommendations for reparations for entitled victims need to be implemented and reinforced if they are to produce lasting effects.

To theorize the efficacy of ritual performativity, another processual model concerned with the construction of critical events as paths for social transformation is drawn upon. Robin Wagner-Pacifici's method of political semiosis identifies the constitutive processes behind the construction of events as turning points. 'Events' are crystallized from the temporal flow of singular acts into an historic event. Emblematic acts of political violence dominate historical events. These range from single acts, such as political assassinations, massacres and terrorist acts, to largescale serial acts produced by mass repression under authoritarian regimes, civil wars or interstate wars. Political semiosis distinguishes between performative, demonstrative and representational acts. Recognition of the ritual structure of transitional justice mechanisms allows us to differentiate between constitutive moments – performative acts – and the mechanisms designed to generate lasting outcomes, e.g. the legitimacy

370 Osiel 2000, o.c., p. 146.
371 Van Damme 2016, o.c., p. 16.
372 Ibid., p. 14.

of the verdict and the punishment, the collective consensus around meaning (culpability for violence) and the institutionalization of the official narrative (memory law, memorialization). The method of political semiosis identifies the constitutive processes behind event construction. Justice rituals involve event construction through the lens of criminal law and, by recognizing their constitutive constituting elements, we can avoid the misrecognition of symbolic performative acts – trial verdicts, commission reports – as a step in the larger process of implementation and normalization.

2.3.4. TURNING POINTS: EVENT ANALYSIS AND POLITICAL SEMIOSIS

The transitional justice four pillars model constructs transition as the product of performative mechanisms which this book refers to these as 'justice measures'. These measures have a tripartite ritual structure moving between three stages – separation, liminality and reaggregation. As legal rituals, they produce closure through the application of the logic of proof, procedures, and adjudication. In other words, trials function as legal rituals with strict procedures and scripts staged as legal dramas to produce a legal truth and closure. Truth commissions stage truth-seeking dramas focused on victim testimonies to produce an official report about human rights violations and the identity of victims. But justice measures are also supposed to generate wider lasting social effects such as the rule of law, reconciliation, democratic government and social inclusion. What if they don't? What if truth –based on legal proof or victim testimony– does not unify the community but divide it; a court decision does not engender trust in the rule of law; reparations recognize only selected victims; or prosecutions engender resentment as scapegoating or victors' justice? What is to be done? Repeat the rituals – more trials of offenders, more hearings and more victim testimonies, strengthen legal technologies, legalize more rights, expand judicialization at the international level, rescale justice under universal jurisdiction and legal norms. In other words, the performative thrust of justice measures can become stuck in the liminal phase and fail to achieve their desired wider goals.

In anthropology, rituals are paradigmatic social events intended to generate change.[373] An event is an assembly of actions which are given a socially constructed set of meanings circulated in the form of a narrative, often in competition with other narrative constructions of events.[374] An 'event' is framed by a particular social and political context and constructed in a narrative that unifies 'a number

[373] D. Hoffman and S. Lubkemann, 'Warscape Ethnography in West Africa and the Anthropology of "Events"' (2005) 78 *Anthropological Quarterly* 315, at 324.

[374] Griffin 1993, o.c., p. 1098.

of past or contemporaneous actions and happenings … into a coherent relational whole' and 'are made up of the raw materials of sequences of social action … in a particular temporal order for a particular purpose'.[375] Historical narratives have a beginning, a middle, and an end constructed as sequences of events which give them force and direction.[376] Rituals, as paradigmatic social events, are temporal markers delineating a before and after signifying either rupture or continuity. They may be used to re-stabilize disrupted social relations, or they may seek to produce new social practices, relations, and subjectivities.[377]

Transitional justice rituals are social events concerned with re-establishing social order based on principles of justice. They can be conceptualized as special legal mechanisms for 'event construction' designed to produce 'significant and durable transformational effects'.[378] Large-scale violence is constructed as an legal 'event' assembled in a chronological sequence of acts with a causal narrative structure. The fulcrum of transitional justice rituals are historical violent events constructed through the interpretative framework of the law – IHL and IHRL. The historical violent events transitional justice rituals are concerned with are the most extreme and socially destructive forms of political violence. They focus on high profile events –assassinations, massacres– or state policies of repression – disappearance, extrajudicial killings, torture, massacres – to construct the meaning of those events in a larger sequence of violent events characterized as periods of pervasive violence –a dictatorship, civil war, or revolution. In Latin America, socially cataclysmic violent events that become universally recognized as historical turning points in collective memory have been signified by the suffix 'azo', for example 'Bogotazo' and 'Caracazo'.[379] In practice, transitional justice translates as crimes acts of extreme violence that have already galvanized public attention, shaped political subjectivities and identities, and generated multiple meanings from the perspective of competing interpretive frameworks.[380] Such dramatic events are widely recognized as crisis events and readily become

375 Griffin 1993, o.c., p. 1097.

376 P. Ricoeur, *Time and Narrative*, University of Chicago Press, Chicago, IL 1984.

377 Hoffman and Lubkemann 2005, o.c., p. 323.

378 R. Wagner-Pacifici, 'Theorizing the Restlessness of Events' (2010) 115 *American Journal of Sociology* 1351, at 1356.

379 Bogotazo refers to the massive riots and urban destruction that followed the assassination in Bogotá, Colombia of Liberal leader and presidential candidate Jorge Eliécer Gaitán on April 9, 1948. The Caracazo is the name given to the wave of protests, riots and looting that started on February 27, 1989 in Guarenas and spread to Caracas. The riots were a response to the brutal repression of protests against neoliberal policies and their impact on an already impoverished marginalized urban population.

380 See Chapter 3 for an analysis of the galvanizing political impact of the assassination of PM Rafik Hariri in Lebanon in 2005. Also, the South African Truth and Reconciliation Commission organized 'event hearings' around events already embedded in the collective memory of repression under the apartheid government – e.g. The 1976 Soweto student uprising; The killing of the 'Gugulethu Seven'; 'The 1992 Bisho Massacre. Truth and Reconciliation Commission of South Africa Report', Macmillan Reference, London, 1999.

constructed as turning points because of their 'generative capacity'.[381] The legal interpretive framework of transitional justice is applied to historical violent events as a superior lens to produce truth based on their claim to objectivity and neutrality. Justice measures inscribe and displace violence through the legal construction of violent events to re-establish state legality and legitimacy. This Section seeks to firstly, recognize the ongoing constitutive process of legal event construction through the method of political semiosis, and secondly, recognize the competing interpretive frameworks of event construction with their distinct liminalities, temporalities and narrativization deployed alongside transitional justice.

Political semiosis identifies three constitutive elements in the construction of historical events: 'a performative feature, a demonstrative feature and a representational feature'.[382] Every transition requires 'a speech act or its performative equivalent that materially changes the world'[383]; a demonstrative act which orients parties in a particular context to 'get their bearings in ongoing situations as relations and identities are in the process of transformation'.[384] Representational acts which mimetically reproduce the event for circulation to wider audiences in order to 'stabilize and sediment the historical transition in the face of uncertainty, distance, and resistance'.[385] Performative, demonstrative and representational acts are all essential for constitution of the historical (violent) event, to orient social actors in context and to circulate a copy to make the event live beyond its occurrence and to have transformative and lasting social effects. An act can also have multiple constitutive aims. A performative act can, at the same time, serve as a demonstrative act – a trial's performative verdict of guilty of crimes against humanity at the same time demonstratively instructs the audience about the wider context of illegality and illegitimacy of the regime. Political semiosis provides a framework to capture 'the restless conveyance of power and meaning in the eventful constitution of history'.[386] In transitional justice, the key performative acts are the justice measures – trials and truth commissions – concerned with serious violations of IHL and IHRL. They produce verdicts and official truth. In the process they are also demonstrative, orienting the community through the interpretive framework of the law to identify which facts are important and how to understand their meaning. Once justice measures have produced their truth, the official version (or legal memory) of the past is circulated through representational narrativization designed to consolidate the

---

381 Hoffman and Lubkemann 2005, o.c., p. 325.

382 Wagner-Pacifici 2010, o.c., p. 1358.

383 Ibid., p. 1358.

384 Ibid., pp. 1359–60. But performative acts have to be acknowledged to be effective. 'The effectiveness of performative speech acts depends on their uptake by social agents (both individual and collective) in structured but essentially open social worlds.'

385 Ibid., p. 1362.

386 Ibid., p. 1358.

outcomes of trials and truth commissions – most commonly these involve forms of memorialization and commemoration. Representational acts themselves signify a radical break with the predecessor regime's violent censorship.[387] While transitional justice rituals are mechanisms designed to enact transition and produce closure, historical violent events remain potentially 'restless events'. A brief example of the application of political semiosis with respect to the phenomenon of disappearance and transitional justice follows.

Michel de Certeau describes writing history as a 'sepulchre' because it 'exorcizes death by inserting it into discourse'.[388] It offers 'soil and a tomb to the dead of the past'.[389] The 'disappeared' became the emblematic absent dead in the transitional justice project because they embodied the erasure of rights, the social trauma of survivors not knowing what happened, and the legal limbo of the disappeared between life and death. Justice measures construct a legal sepulchre to recover the forgotten dead victims, excluded or expelled by the predecessor regime as subversives/enemies, by resuscitating them in a legal narrative about repression.[390] The metaphor of the sepulchre captures the extreme physical and social exclusion of the disappeared, discarded as anonymous victims in clandestine graves. Before they can be made physically visible through exhumation and forensic examination, the disappeared must first become legally visible by strengthening their human rights in international law and the obligation of the state to investigate their disappearance and punish the perpetrators. The mobilization of surviving family and human rights advocates has focused on rescaling justice demands to establish legal remedies under IHL and IHRL – to make prosecutions possible by challenging impunity. The performative potential for justice measures was gradually strengthened by the development of transitional justice soft law and later hard law. In 1986, the IACtHR, in its first decision, addressed the rights of victims of disappearance in the Velásquez Rodríguez case. The Court alleged that the detention and subsequent disappearance of a Honduran student, Angel Manfredo Velásquez Rodríguez by the government of Honduras had violated Articles 4, 5 and 7 of the American Convention of Human Rights.[391] It became a landmark case in the development of IACtHR jurisprudence on the disappeared by the strengthening the rights of the disappeared and their surviving families – the right to know the fate of the disappeared and their right to reparations for harm and loss – in

---

387 E.S. Clemens, 'Toward a Historicized Sociology: Theorizing Events, Processes, and Emergence' (2007) 33 *Annual Review of Sociology* 527, at 541.

388 M. De Certeau, *The Writing of History*, Columbia University Press, New York, NY 1988, p. 100.

389 P. Ricoeur, *Memory, History, Forgetting*, University of Chicago Press, Chicago, IL 2004, p. 369.

390 De Certeau 1988, o.c., p. 47.

391 S.M. Witten, 'Velásquez Rodríguez Case' (1989) 83 *American Journal of International Law*, 361.

transitional justice soft law and eventually hard law.[392] In Latin America, the disappeared became a symbol of the policy of coordinated state terror.[393] The Inter-American Convention on Forced Disappearance of Persons (IACFDP) (1994) followed by the International Convention for the Protection of All Persons from Enforced Disappearance (ICPPED) (2006) established hard lawmaking enforced disappearance a crime against humanity.[394] The legal sepulchre built for the disappeared in Latin America provided the legal scaffolding for local Spanish exhumation movements to challenge the democratic transition Pact of Forgetting (1977) that had consigned the disappeared of the Spanish Civil War to oblivion.[395]

Exhumation and reburial of the disappeared contribute to the performative, demonstrative and representational features of the legal construction of disappearance. Exhumation re-signifies the remains of the disappeared by materially bringing the past into the present; by forensically establishing the cause and circumstances of their deaths; and by reinserting them as individuals into a new inclusive historical narrative about repression. Exhumation of the remains plays an important role in engendering *communitas* in the surviving families and witnessing public as participants in the process of discovery. Exhumation and reburial are also demonstrative acts framing the remains as evidence of a crime, establishing the fate of individual victims and their identities, and engendering public empathy for the suffering of the surviving families. But while memory is the key to the mobilization of surviving families to claim rights and seek legal remedies, memorialization of the recovered remains of the disappeared can be divisive because mourning is individualizing and tends to be depoliticizing. At a minimum, families want personal closure of their mourning by being able to recover, identify, and privately rebury the remains of their disappeared member. Reparations are also almost always awarded to individuals – surviving family members – not communities. In Argentina, the Mothers of the Plaza de Mayo split over a dispute about the ethics of families accepting reparations and recovered remains for reburial when most of the disappeared were yet to be found. The dissenting mothers rejected reparations and the remains because they saw the official recognition of victimhood as individualizing and depoliticizing. They wanted to collectively remember the disappeared by building a monument with all their names inscribed to keep alive the political idealism of the disappeared,

---

392 Klinkner and Davis 2020, o.c.

393 The discovery of the Operation Condor files revealed the conspiracy between the military dictatorships to repress each other's citizens during the 1970s and 1980s. J.P. McSherry, 'Operation Condor: Clandestine Inter-American System' (1999) 26 *Social Justice*, 144.

394 T. Scovazzi and G. Citroni, *The Struggle Against Enforced Disappearance and the 2007 United Nations Convention*, Martinus Nijhoff Publishers, Leiden 2007. See also 'International Convention for the Protection of All Persons from Enforced Disappearance', A/RES/61/177, December 20, 2006.

395 See Chapter 4.4.2. on the role of exhumation movements in Spain.

not to just remember their deaths.[396] The Mothers also wanted to continue their weekly demonstrations in the Plaza de Mayo, a ritual they had initiated during the dictatorship with the aim of finding the disappeared. Because the disappeared became the emblematic victim of transitional justice in Latin America, the claims of the families of the disappeared have often eclipsed and marginalized the claims of other victims of historical injustice. In Chile, the focus of the Rettig Report of the National Commission for Truth and Reconciliation (1991) on the families of the disappeared as 'innocents' – deserving – marginalized the rights claims of political detainees who were seen as undeserving – not innocent.[397] By contrast, in Colombia the disappeared have been a problematic category in the peace process because they could not be uniformly treated as a symbols of state repression. The temporality of the conflict over 50 years, the multiple sources of violence, and the diversity of violent actors has meant that the families of the disappeared were unable to collectively mobilize around historical injustice of state repression and found it difficult to gain official recognition as a victim of enforced disappearance for the purposes of reparations.[398]

In summary, transitional justice measures serve as performative rituals to generate broader social transformation. The fulcrum of these hinge rituals is extreme violence – crimes against humanity – whose unquestionable transgressive horror is seen as a key to engendering community consensus and solidarity to condemn those responsible. These performative justice measures establish what serious crimes were committed; who was responsible; what punishment they should receive; who was harmed; and the reparations they should receive. The force of trials or truth commissions depends on their ability to generate *communitas* expressed as community consensus and unity over their outcomes. But for these justice measures to produce lasting effects, they must move beyond the aspirational and symbolic moment of liminality to institutionalize and normalize the values, rights and law that the justice measures are supposed to uphold. The ritual process can get stuck in the liminal stage for many different reasons: trials are undermined by witness intimidation; truth commission recommendations are not implemented; and the judicial process is delegitimized by opponents' counter-narratives.

The same axial event can be co-opted to generate distinct transition narratives from the perspective of different interpretive frameworks with different temporalities. Lack of progress in one transition narrative – stalled liminality – may look different in another. Take the case of political transition to democracy

---

396 M.E. Burchianti, 'Building Bridges of Memory: The Mothers of the Plaza de Mayo and the Cultural Politics of Maternal Memories' (2004) 15 *History and Anthropology*, 133.

397 B. Loveman and E. Lira, 'Truth, Justice, Reconciliation, and Impunity as Historical Themes: Chile, 1814–2006' (2007) 97 *Radical History Review* 43, at 61–4.

398 M. Humphrey, 'The political lives of the 'disappeared' in the transition from conflict to peace in Colombia' (2018) 19 *Politics, Religion & Ideology*, 452.

after a very repressive military dictatorship in Argentina (1976–1983) and the struggle for accountability for dictatorship era crimes. The same axial event, the atrocities of the Argentine dictatorship, generated at least two competing transition narratives, framed by a distinct legal and political interpretive lens. The first was the criminal justice narrative about the post-dictatorship struggle for criminal accountability for dictatorship era atrocities; the second, the historical narrative about the long struggle for civilian government control over the military. In these narratives the 'transition' has three phases. The first phase (1983–1986) saw the new Alfonsín government initiate transitional justice measures to investigate and prosecute dictatorship era crimes. The second phase (1986–2003), saw the national trials blocked by amnesty laws and, in response, saw the families of the disappeared and human rights advocates rescale their pursuit of justice in the IACtHR and the UN human rights bodies. The third phase (post-2003), saw the amnesty laws annulled and the Kirchner government reactivate prosecutions of dictatorship era crimes.

The criminal justice narrative recounts the long struggle for accountability for dictatorship era crimes. In 1983, the new democratic Alfonsín government used its strong human rights mandate to establish a truth commission (CONADEP) to investigate the fate of the disappeared and then to launch trials of senior military leaders. However, in 1986, in the face of a threatened military rebellion, Alfonsín introduced two amnesty laws (Full Stop Law 1986 and Due Obedience Law 1987) to stop further trials stalling transitional justice. President Menem, Alfonsín's successor, consolidated the military's impunity by pardoning those convicted in the Junta Trials. Blocked in their search for justice by the amnesty laws, the families of the disappeared and human rights advocates turned to the IACHR and UN human rights system to gain recognition for their rights claims. Their international pursuit of justice for the disappeared in the IACHR and IACtHR helped put the serious violations of the Latin American dictatorships on the international human rights agenda and themselves in the vanguard of the development of transitional justice mechanisms and law – Argentina became a signatory to the IACFDP in 1994.[399] The strengthening of human rights protection at the domestic and international levels opened the way for human rights trials to recommence in 2005 under the Kirchner government.[400] The Kirchner government was a strong supporter of the human rights movement and revised the narrative of blame from the 'two demons' to the 'military' as perpetrators of 'genocide'.[401] The criminal justice narrative

399 'ARGENTINA: Legal Memorandum, The Full Stop and Due Obedience Laws, Submitted by Amnesty International and the International Commission of Jurists', *Amnesty International*, December 2003, AMR 13/018/2003.

400 'Argentina: Events of 2021', World Report 2022, Human Rights Watch, https://www.hrw.org/world-report/2022/country-chapters/argentina.

401 Humphrey and Valverde 2016, o.c., p. 132.

demanded accountability for all human rights violations based on the rule of law. Reconciliation was never part of the human rights movement's discourse in Argentina nor was apology ever part of the military's perspective on the 'dirty war'.[402] The military and its supporters continue to question the legitimacy of the trials as partisan – victors' justice, they reject the classification 'crimes against humanity' because they deny there was ever a systematic policy of repression, and they dispute the number (30,000) of disappeared as exaggerated.[403]

The military/civilian government narrative is concerned with democratization and the strengthening of the rule of law in Argentina. The challenge of the return to democracy in 1983 was how to prevent further military coups – the 20th century had seen six coups in 1930, 1943, 1955, 1962, 1966 and 1976.[404] The new Alfonsín government was initially able to assert civilian authority over the military by holding them criminally accountable for their actions during the 'dirty war'. The Junta Trials were possible because the military's legitimacy had been seriously weakened by the disastrous Malvinas war preventing them from negotiating self-impunity in exchange for their return to barracks, as the Uruguayan military had done.[405] The truth commission and trials functioned as hinge rituals which repudiated the military coup and enforced the rule of law to help consolidate the Alfonsín government's democratic authority. However, after the conviction of the most senior military leaders the military grew restless because they feared more extensive prosecutions through the ranks. In response, President Alfonsín was forced to introduce amnesty laws to stop further trials. President Menem, Alfonsín's successor, made peace with the military by pardoning convicted military leaders and forgiving them for their actions in the 'dirty war'. Menem's policy of government reconciliation with the military proved instrumental in their submission to civilian government.[406] He set out to change the internal security focus of the military through initiatives such as their international engagement in UN peacekeeping missions.[407] Menem's accommodation with the military, McSherry argues, was also a strategic partnership to contain popular resistance to his neoliberal economic policies.[408] After the major economic crisis of 2001/2, the new pro-human rights President, Néstor Kirchner, reopened the Junta Trials after Congress annulled the amnesty

---

402 M.D. Goransky, 'Dictatorship Trials and Reconciliation in Argentina' (2018) *FICHL Policy Brief Series*, 1.

403 Ibid.

404 The first four were interim dictatorships while the last two were established as permanent bureaucratic-authoritarian states.

405 See Chapter 2 the Naval Club Pact (1984) and the Expiry Law (1986).

406 Goransky 2018, o.c., p. 2.

407 K.J. Worboys, 'The Traumatic Journey from Dictatorship to Democracy: Peacekeeping Operations and Civil-Military Relations in Argentina, 1989–1999' (2007) 33 *Armed Forces and Society*, 149.

408 J.P. McSherry, 'Strategic Alliance: Menem and the Military-Security Forces in Argentina' (1997) 24 *Latin American Perspectives*, 63.

laws and the Supreme Court had declared them unconstitutional. The Court also struck down the pardons ex-President Menem had granted former convicted military officers.[409] The recommencement of the Junta Trials in 2005 confirmed the successful subordination of the military to civilian authority – 3,493 people were charged, 1,030 convicted, and 159 acquitted of dictatorship era crimes between 2005 and 2021.[410] While there has been a reconciliation between the civilian government and the military, the trials have not produced a consensus about the past between the former protagonists – now the human rights movement and the military.

In these narratives, the role of trials change emphasis across these three stages. In the first stage, trials function as hinge rituals underpinning democratic transition and contrasting the legality of the successor regime and the illegality of the predecessor regime. In the third stage, trials are about the normalization of the rule of law. They assert the superior value of the law in resolving conflicts, the principle of equality before the law and the restorative function of trials. Trials deliver justice to victims in the form of punishment, recognition and reparations. The human rights movement and families have also used the revived trials to morally condemn the Junta by seeking to have them convicted for the worst of all crimes, genocide, through the *querellante* system of plaintiff-prosecutor.[411]

Political semiosis allows us to identify the constitutive features of the multifaceted transitional justice model of the four pillars. In other words, political semiosis helps us understand the relationship between retributive justice and restorative justice measures in producing lasting effects. The headlining of justice measures as performative moments creates the impression that transition has a ritually bounded temporality. Transitions are conceived as moments of rupture and 'instances of strategic action and negotiation' during which immediate accountability was 'imperative because the co-existence of crisis, democratic enthusiasm and new groupings like victim organizations created opportunities that were not possible in ordinary times'.[412] From this perspective, delayed or post-transitional justice signifies a lost opportunity. But McAuliffe questions whether trials and truth commissions really serve as catalysts in transition, arguing that delayed justice is preferable when the political and legal institutions are weak.[413] While the point that the temporality of transitional justice needs to be extended beyond regime transition is well made, the analysis misses the generative potential of transitional justice measures which are embedded

409 *Argentina: Events of 2021*, World Report 2022, Human Rights Watch, https://www.hrw.org/world-report/2022/country-chapters/argentina.
410 Goransky 2018, o.c., p. 1.
411 O'Donnell 2009, o.c., p. 334.
412 P. McAuliffe, 'Transitional Justice, Institutions and Temporality: Towards a Dynamic Understanding' (2021) 21 *International Criminal Law Review* 817, at 823.
413 Ibid., p. 825.

over time through their institutionalization. What McAuliffe describes as the incremental development of state institutions is the ongoing embedding of a model of normalization initiated by the justice measures.

A key representational feature of transitional justice is the institutionalization of collective memory. The generation of an official truth needs to be consolidated through processes of collective memorialization. Transitional justice measures provide a technology for the translation of violence/trauma into a neutral discourse and translate traumatic experience and memory into an official narrative. The need for the state to establish the official historical narrative as hegemonic is also a defensive act to prevent its destabilization by counter memories surviving in the traumatic experience of individuals and communities, or amongst its political opponents as historical denial. Memory laws have been used to sanction counter memories seen as particularly threatening – e.g. to prevent historical denial of the Holocaust or the Armenian Holocaust. The dead are a particularly potent source of symbolization for reconstituting the past in the present. But unlike war memorials that commemorate the dead as patriotic sacrifice, the commemoration of victims of repression cannot render survival meaningful.[414] The role of truth commissions identifying and registering the names of victims of repression, mimicking the democratisation of dead soldiers through their inscription on war memorials, serves as a collective indictment of the wrongs of the predecessor regime. But the suffering of survivors cannot be redeemed in such a transient political project. Instead, it is in the victimhood engendered through the shared experience of trauma that endures as a source of identity and motivation for justice.

2.4. CONCLUSION

Transitional justice is an expression of the evolution of modern international law from its 19th century perspective on the European prerogative of sovereignty, to the sovereignty creating role with the dismantling of empires, to the protection of individuals against abuses of state sovereignty. It is an instrument of external state making that has dominated the 20th century and now 21st century. However, its vision of the role of justice in producing global liberal governance through the integration of states signing onto soft international law and hard international law is not theoretically very developed. Transitional justice intervenes in conflicts with particular genealogies as well as political cultures to manage conflict and bring closure on largescale violence. Elites often resist

414 R. Koselleck, 'War Memorials: Identity Formations of the Survivors' in R. Koselleck (ed.), *The Practice of Conceptual History: Timing History, Spacing Concepts*, Stanford University Press, Stanford, CA 2002, p. 285, at p. 287.

transitional justice measures by asserting sovereignty through measures such as amnesty laws or by subverting transitional justice measures included in political agreements.

Transitional justice is a generative project concerned with producing legal norms as the foundation of the post-conflict social order. Legally, transitional justice promotes post-conflict justice by re-establishing state legality and legitimacy through the harmonization of domestic law with international norms. Politically, transitional justice is integral to the post-Cold War project of liberal global governance in which international law is used to vertically integrate the rehabilitated state. Its focus on atrocity justice – justice for the worst possible (non-derogable) crimes – requires the harmonization of domestic law with IHL and IHRL. The challenge in post-conflict states is their institutional capacity to deliver justice after the judiciary and the law have been weakened through arbitrary repression and impunity. The characterization of transitional justice as a technology – a toolbox – suggests the solution to conflict is the establishment of legal norms and their enforcement. The idea of law as technology is reinforced by the superior authority of international law and logic of rescaling to establish legal norms. This narrow conception of law as the enforcement of norms mistakes the discourse of the rule of law for a much complex and ongoing generative process. Transitional justice is an emancipatory discourse expressed through victims' human rights claiming beyond the state for the administration of justice according to international norms – in domestic or international courts. Human rights claiming by victims and human rights advocates pursues the legalization of human rights to make them justiciable. Rights claiming is generative through the process of crystallization and normalization as soft law in UN human rights reports, declarations, guidance notes. The legalistic and mandatory language of soft law creates momentum towards the consolidation of norms and principles as either customary international law – general consent – or as hard law institutionalized in human rights treaties. In practice, most transitional justice norms persist as soft law and never become hard law. The emancipatory character of human rights changes between the transition and post-transition phases from the victim rights claiming and mobilizing moment to the administration of justice on the basis of international norms. The former embraces the generative processes underlying legalization – grasping the opportunities for civil society participation in international lawmaking – while the latter is about ensuring states meet their obligations under customary international law and as signatories to human rights treaties.

The multifaceted four pillars model is also better understood as a generative model rather than a toolkit. The relationship between retributive and restorative justice measures is both generative and interdependent, not simply alternatives or substitutes. Justice measures are performative legal acts. They establish a legal truth about past violence, deliver verdicts, and produce authoritative reports. However, they need to be contextualized by demonstrative acts and reinforced by representational acts to have lasting effects. Transitional justice, given transitional context, seeks to re-establish legal norms as well as enforce them. Consequently, it has a stronger symbolic lawmaking emphasis more than an instrumental one. Justice measures employ the cultural mechanism of scapegoating to focus guilt on particular individuals – the leaders or the worst offenders – thereby unburdening the rest of society and, through the trial ritual, generating a community consensus and identity (*communitas*) about guilt. But the success of transitional justice in translating political violence into atrocity justice depends on its ability to establish itself as the prevailing interpretive framework. In fact, at transition, there are multiple competing interpretive frameworks with different temporalities and political constituencies. The event-focused and individualized perspectives of atrocity justice identifying victims and perpetrators is primarily concerned with the abuse of state power. However, those events can be articulated in narratives with different temporalities related to the genealogy of conflict which include the history of external state-making and the unresolved conflicts relating to political identity, community and the distribution of power present at the state's foundation.

CHAPTER 3
URUGUAY
Amnesty, Democracy and Reconciliation

3.1. INTRODUCTION

The transitional justice project emerges at the end of the Cold War as a mechanism to support the consolidation of global liberal governance through the expansion of international law. In Latin America, its focus was the violent legacy of Cold War counterinsurgency policies of the authoritarian military regimes, established by coups during the 1960s and 1970s, which were backed by the US National Security Doctrine. The regional military dictatorships had convincingly defeated their local leftist insurgencies using severe repression which included the deniable crimes of forced disappearance and extrajudicial killing to terrorize their populations into submission. When the region's militaries eventually withdrew from power, either because they had been discredited or had negotiated comfortable agreements with elites, they were able to dictate the terms of democratic transition which invariably included amnesty laws. In the Uruguayan case, the military, who had come to power following a creeping coup in 1973, negotiated a pact with political party leaders (Naval Club Pact 1984) on the condition of amnesty and amnesia. The Pact closely resembled the Spanish transition Pact of Forgetting (1977). During Phase II transitional justice the policies of amnesty and amnesia were justified as necessary to achieve peace through democratic consolidation and national reconciliation.[415] Another important factor constraining criminal accountability was the lack of effective international judicial remedies for largescale political crimes at this time. The international codification of human rights was in its early stages; the key human rights treaties were only just coming into force; and most countries in the region only became parties to the America Convention on Human Rights in the 1980s.[416] Moreover, the ICC was only established in 1998 and the IACtHR

---

415 Teitel 2003, o.c., p. 71.

416 N. Roht-Arriaza, 'After Amnesties are Gone: Latin American National Courts and the new Contours of the Fight Against Impunity' (2015) 37 *Human Rights Quarterly* 341, at 348.

did not hear its first case until 1986.[417] In Uruguay, human rights activists and victim families faced an additional barrier to justice, the political authority of democratic consensus in settling contentious issues. Direct democracy was a key ritual of political passage in Uruguay which determined the transition process and the scope of transitional justice policy. Three popular consultations were pivotal in the transition process, which were all defeated. The first was the constitutional plebiscite held on November 30, 1980 through which the military sought to install themselves in power above parliament. The second was the citizen-initiated referendum to repeal the amnesty law held on April 16, 1989. The third was the citizen-initiated plebiscite to repeal the amnesty law 20 years later, on October 25, 2009. This chapter explores the role of rituals of political passage in Uruguay in generating a consensus about transition, democratic restoration, justice, and political legitimacy in Uruguay.

In Uruguay, and in Latin America more broadly, amnesty laws enacted during democratic transitions in the 1980s and 1990s were criticized by the international human rights community as the failure of states to provide human rights protection and to meet their obligation to investigate human rights violations under international law. But the amnesty laws were more than a failure of legality; they disabled the performative character of justice measures – trials and truth commissions – as rituals of political passage to enact transition by generating a community consensus about wrongdoers, wrongdoing and victims. In other words, by sidelining these transitional justice mechanisms, the policy of amnesty and amnesia blocked the performative potential of truth and justice rituals, to generate a national consensus about the past framed by human rights norms. In Uruguay elections and plebiscites were prioritized over truth and justice measures as the rituals of political passage to generate consensus and solidarity to support the successor regime. The Uruguayan case reveals transition as a moment contested by competing political projects with different temporalities and visions, as well as the preference of political elites to use popular mechanisms to generate post-conflict consensus and reconciliation. There were three distinct political projects present at transition in Uruguay, all sharing the minimalist goal of democratic restoration expressed in the anti-dictatorship consensus galvanized by the public rejection of the military-initiated constitutional plebiscite in 1980. This plebiscite was a performative act of direct democracy which upended the military's political ambitions for enduring

[417] The amnesty laws implemented under these transition agreements have been longstanding. In Uruguay the amnesty law lasted 25 years (1986–2011) and 19 years in Argentina (1986–2005). In Spain (1977), Chile (1978) and Brazil (1979), amnesty laws remain in place. As recently as 2019, Guatemala introduced a new amnesty law granting immunity for the perpetrators of gross human rights violations committed during the civil war and repression in the 1980s.

political power and forced them to negotiate the restoration of democracy. The three visions of democratic transition are:

1. democratic transition as restorative, seeking to preserve the pre-dictatorship partidocratic status quo guided by the traditional Uruguayan pactism and clientelism;
2. democratic transition as transformative, seeking to upend the hegemony of the traditional partidocracy that had endured 100 years and fostered the emergence of democratic pluralism – the electoral inclusion of the Left; and
3. democratic transition as the enactment of the post-Cold War project of global liberal governance, founded on the universals of human rights and democracy. In Latin America, the vision of global liberal governance was conceived as the harmonization of domestic political and legal institutions through neo-constitutionalism under the guidance the Inter-American Commission on Human Rights (IACHR) and Inter-American Court of Human Rights (IACtHR).

These three competing visions of democratic transitions premised on distinct sources of legitimacy reveals transitional justice was just one vision of the future.

This chapter explores the dynamic inter-relationship between these three competing visions of democratic transition: the prioritization of popular sovereignty as the basis for political legitimacy; the development of transitional justice in Latin America through human rights activism; and the progressive harmonization of domestic political and legal institutions through the American human rights system and neo-constitutionalism. The chapter provides a genealogy of conflict in Uruguay to contextualize the intervention of transitional justice and its trajectory. It outlines the 100-year dominance of the Uruguayan partidocracy; the political culture of conflict resolution and peacemaking based on elite pactism and amnesty referred to as the 'Uruguayan Way'; the role of direct democracy in settling contentious political issues; the key role of democratic consensus as a source of political legitimacy; and the polarizing impact of military repression on Uruguayan society. The chapter then examines the way in which direct democracy prevailed over transitional justice in generating a consensus about the terms of democratic transition. It looks at three popular consultations: first, the 1980 military-initiated constitutional plebiscite and the elite pact to restore democracy; second, the 1989 citizen-initiated referendum to repeal the Expiry Law and challenge the elite pact; and third, the 2009 citizen-initiated plebiscite to repeal the Expiry Law. Uruguayans experienced democratic transition as a series of popular consultations to accept or reject amnesty and amnesia as the basis for pacification and reconciliation. Dating from the Constitution (1918), direct democracy has been an important constitutional provision enabling popular consultations in Uruguayan democracy. Between 1917 and 2022, there have been 26 popular consultations initiated either by the state or by citizens to support constitutional changes or to repeal laws. The state's use of the plebiscite to mobilize public support for policy reform is a well-established practice in Uruguayan politics. Constitutional plebiscites have been used to determine support for a national executive – *colegiado* – instead of presidential system of government. Political parties have also used popular consultations as a way to distance contentious issues – such as the Expiry Law – from party agendas by transferring responsibility to citizen-initiated referenda/plebiscite campaigns – to enhance their legitimacy as 'grass roots'.[418] They have functioned as democratic mechanisms of political inclusion, political education and for political mobilization, although in practice, outcomes have strongly followed party lines.[419] Nearly half the total number of popular consultations have been held since the coup in 1971. A key element of democratic transition in Uruguay was the way the state represented the dictatorship as an 'authoritarian parenthesis', an exception to the historical norm of Uruguayan democracy.[420] State renewal was popularly understood as the restoration of the natural democratic order, which invoked foundational myths about Uruguayan democratic exceptionalism in Latin America as a secular, modernizing, socially progressive, and consensus-based society.[421]

3.2. POLITICAL CONFLICT AND POLITICAL CRIMES

3.2.1. PARTIDOCRATIC URUGUAY

The two traditional parties, the *Blancos* (*Partido Nacional* – National Party or Whites) and the *Colorados* (*Partido Colorado* – The Red Party), were established soon after independence in 1828 and dominated government until 1971. The political division between the Conservatives and the Liberals was ubiquitous throughout the post-imperial Latin American states in the 19th century. In only two states, Uruguay and Colombia, did their dominance persist into

418 While the terms plebiscite and referendum are often used interchangeably, they have distinct meaning under the Uruguayan Constitution. Plebiscites are used to approve constitutional amendments while non-constitutional laws are decided by referendum. See K. Hite and L. Morlino, 'Problematizing the Links between Authoritarian Legacies and "Good" Democracy' in K. Hite and P. Cesarini (eds.), *Authoritarian Legacies and Democracy in Latin America and Southern Europe*, University of Notre Dame Press, Notre Dame, IL 2004, p. 25.

419 P. Navia, 'Do Plebiscites and Referenda Hinder or Foster Democratic Institutions and Accountability? Evidence from Latin America' (Annual Meeting of the American Political Science Association 2006).

420 J.P. Luna, *Segmented Representation: Political Party Strategies in Unequal Democracies*, Oxford University Press, Oxford 2014, p. 103.

421 J. Rial, 'The Social Imaginary: Utopian Political Myths in Uruguay (Change and Permanence during and after the Dictatorship)' in S. Sosnowski and L.B. Popkin (eds.), *Repression, Exile and Democracy: Uruguayan Culture*, Duke University Press, Durham, NC 1993, p. 59.

the 20th century.[422] Historically, the *Blancos* were the conservatives identified with the rural export-oriented ranching interests and the *Colorados* were the progressive, urban based party that represented the industrial sector protected by the state.[423] Throughout the 19th century, these parties were led by feuding political leaders – *caudillos* – with their own military forces which they used to win power. In 1872, the two parties reached a political power sharing agreement (*Pacto de Abril* – April Pact) decentralizing government by allocating control over four interior departments to the *Blancos* while the *Colorados* controlled Montevideo and the coastal regions.[424] The co-participation formula was subsequently adjusted under *Pacto de la Cruz* (Pact of the Cross) in 1897 which awarded the *Blancos* control over six departments and guaranteed them minority representation on key national bodies. In 1904, the overwhelming defeat of the *Blancos* by the *Colorados* in the last civil war allowed President José Batlle y Ordóñez to centralize government and establish a national army to replace the party militias. He served two terms as president between 1903–7 and 1911–15 and forged Uruguay's modern national identity as a democratic, progressive, secular welfare state premised on the 'protection of individual liberties, civic republicanism and state guided social justice'.[425] His ambition to establish a national executive – *colegiado* – rather than presidential system introduced a permanent point of conflict into Uruguayan politics that saw the design of government oscillate between these systems. A National Council of Government – *colegiado* – was established by constitutional plebiscite in 1916, 1942, and 1952 based on a co-participation formula which allocated the majority party six seats and minority party three seats. Opponents of the *colegiado* managed to re-establish the presidency in 1934 and 1967 through constitutional plebiscites. The 1934 constitutional plebiscite restoring the presidency legitimated a soft coup by *Colorado* President Terra, who established an authoritarian government with the close support of the veteran *Blanco* leader, Luis Alberto de Herrera (1934–38).[426] The historical dominance of the traditional parties and the longevity of the individual political careers of legislators is highlighted by the fact that two legislators were members of both authoritarian administrations established by coups 40 years apart in 1933 and 1973. Alberto Demicheli (*Colorado*) was interim president in 1976 and had been President Terra's Minister

422 M. Coppedge, 'The Evolution of Latin American Party Systems' in S. Mainwaring and A. Valenzuela (eds.), *Politics, Society and Democracy*, Routledge, Oxford 1998, p. 171.

423 C.G. Gillespie, *Negotiating Democracy: Politicians and Generals in Uruguay*, Cambridge University Press, Cambridge 2006.

424 The 'Revolution of the Lances' was precipitated after President Lorenzo Batlle (1968–72) had excluded the *Blancos* from participation in government and was brought to an end by the April Pact.

425 R. Rodd, 'Democratic Citizenship as Uruguayan Cultural Heritage' (2019) 6 *Democratic Theory* 27, at 30.

426 P.B. Taylor, 'The Uruguayan Coup D'état of 1933' (1952) 32 *The Hispanic American Historical Review* 301, at 318.

for the Interior in 1933. Martín Echegoyen (*Blanco*) presided over the Council of State in President Bordaberry's civilian-military (1972–1976) administration and had been Minister for Education (1935–6) and Minister for Public Works (1936–8) in President Terra's administration. He had also been President of the National Council of Government (1959–1960).[427]

From the 1904 election to the 1971 election, the *Colorados* and *Blancos* dominated government through a power-sharing pact, formalized in the 1918 constitution, which saw them consistently secure around 90% of parliamentary votes between them.[428] This 'partidocratic' – the centrality of parties – system based on co-participation and clientelism forged a strong party allegiance and political identity in their supporters and limited the opportunity for any third party to emerge based on programmatic ideas.[429] Between 1918 and 1967, a history of rolling political crises resulted in five constitutions which served to reinforce the primacy of parties, not governments, as the source of legitimacy.[430] Both traditional parties used the state as a redistributive mechanism to secure electoral support through clientelist practices down to the grass roots level. However, by the 1960s, economic stagnation had undermined the state's ability to manage dissent through clientelist policies.[431] Growing strikes and civil unrest and the emergence of the National Liberation Movement – Tupamaros MLN (*Movimiento de Liberación Nacional-Tupamaros*), a movement inspired by the Cuban revolution, escalated into armed confrontations and led to the increasing militarization of the state. At first, the public were bemused spectators of the *Tupamaros*' theatrical politics designed to shame the traditional political parties by exposing their corruption and incompetence. At first, many Uruguayans viewed the MLN actions as a valid critique of the traditional parties from the sidelines but after the state stepped up its counterinsurgency in response to MLN armed actions the population was forced to take sides.

3.2.2. THE SLOW COUP 1972–1973

The 'democratic path to dictatorship' took the form of a slow coup in which the government invited the military under emergency powers to end the widespread

427 K. Eaton, *Politics Beyond the Capital: The Design of Subnational Institutions in South America*, Stanford University Press, Stanford, CA 2020, p. 101.

428 V.P. Bentancur, et al., 'The Case of Uruguay's *Frente Amplio*' in F. Rosenblatt, et al. (eds.), *Diminished Parties: Democratic Representation in Contemporary Latin America*, Cambridge University Press, Cambridge 2021, p. 29.

429 G. Caetano, et al., 'La partidocracia uruguaya. Historia y teoría de la centralidad de los partidos políticos' (1987) 44 *Cuadernos del CLAEH*, 37; A. Barahona De Brito, *Human Rights and Democratization in Latin America*, Oxford University Press, Oxford 1997, p. 18.

430 Gillespie 2006, o.c., p. 17.

431 M. Finch, *A Political Economy of Uruguay since 1870*, Palgrave Macmillan, London 1981, p. 22.

strikes, civil unrest, and the growing armed insurrection. Militarization meant the forcible conscription of strikers into the army which made them subject to the jurisdiction of the military courts – they could be prosecuted in a military court for desertion if they refused to return to work.[432] The military took over the counterinsurgency against the *Tupamaros* from the police and, under the Law of State Security and Public Order (14068) in 1972, prosecuted members of the armed guerrilla movement in military tribunals.[433] When the coup arrived on June 27, 1973, a significant part of the middle class resigned themselves to it as a necessary evil to prevent further chaos while, at the same time, experiencing deep ambivalence over the loss of democracy.[434] Ironically, both the military and the *Tupamaros* claimed the same goal – to 'save the nation' from corrupt politicians.[435]

The Uruguayan military coup formed part of a coordinated US regional response to leftist insurgencies shaped by Cold War geo-politics in the Western Hemisphere. The US National Security Doctrine, dating from the early 1950s, was directed towards eliminating its political enemies. From the 1960s, the US trained the Uruguayan military and police in counterinsurgency strategy and the French provided the military with the 'revolutionary war doctrine' to contain emerging internal threats.[436] The Uruguayan military justified the fight against leftist subversives as fulfilling their historic 19th century founding role as defenders of *la patria* – the nation – and participants in the civil wars known as *patriadas* – wars for the nation.[437] During the 1960s and 1970s, Uruguay served as an important laboratory to test counterinsurgency techniques including the use of torture in interrogations and the deployment of clandestine military and paramilitary operations to hunt leftist insurgents.[438] Once military dictatorships had been established throughout the Southern Cone, the Uruguayan military were integrated into Plan Condor, a secret regional coordination of cross-border state repression of each other's citizens.[439] The implementation of US

---

432 Gillespie 2006, o.c., p. 38. Also, personal interviews with family members who had experienced the practice of being '*militarizado*' in Montevideo July 2015.

433 A. Rico, *Cómo nos domina la clase gobernante. Orden político y obediencia social en la democracia posdictadura. Uruguay 1985–2005*, Ediciones Trilce, Montevideo 2005.

434 N.G. Bermeo, *Ordinary People in Extraordinary Times: The Citizenry and the Breakdown of Democracy*, Princeton University Press, Princeton, NJ 2020, p. 137.

435 E. Kaufman, *Uruguay in Transition: From Civilian to Military Rule*, Transaction Inc., New Brunswick, NJ 1979, p. 36.

436 J.J. Ryan, 'Turning on their Masters: State Terrorism and Unlearning Democracy in Uruguay' in C. Menjívar and N. Rodríguez (eds.), *When States Kill: Latin America, the U.S. and Technologies of Terror*, University of Texas Press, Austin, TX 2005, p. 278, at p. 279; G. Grandin, *Empire's Workshop: Latin America, the United States, and the Rise of the New Imperialism*, Henry Holt and Company, New York, NY 2006.

437 B. Loveman, *For la Patria: Politics and the Armed Forces in Latin America*, Rowman & Littlefield Publishers, Lanham, MD 2004.

438 A.J. Langguth, *Hidden Terrors*, Pantheon Books, New York, NY 1978.

439 The key members of Plan Condor were Chile, Argentina, Uruguay, Bolivia, Paraguay and Brazil. See McSherry 1999, o.c., p. 144.

counterinsurgency methods saw governments rewarded with development aid and their human rights abuses were ignored.[440] Uruguayan citizens did not learn about the existence of Plan Condor until 1992, when the 'archives of terror' from Plan Condor were discovered in Paraguay.[441] Initially, the military justified their counterinsurgency on the grounds of 'national security, the preservation of social discipline and supposed national values, and anti-Marxism'.[442] Because they had already announced the defeat of the *Tupamaros* before their coup, the military justified their rule as transitional, working towards a new state institutional structure.[443] In 1973, the military junta sidelined the politicians by closing Congress, prohibiting all political activity, and disbanding the leftist parties of the Broad Front (*Frente Amplio*).[444] Between 1976 and 1980, they selectively rehabilitated cooperative politicians through the Tribunal of Political Control (*Tribunal de Control Político*) with the aim of changing traditional party politics from the top-down.[445]

3.2.3. *EL PROCESO MILITAR* – DICTATORSHIP 1973–1985

A major obstacle to national reconciliation after dictatorship has been the legacy of repression. Societies are left fragmented and polarized, and individual victims often alienated and isolated. From the perspective of the transitional justice four pillars model, transition is a moment to reverse the effects of repression through truth and justice. The hope that divisions forged by conflict can be overcome and heal society is one of the ambitions of transitional justice. However, the reality of the uneven impact of violence, the gap between the experience and memory of victims of violence and those who were not direct victims, the diversity of the sources of violence and the mistaken belief that trauma can be the basis of collective identity, suggests reconciliation is a very ambitious goal. This section outlines the impact of repression on individuals and collectivities in Uruguay and the way reconciliation was based on a minimalist anti-dictatorship consensus.

The Uruguayan military is considered to have established one of the most repressive dictatorships in Latin America, largely because it was able to establish

440 M. Otterman, *American Torture: From the Cold War to Abu Ghraib and Beyond*, Melbourne University Press, Melbourne 2007; McSherry 1999, o.c., p. 13.

441 K. Zoglin, 'Paraguay's Archive of Terror: International Cooperation and Operation Condor' (2001) 32 *The University of Miami Inter-American Law Review*, p. 57.

442 H. Finch, 'Democratisation in Uruguay' (1985) 7 *Third World Quarterly* 594, at 597.

443 Gillespie 2006, o.c., p. 42.

444 The *Frente Amplio* was established as a coalition of a dozen leftist parties and movements in 1971. The first president of the *Frente Amplio* and its first presidential candidate was General Liber Seregni.

445 Gillespie 2006, o.c., p. 54.

complete control over this small society of around three million inhabitants in a territory of 176, 215 sq kms. It has been described as a totalitarian, not just an authoritarian, regime that completely repressed unions, politicians, leftists, parties, and castrated the university and schools.[446] The dictatorship instituted a form of bureaucratized terror over the entire population by imposing a 'habitus of repression', a form of political subjectivity that sought to make the population complicit in their own submission. *El proceso militar* in Uruguay, the method of civil-military authoritarian governance, was constituted by a regime of pervasive surveillance and control, not ideological indoctrination.[447] Firstly, the dictatorship registered the entire population on a computerized database and classified everyone into three categories (A, B, C) assessed on the basis of their political loyalty according to whether they had agreed to sign the Certificate of Democratic Faith (*el Certificado de Fe Democrática*).[448] Those classified Category A were deemed politically trustworthy and could hold government employment and were able to continue their lives largely unaffected. Those classified Category B were considered politically suspect and prohibited from holding government employment and put under surveillance. Those classified Category C were branded pariahs with no rights and destined for either immediate imprisonment or exile. Secondly, the military used systematic mass imprisonment and torture to force individual submission to authoritarian rule and intimidate the whole society. Close to 20% of the population (500,000) chose to leave for exile and between 1973 and 1977 Uruguay had the highest percentage of political detainees in the world with more than one in every 30 adults detained, interrogated or imprisoned.[449] As Nancy Hollander argues in her study of liberation psychology during the Southern Cone dictatorships, torture inscribed the regime's power on the body leaving a traumatic scar designed to produce 'psychic submission to absolute power of the state'.[450] Their military gaolers taunted political prisoners with the threat that they would destroy them as individuals through 'psychic demolition', not kill them.[451] One legacy of '*los años de plomo*' – the years of lead – and the pervasive use of torture was a collective national memory split

---

446 P.C. Sondrol, '1984 Revisited? A Re-Examination of Uruguay's Military Dictatorship' (1992) 11 *Bulletin of Latin American Research*, 187.

447 J. Yaffé, 'La dictadura uruguaya (1973–1985): nuevas perspectivas de investigación e interpretación historiográfica' (2012) 38 *Estudos Ibero-Americanos* 13, at 19. The term '*el proceso*' was the abbreviation of the Argentine dictatorship project *El Proceso de Reorganización Nacional* but given the level of coordination of repression by the Southern Cone dictatorships under Plan Condor, it can be applied to all of them.

448 N.C. Hollander, *Uprooted Minds: Surviving the Politics of Terror in the Americas*, Routledge, New York, NY 2014, p. 113.

449 Sondrol 1992, o.c., p. 196.

450 N.C. Hollander, *Love in a Time of Hate: Liberation Psychology in Latin America*, Rutgers University Press, New Brunswick, NJ 1997, p. 119.

451 Ibid.

between the majority who wanted to forget the horror of repression, and the minority, the victims, who could not forget, and did not want to.[452]

Repression de-politicized Uruguayan society engendering a pervasive feeling of individual helplessness and normalizing collective paranoia. The individual was made a spectator of authoritarian power unable to control anything and fearful of becoming a victim, leaving them in a state of high anxiety. But the strategy of submission, conformity and anonymity could not guarantee survival imposing in an incalculable burden of anticipation of the unknown.[453] A common defensive psychological response was 'ego regression' whereby the individual became more and more identified with, and reliant upon, a repressive leadership. 'For the witness/victim citizens who survived in the violence of everyday life, identification, at both the unconscious levels with, an arbitrary state power enacting its wrath on the *desaparecidos* permitted them to symbolically choose victims outside themselves to sacrifice – *¡algo habrán hecho!* (they must have done something!)'.[454] The result was a growing refusal to bear witness to events, to engage in self-censorship and to be in denial about what was happening. Families attempted to protect their children by shielding them from the truth of repression leaving the legacy of 'an apolitical and self-censoring generation'.[455]

The military regime required public conformity and compliance but not necessarily their active support. Individual disengagement came with a high personal cost. In Uruguay, '*insilio*' (inward exile) required self-censorship in response to repression, an escape to the inside rather than the outside '*exilio*' (exile). For those politically opposed to the dictatorship, the personal cost was disconnection from people and social reality isolating individuals from each other. For the opposition, de-politicization and the abandonment of political projects was experienced as personal loss and rejection of those values and people once thought important and left stranded in the present.[456] The choice/fate individuals faced was to become exiles, political prisoners or remain hidden as *insiliados* – the internally exiled.[457] Mario Handler, in his film *Decile a Mario que no vuelva* (Tell Mario not to Return), documents the heavy individual

452 M. and M. Viñar, *Fracturas de Memoria Crónicas para una memoria por venir*, Ediciones Trilce, Montevideo 1993, p. 112.

453 Sondrol 1992, o.c., p. 194.

454 Hollander 1997, o.c., p. 114.

455 Hollander 1997, o.c., p. 115.

456 Scott 2013, o.c., pp. 67–8.

457 The neologism '*insilio*' was coined by Diego Pérez Pintos to describe the condition of 'exile within your own frontiers' referring to the relation between an individual and power legitimated through obedience. See A. Trigo, 'Contracultura del insilio en Uruguay (1973–1985)' (1990) 43 *Revista Hispánica Moderna* 228, at 229 and E. Valverde, 'The experience of *Exilio* and Insilio in Reshaping Uruguayan Identity' (2001) III/2 *Bulletin of the Royal Institute for Inter-Faith Studies*, 177.

cost of repression through the experience of education. As one interviewee recounted:

> They destroyed our lives. My generation: they mutilated it ... But they planned this very well, because what they wanted was precisely that. They wanted to control our heads, ideologically ... that creepy fumigation. Because, in reality, they castrated our thoughts ...[458]

The film itself is offered as a space to promote reconciliation or *convivencia* – respectful coexistence – to help forge a new inclusive post-dictatorship subjectivity. The defeat of the 1989 plebiscite to repeal the Expiry Law was not just the product of fear but also the legacy of the erosion of society's moral compass and inability to discern its moral and legal effects.

The dictatorship produced a traumatic social environment designed to make the public feel everything was in jeopardy. The dictatorship produced a 'habitus of repression',[459] a learned way of defensive living under dictatorship to protect oneself which was too readily exposed as futile. Mass imprisonment and routine torture reminded everyone about the reach of the regime and the threat of being reclassified 'C'. The prevailing political subjectivity was fear that at any moment one might have to account for themselves to the military. They came to inhabit a paranoid world in which secret informers drove taxis and travelled in public transport, striking up conversations to uncover subversive opinions. The threat of *allanamientos* – security raids – on private houses justified on the grounds of suspicion of subversion, produced self-censorship leading to a defensive life of *insiliado*, being 'internally exiled' in one's own society. It reinforced the attitude of '*no te metás*' ('don't get involved'):

> The reign of the "just in case" began. One burned the books presumed to be dangerous, just in case another *allanamiento* could take place. One did not visit friends known for their political dissent, just in case they were under surveillance. One did not speak too openly against the new authorities in front of children just in case they might accidentally repeat it to that dangerous "other" at school or in the street.[460]

---

458 *Decile a Mario que no vuelva* (Tell Mario not to Return), Director M. HANDLER, Uruguay, Spain, Twelve Cats SL, 2007.

459 'Habitus' is borrowed from Bourdieu which refers to the process of normalization of patterns of social behaviour. 'The habitus, the durably installed generative principle of regulated improvisations, produces practices which tend to reproduce the regularities immanent in the objective conditions of the production of their generative principle, while adjusting to the demands inscribed as objective potentialities in the situation, as defined by the cognitive and motivating structures making up the habitus'. P. BOURDIEU, *Outline of a Theory of Practice*, Cambridge University Press, Cambridge 1977, p. 78.

460 C. PERELLI, 'Putting conservatism to good use: women and unorthodox politics in Uruguay, from breakdown to transition' in J.S. JAQUETTE (ed.), *The Women's Movement in Latin America: Feminism and the Transition to Democracy*, Routledge, Oxford 1989, p. 95, at p. 102.

The *insiliado* not only loses contact with the present but also with their past and personal identity. As Elizabeth Lira observes:

> The past seems lost within all the losses, symbolized by the dead, the disappeared, the tortured bodies, broken hopes, and the elimination of the future, the exiles, the disenchantment with politics. Each individual is conscious or unconscious of the losses and of the defences that have been utilized to mourn less or to completely evade the necessary mourning.[461]

Rejecting the past was a kind of separation producing a loss of identity and even greater isolation through the avoidance of mourning.

In the transition to democracy there were legacies of different kinds of memories and identities shaping people's expectations about the future. There were the political identities and memories shaped by the utopian and revolutionary social justice movements challenging the state in the pre-dictatorship period. And there were the memories and political identities forged by the experience of repression as victims or as bystanders. For some those memories and identities overlapped but for most people they existed as divergent memories and identities, as different universes.[462] People were left divided by their memories and stranded in the present left with their defeated utopian projects.[463] As Hollander notes: 'while the cause has gone its effects persist and the rupture of interpersonal understanding and alliances that tie people together and sustain social bonds'.[464] The societal legacy of the 'habitus of repression' was played out at the end of the dictatorship between those who had stayed, those who had gone into exile and those who had been imprisoned. Psychotherapists have characterized the dynamics between these groups in the following way:

> Each group believed they had suffered the most or that others had abandoned or betrayed them. Those who had stayed viewed with resentment those who had left, envious of their flight to safety and what they viewed as their self-serving accomplishments abroad. Those who had left were suspicious of those who had stayed, as if they must have colluded with the dictatorship in order to survive. Those who had been imprisoned were suspected of compromising themselves and their *compañeros* in order to still be alive when others were not.[465]

---

461 Elizabeth Lira quoted in Hollander 1997, o.c., p. 112.

462 L. Weschler, *A Miracle, A Universe: Settling Accounts with Torturers*, University of Chicago Press, Chicago, IL 1998.

463 David Scott, writing on transition in Grenada, characterises the disjunction and discontinuity of political identities and memories of the defeated revolutionary movement in Grenada as stranded in transition. Scott 2013, o.c., p. 73.

464 Hollander 1997, o.c., p. 200.

465 Hollander 1997, o.c., p. 191.

These groups inhabited different universes and the depth of their feelings of injustice and resentment towards each other were perpetuated as social divisions.

'All of us were affected', a young therapist named Damian Schroder commented. 'That's why we try to avoid setting up therapy groups exclusively for torture victims, or relatives of the disappeared, or returned expats that would just exacerbate the fragmentation, when what we desperately need are vehicles for reintegration'.[466]

The insidiousness of repression was the way it imposed a shared collective guilt on everyone. Those who stayed were forced into the position of bystander which meant living with anticipatory anxiety that they too could be thrust into the position of victim.[467] Their reaction was 'to dissociate themselves from the persecutory symbol of the disappeared, or to identify with the aggressor by convincing themselves of the rationality or just actions of the repressive state'.[468] Others were directly coerced to cooperate with the military through threats to their jobs or even their liberty. The military would routinely visit workplaces and demand the names of potential 'suspects' from managers as evidence of their loyalty.[469] For the prisoners, the victims of torture, the experience of total vulnerability and inability to retaliate turned aggressive impulses inward. 'Self-blame and guilt are the result: victims reproach themselves for having been caught, for failing to escape, before being weak and showing fear. Guilt is experienced when victims break down under torture or survive it when others do not'.[470] Disappearance left the legacy of frozen grief for the families affected. They were unable to experience a normal process of mourning whereby they detached themselves from the deceased so they could resume life in the present.

The family is caught in a terrible contradiction: a husband, wife, parent, or child cannot mourn without risking intense guilt, for without proof of death, to go on with one's life is tantamount to a kind of murder of a disappeared loved one. Or, 'to go on living and maintain the mental representation of the disappeared, to keep him or her alive, imposes a profound form of mental anguish'.[471]

Trauma cannot serve as a unifying experience because memory is not just an event, but the new meaning given to it.[472] At a minimum, there was an anti-dictatorship consensus for democratic restoration amongst Uruguayans, but no

466 N. Kritz, *Transitional Justice: How Emerging Democracies Reckon with Former Regimes*, United States Institute of Peace, Washington, WA 1995, p. 396.

467 N.C. Hollander, 'Psychoanalysis and the Problem of the Bystander in Times of Terror' in L. Layton, et al. (eds.), *Psychoanalysis, Class and Politics: Encounters in the Clinical Setting*, Routledge, Oxford 2006, p. 154, at p. 156.

468 Ibid., p. 156.

469 Authors' personal interviews in Montevideo with family members to hear their experience of their workplaces under the dictatorship – Montevideo July 2015.

470 Hollander 2006, o.c., p. 131.

471 Hollander 2006, o.c., p. 128.

472 L. D'Orsi, 'Trauma and the Politics of Memory of the Uruguayan Dictatorship' (2015) 42 *Latin American Perspectives* 162, at 171.

unity about how to deal with the past. Those who had been the target of the dictatorship could either embrace political normalization and electoral politics, translate their suffering and trauma into human rights claims and seek justice, or remain isolated and disconnected from the post-dictatorship reality of amnesty endorsed by democratic consensus. The policy of amnesia made 'the memories of victims invisible, marginalizing them and locking them into intimate and private spaces'.[473] In Uruguay, transition was consolidated and political legitimacy re-established through direct democracy and democratic consensus rather than transitional justice measures seeking to institute universal values of human rights and democracy.

3.3. DEMOCRACY, AMNESTY AND PEACE

3.3.1. THE 1980 CONSTITUTIONAL PLEBISCITE AND NAVAL CLUB PACT 1984

The dictatorship can be divided into three phases: (1973–1976) the policing dictatorship (*la dictadura comisarial*) charged with re-establishing public order; (1976–1980) the foundational dictatorship (*la dictadura fundacional*) seeking to restructure political power in the state; and (1980–1985) the transitional dictatorship (*la dictadura transicional*) the military withdrawal from power after the defeat of their constitutional plebiscite designed to install themselves permanently in power.[474] On November 30, 1980, the military held a constitutional plebiscite seeking public support to establish a single party state and secure their permanent role in government through the National Security Council (*Consejo de Seguridad Nacional* – COSENA). The military made voting mandatory, no parties could participate, and only the YES vote got media coverage. To their surprise, and that of most Uruguayans, the plebiscite was defeated when it secured only 42% of the vote.[475] This was in stark contrast to Pinochet's resounding victory with 70% support for his constitutional plebiscite held on September 11, 1980 to establish a National Security Council and install him as President for an eight year term.[476] The military had used the plebiscite to secure the direct support of citizens and marginalize the political parties. However, their defeat revealed that the parties remained key institutions in

---

473 Ibid., p. 165.

474 J. Errandonea, 'Justicia transicional en Uruguay' (2008) 47 *Revista IIDH (Instituto Interamericano de Derechos Humanos)* 13, at 17.

475 Kaufman 1979, o.c., p. 31.

476 The legitimacy of the vote was questioned widely at the time. See R. Barros, *Constitutionalism and Dictatorship: Pinochet, the Junta, and the 1980 Constitution*, Cambridge University Press, Cambridge 2002, p. 172.

political life.[477] It also revealed the new potential of direct democracy as a tool in the dialogue between the citizen and political power.[478] Direct democracy thwarted the Uruguayan military's political ambitions and precipitated the process of democratic transition.

The military staged a one-off Champions' World Cup called the *Mundialito*, scheduled shortly after the 1980 plebiscite, to solicit popular support for their ambition to secure a permanent role in government. Soccer has always been part of the Uruguayan identity, especially since 1930 when they hosted the first Soccer World Cup in Montevideo and Uruguay won. The generals' stratgey was to use soccer to consolidate their referendum win, but this backfired when the constitutional plebiscite was defeated and the *Mundialito* provided the opportunity for a show of public opposition to the dictatorship. The *Mundialito* was held between December 30, 1980 and January 10, 1981 to mark the 50th anniversary of the first World Cup tournament at the same venue in 1930. The six previous winners of the World Cup were invited to participate (Argentina, Brazil, Germany, Holland, Italy and Uruguay). Uruguay beat Brazil in the final 2-1 and the Uruguayans performed in the stadium 'the first public chants against the dictatorship'.[479] This historical moment was recorded by Sebastián Bednarik in the documentary film *Mundialito* (2010).[480]

The referendum defeat triggered the transition process and the engagement between the military, the political parties and human rights activists.[481] While direct democracy provided the internal impetus for democratic transition, the external impetus was provided by US President Jimmy Carter's new regional human rights agenda which increasingly stigmatized and isolated the Southern Cone military regimes.[482] The military established a timeline for elections, determined which parties and candidates could participate in the internal elections scheduled for 1982, which parties could participate in the Naval Club Pact negotiations, and which parties could field candidates in the 1984 national elections.[483] On August 3, 1984, the Naval Club Pact (*El Pacto del Club Naval*) was concluded between the Armed Forces and selected political parties – the *Colorado* Party (*Partido Colorado – Colorados*), the Broad Front (*Frente Amplio*)

---

477 G. Caetano, 'La partidocracia uruguaya: tradicíon y agenda reciente' (1995) 32 *Secuencia: Revisita de historia y ciencias sociales* 103, at 122.

478 J. Rilla, 'Uruguay 1980: Transición y democracia plebiscitaria' (2011) 150 *Nueva Sociedad*, 1.

479 J. Ruffinelli, *Para verte mejor: el nuevo cine uruguayo y todo lo anterior*, Ediciones Trilce, Montevideo 2015, p. 172.

480 *Mundialito* (The Little World Cup), Director Sebastián Bednarik, Spanish, Uruguay, Coral Films, 2010.

481 K. Sikkink, *Mixed Signals: U.S. Human Rights Policy and Latin America*, Cornell University Press, Ithaca, NY 2004, p. 130.

482 Barahona De Brito 1997, o.c., p. 69.

483 L. Roniger, 'How a Shattered Civil Religion is Rebuilt Through Contestation: Uruguay and the Legacy of Authoritarianism' (2016) 36 *Revista de Ciencia Política*, 411.

and the Civic Union (*Unión Cívica*). One of the main traditional parties, the National Party or Whites (*Partido Nacional – Blancos*) was excluded because the military viewed its leader, Wilson Ferreira, as too popular and potentially disruptive. Ferreira subsequently denounced the Pact as 'the embodiment of *continuismo*: the continuity of military rule, and authoritarian economics, behind an electoral façade'.[484] Because of the difficulty all parties faced negotiating in public, the Pact was conducted in secret talks. The Pact established the legal framework for transfer of authority from military to civilian rule, however, the exact details of the agreement remain unclear because no documents were signed nor were there any outside witnesses.[485] The fact that the participating political parties gave tacit approval to military administration's Institutional Act No.19, signed on August 3, 1984, announcing the return to the 1967 Constitution, the reinstitution of elections, and the return of the power to declare a 'state of emergency' to parliament, suggests they had agreed on these points.[486]

Even though amnesty was not mentioned in the Act, it was a major concern for both the military and political parties and had been deliberately kept off the Naval Club agenda because it threatened to derail negotiations.[487] Nevertheless, both sides expected amnesty for different reasons. For the Left and the families of political prisoners, it meant the detainees would be amnestied and released. For the military, it meant they would avoid criminal accountability for human rights violations committed during the dictatorship after the return to democracy. While there was consensus around mutual amnesty, its benefits were very asymmetrical favouring the military. President Sanguinetti's subsequent enactment of the Expiry Law (1985) and his appointment of General Hugo Medina, the key military negotiator in the Pact, as the Commander of the Armed Forces and Minister for Defence in his government suggests he kept the promises to legally shield the military.[488] Before the military left power, they issued another Institutional Act that preserved the positions and jobs of civil servants who had been loyal to the regime.[489] Overall, the Pact was well received by all parties with exception of the *Blancos* whose leader had been excluded from negotiations.[490]

484 C.G. Gillespie, 'Uruguay's Return to Democracy' (1985) 4 *Bulletin of Latin American Research* 99, at 104–5.

485 M.M. Delgado, et al., *"So the People Can Decide": the experience of the referendum against the impunity law in Uruguay: (1986–1989)*, International Human Rights Internship Program, Institute of International Education, Washington 2001.

486 L. Mallinder, 'Uruguay's Evolving Experience of Amnesty and Civil Society's Response' (March 16, 2009), Working Paper No. 4 From Beyond Legalism: Amnesties, Transition and Conflict Transformation, Institute of Criminology and Justice, Queen's University, Belfast, 19, https://ssrn.com/abstract=1387362.

487 Weschler 1998, o.c., pp. 166–7.

488 Mallinder 2009, o.c., p. 21.

489 Gillespie 1985, o.c., p. 104.

490 Gillespie 1985, o.c., p.105.

The Pact reflected the military's vision for the political restoration of the traditional 'partidocratic' government in which parties mobilized their supporters 'on the basis of strong partisan identification, support for individual leaders, and the fractional brokerage, clientelist side-payments and "pork"'.[491] The *Colorados*' electoral victory under President Sanguinetti in 1985 signalled the restitution of the 'normal political order' – in the political discourse of the time '*como siempre fue*' – 'as things always were'.[492] Sanguinetti, from the pro-regime faction of the *Colorados*, had maintained a working relationship with the military during the dictatorship. His post-transition restoration narrative presented the dictatorship as an unfortunate interlude necessary to 'save the nation' from the 'two demons' – the two violent extremes of the *Tupamaros* guerrilla actions on the one side and the military counterinsurgency on the other. A symmetry of blame provided a symmetrical solution.[493] By blaming both sides, Sanguinetti avoided any serious investigation of the cause of the *coup* or the actions taken by both sides. The military and the *Tupamaros* justified their political violence as a response to the violence of the other. The *Tupamaros* justified their resort to armed guerrilla action as a response to the severity of police and military repression against demonstrations and strikes and the practice of mass detentions. The military justified the coup as a response to the armed insurrection against the state instigated by foreign ideologies and parties.[494] For the military, the coup was a patriotic act to defend *la patria* and refound the nation under the military's guardianship.[495] The 'two demons' theory constructed Uruguayan society as the victim of political violence for which the solution was the marginalization of the social forces capable of violence as the way to guarantee the non-repetition of violence.[496] It invoked the myths of the natural civility and consensus of Uruguayan politics and rejected the investigation of human rights violations as inevitably divisive in a society haunted by the past without a common vision of it. Democratic restoration was founded on the historical myth of 'democratic Uruguay' where 'consensus must prevail at all costs' looking back to recovering 'our *paisito*' – 'our dear little country'.[497]

The consensus around amnesty reflected the primacy of party politics and political reconciliation over human rights and justice in the transition in

491 Luna 2014, o.c., p. 87.

492 C. Demasi, 'La partidocracia uruguaya: aportes para la discusión de una hipótesis' (2013) 3 *Contemporánea: Historia y problemas del siglo XX* 267, at 276.

493 A. Buriano, 'A 30 años de la ley de caducidad uruguaya ¿qué y cómo debemos conmemorar?' (2017) 10 *Antíteses* 351, at 357.

494 M. Achugar, *What we Remember: The Construction of Memory in Military Discourse*, John Benjamins, Philadelphia, PA 2008, p. 128; C. Demasi, 'Un repaso a la teoría de los dos demonios' in A. Marchesi, et al. (eds.), *El presente de la dictadura: Estudios y reflexiones a 30 años del golpe de Estado en Uruguay*, Ediciones Trilce, Montevideo 2004, p. 67.

495 Yaffé 2012, o.c., p. 16.

496 Loveman 2004, o.c., p. 234.

497 Rial 1993, o.c., p. 76.

Uruguay. President Sanguinetti's famous phrase, '*no hay que tener los ojos en la nuca*' – 'you must not have eyes in the back of your head' – sums up his policy of looking towards the future. He justified amnesty as part of the 'traditional way' of Uruguayan political peace making. 'Uruguay has always had amnesties to end these situations. This is what Uruguay has done since 1825, at the end of each war, at the end of confrontations .... This is part of our history'.[498] In fact, the political culture of elite pactism and amnesty was not an exclusively Uruguayan 'traditional way' but characteristic of the 19th century mode of political reconciliation between warring *caudillos* in many Latin American countries; the victor determined the terms under which the loser was rehabilitated in national politics.[499] President Sanguinetti bedded down the democratic restoration project by implementing the Naval Club Pact in key laws instituting amnesty and, to a limited degree, restitutive justice, especially the reinstatement of public sector employees dismissed by the military. The Law of National Pacification (*Ley de Pacificación Nacional*), Law 15.737 (March 8, 1985), set out the terms of democratic normalization which included an amnesty for non-state agents, the release of political prisoners – the key issue for the Left opposition, and restitution for the victims of the repression.[500] Under the Law for the Reintegration of the Exonerated (*Ley de Reposición de Destituiduos*) public servants dismissed under military rule and imprisoned or forced into exile had their jobs restored. In total, around 10,500 public employees returned to their former jobs and 6,000 were granted pension benefits.[501] However, democratic restoration without accountability was immediately challenged by opposition political parties and civil society groups. Opposition Deputies established two parliamentary commissions to investigate assassinations and disappearances under the dictatorship with the aim of bringing cases to prosecutors. President Sanguinetti responded by legislating the second amnesty law, the Law of Expiry of the Punitive Claims of the State (*Ley de Caducidad de la Pretensión Punitiva del Estado), Ley* 15.848 of December 22, 1986, which granted the military reciprocal amnesty.[502] To make it law, the *Colorados* had to secure the support

498 Radio Carve. 1986 'Sanguinetti proposes amnesty law for military', *Daily Report, Latin America, FBIS-LAM-86-197*, October 9, cited in F. Lessa, *Memory and Transitional Justice in Argentina and Uruguay: Against Impunity*, Palgrave Macmillan, New York 2013, p. 188.

499 Loveman and Lira 2007, o.c., p. 43.

500 For details of the Law of National Pacification see: A. Barahona De Brito, 'Truth, Justice, Memory, and Democratisation in the Southern Cone' in A. Barahona De Brito, et al. (eds.), *The Politics of Memory: Transitional Justice in Democratizing Societies*, Oxford University Press, Oxford 2001, p. 119, at pp. 127–8; L. Mallinder 2009, o.c., p. 32; Law of National Pacification (Ley 15.737 de 22/03/1985. Ley de Amnistía. Aprobación de la Convención Americana sobre Derechos Humanos llamada Pacto de San José de Costa Rica. Creación de la Comisión Nacional de Repatriación. República Oriental del Uruguay, http://www.impo.com.uy/bases/leyes/15737-1985%20).

501 Barahona De Brito 2001, o.c., p. 128.

502 The Expiry Law was passed with almost unanimous support. See Gillespie 1985, o.c., p. 106.

of the *Blancos*, a significant act of reconciliation by the dominant traditional parties and return to the 'partidocratic' co-participation after their falling out over the *Club Naval Pact* (1984). While amnesty for political prisoners was perhaps the most significant human rights policy implemented by President Sanguinetti there was little truth recovery in this process.[503] At the time, the primary objective of the Left, the target of military repression, in supporting amnesty, was the release of their political prisoners who they regarded as having been unjustly persecuted without due legal process which a subsequent legal review confirmed.[504]

In Uruguay, the Pact sought to restore the political status quo ante through *continuismo*, the return of the partidocratic order.[505] The military gradually rehabilitated the political parties who became the key participants in the restoration process. Human rights NGOs, such as the Service for Peace and Justice (*Servicio de Paz y Justicia* – SERPAJ), played only a limited role and remained largely disconnected from the political parties.[506] In 1983, SERPAJ was further marginalized when it was banned in the lead up to the 1984 election. In the early 1980s, human rights groups lacked international leverage because the IACtHR had only been established in 1979 and its first decision was not made until 1986. In Uruguay, victims and human rights organizations never achieved the prominence they did in Argentina largely because the number of disappeared was very small by comparison.[507] The strong anti-dictatorship consensus amongst Uruguayans revealed through the direct democracy of the 1980 plebiscite was the turning point in the dictatorship and created the momentum for democratic restoration. The military reframed the role of the dictatorship as a necessary interlude for the restoration of democracy during which conflict was neutralized by official mutual amnesty and amnesia.[508] Sanguinetti re-narrated the dictatorship as an interlude, an exception, that could be left behind and forgotten, in the same way the 1933 coup and authoritarian Terra administration (1934–8) had been forgotten as something shameful.[509] Transition to democratic government was achieved through political reconciliation based on a pact between the military and approved

---

503 Barahona De Brito 1997, o.c., p. 76; Mallinder 2009, o.c., p. 34.

504 Weschler 1998, o.c., p. 197.

505 Gillespie 1985, o.c., p. 99.

506 SERPAJ emerged as a regional human rights NGO. See R. Pagnucco and J.D. McCarthy, 'Advocating Nonviolent Direct Action in Latin America: The Antecedents and Emergence of SERPAJ' in S. Zunes, et al. (eds.), *Nonviolent Social Movements: A Geographical Perspective*, Wiley-Blackwell, Oxford 1999, p. 235.

507 According to The Association of Mothers and Families of the Uruguayans Detained and Disappeared (Famidesa) there were 197 disappeared during the 1970s and 1980s. In Argentina the figure was around 30,000 disappeared.

508 Weschler 1998, o.c., p. 197.

509 Taylor 1952, o.c., p. 319.

political parties in which the past was quarantined in order to try to rehabilitate the partidocratic order. But while transition appeared as *continuismo* with the return to government of the *Colorados* as the party of state, disaffected members of the traditional parties and the leftist political parties shifted their agenda from campaigning against the authoritarian regime to democratic reform from below by expanding participation, opening up candidate selection, and renewing their political programmes. The issue of democratic renewal at the grass roots became the major factor shaping public attitudes towards the Expiry Law.[510]

3.3.2. THE REFERENDUM ON THE EXPIRY LAW 1989

The second moment of transition was the citizen-initiated referendum seeking to derogate the Expiry Law held on April 16, 1989. The Expiry Law never actually mentions the term 'amnesty' but delivers it in Article 1, in which the state renounces its right to prosecute members of the military or police with respect to crimes committed until March 1, 1985, and in Articles 3 and 4, which undermine the separation of powers by requiring judges to consult the Executive about exemptions to the Law.[511] The referendum campaign was organized by the National Committee for the Plebiscite (*Comisión Nacional Pro-Plebiscite* – CNP) using the constitutional provision to referendum under Article 79 to derogate a law within a year of its promulgation by collecting the signatures of 25% of the electorate.[512] The CNP campaign was announced by Elisa Dellepiane and Matilde Rodríguez, the widows of two politicians assassinated in Buenos Aires, and María Ester Gatti, a grandmother of a disappeared.[513] The CNP drew its main support from social organizations, SERPAJ, the union movement, and politicians aligned with the *Frente Amplio*, including the *Tupamaros* who were not yet part of this coalition.[514] A split decision of the Supreme Court, in May 1988, upholding the constitutionality of the Expiry Law only added impetus to the CNP campaign.[515] The referendum represented not just a challenge to the Expiry Law but to President Sanguinetti's whole programme of *continuismo* through amnesty and amnesia. While the CNP campaigned for

---

510 Gillespie 2006, o.c., p. 80.

511 F. Lessa, 'Barriers to Justice: The *Ley de Caducidad* and Impunity in Uruguay' in F. Lessa and L.A. Payne (eds.) *Amnesty in the Age of Human Rights Accountability: Comparative and International Perspectives*, Cambridge University Press, Cambridge 2012, p. 123, at p. 126.

512 Hite and Morlino 2004, o.c., p.25.

513 D. Sharnak, 'Uruguay's long transitional decade and a new era of gendered activism' (2017) 23 *Journal of Iberian and Latin American Studies*, 383.

514 M. Humphrey and E. Valverde, 'Peace and Justice Service of Uruguay / El Servicio Paz y Justicia' in L. Stan and N. Nedelsky (eds.), *Encyclopedia on Transitional Justice*, Cambridge University Press, Cambridge 2013, p. 3.

515 J.-M. Burt, et al., 'Civil Society and the Resurgent Struggle against Impunity in Uruguay (1986–2012)' (2013a) 7 *International Journal of Transitional Justice* 306, at 313.

the Green Vote to derogate the Expiry Law in the street, the conservative parties advocated for the Yellow Vote in support of the Law using state television to present their case.[516] The Green Vote argued that equality before the law was a constitutional principle and that truth and justice were essential to consolidate democracy, to strengthen state institutions against military pressures and for national reconciliation.[517] The Yellow Vote argued the Expiry Law should stand because it provided amnesty for both sides, that pacification would be achieved by looking forward not backwards and that the Law's derogation raised the question of 'what next?' and risked political destabilization.[518] The Green Vote campaign was a popular grass roots effort mobilized by the task of collecting the signatures to secure the referendum. The leftist *Frente Amplio* coalition, many of whose members had been imprisoned during the dictatorship, supported the Green Vote but generally kept a low profile to bolster the Green Vote campaign's grass roots image. For the younger generation, involvement in the Green Vote campaign became an important post-dictatorship education in public debate and political participation.

In conjunction with the Green Vote campaign, SERPAJ,[519] the leading human rights NGO, initiated their own *Nunca Más* truth project investigating and documenting state violence which was published just after the 1989 referendum. The Report became the unofficial reference document for human rights violations committed during the dictatorship.[520] It highlighted the failure of the Sanguinetti government to initiate any transitional justice measures to achieve national reconciliation by generating a consensus about the past based on truth and justice. By contrast, the Yellow Vote was based on a political alliance between the traditional parties, most significantly the *Colorados* and *Blancos*. Their collaboration continued the vital support the *Blancos* had given Sanguinetti to pass the Expiry Law in the first place. Nevertheless, the *Colorados* were the most prominent advocates for the Yellow Vote. The *Blancos* remained in the background to avoid the future political risk of being publicly identified with the ratification of the Expiry Law.[521] The Yellow Vote campaign defended the Naval Club Pact and the Expiry Law as the 'traditional way' of

516 S. Christian, 'Uruguay Votes to Retain Amnesty for the Military', *New York Times*, April 17, 1989, https://www.nytimes.com/1989/04/17/world/uruguay-votes-to-retain-amnesty-for-the-military.html.

517 Delgado 2001, o.c., p. 27.

518 Delgado 2001, o.c., p. 27.

519 R. Pagnucco and J.D. McCarthy, 'Advocating Nonviolent Direct Action In Latin America: The Antecedents and Emergence of SERPAJ' in S. Zunes, et al. (eds.), *Nonviolent Social Movements: A Geographical Perspective*, Wiley-Blackwell, Oxford 1999, p. 235.

520 *Uruguay Nunca Más: Informe Violación Derechos Humanos*, SERPAJ: Servicio Paz y Justicia Uruguay Montevideo, 1989.

521 L. Roniger and M. Sznajder, *The Legacy of Human-Rights Violations in the Southern Cone: Argentina, Chile, and Uruguay*, Oxford University Press, Oxford 1999, p. 88.

political reconciliation: 'political compromises that tempered the findings and the politico-legal application of the law in the name of social peace'.[522] Sanguinetti denounced the Green Vote as a political vendetta championed by the Leftist parties and not the grass roots human rights movement it claimed to be.[523] He rejected human rights as something coming from outside the society, in contrast to his own restoration project anchored in historical Uruguayan national practice of tolerance and compromise.[524] He viewed the Expiry Law as 'a political solution to a political problem'.[525] The CNP secured the necessary signatures to hold a referendum but it was defeated 43% to 57%. In response, President Sanguinetti declared: "Uruguay has resolved all the problems of the past. The debate about the dictatorship period is over. The country is facing its future".[526] He saw the poll as a 'demonstration of civility' in the 'Republic's best traditions' of tolerance.[527]

The outcome of the referendum highlighted the competing and irreconcilable perspectives on who was to blame for the dictatorship. For the supporters of the dictatorship, the issue was the betrayal by the revolutionary Left of Uruguayan democratic traditions. For many middle-class Uruguayans, the issue was why had the *Tupamaros* resorted to armed struggle after the good showing of the *Frente Amplio* in 1971 election. For the victims of the dictatorship the issue was the imperative of accountability for the human rights violations they had suffered. Human rights were a divisive, not unifying, discourse in transition. The defeat of the referendum revealed that party affiliation, political reconciliation and democratic consensus took precedence over accountability for human rights violations.[528] Sanguinetti's *continuismo* project juxtaposed order with disorder. The Uruguayan way of pacification produced order by restoring the traditional parties, by compromising with the military over impunity, by retaining the conservative judiciary, and by giving secure tenure to public employees who had been loyal to the dictatorship. Civility and consensus, central to the foundational myth of Uruguayan democracy, were championed as mechanisms for conflict resolution after the legacy of human rights violations.[529] General Hugo Medina viewed the exceptionalism of the Uruguay way of civility as an example to

---

522 Loveman and Lira 2007, o.c., p. 44.

523 Kritz 1995, o.c., p. 400.

524 E. Valverde and J. Hanley, 'Tolerancia y derechos humanos en Uruguay' (2017) 27 *Tabula Rasa* 459, at 477.

525 P. Ford, 'Despite Bitterness, Uruguayans Uphold Army Amnesty', *The Christian Science Monitor*, April 19, 1989, http://www.csmonitor.com/1989/0419/ouru.html.

526 Roniger and Sznajder 1999, o.c., p. 167.

527 L. Roniger, 'Transitional Justice and Protracted Accountability in Re-democratised Uruguay, 1985–2011' (2011) 43 *Journal of Latin American Studies* 693, at 703; Valverde and Hanley 2017, o.c., p. 459.

528 D. Altman, 'Popular initiatives in Uruguay: confidence votes on government or political loyalties' (2002) 21 *Electoral Studies*, 617.

529 Lessa 2013, o.c., p. 164.

all Latin American countries.[530] For Sanguinetti, the human rights agenda opened up uncertainty and the threat of disorder. "What next?" Human rights politics, after all, had arrived only in the transitional dictatorship after the 1980 constitutional referendum had forced the military to commit to the return of democratic government.[531] Moreover, the verdict of popular consultation was a 'sacred and unquestionable citizen ritual for conflict resolution' through the will of the people, providing a mandate for silence and forgetting.[532]

Even though the conservative Yellow Vote prevailed in the 1989 referendum, the traditional party clientelist politics promoting *continuismo* – business as usual – had already begun to erode.[533] Weinstein argues that Sanguinetti and the *Colorados* paid a high price for the referendum victory at the 1989 elections which gave the *Blancos* the presidency and the *Frente Amplio* the government of Montevideo.[534] A study by Buriano argues that the close correspondence between voting for the Law's repeal and votes received in national elections seven months later indicates a strong alignment with party affiliation.[535] As the influence of the traditional parties declined, the popularity of the leftist *Frente Amplio*, whose strong 'partisan identity' had been forged by rank and file members' experience of repression, grew.[536] In a society demobilized by military repression, the *Frente Amplio*'s focus on decentralization, participatory democracy and local mobilization represented an important strategy for re-democratization.[537] The traditional parties' embrace of market policies to manage the crisis of national debt and inflation, allowed the *Frente Amplio* to differentiate itself through a reinterpretation of the traditional *Batllista* statist and redistributive ideology opposing market reforms.[538] The *Frente Amplio* changed politics from protest to participation in 'designing, implementing, and managing community development projects'.[539] They also succeeded in significantly increasing voter turnout, especially in the poor suburbs of Montevideo.

---

530 Roniger and Sznajder 1999, o.c., p. 112.

531 Barahona De Brito 1997, o.c., p. 82.

532 F.L. Caraballo and M.F. Corradi, 'De la "Ley de Caducidad" al "voto verde": Nuevas formas de resistencia en marcos de legalidad. El caso de la Comisión Nacional Pro Referéndum' (2019) 17 *EU-topías: Revista de interculturalidad, comunicación y estudios europeos* 101, at 110.

533 A. Rankin, 'Reflections on the non-revolution in Uruguay' (1995) 211 *New Left Review* 131, at 137.

534 M. Weinstein, 'The Decline and Fall of Democracy in Uruguay: Lessons for the Future' in S. Sosnowski and L.B. Popkin (eds.), *Repression, Exile, and Democracy: Uruguayan Culture*, Duke University Press, Durham, NC 1993, p. 83.

535 A. Buriano, 'Ley de Caducidad en Uruguay y esencia ético-política de la izquierda' (2011) 19 *Perfiles latinoamericanos* 173, at 191.

536 Luna 2014, o.c., p. 87.

537 E. Canel, 'Municipal Decentralization and Participatory Democracy: Building a New Mode of Urban Politics in Montevideo City?' (2001) 71 *European Review of Latin American and Caribbean Studies* 25, at 30.

538 Luna 2014, o.c., p. 88.

539 Luna 2014, o.c., p. 36.

The defeat of the 1989 referendum consolidated the Sanguinetti's amnesty and amnesia policy and kept human rights off the political party agendas for a decade.[540] For the Uruguayan public, the democratic consensus against derogation imposed an enormous political and legal weight on the collective imaginary.[541] The democratic consolidation of amnesty through referendum had contradictory consequences. On the one hand, it entrenched the Expiry Law and removed it from the political agenda, on the other hand, it marked the beginning of the end for the restoration project based on *continuismo* by stimulating the mobilization of a new grass roots Leftist politics focused on citizen participation and the capture of local government. The post-dictatorship civil society mobilization energized political engagement at the local level, which, in turn, saw the Left consolidate political gains in municipal elections and then national elections, with the eventual victory of the *Frente Amplio* government in the 2004 parliamentary and presidential elections. The pacted transition, founded on political party reconciliation and the restoration of democratic government, created the political opportunity for the leftist new *Frente Amplio* coalition to win government. Their electoral constituency was built upon the leftists targeted for repression by the dictatorship and the increasing numbers of voters 'alienated from the traditional parties due to economic and political discontent'.[542]

3.3.3. PLEBISCITE ON THE EXPIRY LAW 2009

If the objective of the Expiry Law was to quarantine the past it failed. Although the defeat of the 1989 referendum removed the Law from the political agenda of the main political parties for a decade, the demand for accountability remained a live issue for the families of the disappeared, human rights organizations and certain politicians. Their post-referendum strategy was to continue to challenge impunity through memorialization of the disappeared, such as in the annual May 20 'March of Silence' (*Marcha del Silencio*) initiated in 1996, and by trying to initiate court investigations into dictatorship era crimes. Until 2000, their efforts to initiate prosecutions were prevented by the combination of the Expiry Law, judicial conservatism and the absence of the right to launch private prosecutions.[543] President Sanguinetti stood firmly against exceptions

540 Roniger and Sznajder 1999, o.c., p. 127.

541 Errandonea 2008, o.c., pp. 64–65.

542 J.P. Luna, 'Frente Amplio and the Crafting of a Social Democratic Alternative in Uruguay' (2007) 49 *Latin American Politics and Society* 1, at 1.

543 Judicial activism was constrained by the financial dependence of the judiciary and the hierarchical structure of the judicial appointments. See E. Skaar, 'Legal Development and Human Rights in Uruguay: 1985–2002' (2007) 8 *Human Rights Review*, 52. In Argentina, where extensive participation rights for victims exists, human rights prosecutions were

to prosecutions. In April 1997, Sanguinetti rejected a request by Judge Alberto Reyes for an exception under Article 4 of the Expiry Law to allow an investigation into the assassination of Deputy Zelmar Michelini in Argentina in 1976 under Operation Condor.[544] The Judge argued the purpose of the investigation was to locate and exhume a clandestine grave and return the remains to the families, not to instigate criminal proceedings against the perpetrators. The Appeals Court overturned the order finding that only the executive could order investigations. President Sanguinetti rejected the petition of Judge Reyes to exercise his presidential power under Article 4 of the Expiry Law to open an investigation. Sanguinetti declared that the Expiry Law 'makes further investigations impossible' … and accused 'those who sought information on disappearances as being "intolerant" and a threat to democratic values'.[545] After Jorge Batlle from the *Colorado* Party became president in 2000, he began to narrow the scope of the Expiry Law by allowing the investigation of cases involving disappeared children.[546] In particular, he ordered DNA tests be conducted to determine the kinship of a girl thought to be the grandchild of Argentine poet, Juan Gelman, whose daughter, María Claudia García Iruretagoyena de Gelman, had disappeared in late 1976 and been secretly transferred to Uruguay where she gave birth to a daughter.[547] In response to lobbying by the Association of Mothers and Families of the Disappeared and Father Aguirre, the then Director of the human rights NGO SERPAJ-Uruguay, President Jorge Batlle began to address the question of the disappeared more systematically. Batlle established the Commission for Peace by presidential Decree 858/2000 (August 9, 2000), presided over by the Archbishop of Montevideo, Monsignor Nicolás Cotugno, to investigate the fate of the disappeared and to find four disappeared children who had not been restored to their families. However, the Commission proved to be very limited with no punitive powers or the capacity to gather evidence for use in future prosecutions.[548] The Commission's final report acknowledged that those who had disappeared in Uruguay – 32 out of the total number of 164 disappeared – had died after being tortured in military barracks, a finding that justified subsequent excavations of military property. The Batlle government

launched into crimes not covered by amnesty such as the abduction of the children of the disappeared. V. Michel and K. Sikkink, 'Human Rights Prosecutions and the Participation Rights of Victims in Latin America' (2013) 47 *Law & Society Review* 873, at 891.

544 Mallinder 2009, o.c., p. 61.

545 Barahona De Brito 2001, o.c., pp. 144–5.

546 Jorge Batlle was the fourth member of the Batlle family to hold the office of President highlighting the dynastic character of the political elite in Uruguay.

547 *Gelman v. Uruguay*, Inter-American Court of Human Rights, Judgment of February 24, 2011 (Merits and Reparations), Costa Rica http://www.corteidh.or.cr/docs/casos/articulos/seriec_221_ing.pdf.

548 E. Skaar, 'Uruguay: reconstructing peace and democracy through transitional justice' in E. Skaar, et al. (eds.), *After Violence: Transitional Justice, Peace, and Democracy*, Routledge, London 2015, p. 67, at p. 73.

adopted the Commission's findings and provided reparations to the families of the disappeared, introduced laws criminalizing torture and forced disappearance and paid compensation to families of victims who had died in detention during the dictatorship and to victims of guerrilla violence.[549]

When the *Frente Amplio* came to power in 2005, President Vázquez set out to increase prosecutions by granting exemptions under Article 4 of the Expiry Law and by trying to narrow the Law's scope. During his presidency (2005–2010), the number of exclusions proceeding to legal prosecution increased significantly to 45 cases focused on actions that occurred outside Uruguay in Argentina and Paraguay.[550] As a result of these exclusions several of the leading political and military figures of the dictatorship were prosecuted. Former President Juan María Bordaberry and former Foreign Minister Juan Carlos Blanco Estradé were prosecuted for the assassinations of Senator Zelmar Michelini and Deputy Héctor Gutiérrez Ruiz in 1976 in Argentina, and Uruguay's last military dictator, Gregorio Conrado Álvarez was prosecuted for the forced disappearance of political prisoners. Bordaberry was convicted, in March 2010, with 30 years' imprisonment for violating the constitution in the coup.[551] Gregorio Conrado Álvarez was convicted in October 2009 for 37 counts of murder and human rights violations.[552] President Tabaré Vázquez also proposed an Interpretative Law designed to exclude particular crimes from amnesty – economic crimes, crimes committed by civilian and military leaders and high ranking official during the dictatorship, crimes committed outside Uruguayan territory such as the illegal appropriation of children – and to transfer responsibility for the determination of exclusions under the Expiry Law from the President to the courts.[553] Vázquez failed to enact the Interpretative Law in the face of strong opposition from the military and traditional parties.

The arrival of the *Frente Amplio* in power in 2005 also opened the opportunity to campaign for a second citizen-initiated plebiscite to repeal the Expiry Law. The families of the disappeared were the driving force behind the second citizen-initiated referendum campaign seeking truth and justice.[554]

---

549 L. Rohter, 'Uruguay: Compensation for Dictatorship' *New York Times*, April 22, 2003, https://www.nytimes.com/2003/04/22/world/world-briefing-americas-uruguay-compensation-for-dictatorship.html.

550 Skaar 2015, o.c., p. 74.

551 W. de León 'Former President Juan Maria Bordaberry is condemned to thirty years of prison and 15 years of precautionary detention for the offenses of "crimes against the constitution", two "political homicides" and the "forced disappearance" of nine citizens', *The National Security Archive*, March 30, 2010, https://nsarchive.gwu.edu/NSAEBB/NSAEBB309/Summary.pdf.

552 See 'Annual Report: Uraguay 2010', *Amnesty International*, May 28, 2010, https://www.amnestyusa.org/research/reports/annual-report-uruguay-2010.

553 Lessa, 2012, o.c., p. 136.

554 Skaar 2007, o.c., p. 52.

They argued the Law needed to be repealed by plebiscite and not through Congress to provide the desired retrospective effects to allow the prosecution of dictatorship era crimes.[555] It was launched in September 2007, with the establishment of the National Coordinator for the Annulment of the Expiry Law, (*Coordinadora Nacional por la Nulidad de la Ley de Caducidad*) and by June 2009 the required number of signatures to put the question to a referendum had been secured.[556] The Supreme Court declaration that the Expiry Law was unconstitutional, just a week before the election/referendum, and strong criticism of the Law by international human rights organizations gave the YES campaign confidence about the outcome.[557] Just before the plebiscite Guadalupe Marengo, Americas Deputy Director at Amnesty International, declared: 'This law was designed as a get-out-of-jail-free card for those who tortured, killed and disappeared people in Uruguay'.[558] Eduardo Galeano, the famous Uruguayan literary figure, had optimistically declared: 'We believe that our country has shown in the first years of the *Frente Amplio* government being in office that we are no longer that country that was paralyzed by fear. It is a sad legacy of the military dictatorship, which has condemned us to pay its debts and to forget its crimes'.[559] The referendum, held on October 25, 2009, the same date as the national election, was again defeated 52% to 48%, even though the leftist *Frente Amplio* retained government and José Mujica, a former MLN *Tupamaro* leader, was elected president. The plebiscite defeat revealed just how polarized the country remained over the question of impunity. Moreover, from the beginning of the campaign, the *Frente Amplio* itself was divided between the grass roots organizations and leadership over whether the party should participate in the signature collection campaign.[560] Many of the *Frente Amplio* leadership felt the

---

555 It would end the statute of limitations as a way to prevent criminal prosecutions. See Bentancur, o.c., p. 44.

556 E. Allier-Montaño and C. V. Ovalle, '"As an Unhealed Wound": Memory and Justice in Post-Dictatorship Uruguay', in E. Allier-Montaño and E. Crenzel (eds.), *The Struggle for Memory in Latin America: Recent History and Political Violence*, Palgrave Macmillan, New York 2015, p. 35, at p. 47.

557 This Supreme Court decision was made with respect to the investigation of Nibia Sabalsagaray, a young activist who was tortured and killed in 1974. See 'Annual Report: Uruguay 2010', *Amnesty International*, May 28, 2010, http://www.amnestyusa.org/research/reports/annual-report-uruguay-2010.

558 'Uruguay must annul law that protects police and military torture suspect', *Amnesty International*, October 20, 2009, https://www.amnesty.org/en/latest/news/2009/10/uruguay-debe-anular-legislacion-protege-autores-tortura-policial-militar-20091020/.

559 The *Frente Amplio* government was a broad coalition of around 12 leftist parties which included the *Movimiento de Liberación Nacional-Tupamaros* or Tupamaros National Liberation Movement, previously the armed guerrilla movement, the military repressed. M. Fox 'Hope and Disappointment in Uruguay's Elections', *Upside Down World*, November 2, 2009, https://upsidedownworld.org/main/content/view/2193/1/.

560 V.P. Bentancur, et al., 'The Case of Uruguay's Frente Amplio' in F. Rosenblatt, et al. (eds.), *Diminished Parties: Democratic Representation in Contemporary Latin America*, Cambridge University Press, Cambridge 2021, p. 29, at p. 45.

Expiry Law had already been settled by the 1989 referendum. José Mujica, in the lead up to the 2004 elections, had expressed that view.[561] In 2005, Mauricio Rosencoff, another former MLN *Tupamaro* guerrilla leader, also emphasized the need to prioritize current social and economic needs of people rather than engage in battles over the Expiry Law and the past – 'We were in a war and we lost!'.[562] Rosencoff's war narrative was shared by the military and many of the *Tupamaros*.[563] Because of these divisions, the *Frente Amplio* did not publicly advocate in support of the referendum campaign.[564]

The Expiry Law was finally repealed by the *Frente Amplio* government with the introduction of Law 18.831 (Punitive Powers of the State: Restoration of punitive powers for crimes committed in the application of state terrorism until March 1, 1985), on October 27, 2011. The Law also harmonized Uruguay's legislation with the Supreme Court's ruling on the *Sabalsagaray* case and its constitutional ruling on Article 72. In October 2010, in anticipation of a critical judgment by the IACtHR in the *Gelman* case, Mujica had proposed a second Interpretative Law to remove Articles (1, 3 and 4) of the Expiry Law considered unconstitutional but he failed to gain the necessary parliamentary support.[565] The repeal of the Law was enacted only after President Mujica came under considerable international legal pressure from the IACtHR judgment in the *Gelman v. Uruguay* case[566] concerning the forced disappearance of an Argentinian citizen in Uruguay and the abduction and change of identity of her daughter to whom she gave birth in captivity. IACtHR judgment reflected the jurisprudence it had developed concerning the systematic repression conducted under Plan Condor, the abduction of the children of mothers disappeared as violence against women, the suppression and substitution of identity and the legal effect of amnesty laws silencing the rights of the victims and their families to know the truth and seek justice.[567] The IACtHR judgment also dismissed the argument that the Expiry Law had twice been endorsed by plebiscites arguing that democratic majorities are 'limited by international norms and obligations related to the protection of HR recognised by the American Convention on

561 J. Mujica, 'En la perspectiva de un gobierno progresista' in J.A. Louis (ed.), *Y si gana el Frente Amplio? Uruguay decide su future*, Capital Intelectual, *Le Monde Diplomatique edición Cono Sur*, Buenos Aires 2004, p. 29.

562 Authors' interview with Mauricio Rosencoff, February 2005.

563 Lessa 2013, o.c., p. 170.

564 Buriano 2015, o.c., p. 185.

565 Skaar 2015, o.c., p. 80.

566 *Gelman v. Uruguay*, Inter-American Court of Human Rights, Judgment of February 24, 2011 (Merits and Reparations), Costa Rica.

567 Y. Gamarra, 'National Responses in Latin America to International Events Propelling the Justice Cascade: The *Gelman* Case' in J.M. Beneyto and D. Kennedy (eds.), *New Approaches to International Law: The European and the American Experiences*, T.M.C. Asser Press, The Hague 2013, p. 75, at p. 89.

Human Rights'.[568] The IACtHR judgment, in part motivated by the failure of the second plebiscite on the Expiry Law, ordered Uruguay to clear the legal obstacles of 'the statute of limitations, the principle of non-retroactivity of criminal norms, the *res juridicata* principle, the *ne bis in idem* principle and any similar ground for exclusion of responsibility that had impeded criminal proceedings in the Gelman case'.[569] In short, it declared that Uruguay had failed to 'comply with its obligation to adapt its domestic law'.[570] Nevertheless, considerable resistance remained from the opposition parties, and some members of the *Frente Amplio*, over the need to annul the Expiry Law. Some argued that the annulment of the Law would be unconstitutional because it would overrule two popular consultations in 1989 and 2009. Moreover, in 2011, the majority of public opinion was still against it.[571] Others argued that the repeal of the Expiry Law had been made largely irrelevant because of its erosion through the exercise of presidential discretion granting exceptions to the Law under Article 4, especially after the *Frente Amplio* came to power in 2005 – Vázquez had granted 45 exceptions under his presidency (2004–2010) and Mujica had granted 80 exceptions in a single decree in 2011.[572] Significantly, the prosecutions that proceeded from these exemptions resulted in the conviction of the most senior figures in the civilian-military dictatorship for long prison terms.[573] Yet, keeping the power of exemptions to prosecute with the executive left justice susceptible to 'political winds' shaped by decisions made 'in the name of political unity and patronage'.[574]

Despite the Expiry Law's repeal, the prosecution of dictatorship era crimes has remained difficult. Since 2011, the Supreme Court has oscillated in its position on the constitutionality of the amnesty laws on the grounds of whether

568 Ibid., at p. 90.

569 H. Olásolo, *International Criminal Law: Transitional Criminal Organizations and Transitional Justice*, Brill Nijhoff, Leiden 2018, p. 143.

570 F. Michelini, 'Reflections on Uruguayan Law No. 18831 a Year After Its Enactment' (2013) 20 *Human Rights Brief*, 2.

571 C. Legrand, 'Uruguay split over ending of amnesty for rights violations under dictatorship', *The Guardian*, April 26, 2011, https://www.theguardian.com/world/2011/apr/26/uruguay-human-rights-amnesty-legrand.

572 Mujica announced the mass exceptions by decree on the 38th anniversary of the military coup (June 27, 1973) after his failure to repeal the law in Congress in May 2011. See 'Uruguay Open to Rights Cases of Dictator Era', *New York Times*, July 1, 2011, https://www.nytimes.com/2011/07/01/world/americas/01uruguay.html.

573 The civilian dictators Juan María Bordaberry (1973–6) was convicted (February 9, 2010) for an attack on the constitutional order, nine crimes of enforced disappearance and two political homicides and sentenced to 30 years of imprisonment and Gregorio Álvarez (1981–85) was convicted to 25 years for disappearance of 37 people (1977–8). The former Foreign Minister Juan Carlos Blanco (1973–76) was also convicted and received a life sentence in 2006 for the aggravated murder of two members of Congress (Zelmar Michelini and Héctor Gutiérrez Ruiz). See Olásolo 2018, o.c., p. 143.

574 D. Soltman, 'Applauding Uruguay's Quest for Justice: Dictatorship, Amnesty, and Repeal of Uruguay Law No. 15.848' (2014) 12 *Washington University Global Studies Law Review* 829, at 845.

a serious human rights violation constitutes a crime or crime against humanity. The underlying issue has been whether dictatorship era crimes should be subject to a statute of limitations. Law 18.831 established that all crimes committed by the military between 1986 and 2011 constituted crimes against humanity according to Uruguay's human rights treaty obligations.[575] However, in February 2013, the Supreme Court declared Law 8.831 unconstitutional because Articles 2 and 3 contradicted the non-retroactivity of criminal norms. The Court decided that the military actions undertaken during the dictatorship were common crimes, not crimes against humanity, which were therefore susceptible to a statute of limitations. The significance of this judgment was the cut-off date of 26 years and eight months for crimes to be investigated and brought to trial was before November 1, 2011 had already passed. The judgment also treated torture as an ordinary crime.[576] Even more controversial was the Supreme Court's reassignment of Judge Motta, an activist judge who had opened more than 50 cases on human rights violations committed during the dictatorship, to a civil court thereby suspending her investigations.[577] A court judgment, on September 25, 2017, supported the defence argument that crimes did not constitute crimes against humanity, but the ruling 'makes no mention of well-recognized rights to truth, access to justice and reparations for victims of the dictatorship'.[578] To draw attention to the ongoing obstacles to justice created by the Supreme Court judgments, a new human rights campaign for justice under the banner 'Justice delayed is justice denied' was launched during the 165th period of hearings of IACHR in Montevideo between 23–27 October 2017.[579]

The uneven decisions of the courts in classifying dictatorship-era crimes as crimes against humanity, or not, reveals ongoing impunity. Recent tensions in civil-military relations has also highlighted the relative autonomy of the military over their affairs including the threat of removal of the generous privileges and entitlements of military officers, military resentment over the alleged lack of fairness in the trials of military officers, and the anachronistic role of the Tribunals of Honour of the Armed Forces (*Los Tribunales de Honor de las*

---

575 Roht-Arriaza 2015, o.c., p. 355.

576 P. Le Goff and F. Lessa, 'Uruguay's Supreme Court of Injustice', *The Argentina Independent*, March 21, 2013.

577 J.-M. Burt, 'Judge's Removal Causes Concerns over Human Rights Investigations in Uruguay', *WOLA*, February 20, 2013, https://www.wola.org/analysis/judges-removal-causes-concerns-over-human-rights-investigations-in-uruguay/.

578 F. Lessa, et al., 'New Ruling by Uruguay's Supreme Court of Justice once again Jeopardizes the Search for Truth and Justice for Dictatorship-Era Crimes', *WOLA*, November 7, 2017, https://www.wola.org/analysis/new-ruling-uruguays-supreme-court-justice-jeopardizes-search-truth-justice-dictatorship-era-crimes/.

579 Ibid.

Fuerzas Armadas) judging the professional conduct of the Uruguayan officer corps.[580] Civil-military tensions came to a head, in March 2019, following a press exposé of the proceedings of a Special Military Tribunal held in 2018 that had exonerated retired senior officers of unethical behaviour after they had testified to committing crimes against humanity before the Special Tribunal.[581] These officers were already serving prison sentences of between 20 and 25 years for convictions in the criminal courts for committing crimes against humanity. In response to the press revelation, President Tabaré Vázquez sacked the Minister for Defence, Jorge Menéndez, and vice-Minister for Defence, Daniel Montiel and six generals, one of whom was the Commander in Chief of the Army, José González, and five others who had been members of two Special Tribunals of Honour.[582] They were dismissed because they had approved decisions that violated human rights and had failed to immediately report these crimes to their superiors and suspend the Tribunal hearings when they became aware of them, as required by law.[583] President Vázquez had only just appointed the Commander in Chief of the Army after dismissing his predecessor, General Guido Manini Ríos, for his public questioning of the impartiality of judicial power by not providing the same guarantees of rights to the military as they had to the guerrillas – the 'enemy'.[584] The most controversial testimony in the Tribunal report was that of the retired General José Gavazzo who admitted responsibility for the disappearance and death of the leftist militant Roberto Gomensoro in 1973.[585] In its report the Tribunal found that Gavazzo had behaved professionally and ethically in his conduct toward Gomensoro despite the fact that he had been found guilty in the criminal courts in 2009 and sentenced to serve 20 years for

580 *El Tribunal Especial de Honor para Oficiales Superiores No. 1* was established for the purpose of hearing the cases of retired military officers. See Ministerio de Defensa Nacional, Expediente No. 2016.01433-0, Tema 226 Tribunales de Honor, https://www.docdroid.net/Ds2ekUz/expediente-completo-del-tribunal-de-honor.pdf.

581 L. Haberkorn, 'Gavazzo admitió que arrojó el cuerpo de Roberto Gomensoro al Río Negro', *El Observador*, March 30, 2019.

582 'Uruguayan president caught on the wrong foot forced to sack six generals and minister of Defense', *Mercopress*, April 2, 2019, https://en.mercopress.com/2019/04/02/uruguayan-president-caught-on-the-wrong-foot-forced-to-sack-six-generals-and-minister-of-defense.

583 Artículo 77 del Decreto 55/985, que dispone "cuando el Tribunal de Honor intervenga en cualquier asunto en el que exista la presunción de un delito, común o militar, su Presidente comunicará de inmediato al Superior que corresponda suspendiendo las actuaciones del Tribunal, hasta tanto el Superior se pronuncie". ('When the Tribunal of Honour intervenes in any matter where there is a presumption of crime, civil or militar, its President will immediately communicate to whoever is its Superior Officer, suspending the functioning of the Tribunal, until the Superior Officer makes a decision'). Reglamento De Los Tribunales De Honor De Las Fuerzas Armadas, Decreto No. 55/985 de 08/02/1985 artículo 1, https://www.impo.com.uy/bases/decretos-reglamento/55-1985.

584 S. Artigas, 'Todos le hicieron el juego a Manini Ríos', *Laizquiarda Diario*, March 13, 2019, https://www.laizquierdadiario.com.uy/Todos-le-hicieron-el-juego-a-Manini-Rios.

585 Haberkorn 2019, o.c.

his crimes.[586] He was one of 20 officers serving between 20–25 years for the crime of enforced disappeared of around 200 Uruguayans, mainly in Argentina, as part of Plan Condor.

The Tribunals of Honour were an anachronistic 19th century Spanish institution reintroduced in 2014 with the support of *Frente Amplio* President, José Mujica and the Minister of Defence, Fernandez Huidobro, both former guerrillas, for members of the military convicted by the criminal courts for human rights crimes.[587] The Tribunals were re-established specifically to try Gregorio Alvarez who had been sentenced to 25 years for human rights crimes, but he died before being brought before a Tribunal. The role of the Tribunals, which are independent from the military justice system, is to judge the moral and ethical conduct of military members. If an officer is judged by their actions not to have upheld the professional ethics of the military a Tribunal can sanction the officer through loss of a pension, the right to wear a uniform, the right to care in a medical hospital or, in the extreme, expulsion from the officer corps. The coexistence of state judicial power with a military jurisdiction for officers already convicted of crimes against humanity is contradictory. It established an inevitable conflict between criminal judgments against convicted military officers and a code of military ethics which undermines them. What the Tribunal decisions highlighted was the officer corps' code of silence in which senior officers could confess to crimes they had not admitted to before the criminal courts. The revelation about the Tribunal decisions was made worse when it became apparent that the Defence Minister and the President – as head of the Army – had signed off on the minutes of the Tribunal without having read them.[588] In April 2019, the *Frente Amplio* government decided to close down the Tribunals altogether.[589]

From a transitional justice perspective, the unresolved legal dispute over whether the dictatorship committed ordinary crimes or crimes against humanity continues to disable the generative potential of truth and justice measures in the reconciliation process. Firstly, it obscures the systemic political and not just individual criminal nature of the violence normalized under authoritarian governance. Secondly, the case-by-case approach to prosecutions, either through the mechanism of executive exemptions prosecutions allowed for under the Expiry Law or through Supreme Court judgments after it's repeal in 2011, has

586 Haberkorn 2019, o.c.

587 C.M. Cerna, 'Honor Tribunals in Uruguay today', *Global Military Justice Reform*, February 2, 2019, http://globalmjreform.blogspot.com/2019/02/honor-tribunals-in-uruguay-today.html.

588 'Uruguayan president caught on the wrong foot forced to sack six generals and minister of Defense', *Mercopress*, April 2, 2019, https://en.mercopress.com/2019/04/02/uruguayan-president-caught-on-the-wrong-foot-forced-to-sack-six-generals-and-minister-of-defense.

589 N. Silva, 'Frente Amplio acordó eliminar los Tribunales de Honor militar', *La Republica*, April 27, 2019.

emphasized individual criminal responsibility thereby avoiding any questions about the systemic and political nature of human rights violations. Thirdly, it highlights the continuing lack of state leadership in generating an inclusive national narrative about the past around which reconciliation could coalesce. By default, the military's narrative of the counterinsurgency as a national war to save the nation from an international revolutionary armed movement has persisted and the question about their responsibility for human rights violations was neutralized by the two demons theory.[590] Fourthly, in Uruguay the rehabilitation of democracy as a political justice measure was given precedence over human rights accountability. Democratic consensus about restoration allowed the dictatorship to be compartmentalized as an 'authoritarian parenthesis', an historical aberration in the myth of the long democratic tradition naturalized as part of Uruguayan national identity. Fifthly, the pact between the military and trusted traditional political elite failed to restore the partidocratic order when the leftist *Frente Amplio* deployed their political victimhood – those targeted by the military – to build a progressive political constituency to gain political power rather mobilize around an identity as human rights victims. In this political equation victimhood based on human rights violations referred back to a defeated revolutionary leftist project which was not politically very useful. In fact, the more the *Frente Amplio* has been able to represent itself as the natural party of government the more their past revolutionary path has been publicly criticized as an unnecessary and counterproductive decision.

In Uruguay, the return to democracy as the 'natural order' sought to put authoritarian repression in the past but also the revolutionary project of the Left. The Uruguayan transition was a particular instance of what Meister refers to as 'transitional liberalism' in which neither the beneficiaries of the dictatorship or its victims were to be judged, punished or acknowledged.[591] The victims – the political prisoners who were tortured/imprisoned and the families of the disappeared – were not redeemable in terms of the original Naval Club Pact that underpinned amnesty in Uruguay because reciprocal amnesty had been framed as reciprocal culpability in the 'two demons' narrative. Moreover, the defeat of the two citizen-initiated popular consultations held 20 years apart demonstrated how deeply polarized the society remained over the issue of amnesty. The beneficiaries of repression – those who had sworn an oath of allegiance to the military to preserve their jobs and were able to continue their normal lives – were also protected against lustration at transition. They supported a 'social peace' narrative founded on the legitimacy of democratic consensus. Reconciliation was not part of the lexicon of transition. In fact, after

590 Achugar 2008, o.c., at p. 202.
591 R. Meister, *After Evil: A Politics of Human Rights*, Columbia University Press, New York, NY 2011, pp. 29–30.

the *Frente Amplio* government held onto power continuously between 2005 and 2020, public opinion surveys on the past regularly questioned the wisdom of the *Tupamaros*' decision to take the route of armed struggle rather than reform through democratic electoral politics.[592] But what these surveys reveal is the gulf between the present post-dictatorship post-Cold War generation, and the 1960s generation whose world was shaped by the US Cold War geopolitics in the Western Hemisphere. Firstly, the question about the decision to resort to revolutionary violence was a continental, not just a national one, and was strongly influenced by the success of the Cuban revolution; and secondly, the prospects for change through legal and peaceful means at that time looked increasingly bleak with the growing number of military *coups* against elected governments in Central America, Argentina and Brazil.[593] It also forgets the fate of the democratically elected Socialist government of President Allende in Chile deposed by military *coup* on September 11, 1973. From the perspective of the victims, especially those from organizations, political parties and sectors targeted for repression, translating the outcome of the conflict into a problem of 'human rights violations' focuses on the individual experience of repression and not its political causes or effects. Traumatic events divided people through their lived experience of time as 'trauma time' and 'linear time', between those who live with the past as ever-present and those who are able to live in historical and narrativized time.[594] The human rights lens optimistically sees justice as the basis for reconciliation while overlooking the obstacles of diverse political subjectivities, social cleavages and divided universes produced by repression as a deliberate strategy of governance through fragmentation. Instead, the consensus underlying the Naval Club Pact was that the restoration of democratic Uruguay as the natural political order, framing the repression as merely an 'authoritarian parenthesis', could be ignored as an aberration.

3.4. CONCLUSION

In Uruguay's transition from an authoritarian to a democratic regime, the political rituals of transition – elections and plebiscites/referenda – were the hinge of transition, not justice rituals – trials, truth commissions – seeking to generate a consensus about how to manage the past based on international legal

592 For an analysis of youth perceptions on the dictatorship see: M. Achugar, et al., 'Re/constructing the past: How young people remember the Uruguayan dictatorship' (2013) 24 *Discourse and Society* 265, at 273.

593 A. Marchesi, *Latin America's Radical Left: Rebellion and Cold War in the Global 1960s*, Cambridge University Press, Cambridge 2018, p. 7.

594 J. Edkins, *Trauma and the Memory of Politics*, Cambridge University Press, Cambridge/New York 2003, p. 229.

norms. This consensus could not be characterized as national reconciliation but a consensus not to address issues that would provoke division. Direct democracy shaped transition and endorsed the Uruguayan way of amnesty and amnesia of a period of almost 30 years. The three instances of direct democracy were: the 1980 military plebiscite, the 1989 citizen-initiated referendum over the Expiry Law and the 2009 citizen-initiated plebiscite to annul the Expiry Law. On these three occasions, democratic consensus decided the military's negotiated withdrawal from power; endorsed the legitimacy of Sanguinetti's transition model based on amnesty and amnesia; and supported the legal status quo in which the Expiry Law allowed for presidential exceptions for prosecutions without risking the politicization of the trials and polarizing society. The defeat of the 1989 referendum to annul the Expiry Law allowed Sanguinetti to establish the hegemony of the narrative of the 'two demons' – both sides were to blame – and of democratic consensus as a sacred expression of the myth of democracy as the natural political condition thereby putting the dictatorship into 'authoritarian parenthesis' which could be forgotten or cleansed. The 2009 plebiscite allowed the *Frente Amplio* government to transfer a divisive issue they were reluctant to take a clear stand on to the citizens.

The eventual repeal of the Expiry Law in 2011 by President Mujica has allowed more prosecutions of dictatorship era crimes but still selectively. The impact of the transition policy of amnesty and amnesia is that justice measures never became mechanisms for a state-led effort to generate a national consensus about the dictatorship and the illegitimacy of its tenure. Political parties, including the *Frente Amplio*, have not sought a political mandate based on compliance with international human rights norms. Both restitutive and retributive justice measures adopted have been on an individual case-by-case basis. The Law on National Pacification (1986) granted political prisoners amnesty and, to help them reintegrate into society, administered restitutive measures such as the restoration of jobs and/or state pensions as a form of compensation. When, after 2005, Tábare Vázquez exercised his power of exception for prosecution under the Expiry Law, they were approached as individual criminal cases not crimes against humanity.

The state has also avoided assuming responsibility for truth seeking to promote national reconciliation. By default, truth seeking was initially taken up by civil society organizations and movements making Uruguay unique in having a civil society-initiated truth commission (SERPAJ) with its *Nunca Más* Report. While President Jorge Batlle established a Peace Commission (2000) which focused on the disappeared, it proved to be a limited exercise in truth seeking, but it did recognize the families of the disappeared through reparations.[595] The

595 E. Allier, 'The Peace Commission: A Consensus on the Recent in Uruguay?' (2006) 81 *European Review of Latin American and Caribbean Studies* 87, at 89.

state has participated in memory projects by establishing the National Archives on Memory, a Museum of memory and a Library of Memory, and declared the annual 'Day of Never Again' *(Día del Nunca Más)* to support the democratization of memory, but these measures do not constitute an official narrative about the past, rather a multiplicity of performative memorializations.[596] The attempts by the Vázquez *Frente Amplio* government to reappropriate General José Gervasio Artigas – the national hero of independence – as a national symbol by resignifying his remains and the commemoration of his birthday were not popular. On the 245th anniversary of Artigas' birth, June 19, 2009, President Vázquez announced he would bring a bill to abrogate the military era decree that the remains of Artigas lie forever in the new mausoleum they built and inaugurated in 1977.[597] Vázquez proposed to close the mausoleum and relocate the remains of Artigas to the *Edificio Nacional.* The military dictatorship had built the mausoleum to entomb Artigas' remains to symbolically create an historical continuity between the founding war of independence and their project of violent renewal of *la patria*.[598] Artigas not only represented the fulcrum of the birth of the nation but also a powerful icon to change the polarity of the military. The 'good' *militar*, the one who had liberated Uruguay, had been returned to dissipate any negative feelings towards the army. However, the citizens were not impressed: they ironically remembered that Artigas had died in exile in Paraguay in 1850, unappreciated by the people for whom he helped gain independence. His remains were repatriated in 1855 and buried in the Central Cemetery of Montevideo where they had remained until 1977. The strong public reaction to Vázquez's attempt to symbolically reappropriate the nation suggested they wanted to let the past, the dictatorship and Artigas, rest.[599]

Vázquez also sought to resignify the anniversary of Artigas' birthday, June 19, 1764, by declaring it would be a day of national remembrance for the victims of the dictatorship (1973–1985) called the Never Again Day [*Día del Nunca Más*]. However the day never established itself as a prominent date on the national calendar.[600] *Crysol*, a human rights organization of former political prisoners, campaigned to have the date of the military coup on June 21, 1973 as day of national remembrance without success.[601] The lack of state-initiated national commemorative dates for the years of dictatorship contrasts with civil society commemorations, especially the March of Silence on 20 May

596 Skaar 2015, o.c., p. 83.

597 J.C. Knarr, 'The New Left and the Nation' (2010) 38 *Latin American Perspectives* 110, at 112.

598 I. Cosse and V. Markarian, *1975: año de la orientalidad: identidad, memoria e historia en una dictadura*, Ediciones Trice, Montevideo 1996, p. 66.

599 Knarr 2010, o.c., p.112.

600 'A diez años, ¿nunca más el Día del Nunca Más?', *El País* (Uruguay), June 19, 2017 https://www.elpais.com.uy/informacion/a-diez-anos-nunca-mas-el-dia-del-nunca-mas.

601 F. Lessa and P.-L. Le Goff, 'A silent anniversary in Uruguay?', *Al Jazeera*, June 27, 2013, https://www.aljazeera.com/opinions/2013/6/27/a-silent-anniversary-in-uruguay.

[*Marcha del Silencio*], initiated in 1996, commemorating the disappeared which now takes place over the whole month of May.[602] Another factor in Uruguay was that human rights activists and victim groups never became the driving force behind demands for accountability and truth seeking as they did in neighbouring Argentina in part because of the relatively small number of disappeared (164) compared with Argentina (30,000).[603] The Left was slow to turn to a universal human rights discourse because they viewed rights as the product of the radical transformation of capitalism.[604] Although political exiles had adopted human rights discourse in their campaigns allying with Amnesty International and petitioning the UNHRC against the dictatorship outside Uruguay, when they returned they found the discourse was largely absent. Many on the Left dropped their radical demands for criminal accountability and deployed human rights as a discourse to present themselves as reliable political actors willing to give up on revenge and embrace electoral politics.[605]

First, the 2009 Supreme Court decision declaring the Expiry Law unconstitutional and then the IACtHR ruling on the *Gelman* case saw Uruguay accept the legal harmonization of national law with international human rights standards under the ACHR and the growing hegemony of *ius constituionale commune* in Latin America with the repeal of the Expiry Law.[606] Civil society groups also helped overturn the law through their advocacy for the *Gelman* case in the IACtHR.[607] Law (18.831) removed the legal effect of the Expiry Law and established that a statute of limitations does not apply for dictatorship era crimes which were now categorized as crimes against humanity.[608] However, despite the repeal of the Expiry Law, accountability for dictatorship crimes remains difficult. Since 2011, there have been a limited number of prosecutions and many appeals.[609] Cases have experienced extensive delays. In 2021, 28 women presented a case to the IACHR concerning sexual violence and rape against 100 people which had made no progress in the Uruguayan courts since 2011 when they submitted it.[610] Activist judges have been penalized by transfer to other jurisdictions for

602 L. Elliott, 'White daisies bloom in Uruguay's streets, in memory of dictatorship missing', *Reuters*, May 21, 2023, https://www.reuters.com/world/americas/white-daisies-bloom-uruguays-streets-memory-dictatorship-missing-2023-05-20/.

603 Sikkink 2007, o.c., p. 130.

604 Moyn 2012, o.c., pp. 141–2.

605 K. Engle, 'Self-Critique, (Anti) Politics and Criminalization: Reflections on the History and Trajectory of the Human Rights Movement' in J.M. Beneyto and D. Kennedy (eds.), *New Approaches to International Law: The European and the American Experiences*, T.M.C. Asser Press, The Hague 2013 p. 41, at pp. 65–6.

606 Burt 2013, o.c., p. 318.

607 Burt 2013, o.c., p. 324.

608 Burt 2013, o.c., p. 322.

609 E. Salgueiro, 'Uruguay: A Law to Benefit Perpetrators of Crimes Against Humanity?', *Justiceinfo.net*, November 30, 2021.

610 'Victims of sexual torture seek justice in Uruguay', *UN OHCHR*, October 28, 2021, https://www.ohchr.org/en/stories/2021/10/victims-sexual-torture-seek-justice-uruguay.

making critical comments about the support for human rights.[611] In 2013, the Supreme Court ruled against the constitutionality of Law 18.831 (2011) to allow for the prosecution of dictatorship era crimes because it was retroactive.[612] The Supreme Court also found that in constitutional matters it had the last word, not the IACtHR.[613] In 2018, a specialized Prosecutor's Office for Crimes Against Humanity was established to improve the progress of prosecutions. However, even those military personnel convicted of dictatorship era crimes have been able to erode the legitimacy of Court verdicts in different ways. One example is the role of the Military Tribunals of Honour undermining the convictions of officers, while another is the initiative of a bill, submitted to the Senate in 2022, to have all persons over 65 released on house detention because of COVID-19 (to the benefit of 26 former military and civilian personnel convicted of crimes against humanity).[614] The search for the disappeared and reparations policy continues to contribute to impunity. A recent UN country report by the *Working Group on Enforced or Involuntary Disappearances* found that Uruguay had failed to make sufficient effort to locate the disappeared.[615] The Uruguay Reparations Law (18.596) 2009 recognized the right of victims to reparations but Article 22 requires victims who accept reparations to waive their right to accountability.[616] State acknowledgement of their responsibility to investigate, prosecute and provide reparations for dictatorship-era crimes still needs to be extracted by the human rights and victims groups. On November 15, 2022, the IACtHR found Uruguay had failed to meet its obligation under the ACHR to investigate and prosecute those responsible for the enforced disappearance of Luis Eduardo González and Óscar Tassino Asteazu and the executions of Diana Maidanik, Silvia Reyes and Laura Raggio. It had also denied the rights of their families to know the truth of what had happened and failed to provide reparations.[617] The NGO CELS (*Instituto de Estudios Legales y Sociales del Uruguay*) and families

---

611 In 2013, the Supreme Court of Justice transferred Judge Mota, who had opened investigations on 50 dictatorship era crimes, to another jurisdiction without clarifying the reasons. See F. Lessa and P-F Le Goff, 'Elusive Justice in Uruguay', *Al Jazeera*, February 13, 2014, https://www.aljazeera.com/opinions/2014/2/13/elusive-justice-in-uruguay. See also C. Liscano and M. C. Díaz, *La impunidad y su relato. El caso Mariana Mota*, Planeta, Montevideo 2022.

612 M. Castaldi, 'Uruguay's Supreme Court rules against dictatorship trials', *Reuters*, February 13, 2013.

613 C.A.V. Sandoval and F.F.C. Veçoso, 'A Human Rights' Tale of Competing Narratives' (2017) 8 *Revista Direito e Práxis* 1603, at 1631.

614 Salgueiro 2021, o.c.

615 'UN experts: Uruguay must step up search for disappeared persons and fight impunity', UN Working Group on Enforced or Involuntary Disappearances, *OHCHR*, July 15, 2022, https://www.ohchr.org/en/press-releases/2022/07/un-experts-uruguay-must-step-search-disappeared-persons-and-fight-impunity.

616 Salgueiro 2021, o.c.

617 Corte Interamericana de Derechos Humanos. Caso *Maidanik y Otros vs. Uruguay*. Sentencia de 15 de noviembre de 2021 *(Fondo y Reparaciones)*, https://www.corteidh.or.cr/docs/casos/articulos/resumen_444_esp.pdf?prm=ep-app.

of the victims had first taken the case to the IACHR in 2007.[618] At a ceremony held in Congress on June 15, 2023, the Uruguayan government – President Luis Lacalle Pou was not in attendance – acknowledged its responsibilities.

Yet a longer historical perspective on transition reveals that democratic restoration in 1985 marked the beginning of democratic transformation in Uruguay. The military did manage to manoeuvre a friendly *Colorado* government into office in 1985 under President Sanguinetti but his government represented the twilight of the partidocratic order that had dominated 100 years of Uruguayan politics until 1971. The *Frente Amplio* very quickly emerged as an important political force, winning the government of Montevideo in 1989 and then the national government in 2005. Their political identity had been forged by military repression. Despite the defeat of the 1989 referendum, the Green Vote campaign provided an important new experience in mobilization and political activism for the youth, giving impetus to *Frente Amplio's* strategy of building a decentralized grass roots organization with Batllista characteristics. In Uruguay, democratic consensus is still prioritized over a judicial consensus based on human rights. The contemporary popular reflection on the *Tupamaros*' historic choice between change through revolutionary insurgency or through parliamentary reform reflects the post-dictatorship hegemony of the discourse of democratic consensus and that the Cold War era is a foreign country for most of those living in post-Cold War Uruguay.

---

618 G.D. Campanella, 'Uruguay reconoce crímenes de la dictadura en un acto oficial sin la presencia del presidente', *El País*, June 16, 2023, https://elpais.com/internacional/2023-06-16/uruguay-reconoce-crimenes-de-la-dictadura-en-un-acto-oficial-sin-la-presencia-del-presidente.html.

CHAPTER 4
SPAIN
The Law of Historical Memory and Justice

4.1. INTRODUCTION

In 2007, Prime Minister Zapatero introduced the Law of Historical Memory (LHM) as a restorative justice initiative to recognize the rights and memory of the Republican victims of the Spanish Civil War (1936–9) and acknowledge their experience of repression and suffering under the Francoist dictatorship (1939–1975).[619] The LHM was introduced to challenge the official censorship of the post-transition investigation of the past imposed by the 'pact of forgetting' (*pacto del olvido*), institutionalized in the Amnesty Law (1977) as a necessary condition for political reconciliation and democratic transition. The LHM was designed to disrupt, but not overturn, the political fix of the Amnesty Law (1977) by introducing a human rights lens on the past in order to help democratize Civil War memory through the inclusion of Republican memory and a recognition of their suffering. Its focus, as a transitional justice initiative, was the recovery from oblivion the estimated 130,000 missing Republicans buried in clandestine mass graves scattered around the country during the Civil War.[620] The LHM in Articles 11–14 legally acknowledge the existence of the 'violently disappeared' and establish the state's role in facilitating their investigation, location and identification.[621] By focusing on the disappeared, the LHM harnessed firstly, the traumatic memory of the surviving relatives of the disappeared to search for their lost members; secondly, the flexibility of the dead body as a cultural

619 Law of Historical Memory, (*Ley 57/2007 por la que se reconocen y amplían derechos y se establecen medidas en favor de quienes padecieron persecución o violencia durante la Guerra Civil y la Dictadura*, (BOE) Núm. 310, de 27 de diciembre de 2007).

620 F. Ferrándiz and C.G.M. Robben, 'Introduction: The Ethnography of Exhumations' in F. Ferrándiz and C.G.M. Robben (eds.), *Necropolitics: Mass Graves and Exhumations in the Age of Human Rights*, University of Pennsylvania Press, Philadelphia, PA 2015, p. 1. To date the Ministry of Justice has identified 2,382 grave sites containing an estimated 45,000 remains of which fewer than 400 have been exhumed. See 'Who are the missing/Spain', *ICMP*, https://www.icmp.int/the-missing/where-are-the-missing/spain/.

621 F. Ferrándiz, 'Subterranean Autopsies: Exhumations of Mass Graves in Contemporary Spain', in E. Schindel and P. Colombo (eds.), *Space and the Memories of Violence: Landscapes of Erasure, Disappearance and Exception*, Springer 2014, p. 61, at p. 68.

technology for signification and resignification of past violence; and thirdly, situated the historical Spanish Civil War disappeared within a transitional justice framework and state obligations in international law towards the disappeared. Through the LHM, the Zapatero government supported the expansion of the emerging 'human rights forensics', a partnership between committed families, human rights advocates, and forensic anthropologists, as the vehicle for recovery of the disappeared and Republican historical memory.[622] The exhumations represented a pedagogic opportunity to publicly remember the disappeared by identifying and resignifying their remains exhumed from mass graves as the forgotten victims of Franco's repression. This chapter examines the LHM as a transitional justice initiative promulgated in response to the internationalization of human rights demands by Spanish grass roots victims' movements to recognize the rights of families to know the fate of the disappeared. The Law was seen as heralding the Second Transition initiated by a new generation of politicians not beholden to the pacts of 1977.[623] The Law sought to erode the pact of amnesia and amnesty made during the democratic transition and thereby forge a more inclusive historical memory of the Spanish Civil War and promote national reconciliation. In October 2022, the LHM was replaced by the Democratic Memory Law (DML) which sought to address its shortcomings by expanding the definition of victims and committing the state to assume greater responsibility for exhumations, forensic identification and DNA archiving.[624]

The foundational violent event of interest is the Spanish Civil War and the evolution of the historical and cultural memory about its meaning and legacy over more than 75 years. The focus is on the 'disappeared' as 'wounds of history' produced by a technology of terror designed to 'erase the memory of violence, and at the same time consolidate regimes of fear that might last for decades'.[625] The grass roots exhumation movement in Spain initiated a new phase in what Katherine Verdery calls 'the political lives of dead bodies': in this case the changing signification and resignification of the Spanish Civil War dead over time. Writing during the Civil War, the famous Spanish poet and playwright Federico García Lorca had noted the vitality of the dead in Spanish political culture: 'a dead man in Spain is more alive than a dead man anywhere else in the world'.[626] The ritual of exhumation of clandestine mass graves and the reburial of

---

622 Smith 2017, o.c., p. 412. Human rights forensics emerged in Argentina in the 1980s as an indictment of the state counterinsurgency policy of secret abduction, murder, and clandestine burial of those the dictatorship identified as subversives.

623 O.G. Encarnación, 'Reconciliation after Democratization: Coping with the Past in Spain', (2008) 123 *Political Science Quarterly* 435, at 455.

624 Law 20/2022 of October 19, 2022, of Democratic Memory, (*Ley 20/2022, de 19 de octubre, de Memoria Democrática*, (BOE) A-2022-17099).

625 Ferrándiz and Robben 2015, o.c., p. 1.

626 F. García Lorca, *Obras completas.* Edición a cargo de Arturo del Hoyo, 2 vols, Aguilar, Madrid, 1974, p. 115.

forensically identified individual remains, constitutes a cultural mechanism for the reinsertion of the dead into history through their symbolic re-coding. The state's control over the posthumous political life of dead bodies involves more than rewriting history to legitimate new polities. As Verdery observes:

> Their political work is to institute ideas about morality by assessing accountability and punishment, to sanctify space anew, to redefine the temporalities of daily life, to line people up with alternative ancestors and thereby to reconfigure the communities people participate in, and to attend to ancestors properly so they will fructify the enterprise of their descendants.[627]

Exhumations engage a community of mourners, engender an affective attachment to the past and compress time by tangibly bringing the past – and the repressed – into the present. Exhumation and reburial are rituals for the political management of the meaning of dead bodies. They are cultural techniques for the social entombment of previously neglected or erased victims in a new historical 'sepulchre'. Michael de Certeau employs the 'sepulchre' as a metaphor to describe the process of writing of history which 'exorcizes death by inserting it into discourse'.[628] History as sepulchre offers 'soil and a tomb to the dead of the past'.[629] Exhumation and reburial recovers the physical remains of those left out of history and then places them in the new 'sepulchre', a transitional justice narrative about victims and victimizers. In Spain, the historical management of the political lives of the Civil War dead through their exhumation and resignification can be divided into four distinct necro-political phases.[630] The first phase of exhumations occurred after 1939 with the purpose of documenting Republican crimes, legitimizing the Franco's regime, honouring the Nationalist dead with state burials and creating 'a commemorative culture of martyrdom that excluded the vanquished and left their unceremonial burying places untouched'.[631] The second phase of exhumations took place in the late 1950s when Franco exhumed and transferred around 300,000 Nationalist and Republican dead from all around Spain and reburied them at the newly completed Valley of the Fallen (VOF), an ambiguous monument symbolizing victory but also reconciliation. The third phase occurred after the death of Franco when family-initiated exhumations occurred spontaneously between 1975 and 1981 across Spain without any material or political support. These exhumations

627 K. Verdery, *The Political Lives of Dead Bodies: Reburial and Postsocialist Change*, Columbia University Press, New York, NY 1999, p. 127.

628 De Certeau 1988, o.c., at 57.

629 Ricoeur 2004, o.c., p. 369.

630 Achille Mbemde defines necropolitics as 'the subjugation of life to the power of death'. See A. Mbembé, 'Necropolitics', (2003) 15 *Public Culture* 11, at 39.

631 Ferrándiz and Robben 2015, o.c., p. 20.

abruptly ceased after the February 23, 1981 failed coup for fear of retributions. The fourth phase began in 2000 when an organized grass roots exhumation movement began openly recovering the Republican disappeared.

Transitional justice deploys the rituals of exhumation and reburial as either a forensic exercise to assist in prosecutions and/or as a cultural technology to discover the truth about missing and forgotten victims of political violence and to reinsert them into a more inclusive historical memory of the Civil War. In fact, the disappeared have become the emblematic 'innocent' victim of political repression and a major focus of transitional justice trials and truth commissions. In Latin America, the search for the disappeared in the context of authoritarian repression galvanized the internationalization of human rights claims to ensure states met their obligations under international law to investigate 'enforced disappearance' and to support the development of international human rights instruments to criminalize it. In 2002 'enforced disappearance' was recognized as a crime against humanity in the Rome Statute of the International Criminal Court (2002) and, in 2010, the International Convention for the Protection of All Persons for Enforced Disappearance (ICPPED) came into effect establishing the right of family members to know the fate of their missing members. The exhumation and reburial of the disappeared is a forensically grounded mechanism to recode their bodies as victims of systemic violence and to renarrate their victimization under authoritarian repression. The 'forensic-led exhumation-of-past-atrocities' has inscribed the disappeared dead body with new political and legal significance, turning it into 'a sort of new scientific memorial relic'.[632] The main reason why the disappeared have remained politically restless bodies is because they have lived on as a private traumatic counter-memory in their surviving families. The traumatic memory of these survivors separated them from regime supporters and bystanders, 'people who either identified uncritically with the dominant ideology or became frightened, disinterested, cynical or alienated by authoritarian control over the political process and discourse'.[633] While the former has been condemned to live in 'trauma time', trapped in disrupted time in which the past constantly intrudes into the present, the latter have been able to live in 'linear time', chronological time lived as historical and narrativized time in which the past is experienced as increasingly distant.[634] The challenge of reconciliation has been the difficulty of generating a politically transcendent consensus about the past to bridge the divide between those living in these temporally different modes. For those living in 'trauma time', the Civil War past must be investigated for reconciliation to be possible; for those living in 'linear time', the past is divisive and its investigation risks its politicization to serve contemporary political agendas.

---

632 Ferrándiz and Robben 2015, o.c., p. 7.

633 Hollander 2006, o.c., p. 24.

634 Edkins 2003, o.c., p. 40.

This chapter examines the political lives of the Civil War dead through their signification and resignification in laws at different moments of political transition since the 1920s. It locates the LHM in a genealogy of laws dealing with the Spanish Civil War dead which institutionalize changing official narratives about historical justice and political legitimacy. In Spanish political history of the 20th century these laws have different names – political responsibilities laws, amnesty laws and historical memory laws – all of which enter into an historical dialogue with earlier transition laws.[635] Hence, the LHM is in historical dialogue with the Amnesty Law (1977), which in turn is in dialogue with the Law of Political Responsibilities (1939) and Decree September 23, 1939, which in turn is in dialogue with the Responsibilities Commission (1931), which in turn is in dialogue with the political 'responsibilities' campaigns for political accountability in the 1920s by which was meant 'retribution for past political offences and for a purge of the state administration'.[636] In the early 1920s, campaigns for political 'responsibilities' were used to mobilize popular support for political reform of the parliamentary monarchy and, in the early 1930s, to reinforce the revolutionary programme of the Provisional Government. The prosecutions of senior conservative military and political figures associated with the Primo de Rivera dictatorship (1923–30) by the Responsibilities Commission established under the Second Republic (1931–1939) contributed to the polarization of political life leading up to the Civil War in 1936. Under the Law of Political Responsibilities (1939), Franco reversed the direction of prosecutions of the original Responsibilities Commission, which he regarded as a case of victor's justice. Fundamentally, these transition laws represent the institutionalization of political fixes for the core unresolved conflicts underlying Spanish nation-state formation. What distinguishes these laws are the lens through which they have constructed political conflict and therefore allocated 'responsibilities'. The Law of Political Responsibilities (1939) employed the victor's lens to blame and punish the – Republican – enemy for the Civil War; the Amnesty Law (1977) used a humanitarian lens to recognize suffering on both sides, to share blame – and thereby politically neutralize – for excesses and to selectively recognize and compensate Republican victims; the LHM (2007) employed a human rights lens to recover the historically silenced and invisible Republican victims, blame Franco for the Civil War and declare his coup and 40 year-long regime politically illegitimate.[637]

---

635 Aragoneses argues that strictly speaking there are no memory laws in Spain that impose 'a particular version of the Francoist past, nor punishing the denial of the crimes of the dictatorship'. A. Aragoneses, 'Legal Silences and the Memory of Francoism in Spain' in A. Gliszczyńska-Grabias and U. Belavusau (eds.), *Law and Memory: Towards Legal Governance of History*, Cambridge University Press, Cambridge 2017, p. 175.

636 C.P. Boyd, "Responsibilities' and the Spanish Republic 1931–6' (1984) 14 *European History Quarterly* 151, at 152.

637 M. Humphrey, 'Law, Memory and Amnesty in Spain' (2014) 13 *The Macquarie Law Journal*, 25.

This chapter analyses the LHM as the legal expression of the latest political fix framed by the rights of victims seeking to rehabilitate excluded Republican memory in the national narrative of the Civil War. The LHM is in historical dialogue with the 1939 and 1977 transition laws, with the aim of bringing about historical reconciliation in Spain, a country still divided over the cultural memory of the Civil War and the historical il/legitimacy of the Franco regime. The Spanish Civil War remains a 'restless event' not only because of the ongoing demands of the surviving families of the disappeared for historical justice, but also because the fundamental political conflicts underlying the Civil War over the character of the Spanish nation-state remain very much alive – i.e. is the state centralizing and unitary or pluralist and regionalist, and is it Catholic or secular?[638] These transition laws have acted as turning points and moments of state renewal which go to fundamental political conflicts about contemporary Spanish national identity, democracy and justice.[639]

By exploring the trajectory of the political lives of the dead and disappeared since the Civil War focusing on the rituals of resignification – exhumation and reburial, the aim is to reveal the limitations of human rights discourse to 'democratize historical memory' without strong state support for, and identification with, the truth and historical justice project. The main reasons the LHM has faced obstacles in generating a new historical consensus and reconciliation are: Firstly, its limited scope as restorative justice focused only on Republican victims. Secondly, the state's decision to franchise the exhumation and historical memory projects to civil society organizations, rather than assuming responsibility for them itself. Thirdly, the LHM's human rights framing of the Civil War as a conflict between victims and perpetrators evokes the historical trope of the 'two Spains' – the idea that Spanish society is divided between modern and progressive and traditional and conservative political forces – reinforcing political polarization, not transcending it, a position that resembles the 'two demons' theory seen in the previous chapter. Fourthly, the

---

638 On December 9, 2018, Santiago Abascal, the leader of Vox, an extreme nationalist right-wing party, announced the Reconquista of Spain from his new parliamentary base in Andalucía. The Vox had taken votes from the People's Party (*Partido Popular* – PP) and *Ciudadanos* to secure 12 seats. Their platform denounced the PP government's corruption, their handling of the Catalan secessionists and their policy on immigrants and refugees. The Vox movement is about the re-establishment of the Francoist unitary Castilian state. See S. Jones, 'Far right breakthrough in Andalucía send shockwave through Spanish politics', *The Guardian*, December 9, 2018, https://www.theguardian.com/world/2018/dec/09/far-right-andalucia-seville-vox-party-shockwave-spanish-politics.

639 The issue of national versus regional identities only intensified in post-imperial Spain after its loss of the last colonies in the Philippines and Cuba as a result of the Spanish-American war of 1898. The Civil War was precipitated by the military rebellion against the Second Republic in July 1936 in response to the Republic's radical programme for social reform – agrarian land reform, anticlericalism, the Catalan statute and the responsibilities commission investigating the political crimes of previous governments – that had increasingly polarized national politics. Boyd 1984, o.c., p. 177.

LHM left unresolved the critical question of the origin of the democratic state. On the one hand, it seeks to recuperate the memory of Republican victims and their defence of the democratic Second Republic and Constitution (1931), while on the other, it locates the democratic origins of the state in the post-Francoist transition (1977) and new Constitution (1978). Fifthly, the LHM has not produced reconciliation through beneficiaries witnessing and acknowledging the 'innocent' victims of past repression but politicized the past and become a lens through which contemporary political agendas are framed. The DML, promulgated in 2022, makes the state responsible for driving the transitional justice agenda but, just as with the LHM, its legal force is contingent on the political commitment of the government in office.

4.2. THE 'TWO SPAINS'

The 'two Spains' trope as an historical binary construction of the Spanish political community persists until today as an obstacle to the nation-state making and the project of national reconciliation. During the 20th century, the 'two Spains' trope was used to refer to the principal divide in the political community and the relationship of the citizen to the state. During the Civil War, the 'two Spains' referred to the Right and the Left, the 'real Spain and the anti-Spain'[640] and the Nationalists and Republicans. With Franco's victory the 'two Spains' referred to the divide between the Nationalist victors and the vanquished Republicans. The trope's binary pairs are not merely opposites but 'asymmetrical counter-concepts' in which the first term negates the second. The binary pairs function as asymmetrically opposed concepts 'to deny the reciprocity of mutual recognition'.[641] Politically, they act as classifications of negation. The LHM, with its universalizing human rights lens, was supposed to transcend these historical binaries of Spanish politics. However, the LHM's focus on Republican victims and their human rights claims quickly evoked the Nationalist/Republican wartime binary in which the Nationalist victors negated the political project of the Republican vanquished. In other words, the human rights framing of the Civil War has functioned as an 'evocative script' transforming the previously unapproved, private and painful Republican memory into the centrepiece of the historical memory movement.[642] Post-Franco, the centre/regions binary continues to function as an asymmetrical counter-concept with some regional

---

640 G. Priorelli, 'The fight against the 'anti-nation' as a historical mission: the delegitimization of the enemy in Italian Fascism and Spanish Fascism' (2018) 18 *Revista História: Debates e Tendências* 449, at 450–1.

641 Koselleck 1985, o.c., p. 160.

642 C. Humphrey, 'Remembering an "Enemy": The Bogd Khaan in Twentieth Century Mongolia' in R.S. Watson (ed.), *Memory, History and Opposition: Under State Socialism*, School of American Research Press, Santa Fe, NM 1994, p. 21.

separatists antagonistic to the very idea of the Spanish nation-state which they see as a phantom of the dictatorship and 'fascist to its core' – the image of the authoritarian unitary Castilian state with which they could not coexist.[643]

4.2.1. MILITARY DEFEAT OF THE SECOND REPUBLIC 1939

Franco's military defeat of the Republican forces divided Spain into the victors and the vanquished, which determined how the survivors and the war dead were to be treated. Estimates of the total number of deaths that occurred during the Civil War and the post-war period vary widely. Based on excess mortality data, there were an estimated 350,000 deaths during the Civil War (1936–39) and 214,000 deaths in the immediate post-Civil War period.[644] Josep Sumalla cites the figure of 190,000 for the number of prisoners who were executed or died in prison during the early years of Franco's regime.[645] Figures for the number of Nationalists killed in the Republican zone during the Civil War range from 49,272 to 85,940. The latter higher figure was reported by the General Proceedings – Report on Criminal Events and Other Aspects of Life in the Red Zone from 18 July until Liberation (*Causa General (Informativa de los hechos delictivos y otros aspectos de la vida en la zona roja desde 18 de julio hasta la liberación)* – Franco's open investigation and prosecution of killings in the Republican zone during the Civil War.[646] The critical difference between the two sides is that the Nationalist victors could act with total impunity in eliminating all resistance at the end of the war and establish a pseudo-legal mechanism for ongoing repression in the context of the outbreak of the WWII.[647]

The differential treatment of the category of missing/disappeared under Franco's transitional justice regime highlighted the initial role of the dead in the political legitimation of the victors and delegitimation of the vanquished. During the Civil War, disappearance had been used by both sides as an instrument of

643 B. Aretxaga, 'Madness and the Politically Real: Reflections on Violence in Postdictatorial Spain' in M-J.D. Good, et al. (eds.), *Postcolonial Disorders: Reflections on Subjectivity in the Contemporary World*, University of California Press, Berkeley and Los Angeles, CA 2008, p. 43, at p. 49.

644 M. Richards, 'From War Culture to Civil Society: Francoism, Social Change and Memories of the Spanish Civil War', (2002) 14 *History and Memory* 93, at 96.

645 J.M.T. Sumalla, *Historical Memory and Criminal Justice in Spain: A Case of Late Transitional Justice*, Intersentia, Brussels 2013.

646 The *Causa General* was established by Decree on April 26, 1940 (*Decreto de 26 abril de 1940 concediendo amplias facultades al Fiscal del Tribunal Supremo para proceder a instruir* <<*Causa general*>> *en la que se reúnan las pruebas de los hechos delictivos cometidos en todo el territorio nacional durante la dominación roja*, (BOE) Núm. 125, 4 mayo 1940).

647 S.G. Biesca, 'El proceso de la recuperación de la 'memoria histórica' en España: Una aproximación a los movimientos sociales por la memoria' (2006) 19 *International Journal of Iberian Studies* 25, at 30–1.

terror to purge enemies from newly conquered territories or to remove 'fifth columnists'. Most historians have judged that the victims of the 'white terror' greatly outnumbered those of the 'red terror' by 3 to 1.[648] One of the coup leaders, General Emilio Mola, described terror as a necessity for victory:

> It is necessary to spread terror. We have to create the impression of mastery eliminating without scruples or hesitation all those who do not think as we do. There can be no cowardice. If we hesitate one moment and fail to proceed with the greatest determination, we will not win. Anyone who helps or hides a Communist or a supporter of the Popular Front will be shot.[649]

The status of 'missing' or 'disappeared' became a metaphor for the historical fate of the Second Republic and its supporters.

Under Decree May 16, 1939, Franco encouraged his supporters to commemorate the Nationalist dead as heroes and martyrs by waiving or reducing fees associated with exhumation and reburial of the remains of victims of 'red barbarism'.[650] By contrast, the Republican dead continued to be stigmatized and criminalized as the enemy and their exhumations, reburials and remembrance prohibited. The estimated number of Republicans disappeared during the Civil War and post-war Francoist repression ranges from 30,000 to 150,000.[651] The Republican disappeared were left abandoned and scattered in clandestine graves across Spain in cemeteries, fields, and in ditches along the sides of roads. They were 'radically excluded from legislation and state funerary practices and became an integral part of a topography of terror'.[652] The Republican disappeared served as a hidden script about the consequences of Franco's victory and ongoing repression of the Republican side. Franco's policy of '*reespañolizar*' (re-Spanicization), 'the process of re-educating the country in patriotism, meant, for the fascist Spain of 1939, de-republicanising it down to the roots'.[653]

---

648 P. Preston, *The Spanish Holocaust: Inquisition and Extermination in Twentieth-Century Spain*, Harper Press, London 2012. The scale and justification of the 'red terror' v. 'white terror' remains historically controversial.

649 P. Preston, *The Spanish Civil War: Reaction, Revolution and Revenge*, Harper Perennial, London 2007, p. 103.

650 Sumalla 2013, o.c., p. 69.

651 These figures are based on the estimated 2000 unmarked graves, the number of bodies found in exhumed graves and the percentage of extrajudicial deaths identified through exhumation See G. F. Etxeberria, 'Exhumaciones Contemporáneas en España: Las Fosas Comunes de la Guerra Civil' (2012) 18 *Boletín Galego de Medicina Legal e Forense,* 13; F. Ferrándiz, 'Mass Graves, Landscapes of Terror: A Spanish Tale' in F. Ferrándiz (ed.), *Necropolitics: Mass Graves and Exhumations in the Age of Human Rights*, University of Pennsylvania Press, Philadelphia, PA 2015, p. 92.

652 Ferrándiz 2015, o.c., p. 92.

653 À. Duarte, 'The Republic, or Spain Freed from Itself' in J. Moreno-Luzón and X.M. Nuñez (eds.), *Metaphors of Spain: Representations of Spanish National Identity in the Twentieth Century*, Berghahn Books, Oxford 2017, p. 63.

The political significance of military victory is its ability to produce effects which outlast its termination. As Elaine Scarry argues, 'a military contest differs from any other contest in that its outcome carries the power of its own enforcement'.[654] War is uniquely able to produce outcomes which appear incontestable, even if defeat is not absolute. Victory gives 'rise to the fiction that its outcome cannot be (or should not be, or must not be) contested'.[655] Victory imposes the hegemony of the victor's narrative and extinguishes the narrative of the vanquished. In the terminology of political semiosis, military victory is performative in enacting political transition, is demonstrative in framing the meaning of the victory, and through representational acts normalizes the political, legal, cultural, and memorial landscape according to the victor's script to ensure no counter-narrative can emerge to destabilize the dominant order. Franco institutionalized his victory narrative of the Civil War as a war of National Salvation in laws which granted impunity, privileges, rewards, and recognition to the Nationalists and criminalized and persecuted the Republicans. Franco's transition laws continued to punish his Republican enemies and purge the state of any traces of the Second Republic because he regarded them as anti-Spain. His Law of Political Responsibilities (February 1939) inverted what he saw as the victor's justice imposed by the Second Republic through the Responsibilities Commission (1931), when it prosecuted conservative politicians and military officers for their role in a colonial military disaster in Morocco and their collaboration with the General Miguel Primo de Rivera dictatorship (1923–30).[656] Franco's Law of Political Responsibilities (February 1939) criminalized the Second Republic and all Republican supporters and launched a legal investigation of the past directed at punishing those the regime blamed for the war.[657] Decree Law September 23, 1939 pardoned all crimes committed by Nationalist supporters during the period of the Second Republic.[658] The logic of these complementary laws reinforced the importance of the victory narrative of National Salvation and ongoing repression as a fundamental source of Franco's

---

654 E. Scarry, *The Body in Pain: The Making and Unmaking of the World*, Oxford University Press, Oxford 1985, p. 99.

655 Ibid., p. 108.

656 The Primo de Rivera dictatorship overturned the political accommodation of the Restoration between the Conservatives and Liberals based on *turno* – taking turns in government. Primo de Rivera introduced authoritarian government to Spain which Franco consolidated after 1939. C. Heath-Kelly and L. Fernández de Mosteyrín, 'The political use of victimhood: Spanish collective memory of ETA through the war on terror paradigm' (2021) 47 *Review of International Studies*, 1.

657 Law of Political Responsibilities, (*Ley de 9 de febrero de 1939 de Responsabilidades Políticas*, (BOE) Núm. 44, de 13 de febrero de 1939).

658 Decree-Law September 23, 1939. (*Ley de 23 septiembre 1939 considerando no delictivos determinados hechos actuación político-social cometidos por personas desde el catorce de abril de mil novecientos treinta y uno hasta el dieciocho de julio de mil novecientos treinta y seis.* (BOE) No. 273, 23 septiembre 1939).

'origin-based legitimacy'.[659] The Law of Political Responsibilities (1939) resulted in the ongoing persecution of Republicans for their 'collaboration' with the Second Republic. From the Republican perspective they were punished for fulfilling their duties towards the legitimate democratically elected government. The Law of Political Responsibilities (1939) ensured that anyone who did not actively take part in the insurgency against the Second Republic could be prosecuted for 'serious passivity'.[660] It imposed fines, impounded possessions, took away land, and stripped Spanish citizens of their nationality. The process of investigation under the Law required judges 'to obtain a report about the conduct of the accused from the local council, another from the *Guardia Civil*, another from the Falange and a fourth from the local priest', resulting in its abuse to arbitrarily impose punishment without charge: torture, imprisonment, execution, exile, fines and professional disqualifications.[661] Women, especially mothers or wives of Republican soldiers or sympathizers, were targeted for 'redemption' and were vicariously punished by imprisonment, rape, torture, and even execution.[662] In the name of purification some 30,000 children were removed from imprisoned Republican mothers and sent to state institutions or to adopting families. To ensure they were legally untraceable, a law allowed the state to change their names.[663]

Another instrument of legal repression in post-Civil War Spain was the *Causa General*, a form of ongoing criminalization and persecution of Franco's Civil War enemies – the republicans, socialists, communists, anarchists, separatists, masons and atheists – by the Supreme Court Prosecutor.[664] Although it was supposed to serve an informative function, it became 'a state instrument for encouraging denunciation and consequently a means for officially sanctioning the social division of post-war Spain'.[665] It was an open prosecution used to punitively denounce 'Red crimes', to commemorate Nationalist sacrifices and to begin the mass collection of the remains of Nationalist dead for burial in the mausoleum, the VOF – Valley of the Fallen.[666] The *Causa General* was

---

659 P. Aguilar Fernández, *Memory and Amnesia: the Role of the Spanish Civil War in the Transition to Democracy*, Berghahn Books, New York/Oxford 2002, p. 35.

660 M. López Lerma, 'What Judicial Memory for the Amnesty Law of 1977?' in D. Gozdecka and M. Kmak (eds.), *Europe at the Edge of Pluralism*, Intersentia, Brussels 2015, p. 191.

661 Sumalla 2013, o.c., p. 48.

662 López Lerma 2015, o.c., p. 192.

663 Brincat Report, Need for international condemnation of the Franco regime, Doc.10737, November 4, 2005, Political Affairs Committee, Parliamentary Assembly of the Council of Europe, http://assembly.coe.int/nw/xml/XRef/X2H-Xref-ViewHTML.asp?FileID=11217&lang=en.

664 Decree April 26, 1940, Political Responsibilities, o.c.

665 A. Cenarro Lagunas, 'Memory beyond the Public Sphere: The Francoist Repression Remembered in Aragon' (2002) 14 *History and Memory* 165, at 170.

666 L. Renshaw, *Exhuming Loss: Memory, Materiality and Mass Graves of the Spanish Civil War*, Left Coast Press, Walnut Creek, CA 2011, p. 80.

nested in a series of laws and special tribunals that facilitated the judicial repression of Franco's political opponents including the Law of the Repression of Freemasonry and Communism (1940); the Law of State Security (1941); the Law of the New Revised Edition of the Penal Code (1944); and the Law of Public Order (1959).[667] The Law of the Repression of Freemasonry and Communism (1940) identified the Communists, Freemasons and Jews as responsible for the criminal decadence of Spain which had culminated in 'the terrible atheistic, materialistic, anti-militaristic and anti-Spain campaign'.[668] Even Franco's brother-in-law referred to the *Causa General* as 'justice upside down'.[669] The ongoing repression of Republicans under the *Causa General* turned Spain into an open prison for all those who opposed Franco and made them subject to the jurisdiction of military courts until 1963.[670] Except for the government party, the Traditionalist Spanish Falange and Offensive of the Unions of the National-Syndicalist (*Falange Española Tradicionalista y de las Juntas de Ofensiva Nacional-Sindicalista* or FET de las JONS) and the official trade union, the Spanish Trade Union Organization (*Sindicato Vertical*), all other political parties and trade unions were declared illegal including the Spanish Socialist Workers' Party (PSOE) (*Partido Socialista Obrero Español*); the Communist Party of Spain (*Partido Comunista de España*), PCE; the Workers' General Union (*Unión General de Trabajadores*), UGT; and the National Confederation of Labor (*Confederación Nacional del Trabajo*), CNT. These parties and trade unions were declared illegal under Francoist Spain and hundreds of militants and supporters were imprisoned or executed.[671] In addition, regional languages (Basque and Catalan) were forbidden and the statutes of autonomy of Catalonia and the Basque Country were abolished.[672]

Franco also inscribed his victory on the memorial and cultural landscape to ensure the public erasure of the Second Republic and silencing of its supporters. The memorial cartography of the war dead was shaped by the 'official narrative of military victory anchored in the concepts of religious crusade, heroism, and

---

667 Law of the Repression of Freemasonry and Communism (*Ley de 1 de marzo 1940 sobre de represión de la masonería y del comunismo*, (BOE) Núm. 204, 22 julio 1944; Law of State Security (*Ley de 4 de enero de 1941 para le seguridad del Estado*, (BOE) Núm. 101, April 11, 1941); Law of the New Revised Edition of the Penal Code (*Ley de 19 julio de 1944 para una nueva edición refundida del Código Penal vigente*, (BOE) Núm. 204, 22 julio 1944); Law of Public Order (*Ley 45/1959, de 30 de julio de Orden Público*), 30 julio 1959, (BOE) Núm. 182, 31 julio 1959.

668 Law of the Repression of Freemasonry and Communism (*Ley de 1 marzo de 1940 sobre de represión de la masonería y del comunismo*, (BOE) No. 204, 22 julio 1944).

669 Sumalla 2013, o.c., p. 59.

670 A. Beevor, *The Battle for Spain; The Spanish Civil War 1936–1939*, Weidenfeld & Nicolson, London 2006, at p. 407.

671 J. C. Santos Juliá et al., *Victimas de la guerra civil*, Ediciones Temas de Hoy, Madrid 1999, p. 395.

672 Ibid., p. 341.

martyrdom – known in Spanish political history as National Catholicism'.[673] Franco's most controversial commemoration of the Civil War dead was the victory monument, the VOF, built outside Madrid. Decree April 1, 1940 stipulated that the Basilica, Monastery, and Military Quarters be erected on land located in the hills of the Escorial (*Guadarrama Sierra*), known as *Cuelga-muros*, to perpetuate the memory of the 'Fallen of our glorious Crusade'.[674] He originally conceived the monument as a commemoration that would defy time: 'The dimension of our Crusade, the heroic sacrifices involved in victory ... cannot be commemorated by simple monuments ... the stones to be erected must have the grandeur of the monuments of old, which defy time and forgetfulness.'[675] By the time the monument was completed in May 1958 the criteria for internment in the VOF had changed from the Nationalist dead to become 'Spanish' and 'Catholic' thereby including Republican dead.[676] Officially, family permission was required to reinter remains in the VOF, but in practice, the remains of both the Nationalists and Republicans were secretly exhumed and transferred to the site without permission, a policy that continued until 1983, eight years after Franco's death. Despite the Francoists officially resignifying the VOF as a symbol of national reconciliation, it remained a potent triumphalist Francoist symbol of victory for many Spaniards. The change of internment criteria, Andrea Hepworth argues, was a Francoist public relations exercise that coincided with the opening of Spain to Europe.[677] This may be the case but what may have looked like a gesture of reconciliation from outside Spain reflected no such political reconciliation inside Spain. In the 1950s, there was no partner in 'national reconciliation'. The VOF merely affirmed the power of the winning side after the war to be able to appropriate the dead of both sides to substantiate their own war aims and the defeat of the losing side's war aims. In other words, the defeated side could no longer publicly signify the meaning of their war dead.

Josep Sumalla argues that the scale and impact of Francoist repression on Spanish society cannot be fully appreciated without first establishing

---

673 F. Ferrándiz, 'Unburials, Generals, and Phantom Militarism: Engaging with the Spanish Civil War Legacy' (2019) 60 *Current Anthropology*, S62, at S65.

674 Law to create a memorial of Our Glorious Crusade at Cuelga-muros, (*Decreto de 1 de abril de 1940 disponiendo se alcen Basílica, Monasterio, Cuartel de Juventudes, en la finca situada en* las *vertientes de la Sierra del Guadarrama (El Escorial), conocida por Cuelga-muros, para perpetuar la memoria de los caídos en nuestra Gloriosa Cruzada* (BOE) Núm. 93, de 2 de abril de 1940, pp. 2240–1).

675 P. Preston, *Franco: A Biography*, Harper Collins, London 1993, p. 35.

676 A. Hepworth 'Site of memory and dismemory: The Valley of the Fallen in Spain' (2014) 16 *Journal of Genocide Research* 463, at 472. Members of both Nationalist and Republican armies were buried under the epitaph '*Caídos por Dios y por España* (The Fallen for God and Spain) 1936–1939. R.I.P'. See Q. Solé i Barjau, 'Inhumados en el Valle de los Caídos. Los primeros traslados desde la provincia de Madrid' (2009) *Hispania Nova: Revista de Historia Contemporánea*, 9, https://www.researchgate.net/publication/41207683_Inhumados_en_el_Valle_de_los_Caidos_Los_primeros_traslados_desde_la_provincia_de_Madrid.

677 Ibid., p. 472.

'how many people died, how many were imprisoned, how many were exiled, how many were professionally disqualified and how many fines were imposed'.[678] While the answers to these questions will probably never be resolved, we do know that at the end of Franco's rule 40 years of repression had produced a public so intimidated by the fear of the past returning that the majority accepted the 'pact of forgetting' (*pacto del olvido*) as necessary for social peace and to allow a successful democratic transition. The dictatorship had produced a Spain divided between Francoist supporters and marginalized political opponents and victims. With no reconciliation, and only limited conditional rehabilitation, Francoism embedded personal grievances and traumatic memories of defeat in the Republican survivors. To survive under Franco's repression, the defeated were forced to 'renounce their past, experiences and identity' and accept the subject position of 'defeated' imposed on them by the victors.[679] The longevity of the dictatorship imposed deep and lasting scars on families and caused some members to become alienated from each other when they subsequently changed sides after negatively re-evaluating their Republican allegiance during the Civil War. By the time of Franco's death in 1975, the regime had shifted from origin-based to performance-based legitimacy, arguing that democratic transition had been possible only through the peace and economic progress achieved under Francoism. As part of the depoliticization process, late-Francoism instilled the ideological acceptance of technocratic government as the business of infrastructure and material development.[680] As a consequence, transition brought no demand for a 'responsibilities commission' or a purge of the state administration because of the process of de-politicization on one hand, and the pervasive presence of Francoist supporters throughout government, the administration and the judiciary on the other. In fact, a key demand of the Franco regime's political opponents – secularists, socialists, regionalists, separatists – was amnesty for political prisoners as a priority in negotiations marginalizing those victims who wanted some form of accountability. Democratic transition did not generate a 'human rights forensics' partnership in search of the disappeared, as had occurred in Argentina in the 1980s as an indictment of the dictatorship's counterinsurgency policy of secret abduction, murder and clandestine burial of those the dictatorship identified as subversives.[681] It was not until 2000 that a human rights partnership emerged in Spain, inspired by the success of Latin American human rights organizations prosecuting Latin American human rights violators under universal jurisdiction in Spanish courts.

---

678 Sumalla 2013, o.c., 48.

679 Cenarro Lagunas, o.c., at p. 167.

680 A. Gómez López-Quiñones, 'A Secret Agreement: The Historical Memory Debate and the Limits of Recognition' (2012) 11 *Hispanic Issues On Line* 87, at 106–7.

681 Smith 2017, o.c., pp. 400–401.

4.2.2. PACTISM, DEMOCRATIC TRANSITION AND AMNESTY 1977

The impetus behind the promulgation of the LHM in 2007 was the failure of the post-Franco democratic governments to address the grass roots movement's demands for the recognition of the rights of Republican victims of Francoist repression during the Civil War and under the dictatorship. The Amnesty Law (1977) was the first piece of legislation passed by the new democratic government on October 15, 1977 and its effect was to grant amnesty/pardon to all sides and to prevent any legal investigation into the past human rights violations. In fact, the bill for blanket amnesty had been put forward by the Communist Party as a way to promote national reconciliation.[682] It demanded 'amnesty for all political crimes, without exception, arguing that amnesty was the only way to achieve national reconciliation and peace' and 'open the way for peace and freedom'.[683] This statement was not merely an expression of political pragmatism but the politically transformative consequences of democratic transition after 40 years of Francoism. Just as in the colonial struggles for national independence where suffering and loss was politically redeemed in the irreversible end to colonial rule, democratic transition in Spain signified the definitive end to Franco's anachronistic authoritarianism. The Amnesty Law 1977 institutionalized the 'pact of forgetting' in which political party elites agreed to amnesia and amnesty as the best way to move towards democratic elections and a new future. The Amnesty Law was approved by 93.3% of parliamentarians and supported by the majority of Spaniards in opinion polls.[684] The political agreement underpinning the Amnesty Law included the redistribution of democratic power between the centre and the region which was formalized in the Constitution (1978) and the suppression of the Republican collective memory. Political support for the Law was based on firstly, political reconciliation between the main parties and secondly, a largely politically demobilized public. The Amnesty Law was reinforced by an official political gag in parliament on debate about the past to enforce official amnesia. The Law ruled out any form of transitional justice in large part because none of the key political actors demanded it.[685] The success of

---

682 R. Jimeno, *Amnesties, Pardons and Transitional Justice: Spain's Pact of Forgetting*, Routledge, Oxford 2017, p. 64.

683 López Lerma 2015, o.c., p. 195.

684 A.G. Gil, 'Spain as an Example of Total Oblivion with Partial Rehabilitation' in J. Almqvist and C. Espósito (eds.), *The Role of Courts in Transitional Justice: Voices from Latin America and Spain*, Routledge, London 2013, p. 108. See also O.G. Encarnación, 'Justice in Times of Transition: Lessons from the Iberian Experience' (2012) 56 *International Studies Quarterly* 179, at 187.

685 C. Powell, 'Revisiting Spain's Transition to Democracy' in S. Florensa (ed.), *The Arab Transition in a Changing World. Building Democracies in the Light of International Experiences: A Critical and Demanding Challenge for the Arab World*, iMED, Barcelona 2016, p. 38, at p. 48.

the constitutional process was attributed to the demobilization of street protest, the inclusion of all main political parties, the conduct of negotiations in private and mutual respect between elites.[686]

During the political transitions in the 1920s and 1930s, demands for accountability had been the political norm. Each new regime sought to legitimize its mandate through an investigation into the former regime's 'political responsibilities' – their alleged political crimes and/or corruption – and a purge of the state as an act of renewal and purification. The Amnesty Law 1977, by contrast, facilitated the continuity between – not rupture with – the Francoist regime and the democratic state. There was no accountability, no lustration, and no popular mobilization for justice and victims' rights. Impunity was reinforced by an official amnesia expressed in a new transition narrative designed to politically neutralize the past by creating symmetry between the Civil War winners and losers in their suffering and responsibility. A humanitarian lens created an equivalence between victims based on the recognition of their shared bodily suffering, not their political or moral attributes.[687] The Francoist victory narrative of Republican responsibility for causing the Civil War was superseded by a narrative blaming both sides. Their shared past suffering was to be redeemed in the new democratic Spain with the promise of a unifying future, not a divisive past. Yet the historical recoding of Nationalist and Republican Civil War victims as equivalent, was very selective as revealed in the entitlement for reparations. Firstly, the criteria for entitlement to reparations was restricted to former Republican officials and military dismissed under Franco; secondly, these 'administrative reparations' placed the burden of proof of eligibility on individuals; and thirdly, the largest category of victims – the families of the disappeared and those condemned under the Councils of War and the military tribunals – were excluded.[688]

The transition formula of amnesty, amnesia and victim equivalence was complemented by the narrative of the 'good memory' (*la buena memoria*), the myth of the model Spanish democratic transition.[689] The 'good memory' eschewed the past and constructed Civil War memory as divisive and a threat to the peace achieved under 40 years of Francoism which had made coexistence possible.[690] The past risked a return to the politics of the 'two Spains', the war narrative of the Nationalist v. Republicans. But behind the myth of the 'good

686 Ibid., p. 49.

687 M. Humphrey, 'The Politics of Trauma' (2010) 32 *Arts: The Journal of the Sydney University Arts Association* 37, at 40.

688 Jimeno 2017, o.c., p. 166 and S.R. Golob, 'Volver: The Return Of/To Transitional Justice Politics in Spain' (2008) 9 *Journal of Spanish Cultural Studies*, 127.

689 R. Vinyes, 'La memoria del estado' in R. Vinyes (ed.), *El estado y la memoria: gobiernos y ciudadanos frente a los traumas de la historia*, RBA Libros, Barcelona 2009, p. 23, at p. 35.

690 Duarte 2017, o.c., p. 81.

memory' was the unstated culture of fear produced by the repression. As Aguilar observes, 'only a nation so traumatized by war could be so devoted to peace, and not only during the post-war period, but throughout the Franco era and beyond'.[691] Republican traumatic memory had to be excluded from the 'good memory' in order not to destabilize it. The political aversion to the past and manufactured ignorance of it was a legacy of repression which, at transition, made civil society complicit by making no demands for any debate about past injustice, for a search for the graves of the disappeared, or for compensation for Republican victims.[692] The legacy of the political subjectivities produced by Francoist repression was a population for whom the past had been so demonized that they were willing to accept the promise of a democratic future rather than risk exploring the authoritarian past. In practice, the myth of the 'good memory' meant that the hegemonic Francoist narrative that the Civil War was caused by Republican excesses and authoritarian rule were left officially unchallenged, justified as necessary to achieve peace. The opposition accepted the 'good memory' narrative not merely out of fear, but also out of political pragmatism to bring an end to Francoism. The demand for political amnesty had galvanized anti-Franco forces from the late 1960s and the opposition slogan 'amnesty and liberty' championed the release of all political prisoners.[693] For them, amnesty helped consolidate the political goal of democratic transition which signified Europeanization, progress and the embrace of the European Social Model.[694] It also implicitly stigmatized Francoism as historically illegitimate authoritarian and a fascist hangover from the 1940s.[695] Nevertheless, there was no reference to the Second Republic in the Constitution (1978) or Amnesty Law (1977) and commemorations of the April 14 proclamation of the Second Republic in 1931 were banned until the end of the 1970s.[696]

The political acquiescence in forgetting at transition perpetuated the culture of silence normalized under Franco's authoritarian rule. His victory narrative was gradually supplemented by the narrative of 'Franco's peace' based upon harsh disciplining. Punishment provided a mechanism for post-war reintegration of Republicans. As the living memory of the Civil War lost its capacity to bind successive generations together, authoritarian discipline replaced it. In the 1950s and 1960s the culture of repression produced an 'obedient generation' manifested in their silent compliance. Michael Richards argues their silence was the result

691 Aguilar Fernández 2002, o.c., p. 135.

692 Biesca 2006, o.c., p. 25.

693 Duarte 2017, o.c., p. 80.

694 The European Social Model (ESM) is based on sustainable economic growth, social cohesion and participatory democracy. See L. Moreno, 'Europeanisation and Catalonia's in(ter) dependence' (2017) 6 *Global Constitutionalism* 218, at 223.

695 Brincat Report, o.c.

696 Duarte 2017, o.c., p. 80.

of evasion and apathy, rather than consent or support.[697] Evasion reflected the strategy of self-censorship or *prudencia*, 'making careful judgements about what was permissible and what could not be done was part of everyday existence'.[698] The attitude conveyed by '*no hay que meterse*' (one mustn't get involved in anything) was also a common response to state terror under the Latin American dictatorships. Out of punishment and self-censorship there emerged in the 1960s and 1970s an acceptance that individual and collective amnesia was the best medicine for Spain and that the Civil War had been a collective tragedy for which both sides were to blame.[699] In other words, amnesia was not merely a solution produced by elite reconciliation in the pact of forgetting at transition, but a normalized way of existence generated by Francoism.

The 'pact of forgetting' obscured the historical conflicts over the character of the state dating back to the 19th century. In the 1920s, the core political conflict was over whether Spain would continue to be a parliamentary monarchy, Catholic and unitary and, in the 1930s, over whether the state could be consolidated as a secular and more pluralist/regionalist republic. Franco was strongly anti-communist and anti-separatist and his war aims were to dismantle the secular, democratic and republican pluralist state and replace it with an authoritarian, centrist, unitary, Castilian, and Catholic one. At transition, the 'pact of forgetting', and the revisionist narrative of the war as a 'collective tragedy' concealed the irreconcilable political objectives over which the Civil War was fought. The victims from both sides were collectively redeemed in the 1978 constitutional pact as the sacrifice founding the new democratic state. However, Republican memory contradicted this myth of democratic origins. After all, they had fought and sacrificed themselves in the Civil War in the name of the legitimate democratically elected government established under the 1931 Constitution. Post-1977, the political reconciliation reflected in the constitutional pact was sustained by the principle of *bipartidismo*, the peaceful alternation of power between the PSOE and the conservative People's Party (*el Partido Popular* – PP) sharing the spoils of office, especially during the 1980s and 1990s.[700] Moreover,

697 Richards 2002, o.c., p. 110.

698 Ibid., p. 110.

699 Ibid., p. 111.

700 Hunt argues *bipartisdismo* was possible because the PSOE was not a radical left party. See W. Hunt, 'The Ghost in The Ballot Box: Catalonia's Crisis in Context', *Dissent*, October 10, 2017, https://www.dissentmagazine.org/online_articles/catalonia-independence-referendum-crisis-history-franco. In fact, the practice of elite powersharing dates back to the late 19th century during the Restoration period (1875–1923). There was an unofficial system of *turno* (turn taking) alternating between Liberal and Conservative governments until the Primo de Riviera coup in 1923. Both parties were effectively conservative – monarchist, elitist, defenders of constitutional order and *caciquismo*. Nevertheless, the Liberal party agenda was more progressive, seeking to extend suffrage, broaden civil rights, reform law codes and judicial procedures, less protectionist, increasingly anticlerical, and opposed to civil repression by increased police power. See S.G. Payne, 'Spanish Conservatism 1834–1923' (1978) 13 *Journal of Contemporary History* 765, at 779.

in the 1980s, the Spanish democratic transition acquired the international status as an example of 'third wave' democratization when the transitologists adopted it as a model of democratization contingent on elite agency rather than on structural pre-conditions.[701]

The ambiguous character of the Spanish state is embodied in the Constitution (1978) which includes 'both the idea of the indivisible nation and Spain as a plural ensemble of diverse peoples, historic nationalities and regions'.[702] On the one hand, the Constitution establishes a centralist and unitary state symbolized in the parliamentary monarchy, on the other it recognizes the state of autonomies (*estado de autonomías*) consisting of 17 autonomous communities (*comunidades autónomas*) which serve as administrative units with devolved powers.[703] What varies between *autonomías* is the extent of the devolution powers shaped by the strength of regionalist nationalisms with the most radical voices – Basque and Catalan separatists at different times – demanding complete independence. For some of the separatist parties the democratic state is a phantom Francoist state.[704] In other words, for the separatists, the binaries Spain/Basque Country or Spain/Catalonia constitute asymmetrical counter-concepts which are mutually exclusive and negate each other. Since the transition, the centrist state has been destabilized by the experience of cycles of economic crisis and unstable democratic majorities which regional politicians have increasingly denounced as authoritarian. As Ignacio Echevarría observes: 'Thanks to Francoism, at least two generations of Spaniards were thoroughly "vaccinated" against Spain'.[705] The resistance of Autonomous Communities to the political choices of the national governments has exacerbated the central/regional tensions. After 2011, the PP government under PM Rajoy (2011–2015) increasingly ruled by decree and used the Constitutional Court as an upper chamber against the Autonomous Communities.[706] In the case of Catalonia, the Court refuted many pieces of legislation passed by the Catalan parliament. The PP national government increasingly assumed authority over the Catalan parliament and in 2017, in response to the 'illegal' Catalan independence referendum, it suspended the Catalan parliament's authority under Article 155 of the Constitution and

---

701 Powell 2016, o.c., p. 38.

702 L. Moreno, 'Federalization in multinational Spain' in M. Burgess and J. Pinder (eds.), *Multinational Federations*, Routledge, London 2007, p. 86, at p. 96.

703 Spain has been described as a 'federation without federalism'. See G. Sala, 'Federalism without Adjectives in Spain' (2013) 44 *Publius: The Journal of Federalism* 109, at 109.

704 Aretxaga 2008, o.c., p. 49.

705 S. Faber, *Exhuming Franco: Spain's Second Transition*, Vanderbilt University Press, Nashville, TN 2021, p. 70.

706 M. Clua-Losada and O. Ribera-Almandoz, 'Authoritarian Neoliberalism and the Disciplining of Labour' in C. B. Tansel (ed.) *States of Discipline: Authoritarian Neoliberalism and the Contested Reproduction of Capitalist Order (Transforming Capitalism)*, Rowman & Littlefield Publishers, London/New York 2017, p. 33.

detained leading Catalan independence politicians. The Catalan separatists denounced these actions as undemocratic and authoritarian.[707]

4.3. THE ANTI-IMPUNITY MOVEMENT IN SPANISH DEMOCRATIC POLITICS

4.3.1. FAMILIES OF THE DISAPPEARED AND THE EXHUMATION MOVEMENT

The main challenges to the policy of amnesty and amnesia at transition did not come from the conservative judiciary but from civil society movements associated with historical memory and the recovery of the disappeared. The Amnesty Law (1977) had blocked any official criminal investigation of the past and amnesia had left the legacy of the official Francoist narrative of victory and technocratic pacification unchallenged. The aim of the historical memory movement was to undermine the hegemony of the official Francoist cultural memory of the Civil War, embedded by the authoritarian state over 40 years, through the recuperation of 'Republican memory' silenced and stigmatized by Franco. After all, the movement was anchored in a watershed moment, the Civil War, that was politically catastrophic, transformative, left a 'social memory of collectively life-shattering events' and was indelible for those who had suffered from it.[708] By 2006, just before the promulgation of the LHM, there were 165 local and state associations and foundations advocating for justice for the Republican victims of the Civil War and repression under the Francoist dictatorship.[709] While these groups had different goals and were only minimally coordinated, they shared common perspectives and tactics on how to promote awareness of a more inclusive historical memory of the Civil War. They represented themselves as non-political and claimed humanitarian motives for investigating the historical memory of Republican victims who had been the target of political crimes and institutional silencing. They justified their demand for official historical accountability for Civil War political crimes as a moral question concerned with the human dignity of victims, not political differences.[710] In Spain, 'historical memory' referred to specific issues about the Civil War concerned with the exhumations of the disappeared, economic

707 'Generalitat denuncia "agresiones fascistas" a independentistas', *HISPANTV*, August 4, 2018, https://www.hispantv.com/noticias/espana/384415/torra-catalunya-agresion-fascistas-independentistas.

708 M. Richards, *After the Civil War: Making Memory and Re-Making Spain since 1936*, Cambridge University Press, Cambridge 2013, p. 363.

709 Biesca 2006, o.c., at 34.

710 Gómez López-Quiñones 2012, o.c., pp. 92–3.

reparations for victims, and overturning convictions issued by Franco's military tribunals.[711]

The recuperation of Republican 'historical memory' drew on the 'embodied memory' of the surviving Republican victims. For the survivors, the Civil War remained a 'restless event' because of its unforgettable personal impact. The historical memory movement emerged as the most important grass roots truth seeking initiative to challenge the transition policy of amnesty and amnesia. As Alison Ribeiro de Menezes shows, their memory practices were multifaced. The movement used the 'collected memory' of surviving Republican victims and families to destabilize the – official – 'cultural memory' of the Civil War and dictatorship. 'Cultural memory' refers to historically fateful events whose memory is institutionalized through texts, commemorations, and monuments by the state.[712] 'Collected memory' refers to aggregated individual memories of a group about their personal experiences of 'persecution, injustice and victimhood'. It offers the possibility of historical and legal accountability that restore to victims 'individual agency that discourses of victimhood, trauma and suffering remove'.[713] Other forms of memory include 'collective memory' which refers to generational memory constituted by a shared archive or set of remembrances which is often diverse and fragmented, and 'post-memory', which refers to the inter-generational transfer of memory to those who cannot recollect past traumatic events but have grown up saturated by the narratives of the previous generation who do remember them.[714] The challenge of the historical memory movement has been to mobilize different forms of memory in order to re-establish generational transmission of a more comprehensive collective memory. Its strategy was to raise public consciousness about the silenced Republican victims; to recover individuals from clandestine graves for reburial by surviving family; to democratize and pluralize memory thereby destabilizing the legacy of the hegemonic cultural memory of the Civil War; to denounce the political crimes of Franco; and to seek recognition for the Republicans victims. In response, the conservative establishment pushed back against the Republican narrative of victimhood with a revisionist account of pacification and coexistence strongly supported by dominant media corporations, the Catholic Church, and the PP.[715]

From 2000, the 'new memory debates' in Spain intersected with the victim-centred exhumation movement framed by a human rights lens focused 'on images

---

711 Gómez López-Quiñones 2012, o.c., p. 93.

712 A. Ribeiro de Menezes, *Embodying Memory in Contemporary Spain*, Palgrave MacMillan, New York, NY 2014, p. 37.

713 Ibid., p. 37.

714 Ibid., p. 60.

715 Biesca 2006, o.c., pp. 30–1.

of ruined bodies and ruptured genealogies'.[716] The victim-centred focus points to another dimension of the new memory debates: the impetus created by the embodied traumatic memory of surviving Republican families to know the truth about the fate of the disappeared. After the transition to democracy, there was a prolific production and publication of memoirs, autobiographies, oral histories, and family recollections made by victims and surviving relatives of victims. There were also isolated spontaneous exhumations of mass graves initiated by individual families between 1975–1981. However, the emergence of organized exhumations of Republican mass graves did not happen until 2000.[717] Civil society initiated exhumations represented a radical rupture of memory politics described by Fernández de Mata as a 'mass grave phenomenon'.[718] The principal civil society organizations involved in the exhumation movement have been the Association for the Recovery of Historical Memory (ARMH – *Asociación para la Recuperación de la Memoria Histórica*) founded by Mario de Silva in 2000; Forum for Memory (*Foro por la memoria*) associated with the Communist party, along with numerous regional affiliates and other autonomous local groups. ARMH publicly introduced the human rights lens to frame Civil War and dictatorship memory, and through its title, it brought to public consciousness the idea of the 'recuperation of historical memory'. However, despite the exhumation movement's shared human rights perspective and emphasis on enforced disappearance, it has remained diverse and fragmented along national, regional, and local lines with quite different agendas and exhumation protocols.

In the early stages, the exhumation movement was divided over the purpose and meaning of the exhumation of Republican remains. Some criticized these local exhumations as an 'erasure of genocide', arguing that 'exhumations performed without judicial mandate and any legal criminal framework amounted to the "destruction" of "historical patrimony" and, indirectly, to the whitewashing of the crimes of Francoism'.[719] Gradually, opposition to the exhumations faded away as the 'body-centred regime of memory, justice and truth-seeking' became the dominant methodology to recover the past.[720] The humanitarian logic of transitional justice constructed the disappeared as 'innocent suffering' bodies whose stories needed to be heard to save them from the oblivion of Agamben's 'bare life', victims 'whose killing was neither

[716] F. Ferrándiz and A. Baer, 'Digital Memory: The Visual Recording of Mass Grave Exhumations in Contemporary Spain' (2008) 9 *Forum Qualitative Social Research*, art. 35, https://www.qualitative-research.net/index.php/fqs/article/view/1152.

[717] Ferrándiz 2015, o.c., p. 93.

[718] I. Fernández De Mata, 'The "Logics" of Violence and Franco's Mass Graves: An Ethnohistorical Approach' (2004) 2 *International Journal of the Humanities*, 2527.

[719] F. Ferrándiz, 'Exhuming the defeated: civil war mass graves in 21st-century Spain' (2013) 40 *American Ethnologist* 38, at 43.

[720] Ibid.

prohibited as murder nor celebrated as sacrifice'.[721] For the surviving families, exhumations served the moral purpose of saving the disappeared from a meaningless death through their symbolic social reintegration by reburial. Exhumations functioned as performative rituals to recover the Republican disappeared, body by body, from clandestine graves and thereby changing their status from victimage to victimhood. Victimage refers to those scapegoated and those collectively blamed and 'justly' made to suffer – sacrificed – for the catastrophe visited on the community/society. Victimhood refers to the 'innocent' victims of human rights violations committed by the perpetrator who is justly punished – perpetrators of human rights violations cannot be seen as scapegoats because they are not innocent. It reverses the moral relevance of the disappeared from victims ritually cleansed as polluting to the victims of historical injustice whose neglect stains society.[722]

After 2000 the grass roots exhumation movement evolved into a 'human rights forensics' partnership between families of the disappeared, human rights advocates and forensic anthropologists working independently of the state.[723] This partnership in the search for the disappeared championed the campaign for transitional justice legislation to recognize and protect the rights of victims to learn the truth about the fate of their family members.[724] The organized exhumation movement had been initiated into international human rights activism through the role of the Spanish Judge Baltasar Garzón opening prosecutions of Chilean and Argentine human rights violators under universal jurisdiction at the request of of Chilean and Argentinian human rights organizations. He unsuccessfully attempted to extradite General Pinochet, the former Chilean military dictator, from the United Kingdom to Spanish courts universal jurisdiction in 1998;[725] he successfully prosecuted Adolfo Scilingo, a former Argentine naval officer, in a Spanish court for the murder of political prisoners during the Argentine dictatorship in 2005.[726]

721 R. Meister, *After Evil: A Politics of Human Rights*, Columbia University Press, New York, NY 2011, p. 169.

722 Ibid., p. 287.

723 Smith 2017, o.c., p. 402.

724 E. Valverde, 'Constructing victimhood in post-Franco's Spain: the recovery of memory by the grandchildren of victims of the Civil War and dictatorship' ('Konstruisanje žrtve u Španiji nakon Franka:obnovljeno sećanje unuka žrtava građanskog rata i diktature'), (2012) 15 *Temida. The Journal of Victimization, Human Rights and Gender*, 77.

725 C. Krauss, 'Britain Arrests Pinochet to Face Charges by Spain', *New York Times*, October 18, 1998, https://www.nytimes.com/1998/10/18/world/britain-arrests-pinochet-to-face-charges-by-spain.html. In 1998, Judge Baltasar Garzón sought the extradition of Pinochet who was visiting Britain for health care. He also issued a warrant for the arrest of Argentine general for crimes against humanity in the judicial investigation of Plan Condor which saw the southern cone dictatorships cooperate in the repression of each other's citizens.

726 Scilingo was convicted for crimes against humanity in the *Audencia Nacional* in Spain and sentenced to 640 years imprisonment for his role in the notorious ESMA death flights which dumped drugged disappeared prisoners from aircraft into the sea. A confessional account

The exhumation movement, led by ARMH, asked PM José María Alfredo Aznar, head of the PP government, to establish a truth commission to investigate the fate of the disappeared. When PM Aznar refused, ARMH referred Spain to the UN Working Group on Enforced or Involuntary Disappearance which resulted in Spain's inclusion on the list of countries with unresolved disappearances. In 2002, the PP government agreed to support a non-binding resolution put forward by the opposition parties 'condemning Franco's military uprising and proclaiming moral recognition of victims of the civil war and dictatorship'.[727] But it was only when the PSOE government of PM Zapatero came to office in 2004 that the demands of the exhumation movement were addressed for the first time with the establishment of the Commission for the Study of the Situation of Victims of the Civil War and Francoism.

The rise of the human rights idiom in Spain resulted in victimization becoming the focus of the historical memory movement. On the one hand, it constructed individual victims as the repository of rights and positioned them in a transitional justice framework which rejected impunity, prioritized state accountability and supported their inclusion in historical memory.[728] Human rights empowered the subject position of the victim as the most effective position from which to express political demands on governments. On the other hand, the historical memory emphasis on victimization was depoliticizing in two ways. Firstly, Republican victims of the Civil War had been depoliticized by Francoist repression of all oppositional political activity – being *politico*, then by the 'Pact of Forgetting' at democratic transition.[729] The historical memory movement produced a new kind of depoliticization by reconstituting Republican victims as victims of human rights violations stripped of their Civil War political affiliations and ideologies. Secondly, the historical memory movement depoliticized Republican victims through the process of privatization and individualization of Civil War atrocities 'as tragic events that fundamentally concern the affected families and their private feelings'.[730] Narotzky and Smith point out that the 'forced privatisation of past memories' erodes their 'social' dimension and thus their potential to link the past and present and create a framework for political agency.[731] The privatization and individualization of memories as trauma has also contributed to the 'pathological recoding of history

of his role in the 'death flights' is published in H. Verbitsky, *The Flight: Confessions of an Argentine Dirty Warrior*, The New Press, New York, NY 1996. For an analysis of the impact of his confessions on the Argentine military and society see M. Feitlowitz, *A Lexicon of Terror: Argentina and the Legacies of Torture*, Oxford University Press, New York, NY 1998.

727 López Lerma 2015, o.c., p. 198.

728 Golob 2008, o.c., p. 127.

729 S. Narotzky and G. Smith, '"Being politico" in Spain: An Ethnographic Account of Memories, Silences and Public Politics', (2002) *History & Memory: Studies in Representation of the Past* 189, at 200–3.

730 Gómez López-Quiñones 2012, o.c., p. 93.

731 Narotzky and Smith 2002, o.c., p. 219.

as trauma'.[732] Victimhood, arising from the shared past experience of human rights violations, conferred a new political identity and unity.[733]

4.3.2. LAW OF HISTORICAL MEMORY 2007

In its preamble, the LHM embraced the 'spirit of reconciliation and concord and of respect to pluralism and peaceful defence of all ideas' which had underpinned the 1977 transition and was given expression in the Constitution 1978 described as 'the most productive constitutional model of coexistence we have enjoyed'.[734] The LHM was a limited transitional justice measure concerned with restorative justice. It set out to firstly, promote moral reparations for victims who had suffered persecution or violence for reasons of political, ideological, or religious belief during the Civil War and dictatorship, and secondly, to overcome the division between citizens within and across generations by encouraging social cohesion and solidarity. The articles of the LHM establish state support for the neglected victims of repression during the Civil War and Francoist dictatorship by the recognizing Republican memory; by providing financial support to civil society organizations seeking to locate and exhume the disappeared and give them a dignified reburial; by the recovery of Spanish citizenship for Civil War exiles; by opening up historical archives on the Civil War for researchers; by respecting the dignity of the Republican victims through the removal of Francoist symbols exalting military victory and the dictatorship; by declaring illegitimate the decisions of the Francoist tribunals and courts; and by providing reparations to the families of those who had lost their lives fighting for democracy – the Second Republic.[735] The LHM obligates the Spanish administration only to 'provide assistance' to individuals and families for the identification of corpses in unidentified graves, leaving the task of location and exhumation of bodies in the hands of private citizens and their families.[736]

The LHM was framed by the universalizing discourses of human rights and humanitarianism, inclusive on the basis of our shared humanity in the former and our shared sentient – suffering – bodies in the latter.[737] Reconciliation,

---

732 Ribeiro de Menezes 2014, o.c., p. 111.

733 Gómez López-Quiñones 2012, o.c., p. 96.

734 Law of Historical Memory (*Ley 52/2007, de 26 de diciembre, por la que se reconocen y amplían derechos y se establecen medidas en favor de quienes padecieron persecución o violencia durante la guerra civil y la dictadura.* (BOE) A-2007-22296), https://www.boe.es/eli/es/l/2007/12/26/52/con.

735 Ibid.

736 D. Barcala and L. Calvo, 'El Estado no asumirá las exhumaciones de las fosas franquistas', *publico.es*, March 11, 2009, https://www.publico.es/actualidad/no-asumira-exhumaciones-fosas-franquistas.html.

737 Humphrey 2010, o.c., p. 40.

conceived as a product of an enlightenment project, assumes that the forensic – objective – truth revealed in bodies, reinforced by the empathetic truth revealed in suffering, can generate a consensus about what happened in the past was wrong. It imagines that by producing a more inclusive narrative about the past one can produce a more inclusive future.[738] However, the LHM as a transitional justice initiative was an instrument to facilitate support for exhumations and the democratization of memory, not to make the state responsible for driving transitional justice as a project of national reconciliation. The human rights forensics partnership that had driven the demand for the state legislation to recognize rights of the victims of Francoist repression was now given responsibility to search for the mass graves of the disappeared. Through the LHM, the PSOE government under PM Zapatero politically legitimated the exhumation movement and gave it legal and financial support to continue their search. This strategy of franchising responsibility for human rights forensics was anchored in the traumatic memory of families in which the state invested as the engine of the exhumation movement and vehicle for the implementation of their transitional justice policy democratizing memory.

The PSOE decision to support human rights forensics partnerships only served to amplify firstly, its Republican focus and secondly, the traumatic memory of families as a source of counter-memory. Even though the LHM was framed as a human rights law it was explicitly concerned with Republican victims of repression – the disappeared, those executed after summary military trials – and the displaced – those who lost their government positions: administrative, teaching, judicial, military – and the recovery of Republican memory. In the LHM, 'historical memory' was code for Republican historical memory. Hence, the exhumation movement's demands for human rights accountability enacted in the LHM, functioned as an evocative script because it was 'intended to elicit or evoke a particular interpretation beyond the surface meaning'.[739] Caroline Humphrey coins the term 'evocative script' to refer to shared memory that exists in silent disagreement with the official or normalized narratives of the past. The LHM became the vehicle through which Republican memory and victimhood were ritually revealed through exhumation and reburial as historically excluded memory. The victim of human rights violations was code for the Republican victim who in turn was historically bound to the 'two Spains' narrative framed by the asymmetrical counter-concepts Nationalist/Republican and victors/vanquished in which they were on the negated side of the binary. The LHM human rights framing of Civil War history served as an evocative script because it functioned as code for Republican memory and victimhood. By handing over the search for the disappeared to the exhumation movement, the state

738 Ribeiro De Menezes 2014, o.c., p. 57.
739 C. Humphrey 1994, o.c., p. 23.

had effectively handed over the resignification of the disappeared, and their reinsertion in Civil War historical memory to them. It raises the question of whether the recovery of Republican memory as victimhood can serve as the basis for generating a more inclusive cultural memory to promote national reconciliation. Rather than the democratization of Civil War memory opening a new national perspective, it has largely evoked historically entrenched counter memories. The struggle over memory has also been played out in the courts over the priority of constitutional rights in the Spanish Constitution 1978, between Article 18.1 on 'the right to honour', and Article 20.1 on 'the right to the freedom of expression'.[740] In response to Republican survivors' – families – published accounts of historical memory, Nationalist families have legally asserted their right to protect their family reputations. The limits of the 'right to know' opened by the LHM were revealed when Judge Garzón's attempt to launch a *causa general* against Francoism to investigate Civil War mass graves for evidence of crimes against humanity was blocked for exceeding his jurisdiction in contravention of the Amnesty Law 1977.[741]

The LHM, by franchising the conduct of exhumations to civil society groups, has emphasized the role of traumatic memory in the construction of collective memory and the promotion of national reconciliation. As Jenny Edkins points out, 'trauma time' can rupture 'linear time' because it is 'the disruptive, back-to-front time that occurs when the smooth time of the imagined or symbolic story is interrupted by the real (time – *sic*) of "events"'.[742] The conflict between the survivors and the state over historical memory is precisely because survivors' testimony in trauma time threatens to destabilize state power by revealing the hidden founding acts of political violence of the authoritarian regime. In Spain, the historical memory movement turned to the traumatic memory of survivors as a source of authentic counter-memory to challenge the neutralizing transitional Civil War narrative that there was blame and suffering on both sides. Yet ironically, while traumatic memory is a potentially disruptive source of counter-narrative, it must be reinscribed in a linear narrative to be told. It needs to be 'tamed' by strategies of closure, turning victim testimony into lessons about the past and by producing an official – linear – narrative, the homogenizing time of the state, the political purpose of which is to 'return sovereignty to the domain of the government and the state'.[743] The process of re-inscription of traumatic memory in a linear narrative – of survivor stories – about past injustice is necessarily

740 F. Espinosa-Maestre, *Shoot the Messenger? Spanish Democracy and the Crimes of Francoism*, Sussex Academic Press, Brighton/Portland/Toronto 2013, p. 178.

741 Jimeno 2017, o.c., p. 173; J. Yoldi, 'El fiscal acusa a Garzón de abrir una "causa general" por el franquismo', *El País*, October 20, 2008, https://elpais.com/diario/2008/10/21/espana/1224540007_850215.html.

742 J. Edkins 2003, o.c., pp. 229–30.

743 J. Edkins 2003, o.c., p. 228.

depoliticizing by individualizing both the injury and responsibility. The goal of national reconciliation, based on a liberal consensus, can only be achieved by neutralizing potentially disruptive and accentuating inclusive aspects of the past.[744] Politics is 'evacuated of antagonism' and takes place in the context of the space of the nation-state as the inclusive imagined community.[745] Yet, in Spain, it has been the exhumation movement, not the state, that has taken charge of the resignification of the disappeared and their reinscription into historical memory. In other words, exhumation has involved the recovery of an evocative script about Republican victimhood by different organizations, each with their own politically inflected meaning for the recovered disappeared. The result is that the recovery of the historical memory of Republican victimhood cannot be redeemed through the universalizing discourse of human rights because it acts as an evocative script about the 'two Spains' – the conflictive tensions between the nation-state as unitary, centralised, and Castilian, and the nation-state as federal, decentralised, and pluralist. The state's memorialization of the recovered disappeared is unresolved because, beyond symbolizing Franco's repression, the disappeared have not been able to be reinscribed in a smoothed-out national historical memory. To repeat a point made earlier, the idea that a more inclusive future can be produced by a more inclusive view of the past misunderstands the problem of reconciliation in Spain.[746] Reconciliation requires a consensus about how to redeem politically inflicted suffering. It also requires the generation of a new post-dictatorship subject position which transcends yesteryears' perpetrators and victims because the recovery of memory fragments into different ethnic, national, regional, and political identities. Unlike in the transition in 1977, the promise of post-dictatorship democratic citizenship is no longer sufficient as the basis for equality and inclusion. As noted earlier, there is an inherent conflict within the LHM which constructs the origins of democracy as the Constitution of 1978 and not the Constitution of 1931 that established the Second Republic. Moreover, Republican memory sees the sacrifices and repression they suffered in Civil War for the Second Republic as made in the name of democracy. Thus, an important step in the recognition of their suffering is not merely their inclusion in cultural memory but their redemption as victims arising from their historical defence of a democratically elected government. In other words, the Francoist narrative of authoritarian pacification as the foundation for post-transition democracy needs to be displaced by the narrative that democracy in modern Spain was founded by the Second Republic and the Constitution 1931.

The LHM did not advance criminal justice because it did not attempt to annul the Amnesty Law (1977) or even open investigations to establish the

---

744 A. Gómez López-Quiñones 2012, o.c., p. 90.

745 J. Edkins 2003, o.c., pp. 229–30.

746 Ribeiro De Menezes 2014, o.c., p. 57.

facts around the deaths of the disappeared. In response to legal claims from NGOs, Judge Garzón – renowned for his attempt to extradite the Chilean dictator Augusto Pinochet from London for genocide, international terrorism, torture, and forced disappearances in 1998 – unsuccessfully attempted to push the judicial boundaries of the LHM by opening an investigation, in 2008, into 'enforced disappearance' and 'crimes against humanity' focused on clandestine Civil War era mass graves.[747] His investigation was halted by the Spanish High Court and subsequently the Supreme Court for acting beyond his judicial authority and ignoring the Amnesty Law 1977. Nevertheless, Garzón's investigation contributed to a new public awareness of the victims of Francoist repression by framing it in the legal language of universal rights and non-derogable crimes – 'enforced disappearance' and 'crimes against humanity'. He contextualized Francoist repression with more recent authoritarian repression in the Southern Cone countries in which the term 'enforced disappearance' had crystalized as legal concept. Garzón's judicial investigation helped generate what Ferrándiz refers to as 'social jurisprudence', the generation of a public imaginary which catches on in public discourse.[748] It helped catalyze widespread demonstrations for universal justice and against the impunity of Francoism in response to the judicial, political and media obstacles, including the example of Judge Garzón's, they had encountered.[749] Nevertheless, the case of the Spanish Civil War disappearances fall into a legal black hole in international law. The European Court of Human Rights ruled that the Spanish cases of enforced disappearance were inadmissible because the victims had not acted 'without delay' in bringing it before the Court.[750] The Committee on Involuntary and Enforced Disappearances has determined that, while the cases met the definition of enforced disappearance, they fall outside its mandate because they occurred before the UN was established in 1945.[751]

The LHM helped decriminalize the past and democratize historical memory but not recognition of victims and reconciliation in a population whose political subjectivities were profoundly differentiated by their experience of Francoist repression. These political subjectivities have persisted in the asymmetrical

---

747 F. Ferrándiz, 'De las fosas comunes a los derechos humanos: El descubrimiento de las *desapariciones forzadas* en la España contemporánea', (2010) 19 *Revisita de Antropología Social* 161, at 167.

748 Historians dispute the applicability of the term 'enforced disappeared' to refer to all missing and seek to restrict its use to characterize particular phases of Nationalist repression. Ibid., p. 173.

749 Ibid., p. 184.

750 L. Vicente and M. Melón, 'A European Court of Human Rights' Decision Devoid of Justice', *IJ Central*, December 14, 2012, https://www.foroporlamemoria.info/2012/12/a-european-court-of-human-rights-decision-devoid-of-justice/.

751 P. de Greiff, 'Report of the Special Rapporteur on the promotion of truth, justice, reparation and guarantees of non-recurrence: Mission to Spain', A/HRC/27/56/Add.1, July 22, 2014.

counter-concepts of the 'two Spains' – the Nationalists/Republicans and victors/vanquished – upon which the Francoist state was founded. There is the 'collective memory' of the generation who experienced the civil war and Francoist years whose shared memory is diverse, fragmented and polarized. There is also the post-memory produced by the failure of generational transmission of memory stalled by the political silencing of traumatic memories but with residues conveyed through family stories about events they have no experience of and little knowledge about.[752] The almost total lack of concern with justice for past crimes at transition was, in part, an expression of the hold of the hegemonic Francoist narrative about the necessity of the Civil War to save Spain and the benefits of authoritarian pacification encapsulated in the pact of forgetting. Democratic transition rested on the foundational exclusion of the Republican memory and concealment of the illegal founding violence of the Francoist regime and its sacrificial victimage. But the democratization of memory has been pluralizing and fragmenting, not unifying. Because the recovery of Republican memory is driven by the politically diverse historical memory movement with no shared vision of national reconciliation, not least because often their perspectives on the Spanish nation-state project diverge. With the intensification of centrifugal forces of regionalism after the post-Great Financial Crisis (2008) centre-region relations have given impetus to strong secessionist movements which construct the Spanish state as a phantom authoritarian state – i.e. as if 'Madrid' were still the Francoist regime.

After the PSOE lost government in 2011, it quickly became apparent that the force of the LHM depended on which political party was in government.[753] The new PP government under PM Mariano Rajoy immediately withdrew support for the LHM provisions, especially financial support for exhumations. It was only when the PSOE returned to government in 2018, led by PM Pedro Sánchez, that the LHM was reactivated. PM Sánchez signalled a more activist role in transitional justice promising to establish a truth commission, to undertake a victim census of Civil War victims, and to take charge of the search for the disappeared.[754] On October 21, 2020, PM Sánchez promulgated the Democratic Memory Law and established a Public Prosecutors Office for human rights and democratic memory to investigate past violations during the Civil War and Franco's dictatorship in response to criticisms by different UN reports and by the

---

752 Ibid., p. 99.

753 E. Valverde, 'What's happening in Spain? Can the Indignados resurrect the Spanish left?' *Australian OPTIONS* (South Australia), 2013.

754 122/000157 Proposición de Ley para la reforma de la Ley 52/2007, de 26 de diciembre, por la que se reconocen y amplían derechos y se establecen medidas en favor de quienes padecieron persecución o violencia durante la guerra civil y la dictadura, Congreso de los Diputados, December 22, 2017, Nos. 190-1, http://ctxt.es/es/20180620/Politica/20301/documentos-ctxt-memoria-historica-psoe-propuesta-de-ley-politica-espa%C3%B1a-guerra-civil-dictadura.htm.

Working Group on Enforced or Involuntary Disappearance that criticized the failure of the Spanish state to deal with enforced disappearance within human rights law and transitional justice frameworks.[755] The bill takes responsibility for acts of the past, recuperating the memory of victims, exhuming mass graves and identifying the disappeared, establishing a national DNA providing reparations and guaranteeing to prevent the circumstances that could allow a return to a totalitarian regime. It declares Franco's *coup d'état* illegal and opens the possibility of investigating past crimes, but did not repeal the Amnesty Law (1977) and provided only for symbolic reparations, not economic ones. The PP responded by declaring they would repeal the DML when they returned to office. From their perspective, the DML was only passed with the support of minority leftist and nationalist/secessionist parties. Particularly controversial was the provision to investigate human rights crimes committed between 1978 and 1983, an amendment proposed by EH Bildu, a far-left Basque pro-independence party. It wanted the post-transition state repression against ETA (Basque Homeland and Liberty – *Euskadi Ta Askatasuna*) and Basque activists investigated.[756]

The Sánchez government's initiative to strengthen the judicial investigation of the past has occurred in the context of other attempts to open criminal investigations into the crimes of the dictatorship. Firstly, there are the ongoing criminal investigations launched by Judge Servini de Cubría in Argentine courts under universal jurisdiction relating to enforced disappearance under Franco, and secondly, the criminal prosecution in Spanish courts of doctors and religious officials for child trafficking during the dictatorship.[757] Moreover, the new revelations about the scale of post-Civil War repression has given impetus to replacing the term 'political crimes' with 'crimes against humanity'. For example, the exhumation of the remains of 2,238 victims of post-civil war repression in the Paterna Cemetery in Valencia by the Department of Valencia has only intensified the demands for the state to meet its legal obligations to investigate the fate of the disappeared even if they cannot result in prosecutions because those responsible are deceased.[758]

---

755 C. Fernandez-Torne and P. Ouziel, 'Democratising and Decolonising Spain: The Limits of The New Law on Memory' *Justiceinfo.net*, December 5, 2022, https://www.justiceinfo.net/en/109817-democratising-decolonising-spain-limits-new-law-memory.html.

756 G. Hedgecoe, 'Spain's controversial attempt to confront its painful past', *Politico*, July 14, 2022, https://www.politico.eu/article/francisco-franco-eta-pedro-sanchez-spain-controversial-attempt-to-confront-its-painful-past/.

757 R. Minder, 'In Spain's 'Stolen-Babies' Scandal, Doctor Escapes Punishment', *New York Times*, October 8, 2018. https://www.nytimes.com/2018/10/08/world/europe/spain-stolen-babies-ines-madrigal.html.

758 'El secretario de Justicia del PSOE pide que se trate la memoria histórica sin tapujos', *El País*, August 6, 2017, https://elpais.com/ccaa/2017/08/06/valencia/1502011110_876636.html; 'Comienzan los trabajos de exhumación de la fosa 112 de Paterna' *El País*, August 21, 2018, https://www.lavanguardia.com/local/valencia/20180821/451398864197/exhumacion-fosa-112-paterna-valencia-fusilados-franquismo.html.

4.3.3. VALLEY OF THE FALLEN

An important focus of the LHM was the resignification of the Francoist public places, institutions, and monuments. LHM Article 15 (Symbols and Public Monuments) required the removal of commemorative symbols and monuments that glorified the military uprising, the Civil War and of the repression of the dictatorship.[759] LHM Article 16 (VOF) required the VOF to be managed in accordance with regulations governing places of worship and cemeteries and was not to be used for political purposes. In practice, the renaming of public places and monuments throughout Spain required by the LHM has been very uneven, largely contingent on the willingness of local administrations to cooperate. At the national level, LHM Article 16 (VOF) represented the most controversial and difficult site to resignify because of the presence of Franco's grave in the mausoleum. In 2011, PM Zapatero set up a Commission of Experts on the Future of the VOF, under the auspices of the LHM, to give advice about converting the VOF into a national memorial site that dignified and rehabilitated the victims of the Civil War and Franco regime. The Commission's Report recommended that Franco's remains be exhumed and reburied elsewhere because he had not 'fallen' during the Civil War.[760] Moreover, the Report argued the VOF could not be reinterpreted as a site of national reconciliation without dismantling the existing Francoist funerary hierarchy on which it was built.[761] The proposal to resignify the VOF by exhuming and reburying Franco's body elsewhere, while politically sensitive, was not out of character with the way the VOF had been assembled as an enormous military mausoleum containing around 34,000 bodies through an ongoing process of exhumation and reburial of the Civil War dead from all over Spain.[762] The VOF was originally conceived by Franco as an eternal monument to his victory. The Nationalist dead were the first mass exhumations reburied at the VOF as a tribute to their sacrifice for the Nationalist cause and victory. By law, the relocation of the dead to the VOF required the permission of family members, however many remains were secretly exhumed and reburied in the VOF without permission. Subsequently, Republican dead were also secretly entombed in the VOF to fill the mausoleum and collectivize the casualties to signify the cost of victory – i.e. their collective deaths were used to substantiate the enormity of Franco's victory.[763] The honourable relocation through exhumation and reburial

---

759 Preamble to 'The Law of Historical Memory', o.c.

760 The Commission was established very late in the Zapatero government's term and had only five months to complete its Report which was handed down only after the elections had been won by the PP who then refused to implement its recommendations. *Informe: Comisión de Expertos para el Futuro del Valle de los Caídos*, Entrega al Ministro de la Presidencia En Madrid, November 29, 2011.

761 Ferrándiz 2019, o.c., p. S70.

762 Ferrándiz 2019, o.c., p. S65.

763 Hepworth 2014, o.c., p. 470.

of Nationalists killed during the Civil War took place all over Spain with the most esteemed reburied in a funerary pantheon at the VOF. The most prominent reburial in the basilica was the founder of the Falange, José Antonio Primo de Rivera. However, by the time the VOF was completed in 1958, Franco publicly resignified the monument as a symbol of national reconciliation achieved through pacification/repression.

The PP strongly opposed the Commission's recommendation to remove Franco's remains from the VOF and when they came to power in 2012, PM Mariano Rajoy refused to implement it on the grounds that the Commission was partisan.[764] Despite the PP's refusal to act, regional political parties such as the Basque National Party (2012) and the Catalan Agreement of Progress (2013) continued to put forward motions in the Senate to implement the Report's recommendation without success. The PP refused to allow any changes at the VOF in the absence of a social or political consensus. In May 2017, the PSOE opposition successfully introduced a non-binding motion into Congress calling for the removal of Franco's remains from the VOF, the relocation of Primo de Rivera in the Basilica, and the creation of a truth commission to investigate the Franco regime (1939–1975). The PP abstained from the vote and PM Rajoy refused to act on the motion on the grounds that they considered the VOF no longer to be a Francoist monument and that laws already prohibited the use of the site for political commemoration. When the PSOE returned to government in 2018, PM Pedro Sánchez brought a new willingness to revise the LHM in order to strengthen victims' rights by taking charge of the search for the disappeared and establishing a truth commission on the Civil War and Francoism.[765] PM Sánchez also made the removal of Franco's remains from the VOF a priority and immediately approved a Decree to modify the LHM to permit the exhumation.[766] This Decree was subsequently passed by Congress in September 2018 with the abstention of the conservative parties, the PP and the Citizens Party (*Ciudadanos*).

The struggle over memorialization at the VOF has been trapped in the 'two Spains' trope with respect to the Spanish Civil War. Franco built the VOF as an 'avowedly nostalgo-triumphalist' Nationalist monument. Surviving Republican families of victims buried at the VOF have now recoded it as a site for the recollection of suffering.[767] This resignification reflects broader trends in official

---

764 A. Guede, 'Críticas a Zapatero por crear la comisión del Valle de los Caídos poco antes del 20N', *El País*, February 1, 2012, https://elpais.com/politica/2012/02/01/actualidad/1328106053_049636.html.

765 122/000157 Proposición de Ley para la reforma de la Ley 52/2007, o.c.

766 C.E. Cué, 'Government to use decree to give legal coverage to plans to exhume Franco's body', *El País*, August 21, 2018, https://english.elpais.com/elpais/2018/08/21/inenglish/1534840526_621180.html.

767 T. Judt, 'What Have We Learned, If Anything?', *New York Review of Books*, May 1, 2008, https://www.nybooks.com/articles/2008/05/01/what-have-we-learned-if-anything/.

memorialization in Europe 'moving from winners' history to victims' history'.[768] However, the official memorialization of war from these perspectives, Tony Judt argues, does not enhance our understanding of the past but acts as a substitute or surrogate for it. Hence, as the VOF is recoded as an official site of different victimhoods, it will only further fragment identities each seen through 'the vector of their ancestors' suffering'.[769] While the leverage of human rights in the recovery historical victims has been very important, the linear narrative about Civil War will have to draw lessons beyond cruel and unjust suffering. As Judt observes, 'war – total war – has been the crucial antecedent condition for mass criminality in the modern era'.[770] In Spain, any national reconciliation narrative will have to address fundamental political questions underlying the Civil War about the formation of the nation-state, including the origins of Spanish democracy, the distribution of power between the centre and the periphery, and the constitutive parts of Spanish society.

4.4. CONCLUSION

The Spanish transition to democracy has been characterized as 'delayed transitional justice' because of the political failure of post-dictatorship governments to annul Amnesty Law (1977). The Law represented the institutionalization of a political pact based on the understanding that the transition would mark the end of authoritarian rule and the beginning of a plural liberal democracy. The Law was the product of political reconciliation between political party elites formalized in a constitutional pact under the rhetoric of 'no victor, no vanquished'. But the adoption of the policy of amnesia and amnesty to manage the 1977 democratic transition by closing investigation of the past was the historical exception in the 20th century in Spain. Previous political transitions after elections or *coups d'états* in the 1920s and 1930s were accompanied by victors' justice in the form of demands for 'political accountability' for political crimes of commission and omission of the predecessor regime. The successor regime pursued the criminal prosecution, punishment and purging of their enemies to legitimate its authority. While the 'pact of forgetting' underpinning the transition to democracy in 1977 avoided demands for political responsibility, it did reflect the political asymmetry between the parties. Francoism had not been defeated, just made an anachronism in modern democratic Europe. The outgoing Francoist regime was able to dictate the terms of the democratic restoration and foreclose on the question

---

768 Ibid.

769 Ibid.

770 Ibid.

of accountability by politically neutralizing Nationalist and Republican Civil War victims as equivalent – i.e. both sides shared loss and suffering. The Law perpetuated a culture of silence that Francoism had imposed through a culture of repression and public complicity through evasion and self-censorship. The fact the Amnesty Law could establish the political parameters of democratic transition was a measure of the historical effectiveness of Franco's 1939 victory in erasing Republican Spain from the political and cultural landscape and marginalizing Republican supporters in internal exile or *insile* – to coin the Uruguayan expression. It is not surprising that after 40 years of authoritarian rule a negotiated transition to democracy was still dictated by Francoism. The political unification of Spain in 1939 was achieved through military victory and the exclusion of Republicans from any political or cultural role in Spain's future. In 1977, the Amnesty Law quarantined the past and sought to politically unify citizens around an anti-dictatorship and pro-democracy agenda. The Pact of Forgetting officially obscured the founding violence of the new democratic state by perpetuating the exclusion of Republican memory. By default, the Francoist narrative of democratization prevailed – i.e. that Franco's victory in 1939 and successful authoritarian pacification of Spanish society created the conditions for peaceful co-existence which had made democracy possible. Political reconciliation was founded on two unifying moments – the rejection of the authoritarian past and the embrace of a modern democratic future through integration into the eurozone and European Community based on the policy of 'democratic conditionality'.[771]

Another distinctive feature of the democratic transition in 1977 was the lack of civil society mobilization around demands for transitional justice.[772] At that time, the globalization of human rights was still in its early phase and the Spanish democratic transition was being held up internationally as a model to emulate, especially by the post-authoritarian governments in Latin America. The linkup of the grassroots Spanish exhumation movement with the international human rights networks, and with activist Spanish judges willing to pursue the prosecution of crimes against humanity under universal jurisdiction, provided the impetus for a Spanish human rights forensics partnership to emerge. Despite the success of the exhumation movement in getting the Socialist government of PM Zapatero to promulgate the LHM (2007), the Law proved to be a limited transitional justice measure except as a denunciation of the impunity of Francoism in the language of universal law. The LHM provided permission for, and limited support to, civil society organizations to conduct the exhumation of mass graves and the forensic investigation of the remains. As a human rights law

---

771 C. Powell, 'The Long Road to Europe: Spain and the European Community 1957–86' in J. Baquero Cruz and C. Closa Montero (eds.), *European Integration from Rome to Berlin 1957–2007*, PIE Peter Lang, Brussels 2009, p. 39, at pp. 51–3.

772 Powell 2016, o.c., p. 48.

supporting the right to know and the right to remember, the LHM rhetorically included all victims, but in practice it served as an evocative script about Republican victimhood framed by the 'two Spains' trope. The human rights forensics partnership in Spain produced a supportive, not activist, state under the Zapatero government. The state did not assume responsibility for the search for the disappeared. Instead, it left the process of exhumation of clandestine graves, the identification of remains, and the resignification of the disappeared in the hands of the different civil society organizations involved. Pablo de Greiff, the Special Rapporteur on the promotion of truth, justice, reparations and guarantees of non-recurrence (2012–2018), characterized this policy of 'privatization of exhumations' as the state's indifference towards 'officializing the truth' and a failure to meet its obligations under international law to investigate enforced disappearance and crimes against humanity.[773] The ongoing exhumations have produced a continuous procession of the dead making visible and serving as symbolic reminders of the hidden horror, scope, and scale of Francoist repression and Republican victimhood, and the ongoing impunity of Francoism in Spain's mass graves.[774] The human rights objectives of the LHM may have unified the exhumation organizations in their shared goals of recovering the Republican disappeared and dignifying them through proper burial, but it did not provide a unifying narrative about victimhood, only plural and fragmented ones. In other words, the LHM provided no performative transitional justice measures such as a trial verdict or truth commission report around which to consolidate an official account of the past. The effect of the democratization and pluralization of historical memory was to destabilize and erode the legacy of Francoist cultural memory about war and peace. The LHM project to rename public places, what Ferrándiz refers to as the de-militarization by 'dismantling war-derived cartographies of death', was only unevenly implemented, especially in the rural areas.[775] When the Zapatero government lost office in 2011, the future of the VOF and the removal of Franco's remains were still unresolved. The polarizing impact of the LHM was demonstrated by the decision of PM Mariano Rajoy, head of the new PP government, to withdraw support for exhumations and the removal of Francoist symbols from public places. The LHM was only reactivated with the return, in 2018, of the PSOE government under PM Pedro Sánchez. He strengthened the LHM by passing the DML in 2020

---

773 de Greiff 2014, o.c., p. 15.

774 Ferrándiz 2010, o.c., p. 167. There continues to be almost daily reporting of exhumations in Spain. E. Saiz, 'La fosa común de Pico Reja se cierra tras ser recuperados los cuerpos de 1.800 víctimas del franquismo', *El País*, February 21, 2023, https://elpais.com/espana/2023-02-21/la-fosa-de-pico-reja-el-mayor-osario-de-las-victimas-del-franquismo-pendiente-del-adn.html; S. Jones, 'Remains of anti-Franco activist who died in 1973 recovered in Catalonia', *The Guardian*, February 22, 2023, https://www.theguardian.com/world/2023/feb/22/remains-cipriano-martos-anti-franco-activist-who-died-in-1973-recovered-catalonia.

775 Ferrándiz 2019, o.c., p. 362.

which expanded the role of the state in the administration of exhumation, the recognition of victims, symbolic reparations and annulling the decision of the Francoist military tribunals. PM Sánchez has embraced a more comprehensive transitional justice policy in accordance with the recommendations of UN bodies and Special Rapporteurs. However, the promise to establish a truth commission has been met with scepticism. The historical facts are already well known, the amount of material to cover is vast, and there is no likelihood of an official consensual truth emerging as a unifying cultural memory of the Civil War. Ricard Vinyes, a prominent Spanish historian, is critical of the promotion of truth commissions by the UN Rapporteurs, who he describes as part of the 'gentry of memory management'.[776] He argues in Spain there is a lack of understanding about the role truth commissions have played in the transmission of knowledge about the past. In Latin America, the case often cited by Spanish politicians, truth commissions were designed to prevent prosecutions. In Spain, truth commissions will reflect the political failure to annul the Amnesty Law (1977). Vinyes argues victims' memories and testimonies cannot substitute for a state policy for the transmission of knowledge about the past based on academic research and scholarship.[777] The main role of a truth commission in Spain will be the visibilization of the surviving victims through their collected memories and, to a limited extent, recognition as a form of symbolic reparation. The truth commission will extend the exhumation movement's ongoing procession of the dead victims which evokes the 'two Spains' trope. The start of exhumations at the VOF in June 2023, long demanded by Republican families trying to find their relatives who were reburied at the VOF without their knowledge, will extend the procession of the dead victims for many years to come.[778]

While some regard the DML as a radical break with 1977 heralding a Second Transition, politically it has had a polarizing impact galvanizing unexpected coalitions in the context of the erosion of the main political parties and the rise of regional nationalism and secessionist parties. Ribeiro de Menezes has introduced an important counterpoint to the memory debates and transitional justice project in Spain. She argues the idea that it is out of 'a more inclusive view of the past that we create a more inclusive future is in danger of sounding like a disillusioned left-liberal hope rather than a concrete vision: at best it puts the emphasis on the victims of history to fill in our lost utopianism, rather than on us to be the agents of its realization'.[779]

---

776 S. Faber 2021, o.c., p. 202–3.

777 Ibid, p. 202.

778 The DML provision to develop a national DNA database creates the possibility of the identification of the 34,000 anonymous remains entombed in the VOF. See S. Jones, 'Exhumation of civil war dead from Spain's Valley of Cuelgamuros begins', *The Guardian*, June 12, 2023, https://www.theguardian.com/world/2023/jun/12/exhumation-of-civil-war-dead-from-spain-valley-of-cuelgamuros-begins.

779 Ribeiro De Menezes 2014, o.c., p. 57.

CHAPTER 5
LEBANON
Fragmented Sovereignty, Impunity and Legal Intervention

5.1. INTRODUCTION

On February 14, 2005, former Prime Minister Rafiq Hariri was assassinated by a massive car bomb in the hotel district of Beirut, the very area with which he himself had become so closely identified because of his prominent role in rebuilding post-war Beirut. Known as 'Mr. Lebanon', Rafiq Hariri was a larger-than-life figure in Lebanese business and politics serving as Prime Minister between 1992–1998 and 2000–2004.[780] He had earned his enormous wealth in the business of construction and infrastructure development in Saudi Arabia.[781] In death, he became the focus of a mass outpouring of public grief with around one million people gathering in Martyr's Square in Beirut to mourn their loss. The shock event was collectively experienced as an historical turning point in Lebanese politics. His dramatic death galvanized political movements for and against the UNSC's international investigation into the Hariri assassination, known respectively as the March 14 Movement and the March 8 bloc. The March 14 Movement, led by Sa'ad Hariri, the son of the assassinated ex PM Rafiq Hariri, accused Syria of being behind the assassination and demanded its immediate military withdrawal from Lebanon in accordance with UN Security Council Resolution (UNSCR) 1559 (September 2, 2004).[782] It also called for the establishment of an international tribunal to prosecute those responsible for his murder. From the beginning, the March 8 bloc opposed the UNSC resolutions establishing the United Nations

---

780 R. Fisk 'Who killed Mr Lebanon?: The hunt for Prime Minister Rafiq Hariri's assassins', *The Independent*, January 11, 2009, http://www.independent.co.uk/voices/commentators/fisk/who-killed-mr-lebanon-the-hunt-for-prime-minister-rafiq-hariris-assassins-1231542.html.

781 Forbes records Rafiq Hariri was in the top 100 richest people in 2004, https://www.forbes.com/maserati/billionaires2004/LIRSKVY.html?pass=.

782 The Syrian military presence dates from their intervention in the Lebanese Civil War in 1976. See F. H. Lawson, 'Syria's Intervention in the Lebanese Civil War, 1976: A Domestic Conflict Explanation' (1984) 38 *International Organization*, 451.

International Independent Investigation Commission (UNIIIC) under UNSCR 1595 and the Special Tribunal on Lebanon (STL) under UNSCR 1757 which they saw as just the latest attempt by the US to reduce Syria's influence over Lebanese affairs and increase its own. They regarded the reports of both the UNSC Fact-Finding Mission (Fitzgerald Report 2005) and the UNIIIC (Mehlis Report 2006) implicating Syria in the assassination, as just further proof of UN bias against Syria.[783] Hariri's death caused a political earthquake which radically destabilized the Syrian hold over Lebanon and opened the way for international judicial intervention.[784] These political forces shaped the potential and limits for transitional justice in Lebanon.

The national and international impact of the assassination of Hariri saw the United Nations Security Council (UNSC) rush to organize an internationally supervised legal investigation into those responsible for Hariri's murder. The UN Secretary-General Ban Ki-Moon condemned the attack as a terrorist act linking it to the international 'fight against terrorism' and dispatched a fact-finding mission to Beirut headed by an international investigator, Peter FitzGerald, on February 25, 2005.[785] The Mission reported that while responsibility for the crime could only be determined through criminal prosecutions, the Syrian government, whose military occupation had allowed it to dominate Lebanese affairs, was largely responsible for the political tensions leading up to the assassination.[786] Specifically, the Mission report identified the Syrian government as the cause of the political stalemate through their support for an extension of the incumbent pro-Syrian President Lahoud for a third term in contravention of the Lebanese Constitution. The Mission also concluded that the ongoing Lebanese criminal investigation into Hariri's assassination was flawed and unlikely to be able to reach a credible conclusion. Because of the absence of an effective investigation at the national level, the UNSCR 1595 (April 7, 2005) established the United Nations International Independent Investigation Commission (UNIIIC) to gather evidence to assist Lebanese authorities in their investigation of the Hariri assassination.

---

783 P. FITZGERALD and K. ANNAN, Report on the Mission of Inquiry into the Circumstances, Causes and Consequences of the February 14 Beirut Bombing, 9–10, delivered within a Letter from the Secretary-General to the Security Council, U.N. Doc. S/2005/203 (March 24, 2005, 2). It became known as the Fitzgerald Report.

784 Historically Damascus had dominated the Syrian coast both politically and economically for centuries. This changed in the 19th century when the focus of trade shifted from the East to the West making Beirut more important. From the 1860 civil war in Mount Lebanon until the outbreak of the 1975 civil war in Lebanon, Beirut dominated Damascus. Between 1975 and 2005 Syria once again dominated Beirut. See L. FAWAZ, 'The changing balance of forces between Beirut and Damascus in the nineteenth and twentieth centuries' (1990) 55–6 *Revue des mondes musulmans et de la Méditerranée* 208, at 210.

785 Kofi Annan The Secretary – General, Statement of the Secretary-General on the Situation in the Middle East, 5, delivered to the Security Council, UN Doc. S/PRST/2005/4 February 15, 2005.

786 Fitzgerald Report, o.c., p. 2.

On May 30, 2007, the UNSC, acting under Chapter VII of the Charter, adopted resolution 1757 authorizing the creation of the Special Tribunal for Lebanon (STL) to investigate the assassination of ex-PM Rafiq Hariri on February 14, 2005 and other related assassinations. The STL is a treaty based jurisdictional organ, like the Special Court for Sierra Leone and the Extraordinary Chambers in the Courts of Cambodia. It is better understood as a subsidiary organ of the UNSC, like the International Criminal Tribunal for the former-Yugoslavia (ICTY) and the International Criminal Tribunal for Rwanda (ICTR), whose statute had to be enforced by the UNSC.[787]

The creation of the STL, a hybrid Lebanese-international court, is an instance of the judicialization of international relations, the resort to international law and courts to try to manage political crises by turning them into what can be called 'legal emergencies', urgent international legal interventions to get international investigators to the scene of unfolding mass crimes in 'real-time' to bring international attention to atrocities, to deter further atrocities, and to maximize the opportunity to establish the evidentiary grounds for legal prosecutions.[788] International Humanitarian Law (IHL) and International Human Rights Law (IHRL) are deployed to investigate crimes against humanity, genocide or war crimes as 'emergency law', a form of legal triage to manage critical political events. In the case of the Hariri assassination, the 'international' crime targeted was controversially framed as 'international terrorism', which had an ambiguous status in international law.[789] The increasing international resort to 'emergency law' is an index of the crisis of sovereignty in many postcolonial and/or post-authoritarian states and the expansion of transnational governance through international legal intervention as a solution through the consolidation of the global rule of law. Emergency law, as an arm of transnational governance, is an expression of legal globalization, the progressive expansion of transnational liberal legal structures and discourses. Legal globalization rests on the idea that the legitimacy of law is no longer based solely on state sovereignty but on universalized legal principles, concepts and values. In other words, law itself becomes a source of legitimacy in a globalizing world where 'sovereignties are found in multiple and layered forms'.[790] The expansion of international criminal law represents a 'new international legalism' that has grown with the increased

---

787 M. Wählisch, 'Legitimacy Defects and Legal Flaws of the Special Tribunal for Lebanon: Dilemmas of the 'Peace Through Justice Theorem'' in N. Hayashi and C.M. Bailliet (eds.), *The Legitimacy of International Criminal Tribunals*, Cambridge University Press, Cambridge 2017, p. 297, at p. 415.

788 M. Humphrey, 'The Special Tribunal for Lebanon: emergency law, trauma and justice' (2011) 33 *Arab Studies Quarterly* 4, at 5.

789 N.N. Jurdi, 'The Crime of Terrorism in Lebanese and International Law' in A. Alamuddin, et al. (eds.), *The Special Tribunal for Lebanon: Law and Practice*, Oxford University Press, Oxford 2014, p. 73, at p. 82.

790 T.B. Hansen and F. Stepputat, 'Sovereignty Revisited' (2006) 35 *Annual Review of Anthropology* 295, at 307.

institutionalization of international law and the weakened nation-state.[791] Emergency law subordinates national courts to international legal authority and jurisdiction with an ambitious agenda of recovering state sovereignty. By translating political crises into legal matters, emergency law seeks to strengthen national legal authority and the rule of law to challenge political impunity and deliver victims' justice.[792] As Antonio Cassese, Judge and President of the STL, outlined in his statement in August 2011,

> Any claim that the Tribunal is under the influence of some countries is simply preposterous. We are only acting in the interest of Lebanon; our only motivation is the pursuit of justice. Our exclusive aim is to find the truth about the assassination of 14 February 2005 and other possibly connected criminal cases, while upholding the highest international standards of criminal law. For the Lebanese public, this mission means that our work will help put a stop both to the use of assassination in the context of Lebanese political disputes, and to the tendency to forgo accountability, which in fact perpetuates the vicious cycle of assassinations and instability.[793]

The STL's ambitious aim was not just to establish the criminal responsible for the assassination but to help re-establish the rule of law and to rehabilitate the Lebanese state sovereignty. It hinged on one trial, the successful prosecution, conviction, and punishment of those responsible for Hariri's assassination. By framing the political act as an international crime, the STL hoped to generate a moral consensus and unity in a deeply politically polarized community.

To resort to 'emergency law' in Lebanon to end political conflict through a hybrid tribunal, challenged the usual way Lebanese political elites managed political crises through negotiated elite pacts conditional on amnesty and amnesia. Political violence and a culture of impunity have long been normalized in Lebanese confessional politics. Since independence in 1943, there have been two civil wars in 1958 and 1975–1989, and many political assassinations. Between 1950 and 2022, there have been 104 political assassinations and 94 attempted assassinations of political and religious leaders, including presidents, prime ministers or ex-prime ministers, with rarely any prosecutions.[794]

---

791 Teitel 2002, o.c., p. 365.

792 M. Bluhm, 'Cassese hopes tribunal's work will instil 'culture of accountability' in Lebanon', *The Daily Star*, May 17, 2010.

793 Statement of Judge Antonio Cassese, President of the Special Tribunal for Lebanon August 11, 2011, News, Special Tribunal for Lebanon, https://cldhpressreview.blogspot.com/2011/08/iloubnan-cassese-issues-letter-for-4.html?m=0.

794 G. Lenoir, 'In Lebanon, the Lokman Slim Foundation Will Keep the Memory of Political Assassinations', *Justiceinfo.net*, February 3, 2022, https://www.justiceinfo.net/en/87214-lebanon-lokman-slim-foundation-keep-memory-political-assassinations.html. On political assassination in Lebanon see A. Knudsen, 'Acquiescence to Assassinations in Post-Civil War Lebanon?' (2010) 15 *Mediterranean Politics*, 1, and W. Harris, 'Investigating Lebanon's Political Murders: International Idealism in the Realist Middle East?' (2013) 67 *Middle East Journal*, 9.

In response to each crisis, the political elite have sought to bring cycles of violence to an end through pacts underwritten by amnesties – i.e. no legal or political accountability.[795] Since Lebanese independence, there have been 13 general amnesty laws, the most recent of which in 2020 proposed amnesty for citizens convicted of serious crimes including murder, terrorist acts, kidnapping and drug offences. The latest proposal for general amnesty was viewed cynically by the public who interpreted it as the political elite granting immunity for many different offences, including some not yet prosecuted, to protect themselves from prosecution for corruption.[796] Historically, elites have used the general amnesty law to quarantine justice and forget the victims of political violence. The Amnesty Law 1991, legislated at the end of the Civil War as part of the Ta'if Agreement, absolved sectarian political elites from taking responsibility for initiating any transitional justice measures to prosecute perpetrators, establish the truth about the civil war and recognize the victims.[797] Lokman Slim, a human rights advocate, described the Amnesty Law (1991) as symptomatic of the Lebanese culture of impunity, 'the habit of fast forgiveness [in which] every time we fight, we end it with an amnesty law … [hence] we are dealing in a light way with history'.[798] The practice of amnesty creates two kinds of victims: 'the political or religious elite whose assassination is considered 'unpardonable', and a second-rate category that comprises the 'ordinary people, victims of massacres, expulsions and forced disappearances'.[799] In other words, the religious and political elite were exempt from the law.

Prior to the establishment of the STL, numerous non-judicial international commissions of inquiry had been established to investigate serious acts of political violence, including massacres, terrorism, disappearances and war crimes, committed in Lebanon over decades. The UN, Israel and the US had all initiated non-judicial inquiries into IHL violations committed during different

795 The peace treaty between Maronite and Druze notables after the 1860 massacres in Mount Lebanon during Ottoman rule was also premised on amnesty and amnesia. See U. Makdisi, *The Culture of Sectarianism: Community, History, and Violence in Nineteenth-Century Ottoman Lebanon*, University of California Press, Berkeley, CA 2000.

796 There were many different versions of the General Amnesty Bill for the release of prisoners motivated by different political events. See N. Houssari, 'Lebanese MPs fail to reach agreement on draft amnesty law', *Arab News*, May 29, 2020, https://www.arabnews.com/node/1681471/middle-east. The latest version was framed by health concerns for COVID-19. N. Saghieh, 'Lebanon's General Amnesty in the Age of Corona: The Right to Health as a Tool for Political Ends', *The Legal Agenda*, January 29, 2021, https://english.legal-agenda.com/lebanons-general-amnesty-in-the-age-of-corona-the-right-to-health-as-a-tool-for-political-ends/. The beneficiaries of the bill are not just prisoners but also pardons for those who have not yet been prosecuted and includes effectively self-pardon for crimes committed by the people proposing the laws.

797 Law No. 84 of August 26, 1991, Granting General Amnesty to Crimes Committed before March 28, 1991 (Beirut: Dar al-Manshourat al-Houquouquiya-Matbaat Sader, Vol. 3), 3532.

798 M. Wierda et al., 'Early Reflections on Local Perceptions, Legitimacy and Legacy of the Special Tribunal for Lebanon' (2007) 5 *Journal of International Criminal Justice* 1065, at 1071.

799 Ibid.

wars in Lebanon. The UN had conducted investigations into the Palestinian camp massacres in Sabra and Shatila that occurred during the Israeli military invasion to evict the PLO from Lebanon in (1982),[800] the Qana massacre at the UN Peacekeeping post in South Lebanon (1996)[801] resulting from Israeli military action, and the extensive civilian casualties and urban destruction caused by Israeli war in Lebanon (2006).[802] The Israeli government held its own commissions of inquiry into the Sabra and Shatila camps massacre (1982)[803] and the 2006 war in Lebanon.[804] The US Department of Defence held an inquiry into the terrorist bombing of the US Marine force in Beirut in 1983.[805] The purpose of these earlier international commissions of inquiry was to establish the facts about what had happened, not to establish criminal responsibility or compensate victims. The recommendations of these commissions of inquiry were largely directed towards strengthening rules governing the conduct of military operations or reviewing the chain of military command to avoid repetition of command failures. Politically, their purpose was to contain ongoing internal conflict and prevent its regional escalation, not try to resolve it. The most conspicuous transitional justice failure has been the lack of accountability for nearly all the political assassinations, abductions and massacres committed during the Lebanese Civil War (1975–1989) or any acknowledgement of its victims. Notably, the Lebanese Civil War hardly features in the official documents of the UN investigative bodies.[806] Instead, Lebanese political reconciliation at the end of the war accepted the popular characterization of the Civil War as the

800 S. MACBRIDE, et al., *Israel in Lebanon: Report of International Commission to enquire into reported violations of International Law by Israel during its invasion of the Lebanon*, Ithaca Press, London 1983. The only prosecution attempted was under universal jurisdiction in the Belgium courts, but it was unsuccessful. See C. MALLAT, 'Special Dossier on the "Sabra and Shatila" case in Belgium' (2002–3) XII, *The Palestinian Yearbook of International Law*, 183.

801 The UN Secretary-General reported to the UN Security Council that it was 'unlikely that the shelling of the United Nations compound [at Qana] was the result of gross technical and/or procedural errors'. UN Security Council, 'Letter dated 7 May 1996 from the Secretary-General addressed to the President of the Security Council', https://digitallibrary.un.org/record/212595?ln=ar&v=pdf.

802 See Human Rights Council Resolution S-2/1, 'The grave situation of human rights in Lebanon caused by Israeli military operations', August 11, 2006, www2.ohchr.org/english/bodies/hrcouncil/specialsession/2/; *Report of the Commission of Inquiry on Lebanon Pursuant to Human Rights Council Resolution* S-2/1, November 23, 2006, http://www.refworld.org/docid/45c30b6e0.html.

803 L.A. MALONE, 'The Kahan Report, Ariel Sharon and the Sabra-Shatila Massacres in Lebanon: Responsibility under International Law for Massacres of Civilian Populations' (1985) 2 *Utah Law Review*, 373.

804 See R. COHEN-ALMAGOR and S. HALEVA-AMIR, 'The Israel-Hezbollah War and the Winograd Committee' (2008) II *Journal of Parliamentary and Political Law*, 113.

805 *Report of The DOD Commission on Beirut International Airport Terrorist Act*, October 23, 1983, https://fas.org/irp/threat/beirut-1983.pdf.

806 H. VAN DER WILT, 'The Legacy of the Special Tribunal for Lebanon' in A. ALAMUDDIN, et al. (eds.), *The Special Tribunal for Lebanon: Law and Practice*, Oxford University Press, Oxford 2014, p. 268.

'war-of-others' – i.e. Lebanon was the victim of a regional proxy-war conducted on its territory. The 'war-of-others' narrative absolved the Lebanese of any responsibility for the war while ignoring the fact that external intervention was inherent to the Lebanese confessional system in which each sect solicited the support of external patrons to defend or increase their relative power vis-à-vis other sects. The Lebanese civil war was a 'war-of-others' in two senses: firstly, external actors intervened militarily and financially to support Lebanese militias and political parties. The Israelis, Syrians, Palestinians, and briefly the United States and France, all had an armed presence in the country at different times. The Syrian military occupied large parts of Lebanon between 1975–2005 and the Israeli military controlled much of South Lebanon between 1982–2000 as well as conducting major military incursions into Lebanon in 1978 and 2006 and many other limited ones. Secondly, it was a 'war-of-others' because there was only limited Lebanese popular participation and support for the different militias during the war.[807] With the exception of a non-judicial commission in 2000 created by the Lebanese parliament to investigate the disappearance of some 17,000 persons as an ongoing crime, the victims of the Civil War (1975–89) have been officially ignored.[808] The official failure of any transitional justice measures to recognize and commemorate the victims means the scale of phenomenon such as enforced disappearance remain unknown, except by the victims themselves and/or their surviving families.[809] In 1983, a survey found that 36% of respondents indicated they had had a relative or a family member killed, 5% had been kidnapped, while 30% had a family member or a close friend kidnapped who had gone missing during the civil war.[810] The attempts by families to prosecute instances of disappearance in the national courts has had very limited success.[811] The main barrier they have encountered has been an enduring 'institutionalized silence'.[812]

---

807 S. Haugbolle, *War and Memory in Lebanon*, Cambridge University Press, Cambridge 2010, p. 16. One measure of armed participation in the civil war was the relatively small number of militiamen demobilized at the end of the war. See E. Picard, *The Demobilization of the Lebanese Militias*, Centre for Lebanese Studies, Oxford 1999. Based on surveys conducted in the 1980s Salim Nasr concluded that less than 20% of the population was in the 'war society' – i.e. actively involved in supporting a faction or militia. Cited in M. Johnson, *All Honourable Men: The Social Origins of War in Lebanon*, IB Tauris, London and New York 2001, p. 227.

808 Smaira and Cassehgari 2014, o.c., pp. 16–18.

809 In 1991, a Lebanese police report stated there were 17,415 disappeared. See 'Never Forgotten: Lebanon's Missing People', *Amnesty International*, April 14, 2011, https://reliefweb.int/report/israel/never-forgotten-lebanon's-missing-people.

810 S. Khalaf, *Civil and Uncivil Violence in Lebanon: A History of the Internationalization of Communal Conflict*, Columbia University Press, New York, NY 2002, pp. 254–5.

811 D. Smaira and R. Cassehgari, 'Failing to Deal with the Past What Cost to Lebanon?', Report, International Center for Transitional Justice, New York, 2014, 6.

812 I. Kovras, 'Institutionalized Silences for the Missing in Lebanon' in I. Kovras (ed.), *Grassroots Activism and the Evolution of Transitional Justice: The Families of the Disappeared*, Cambridge University Press, Cambridge 2017, p. 129, at p. 131.

From the perspective of international criminal justice, the UNSCR 1595 to investigate the assassination of Hariri, and the UNSCR 1757 establishing the hybrid Tribunal to prosecute those responsible, were supposed to mark an historical turning point ending impunity for political crimes in Lebanon. For the UNSC, the STL mandate was an important opportunity to address longstanding impunity in Lebanon where political assassination went unsolved and the amnesty law (1991) prevented any investigation of serious IHL and IHRL violations committed during the Civil War (1975–1989). However, the broader goals of international justice to end impunity constituted mission-creep going well beyond its limited mandate to investigate a specific crime, the bombing of ex-PM Rafiq Hariri's motorcade and the deaths and injuries arising from it.[813] As a consequence, from its inception, the STL became vulnerable to de-legitimation in domestic politics. Opposition to the STL was not merely a reflection of self-interested avoidance of legal prosecution by the political leadership but the preservation of the confessional status quo based on elite pactism and contingent sovereignty. From the perspective of the pro-Syrian forces, the STL represented partisan intervention in the interests of its opponents. Their response was to try to bring the judicial processes under full Lebanese control so they could shape an outcome guided by elite pactism. While the STL sought to re-found Lebanese sovereignty through justice and the rule of law, the political elite sought to re-found sovereignty on the basis of pactism. In the process, the victims of violence were turned into sacrificial victims or scapegoats whose rights and suffering were forgotten in favour of the elite's interest in reconstituting peace through a renewed confessional power sharing formula.[814]

The UNSC support for international criminal justice as a vehicle for the recovery of Lebanese sovereignty and the rule of law misunderstands the historically contingent nature of Lebanese sovereignty and therefore the limited potential for international criminal justice to generate national consensus and unity through prosecutions. Rather than simply being weak, and therefore needing strengthening with external support, Lebanese state sovereignty is contingent because it rests upon a balance between internal power-sharing by corporate sectarian groups guaranteed by external patrons. Historically, the Lebanese sectarian power-sharing system, referred to as confessionalism, has proven to be very sensitive to changes in the balance between internal and external power. The Lebanese state has a 'hybrid sovereignty' in which it forfeits or outsources sovereignty to other state and non-state actors to preserve itself.[815] Elite pactism seeks to reconstitute sovereignty, after the breakdown of

---

813 Wählisch 2017, o.c., p. 309.

814 R. Girard, *Violence and the Sacred*, John Hopkins University Press, Baltimore, MD 1977.

815 W. Hazbun, 'Assembling security in a 'weak state': the contentious politics of plural governance in Lebanon since 2005' (2016) 37 *Third World Quarterly* 1053, at 1054.

the previous elite pact, through a new elite pact that re-establishes the law by deferring justice.[816] Each new pact is constructed as exceptional, an emergency, but in practice is just another instance of an historically reiterative process of a crisis management driven strategy to de-escalate political violence in order to preserve the elite dominated confessional system. From the perspective of Lebanese elite pactism, the STL's legal intervention is less about strengthening state territorial sovereignty through the instrumental use of international criminal justice than the recruitment of a powerful external ally to shift the internal balance of power to the benefit of a particular corporate sectarian group or groups. From the perspective of the Lebanese opponents of the STL, UNSC legal intervention creating the STL under Chapter VII was simply a form of judicialized international politics seeking to empower the pro-Western side of the Lebanese political elite to the detriment of the pro-Syrian/Iran side – the Axis of Resistance. Two mass movements, known as March 14 and March 8, mobilized in response to the assassination, articulating the competing narratives for and against the UN-initiated international criminal investigation into Hariri's assassination. The March 14 bloc (led by Saad Hariri, Rafiq Hariri's son) supported the internationalization of justice while the March 8 bloc (led by Hizbullah representing the Axis of Resistance in Lebanon) opposed it.[817] The March 14 bloc argued that an international tribunal was essential to deliver justice because Lebanon's judicial institutions were weak and vulnerable to political manipulation. They reasoned international criminal justice would strengthen Lebanese legal institutions, act as a deterrent against future assassinations, and would strengthen the rule of law and Lebanese sovereignty. Conversely, the March 8 bloc argued that the STL infringed Lebanese sovereignty, politicized justice and was unconstitutional and corrupt.[818] These competing narratives were framed by very different event constructions of Hariri's assassination. While both the March 14 bloc and the March 8 bloc accepted the assassination was an international crime, the former suspected Syria was responsible while the latter suspected by a hidden hand was responsible – Israel. The March 8 bloc believed the assassination was designed to implicate Syria so as to weaken its influence over Lebanese affairs and the position of its key allies – Hizbullah – in the confessional order.

---

816 J. Derrida, 'Force of Law: The "Mystical Foundations" of Authority' in G. Anidjar (ed.), *Acts of Religion*, Routledge, New York, NY 2002, p. 358.

817 These two blocs constituted the two main political factions. The March 8 Bloc rallied less than a month after Hariri's assassination while the March 14 bloc was named after the date of the Cedar Revolution, one month after the date Hariri's assassination. See M. Burgis-Kasthala, 'Defining Justice during Transition? International and Domestic Contestations over the Special Tribunal for Lebanon' (2013) 7 *International Journal of Transitional Justice* 497, at 504.

818 M. Burgis-Kasthala and A. Saouli, 'The Politics of Normative Intervention and the Special Tribunal for Lebanon' (2022) 16 *Journal of Intervention and Statebuilding* 79, at 88–9.

The assassination of Hariri is approached here as a violent event framed by competing narratives/frameworks. The focus of these narratives has been the legitimacy of international justice intervention when national justice fails or is severely compromised. Seen through the lens of political semiosis, competing narratives about violent events are established and sustained by performative, demonstrative and representational acts which determine their public acceptance and lasting effects. Galvanized by Hariri's assassination, the March 14 and March 8 blocs played the dominant role in framing the justice narratives designed to shape public opinion about the prosecutions, the charges, the impartiality of international justice, and the legitimacy of the STL its verdicts. The narrow mandate of the STL focused on a single case, and the centrality of the trial unsupported by any broader transitional justice initiatives, made the goal of generating a consensus to challenge elite impunity very ambitious. The STL also became burdened by the expectations for justice it raised in the neglected past victims of the Civil War. The high-profile assassination was experienced as a national public shock and crisis which further polarized not unified Lebanese society. The meaning of the assassination emerged from blending the event into salient post-Civil War narratives about the Civil War as unfinished.[819]

The chapter first contextualizes the Hariri assassination in the history of recurrent political crises and the process of external state formation in Lebanon. It outlines the Lebanese conflict management model based on elite pactism, confessionalism, amnesty and amnesia the international criminal justice intervention had to contend. The chapter then examines in detail the political assassination of Hariri, the intervention of international justice and the domestic resistance to it. The chapter argues that, from the outset, the STL was seen through the prism of internal confessional competition and partisan external intervention in the internal balance of power. Indeed, the March 8 bloc denounced both the UNIIIC and the STL as partisan external actors, not impartial arbiters of international criminal justice. By the time the STL had delivered its verdict in 2021 and was effectively closed down in July 2022, other crises had come to dominate Lebanese politics and expose the limitation of judicial processes in re-establishing state legality and protecting the rights of citizens. Firstly, the Syrian civil war imposed itself on Lebanese politics and the failure of the UNSC to investigate the large-scale IHL and IHRL violations in Syria highlighted the limited character of the STL mandate. Secondly, the constant political interference in the judicial investigation of the Beirut Port explosion (2020) prompted demands by victims for an international investigation at the very moment the STL was being wound down.

---

819 S. Haugbolle, 'The historiography and the memory of the Lebanese civil war', *SciencesPo*, October 25, 2011, https://www.sciencespo.fr/mass-violence-war-massacre-resistance/fr/document/historiography-and-memory-lebanese-civil-war.

5.2. PACTISM, CONTINGENT SOVEREIGNTY AND IMPUNITY

Lebanon remains a state under construction. It was created by the League of Nations Mandate system under French supervision from which it emerged to become an independent state during WWII in 1943. It was the product of external state-making by France who carved Lebanese territory out of its Syrian mandate, thereby fulfilling its longstanding historical role as a protector of the Maronites in the Levant. The 1926 Constitution, introduced during the Mandate period, adopted confessional power-sharing as a temporary political arrangement to work towards secular political institutions. The inclusion of the power-sharing principle in the Constitution produced a permanent state of transition or permanent liminality in which each successive political crisis has remained trapped. Since Lebanon's independence in 1943, each major political crisis has been accompanied by calls for confessionalism to be replaced by a secular system. This section argues that the mandate model of external state-making created a Lebanese state based on a contingent sovereignty shaped by sectarian power-sharing, elite pactism, and external patronage. Three key examples of elite pacts as political fixes are examined here – the National Pact 1943; the 1958 civil war and the Lebanese Civil War (1975–1989); and the Ta'if Agreement. These political events constitute major historical turning points in post-independence Lebanon. They illustrate the way political crises have been fixed by elite pactism refounding and renewing the state based on the formula of recalibrated power-sharing, amnesty and amnesia. There are many other events political crises that could be chosen to illustrate the relationship between elite pactism and state renewal because, in Lebanon, local disputes have had the potential to rapidly escalate to become national crises, mobilizing coalitions along the conduits of clientelism and communalism.[820] Unlike the traditional 'damage-limitation exercise' of the feud in local communities, there were few possibilities for mediation to contain conflict in Lebanese politics except the sectarian leaders.[821]

5.2.1. THE NATIONAL PACT 1943 – ELITE PACTISM AND EXTERNAL STATE FORMATION

Lebanon became an independent state on November 22, 1943, with the declaration of the National Pact terminating the French Mandate established

[820] M. Johnson, 'Factional Politics in Lebanon: The Case of the 'Islamic Society of Benevolent Intentions' (Al-Maqāṣid) in Beirut' (1978) 14 *Middle Eastern Studies*, 56.

[821] Johnson 2001, o.c., p. 233.

in 1920.[822] The French had carved out the territory of Greater Lebanon as a Christian majority state from their post-WWI Mandate in Syria and Lebanon agreed to under the secret Sykes-Picot agreement in 1916 and formalized by the League of Nations in 1923. Lebanon is a case of external state-making via the League of Nations Mandate system which established the principle of self-determination for the peoples formerly part of the Ottoman Empire. The confessional power-sharing model enshrined in the National Pact, an unwritten gentlemen's agreement between members of the dominant Maronite Christian and Sunni Muslim political elites, had been set out in the Constitution of 1926 and the proportional allocation of Parliamentary seats and key political posts fixed by a 1932 population census on the ratio of 6:5.[823] The consociational power-sharing principle borrowed from the Ottoman system of the *Mustassarifiya*, 'an administrative council that reserved seats for sects based on their demographic size'.[824] The French creation of a separate Mandate in Lebanon had its origins in their self-appointed historical role as European protector of the Maronite Catholic minority in the Ottoman Empire dating back to the 16th century.[825] During the 19th century the French expanded their political, commercial and cultural roles in the Levant. First, in 1860, France intervened to protect the Christian communities after largescale communal violence in Syria and Mount Lebanon and negotiated the creation of the small Ottoman autonomous district of Mount Lebanon –*sanjak*– as a Christian haven.[826] The Ottoman Organic Law (*Règlement Organique*) (1861) set out a sectarian power-sharing formula for the Mount Lebanon *sanjak* whose administration was overseen by an international commission to 'fix responsibility, determine guilt, estimate indemnity, and suggest reforms for the reorganization of Mount Lebanon'.[827] Second, the French expanded their presence in the Ottoman territories by establishing French religious schools,

---

822 The French were granted the right to rule the autonomous province of Mount Lebanon (sanjak) on behalf of the League of Nations at the San Remo Conference on April 28, 1920. On September 1, 1920, Mount Lebanon was enlarged to include four other regions to create the Mandate of Greater Lebanon. See R. Maktabi, 'The Lebanese census of 1932 revisited. Who are the Lebanese?' (1999) 26 *British Journal of Middle East Studies* 219, at 225.

823 Maktabi 1999, o.c., pp. 234–5.

824 J. Nagle and M-A. Clancy, 'Power-sharing after Civil War: Thirty Years since Lebanon's Taif Agreement' (2019) 25 *Nationalism and Ethnic Politics* 1, at 2.

825 The French role of protector of the rights of Christian minorities in the Levant dates back to the Franco-Ottoman Treaty of 1523. See D.L. Jensen, 'The Ottoman Turks in Sixteenth Century French Diplomacy' (1985) 16 *The Sixteenth Century Journal* 451, at 453.

826 Estimates of the massacre of Christians in Mount Lebanon (11,000) and Damascus (12,000). See L.T. Fawaz, *An Occasion for War: Civil Conflict in Lebanon and Damascus in 1860*, University of California Press, Berkeley, CA 1994, p. 226.

827 S. Khalaf, *Persistence and Change in 19th Century Lebanon: A Sociological Essay*, American University of Beirut, Beirut 1979, p. 93.

hospitals, asylums and orphanages and became heavily involved in Ottoman financing and development, especially the railways.[828] When the Ottoman Empire collapsed at the end of WWI, the French historical role as protector of Maronite communities evolved into external state-maker derived from the Mount Lebanon *sanjak* confessional power-sharing model. The so-called 'Greater Lebanon' was constituted by the expansion of the Mount Lebanon *sanjak* to include coastal territories. The principle of confessional power-sharing set out in the 1926 Constitution was seen as a temporary measure to facilitate transition to a fully independent state.[829] In 1943, the National Pact reconfirmed confessional power-sharing and political communalism as the basis of the new independent Lebanese state.

The contingent character of the sovereignty of the new Lebanese nation-state was reflected in the unresolved question of national identity in the National Pact in 1943. The Maronite-Sunni political partnership between Bechara al-Khoury and Riad al-Solh agreed that Lebanon was 'not East, not West' but, at the same time, had an 'Arab face'.[830] The Lebanese national independence project was forced to accommodate itself to the wider regional project of Arab nationalism through the Lebanization of the Sunni elite and the Arabization of the Maronite elite brokered with the support of the Syrians, the British and the Egyptians. These centrifugal tensions created the historical predicament in which, according to Robert Fisk, 'Lebanon will always be a nation in waiting'.[831] From its inception, the National Pact (1943) was unstable because it was based on two faulty assumptions. First, an internal one based on the belief that elite consensus reflected grass-roots communal support; and second, an external one that assumed the balance-of-power in the region would remain unchanged and always reflect the value system of the first generation of conservative pro-Western Arab nationalists.[832] In practice, the National Pact was constantly threatened with destabilization arising from internal competition amongst the Lebanese political elite and/or the external impact of turbulent regional geo-politics. Despite the

---

828 W.I. Shorrock, 'The Origin of the French Mandate in Syria and Lebanon: The Railroad Question, 1901–1914' (1970) 1 *International Journal of Middle East Studies*, 133.

829 Article 95 of the 1926 Constitution stipulates that 'in the transition period [which has persisted since 1926] … the communities shall be equitably represented in the ministries'. Quoted in E. Picard, 'Post-war Lebanese communities in search of reconciliation' in V. Makrides and J. Rüpke (eds.), *Religionen im Konflikt*, Aschendorff Verlag, Münster 2005, p. 127, at p. 128.

830 F. AL-Khazen, 'The Communal Pact of National Identities: The Making and Politics of the 1943 National Pact', Papers on Lebanon 12, Centre for Lebanese Studies, Oxford, 1991, p. 38.

831 R. Fisk 'Lebanon is a sectarian nation, yet it has avoided civil war while the Middle East burns – here's why', *The Independent*, October 20, 2016, http://www.independent.co.uk/voices/lebanon-civil-war-avoided-peaceful-nation-middle-east-syria-turkey-israel-conflict-robert-fisk-a7371326.html.

832 F. AL-Khazen 1991, o.c., p. 39.

destabilizing interdependent internal and external dynamics, the confessional system has been able to survive many political crises by renewing elite pacts founded on their agreement to recalibrate sectarian power-sharing, their recommitment to national unity and the preservation of their role as patrons and powerbrokers. Because of the multipolarity of external patronage no single external power has been able to successfully broker peace between elites. Pacts required multilateral efforts. Ironically, while internationally brokered power-sharing may have succeeded in ending conflict it also kept 'alive incompatible myths and hopes of victory'.[833] Because the National Pact founded sovereignty as a constitutional pact, each time the Lebanese state's authority broke down Lebanese sovereignty has had to be refounded with a new constitutional pact to unite the country.

The sectarian power-sharing formula and elite pactism are at the heart of the in/stability of Lebanese confessional system. While sectarian power-sharing institutions in multi-ethnic and multi-sect societies are, in theory, supposed to reduce conflict by ensuring proportional representation of all communities, they can also intensify competition and conflict. Consociational systems are supposed to enhance equality by preventing domination by majoritarian rule in multiethnic/religious societies.[834] But rather than enhance a pluralist democracy, sectarian power-sharing institutions can also limit democracy because the conservative interests of ethnic elites act to preserve the power-sharing status quo by block veto and by privileging issues of inter-ethnic allocation of power and resources, which push to the forefront 'fundamental issues of renegotiating the rules of power sharing'.[835] The dominant ethnic/sectarian groups become less concerned with compromise or conciliation and more interested in preserving their power. They tend to be inflexible and unable to adapt to rapidly changing social conditions. If sanctions against power-sharing rule breakers are ineffective and external guarantors fail to intervene to preserve the internal status quo, rapid change can escalate conflict.[836] In Lebanon, politics is constituted by elite pactism and political history is the story of serial political fixes reached through political reconciliation between elites claiming to act as representatives of sectarian corporate groups. These groups are corporate in two senses: firstly, constitutionally all citizens must be members of a sectarian community prior to their membership in the nation. The almost exclusive jurisdiction of the

---

833 P.G. Roeder and D.S. Rothchild, 'Conclusion: Nation-State Stewardship and the Alternatives to Power Sharing' in P.G. Roeder and D.S. Rothchild (eds.), *Sustainable Peace: Power and Democracy After Civil Wars*, Cornell University Press, Ithaca, London 2005, p. 319, at p. 323.

834 C. Bell, 'Power-sharing and human rights law' (2013) 17 *The International Journal of Human Rights* 204, at 205.

835 O. Geukjian, *Lebanon After the Syrian Withdrawal: External Intervention, Power-Sharing and Political Instability*, Routledge, London 2016, p. 37.

836 Roeder and Rothchild 2005, o.c., pp. 36–41.

religious courts over marriage and divorce reinforces the corporate character of the sectarian community. Secondly, sectarian communities are corporate in the political sense that members are beneficiaries of political elite patronage who expect in return their allegiance in the form of votes. However, elite pacts are characteristically temporary political fixes that do not seek to address the underlying structures of power and inequality that generate the conflicts. In his study of pactism in Italian city-states, Tarrow observes: 'pacts have the property that they do not produce long-term reconciliation between interests; they only mediate them. Pact-like institutions are both susceptible to breaking down under external pressure and to spilling easily into non-institutional contention'.[837] Lebanese pactism has evolved from the historical role of elite families as mediators between subjects and political authority under Ottoman rule. The status and power of elite families (*za'im, zu'ama pl.*) grew with their appointment as community leaders responsible for tax-collecting on behalf of the Ottoman authorities as well as serving as go-betweens for local clients. The Lebanese historian Albert Hourani charts the evolution of the *zu'ama'* and patron-client relations by identifying three types: 'the feudal *za'im*'; 'the popular political leader'; and 'the urban *za'im*'.[838] In Lebanese confessional politics, the *za'im* exchanged services and benefits for his client's vote in parliamentary elections. Success in gaining political office provided access to state resources and the opportunity for a *za'im* to expand his patronage. While the confessional system is often denounced as corrupt and an obstacle to political reform, the mutual interests of *zu'ama* in preserving their relative power and clientelist relations have contributed to its resilience. Elites have been able to preserve their role as patrons internally by responding to the changing moods and attitudes of their constituencies, and externally, by acting as intermediaries between external powerbrokers and their sectarian constituencies in the context of a weak state.[839]

5.2.2. THE CIVIL WAR 1958 – POWER-SHARING AND GEOPOLITICS

The recurrent catalyst for political crises and outbreaks of violence has been the breakdown of pact agreements over sectarian power-sharing precipitated by internal conflict exacerbated by external geopolitical forces. The go to solution for these crises has been exceptionalism – one-off solutions to preserve the confessional system by forging a new elite pact underpinned by amnesty

---

837 S. Tarrow, 'From comparative historical analysis to "local theory": The Italian city-state route to the modern state' (2004) 33 *Theory and Society* 443, at 454.

838 A. Hourani, 'Ideologies of the Mountain and City' in R. Owen (ed.), *Essays on the Crisis in Lebanon*, Ithaca Press, London 1976, p. 35.

839 D. Noar, 'The Arena of the *Zu'ama* – Reviewing Hizballah's Role in Lebanon' (2014) 18 *Middle East Review of International Affairs*, 8.

and amnesia.[840] New elite pacts re-enact the founding of the state which amnesty as forgetting is the historical norm. Hall makes the point that 'both violence and amnesty are constitutive of the law and the state'.[841] Thus amnesty, which Hall characterizes as the suspension of the law in the name of justice, and the amnesia on which it is premised, are integral to founding nation-states which forget the violence and victims – the price paid and sacrifice made – on which the state and rule of law have been established.[842] The violence that refounds the state is in excess of law which is itself founded upon the violence of the state. The most serious political crises leading to outbreaks of violence since independence have been the brief 1958 Civil War and the protracted Lebanese Civil War (1975–1990). The 1958 crisis erupted over the clash between the pro-Western orientation of President Chamoun and the popular regional support for Arab nationalism under the leadership of President Nasser. The outbreak of civil war in 1975 was precipitated by the growing militarized Palestinian presence from the late 1960s and the radical mobilization of the pro-Arab nationalist Lebanese National Movement which threatened to completely dismantle the confessional system. In both cases, the crises were precipitated by changes in the balance of political power internally between sects and externally in the influence of outside states as brokers/patrons. Even after the breakdown of government and territorial fragmentation during the Lebanese Civil War (1975–1990), the key to political reconciliation was recalibration of confessional power-sharing brokered by the elite.

Since its founding with National Pact (1943), the stability of the Lebanese confessional system has been regularly tested by the turbulent regional geopolitics that penetrated and divided different Lebanese political constituencies into pro-Arab and pro-Western camps. The first test of the National Pact occurred when Lebanon participated in the Arab-Israeli war in 1948 but on that occasion the prevailing cross-sect pro-Arab consensus preserved national unity. However, growing Sunni Muslim grievances over the concentration of power in the office of the Maronite President and the assassination of Sunni Muslim Prime Minister Riyad as-Sulh in 1951 shortly after leaving office weakened their influence in confessional politics. By the mid-1950s, the regional geopolitical division between the Iraqi led pro-Western and Egyptian led anti-imperialist camps became articulated in Lebanese politics in the opposition between pro-Western policies of President Chamoun and the pro-Arab Nationalist position of Sunni Muslim leaders and the Muslim 'street'. A series of regional events polarized domestic politics – the Suez crisis 1956; the creation by President Nasser of

---

840 M. Mugraby, 'The Syndrome of One-Time Exceptions and the Drive to Establish the Proposed Hariri Court' (2008) 13 *Mediterranean Politics*, 171.

841 J. Hall, 'Displacing Evil: The 1991 Lebanese Amnesty, the City and the Possibility of Justice' in S. Dam and J. Hall (eds.), *Inside and Outside the Law: Perspectives on Evil, Law and the State*, Inter-Disciplinary Press, Oxford, 2009, p. 61, at p. 61.

842 Ibid.

the United Arab Republic (UAR) by the Egyptian–Syrian union on February 1, 1958; and the July 14, 1958 revolution in Iraq, resulting in the overthrow of the Hashemite dynasty with the execution of King Faisal II and Prime Minister Nuri al-Said. In this climate, Chamoun's ambition to extend his presidency for another term, and his endorsement of the Eisenhower Doctrine (March 16, 1957), precipitated a domestic rebellion against his presidency and his pro-Western alliance.[843] In response to the armed rebellion against Chamoun's government, the US activated the Eisenhower Doctrine and landed US Marines in Beirut on July 15, 1958. The crisis was quickly resolved through an agreement between Cairo and Washington to support the election of the Lebanese army commander General Fouad Shihab as a consensus president.[844] An important contribution to help de-escalate the conflict was made by the Arab states at the UN in their affirmation of their adherence to Article 8 of the Arab League Pact which required Arab states not to intervene in other Arab states to change their systems of government support.[845] President Shihab (1958–1970) set out to restore national unity around loyalty and allegiance to Lebanon as a 'final indisputable country' and, at the same time, marginalize the traditional confessional elite.[846] In order to re-establish the confessional status quo, the Shihab government promoted national reconciliation based on "no victor, no vanquished", which allowed the US to withdraw its military forces.[847] Shihab pursued an agenda of state modernization built upon a new coalition of progressive members of the traditional confessional elite and the newly educated professional class of technocrats and military officers who owed loyalty to Shihab personally. Shihab's trans-sectarian agenda for state modernization and national unity did not survive the Presidency of Suleiman Frangieh (1970–76), an embodiment of the traditional confessional elite style of politics. The key to the resolution of the 1958 Civil War was the agreement amongst external patrons that the Lebanese had to find a political solution. The Lebanese elite agreed that President Chamoun had to be replaced by General Shihab.

5.2.3. LEBANESE CIVIL WAR 1975–1989 AND THE TA'IF AGREEMENT

By the 1970s, the escalation of violent confrontations between sectarian and ideologically based armed groups resulted in the complete breakdown of the

843 B.F. Salloukh, et al., *The Politics of Sectarianism in Postwar Lebanon*, Pluto Press, London 2015, p. 18.

844 Ibid.

845 K.R. Sorby, 'Lebanon: The Crisis of 1958' (2000) 9 *Asian and African Studies* 76, at 107.

846 Ibid., p. 19.

847 M.M. Labelle, 'A New Age of Empire? Arab 'Anti-Americanism', US Intervention, and the Lebanese Civil War of 1958' (2013) 35 *The International History Review* 42, at 61.

confessional system. The causes of Lebanese Civil War are disputed but the key issues were firstly, the historical injustice of the confessional power-sharing formula which politically privileged Maronites and Sunnis over the other sects, and secondly, the right of the Palestinian resistance to run its own refugee camps and conduct military operations against Israel from Lebanese territory conceded under the –undocumented– Cairo Agreement in 1969 between the Lebanese Army and the PLO.[848] Since the arrival of the Palestinian refugees in Lebanon in 1948, many Maronite Lebanese regarded them as a demographic threat to the confessional balance in favour of the Muslims and a lightning rod for pro-Arab Nationalist politics. By the early 1970s, the consensus of the Lebanese elite expressed in the National Pact (1943) had eroded and each leader recruited their own militia in a bid to preserve sectarian power.[849] What is referred to as the 'Lebanese Civil War' is more accurately described as a series of related conflicts between shifting alliances of sectarian groups, political parties, and external actors. There were five phases: 'the two-years war from April 1975 to November 1976; the long interlude of failed peace attempts, Israeli and Syrian intervention and a host of internal armed conflicts between November 1976 and June 1982; the Israeli invasion and its immediate aftermath from June 1982 to February 1984; the internal wars of the late 1980s; and finally the intra-Christian wars of 1988–90, which led to the end of the war'.[850] Each period is associated with notorious massacres and assassinations: the Black Saturday, Tal al-Za'tar and Damour massacres between 1975–76; the War of the Mountain between Druze and Christian forces during 1982–83; Israeli bombardment of West Beirut in August 1982, and the Sabra and Shatila camp massacres that followed; the War of the Camps between Palestinian and Shiite forces from 1985 to 1987; and Michel Aoun's war with Samir Ja'ja's Lebanese Forces and the Syrian army in 1989 and 1990. The human cost of the war was approximately 150,000 killed, hundreds of thousands injured, hundreds of thousands internally displaced and a million left the country.[851] The many attempts to end the Civil War all revolved around plans to reinstitute a modified confessional power-sharing agreement backed by different external brokers – primarily the Syrians, the Israelis and the Saudis.[852] By the end of the Civil War in 1990, the Syrian government had established itself as the dominant external powerbroker in Lebanon. After the Israeli military eviction of the PLO in the 1982 war, the attempt by the US and Israel to install a pro-Western government able to sign a peace treaty with Israel

848 R. El-Husseini, *Pax Syriana: Elite Politics in Postwar Lebanon*, Syracuse University Press, Syracuse, NY 2012, p. 11.

849 Johnson 2001, o.c., p. 56.

850 Haugbolle 2011, o.c., p. 3.

851 M. Wenger, 'Primer: Lebanon's 15-Year Civil War 1975–1990' (1990) 162 *MERIP*, https://merip.org/1990/01/primer-lebanons-15-year-war-1975–1990/.

852 B. Salloukh, 'Syria and Lebanon: A Brotherhood Transformed' (2005) 236 *MERIP*, http://www.merip.org/mer/mer236/syria-lebanon-brotherhood-transformed.

failed when the US withdrew its military presence after the bombing of the US Marine base in Beirut in October 1983 resulting in the death of 241 US Marines and 58 French military personnel.[853]

The Ta'if Agreement, officially known as the National Reconciliation Accord, was signed in September 1989 in Saudi Arabia and approved by Lebanese parliament on November 4, 1989. It marked the end of the protracted Civil War and the founding of the Second Lebanese Republic based on a modified confessional power-sharing formula. It was negotiated by the surviving members of the 1972 Lebanese parliament, mediated by the Saudis, and strongly influenced by Syria. Rafiq Hariri, as a former Saudi diplomatic representative, played an important role in negotiations.[854] The Agreement occurred at a moment when there was a broad consensus over ending the Israeli military occupation of South Lebanon and the acceptance of a transitional role for Syria in Lebanon. It delivered Syrian dominance, peace, and no reconciliation. Ta'if recalibrated the sectarian formula from 6:5 to 1:1 Christian to Muslim, establishing a balance between Christian and Muslim appointments to the bureaucracy and shifting power away from the office of the president –Maronite– to the parliament where the Sunni –Prime Minister– and Shi'a –Speaker– communities had greater influence. The 1:1 recalibration in no way reflected the new demographic reality in which Christians represented less than 40% of the population.[855] The recalibrated sectarian power-sharing formula was understood as a transitional arrangement that would eventually be replaced by a non-sectarian bicameral system of government.[856] Despite the Agreement's explicit goal of abolishing confessionalism, the post-war confessional system became more entrenched because firstly, the traditional political elite – the surviving Deputies from the last elected government in 1972 – were included as parties to the Ta'if agreement, and secondly, because Syrian overlordship preserved confessionalism as a vehicle for their continued clientelist influence over Lebanese affairs. Syria subsequently entrenched its institutional dominance over Lebanese affairs through the Treaty of Brotherhood and Cooperation signed with the Lebanese government on May 22, 1991.[857] The Ta'if Agreement did not resolve the main conflicts of the war – the future of confessional power-sharing; the Palestinian refugee issue; the hegemonic Syrian presence and control over Lebanese affairs; and the status of Hizbullah as the only armed militia after the others had agreed to demobilize.

853 N. Shehadi, 'The Special Tribunal for Lebanon: The UN on Trial?' (2007) MEP/IL BP 07/01, Chatham House, *Middle East/International Law Briefing Paper*, 3.

854 M.W. Neal and R. Tansey 'The dynamics of effective corrupt leadership: Lessons from Rafik Hariri's political career in Lebanon' (2010) 21 *The Leadership Quarterly*, 33.

855 Picard 2005, o.c., p. 136.

856 S. Rosiny, 'A Quarter Century of 'Transitory Power-Sharing'. Lebanon's Unfulfilled Ta'if Agreement of 1989 Revisited' (2015) 17 *Civil Wars* 485, at 492.

857 J. Slomich, 'The Ta'if Accord: legalizing the Syrian occupation of Lebanon' (1999) 22 *Suffolk Transnational Law Review* 619, at 624.

Moreover, the kidnappings, disappearances, assassinations and massacres of the Civil War were closed to investigation under the Amnesty Law (1991) for crimes committed before March 28, 1991.

The Ta'if Agreement's pragmatic preservation of confessionalism as a temporary political fix to achieve political reconciliation only perpetuated the negative liminality – the unresolvable politics of sectarian entitlement and grievance – inaugurated with the adoption of confessional power-sharing as a transitional measure in the 1926 Constitution. It repeated the formula of political reconciliation under the rhetoric of 'no victor, no vanquished'. In practice, the Second Republic only entrenched sectarian leadership and political constituencies. It did, however, change the dynamics of sectarian power-sharing by reducing the power of the Maronite President, who could no longer dismiss the Sunni Prime Minister, and effectively gave veto power to the Sunni Prime Minister and the Shi'a President of Parliament. Moreover, the role of Syria as arbiter in Lebanese affairs only intensified elite competition to solicit Syrian intervention in support of their interests. Consequently, communalism deepened the divide between communities and strengthened political sectarian constituencies. The Hariri assassination occurred in the political context of this ebb and flow of rivalry between elites to gain Syrian support.[858] It was hoped that the shared experience of the tragedy of the Civil War had at last forged a Lebanese national identity and created impetus towards national reconciliation. But the transitional justice policy of amnesty and amnesia left ordinary Lebanese divided by their experiences of the war and despaired that forgetting was the only way to move forward. The war lacked any heroic or redemptive character, nor was there any consensus about its origins or consequences. Amnesia suited the sectarian leaders, especially the new generation of former militia leaders, allowing them to avoid public debate about the war and any uncomfortable discussions about their own involvement.[859] Post-war elections as a transitional mechanism for generating consensus about the past and national unity, pivotal in the Uruguayan case, did not serve that unifying function in Lebanon.[860] The disillusionment with the new political order and opposition to Syrian military occupation saw low participation in the 1992 election. The results reflected the gerrymandering of electorates to guarantee the election of the warlords-cum-parliamentarians and the Christian boycott of the elections only reinforced the dominance of Syrian-endorsed candidates.[861] Nor did the selective use of criminal justice to prosecute Samir Geagea, leader of the Christian Lebanese Forces, for the murder of political opponents and bombing of a church was

858 Johnson 2001, o.c., p. 280.
859 Haugbolle 2010, o.c., pp. 74–84.
860 See Chapter 3.3.1 on the role of elections in Uruguay in 1984.
861 Johnson 2001, o.c., pp. 236–8.

widely viewed as retribution against anyone opposing Syrian control over Lebanese affairs.[862]

Syria was able to establish its post-war hegemony in Lebanon through its reproachment with Saudi Arabia and the US which allowed it to become the external arbiter of Lebanese affairs and forced all sides to seek Syrian approval of their political agendas. After 2000, Syria's dominance was gradually eroded by changing regional geopolitics. First, Syrian relations with Israel deteriorated. After Israeli forces voluntarily withdrew from South Lebanon in 2000 under pressure from resistance groups led by Hizbullah, Syria also came under pressure to withdraw. The Syrian-Israeli peace process focused on the Golan Heights broke down and Syria's ongoing support of rejectionist organizations like Hizbullah and Hamas only worsened their relations with Israel. Second, Syria's relations with the US also deteriorated, bringing US pressure on Syria to withdraw from Lebanon. Relations between the US and Syria had long been problematic. In 1979, the US State Department had criminalized the Assad regime by including Syria on its list of State Sponsors of Terrorism.[863] In 1989, the US had accepted the Syrian role in the Ta'if Agreement to end the Civil War. In 2001, Syria had cooperated with the US by providing intelligence on Al Qaeda after the 9/11 terrorist attacks. In 2002, the US Congress brought pressure on Syria to withdraw from Lebanon by passing the Syrian Accountability and Lebanese Sovereignty Act.[864] In 2003, Syria opposed the US invasion of Iraq and supported Saddam Hussein. In 2004, the Syrian government sought to assert its control over Lebanon by supporting President Lahoud, a political ally, for a third presidential term. They also sought to marginalize PM Hariri whose privatization of state-controlled enterprises threatened to weaken pro-Syrian ministers by removing from their control ministries they used as sources of patronage. The rising tension between the US and Syria undermined Hariri's relationship with Damascus and with the pro-Syrian forces in Lebanon. For the Syrian regime, Hariri became the enemy because they believed he was behind the Franco-US sponsored UN Security Council Resolution 1559 which opposed the extension of President Lahoud's term of office, called for the disarmament of Hizbullah, and demanded the withdrawal of Syria from Lebanon. Hariri became the hinge connecting domestic opposition with the French and US sponsored resolution pressuring Syria.[865] By 2004, Hariri had become closely associated with UNSC Resolution 1559 (September 2, 2004), because of his close ties with

---

862 Ibid., p. 240.

863 US Department of State, 'State Sponsors of Terrorism', https://web.archive.org/web/20090610080648/http://www.state.gov/s/ct/c14151.htm.

864 *Syria Accountability and Lebanese Sovereignty Restoration Act of 2003*, PUBLIC LAW 108-175-(108th Congress) Dec. 12, 2003.

865 H. Baumann, 'Citizen Hariri and neoliberal politics in postwar Lebanon', PhD Thesis, SOAS, University of London, 2012, p. 267, http://eprints.soas.ac.uk/14240.

the US, France and Saudi Arabi.[866] UNSCR 1559 called for the 'strict respect for Lebanese sovereignty, territorial integrity, unity and political independence under the sole and exclusive authority of the Government of Lebanon throughout the country' and 'the disbanding and disarmament of all Lebanese and non-Lebanese militias'.[867] He was assassinated a few months later in February 2005.

The Ta'if Agreement established a new sectarian power-sharing formula which created the conditions for government paralysis through the veto power in the Cabinet to one of the three aligned blocs of ministers – those of the president, the speaker of parliament and the prime minister.[868] It also confirmed Syria as the external arbiter of internal Lebanese domestic politics. However, after the Israeli military withdrawal from South Lebanon, external pressure mounted on Syria to also withdraw its military presence from Lebanon and other external actors increased their role in Lebanese domestic politics. As PM Rafiq Hariri's relations with Syria became more strained, he sought external support to reduce Syrian dominance of Lebanese affairs and to bring about the disarmament of Hizbullah. The assassination of Hariri and other pro-Syrian politicians and journalists during the UNIIIC investigations strongly suggest that Syria was unwilling to let go of its role as arbiter of Lebanese affairs.

5.3. INTERNATIONAL CRIMINAL JUSTICE AND THE HARIRI ASSASSINATION 2005

5.3.1. THE UNITED NATIONS INTERNATIONAL INDEPENDENT INVESTIGATION COMMISSION 2005–2009

What distinguished the assassination of Rafiq Hariri from the all-too-common practice of political assassination in Lebanese political life was its transformation into a matter for international criminal justice. The UNSC immediately sent a fact-finding mission to Lebanon and quickly established the UNIIIC transforming the legal and political significance of the assassination by framing it as an international terrorist crime. Even though 'terrorism' was not recognized as an international crime in law, and therefore not strictly a matter for international criminal justice, framing the assassination as international terrorism situated it politically in the regional context of the conflict over Syrian

866 Shehadi 2007, o.c., p. 3.

867 Shehadi 2007, o.c., p. 3. And also S. Fregonese, 'Beyond the 'Weak State': Hybrid Sovereignties in Beirut' (2012) 30 *Environment and Planning D: Society and Space* 655, at 662–3.

868 J. Bahout, 'The Unraveling of Lebanon's Taif Agreement: Limits of Sect-Based Power Sharing' (2016) Carnegie Endowment for International Peace, https://carnegieendowment.org/files/CP_271_Bahout_Taif_Final.pdf.

dominance of Lebanese affairs and the international context of the 'War on Terror'. The international security lens of the War on Terror internationalized the significance of terrorism as a threat to regional peace and stability. Several UN counter-terrorism resolutions had put the threat of terrorism high on the international security agenda after 9/11. UNSC resolution 1377 (2001) on the Declaration on the Global Effort to Combat Terrorism characterized international terrorism as 'one of the most serious threats to international peace and security in the twenty-first century'.[869] The fact that Syria, a state included on the US State Department's list of 'State Sponsors of Terrorism' since 1979, had been implicated in the assassination by the Fitzgerald Report and the UNIIIC reports only reinforced the characterization of the assassination as a crime of international terrorism.[870] In Lebanon, the effect of the judicial internationalization of the Hariri investigation was to shift the political focus of competition between the March 8 and March 14 blocs into the legal arena. Lebanese politics became polarized over the conduct of the UNIIIC investigation, the establishment of the STL as a UN treaty-based tribunal, and the legitimacy of the STL prosecutions. The international investigation and prosecutions encountered opposition ranging from non-cooperation, public campaigns questioning their impartiality and legitimacy, and a terror campaign assassinating prominent Lebanese figures opposed to the Syrian control of Lebanese affairs. The March 8 bloc challenged the dominant legal framing of the Hariri assassination, promoted an alternative conspiratorial account, and sought to delegitimize the STL trials and verdict. They often used highly legalized speech to discredit the STL.[871] The March 14 bloc sought to maintain government commitment to the investigation and prosecution and instrumentalize the STL as a political weapon against their opponents. The acceptance of international legal norms by both sides established the legal terrain of the contest but not necessarily their internalization.[872] The ultimate political significance of the STL mandate rested with the verdicts it reached and their lasting effects on the rule of law and impunity in Lebanon. Would its judgments be seen as justice? Would the trials strengthen the rule of law and challenge the culture of elite impunity? Would justice for the Hariri assassination generate a demand for criminal

---

869 UNSC Resolution 1377 of November 12, 2001, Declaration on the Global effort to Combat Terrorism, https://documents-dds-ny.un.org/doc/UNDOC/GEN/N01/633/01/PDF/N0163301.pdf?OpenElement. Subsequent counter-terrorism resolutions reinforced international criminalization: UNGA Res/60/288, adopted on September 8, 2006, Global Counter-Terrorism Strategy; UNGA Res/68/119, adopted on December 16, 2013, Measures to eliminate international terrorism.

870 US State Department list of State Sponsors of Terrorism, https://www.state.gov/state-sponsors-of-terrorism/.

871 Burgis-Kasthala and Saouli 2022, o.c., p. 84.

872 K. Kees Van and B. Verbeek, 'The Politics of International Norms: Subsidiarity and the Imperfect Competence Regime of the European Union' (2007) 13 *European Journal of International Relations* 217, at 234.

accountability for the many uninvestigated past political assassinations, war crimes and crimes against humanity?

After the Fitzgerald fact-finding mission reported to the UNSC that the Lebanese investigation into Hariri's assassination lacked the capacity or commitment to reach a satisfactory conclusion. UNSC Resolution 1595 on April 7, 2005 established the UNIIIC under Chapter VII to support the Lebanese investigation of the Hariri assassination and 'to help identify its perpetrators, sponsors, organizers and accomplices'.[873] The UNIIIC was different from previous UN commissions in that it dealt with terrorism, had the mandate of a domestic law enforcement authority and could designate individuals as suspects and impose sanctions on their investigation.[874] The UNIIIC also uniquely transitioned into a hybrid tribunal. It transferred its operations to the Office of the Prosecutor of the Special Tribunal for Lebanon on March 1, 2009. The UNIIIC operated under the jurisdiction of Lebanese law and was able to determine its own procedures, collect documentary and physical evidence, and interview any civilian or state official in Lebanon.[875] It was led by the senior German Prosecutor Detlev Mehlis who issued his first report in October 2005. UNSCR 1595 required member states to meet their international obligations to cooperate with the UNIIIC investigation, but UNSC was forced to adopt Resolution 1636, in October 2005, to provide the UNIIIC with the ability to conduct investigations with coercive powers in Syria. The UNIIIC operated under domestic jurisdiction but because the path to prosecution was unclear, it conducted the investigation, collected evidence and testimonies, and interpreted the law according to international standards. From the perspective of the UNIIIC, the investigation sought to contribute to the larger transitional justice aims of inculcating in Lebanese institutions higher standards of accountability to strengthen democratic institutions and the rule of law.

Initially, Hariri's assassination produced a political environment favourable for the UNIIIC international criminal investigation. Firstly, the Syrian army was forced to withdraw from Lebanon (April 26, 2005) after 29 years of occupation in the face of mass public protest and international condemnation over its alleged role in the assassination; and secondly, the anti-Syrian and pro-UNIIIC/STL March 14 bloc won the 2005 and 2009 parliamentary elections. However, parliamentary support for the international justice project did not last.[876] The March 8 bloc quickly characterized the UNIIIC as an instrument

---

873 UNSC Resolution 1595 (2005) [on establishment of an international independent commission to assist in investigation of the terrorist bombing in Lebanon], https://digitallibrary.un.org/record/545254?ln=en.

874 A. Alamuddin and A. Bonini, 'The UN Investigation of the Hariri Assassination' in A. Alamuddin et al. (eds.), *The Special Tribunal for Lebanon*, Oxford University Press, Oxford 2014, p. 50, at p. 56.

875 Ibid., p. 52.

876 Harris 2013, o.c., p. 20.

of US intervention in support of the anti-Syrian political forces in Lebanon. Between 2005–2014, the key issue over which Lebanese governments either fell or became paralyzed was over the international investigation and prosecution of those responsible for Hariri's assassination. Its opponents set out to delegitimize the UNIIIC for its narrow mandate which they argued was politically selective – why this and not other assassinations? The narrowness of its mandate was particularly apparent after the Israel-Lebanon war in July 2006 during which hundreds of Lebanese were killed.

5.3.2. THE CREATION OF THE SPECIAL TRIBUNAL FOR LEBANON

As the security situation worsened with the growing number of political assassinations of leading anti-Syrian politicians, intellectuals and journalists, PM Fuad Siniora asked the UN Secretary General to broaden the UNIIICs mandate to investigate related these political crimes and to expand the UNIIIC by establishing an ad hoc international tribunal.[877] In response, the UNSC adopted Resolution 1644 (December 15, 2005) to expand the UNIIIC mandate and create a hybrid tribunal.[878] But when PM Siniora brought the resolution to the Cabinet for ratification the March 8 bloc members resigned their Cabinet posts to prevent a vote.[879] To overcome the political stalemate PM Siniora requested that the UNSC use its authority under Chapter VII to unilaterally establish the STL which it did with Resolution 1757 (May 30, 2007) 18 months later.[880]

---

877 Assassinations and attempted assassinations of anti-Syrian public figures from late 2004 leading up to PM Rafiq Hariri's murder (February 14, 2005): Druze MP Marwan Hamadeh (October 1, 2004); (attempted) Ali Ramez Tohme, leading journalist (September 15, 2005); Samir Kassir leading journalist (June 2, 2005); George Hawi, former leader of Communist Party (June 21, 2005); (attempted) Defence Minister Elias Murr (July 12, 2005); (attempted) May Chidiac, leading journalist (September 25, 2005); Gebran Tueni, journalist and lawyer (December 12, 2005); Pierre Amine Gemayel, son of Kataeb leader Amin Gemayel (December 21, 2006); MP Walid Eido (June 13, 2007); MP Antoine Ghanem (September 19, 2007); Brigadier General François al-Hajj (December 12, 2007); Captain Wissam Eid, investigator working on Hariri assassination (January 25, 2008); Druze politician Saleh Aridi (September 10, 2008); Druze politician Saleh Aridi (September 10, 2008); Kamal Naji, deputy representative of the PLO (March 23, 2009); Brigadier General Wissam al Hassan, Head of Internal Security Forces and patron of March 14 Alliance (October 19, 2012); Mohamad Chatah, former Finance Minister and advisor to Sa'ad Hariri (December 27, 2013).

878 The UN Secretary-General was very aware that the focus on a single murder would be controversial. See Report of the Secretary-General on the Establishment of a Special Tribunal for Lebanon Doc S/2006/893, para. 18.

879 B. Berti, 'Balancing Justice, Stability and Legitimacy: Lebanon and the UN Special Tribunal – Understanding the Domestic Impact of International Criminal Justice' (2014a) 19 *Mediterranean Politics* 117, at 123; See also UNSC Resolution 1664 (March 29, 2006) S/RES/1664.

880 Annex "Letter dated 15 May 2007 from the President of Lebanon addressed to the Secretary-General" [from President Lahoud] UN Doc S/2007/286.

The March 8 bloc immediately denounced UNSCR 1757 as an external imposition on Lebanese sovereignty and boycotted the government paralyzing it for 18 months.[881] During this political stalemate, the March 14 bloc government came under political siege through the escalating assassination of its Deputies and barely survived in government.[882] The deadlock was resolved only after the Lebanese National Dialogue Conference supported the formation of a national unity government formalized in the Doha Agreement on May 21, 2008.[883] The political effect of this recalibration of sectarian power was to give the March 8 bloc a permanent veto in Cabinet.[884] The Doha agreement reflected Hizbullah's enhanced political influence and prestige after its prominent military role in the 'resistance' against the IDF in the 2006 Israel-Lebanon war. It was widely expected that the March 8 bloc would win the 2009 parliamentary elections, because of the support they won for their role in the war against Israel, and then withdraw their cooperation with the STL. But surprisingly, the March 14 bloc won and Sa'ad Hariri, the son of assassinated PM Rafiq Hariri, became Prime Minister. President Bashir al-Assad and the March 8 bloc immediately demonstrated their control over Lebanese affairs by pressuring PM Sa'ad Hariri to publicly denounce the STL as a tool of US and Israel imperialism and withdraw his cooperation with it. While his close Druze ally, Walid Jumblatt, changed sides and signed the declaration denouncing the STL, PM Sa'ad Hariri refused.[885] In response, Hizbullah withdrew support from the Hariri government causing its collapse and forcing Sa'ad Hariri to flee into exile in fear of his life for three years from January 2011 to August 2014.[886] It took six months for the March 8 bloc to negotiate the formation of a new government under PM Najib Miqati.

Article 1 of the STL Statute stipulates that the Tribunal has jurisdiction over persons responsible for attacks in Lebanon between October 1, 2004 and December 12, 2005 that are connected to the attack on February 14 of the former PM Rafiq Hariri.[887] Despite its narrow jurisdiction, international

---

881 W. Harris, 'Investigating Lebanon's Political Murders: International Idealism in the Realist Middle East?' (2013) 67 *Middle East Journal* 9, at 12.

882 The March 14 Alliance government was reduced from 72/128 deputies to 68/127 deputies by assassinations (4) and defection (1). P. Brookes, 'The Siege of Lebanon', *The New York Post*, June 18, 2007, http://nypost.com/2007/06/18/the-siege-of-lebanon/.

883 Doha Agreement 'On the Results of the Lebanese National Dialogue Conference', May 21, 2008. https://peacemaker.un.org/sites/peacemaker.un.org/files/Lebanon_DohaAgreement2008_Engl.pdf.

884 Letter dated May 22, 2008, from the Permanent Observer of the League of Arab States to the United Nations addressed to the President of the Security Council, S/2008/392, 10.

885 A. Shadid, 'Ousted Lebanese Leader Swallows Rivals' Bitter Pill', *New York Times*, January 25, 2011, www.nytimes.com/2011/01/26/world/middleeast/26lebanon.html.

886 B. Berti and D. Lee, 'Lebanon and the United Nations Special Tribunal: Between (Un)Accountability and (In)stability' (2014) 17 *Strategic Assessment* 95, at 99.

887 Statute of the Special Tribunal for Lebanon, Documents, Special Tribunal for Lebanon, https://www.legal-tools.org/doc/da0bbb/.

support for the STL reflected the optimism that international criminal justice would help bring about the domestic transformation of justice and the rule of law in Lebanon. Internationally, the Tribunal was justified on the grounds that 'a court with international participation, could serve a symbolic and exemplary function to promote the rule of law domestically'.[888] It brought international criminal justice to a post-conflict state with the aim of preventing future crimes and achieving social integration and rehabilitation.[889] The Fifth Annual Report of the STL explicitly states that prosecutions support 'the strenuous efforts of the Government and people of Lebanon to reinforce the rule of law through due process'.[890] In the words of one defence lawyer at the Tribunal: "The STL, your Honours, as we see it, is the lever of justice. By ending impunity and restoring basic human rights to people of Lebanon, by applying principles of international justice, this tribunal can change history". The defence lawyer continued: "Your Honours will be issuing the ruling. You will be pushing the button that will help stop the mountain of terror, not just in Lebanon but in the entire world. This tribunal is a world tribunal".[891] Antonio Cassese, judge and President of the STL (2009–2011), had a similarly expansive view of the goals of international tribunals which he argued were 'not only [about] putting a stop to impunity and … alleviating the suffering of the victims, but also … bringing about reconciliation and the establishment of peace and the rule of law'.[892] The STL was established as a treaty-based Lebanese tribunal with national and international judges administering the Lebanese Criminal Code. Hybrid tribunals, as alternative judicial mechanisms to apply international standards of justice, are supposed to benefit from greater domestic legitimacy when states assume a share of responsibility for prosecutions and they are conducted in the communities in which the crimes occurred.[893] Under the STL Rules of Procedure and Evidence, the Tribunal was required to conduct outreach activities to enhance its public acceptance and credibility.[894] However, from its inception the STL suffered

---

888 C.L. Sriram, 'The Special Tribunal for Lebanon, Promoting Justice or Prolonging Conflict?' (2012) 24 *Reconciliation, Reform and Resilience: Positive Peace for Lebanon, Reconciliation Resources*, 49, https://www.c-r.org/accord-article/special-tribunal-lebanon.

889 Burgis-Kasthala 2013, o.c., pp. 514–5.

890 Special Tribunal for Lebanon, Fifth Annual Report, 2013–2014, 7, https://www.legal-tools.org/doc/7cdb46/.

891 STL proceedings, Live Coverage – Day 2, January 17, 2014, https://now.mmedia.me/lb/en/NewsReports/530848-live-coverage-stl-proceedings.

892 A. Cassese, 'The Legitimacy of International Criminal Tribunals and the Current Prospects of International Criminal Justice', (2012) 25 *Leiden Journal of International Law*, 491, at 497.

893 E. Nielsen, 'Hybrid International Criminal Tribunals: Political Interference and Judicial Independence' (2010) 15 *UCLA Journal of International Law and Foreign Affairs* 289, at 292.

894 International tribunals expanded public outreach activities after the widespread public dissatisfaction with the outcomes of the ICTY and ICTR prosecution which were interpreted as, in part, the result of their neglect of public education about the judicial process. M. Klarin, 'The Impact of the ICTY Trials on Public Opinion in the Former Yugoslavia' (2009) 7 *Journal of International Criminal Justice* 89, at 90.

from a 'domestic legitimacy deficit' because its opponents denounced it as internationally imposed.[895]

On January 16, 2014, the STL trials against five indictees – Mustafa Amine Badreddine, Salim Jamil Ayyash, Hassan Habib Merhi, Hussein Hassan Oneissi and Assad Hassan Sabra (all allegedly members of Hizbullah) – charged with responsibility for Hariri's assassination, opened in The Hague.[896] The charges against the defendant, Badreddine, were subsequently withdrawn after his reported assassination in Syria in May 2016.[897] Because Hizbullah refused to cooperate with the STL by handing over the indictees, the trials were conducted *in absentia*. The menace of the ongoing campaign of political assassinations in Lebanon hung over the opening. Only a few days before the trial began, Sa'ad Hariri's close political advisor and leading political figure, Mohamed Chatan, was assassinated in Lebanon. In an interview given at the opening trial in The Hague Sa'ad Hariri defiantly stated:

> The STL trial should be seen as an instrument in the war on terror. … We believe impunity for political murder should and will stop. But yes, the assassins still believe they can keep killing, as they did with Mohamed Chatan. They still believe they can do what they want. But we still believe in justice, and March 14 still believes that good will always prevail over evil.[898]

Sa'ad Hariri's presence at the Tribunal symbolized the painful contradiction that in exile he could attend the trial's opening because it was in The Hague. Mohamed Chatan's assassination and the threats against Sa'ad Hariri's own life demonstrated that the opponents of the STL were still willing to use political assassination in the struggle for political power in Lebanon and expose the powerlessness of the Tribunal to prevent further assassinations.

The aim of the STL prosecutions was to generate a national consensus about the Hariri assassination by reaching a verdict based on legal evidence about who was responsible. By holding those responsible for the crime accountable the STL sought to achieve justice for the victims, survivors, and society as a whole. However, the performative promise of the STL prosecutions to reach verdicts, bring closure, and strengthen justice were all contested by their opponents.

---

895 S. Hanafi, et al., 'Trial of the Status Quo: the politics of mediated justice in the Special Tribunal for Lebanon' (2016) 24 *Arab Studies Journal* 68, at 71.

896 M. Kersten, 'Trials and Tribulations at the Special Tribunal for Lebanon', *Justice in Conflict*, January 28, 2014, https://justiceinconflict.org/2014/01/28/trials-and-tribulations-at-the-special-tribunal-for-lebanon/.

897 M. A. Badreddine, Order Terminating Proceedings Against Mustafa Amine Badreddine Without Prejudice and Ordering the Filing of an Amended Consolidated Indictment, Trial Chamber, STL-11-01, July 7, 2016, http://www.legal-tools.org/doc/0b7008/.

898 L. Smith, 'Hariri's Moderate Awakening', *The Weekly Standard*, January 17, 2014.

The STL's demonstrative framing of the crimes as an international crime –terrorism– to be judged according to international norms under international jurisdiction were challenged by the opposition's demand to fully repatriate the trials to the Lebanese courts. The STL narrative of international justice and accountability met with the counternarrative of imperialist intervention in the interests of their geo-political rivals.

5.3.3. POLITICAL ASSASSINATION AS AN ACT OF INTERNATIONAL TERRORISM

In the post-9/11 era of the War Against Terrorism, the assassination of Rafiq Hariri was quickly framed as an act of international terrorism. After the preliminary investigation of the Hariri assassination by a Lebanese judge, the Lebanese government described the crime as 'a terrorist act targeting the Republic' and transferred jurisdiction to the Justice Council.[899] On February 15, 2005, the President of the Security Council requested the Secretary General 'to follow closely the situation in Lebanon and to report urgently on the circumstances of this terrorist act'.[900] The Report of the Fact-Finding Mission (Fitzgerald Report) recommended the creation of the UNIIIC (UNSC Resolution 1595, April 7, 2005) to investigate all aspects of the 'terrorist act' which included the role of Syria.[901] UNSC Resolution 1757 establishing the STL identified terrorism as a distinct crime and a 'threat to international peace and security'. The broad legal definition of terrorism applied by the STL was based on Lebanese law which refers to terrorism as the use of means that are 'liable to create a public danger' (Article 314 of the Lebanese Criminal Code).[902] The Appeals Chamber of the STL, in an advisory opinion on Article 314, controversially sought to clarify the definition of transnational terrorism according to the means used to 'create public danger' and thereby open up the opportunity for terrorism to be included in the list of crimes able to be prosecuted under international law.[903] In summary, the Hariri assassination was legally constructed as a 'terrorist act' perpetrated by, or with the support of, an external state that threatened the stability and peace of the Lebanese state. The crime was to be adjudicated by a hybrid international tribunal applying Lebanese domestic law.

The STL focus on the prosecution of a single terrorist act has been unique in international tribunals and was seen as an both an innovative and

899 Report of the International Independent Investigation Commission established pursuant to UNSCR 1595 (2005), S/2005/662, October 19, 2005, 3. It is also referred to as the Dertlev Mehlis Report.
900 STL Timeline of Events, Special Tribunal for Lebanon.
901 Fitzgerald Report, o.c.
902 STL Close-Up.
903 Jurdi 2014, o.c., p. 82.

problematic attempt to test the concept of a 'terrorist act' as an international law concept.[904] Firstly, international terrorism has yet to be defined in international law as a crime. The Ad Hoc Committee on Terrorism to negotiate the Draft Comprehensive Convention on International Terrorism (CCIT) was established by UNGA Resolution 51/210 of December 17, 1996 but has not yet been able to reach a consensus. In addition, terrorism is not included as a core offence in the ICC Statute. Secondly, the STL mandate was not based on universal jurisdiction, did not have jurisdiction over crimes against humanity, and was only able to implement Lebanese national law. Nevertheless, several Articles of the STL Statute served to internationalize its jurisdiction. Article 2 includes reference to 'acts of terrorism, crimes and offences against life and personal integrity' and 'illicit associations and failure to report crimes and offences' and Article 3 adds a form of liability normally known only in international criminal law 'superior responsibility and the doctrine of joint criminal enterprise' opening up the possibility of charging 'high-ranking defendants' for plans such as 'maintaining Syrian influence in Lebanon'.[905] The provision in Article 22 in the STL Statute to be able to hold trials *in absentia* anticipated the resistance the Tribunal was likely to face getting the cooperation to detain indictees. Article 22 addresses the political reality of the limited territorial sovereignty of the Lebanese government undermined by the continued influence of Syria in Lebanese affairs and an electorate polarized between anti-Syrian and pro-Syrian camps. Even though the Lebanese courts, the UNSC, and the STL legally framed Hariri's assassination as a 'terrorist act' it was in fact not an exceptional crime but an instance of the all too familiar pattern dating from the founding of the Republic in 1943 resorting to political assassination as a way of eliminating rivals or critics.[906] The STL, by focusing on a single crime and others related to it that had occurred between October 1, 2004 and December 12, 2005,[907] decontextualized the assassination and prevented it from potentially being viewed as a crime against humanity – i.e. part of a pattern of systematic attacks against the civilian population in Lebanon directed by a foreign state.[908] Moreover, Article 1 of the STL Statute framing the assassination as a terrorist act had the effect of politicizing the STL because it focused on the crimes of the Syrian state and its allies, not on any pro-Western

---

904 C. Damgaard, *Individual Criminal Responsibility for Core International Crimes: Selected Pertinent Issues*, Springer Berlin, Heidelberg 2008, p. 400.

905 B. Elberling, 'The Next Step in History-Writing through Criminal Law: Exactly How Tailor-Made Is the Special Tribunal for Lebanon?' (2008) 21 *Leiden Journal of International Law* 529, at 534.

906 Knudsen 2010, o.c., p. 1.

907 These dates refer to specific attacks, first, October 1, 2004 the attempted assassination of Druze MP Marwan Hamadeh and second, December 12, 2005 the assassination of journalist and lawmaker Gebran Yueni. See Elberling 2008, o.c., p. 532.

908 B. Saul, *Defining Terrorism in International Law*, Oxford University Press, Oxford 2006, p. 221.

groups.[909] The STL became the laboratory for testing the viability of terrorism as a legal concept in international criminal law in the context of the geo-political contest to reduce Syrian influence over Lebanese affairs.

To ensure the indictments were confirmed on 'sound and well-founded grounds' the pre-trial judge requested an advisory opinion from the Appeals Chamber about the jurisdiction of the Tribunal, its legality, and the status of terrorism in international criminal law.[910] The Appeals Chamber ruled that the STL mandate required it to apply Lebanese law as interpreted and applied by Lebanese courts unless it was unreasonable, or result in injustice or is not consistent with international principles and rules binding Lebanon.[911] The Appeals Chamber adopted an 'internationalist approach' granting international law a more autonomous role in interpreting and applying the definition of terrorism in Lebanese law.[912] The Appeals Chamber ruling on the status of terrorism as a crime in customary international law was regarded as controversial.[913] While acknowledging there was no international consensus on the definition of terrorism, it argued one had emerged with customary international law status. Based on treaties, UN resolutions and legislative and judicial practices, three key elements can be identified: 1) the perpetration – or intent to perpetrate – of a serious criminal act including murder, kidnapping, hostage-taking, arson; 2) the intent to spread fear in a population or directly or indirectly coerce a national or international authority to take some action or refrain from taking action; 3) the act has a transnational dimension.[914] The ruling found there is an international customary rule forbidding the crime of terrorism and binding the states to prosecute on its territory those responsible.[915] Several leading legal scholars have criticized the STL Appeals Chamber ruling constructing terrorism as a crime in customary international law as overreach.[916]

909 Elberling 2008, o.c., p. 533.

910 L. Mareček, 'Terrorism as a Crime Under International Customary Law Introduced by Special Tribunal for Lebanon' (2017) 7 *The Lawyer Quarterly: International Journal for Legal Research* 73, at 74.

911 UN Special Tribunal for Lebanon (Appeals Chamber), Interlocutory Decision on the Appliable Law: Terrorism, Conspiracy, Homicide, Perpetration, Cumulative Charging, STL-11-01, February 16, 2011.

912 E. Van Sliedregt and L. Van Den Herik, 'Introduction: The STL Interlocutory Decision on the Definition of Terrorism – Judicial Ingenuity or Radicalism?' (2011) 24 *Leiden Journal of International Law* 651, at 652.

913 A. Blick, 'The Special Tribunal for Lebanon: How did it survive for so long?', *EJIL: Talk!*, September 20, 2021, https://www.ejiltalk.org/the-special-tribunal-for-lebanon-how-did-it-survive-for-so-long/.

914 Case STL -11-01/1, February 16, 2011, para. 85.

915 Mareček 2017, o.c., p. 73.

916 B. Saul, 'Legislating from a Radical Hague: The United Nations Special Tribunal for Lebanon Invents an International Crime of Transnational Terrorism' (2011) 24 *Leiden Journal of International Law*, 677; K. Ambos, 'Judicial Creativity at the Special Tribunal for Lebanon: Is There a Crime of Terrorism under International Law?' (2011) 24 *Leiden Journal of International Law*, 655.

Despite the pre-trial judge's precaution in seeking an advisory opinion from the Appeals Chamber to ensure the indictments were secure, the defence counsel for Ayyash et al. immediately challenged the jurisdiction and legality of the Tribunal at the beginning of the trial. The Trial Chamber dismissed the defence motions, as did the Appeals Chamber, that found because the Tribunal had not been established by an international agreement or treaty but UNSC Resolution 1757 under Chapter VII powers, the Lebanese Constitution had not been violated.[917]

5.3.4. THE EROSION OF THE LEGITIMACY OF THE STL

The pivotal legal significance of a trial is its performative character determining the guilt or innocence of the accused. The verdict brings closure to the trial as a legal ritual conducted within the procedures and rules of criminal justice. A guilty verdict produces a legal narrative and institutionalizes memory about responsibility for the crime, punishes those convicted and its victims. Because of the centrality of the trial to the success of international criminal justice, it is not surprising the Lebanese opponents of the UNIIIC and STL sought to obstruct the judicial process and limit the impact of any trial verdict. The very thing that conferred legitimacy on the UNIIIC and STL, their international character, was the source of their illegitimacy in the eyes of their Lebanese opponents. From the perspective of global liberal law, Antonio Cassese, Judge and President of the STL, observed that the legitimacy of international criminal justice, rests 'on *universal values legitimacy*, for it pursues goals (justice, peace and reconciliation) shared by the whole world community'.[918] At each stage in the development of the investigations and prosecutions, the March 8 bloc sought to obstruct and delegitimize the international criminal justice process. It refused to cooperate with the UNIIIC accusing it of being partisan because of its focus on Syria. It refused to endorse the treaty-based agreement between UNSC and Lebanese government to establish the STL which forced the UNSC to establish the STL under Chapter VII. It refused to hand-over the indicted Hizbullah members and forced the trials to be conducted *in absentia*. In addition, the March 8 bloc opposition to the UNIIIC occurred against the backdrop of an ongoing terror campaign of assassination and bombings by unknown hands targeting high profile anti-Syrian Lebanese and Lebanese UNIIIC investigators.[919] The terror campaign of assassinations had a direct impact on the work of the UNIIIC

917 B. Tabbarah, 'The Legal Nature of the Special Tribunal for Lebanon' in A. Alamuddin, et al. (eds.), *The Special Tribunal for Lebanon: Law and Practice*, Oxford University Press, Oxford 2014, p. 32, at p. 46.

918 Cassese 2012, o.c., p. 497.

919 Statute of the Special Tribunal for Lebanon, Documents, Special Tribunal for Lebanon, https://www.legal-tools.org/doc/da0bbb/.

when, in January 2008, Captain Wissam Eid, a lead investigator into the electronic records evidence, was killed by car bomb in Beirut. Because of their extreme vulnerability to attack the UNIIIC Lebanese investigators handed the investigation over to the international team in The Hague.[920]

Following Hariri's assassination, the population was polarized over the questions about who was responsible and what should be done.[921] After the UNIIIC was established it became the focus of the March 8 bloc's opposition to the international criminal investigation. Initially, the UNIIIC investigation, headed by the prosecutor Mehlis, actively used the media to raise the public profile of their investigation in Lebanon and internationally to enhance its legitimacy.[922] But the complex Lebanese media landscape dominated by privatized outlets aligned with antagonistic political elites, their conflicting agendas, and sectarian constituencies meant the media activism of Prosecutor Mehlis was quickly portrayed as politicizing the Tribunal.[923] Olga Kavran, the former head of the STL Outreach and Legacy Section (2010–2020), argues that the STL's powerful opponents successfully shaped public opinion toward the STL through a disinformation campaign alleging the unconstitutional establishment of the STL, the Tribunal's narrow mandate focused on Syria, the UNIIIC's biased reliance on false witnesses, the STL's deliberate leaks of confidential information to the media, and the role of the STL in an American-Israeli plot.[924] Of these, the 'false witnesses' controversy had the greatest impact on the credibility of the STL and the promise of international criminal justice. In his first Report, Prosecutor Mehlis had relied heavily on the testimonies of two witnesses to draw the conclusion that 'there is now evidence pointing at both Lebanese and Syrian involvement in the terrorist act'.[925] Their testimony was an important factor in the arrest and detention of four high-ranking members of the military

---

920 C. Harwood, 'The UN International Independent Investigation Commission in Lebanon' in J. Meierhenrich (ed.), *The Law and Practice of International Commissions of Inquiry*, Oxford University Press, Oxford 2017, p. 20.

921 S. Hanafi, et al., 'Trial of the Status Quo: the politics of mediated justice in the Special Tribunal for Lebanon' (2016) 24 *Arab Studies Journal* 68, at 71.

922 C. Mallat, 'The Special Tribunal for Lebanon, the staring abyss and what must be done about it in the STL, the UN and Lebanon must all contribute to avert an explosive situation in the country', *Daily Star*, October 7, 2010, http://cdmbuntu.lib.utah.edu/cdm/ref/collection/utlawrev/id/598.

923 Hanafi, et al., 2016, o.c., p. 68.

924 O. Kavran, 'The Special Tribunal for Lebanon and its Outreach Programme' (2022) 20 *Journal of International Criminal Justice* 81, at 86–7.

925 Report of the International Independent Investigation Commission established pursuant to UNSCR 1595 (2005), S/2005/662, October 19, 2005, 3. Muhammad Zuhair Saddik and Hussam Taher Hussam allegedly provided 'false witness' to the UNIIIC in 2005 about the involvement of high-level Syrian and Lebanese officials. See 'Trial by Fire: The Politics of the Special Tribunal for Lebanon', Middle East Report No. 100, International Crisis Group, December 2, 2010, 18.

by the UNIIIC which boosted its image as an effective judicial body.[926] The detention of four senior Lebanese security officials (August 2005) for almost four years without charge fuelled the resentment over the 'false witness' affair throughout the life of the STL.[927] It became the main issue used by the March 8 bloc to turn public opinion against the STL in order to undermine its legitimacy. Declining support for the STL between 2005–2011 in opinion polls suggest they were successful.[928] The March 8 bloc used 'inoculation as a tool of political communication' by priming a target population to be unreceptive to new charges and reject the credibility of first the UNIIIC and subsequently the STL.[929] The March 8 bloc counter-narrative represented the STL as a conspiracy concealing the responsibility of Israel, the real enemy of Lebanon, for the clandestine assassination.[930] Blaming Israel, not Syria, tapped into a longstanding historical view of Israel as Lebanon's real enemy.[931] Firstly, the Israel Boycott Law (June 23, 1955), which prohibited Lebanese contact with Israeli individuals or institutions, had institutionalized Israel as the historical enemy;[932] and secondly, Lebanese memory of the many Israeli military incursions and wars against Lebanon (1978, 1982, 2006) and the IDF occupation of South Lebanon between 1982 and 2000 had been deeply embedded in the national consciousness. These competing narratives about criminal responsibility were underpinned by conflicting geo-political perspectives about the necessary conditions for future peace in Lebanon; one side held that peace would flow from the recovery of sovereignty and democracy guaranteed by a US-Saudi axis, the other side argued that peace necessitated the recovery of sovereignty guaranteed by the Syrian and Iranian nexus against the imperialist interests of the US and Israel.

In 2009, after newspaper reports had implicated Hizbullah party members in the assassination of Hariri, Hizbullah intensified its attacks against the legal professionalism and reputation of the STL. Their focus was the issue of the detention of the four Lebanese generals in security and intelligence on false testimony by Lebanese authorities at the request of the UNIIIC.[933] Hizbullah

---

926 Berti 2014, o.c., p. 128.

927 Generals arrested on August 30, 2005: General Ali al-Hajj (Internal Security Forces); Gen Raymond Zara (Military Intelligence); Brigadier General Jamil al-Sayyed (Sûreté Générale); and Mustafa Hamdan (Presidential Guard). See "The Special Tribunal for Lebanon. Selective Justice?", *Amnesty International*, 2009.

928 Wählisch 2017, o.c., p. 316.

929 Ibid., p. 71.

930 Berti and Lee 2014, o.c., p. 98.

931 Wählisch 2017, o.c., p. 300.

932 G. Sebaali, 'Lebanon and Israel: Agreements, Resolutions, and Local Laws', *Lebanon Law Review*, May 28, 2020.

933 Generals arrested on August 30, 2005: General Ali al-Hajj (Internal Security Forces); Gen Raymond Zara (Military Intelligence); Brigadier General Jamil al-Sayyed (Sûreté Générale); and Mustafa Hamdan (Presidential Guard). See "The Special Tribunal for Lebanon. Selective Justice?", *Amnesty International*, February 25, 2009, London, https://www.amnesty.org/download/Documents/48000/mde180012009en.pdf.

called for an ad hoc national commission to investigate who had provided fabricated evidence to the UNIIIC. The continued detention of the four the high-ranking security officials, the disagreement between the UNIIIC and Lebanese authorities over who had legal responsibility for their detention, and the lack of accountability mechanisms for relief had left the detainees in a legal black hole. Soon after the UNIIIC handed jurisdiction over to the STL in 2009, the decision by Pre-Trial Judge, Daniel Fransen, to direct the Lebanese authorities to release the four pro-Syrian generals after four years of detention without charge on the grounds that witness statements were unreliable, had an enormous negative impact on public confidence in the STL and the prospects for international criminal justice.[934] In a counter legal action in 2010, a Syrian judge issued arrest warrants for 33 Syrian and Lebanese citizens on the charge of giving false testimony against Syria to the UNIIIC.[935] General Jamil al Sayed, one of the four pro-Syrian generals detained by the UNIIIC in pre-trial detention, made an application to the STL for the disqualification and withdrawal of Judge Afif Chamseddine on the grounds that he was biased.[936]

In response to March 8 bloc attacks, the STL adopted an unofficial policy of secrecy and opaqueness to avoid further politicization of its activities withdrawing behind bland bureaucratic communication routinizing reporting and press releases that provided limited information.[937] But the failure of Sa'ad Hariri and the March 14 to effectively respond to the March 8 anti-STL media campaign allowed the counter-narrative of the 'false witnesses' and the US-Israeli conspiracy theory to dominate public opinion.[938] Eventually the STL reversed its low-profile media policy and developed outreach activities, especially engagement with the legal profession and university law students, to try to counter its detractors.[939] Its focus was not the Tribunal's jurisdiction of the 'factual truth' but international criminal justice and the 'meta-normative truths' – universals – concerned with human suffering and the immorality of certain behaviour.[940] But, in reality, no amount of STL outreach through legal education was able to overcome the situation where the STL was used by the anti-Syrian

---

934 Berti 2014, o.c., p. 128.

935 Ibid., p. 127.

936 Application for the disqualification and withdrawal of Judge Afif Chamseddine, Case No. OTP/AC/2010/01, Filed Before: The President, Mr Antonio Cassese by General Jamil El Sayed, October 20, 2010, Special Tribunal for Lebanon.

937 A. Knudsen and S. Hanafi, 'Special Tribunal for Lebanon (STL): Impartial or Imposed International Justice?' (2013) 31 *Nordic Journal of Human Rights* 176, at 198.

938 'Who's Afraid of a False Witness?', posted by Qifa Nabki, https://qifanabki.com/2010/10/06/lebanon-false-witness/comment-page-1/.

939 B. Berti, 'Balancing Justice, Stability and Legitimacy: Lebanon and the UN Special Tribunal – Understanding the Domestic Impact of International Criminal Justice' (2014a) 19 *Mediterranean Politics* 117, at 131. See Special Tribunal for Lebanon, Third Annual Report (2011–2012), p. 26. https://www.legal-tools.org/doc/272706/pdf/.

940 Kavran 2022, o.c., pp. 89–90.

forces to attack the Hizbullah-led coalition, and where Hizbullah had made the rejection of the Tribunal the core element of its domestic policy.[941] The STL Registrar Herman von Hebel (2010–2013) tried to counter the claim that the STL was conducting political trials by explaining that 'an indictment is really only the beginning of the process and not the final determination of responsibility but it has been turned into the issue which has determined public opinion about the credibility and legitimacy of the Tribunal'.[942] In 2011, shortly before the STL indictments implicating them, Hizbullah intensified the campaign against the STL describing it as a 'last ditch effort, the last weapon, the last shot to be fired at 'The Resistance' (*sic* the Syrian-Iranian-Hizbullah axis allied against Israel), its symbols and its movement in Lebanon'.[943] For Hizbullah, the jury was the court of public opinion which included Lebanon's Shiite community, Hizbullah's Christian allies – Aoun's constituency and the wider Arab public. Hizbullah denounced the STL proceedings as an attack on Lebanese sovereignty. They proposed the repatriation of justice by establishing alternate commissions and prosecutions in the Lebanese courts with which they promised to fully cooperate.[944] Hizbullah used the 'false witness' affair to try to force the Cabinet to refer the issue to the Lebanese Judicial Council and thereby cast doubt on the STL's impartiality.[945] The ability of Hizbullah to saturate media coverage of the 'false witness' issue contrasted with March 14 bloc's reliance on the STL to challenge the counter-narrative. However, with the indictments pending the STL kept its public commentary to a minimum.[946] In reality, Hizbullah's strategy to repatriate of justice was less about legal sovereignty than the subordination of the judicial process to the Lebanese executive where Hizbullah could exert political influence.[947] Hizbullah had already managed to recalibrate the sectarian balance of power under the Doha Agreement (2008) which effectively gave them a veto over Cabinet decision-making. The logic of pactism was invoked to undermine the impact of the anticipated indictments against Hizbullah members in 2011. As mentioned earlier, the attempt by Hizbullah to pressure PM Sa'ad Hariri to

---

941 Ibid., p. 95. Olga Kavran argues that the STL's restrictive electronic media communications policy impacted negatively on its capacity to reach the Lebanese public. The Registrar decided that outreach staff in Lebanon were not to engage with the media leaving that role to the Tribunal's only Spokesperson in The Hague.

942 C. Blum, 'No Details on the Indictment for Months: Registrar', *The Daily Star*, December 7, 2010.

943 R. Slim, 'Hezbollah's campaign against the Special Tribunal for Lebanon', *Foreign Policy*, August 13, 2010.

944 Burgis-Kasthala 2013, o.c., p. 512.

945 'Trial by Fire: The Politics of the Special Tribunal for Lebanon', *Middle East Report*, No. 100, December 2, 2020, International Crisis Group, p. 18.

946 Ibid., pp. 17–18. The STL rejects the phrase 'false witness' because no witness had testified before the court at that stage and because they had no bearing on the credibility of the indictments.

947 See Section 5.4.3 on the Beirut Port explosion and political interference in the judicial investigation.

disassociate himself with the STL revealed the extent of the reassertion of Syrian dominance over Lebanese affairs.[948] Hizbullah sought to leverage improved external relations between Syria and Saudi Arabia to bring pressure to bear on the March 14 movement to distance itself from the STL.[949]

The impact of the March 8 campaign against the STL was to delay and constrain the judicial processes. After Hizbullah refused to hand over its members indicted for trial the STL was forced to conduct trials *in absentia.* Historically, *in absentia* trials have been regarded as unacceptable in international trials because they deprive the accused of an effective defence.[950] Public confidence in the STL and international criminal justice had been undermined by the March 8 campaign over the 'false witness' affair which, in the court of public opinion, was vindicated by the STL decision to release the high-ranking military detainees without charge after four years. Through their attacks on the credibility and legitimacy of the STL the March 8 bloc effectively minimized the potential legal and political impact of the STL trials in Lebanon.[951] The STL was unable to escape its politicization by both sides. Its vulnerability to politicization was illustrated by the case of the Registrar, Judge Robert Roth, who decided to resign in 2014 after a Lebanese newspaper published that he was a 'Zionist' and questioned his impartiality. For Judge Roth, the STL has been unable to meet the challenge on which international criminal justice is based – i.e. delivering justice independently of the political expectations of founders, donors, and opponents.[952] It is important to remember the dysfunctional political backdrop against which the STL proceedings took place. Between 2013 and 2017, 44 parliamentary sessions failed to elect a new president, saw national elections postponed three times (2013, 2014 and 2017) and appointments to the head of the military, central bank, and judiciary deferred because of disputes over the positions as sectarian entitlements.[953]

5.3.5. THE STL VERDICTS

On August 18, 2020, the STL issued its verdict in the case of Ayyash et al. It found Salim Jamil Ayyas 'guilty beyond reasonable doubt' in his role in perpetrating

---

948 C. Wieland, 'Syrian-Lebanese relations. The impossible dissociation between Lebanon and Syria' in M. Felsch and M. Wählisch (eds.), *Lebanon and the Arab Uprisings: In the Eye of the Hurricane*, Routledge, Oxford 2016.

949 'Trial by fire', o.c., 22.

950 Wählisch 2017, o.c., p. 310.

951 Blick argues that the fact Hizbullah did not veto government funding of the STL after the indctments is an indication they were able to live with these now unthreatening STL proceedings. See Blick 2021, o.c.

952 R. Roth, 'Tribunal spécial sur le Liban: retour sur une expérience' (2017) XLX: 1 *Revue belge de droit international*, 290, https://archive-ouverte.unige.ch/unige:104034.

953 Nagle and Clancy 2019, o.c., p. 6.

an explosion which killed 22 people including the former PM Rafiq Hariri and sentenced him to life imprisonment. The other three defendants were acquitted of all charges. The judgment found that 'Syria and Hizbullah may have had motives to eliminate Mr Hariri, and some of his political allies', but that '[t]here is no evidence that the Hezbollah leadership had any involvement in Mr Hariri's murder and […] no direct evidence of Syrian involvement in it'.[954] On March 10, 2022 the Appeals Chamber reversed the acquittals of Merhi and Oneissi finding them guilty on charges of terrorism and murder.[955] The trial verdicts were largely seen as a disappointment. The trials delivered judgments but only limited justice. Firstly, the initial hope that international criminal justice would be able to deliver justice and challenge impunity for political assassination independent from political pressure and interference was not realized. Instead of reducing the impunity for political assassination the international judicial process itself became subject to an ongoing campaign of political assassinations against its Lebanese supporters as well as prosecutors and investigators. The outcome, the conviction of three low-level operatives, was experienced as an anticlimax after an international judicial process that took 15 years and cost almost a billion dollars.[956] The verdict did not deliver justice for the victims.[957] Firstly, the long prison sentences for those found guilty were very unlikely to ever be served because none were in custody. Secondly, command responsibility for the assassination was not identified. Thirdly, most victims received no reparations, except a few who received money from a state body and others from the Hariri family, because the Trial Chamber did not have the power to order reparations.[958] The Trial Chamber could only remind the Lebanese Government of its obligations under the UN Declaration of Basic Principles of Justice for Victims of Crime and Abuse of Power to have an adequate compensation scheme for victims. Habib Nassar, Director of Policy and Research at Impunity Watch, argues that STL failed to make full use of its strong Statute to expose the system that had enabled political assassinations and the chain of command behind them.[959]

954 *Prosecutor v. Salim Jamil Ayyash, Hassan Habib Merhi, Hussein Hassan Oneissi, Assad Hassan Sabra*, STL-11-01/TC, August 18, 2020.

955 J.H. Anderson, 'Special Tribunal for Lebanon's "Second Best Justice"', *Justiceinfo.net*, March 22, 2022, https://www.justiceinfo.net/en/88918-special-tribunal-for-lebanons-second-best-justice.html.

956 Blick 2021, o.c.

957 M. Young, 'Hariri verdict: Is the UN capable of delivering justice?', *The National News*, August 25, 2020, https://www.thenationalnews.com/opinion/comment/hariri-verdict-is-the-un-capable-of-delivering-justice-1.1068280.

958 A. Meijknecht, 'Hague Case Law: Latest Developments' (2020) 67 *Netherlands International Law Review*, 581.

959 H. Nassar, 'Special Tribunal for Lebanon: The Mountain That Gave Birth to a Mouse', *Justiceinfo.net*, January 8, 2021, https://www.justiceinfo.net/en/46418-special-tribunal-for-lebanon-the-mountain-that-gave-birth-to-a-mouse.html.

According to STL General Prosecutor, Norman Farrell, the STL had several successes as a hybrid tribunal. First, the convictions based on an extensive analysis of technical data were historically unique in international justice. Second, the electronic telecommunications data revealed the different interconnected networks behind the planning and execution of the attack. Third, the convictions were accepted by the Appeals Chamber as being in accordance with the highest standards of international justice.[960] To these can be added that the Tribunal was the first to prosecute terrorism as an international crime, the first to allow victims to participate in proceedings,[961] and the first to charge a corporate – media – entity with contempt and obstruction of justice.[962] But Prosecutor Farrell also acknowledged *in absentia* trials delivered only second best justice. The Appeals judgment contributed to 'the historical record as the factual narrative' of what happened (on February 14, 2005) but it was only a form of justice. It represents an incomplete remedy which 'requires that the convicted persons, who have evaded justice be arrested'.[963] Prosecutor Robert Roth (2012–13) argued that convictions were not enough:

> Legitimacy does not rely on convictions. The real challenges to the legitimacy of the STL are still open: does it make sense to adjudicate seventeen years after the event? Have the real responsible been prosecuted? The suspicion of Syrian involvement, on which the Trial Chamber has expressed itself briefly but with strong words, is still on the table and will probably never be addressed.[964]

Roth argues the STL as a hybrid tribunal was too vulnerable to politicization, as his own experience showed. A few examples illustrate the kind of political interference experienced by the UNIIIC investigations and STL prosecutions: the resignation of Prosecutor Detelf Mehlis who, after taking a high profile and activist approach, was told he had to continue his work from Germany not Beirut because of security concerns; the slowness of the UNIIIC under Serge Brammertz was attributed to his over cautious approach not to precipitate political unrest by pushing too hard; the neglect of critical telecommunications data and delay in its analysis which proved so vital the Lebanese investigators

960 J.H. Anderson, 'Special Tribunal for Lebanon's "Second Best Justice"', *Justiceinfo.net*, March 27, 2022, https://www.justiceinfo.net/en/88918-special-tribunal-for-lebanons-second-best-justice.html.
961 Journey to Justice: Victims Participation at the STL, STL Documentary, 2020, https://www.youtube.com/@STLebanon.
962 J. Rikhof, 'Analysis: The Special Tribunal for Lebanon: a Unique Institution', (2018) 2 *PKI Global Justice Journal*, 22.
963 J.H. Anderson, 'Special Tribunal for Lebanon's "Second Best Justice"', *Justiceinfo.net*, March 27, 2022, https://www.justiceinfo.net/en/88918-special-tribunal-for-lebanons-second-best-justice.html.
964 Ibid.

responsible were either assassinated or seriously injured;[965] the resignation of Prosecutor Roth; the withdrawal of the UNIIIC and STL from media engagement except through official reporting mechanisms and their failure to challenge the wild conspiratorial counter-narratives; the chronic lack of cooperation by Hizbullah and the Syrian government with the UNIIIC and STL; the lack of political commitment by international supporters of the STL to impose sanctions on failure to cooperate with it.

The most consequential response to the STL verdicts was the decision by the international donors not to continue funding the STL and therefore its mandate. The international funding crisis had increasingly limited STL activities which came to a head in July 2021. At that point it received a further $7 million for 2022 to complete the appeals in the Appeals Chamber. On July 1, 2022 the Tribunal entered a residual phase to preserve its records, to archive and to address remaining obligations to victims and witnesses and will close its doors at the end of 2023.[966] The impact of UN failure to secure ongoing funding was the second Ayyash trial did not go ahead and the trial of Hammdeh, Hawi and El-Murr (STL-11-02) on the related assassinations of Lebanese politicians was suspended two weeks before it was due to begin.[967] The STL outreach obligations under its Statute and Rules of Procedure and Evidence to inform the public about its work was also force to suspend further activities.[968] Particularly significant is the outreach role the STL was supposed to play in educating the public about the judgments of the Trial Chamber and Appeals Chamber in the Ayyash et al. case. In other words, the outreach role –representational acts– of the STL aimed at embedding the legal and political narrative and challenging a culture of impunity for political assassinations was abandoned. The gradual erosion of the legitimacy of the STL over 17 years has only been exacerbated by neglecting the work to provide an accounting of international criminal justice and its successes and limitations. The decision to close the Tribunal fails to appreciate the importance of outreach – representational acts – in ensuring verdicts – performative acts – have the intended enduring legal and political effects. By default, the verdicts

965 For a discussion of the vital role of the Lebanese investigator's success in the analysis of electronic communities to identify suspects see N. Macdonald, 'CBC Investigation: Who killed Lebanon's Rafik Hariri?', *CBC News*, November 22, 2010, https://www.cbc.ca/news/world/cbc-investigation-who-killed-lebanon-s-rafik-hariri-1.874820.

966 Statement attributable to the Spokesperson for the Secretary-General – on the Special Tribunal for Lebanon, UNSG, January 12, 2023, https://www.un.org/sg/en/content/sg/statement/2023-01-12/statement-attributable-the-spokesperson-for-the-secretary-general---the-special-tribunal-for-lebanon.

967 N. Shehadi, 'Shutting down Hariri tribunal a reckless move', *Arab News*, June 25, 2022, https://www.arabnews.com/node/2110686. See 'Hammdeh, Hawi and El-Murr STL-11-02' in L.E. Jreissati, UPDATE: Researching the Special Tribunal for Lebanon (STL), *GlobaLex*, March/April 2022, https://www.nyulawglobal.org/globalex/Special_Tribunal_Lebanon1.html#cases-hamadeh-hawi-and-el-murr-2011.

968 Kavran 2022, o.c., at 96.

are now eclipsed by the conspiratorial counter narratives that came to dominate Lebanese public opinion about the STL proceedings.

5.4. THE STL AND CONTINUING IMPUNITY IN LEBANON

The UNSC intervention in the criminal investigation of the Hariri assassination hoped that international criminal justice would hold accountable those responsible for the assassination, strengthen the rule of law in Lebanon, and challenge the culture of impunity for political assassination. However, the initial optimism that international criminal justice could realize its goals was increasingly eroded. Three issues reveal the ongoing impunity in Lebanon post-2005. The lack of justice for the families of the disappeared from the Lebanese Civil War, the victims of the Syrian Civil war (2011–ongoing), and the victims of the Beirut Port explosion (2020). They demonstrate that the victims of the Lebanese Civil War continue to be denied any justice, Syria still dominates Lebanese affairs, and the Lebanese political class continue to have immunity from legal accountability.

5.4.1. THE FAMILIES OF THE DISAPPEARED

The tens of thousands of victims of political crimes and/or their surviving relatives dating back to the 1950s, especially the victims of the Lebanese Civil War (1975–1990) have lost confidence in the capacity of international criminal justice to challenge impunity.[969] In Lebanon, amnesties have 'allowed past acts of violence to be lived in the present and transitioned into the future, as people recall them and create the conditions for an intensification of memory'.[970] The Ta'if Agreement silenced the victims of the Civil War by only recognizing the crimes committed against leaders, not the crimes against innocent victims. Amongst these forgotten and silenced victims who were treated as collateral damage of war with no rights, the establishment of the STL created big expectations for justice. For first time ever victims of alleged terrorism were able to present their case before an international tribunal.[971] But the expectation that international justice would reach back to investigate Civil War-era crimes and bring justice to innocent victims began to fade when the STL came under relentless attack

969 H. Hobbs, 'Hybrid Tribunals and the Composition of the Court: In Search of Sociological Legitimacy' (2016) 16 *Chicago Journal of International Law*, 482.

970 S. Hermez, *War Is Coming: Between Past and Future Violence in Lebanon*, University of Pennsylvania Press, Philadelphia, PA 2017, p. 174.

971 Victims' case in the *Ayyash et al.* trial, *STL Bulletin*, August 28–September 8, 2019.

by pro-Syrian leaders and the international commitment to continue funding its operations began to decline – the annual cost of running the STL (around $40 million) was more than the annual cost of running the whole Lebanese legal system (around $30 million).[972] The neglected and largely invisible victims of Lebanese political life continue to exist as phantoms, 'the presence of an absence, the presence of a traumatic history that remains not altogether resolved'.[973] A law to establish a national commission on the 17,000 disappeared was only legislated in November 2018, almost 30 years after the end of the civil war.[974] However, the selectivity of the STL's mandate prosecuting a single crime likely to implicate Syria and its allies limited the possibility of producing a more inclusive history of criminal responsibility for political violence over decades and the opportunity for national reconciliation.[975] Victims of the Civil War violence may have been able to identify with the suffering of the victims and families of the Hariri assassination but their own suffering has not received any recognition. They remain the hidden collateral sacrifice of the peace agreed to between elites, to refound a new constitutional pact. Nevertheless, the STL discourse on victims did speak to an emerging politics of memory against the state. The state's claim to national subjectivity is re-articulated 'in a new discourse about the individual as victim, not (subsumed) national citizen'.[976]

5.4.2. THE IMPACT OF THE SYRIAN CIVIL WAR 2011–2020

Even before the STL trials opened in 2014, the impact of Syria on Lebanese affairs had taken a new turn. In 2011, ripples of the Arab Spring brought popular demonstrations against the Assad regime which precipitated a civil war. The immediate effect on Lebanon was a very large refugee influx which grew to constitute an increase of the population by 25%.[977] The Syrian Civil War only amplified the divisions between the pro- and anti-Syrian alignments in Lebanese politics which threatened to spill over into armed clashes in Lebanon as Sunni and Shi'a militias became involved in the civil war in Syria. A Syrian judge issued

---

972 Mugraby 2008, o.c., p. 172.

973 B. Aretxaga, 'Madness and the Politically Real: Reflections on Violence in Postdictatorial Spain' in M.-J.D. Good, et al. (eds.), *Postcolonial Disorders: Reflections on Subjectivity in the Contemporary World*, University of California Press, Berkeley and Los Angeles, CA 2008, p. 43, at p. 49.

974 'Lebanon to form body to probe civil war disappearances', *Arab News*, November 12, 2018, http://www.arabnews.com/node/1403736/middle-east.

975 Elberling 2008, o.c., p. 533.

976 S. Haugbolle and A. Hastrup, 'Introduction: Outlines of a New Politics of Memory in the Middle East' (2008) 13 *Mediterranean Politics* 133, at 144.

977 UNHCR Lebanon: Fact Sheet, September 2021, *Relief Web*, November 26, 2021, https://reliefweb.int/report/lebanon/unhcr-lebanon-fact-sheet-september-2021.

a warrant for the arrest of PM Sa'ad Hariri for his role in the terrorist crimes of financing and arming rebels fighting President Bashar a-Assad.[978] Hariri was accused of funding Saudi-backed Sunni jihadist fighters in Lebanon. Fearing a spillover of the Syrian conflict into Lebanon and the complete breakdown of the confessional pact, the Lebanese political elite agreed to neutralize Lebanon from the regional and international conflicts in the Baabda Declaration (2012).[979] It banned military involvement in the Syrian conflict allowing only humanitarian aid and political expressions of solidarity. However, Hizbullah soon ignored the agreement and sent its armed militia to fight alongside the Syrian army in Syria.[980] The hoped-for symbolic and legal effects of the STL to strengthen Lebanese sovereignty and state institutional authority were eclipsed by the Syrian Civil War reasserting the influence of the Syrian-Iranian-Hizbullah axis in Lebanese affairs and by the international legal demands to investigate the large-scale atrocities committed by the Assad regime. The Syrian war deepened the division between the March 8 and March 14 movements because Lebanese political parties aligned themselves with the pro-regime and anti-regime forces respectively.[981] While Hizbullah's military support of the Assad regime strengthened it politically in Lebanon, Sa'ad Hariri's Future Movement's support for the Syrian opposition backfired with the ascendancy of the Assad regime's influence in Lebanon. Sa'ad Hariri was politically humiliated, firstly, by his apology to President Assad for originally blaming Syria for his father's assassination, and secondly, by his summons to Riyadh and forced resignation as PM because of his failure to counter the influence of the Syrian-Iranian-Hizbullah axis over Lebanese affairs.[982]

International criminal justice has made little progress in advancing accountability for crimes against humanity and war crimes in Syria. At the international level the Independent International Commission of Inquiry on the Syrian Arab Republic was established by Human Rights Council resolution S-17/1 in March 2011 to assist in the investigation and prosecution of those responsible for the most serious crimes under international law committed in Syria since March 2011. But because Syria is not a Party to the Rome Treaty, the ICC does not have territorial jurisdiction, and the UNSC attempts to initiate

---

978 D. Evans, 'Syria seeks arrest of Lebanese former PM Hariri', *Reuters*, December 12, 2012, http://uk.reuters.com/article/uk-syria-crisis-lebanon-idUKBRE8BB1EV20121212.

979 Hazbun 2016, o.c., p. 1063.

980 B. Hubbardaug, 'Iran Out to Remake Mideast With Arab Enforcer: Hezbollah', *New York Times*, August 27, 2017, https://www.nytimes.com/2017/08/27/world/middleeast/hezbollah-iran-syria-israel-lebanon.html.

981 'Lebanon's Self-Defeating Survival Strategies', *Middle East Report*, No. 160, July 20, 2015, International Crisis Group, p. ii.

982 B. Hubbard and H. Saad, 'Lebanon's Vanishing Prime Minister Is Back at Work. Now What?', *New York Times*, November 25, 2017, https://www.nytimes.com/2017/11/25/world/middleeast/lebanon-saad-hariri-iran-saudi-arabia.html?searchResultPosition=4.

international criminal justice measures have been vetoed.[983] As an alternate route to international justice, Syrian victims in diaspora communities have pursued justice under universal jurisdiction in German and Swedish courts with some success.[984] But for international criminal justice to prosecute the leadership, international accountability mechanisms will have to be autonomous and not constrained by the political interference experienced by the STL. What the STL demonstrated is that in politically polarized contexts like Lebanon and Syria, international courts and judicial mechanisms alone are not enough. Accountability must be approached as a multi-faceted project which includes the use of other jurisdictions under universal jurisdiction and transitional justice measures which strengthen a discourse of rights, the truth about crimes and a robust justice narrative able to contest counter narratives seeking to delegitimize international justice initiatives.

5.4.3. THE BEIRUT PORT DISASTER 2020

The hope that the STL would strengthen the rule of law and help end impunity for the political elites in Lebanon has turned out to be wishful thinking. On August 4, 2020 a massive explosion at the Beirut Port killed 210 people, injured around 6,500, and displaced more than 300,000. Some 2,750 tonnes of highly explosive ammonium nitrate stored in a warehouse since 2014 caused the blast. For six years authorities from customs, the military, the security agencies, and the judiciary had all raised the alarm about the extremely risky storage of highly explosive ammonium nitrate at the Port.[985] The cataclysmic event, described by UN experts as the largest non-nuclear explosion in history, shocked the country and galvanized mass demonstrations and demands for justice for the

---

983 Prosecutor Bensouda argued that in the case of ISIS, crimes in Syria and Iraq, the ICC could exercise personal jurisdiction over alleged perpetrators who are nationals of a State Party. 'Statement of the Prosecutor of the International Criminal Court, Fatou Bensouda, on the alleged crimes committed by ISIS', ICC, April 5, 2015, https://www.icc-cpi.int/news/statement-prosecutor-international-criminal-court-fatou-bensouda-alleged-crimes-committed-isis.

984 'Universal Jurisdiction in Sweden: Victims of Syria's Chemical Weapons Attacks Demand Justice', *Civil Rights Defenders*, April 2021, https://www.justiceinitiative.org/uploads/c3cda961-388f-4d50-b8b7-e28e5598d1e2/faq_chemical-weapons-criminal-complaints-in-sweden_04192021.pdf. C. Schaer, 'Prosecuting Syrian War-Crimes Suspects from Berlin', *The Atlantic*, July 31, 2021, https://www.theatlantic.com/international/archive/2019/07/can-germany-convict-syrian-war-criminals/595054/.

985 F L. Fouad, 'Criminal responsibility and legal proceedings in the aftermath of the Beirut blast: throwing (more) dust in the eyes of the Lebanese?', *Revue des Juristes de Sciences Po*, February 25, 2021, https://www.revuedesjuristesdesciencespo.com/index.php/2021/02/25/criminal-responsibility-and-legal-proceedings-in-the-aftermath-of-the-beirut-blast-throwing-more-dust-in-the-eyes-of-the-lebanese/.

victims.[986] It was a violent event collectively experienced by the Lebanese public as a tipping point, the last straw after the political crisis in October 2019 which had produced largescale protests demanding the fall of the government for mismanagement, corruption, and unfairly burdening the poor with more taxes to pay the huge national debt.[987] The shattered towering grain silos at the Port became a symbol of state corruption and mismanagement. Within a week of explosion, the government of PM Hassan Dib, who declared the disaster was the result of endemic corruption, was forced to resign after a third of his Ministers quit their posts.[988] Shortly after the lethal explosion a joint statement by 38 UN experts expressed concern about the effectiveness of a state investigation into the explosion because of widespread state corruption and impunity.[989] They called for the UNHRC to deliver justice for the victims, guarantee non-repetition through systemic reforms, and provide humanitarian assistance.[990] Rejecting these calls the government referred the investigation to the Judicial Council (August 10, 2020).[991]

The obstacles faced by the investigation into the Beirut Port blast highlight the convoluted and layered immunity that still protects the political elite.[992] What has been referred to as the 'red lines' for investigators by parliamentarians are Articles 39–40 of the Lebanese Constitution which provide parliamentary immunity from criminal arrest or prosecution for all members of parliament, except if they are caught in the act or parliament votes to lift their immunity.[993] Parliamentary immunity has only been amplified by the indeterminacy of the law which parliamentarians have weaponized to prevent the legal progress of Judicial Council investigations.[994] Each time an investigator has tried to prosecute

---

986 'UN rights experts call for accountability following Beirut's 'unprecedented' lethal explosion', UN News, *OHCHR*, August 13, 2020, 'UN rights experts call for accountability following Beirut's 'unprecedented' lethal explosion', UN News, *OHCHR*, August 13, 2020; 'Lebanon: Only an international investigation can ensure Beirut explosion victims' rights to truth, justice and remedy, Amnesty International', September 7, 2020, https://www.amnesty.org/en/documents/mde18/2997/2020/en/.

987 M. Chulov, 'Lebanon's mass revolt against corruption and poverty continues', *The Guardian*, October 23, 2019.

988 M. Chulov, 'Lebanese government quits following Beirut port explosion', *The Guardian*, August 11, 2020.

989 'UN human rights experts call for justice and accountability in response to Beirut explosion', *UN News*, August 13, 2020, https://www.ohchr.org/en/press-releases/2020/08/un-human-rights-experts-call-justice-and-accountability-response-beirut?LangID=E&NewsID=26163.

990 Ibid.

991 Fouad 2021, o.c.

992 T. Graham and E. Hodges, '"Red Lines" in Beirut Blast Investigation: How Exactly Lebanese Politicians Escape Accountability', *Just Security*, March 6, 2021, https://www.justsecurity.org/75252/red-lines-in-beirut-blast-investigation-how-exactly-lebanese-politicians-escape-accountability/.

993 Ibid.

994 The Bar Association and Lebanese Judge's Association argued that the crime of killing or causing the death of citizens is not subject to immunity. The conservative argument that

Ministers for criminal negligence in the management of the Port they have been blocked and eventually removed or sidelined from their positions through executive pressure on the Judicial Council. The fate of the investigators reveals the lack of independence of the judiciary from the executive. The appointments to Judicial Council are made by decree of the Justice Minister but the head of the Judicial Council and head of the Supreme Judicial Council are the same person.[995] The International Commission of Jurists found the Supreme Judicial Council, the body responsible for recommending the appointment of judges, lacked independence and impartiality – eight of its 10 members are appointed by the executive.[996] In other words, the judiciary is subject to same clientelist networks that have penetrated the rest of the state 'to reward and punish its constituents – lawyers, judges, and citizens seeking justice – according to their placement within this system of power'.[997] The judiciary has become subject to extensive political gatekeeping and interference, so they provide a veneer of impartiality and legitimacy to entrenched interests of the political elite.[998]

The judicial crisis over the investigation of the Beirut Port explosion highlights the continuing problem of impunity in post-war Lebanon described by Sami Hermez as the 'politics of protracted conflict'.[999] The Ta'if Agreement (1989) had allowed the project of post-war state renewal to be co-opted by a new elite and their constituencies forged during the war. The adjusted 50:50 power-sharing between Christian and Muslims intensified communal clientelism throughout state institutions and shifted from sectarian competition to control over state positions and resources. The Ta'if narrative of 'no victor, no vanquished' meant that no-one was responsible for the war and allowed everyone to claim the status of victim, even collectively, as expressed in the Lebanese narrative of the 'war of others'.[1000] The Ta'if agreement served the goal of elite reconciliation only to burden the rest of society.[1001] As a consequence, the end of the Civil War did not mean the return of the state but the transfer of war-time systems of

ministers can only be prosecuted by the Supreme Council for Trying Presidents and Ministers was impossible in the context of sectarian polarization and the lack of any record of prosecutions in parliament. See '"They Killed Us from the Inside": An Investigation into the August 4 Beirut Blast', *Human Rights Watch*, August 2021, p. 51, https://www.hrw.org/sites/default/files/media_2021/08/lebanon0821_web.pdf.

995 Ibid.

996 'The Lebanese High Judicial Council in Light of International Standards', A Briefing paper, February 2017, International Commission of Jurists, Geneva.

997 Graham and Hodges 2021, o.c.

998 Graham and Hodges 2021, o.c.

999 Hermez 2017, o.c., at p. 173.

1000 The prominent diplomat and journalist Ghassan Tueni published a book with this title. G. Tueni, *Une guerre pour les autres*, J.C. Lattes, Paris 1985.

1001 R. Saadeh, 'On Justice Denied: Interrogating Amnesty and Amnesia in Post-conflict Lebanon', *Yale Journal of International Affairs*, November 23, 2021, https://www.yalejournal.org/publications/on-justice-denied-interrogating-amnesty-and-amnesia-in-post-conflict-lebanon.

governance overseen by warlords into the state. Former warlords retained their sectarian control over social services and state-like functions for their Civil War constituencies as political clients in electoral politics.[1002] The unresponsiveness of the judicial system to civil society's demands for justice and accountability is symptomatic of its penetration by these 'beneficiaries-of-war-*cum*-politicians'. The Beirut Port Authority itself is a microcosm of the dysfunctional Lebanese state lacking accountability and suffering from organizational paralysis. During the war, Lebanese ports were highly profitable sinecures controlled by warlords to tax imports and exports and for smuggling. After the war, the Port Authority was managed by a 'Temporary Committee for Management and Investment of the Port of Beirut' because the former warlords and politicians with a financial stake in the Port were unable to reach agreement. The Temporary Committee remains in charge. In a scathing critique of the Port Authority the World Bank found it lacked accountability, status as a legal entity, financial records, and operational transparency, resulting in poor planning, safety, and efficiency in its management.[1003]

The executive's influence over the Supreme Judicial Council and Judicial Council has resulted in the removal or sidelining of two lead investigators into the Port explosion. First, Judge Sawan, who was appointed lead investigator on August 13, 2021, brought charges against 37 people who were mainly low-level customs, Port, and security officials. After the parliament refused to act on Judge Sawan's request to investigate 12 current and former Ministers, he charged the Caretaker Prime Minister, Hassan Dib, and three former ministers (Ghazi Zeaiter, former Minister of Public Works and Transport; Ali Hassan Khalil, former Minister of Finance; and Youssef Fenianos, former Minster of Public Works and Transport) with criminal negligence. Two of the former Ministers filed a complaint before the Court of Cassation for Judge Sawan to be removed from the case.[1004] In February 2021, Judge Sawan was removed by the Court and replaced by Judge Tarek Bitar who has faced the same difficulties as his predecessor with the 'red lines' of parliamentary immunity. When he requested parliament lift the parliamentary immunity of two former Ministers and tried to prosecute several senior military officers in charge of security, he too was subjected to lawsuits seeking to remove him. Supporters of the Shi'a Amal Movement protested near the Palace of Justice demanding Judge Bitar be removed which led to an armed clash between rival political parties in which seven people died. In response, Ministers from Hizbullah and Amal boycotted Cabinet meetings paralyzing

1002 Graham and Hodges 2021, o.c.

1003 Cited in '"They killed us from the inside": An Investigation into the August 4 Beirut Blast', *Human Rights Watch*, August 3, 2021, p. 12, https://www.hrw.org/sites/default/files/media_2021/08/lebanon0821_web.pdf.

1004 Ibid.

government and demanded Judge Bitar be removed to guarantee their right to immunity.[1005] Another lawsuit was filed against Judge Bitar in the Court of Cassation, but the case was left in limbo because of the retirement of the judge examining the lawsuit in January 2022 and the highly politicized character of judicial appointments. In addition, there has been ongoing criticism of Judge Bitar by Hizbullah who have called his investigation a 'big' mistake' and biased.[1006] In September 2022, with Judge Bitar's future role in the investigation still unresolved, the Justice Minister, Henry Khoury, asked the Supreme Judicial Council to appoint another investigator to temporarily takeover the investigation but without the power to issue charges.[1007] By August 2022 a total of 25 requests had been made to dismiss the lead judges.[1008]

In response to the judicial paralysis caused by the lack of independence of the Judicial Council, there have been growing calls for an international investigation. In 2021 a Human Rights Watch report on the Port investigation recommended the UNHRC adopt a resolution establishing an independent international investigative mission into the Beirut Port explosion with a mandate to take the necessary measures to guarantee full accountability of those responsible and to address the underlying systemic failures that led to the explosion and the failure of the domestic investigation.[1009] A UNHRC working group on the Universal Periodic Review expressed concern about the lack of impartiality and independence of the Beirut Port blast investigation and called for an international investigation to overcome the judicial paralysis.[1010] At present, the prospect of international criminal justice is slight because Lebanon is not a signatory to the Rome Statute and it remains unclear as to whether criminal neglect can be prosecuted as a crime against humanity without proof of criminal intent or international criminal liability for state recklessness in not responding to the high risk of an explosion.[1011] Unless the more conspiratorial accounts related to the war in Syria about why so much ammonium nitrate was stored at the Port are substantiated by proof, then an international criminal investigation is unlikely.

1005 K. Merhej, 'The Beirut Port Blast and Lebanon's Legacy of Impunity', *ISPI Online*, May 10, 2022, https://www.ispionline.it/en/pubblicazione/beirut-port-blast-and-lebanons-legacy-impunity-34960.

1006 M. Hadchiti, 'Judicial Disputes Over Appointing Alternative Judge In The Beirut Blast Case', *The 961*, September 22, 2022, https://www.the961.com/judicial-disputes-over-alternative-judge-beirut-blast-case/.

1007 'Lebanon's judiciary seeks to name second investigator to stalled Beirut blast probe', *Alarabiya*, September 11, 2022, https://english.alarabiya.net/News/middle-east/2022/09/07/Lebanon-s-judiciary-seeks-to-name-second-investigator-to-stalled-Beirut-blast-probe.

1008 T. Fox, 'Two years after Beirut blast, lawsuits raise hopes for justice', *Al Jazeera*, August 4, 2022, https://www.aljazeera.com/news/2022/8/4/lebanon-beirut-port-explosion-two-years-on-fight-for-justice-lawsuits.

1009 "They Killed Us from the Inside", o.c.

1010 J. Elias, 'Beirut Blast: International Investigation?', *Lebanon Law Review*, April 2, 2021.

1011 Fouad 2021, o.c.

Nevertheless, international civil actions have been launched in domestic courts in the United States and Europe in relation to dual citizens and diplomats injured or killed in the explosion. The Swiss-based organization, Accountability, filed a civil case in the United States in mid-July seeking $250m in damages for the survivors. Another legal action is seeking damages from Texas-based TGS, a US-Norwegian geophysical services group which owns the British firm, Spectrum, the company that chartered the Moldovan-flagged Rhosus to ship the ammonium nitrate in 2013 – allegedly destined for Mozambique.[1012] The Beirut Bar Association filed a major international lawsuit in mid-2022 in the United Kingdom's High Court of Justice regarding Savaro Ltd, the company suspected of importing the ammonium nitrate from the Georgian chemicals factory Rustavi Azot. In addition, there are local prosecutions in France, Germany, and the Netherlands regarding the death of diplomats in the explosion. Because all these legal actions are dependent on the progress of the domestic investigation to reveal findings, they too would benefit from a separate UNHRC fact-finding mission.[1013]

The deep crisis in the judiciary over the issue of its independence from the executive has led to an unprecedented strike by most of the judiciary. One official commented: "Lebanese judges are qualified, but the political class is using its power to subject them to their interests. One of the main examples is what happened with the file of the Beirut Port explosion and the removal of Judge Tarek Bitar just because he accused politicians of negligence."[1014] Just as STL is abandoned by international donors, the urgency for transparency and accountability over the Beirut Port explosion, the same values that drove the establishment of the STL, is greater than ever.

5.5. CONCLUSION

The establishment of the STL by the UNSC to prosecute those responsible for the Hariri assassination was meant to signal a turning point to end Lebanon's endemic culture of impunity, corruption, and political assassination. International legal intervention rescaled justice by creating an independent hybrid tribunal with superior jurisdiction administering national law to prosecute those responsible for the assassination of ex-PM Rafiq Hariri. Its broader political aim was to reinstall state sovereignty and the rule of law in Lebanon through justice for the victims. However, in Lebanon, international criminal justice has not provided

---

1012 Fox 2022, o.c.

1013 Fox 2022, o.c.

1014 N. Houssari, 'Lebanon faces judicial paralysis as judges refuse to work', *Arab News*, August 23, 2022, https://www.arabnews.com/node/2148881/middle-east.

a viable solution to entrenched political obstacles.[1015] PM Siniora's strategy to outsource difficult political problems to the STL failed. The STL was confronted by a post-war society polarized between competing confessional alliances who became its supporters and opponents. Although conceived as a hybrid tribunal with Lebanese government support, the logic of Lebanese pactism and confessionalism saw the March 8 movement denounce the UNIIC and the STL as instruments of the US-Saudi axis of influence in Lebanon and worked to undermine its legitimacy. For the STL to successfully bring an end to impunity in Lebanese politics it had to overturn the Lebanese formula for managing political crises – elite pactism, amnesty and amnesia. In this model, conflict is imagined as the product of elite competition which can be turned on and off by deals between them. On the condition of mutual amnesty, the expectation is that political elites can be reconciled, their supporters can be pacified, and the conflict ended. Elite pactism, founded Lebanese sovereignty in 1943, has remained the cornerstone of Lebanese politics until today. Every political crisis since independence has been resolved by a constitutional pact renewing power-sharing agreements to refound the equilibrium of the confessional state. The formula of amnesia and amnesty, formal or informal, to deal with serious political violence and political crises has shaped the parameters of each successive pact.[1016] But Lebanese pactism as a solution for conflict does not actually recover sovereignty, only the latest iteration of contingent sovereignty on which the internal/external balance of power-sharing is reconstituted. There is an inherent instability to power-sharing which instead of reducing conflict, ironically creates the conditions to intensify it. Power-sharing increases competition between groups. It keeps alive, and to the forefront, the original founding conflict over ethnic proportionality and fairness in the distribution of power and opportunities between sects. It advantages dominant groups and, instead of enhancing representation and inclusive decision-making, produces patterns of vetoes.[1017]

From the start, two key issues have worked against the STL fulfilling its ambitious legal aim of conducting successful prosecutions and political aim of recovering sovereignty and the rule of law in Lebanon. First, its narrow mandate focused on a single crime –a time-specific event– and second, the politicization of the Tribunal by its opponents characterizing it as just the latest partisan intervention by an external actor seeking to change the internal/external balance of power-sharing. Ironically, the Tribunal's hybrid character did not enhance justice in Lebanon. Instead, it created a new opportunity for the politicization of justice. STL Prosecutor Robert Roth argues the essential independence of

---

1015 A. Dworkin, 'Protracted, neglected, and ineffective: Lessons from the Lebanon tribunal', *European Council on Foreign Relations*, September 4, 2020, https://ecfr.eu/article/commentary_protracted_neglected_and_ineffective_lessons_from_the_lebanon_tr/.

1016 J. Hall 2009, o.c.

1017 Roeder and Rothchild 2005, o.c., pp. 36–41.

international criminal justice is compromised in hybrid tribunals because of their vulnerability to politicization.[1018] For those victims historically denied justice by elite pactism, the STL became a symbol of the hope of international criminal justice to overturn elite impunity at home. However, the relentless delegitimation of the Tribunal by the Hizbullah-led opposition made it almost impossible to conduct effective trials and reach a verdict that would not be seen as partisan. The opponents of the STL conducted a relentless campaign and counter-narrative of partisanship to undermine public confidence in the Tribunal and its legitimacy. The Tribunal was never able to effectively counter the Hizbullah accusations that it was biased against Syria and had manipulated evidence to conceal the real perpetrator. The STL lost out in the contest to communicate with the Lebanese public and have their claim to be delivering impartial international justice prevail. Hizbullah's demands for the repatriation of justice and its criticism that the STL was destabilizing Lebanon were designed to bring the judicial process under the political influence of Lebanese elite pactism. When PM Sa'ad Hariri refused to submit to Syrian pressure for him to denounce the Tribunal, he was refusing to accept a return to Syrian hegemony over Lebanese affairs with the result that his government fell and he was forced into exile. Six years later, in 2017, PM Sa'ad Hariri, fighting for his government's political survival, apologized to President Assad for originally blaming Syria for his father's assassination.[1019] As the recent stalled judicial investigation into the Beirut Port explosion has demonstrated, repatriation would have only exposed the Hariri investigation to even greater political veto and impunity because of the executive's extensive interference in the judicial system. The impact of the Syrian civil war on the STL has been to diminish its legal and political significance in Lebanon and internationally due to the scale of crimes against humanity and war crimes allegedly committed there. The failure of the UNSC to refer to the ICC for investigation the alleged war crimes and crimes against humanity committed in Syria demonstrated the barriers to international criminal justice through the UNSC. With Assad's total military victory in sight, it seems the prospect of any international criminal prosecution seems very slight. The only successful prosecutions to date have been of Syrian immigrants/refugees in courts in Germany and Sweden under universal jurisdiction.[1020]

1018 Roth, o.c., p. 290.

1019 B. Hubbard and H. Saad, 'Lebanon's Vanishing Prime Minister Is Back at Work. Now What?', *New York Times*, November 25, 2017, https://www.nytimes.com/2017/11/25/world/middleeast/lebanon-saad-hariri-iran-saudi-arabia.html?searchResultPosition=4.

1020 J. Crawford, 'Is Syria giving universal jurisdiction new life?', *Justiceinfo.net*, March 4, 2019, https://www.justiceinfo.net/en/tribunals/national-tribunals/40483-is-syria-giving-universal-jurisdiction-new-life.html; J. Macey, et al., 'A War Crimes "Wiki": The Need for an Open Database to Ensure Syrian Accountability', *Yale Journal of International Law*, December 4, 2017, http://www.yjil.yale.edu/a-war-crimes-wiki-the-need-for-an-open-database-to-ensure-syrian-accountability/.

In the face of ongoing impunity in Lebanon, the burden of justice falls on the victims. Through the NGO, UMAM Documentation and Research, Lokman Sim and his wife, Monika Borgmann, had worked to preserve the memory of the Lebanese Civil War. In a programme entitled 'Who killed whom?', he documented the political assassinations of intellectuals, researchers, journalists and opponents in the Middle East region. He himself tragically became an object of his own programme for justice when he was murdered on February 3, 2021, for which no-one has been held accountable.[1021] On the first anniversary of his death his widow, Hanna Jaber launched the Lokman Slim Foundation to investigate political assassinations in the Middle East. The work the Foundation is doing is the work the judiciary and the state should be doing to pursue justice for the victims.

The Hariri assassination was widely constructed as a turning point internationally, a galvanizing experience available to generate the transformation of chronic political crisis in Lebanon. The assassination was framed as an international terrorist act. In the form of the STL, international criminal justice was overburdened by the expectation that a single international trial could provide the beginnings of a solution to impunity for political assassination in Lebanon. The idea that the framing of political assassination as a crime could generate moral unity around the transgression through the verdict was overly ambitious. Through its campaign of institutional delegitimation of the STL, March 8 attacked the very base of international criminal law as justice, the value underpinning it. For them, justice was partisan and the outcome would be biased because of the superior political manipulation of the judicial STL process. The unsatisfactory verdict – three life convictions for individuals that would probably never serve the time – produced a state of permanent liminality, an incomplete outcome with no possibility of closure. The victims of the Beirut port explosion have shared the same experience of justice as a state of permanent liminality after the serial undermining and sidelining of judge investigators by politicians, guaranteeing their immunity from prosecution. The victims are treated as unfortunates, the cost of negligence, for which there will be no accountability. Justice is debased because there is no state institution or authority that can escape politicization. Judicial proceedings are co-opted as a ritual legal mechanism of closure able to produce judgments but not justice.

[1021] Lenoir 2022, o.c.

CHAPTER 6

KENYA

Rescaling Justice, Elite Pactism and Impunity

6.1. INTERNATIONAL LAW, HUMAN RIGHTS AND ANTI-COLONIALISM

In 2010, two international legal cases addressed impunity and serious human rights violations in Kenya. The first case involved the decision by the UK High Court in London to hear a case against the British Foreign and Commonwealth Office (FCO) brought by Mau Mau veterans for compensation for serious human rights violations suffered during the colonial Kenyan Emergency (1952–1960). The second case involved the ICC preliminary investigation into the responsibility of Kenyan political leaders for the 2007 post-election violence. Together these cases represented a human rights framing of political violence which the Kenyan Human Rights Commission (KHRC) constructed as an historical catalogue of crimes – human rights violations, crimes against humanity – and impunity dating back the colonial state and continuing into the postcolonial state.[1022] This chapter explores the impact of the resort to international courts to challenge elite impunity in Kenya by addressing serious human rights violations. It asks: has international criminal justice contributed to political justice in Kenya? The rescaling of justice to the UK High Court and the ICC represents the judicialization of politics arising from the chronic failure of the postcolonial state of Kenya to resolve fundamental conflicts over elite pactism, elite impunity, ethnic representation, land inequality, and the centralization of political power since independence. The UK High Court and the ICC emerged as new judicial arenas to pursue justice for the victims of state violence committed by the colonial and then the postcolonial state respectively, and at the same time, serve as an instrument to exert political leverage in the struggle for political reform and recognition in Kenya. The Mau Mau veterans' claims reached the UK High Court with the support of Kenyan civil society

[1022] D. Malombe, *Justice Delayed: A Status Report on Historical Injustices in Kenya*, Kenya Human Rights Commission, Nairobi 2011.

organizations' (CSOs) human rights campaigns and the advocacy of the KHRC, but only after President Mwai Kibaki unbanned the Mau Mau organization in 2003 when he came to power. From the time of the Colonial Emergency regime in the 1950s until 2003, the Mau Mau remained a banned and illegal organization officially despised and forgotten as terrorists in the postcolonial state. The KHRC 'Mau Mau Project' aimed to break the conspiracy of silence about the Mau Mau as victims of colonial repression, to secure them reparations, and to help politically rehabilitate them as heroes of the struggle for national liberation instead of remaining stigmatized and ostracized as despised and forgotten terrorists. The KHRC viewed the 'Mau Mau Project' as a way to address the long standing problems of impunity for past abuses in Kenya, develop transitional justice measures, and support the litigation of colonial era atrocities.[1023] The ICC intervention in 2011 occurred only after Kenyan politicians had failed to establish a Special Tribunal to initiate prosecutions against those responsible for the 2007 post-election violence, as stipulated by the National Accord and Reconciliation Process. Nevertheless, CSOs had played an important role in insisting on international trials because they had no faith in the independence of the Kenyan judicial system. The political aim of the ICC prosecutions was to secure judgments against ethnic leaders responsible for the post-election violence to challenge impunity and strengthen the rule of law in Kenya. Both cases used anti-imperialist discourse to mobilize support, although in opposite directions. The Mau Mau veterans invoked the anti-colonial struggle for independence to denounce British colonial state repression during decolonization. The Kenyan government invoked anti-imperialist discourse to oppose the ICC prosecutions as undermining state sovereignty.

6.2. DECOLONIZATION, PACTISM AND DEMOCRATIZATION

While these international legal cases signify the recent expansion of international law to redress the grievances of victims of colonial state and post-independence state political violence, they are also indicators of the ongoing crisis of state formation in Kenya where chronic elite impunity and the marginalization of victims of historical violent events persists. These international legal cases address the continuity in the use of political repression as a mode of governance, firstly under the authoritarian British colonial state, and secondly, in the postcolonial state, especially under the authoritarian presidencies of Jomo Kenyatta (1964–1978) and Daniel arap Moi (1978–2002). The managed process of political transition to independence has been characterized as 'consensual

[1023] R. Carina, 'The Empire's Ghosts Return' (2009) 487 *New African* 18.

decolonization', a bargaining process 'oriented to integrating a potentially disruptive nationalist movement into the structures and requisites of the colonial political-economic system'.[1024] In Kenya, 'consensual decolonization' produced continuity in modes of governance between colonial and post-independence states through the transfer of power to trusted Kenyan elites who were able to monopolize political power after independence in the 1963 Constitution. Writing in 1995, Ochieng' and Atieno-Odhiambo characterized Kenya as a 'neo-colonial state' because of the continuity between the colonial and post-colonial state, in which all that had happened was the expansion of the colonial administrative and economic structures.[1025] In post-independent Kenya, the five year cycle for national elections has served as a catalyst for political violence which has been managed by elite pacts, As Muhula and Ndegwa observe, in Kenya, pacts are 'institutionalized as a solution to the problem of weak aggregation, adjudication and execution institutions, and have become the preferred method for resolving conflicts that the established institutions are unable to solve'.[1026] Each new pact reflected political realignments institutionalized in serial constitutional amendments. There have been 32 constitutional amendments since independence.[1027] The Constitution 'became a central cog in elite machinations to reproduce their position in the postcolonial state' which they used to further centralize power.[1028]

This chapter explores how the international legal cases in the High Court and ICC addressing accountability have come up against the assertion of judicial sovereignty – the former colonial state (FCO) denied it had liability because of the statute of limitations and the postcolonial state claimed it had prior judicial sovereignty over the crimes. What has been the impact of criminal justice, at both the national and international levels, on elite impunity in Kenya? Mahmood Mamdani makes the point that the distinction between political and criminal violence is qualitative. Political violence requires more than just criminal agency; it needs a political constituency. More than just perpetrators; it needs supporters. A political constituency, in turn, is held together and mobilized by an issue. More than criminal violence, political violence is

1024 G. Wasserman, *Politics of Decolonization: Kenya Europeans and the Land Issue 1960–65*, Cambridge University Press, Cambridge 1976, p. 5.

1025 W.R. Ochieng and E. S. Atieno-Odhiambo, 'Prologue: On Decolonization' in B.A. Ogot and W.R. Ochieng' (eds.), *Decolonization and Independence in Kenya 1940–93*, James Currey, London 1995, p. xi.

1026 R. Muhula and S.N. Ndegwa, 'Instrumentalism and constitution-making in Kenya: triumphs, challenges and opportunities beyond the 2013 elections' in G.R. Murunga, et al. (eds.), *Kenya: The Struggle for a New Constitutional Order*, Zed Books, London 2014, p. 79, at p. 93.

1027 L. Nichols, *The International Criminal Court and the End of Impunity in Kenya*, Springer, Heidelberg 2015, p. 51. See *Truth, Justice and Reconciliation Report*, Volume IIA, TJRC, Nairobi 2013, for selected amendments between 1963–1969, 1982–91, 21 and 25.

1028 Murunga 2014, o.c., p. 146.

issue driven.[1029] These international legal cases intervened in long-standing unresolved conflicts concerned with inter-ethnic grievances about post-independence political injustice arising from disputes over who should be the beneficiaries of decolonization, over the centralization of political power, over ethnic domination in a multiethnic society, and over the uneven distribution of land ownership.[1030] Political violence associated with electoral cycles has been symptomatic of the ethnicization of political constituencies for political power and clientelism.

Our approach to the analysis of these international judicial interventions to hold the state accountable for political violence – core human rights violations – is to contextualize events in three key historical transitions in Kenya following periods of political violence: 1) the independence Act in 1963; 2) the national investigation of post-election violence in 2007 (the Waki Report); and 3) the ICC intervention in 2010 triggered by national political failure of the Kenyan parliament to fulfill a UN-negotiated agreement to establish a Special Tribunal to investigate criminal responsibility for the 2007 post-election violence. These transitions correspond to Kenyan political periodization: the beginning (1963) and end of the 'First Republic' (2007), and the birth of the 'Second Republic' with the new Constitution' in 2010 and the struggle to enact it as law.[1031] They represent historical turning points in which fundamental political conflicts over citizenship, land ownership, and political representation are the continuing threads. Each transition is constituted by a political fix reached through a political pact institutionalized in constitutional amendments and justified in an official narrative about past violence. Each political fix establishes the parameters of the next political crisis and elite pact. The introduction of a human rights framing of political violence by the KHRC integrated both colonial and postcolonial history in a continuous narrative of state abuse and impunity. In the KHRC Report *Justice Delayed* (2011), state repression is constructed as 'systemic injustice (human rights violations and economic crimes) … committed by both the colonial and post-independence regimes in Kenya'.[1032] The Report catalogues the historical pattern in the use of political violence – it is targeted against specific groups, it happens in specific places, it uses similar methods, it is associated with public events, it is committed by organized groups – state and

---

1029 M. Mamdani, 'Beyond Nuremberg: The Historical Significance of the Post-apartheid Transition in South Africa' (2015) 43 *Politics & Society* 61, at 63.

1030 While no ethnic group is numerically dominant the five biggest tribes have had the most influence over who is elected. According to Kenya's National Bureau of Statistics (1989 census), the largest native ethnic groups are the Kikuyu (6,622,576), the Luhya (5,338,666), the Kalenjin (4,967,328), the Luo (4,044,440) and the Kamba (3,893,157).

1031 P.T. Zeleza, 'The protracted transition to the Second Republic in Kenya' in G.R. Murunga, et al. (eds.), *Kenya: The Struggle for a New Constitutional Order*, Zed Books, London 2014, p. 17, at p. 17.

1032 Malombe 2011, o.c., p. 8.

non-state – and it results in impunity.[1033] The Report's human rights framing finds that political violence is fuelled by recurrent disputes over authoritarian and centralized power, inequitable land distribution, unequal distribution of ethnic power and the differentiation of citizenship by ethnicity. The international legal rescaling of accountability and claims for reparations is symptomatic of the chronic problem of elite impunity in Kenyan politics and dysfunctional state institutions. The human rights claims presented to the UK High Court and the ICC were driven by civil society movements. But while the human rights claims of Mau Mau veterans in the UK High Court were leveraged by Mwai Kibaki to mobilize party political support by invoking the independence struggle, the human rights claims of the victims of post-election violence (2008) in the ICC were undermined by the indicted political leaders who labelled the prosecutions a neo-colonial intervention in Kenyan sovereignty. The relationship between human rights and neo/colonialism was shaped by political agreements at independence and elite resistance to the reform of the Kenyan state and society according to the template of the new Constitution (2010).

6.2.1. KENYA INDEPENDENCE ACT 1963

On the December 12, 1963, the Independence Act established Kenya as an independent state based on the borders of the British Colony and Protectorate of Kenya originally created in 1920. The Act represented an historical turning point marking the transition from a colonial to post-independence state and an act of historical political justice. The independence narrative was framed as the achievement of 'consensual decolonization', the successful outcome of negotiations taking place over nine years and progressively institutionalized in the Lyttleton Constitution of 1954, then the Lennox-Boyd Constitution of 1954, and finally the Lancaster House Conferences held between 1960 and 1963.[1034] Wasserman argues that consensual decolonization emerged as a strategy adopted by the colonial state to manage the transfer of sovereignty through elite pacts and popular demobilization. Firstly, the colonial elites are prepared for the 'removal of colonial authority'; secondly, the nationalist elites are co-opted into the colonial system; and thirdly, mass discontent is pre-empted or controlled to ensure 'the acquiescence of the masses to the process of consensual decolonization'.[1035] In Kenya, the British Colonial state groomed Jomo Kenyatta as the nationalist leader to whom power was transferred at independence, despite the fact he had been imprisoned as an anti-colonial activist, mistakenly

[1033] Ibid., p. 8.
[1034] Wasserman 1976, o.c., p. 4.
[1035] Wasserman 1976, o.c., p. 5.

as a Mau Mau leader, between 1954–1961. Kenyatta and his party, the Kenyan African National Congress (KANU), presented independence as the realization of national unity and independence (*uhuru*) through the creation of a centralized postcolonial state. Once he was elected as President in 1964, Jomo Kenyatta quickly consolidated his own personal power by establishing a single party state and centralized executive power. However, the official version of independence as 'consensual decolonization' omitted the details about the processes of co-option and popular demobilization that the British used to manage the struggle for independence. The consensual decolonization narrative omits three key political conflicts: firstly, the defeat and criminalization of the Mau Mau movement during the lead up to decolonization; secondly, the marginalization of *majimboism* or push for decentralized federalism; and thirdly, the issue of Somali ethnic identity and the Shifta secessionist movement in the north east region.[1036] These unresolved political tensions continued to shape post-independence state formation in Kenya and were expressed in the long delayed official rehabilitation of the Mau Mau as heroes in the national liberation/struggle; in the intensification of ethnicized electoral politics and ongoing demands for decentralized governance; in the practice of elite pactism to sabotage constitutional reforms; in the recurrence of militarized governance of north Kenya; in the intervention in the civil war in Somalia; and in the securitization of Somalis in response to *al-shabaab* terrorism and the risk of radicalization of Kenyan Muslim youth.

The first theme omitted from the independence narrative was the role of the Mau Mau in the struggle for independence. During the decolonization negotiations both the British colonial state and President Kenyatta excluded the Mau Mau from the independence narrative, firstly because the civil war had deeply polarized the population and secondly, because the movement contradicted Kenyatta's national independence narrative of consensual decolonization and national unity. The negotiated independence agreement was concluded between the British colonial state and chosen Kenyan nationalist elites. In 1952, the colonial state declared a State of Emergency to defeat the Mau Mau insurgency by dividing the Kikuyu, the tribal origin of the Mau Mau, into loyalists and militants. British counter-insurgency policy punished the Mau Mau and their supporters and rewarded the loyalists which, by 1955, had succeeded in creating a civil war amongst the Kikuyus. Suspected Mau Mau members were detained, tortured and subjected to capital punishment – between 1952 and 1958 around 3,000 Mau Mau were put on trial for capital crimes and 1090 were executed.[1037] Suspected Mau Mau sympathizers were

[1036] D. Branch, *Kenya Between Hope and Despair, 1963–2011*, Yale University Press, New Haven and London 2011, pp. 31–4.

[1037] D. Anderson, *Histories of the Hanged: Britain's Dirty War in Kenya and the End of Empire*, Weidenfeld & Nicholson, London 2005a, p. 7.

also subjected to collective punishment through enforced villagization which concentrated 1,050,899 Kikuyu in 804 villages enclosed with barbed wire, and through seizures of Kikuyu land.[1038] The colonial authorities rewarded Loyalist Kikuyu through patronage in the form of jobs in the Home Guard, the civil service and provincial administration, as well as access to land through land consolidation, cash-cropping and private ownership introduced under the Swynnerton Plan.[1039] Those Kikuyu who remained in detention as Mau Mau militants or as sympathizers were doubly punished by their exclusion from these schemes. The counterinsurgency strategy rewarding supporters and punishing militants had a polarizing impact on their identities 'fired in a kiln of violence' seeking protection or revenge which continued into post-independence Kenyan politics.[1040]

Colonial pacification of the Kikuyu through repression and reward was continued under the post-independence state building project. Despite he himself being gaoled as a political prisoner and alleged Mau Mau leader, President Jomo Kenyatta erased the Mau Mau from the independence narrative. He represented himself as a reconciliator and national centralist politician who reassured white settlers that he believed people had to work to get land and not simply be beneficiaries of its expropriation by the newly independent state, as the Mau Mau had demanded. His stigmatization of the Mau Mau movement was a key element in his nationalist and centralist project: "We are determined to have independence in peace, and we shall not allow hooligans to rule Kenya. We must have no hatred towards one another. Mau Mau was a disease which had been eradicated and must never be remembered again".[1041] Kenyatta articulated his amnesia policy of 'forgive and forget' on Kenyatta Day in 1964:

> "Triumph in a struggle of this kind cannot be achieved without a long history of setbacks and sufferings, of failures and humiliation. But all this is worthwhile, and all can be forgotten, when its outcome is the foundation on which a future can be built. It is the future, my friends, that is living, and the past that is dead".[1042]

President Kenyatta saw the Mau Mau ex-detainees as a political threat to his presidency and project of national unity and set out to marginalize them. Despite the ongoing criminalization of Mau Mau organizations, the ex-detainees quickly became politically influential at local government level displacing Kikuyu

---

1038 Elkins 2005, o.c., p. 235.

1039 D. Branch, *Defeating Mau Mau, Creating Kenya: Counterinsurgency, Civil War, and Decolonization*, Cambridge University Press, Cambridge 2009, p. 121.

1040 Ibid., p. 97.

1041 M.S. Clough, 'Mau Mau and the Contest for Memory' in E.S.A. Odhiambo and J. Lonsdale (eds.), *Mau Mau & Nationhood: Arms, Authority & Narration*, James Currey, Oxford 2003, p. 251, at p. 255.

1042 Ibid., p. 256.

loyalists and active local party members in KANU. On their release, they formed the Land and Freedom Army (LFA) demanding reparations as ex-detainees and the right to the land that they had fought for, not the right to buy white settler properties.[1043] The LFA was set up as an organization ready to govern all of Kenya if the new government 'betrayed their cause of land and freedom'.[1044] Kenyatta feared that the Mau Mau demand for land was potentially too revolutionary and, although he made symbolic gestures of rehabilitation by pardoning Mau Mau prisoners in custody and offering amnesty to Mau Mau fighters in the forest, he ignored their expectations for the return of their seized land and new employment opportunities. Kenyatta's response was: "We all fought for *Uhuru*". But the difference was that Mau Mau veterans got no medals and their graves were left unmarked. For Kenyatta, they were a 'political embarrassment'.[1045] The narrative of 'consensual decolonization' promoted the myth of peaceful transition built on a partnership between the British government and Kenyatta. It was designed to erase the memory of the Emergency and the role of the Mau Mau in the violent struggle for independence. British concern that their colonial rule should be remembered favourably, especially their exit, saw them pressure political leaders such as Kenyatta to publicly denounce the Mau Mau.[1046] The British wanted the Mau Mau to remain stigmatized as terrorists not remembered as national heroes 'fighting for land and freedom'.[1047] In order to obscure the methods employed in the counterinsurgency campaign the colonial government expurgated the official memory of the Emergency by transferring a large number of colonial administrative archives to Britain. These buried archives were only recently discovered in the UK by historians while working in support of the Mau Mau veterans' cases in the UK courts filed in 2009.[1048]

Although the official annual commemoration of independence on *Uhuru* Day on December 12, suppressed Mau Mau memories of detention camps, massacres, punishments, and dispossession remained just below the surface as a topic of popular conversation and the focus of memory work in local communities. Dozens of Mau Mau associations were established; Mau Mau were remembered as victims in local memorials; and heroes such as Dedan Kimathi were celebrated. Opposition intellectuals and pro-democracy activists embraced the Mau Mau as the embodiment of an heroic narrative of national liberation and leveraged support against the Jomo Kenyatta (1964–1978) and Daniel arap

---

1043 R.B. Edgerton, *Mau Mau: An African Crucible*, Collier MacMillan Publishers, London 1989, p. 215.

1044 Ibid., p. 215.

1045 Ibid., p. 232.

1046 C. Elkins, *Imperial Reckoning: The Untold Story of Britain's Gulag in Kenya*, Henry Holt and Company, New York 2005, p. 244.

1047 Edgerton 1989, o.c., p. 57.

1048 C. Elkins, 'Alchemy of Evidence: Mau Mau, the British Empire, and the High Court of Justice' (2011) 39 *The Journal of Imperial and Commonwealth History*, 731.

Moi (1978–2002) presidencies for their mistreatment of them. Ali Mazrui, the leading Kenyan intellectual and critic of colonialism, had foreseen at the time of independence their official rehabilitation asking whether 'the old "title of ridicule" would now be invested with honour?'.[1049] However, it was not until the election of President Mwai Kibaki and the National Alliance Rainbow Coalition (NARC) in 2002 that the Mau Mau received support for their claims for historical justice promoting the 'democratization of the past' to redeem the Mau Mau as national liberation heroes.[1050] President Kibaki rescinded the ban on Mau Mau as an illegal organization, officially memorialized the Mau Mau leader Dedan Kimathi, and supported the legal case of Mau Mau veterans for reparations in UK courts.[1051] Kibaki's embrace of the Mau Mau as national liberation heroes also served his political agenda to secure his own Kikuyu power base and to counter the influence of the popular Kikuyu Mungiki youth movement who acted as political vigilantes for his political opponents and claimed to be the heirs of Mau Mau. The veterans' claims for reparations in the UK High Court functioned as a mechanism for their political rehabilitation at home as a symbol of national unity forged in the anti-colonial struggle.[1052]

The second theme excluded from the independence narrative of national unity was *majimboism*, the idea of the devolution of government through regionalism or federalism. The tension between centralized and decentralized government has remained at the core of conflicts over constitutional reform, electoral competition, and the ethnic distribution of political power in Kenya. The erosion of *majimboism* in the third Lancaster House negotiations in 1963 signified the victory of KANU over the rival Kenyan African Democratic Union (KADU) in the constitutional struggle leading up to independence. While KADU had championed regionalism to counter the ethnic domination of the Kikuyu and Luo, KANU, under Jomo Kenyatta's leadership, had supported centralized government and national unity. The ethnic minorities also understood *majimboism* as a mechanism for historical justice through which their pre-colonial rights would be restored, especially land lost to white settlers and to other ethnic groups, in particular the dominant Kikuyu. At the end of the colonial period, the white settlers represented about 1% of the population and controlled about one third of the national income; the Asian settlers represented 2% of the population and controlled another third; while the Africans represented 97% of the population and controlled another third.[1053] Land rights and control

---

1049 A. Mazrui, 'On Heroes and Uhuru-Worship' (1963) 11 *Transition*, 24.

1050 Branch 2011, o.c., p. xiii.

1051 Anderson 2005a, o.c., p. 343.

1052 J.L. Balint, 'The "Mau Mau" Legal Hearings and Recognizing the Crimes of the British Colonial State: A Limited Constitutive Moment' (2016) 3 *Critical Analysis of Law* 261, at 271.

1053 B. van Arkadie, 'Reflections on land policy and the independence settlement in Kenya' (2016) 43 *Review of African Political Economy* 60, at 63.

over the post-independence land redistribution scheme was the major issue dividing KANU and KADU. Regionalism was also the preferred liberal agenda for the departing colonial government because they saw in it the best policy to protect privileged white settler property rights and British interests in the post-colonial state.[1054] The colonial state had deliberately reinforced the local territorialization of ethnic identities by only allowing political organization and representation at the regional and local level, not at the national level. However, as Maxon argues, white settler support for *majimboism* was concentrated in the white highlands where they imagined they could establish European control in the context of a long transition to independence.[1055] At the second Lancaster House conference (1960), a *majimboist* draft constitution which devolved significant political power to the regions favoured by KADU won out. At the time the draft was seen as a victory for the ethnic minorities, white settlers, and colonial government. The Independence Constitution (1963) preserved the *majimboist* agenda through the distribution of power between the centre and the regions and the creation of a bicameral federal legislature providing checks and balances, but it was quickly eroded by subsequent constitutional reforms pushed by Jomo Kenyatta. By the time of the first presidential elections in 1964, Kenyatta had managed to seize control under a one-party state by incorporating KADU – the pro-devolutionists – into KANU and erasing the remaining elements of regionalism by constitutional amendment in 1964. These constitutional reforms included merging the role of the President and Prime Minister as head of state and head of government, the takeover of regional legislative competencies by the central parliament, and the incorporation of the Senate, which represented the regions, into the National Assembly.[1056] Kenyatta's independence meta-narrative was the rise of Kenyan nationalism.[1057] His centralizing project emphasizing national identity and unity was designed to counter the historical impact of the colonial policies of ethnic differentiation, regionalization of administration, discriminatory labour laws, and the displacement of Kenyans from the best arable land. He opposed *majimboism* firstly, because he believed ethnic minority representation would preserve colonial influence in the independent state, and secondly, because it risked ethnic radicalization already witnessed in the Mau Mau uprising in response to the Kikuyu experience of displacement and landlessness. Kenyatta stigmatized the *majimboists* as 'tribalists' opposed to

---

1054 D.M. Anderson, "Yours in Struggle for Majimbo'. Nationalism and the Party Politics of Decolonization in Kenya, 1955–64' (2005b) 40 *Journal of Contemporary History* 547, at 553.

1055 R.M. Maxon, *Kenya's Independence Constitution: Constitution-making and End of Empire*, Fairleigh Dickinson University Press, Plymouth 2011, p. 229.

1056 C. Glinz, 'Kenya's New Constitution: a Transforming Document or Less than Meets the Eye?' (2011) 44 *Verfassung und Recht in Übersee/Law and Politics in Africa, Asia and Latin America* 60, at 62.

1057 Anderson 2005b, o.c., p. 547.

the independent new nation.[1058] Independence was 'a compromise between a decolonizing Britain and moderate nationalists at the expense of White settlers and Mau Mau militants, the immediate adversaries at the start of the Mau Mau war'.[1059]

Although the independence meta-narrative promoted national unity based on majoritarian rule, what emerged was an authoritarian one-party state that politicized ethnicity through the Kikuyu elite's monopolization of power in alliance with the Kalenjin elite. Between 1963 and 2007, politicians politicized and mobilized constituencies around their ethnic identities to defend them from a perceived attack of other groups, to contest the distribution of resources, or to consolidate the power of a dominant group.[1060] These political contests revolved around control of the postcolonial state, itself a replica of the colonial state. In practice, Jomo Kenyatta continued the colonial policy of centralization concentrating power in the presidency and producing a 'bureaucratic-executive state' which combined administrative and executive power in the postcolonial state underpinned by 'an alliance of elites'.[1061] The management of conflict through elite pacts also helped to perpetuate the authoritarian one-party state by buying off ethnic minority leaders with promises of access to KANU patronage before and after elections. Centralized government produced co-existing national and ethnic citizenships, one constructed as a legal definition and the other as a social definition of belonging.[1062] One is a 'liberal vision' and the other is a 'civic-republican vision' of citizenship. In the former, 'rights inhere in individuals, exist prior to the community, and are guaranteed with minimal obligation to the community'.[1063] In the latter, rights are not seen as 'inherent but as acquired through civic practice that upholds obligations to the community'.[1064] However, civic-republican citizenship undermines liberal citizenship when ethnic elites capture the state by mobilizing electoral support from their own ethnic constituencies. While electoral success delivers government authority over all citizens, their political obligations are limited to their own ethnic group or supporters. In other words, allegiance based on elite patronage of ethnic/tribal clients created the expectation that the fruits

1058 Anderson 2005b, o.c., p. 547.

1059 M. Mamdani, 'Mau Mau: Understanding Counter-Insurgency' (2006) 2 *Africa Review of Books* 7, at 9.

1060 R. Ajulu, *Post-Colonial Kenya: The Rise of an Authoritarian and Predatory State*, Taylor & Francis, Milton 2021, pp. 3–6.

1061 D. Branch and N. Cheeseman, 'The politics of control in Kenya: Understanding the bureaucratic-executive state, 1952–78' (2006) 33 *Review of African Political Economy* 11, at 12.

1062 S.N. Ndegwa, 'Citizenship and Ethnicity: An Examination of the Two Transition Moments in Kenyan Politics' (1997) 91 *The American Political Science Review* 599, at 601.

1063 Ibid., p. 602.

1064 Ibid., p. 602.

of electoral victory delivered benefits – or in the vernacular 'it's our turn to eat'.[1065] Elections were fiercely contested by parties with ethnic and clientelist constituencies in which the winner took all.[1066] In Kenya, the co-existence of national and ethnic citizenship preserved *majimboism* as a counter-narrative to the post-independence centralist paradigm and ethnic dominance of Kikuyu and Kalenjin in government. Both President Kenyatta and President Moi denounced 'tribalism' but in practice they governed through one-party authoritarianism and exploited ethnicity for political and economic advantage, producing weak and dysfunctional state institutions.[1067] In the 1992, 1997, 2002, and 2007 elections *majimboism* remained a constant theme as a demand by ethnic communities for greater control over resources at the local level. The emergence of multiparty elections in 1991 changed the way *majimboism* was used in an exclusionary way. The politicization of localism during elections contributed to the use of ethnic violence directed at the eviction of ethnic and political opponents from particular regions/electorates and the appropriation of their properties and land. *Majimboism* was invoked as an ethnic minority counter-narrative to the entrenchment of ethnic citizenship and ethnic elite patronage by the centralists whose nationalist discourse concealed their ethnic monopolization of government. The elite also deployed *majimboism* to shore up their local constituencies when they feared the loss of state power. These dynamics are explored further below.

The third theme omitted from the independence narrative was the Shifta rebellion pursing ethnic regionalism and secession in north Kenya. In the lead up to independence, the Regional Boundaries Commission consulted ethnic groups to identify which region they wanted to belong in the post-independence state. It resulted in the creation of an eighth region for the secessionist Somali population.[1068] For Jomo Kenyatta Somali irredentism was yet another expression of the dangers of ethnic regionalism opposed to a strong central state and national unity. The use of the term 'Shifta', like 'Mau Mau', was originally coined by British colonial officials to stigmatize lawless groups – in this case marauding bandits or cross-border cattle raiders from Ethiopia and Somalia. The Muslim 'Shifta' resisted the idea of political inclusion in a pagan government and formed the Northern Frontier Districts Liberation Army (NFDLA) to oppose it.[1069] Only weeks after the declaration of independence, the NFDLA took up

---

1065 M. Wrong, *It's Our Turn to Eat: The Story of a Kenyan Whistleblower*, Harper Perennial, London 2009, p. 52.

1066 D. Branch and N. Cheeseman, 'Democratization, sequencing, and state failure in Africa: Lessons from Kenya' (2008) 108 *African Affairs* 1, at 13.

1067 W.K. Shilaho, *Political Power and Tribalism in Kenya*, Palgrave MacMillan, London 2018, p. 51.

1068 Ndegwa 1997, o.c., p. 605.

1069 T. Scharrer, '"Ambiguous citizens": Kenyan Somalis and the question of belonging' (2018) 12 *Journal of Eastern African Studies* 494, at 498.

arms against the new state. In response, President Jomo Kenyatta declared a state of emergency and requested British military support to suppress the Shifta because he distrusted the influence of his political rivals in the new Kenyan military. In order to isolate and control the NFDLA and the Somali population, Kenyatta employed the same villagization policy as the British colonial state had used during the Emergency to control the Mau Mau and Kikuyu population.[1070] Kenyatta justified villagization of ethnic Somalis as a necessary national security response to counter the new Cold War threat of Soviet expansion in Somalia.[1071] The northern region remained under military government and emergency regulations until 1991. Since then, underdevelopment and government neglect of the northern region has only served to reinforced ethnic grievances and the status of Somalis as 'ambiguous citizens'.[1072] Civil war in Somalia in the 1980s and the UN peacekeeping intervention in the 1990s only reinforced the perception of the northern region as a zone of insecurity. In 2011, the Kenyan army along with Ugandan and Ethiopian forces, invaded southern Somalia to defeat *al-Shabaab*. The rationale of the military invasion was to enhance security in the north; to develop newly discovered oil reserves; and to police the more than 400,000 Somali refugees in the region where state control was weak.[1073] The blowback from Kenyan military intervention in Somali has been increased terrorism in Kenya, introducing a new source of ethnic and religious division especially in the North East and Coastal Provinces.[1074] The securitization of Muslims in response to terrorism has only served to further alienate Muslim communities and make some youth more receptive to *al-Shabaab's* defence of them as politically marginalized and socially oppressed.[1075]

The Kenya Independence Act 1963 established an independent sovereign state which was deliberately forward-looking and closed the door on past conflicts. Independence enacted as consensual decolonization was a top-down process based on a partnership between the British colonial state and selected nationalist elites both of whom benefited from its characterization as the product of peaceful transition legitimizing the British transfer of power to the nationalist elite and promoting the legacy of the British as benign rulers. In practice, independence did not represent a break with the centralized mode of colonial

---

1070 H. Whittaker, 'Legacies of Empire: State Violence and Collective Punishment in Kenya's North Eastern Province, *c.* 1963–Present' (2015) 43 *The Journal of Imperial and Commonwealth History* 641, at 646.

1071 D. Branch, 'Violence, decolonisation and the Cold War in Kenya's north-eastern province, 1963–1978' (2014) 8 *Journal of Eastern African Studies* 642, at 643.

1072 Scharrer 2018, o.c., p. 495.

1073 D.M. Anderson and J. McKnight, 'Kenya at War: Al-Shabaab and its Enemies in Eastern Africa' (2014) 114 *African Affairs* 1, at 25.

1074 Whittaker 2015, o.c., p. 642.

1075 Anderson and McKnight 2014, o.c., p. 26.

state governance. As Yash Pal Ghai observes, the authoritarian postcolonial state established under Kenyatta was founded on the authoritarian colonial state:

> There was no accountability of government to the people they ruled. There was virtually legal immunity for the colonial administration under the Act of State doctrine, especially in respect of liability to local people. The government was free to change the law when it suited it. Nor was the judiciary independent, since the power of appointment and dismissal rested with the governor, who, for a period, also personified legislative and executive powers – and certainly dominated these institutions until independence.[1076]

The postcolonial state was not an expression of a liberation struggle for democratic ideals but 'a counter-insurgent path towards bureaucratic authoritarianism'.[1077] President Kenyatta quickly consolidated his personal power in the centralist state immediately after independence by creating a one-party authoritarian state. Yet this top-down consolidation of the postcolonial state did not prevent the three key conflicts omitted from the independence narrative from remaining restless. Firstly, there was the legacy of internal division amongst the Kikuyu produced by the colonial counterinsurgency policy of co-option and repression; secondly, the ongoing resentment of ethnic minorities over the constitutional erasure of *majimboist* claims against the authoritarian centrist state and ethnic power; and thirdly, the prolonged and recurrent militarized governance of northeast Kenya and the stigmatization and marginalization of the ethnic Somalis.

6.2.2. CONSTITUTIONAL REFORM MOVEMENT AND DEMOCRATIZATION 1991

Between the 1991 and 2007 elections, the struggle for democratization in Kenya revolved around multiparty elections and demand for constitutional reforms. Far from subordinating ethnic identity to national identity and forging national unity, the experience of the authoritarian one-party (KANU) state increasingly politicized ethnicity as a grievance. Consequently, the centralist and authoritarian governments of President Kenyatta (1964–1978) and then President Moi (1978–2002) became the focus of growing demands for constitutional reform of the colonial era Lancaster House Constitution (1963) to democratize politics and create a more inclusive society. These demands for constitutional reform were articulated either as minority rights by ethnic leaders or as human rights by

---

1076 Y.P. Ghai, 'Constitutions and constitutionalism: the fate of the 2010 constitution' in G.R. Murunga, et al. (eds.), *Kenya: The Struggle for a New Constitutional Order*, Zed Books, London 2014, p. 119, at p. 121.

1077 Branch 2009, o.c., p. 97.

civil society organizations (CSOs). Political elites sought to strengthen minority rights to consolidate their ethnic political constituencies while CSOs sought to strengthen individual rights, democratize politics, expand citizenship rights and challenge impunity through radical constitutional reform. The most urgent demand by the opposition parties and CSOs was for constitutional reform to allow multiparty elections to break KANU's monopoly control of political power. Their demands coincided with the end of the Cold War and global political liberalization. Faced with pressure from Western aid donors making funds conditional on political liberalization and growing internal dissent over authoritarian one-party rule, President Moi introduced constitutional amendments to allow multiparty elections in the 1991 elections.[1078] He repealed Section 2(A) of the 1963 Kenyan constitution which legalized the formation of political parties and introduced a new era of competitive electoral politics.

President Daniel arap Moi, Kenyatta's successor from the minority Kalenjin ethnicity, immediately set about countering the threat of multiparty electoral politics to KANU's monopoly of power by pursuing a policy of ethnic mobilization under the rhetoric of *majimboism*. Paradoxically both the supporters and opponents of multiparty elections were ethnically motivated but for different reasons. The former advocated ethnic representation based on demography allowing the largest ethnic groups to dominate majoritarian politics, while the latter advocated ethnic representation based on territory favouring the geographical ethnic concentrations. In the 1990s, *majimboism* ceased to be a policy of regionalism and became a discourse used by pro-establishment tribes/ethnicities to claim the status of 'native' or 'indigenous' landowners of the Rift Valley and brand the pro-opposition, the multiparty supporters, as an 'alien' and 'foreign' presence. The Akiwumi Report, the 'Report of the Judicial Commission Appointed to Inquire into Tribal Clashes in Kenya 1998', describes *majimboism* as 'an arrangement in which each community would be required to return to its ancestral district or province and if for any reason they would be reluctant or unwilling to do so, they would by all means be forced to do so'.[1079] Moi advocated *majimboism* to consolidate his Kalenjin ethnic homelands by discriminating against the rights of ethnic outsiders, especially their access to land and their local registration to vote on electoral rolls. The expression '*madoadoa* (spots) and *kwekwe* (blemishes)' referred to the idea of the 'contamination' of ancestral lands of the Kalenjin and Maasai in the Rift Valley region by migrant ethnic groups,

1078 S. Brown, 'Authoritarian leaders and multiparty elections in Africa: How foreign donors help to keep Kenya's Daniel arap Moi in power' (2001) 22 *Third World Quarterly* 725, at 726.

1079 The Akiwumi Report was the Report of the Commission of Inquiry into Tribal Clashes appointed on July 1, 1998. Its mandate was to investigate the causes of tribal clashes that had occurred in different parts of Kenya between 1991–98. The Judicial Commission of Inquiry was composed of judges.

especially Kikuyu.[1080] President Moi had begun disenfranchising his opponents to consolidate his Kalejin ethnic base in 1985 when he enacted a constitutional amendment to remove rights to citizenship based on birth and replace it with a purely descent based system with retroactive effect to the date of independence.[1081] He also promoted state informalization by deinstitutionalizing the state's control over violence, covertly deploying ethnic militias, which allowed the government plausible deniability, to coerce and displace populations considered outsiders to consolidate Kalenjin ethnic hegemony.[1082] In multi-ethnic areas the land issue was used to politically mobilize against multipartyism.[1083] The economy of violence linked criminal and political actors to produce a shadow state. The case of the Mungiki youth movement, predominantly poor Kikuyu, highlights the complex intersection between religious cult, violent criminal gang, political enforcers and radical political movement that identified with a rebirth of the Mau Mau and their struggle for 'land and freedom' in political competition.[1084] In the 1990s, the Mungiki recruited extensively from the large number of Kikuyu IDPs in the central Rift Valley by promising followers they would reclaim their 'forefathers' land from the Kikuyu political and landed elite and redistribute it to them.[1085] Moi transformed *majimboism* into a policy of ethnic cleansing for voter suppression.[1086]

The opposition parties and CSOs had hoped that multiparty elections would help dislodge KANU from monopolizing government, but KANU won the 1992 and then the 1997 elections. The opposition parties lost because they lacked the unity needed to defeat KANU, on the one hand, and KANU was able to preserve its dominance over government by using both co-option and repression of opposition parties and CSOs. Post-1991, President Moi was able to co-opt minority leaders through pacts which granted them a share in the benefits of power.[1087] As Muhula and Ndegwa point out, elite pacts 'tend to reduce competitiveness as well as conflict; they seek to limit accountability to wider publics; they attempt to control the agenda of policy concerns; and they deliberately distort the principle of citizen equality'.[1088] In Kenya, political elites preferred pact-making rather than risk the violent rupture of the status

1080 Ndegwa 1997, o.c., p. 610.

1081 B. Manby, *Citizenship in Africa: The Law of Belonging*, Bloomsbury Publishing, London 2018, p. 182.

1082 Branch and Cheeseman 2008, o.c., p. 13.

1083 P.M. Kamungi, 'The politics of displacement in multiparty Kenya' (2009) 27 *Journal of Contemporary African Studies* 345, at 348.

1084 D.M. Anderson, 'Vigilantes, violence and the politics of public order in Kenya' (2002) 101 *African Affairs* 531, at 535.

1085 Kamungi 2009, o.c., p. 348.

1086 Shilaho 2018, o.c., p. 99.

1087 Muhula and Ndegwa 2014, o.c., p. 79.

1088 Muhula and Ndegwa 2014, o.c., p. 81.

quo that might 'threaten a break-up of their collective privilege'.[1089] Because the Kenyan state remains the 'primary source of power and wealth in society' acquiring and retaining government has been the main driver of elite political competition and corruption.[1090] The introduction of multiparty elections was not enough by itself to bring about democratic transformation. In 1997, a growing mass movement for constitutional reform led by the National Convention Executive Council (NCEC) resulted in civil disobedience and mass demonstrations to get the government to commit to major constitutional reforms under the slogan 'No reforms, No elections'.[1091] From their perspective, the 1991 electoral reforms had only benefited the political elites and neglected the major issues around inequalities in land distribution and tenure, security, employment and education.[1092] In response, the government denounced the NCEC as 'a lawless organization bent on violence' and entered into another pact, the so-called Inter-Parties Parliamentary Group agreement, to take the agenda for constitutional reform away from the CSOs and allow the 1997 elections to proceed.[1093] Parliament finally enacted the Constitution of Kenya Review Act in 1999, establishing the Constitution of Kenya Review Commission (CKRC), which was to survey Kenyans on their views and make recommendations to parliament. This was followed up by the Constitution of Kenya Review Act of 2000 to formally institute a process to write a new constitution.

6.2.3. KIBAKI AND THE PROMISE OF REFORM

In 2002, Mwai Kibaki and the National Rainbow Coalition (NARC), with the support of the CSOs, defeated the Moi backed KANU candidate, Uhuru Kenyatta, the son of the founding president Jomo Kenyatta. The outcome brought the promise of the major constitutional reform the NARC had campaigned on. The level of violence had been greatly reduced because the defeat of the KANU candidate, Uhuru Kenyatta, was widely anticipated by the political leaders who pragmatically gambled on Kabiki not to investigate abuses of power committed during the Moi presidency and to be open to new alliances/pacts to their benefit. Once in government, the NARC electoral pact between Mwai Kibaki and Raila Odinga quickly broke down when Kibaki failed to deliver on the agreed ethnic

1089 Muhula and Ndegwa 2014, o.c., p. 82.

1090 Ghai 2014, o.c., at p. 127.

1091 W.S. Nasong'o, 'Revisiting 'the two faces of civil society' in constitutional reform in Kenya' in G.R. Murunga, et al. (eds.), *Kenya: The Struggle for a New Constitutional Order*, Zed Books, London 2014, p. 97, at p. 102.

1092 J.M. Mati, 'Antinomies in the struggle for the transformation of the Kenyan constitution (1990–2010)' (2013) 31 *Journal of Contemporary African Studies* 235, at 239.

1093 Nasong'o 2014, o.c., p. 104.

distribution of ministerial posts and the promise to appoint Odinga to the position of prime minister. In office, Kibaki expanded civil liberties and political freedoms but also launched a sustained attack on CSOs like the KHRC. He did not fulfil his promise to act on the Akiwumi Report and attempt to hold President Daniel arap Moi accountable for the electoral violence in 1998.[1094] The breakdown of the Kibaki and Odinga election pact manifested itself in the growing internal division over the proposed 2005 referendum on a draft Constitution. Although the initial Bomas draft of the Constitution included the provision for an executive prime minister to be head of government, the revised Wako draft submitted to referendum only provided for a prime minister who would be appointed by the president, be accountable to him, and merely be leader of government business in the house.[1095] Kibaki undermined the role of CSOs in the citizen-led campaign for constitutional reform by firstly, recruiting a significant number of 'seasoned CSO leaders' into the ranks of the new government; secondly, adopting a human rights discourse and social justice programmes previously championed by the CSOs; and thirdly, by preventing them playing a watchdog role after they had been recruited to support the NARC in the 2002.[1096] The Banana and Orange factions, the electoral symbols used in the referendum 'for' and 'against' the draft Constitution (2005) respectively, established the polarized lines of ethnic competition along which the 2007 election was subsequently contested. Kibaki mobilized the Kikuyu community in his support while Odinga sought the support of the Luo and the other ethnic minorities. The 2005 referendum campaign polarized society along ethnic lines and shaped the intense contest between Odinga's Orange Democratic Movement (ODM) and Kibaki's Party of National Unity (PNU) for government and the presidency in the 2007 election. To shore up his support in the cosmopolitan Rift Valley province, Raila Odinga promised the new constitution would guarantee the devolution of financial resources and governance structures to support regional development. It was here in the Rift Valley where violence erupted after the announcement of the 2007 election results for the parliament and the presidency. The Electoral Commission of Kenya (ECK) determined that ODM gained the largest number of parliamentary seats but Kibaki defeated Odinga 46% to 44% to win the presidency.

The period of the First Republic (1963–2007) was characterized by a struggle between political elites who had increasingly ethnicized electoral politics to consolidate their ethnic constituencies and retain the centralized state as their primary source of patronage even after the introduction of multiparty politics.

1094 J.-C. Servant, No Safe Haven in Kenya, *Le Monde Diplomatique*, February 2008, http://mondediplo.com/2008/02/06kenya.

1095 Muhula and Ndegwa 2014, o.c., p. 82.

1096 Nasong'o 2014, o.c., p. 106.

The opposition parties and CSOs had put their faith in the constitutional reform of the colonial era Constitution to dismantle the authoritarian one-party state through the decentralization of power and introduction of multiparty elections. However, elite pactism was able to limit demands for constitutional reform by manipulating the interest of minority ethnic leaders to gain access to patronage and preserve the ethnic clientelist system that underpinned their electoral base. Between 1963 and 2002, ethnic pactism preserved the status quo through political agreements associated with deal-making during elections which were institutionalized in Constitutional amendments.[1097] Hence, KANU was able to preserve its dominance even after the introduction of multiparty elections in 1991 through pacts with minority ethnic leaders for the benefits of state patronage for their ethnic minority supporters. The ethnic polarization of politics that created the conditions for the post-election violence in 2007 grew out of the breakdown of the pact between Kibaki and Odinga. In the 2007 election, Raila Odinga's ODM advocated for *majimboism* aimed at strengthening ethnically based regionalism and the devolution of political authority and resources to the local level.[1098] Different regions were promised benefits addressing their particular historical grievances and demands which they saw as a local righting of historical wrongs. The ODM campaign intensified its regional strategy to counter what was perceived as a plot by President Kibaki to entrench Kikuyu and Kalenjin dominance in power by promising dynastic succession to the sons of Kenyatta and Moi, the first two presidents, in the next election in 2012.[1099] The persistence of the *majimboism* counter-narrative in fact highlighted the priority of ethnic over national citizenship in Kenya despite the centralist's assertion of national unity and identity.

6.3. POST-ELECTION VIOLENCE AND INTERNATIONAL INTERVENTION 2007–2008

6.3.1. ROUTINIZATION OF ELECTORAL VIOLENCE

The post-election violence that triggered international intervention in 2008 was not a new phenomenon in the Kenyan electoral cycle. After the introduction of multiparty elections in 1991, political violence became a routinized feature

---

1097 P.T. Zeleza, 'The protracted transition to the Second Republic in Kenya' in G.R. Murunga, et al. (eds.), *Kenya: The Struggle for a New Constitutional Order*, Zed Books, London 2014, p. 17.

1098 J. MacArthur, 'How the West was Won: Regional Politics and Prophetic Promises in the 2007 Kenya Elections' (2008) 2 *Journal of Eastern African Studies* 227, at 228.

1099 Ibid., p. 234.

of electoral competition making it 'acceptable, dismissible, and forgettable'.[1100] Klopp characterizes governance through routinized violence at the local level as 'decentralized despotism', the way the ruling elite was able to benefit from localized ethnic clashes to secure their hold on power.[1101] For example, cattle stealing funded elections campaigns and outsiders were displaced to grab their land and property to give to supporters for the electoral benefit of the political elite.[1102] In the 1990s, President Moi used the discourse of *majimbo* to deploy violence along ethnic lines to intimidate the opposition, suppress the vote, and create homogeneous 'KANU zones'. To counter the threat that political liberalization represented to his hold on the presidency, Moi employed ethnic cleansing.[1103] In 1992, pre-election ethnic violence targeting opposition parties killed 1,500 people and expelled 300,000 from their homes. Moi also suppressed the vote by preventing between 500,000 and 3,000,000 voters receiving registration cards in the 1992 and 1997 elections.[1104] While the Moi government instituted official inquiries into the 'tribal clashes' during the 1992 election violence (Kiliku Report) and the 1998 election violence (Akiwumi Report), neither Report led to prosecutions even though both Reports identified individuals to be investigated.[1105] The Moi government's inaction on these Reports merely underlined the culture of impunity which allowed political leaders and parties to deploy violence for their electoral benefit without fear of sanctions.[1106]

When KANU lost power to Mwai Kibaki and the NARC alliance in the 2002, it was expected that Kibaki would fulfil his election promises to introduce transitional justice measures to prosecute those named in the Akiwumi Report (1999) and to establish a truth commission. Instead, Kibaki demonstrated his political pragmatism by avoiding the question of accountability for past electoral violence. He ignored the Akiwumi Report recommendations for prosecution in part because the NARC coalition itself included KANU defectors who had been mentioned in the Report. Kibaki established a taskforce to explore public support for a truth commission and, despite its strong recommendation, he shelved the

1100 B. Straight, 'Making Sense of Violence in the "Badlands" of Kenya' (2009) 34 *Anthropology and Humanism* 21, at 26.

1101 J.M. Klopp, '"Ethnic clashes" and Winning Elections: The Case of Kenya's Electoral Despotism' (2001) 35 *Canadian Journal of African Studies* 473, at 475.

1102 Straight 2009, o.c., p. 27.

1103 Branch and Cheeseman 2008, o.c., p. 14.

1104 Brown 2001, o.c., p. 727.

1105 The Kiliku Report refers to The Report by the Parliamentary Select Committee to Investigate Ethnic Clashes in Western and other parts of Kenya, National Assembly, Kenya, 1992. See also '*Lest We Forget: The Faces of Impunity in Kenya*', Kenyan Human Rights Commission, Nairobi, 2011.

1106 M. Mutua, 'Justice under Siege: The Rule of Law and Judicial Subservience in Kenya' (2001) 23 *Human Rights Quarterly*, 96.

plans for it. The breakdown of the pact between Kibaki and Odingo over power-sharing contributed to deepening the ethnic polarization of politics played out in the referendum for the new Constitution (2005) and the growth in the use of party militias to control votes in their districts.[1107] The largescale post-election violence in 2008 was the culmination of the ethnicized struggle between the Party of National Unity (PNU) and the Orange Democratic Movement (ODM) to capture Kenya's highly centralized state. Odinga accused Kibaki (PNU) of manipulating the election results to stay in power.[1108] In response to the election outcome, ODM supporters launched violent protests and attacked members of the Kikuyu ethnic group and their property. This initial more spontaneous violence was followed by more systematic violence in January 2008 when elites opportunistically exploited the dissent over the election to attack rivals. Raila Odinga (ODM) used Kalenjin militias to systematically kill and displace non-Kalenjin communities in the Rift Valley. Members of the Kikuyu community organized retaliatory attacks against Kalenjin and Luo communities in the Rift Valley.[1109]

6.3.2. THE KRIEGLER COMMISSION AND WAKI COMMISSION

The 2007 post-election violence became a political turning point because, unlike previous instances of post-election violence, it led to international diplomatic intervention to halt the ethnic violence and introduce transitional justice measures to bring an end to these cycles of election violence. Even though the casualties and displaced people – over 1,300 killed, 663,921 displaced and 12,000 refugees[1110] – were relatively small when compared with the scale of ethnic cleansing in the Balkans or genocide in Rwanda, the event was nevertheless seen by the UN as a crisis which justified R2P intervention.[1111] The 'post-Rwanda genocide' sensitivity to state sponsored ethnic violence in Africa engendered considerable international concern about the Kenyan state unravelling. After intense international diplomatic negotiations, the African Union appointed a

---

1107 H. Maupeu, 'Revisiting Post-Election Violence' (2008) 38 *Les Cahiers d'Afrique de l'Est/The East African Review* 193, at 201.

1108 The integrity of the elections results was questioned by international observers from the EU, Commonwealth and East African Community. See Nichols 2015, o.c., p. 49.

1109 Nichols 2015, o.c., p. 50.

1110 Kamungi 2009, o.c., p. 345.

1111 Intervention was justified on humanitarian grounds. Through international mediation by the African Union Panel of Eminent Personalities led by Kofi Annan, the former UNSG, supported by the UN, neighbouring states, donors, and civil society the resolution of the crisis was claimed in the name of R2P. N. Crossley, 'A Model Case of R2P Prevention? Mediation in the Aftermath of Kenya's 2007 Presidential Elections' (2013) 5 *Global Responsibility to Protect* 192, at 195.

Panel of Eminent Personalities headed by former UN Secretary General Kofi Annan to mediate talks between the PNU (Kibaki) and ODM (Odinga).[1112] What became known as the National Dialogue and Reconciliation Process agreed on a four point agenda: 1.) end the violence and restore fundamental rights and liberties; 2.) address the humanitarian crisis and promote reconciliation, healing and restoration; 3.) overcome the political crisis through negotiations; 4.) work on long-term strategies to establish a durable peace.[1113] The violence was officially ended with the signing of a National Accord and Reconciliation Act between Mwai Kibaki and Raila Odinga on February 28, 2008, which established a Government of National Unity (GNU) and introduced transitional justice measures to promote reconciliation, restoration and combat impunity. It constituted a defensive elite pact between party leaders forged in response to international intervention in Kenya's internal affairs. The agreement led to the establishment of two non-judicial commissions of inquiry, one into the electoral process – the Independent Review Committee also known as the Kriegler Commission – and the other into the cause of the post-election violence – the Commission of Inquiry into Post-Election Violence (CIPEV) also known as the Waki Commission.[1114] A non-judicial Truth, Justice and Reconciliation Commission (TJRC) was also established. To ensure that the Kenyan government established these commissions they were jointly funded by the Government of Kenya and the multi-donor Trust Fund for Kenyan National Dialogue and Reconciliation managed by the United Nations Development Programme (UNDP).[1115] The logic of the Waki Report was that justice would follow from the National Accord embodied in the post-conflict government of national unity which included the main protagonists. It was hoped that the government of national unity would take responsibility for the investigation and prosecution of those responsible for the election violence, would establish a truth commission to find out what had happened, who was responsible, and who were the victims, and it would initiate a constitutional reform process.

The Waki Commission investigation into the causes of the post-election violence provided a scathing indictment of the prevailing culture of impunity and

1112 The OHCHR deployed a 'Fact-Finding Mission to Kenya' to investigate the violence and alleged grave human rights violations. It recommended the creation of a special prosecutorial body and a truth commission. Report from OHCHR Fact-Finding Mission to Kenya between 6–28 February 2008, OHCHR February 28, 2008, https://www.ohchr.org/sites/default/files/Documents/Press/OHCHRKenyareport.pdf.

1113 Kenyan National Dialogue and Reconciliation, 'Annotated Agenda and Timetable', February 1, 2008.

1114 *Revised Kriegler and Waki Commission Reports*, Dialogue Africa Foundation 2009, https://www.kas.de/c/document_library/get_file?uuid=d8aa1729-8a9e-7226-acee-8193fd67a21a&groupId=252038.

1115 *Commission of Inquiry into Post-Election Violence (CIPEV) (Waki Report)*, The Government of Kenya, Nairobi, 2008, p. 1, http://www.kenyalaw.org/Downloads/Reports/Commission_of_Inquiry_into_Post_Election_Violence.pdf.

endemic political violence in Kenya. It characterized the post-election violence as the product of the ethnicization of politics and the chronic impunity of the political elite. The Report attributed the election violence to the intensification of electoral competition arising from the introduction of multiparty elections; the increasing concentration of power in the hands of the executive-president; the marginalization of ethnic minorities from power; and the institutionalization of electoral violence using youth gangs, themselves marginalized by chronic unemployment. It found that the violence had been planned by politicians and businessmen and identified the perpetrators as overwhelmingly state agencies and political gangs, not civilians.[1116] The Report approached electoral violence as a criminal justice matter stipulating that parliament establish a Special Tribunal to investigate and prosecute the ethnic leaders it had identified as most responsible.[1117] The Special Tribunal was to conduct an event-specific investigation of persons responsible for serious crimes between December 27, 2007 and February 28, 2008.[1118] However, because of the previous poor record of Kenyan governments failing to implement the recommendations of previous official investigations into human rights violations, the Waki Report included an innovative time trigger of 60 days after the Report being made public to escalate criminal investigations to the ICC if the Kenyan government failed to establish a Special Tribunal.[1119] As anticipated, the national accountability agenda of the Waki Report was resisted by both the political elite and civil society organizations, but for very different reasons. The political elite resisted accountability in a national tribunal to protect themselves from investigation; the CSOs resisted national accountability because of their longstanding distrust of the national courts to deliver justice. Consequently, the CSOs prioritized international justice at the ICC over a national Special Tribunal.[1120] In fact the national accountability and reform programme of the Waki Report represented a radical challenge to the political elite's impunity and their control over the judiciary and police.[1121] It quickly became apparent that the political elite would resist the creation of the Special Tribunal after legislation to establish it was blocked three times by parliament between 2008 and December 2009, well beyond the Report's stipulated 60 days before the referral of the sealed names

1116 Ibid., p. 5.

1117 *Securing Justice – Establishing a domestic mechanism for the 2007/8 post-election violence in Kenya*, Kenyans for Peace with Truth and Justice, https://kptj.africog.org/securing-justice-establishing-a-domestic-mechanism-for-the-2007-8-post-election-violence-in-kenya/.

1118 G.M. Musila, 'Options for Transitional Justice in Kenya: Autonomy and the Challenge of External Prescriptions' (2009) 3 *The International Journal of Transitional Justice* 445, at 454.

1119 S. Brown and C.L. Sriram, 'The Big Fish Won't Fry Themselves: Criminal Accountability for Post-Election Violence in Kenya' (2012) 111 *African Affairs* 244, at 258.

1120 Mutua 2001, o.c., p. 107.

1121 C. Bjork and J. Goebertus, 'Complementarity in Action: The Role of Civil Society and the ICC in the Rule of Law Strengthening in Kenya' (2011) 14 *Yale Human Rights and Development Law Journal* 205, at 214.

for potential prosecution to the OTP. The measures recommended by the Waki Report confronted the political reality that justice was not possible in national courts without a real political transition enacted through radical constitutional reform. The National Accord and government of national unity turned out to be obstacles to justice because they preserved the power of the political elite to resist accountability and law reform.

The CSOs supported the Waki Report's justice and reform agenda but prioritized international prosecutions over national prosecutions as the best way to challenge impunity. On the release of the Waki Report in February 2008, the CSOs immediately lobbied the ICC to open an investigation into high profile politicians through the 'preliminary examination' powers of the Office of the Prosecutor (OTP).[1122] The 'preliminary examination' powers under Article 15 of the Rome Statute allow the OTP to initiate investigations with the aim of pressuring national courts to investigate international crimes themselves – i.e. 'positive complementarity'.[1123] One of the objectives of Article 15 is to strengthen domestic legal institutions to consolidate the rule of law. In the Kenyan case, the OTP, Luis Moreno-Ocampo, had proposed a 'three-pronged strategy' which included two domestic mechanisms – a truth commission and special tribunal – as well as the ICC investigations.[1124] However, Kenyan CSOs approached the 'preliminary examination' powers not to ensure national investigations but to promote international investigations and prosecutions by the ICC. To achieve their goal, they set out to demonstrate that the Kenyan government was '"unwilling or unable" to prosecute crimes domestically'.[1125] The CSOs, already largely alienated from the state, developed a counter-narrative about legitimacy of the ICC over national courts.[1126] They juxtaposed the international justice embodied in the ICC as transparent and legitimate with national courts as corrupt and politicized. The Kenyan CSOs became a *de facto* outreach arm of the ICC by educating communities about the Court and the legitimacy of prosecution cases even before the OTP had initiated preliminary investigations. Other CSOs helped communities 'create and accept a collective narrative around the fact that the post-election violence implicated perpetrators and victims of all ethnicities in Kenya, and therefore, that those held responsible will (and must) come from all ethnicities'.[1127] By building up the legitimacy of the ICC the CSOs were able to advance their causes and leverage ICC attention. For some, the ICC became an important vehicle for renewal of the whole political system because

---

1122 Ibid., p. 205.

1123 Nichols 2015, o.c., p. 79.

1124 C. L. Sriram and S. Brown, 'Kenya in the Shadow of the ICC: Complementarity, Gravity and Impact' (2012) 12 *International Criminal Law Review* 219, at 211.

1125 Bjork and Goebertus 2011, o.c., p. 205.

1126 Bjork and Goebertus 2011, o.c., p. 216.

1127 Bjork and Goebertus 2011, o.c., p. 227.

they believed successful ICC prosecutions would remove the old political elite from power. Others supported ICC prosecutions because their profile and impact would be much greater at home than domestic prosecutions.[1128] The CSOs success in establishing the superior legitimacy of international over national justice eventually burdened the ICC with the expectation that it could solve social injustice in general including the 'lack of water, lack of food, lack of housing, corruption in the political class and lack of political accountability'.[1129] Nichols argues that the enhanced public status of the ICC and reliance on its prosecutions to bring justice had the negative effect of devaluing local courts even further.[1130]

6.3.3. ACCOUNTABILITY: NATIONAL OR INTERNATIONAL?

It quickly became apparent that the fulfilment of the NDR four agenda items would be conditional on the support of the political elite. The electoral protagonists, Kibaki and Odinga, established a government of national unity which brought an end to the violence. Parliament passed the Constitution Review Act (2008) which sought to shield Constitutional reform from political maneuvering inside the parliament by requiring a two-thirds vote to make any constitutional change. Then the two leaders, Kibaki and Odinga, who had been on opposite sides in the 2005 constitutional referendum, now both supported the 2010 constitutional referendum.[1131] Muhula and Ndegwa point out that despite the rhetoric of a 'people-driven' constitutional process, the 2010 constitution was essentially an elite compact.[1132] The new constitution was supposed to end the 'winner takes all' electoral system which had helped fuel the electoral violence. However, the final draft of the constitution that went to referendum, and was approved by two thirds of voters, provided only limited devolution of government and the power of the president. The continuation of politics as usual based on elite pacts was most evident in the failure of the parliament to establish the Special Tribunal stipulated by the Waki Commission. The two pieces of required legislation, the Special Tribunal for Kenya Bill 2009, which set out its structure and jurisdiction, and the Constitutional amendment Bill, designed to ensure its constitutionality and insulate it from the local courts, were not passed. The vote was either procrastinated or sabotaged, including parliamentary boycotts, to prevent a quorum.[1133] The attitude of the political elite towards the prospect

---

1128 Bjork and Goebertus 2011, o.c., p. 224.
1129 Bjork and Goebertus 2011, o.c., p. 226.
1130 Nichols 2015, o.c., p. 244.
1131 Muhula and Ndegwa 2014, o.c., p. 89.
1132 Muhula and Ndegwa 2014, o.c., p. 82.
1133 Sixty CSOs sent open letter to Kibaki condemning the Cabinet decision. See Nichols 2015, o.c., p. 75.

of accountability at the ICC was revealed at the international signing ceremony for the new Constitution on August 4, 2010. The government invited President Omar al-Bashir to attend the international ceremony but did not execute an ICC warrant for his arrest.[1134] While the Kenyan political elite constantly assured international observers they would hold both low and high level offenders to account, there was little progress. By January 2012, official figures show that of 'the 8,869 reported post-election violence cases, just 258 resulted in a conviction' representing around 3% of cases.[1135] This low level of national prosecutions occurred despite the pressure exerted by the OTP over a period of two years to initiate prosecutions.[1136]

6.3.4. ICC INTERVENTION

After the Kenyan parliament failed to establish the Special Tribunal as required by the Waki Commission, the Pre-Trial Chamber II authorized the OTP, on March 31, 2010, to initiate investigations into the 2007 post-election violence.[1137] In December 2010, the OTP presented two cases against six individuals for trial: William Samoei Ruto, Henry Kiprono Kosgey, Joshua arap Sang, Francis Kirimi Muthaura, Uhuru Muigai Kenyatta and Mohammed Hussein Ali for crimes against humanity.[1138] These ICC indictments were divided equally between Kikuyu and Kalenjin ethnic groups, the main protagonists in the conflict. The political impact of the ICC's intervention was to help break the 'business as usual' model bringing the end of the 'First Republic'.[1139] But far from stigmatizing and politically marginalizing these antagonistic and indicted political leaders, they joined forces and mobilized against the ICC with the aim of discrediting the Court by denouncing its legal intervention as a neo-colonial exercise transgressing Kenyan sovereignty.[1140] The indicted leaders set out to delegitimize the ICC, firstly, by launching an international diplomatic campaign against the ICC with the support of the African Union; secondly, by forming an electoral alliance forged out of their opposition to the Court as neo-colonial; thirdly, by stigmatizing CSOs working with the Court as the enemy, and fourthly, by undermining the ICC prosecution of cases.

1134 S. Kendall, '"UhuRuto" and Other Leviathans: The International Criminal Court and the Kenyan Political Order' (2014) 7 *African Journal of Legal Studies* 399, at 413.

1135 Nichols 2015, o.c., p. 98.

1136 Nichols 2015, o.c., p. 102.

1137 'ICC judges grant the Prosecutor's request to launch an investigation on crimes against humanity with regard to the situation in Kenya', International Criminal Court, March 31, 2010, ICC-CPI-20100331-PR512.

1138 Nichols 2015, o.c., p. 83.

1139 Branch 2011, o.c., p. 288.

1140 G. Lynch, 'Electing the 'alliance of the accused': the success of the Jubilee Alliance in Kenya's Rift Valley' (2014) 8 *Journal of Eastern African Studies* 93, at 106.

Firstly, the political elite sought to delegitimize the ICC by challenging its jurisdiction and demanding the repatriation of the prosecutions. They used the African Union (AU) to represent their case at the UN Security Council moving a motion under Article 16 to defer the ICC proceedings.[1141] The Kenyan parliament also passed a non-binding motion calling for Kenya's withdrawal from the Rome Statute. In support of Kenya's criticisms of the Court the AU denounced the ICC as politicized by pointing to the fact that the Court had only, up to that time, intervened to prosecute African leaders.[1142] Geoffrey Lugano refers to this strategy as the politics of counter-shaming through the mobilization of national and regional support.[1143] The political elite's claim that national courts could effectively prosecute those responsible for the post-election violence ignored the fact that the Waki Report had recommended a Special Tribunal be established precisely because of concerns about the lack of independence of the judiciary. Moreover, the repatriation of prosecutions only risked perpetuating impunity because the Kenyan Directorate of Public had prosecuted very few cases relating to the 2007 electoral violence with thousands of cases stalled by lack of evidence or reliable witnesses.[1144]

Secondly, the key indictees and protagonists, Uhuru Kenyatta (The National Alliance) and William Ruto (United Republican Party), joined together to form the 'Jubilee Alliance' for the 2012 election to campaign against the Court's legitimacy. 'Uhuruto', as the election alliance was referred to in campaigning, represented the renewal of an old KANU alliance between the Kikuyu and the Kalenjin – Uhuru Kenyatta was the son of President Jomo Kenyatta and Raila Ruto was a fixer for President Moi.[1145] The leaders represented themselves as victims of ICC persecution and claimed a vote for them was a vote against the ICC. They portrayed their coalition – the Jubilee Alliance – as a 'party of reconciliation' while their opponents, those supporting the ICC prosecutions, were stigmatized as a 'party of vengeance'.[1146] They sought to deepen ethnic divides by suggesting that the Luo, in cooperating with the OTP, had been responsible for taking them to the ICC.[1147] The election-winning Jubilee Alliance framed ICC justice as 'a performance of injustice, neo-colonialism and a threat to the country's sovereignty, peace and stability'.[1148] After all, they asserted, the

---

1141 Nichols 2015, o.c., p. 159.

1142 Kendall 2014, o.c., p. 417.

1143 G. Lugano, 'Counter-Shaming the International Criminal Court's Intervention as Neocolonial: Lessons from Kenya' (2017) 11 *International Journal of Transitional Justice*, 9.

1144 Perceptions and Realities: Kenya and the International Criminal Court, *Human Rights Watch*, November 13, 2014, https://www.hrw.org/news/2013/11/14/perceptions-and-realities-kenya-and-international-criminal-court.

1145 R. Ajulu, *Post-Colonial Kenya: The Rise of an Authoritarian and Predatory State*, Taylor & Francis, Milton 2021, p. 181.

1146 Kendall 2014, o.c., p. 410.

1147 G. Lynch 2014, o.c., p. 106.

1148 G. Lynch 2014, o.c., p. 95.

electoral alliance between key protagonists was itself evidence of reconciliation. Their supporters were readily mobilized and unified against the Court because they saw the violence as a tribal war in which their leaders had protected them, and they were proud of them for doing it.[1149]

Thirdly, the Jubilee Alliance also sought to discredit CSOs as opponents of the state serving to deepen the rift between them.[1150] Some of President Uhuru Kenyatta's senior aides referred to civil society as 'evil society'.[1151] The Alliance set out to stigmatize the CSOs involvement with the ICC as a threat to the national sovereignty and accused them of being 'unelected' agents of 'foreign interests or powers' and simply interested in money.[1152] It targeted CSOs supporting the ICC's outreach work and helping with the identification of potential victim participants, especially CSOs in the Kenyans for Peace, Truth and Justice coalition.[1153] The anti-CSO stance by President Uhuru Kenyatta reflects an historically antagonistic relationship between the state and civil society groups dating back to independence. Human rights CSOs had been in the vanguard of social movements demanding multiparty elections and major constitutional reform. From 2009, the Civil Society Organizations Reference Group, an umbrella CSO organization, lobbied for major reform of the CSO sector which resulted in the Public Benefit Organization Act in 2012. The aim of this legislation was to provide a new regulatory framework and improve the relationship between the state and civil society. However, the arrival of the Jubilee Alliance in power in 2013 delayed the implementation of the law until 2016. During those three and a half years President Uhuru Kenyatta took the opportunity to restrict further the civic space in which CSOs could operate. In 2014, the NGOs Coordination Board closed hundreds of CSOs on the grounds of non-compliance. National security was also used to justify even greater control over CSOs in the context of *al-Shabab* terrorist attacks. Hence, in 2015, the government froze the accounts of Muslim human rights organization – Muslims for Human Rights (Muhuri) and Haki-Africa – alleging they were funding terrorist activities but Supreme Court reversed the decision finding they had no case to answer.[1154] When the Public Benefits Organizations (PBO) Act was finally implemented, it did not improve relations between the state and the CSOs but was instead used against them. The Act restricted foreign funding to 15%, undermined self-regulation, imposed

1149 J. Verini, The Prosecutor and the President, *The New York Times Magazine*, June 22, 2016, https://www.nytimes.com/2016/06/26/magazine/international-criminal-court-moreno-ocampo-the-prosecutor-and-the-president.html.

1150 Kendall 2014, o.c., p. 405.

1151 L. Madowo, 'Kenya is sliding into a dictatorship', *The Washington Post*, February 7, 2018, https://www.washingtonpost.com/news/global-opinions/wp/2018/02/07/kenya-is-sliding-into-a-dictatorship/?noredirect=on.

1152 Kendall 2014, o.c., p. 420.

1153 Kendall 2014, o.c., p. 421.

1154 N. Kabeberi, 'The role of the state in shrinking political spaces for CSOs in Kenya' (2016) 3 *Perspectives Africa: Political Analysis and Commentary*, 28.

excessive national executive regulations on the CSOs and led to an increasing number of CSO de-registrations. Their de-registration has increasingly been justified on national security and counter-terrorism grounds.[1155] The 2017 elections also saw the government act against civil society groups involved in campaigning and election monitoring, especially after the Supreme Court annulled the presidential election result. In response, President Uhuru Kenyatta tried to shut down through de-registration the activities of some high profile CSOs – the Africa Centre for Open Governance (AfriCOG), the International Development Law Organization (IDLO) and the Kenya Human Rights Commission (KHRC), one of the oldest human rights groups in Kenya.[1156] The withdrawal of the ICC prosecutions only served to weaken further the position of the CSOs and embolden an increasingly authoritarian government.[1157]

Fourthly, the political elite sought to discredit and undermine ICC prosecution cases through its election campaign turning it into a referendum on the Court's intervention.[1158] According to reports from the OTP, security threats were made 'to ICC witnesses, conflict-affected communities and CSOs that support the court's work'.[1159] The OTP found they had to try to find ways to preserve evidence in cases where witnesses had recanted or refused to testify in court. In the cases of Deputy President William Samoei Ruto and former journalist Joshua arap Sang, the OTP applied to the ICC to include as evidence original recorded witness statements alleging that bribery and intimidation had been used to stop them cooperating with the Court.[1160] The ICC was forced to directly counter the charge that the Court had been externally imposed and the indictees' co-option of the language of victimhood. The ICC Prosecutor Fatou Bensouda declared that neither Kenya nor its people were on trial, and the Court's aim was to obtain 'justice for the many thousands of victims of the post-election violence and ensuring that there is no impunity for those responsible, regardless of power or position'.[1161]

Two contradictory political processes flowed from the 2007 post-election violence.[1162] The first was the mobilization of widespread support for radical constitutional reform. The second was an elite led counter-movement against

---

1155 A. Abdi, 'Kenya, Again, Represses Civil Society: Government Board Targets Groups Critical of Elections Process', *Human Rights Watch*, November 7, 2017, https://www.hrw.org/news/2017/11/07/kenya-again-represses-civil-society.

1156 Ibid.

1157 Madowo 2018, o.c.

1158 Kendall 2014, o.c., p. 410.

1159 Kendall 2014, o.c., p. 405.

1160 T. Maliti, 'ICC Prosecutor Asks Court to Admit as Evidence Statements of Witnesses Who Recanted', *International Justice Monitor*, June 4, 2015, https://www.ijmonitor.org/2015/06/icc-prosecutor-asks-court-to-admit-as-evidence-statements-of-witnesses-who-recanted/.

1161 Kendall 2014, o.c., p. 423.

1162 M. Mamdani, 'How land issues, the ICC played out in the election', *Daily Nation*, March 17, 2013.

the ICC indictment of six political leaders. The ICC prosecutions supported the thrust of the 2010 constitution to establish the Second Republic founded on human rights and democracy. However, to fulfil the promise of the constitution, a very large amount of implementing legislation was needed to establish new values, institutions, and structures of power. But, as Ghai argued, unless the radical makers of the radical institutions are in charge of the state, its implementation will be politically and bureaucratically obstructed by those who presently occupy the state.[1163] The very same elites who had campaigned against the Constitution won the 2013 election and became responsible for implementing it.[1164] Moreover, the preoccupation of the Jubilee Alliance was not the implementation of the Constitution but the delegitimation of the ICC trials. As Ghai observed, the Constitution (2010) had 'changed the form but not the reality of the state: its colonial legacy. It is still dominated by a small class, dependent heavily on armed force'.[1165] The elite pact expressed in the Jubilee Alliance forged for the 2013 elections established the basis for the continuity of Kikuyu and Kalenjin power in the 2017 and 2022 elections. In 2017, Kenyatta and Ruto merged their alliance into the Jubilee Party to consolidate a transactional electoral pact by locking in Kalenjin votes for Kenyatta in 2017 for Kikuyu support for Ruto in the 2022 election.[1166]

If the measure of the ICC's success in challenging impunity in Kenya is the number of guilty convictions, then it failed. None of the indictees were found guilty. However, if the role of international courts – in the case of both the ICC and the UK High Court – is understood as a new mechanism to enact political transitions, then they have a much wider legal and political significance. International jurisdictions have emerged as multi-scalar institutions integral to the strategic judicialization of politics at different levels. In Kenya, the impact of international courts has been to open up a new political arena for CSOs to mobilize support to pursue justice, to reform politics, and to change constitutions; to help rehabilitate stigmatized and excluded groups – e.g. the Maua Mau veterans; to assist ethnic minorities to try to realize electoral justice – e.g. the ODM. Through their intervention in conflict settings international courts have 'become political agents themselves, in the sense that they form alliances with some actors (often states whose support they rely upon) and designate others as alleged criminals, producing domestic political effects'.[1167] It can be argued that the shadow of the ICC has reinforced the electoral dispute resolution mechanisms recommended by the Kriegler Commission and included in the new Constitution (2010).

1163 Ghai 2014, o.c., p. 130.
1164 Ghai 2014, o.c., p. 130.
1165 Ghai 2014, o.c., p. 138.
1166 'Kenya's Rift Valley: Old Wounds, Devolution's New Anxieties', *Africa Report*, No. 248, May 30, 2017, International Crisis Group, Brussels, p. 5.
1167 Ghai 2014, o.c., p. 404.

The mechanism has been invoked after every presidential election since the Law was introduced in 2013, 2017 and 2022 to contest the result in the Supreme Court. Most significantly the decisions of the Court have been accepted, even the Supreme Court decision in 2017 to annul the presidential election and hold new elections.[1168] While doubts about the integrity of the elections remained, the loser Odinga accepted the Court's decision and did not resort to mass protests and violence to challenge the result as had happened in 2007.[1169] But while expanding the judicial arena, the intervention of international law has also had a polarizing impact on domestic politics where opponents have re-ethnicized communities deepening societal divisions as a strategy of power. The criminalization of political elites resulted in the most powerful of them closing ranks to retain power through elite pactism.[1170]

6.4. CONCLUSION

The ICC intervention in Kenya under Article 15 of the Rome Statute was triggered by the positive complementarity provision when the Kenyan parliament failed to establish a Special Tribunal as required by the Waki Commission Report into post-election violence. The Special Tribunal and the TJRC were the key transitional justice measures prescribed by the Waki Report, but they were continually obstructed by the political elite. In 2014, the Civil Society Coalition on Kenya's second universal periodic review observed that 'Kenya appears non-committal to the successful implementation of various processes within the transitional justice agenda as articulated in the Kenya National Dialogue and Reconciliation Accord of 2008'.[1171] Initially, the ICC intervention had been widely welcomed because the Kenyan crisis seemed like the very case the ICC was designed to hear – 'a member state, stymied by self-interested politicians, was suffering a justice deficit in relation to violations of core crimes'.[1172] However, the ICC prosecutions were thwarted by the indicted Kenyan political leaders who set out to delegitimize the Court by mobilizing domestic and regional support against it as a neo-imperialist institution. Nearly seven years after the ICC first

1168 The Supreme Court decision was considered controversial because it focused on the validity of the process rather than the outcome of the election. See K. Mutuma, 'Kenya's annulled presidential election: A step in the right direction?' (2021) 35 *Speculum Juris*, 92.

1169 Musila 2009, o.c., p. 448.

1170 M. Mamdani, 'Kenya: you cannot solve political problems through the courts' (2013) 51 *The Africa Report*, 25.

1171 Civil Society Coalition on Kenya's second universal periodic review (ASCK_UPR) June 14, 2014, KHRC, Nairobi, 3.

1172 K.B. Carlson, 'ICC case against Kenyan lawyer Gicheru: it matters, but not for victims of the violence', *The Conversation*, March 15, 2022, https://theconversation.com/icc-case-against-kenyan-lawyer-gicheru-it-matters-but-not-for-victims-of-the-violence-178938.

initiated investigations in 2009, the Court was forced to dismiss the cases against all six indictees because of insufficient evidence denied it by alleged witness intimidation and lack of access to official documents.[1173] When the ICC issued arrest warrants in March 2015 against two Kenyans alleging they had bribed or tried to bribe six prosecution witnesses to withdraw as witnesses in the trial of Deputy President Ruto and Joshua arap Sang, Kenya's High Court reported it was unwilling to prosecute them.[1174] The OTP Fatou Bensouda, in reference to the case against President Uhuru Kenyatta, strongly criticized the Kenyan government for its lack of cooperation with the Court:

> Contrary to the Government of Kenya's public pronouncements that it has fully complied with its legal obligations in this case, the ruling has confirmed that in fact it has breached its treaty obligations under the Rome Statute by failing to cooperate with my investigation.[1175]

Instead of challenging the problem of chronic elite impunity the ICC found it had been turned into a new arena for domestic political competition and conflict by the political elites. International intervention under R2P discourse had resulted in the judicialization of Kenyan politics through the human rights framing of the 2007 post-election violence followed by the contest, championed by CSOs, to rescale and internationalize justice. In response, the Kenyan government signalled its intention to withdraw from the jurisdiction of the ICC just days before Vice President Samoei Ruto was to face trial at The Hague in September 2013. After the Court had dismissed all the cases, the Kenyan government decided to remain in the Rome Statute declaring its commitment to international justice and accountability.[1176]

The failure of the ICC to successfully prosecute any of the indicted political leaders revealed some major limitations in the role of international criminal

---

1173 O. Bowcott, 'International criminal court abandons case against William Ruto', *The Guardian*, April 5, 2016, https://www.theguardian.com/world/2016/apr/05/international-criminal-court-william-ruto-kenya-deputy-president-election-violence.

1174 T. Maliti, 'Senior Prosecutor Says Kenya Unwilling to Prosecute Two Kenyans Wanted by ICC', *International Justice Monitor*, July 28, 2017, https://www.ijmonitor.org/2017/07/senior-prosecutor-says-kenya-unwilling-to-prosecute-two-kenyans-wanted-by-icc/. The trial against Paul Gicheru accused of witness interference opened on at the ICC February 15, 2022. The trial was closed when the defendant died. *The Prosecutor v. Paul Gicheru* ICC-01/09-01/20, Decision Terminating the Proceedings against Paul Gicheru, October 14, 2022, https://www.icc-cpi.int/court-record/icc-01/09-01/20-337.

1175 'Statement of the Prosecutor of the International Criminal Court, Fatou Bensouda, on the status of the Government of Kenya's cooperation with the Prosecution's investigations in the Kenyatta case', *International Criminal Court*, December 4, 2014, https://www.icc-cpi.int/Pages/item.aspx?name=otp-stat-04-12-2014.

1176 J. Ndunda, 'Kenya will not withdraw from ICC, says Githu Muigai', *The Star*, February 27, 2018, https://www.the-star.co.ke/news/2018-02-27-kenya-will-not-withdraw-from-icc-says-githu-muigai/.

justice as a mechanism to help overturn impunity, resolve political conflict, and bring about state renewal. Firstly, the ICC is vulnerable to de-legitimation at the local level. In Kenya, the 'Uhuruto' Jubilee Alliance evoked the collective memory of colonial state violence to delegitimize the intervention of the ICC as neo-colonial and win a critical election. Secondly, in this highly polarized context the Court outcome risked criminalizing one side in an ethnic conflict, according to the relative merits and strengths of a case, when often both sides shared responsibility.[1177] The ICC had attempted to signal its impartiality by prosecuting an equal number of indictees on both sides. However, its dismissal of all cases allowed the accused to represent the outcome as proof of their innocence and to attack the supporters of the ICC prosecutions as the one's rejecting peace.[1178] The challenge for the ICC was how to overcome the inertia of the normal way of doing business – conflict managed by elite pactism and impunity. The very failure of the Kenyan government to establish a Special Tribunal, as agreed to under the National Accord and Reconciliation Act (2008), was a measure of the entrenched power of the political elites to block all transitional justice measures. The CSO strategy to prioritize international over national trials, for good reasons, backfired in the end when the Jubilee Alliance stigmatized them as anti-peace and undermined the legitimacy of their human rights advocacy.

The ICC intervened in Kenya with the ambitious goals to rehabilitate state authority and the rule of law through the prosecution of the abuse of state power. The OTP, Luis Moreno-Ocampo, declared his aim was to prosecute those responsible for the 2007 post-election violence in Kenya to end impunity. He observed that "you can't measure [the ICC's] success only by trials. We must be judged by our impact on the conflict". The OTP claimed the Kenya intervention would serve as a 'world example of managing violence'.[1179] Yet, as Prunier argues, the Court's human rights framing was a far too neat and tidy construction of the causes of contemporary violence in Kenya which has turned into an expression of complex social war. Unlike earlier post-election violence in 1992 and 1997 which could be switched on and off by the political elites behind it, violence has become more democratic and has escaped the control of the ethnic leaders who nevertheless continue to manipulate it for their own purposes.[1180] Part of the urgency behind the need for the NDR to reach an agreement in 2008 was precisely the fear violence was escalating beyond the control of the political leaders and into the hands of the militias.[1181] The idea that reconciliation and

---

1177 Mamdani, 2013, o.c., p. 25.

1178 M. Mutiga 'Fumbling for Justice for Kenya', *New York Times*, December 26, 2014, https://www.nytimes.com/2014/12/27/opinion/mutiga-fumbling-justice-for-kenya.html?_r=0.

1179 Nichols 2015, o.c., p. 2.

1180 G. Prunier, 'Kenya: histories of hidden war', *Democracy Now*, February 29, 2008, https://www.opendemocracy.net/en/kenya_behind_the_crisis/.

1181 G.M. Khadiagala, 'Forty Days and Nights of Peacemaking in Kenya' (2008) 7 *Journal of African Elections*, 17.

the rule of law could flow from a renewed elite pact between ethnic leaders, such as the post-2007 national unity government between Mwai Kibaki and Raila Odinga, ignored the systemic nature of the violence in Kenya. Another factor fuelling the social war was the fragmentation of sovereignty as the state ceded full control over its peripheral areas and borders resulting in a mediated governance relying on 'clan elders, local NGOs, business people, clerics and others' to project its authority.[1182]

The impact of international courts on conflicts are multi-scalar and cannot be judged simply by their decisions. In the case of Kenya, ICC intervention represented one element in the broader legal and political reforms institutionalized in the 2010 Constitutional agenda to establish the Second Republic based on 'inclusive citizenship, good governance, devolution of power and more equitable development'.[1183] The consequences of the intervention of the ICC were firstly, to impose a human rights framing on electoral political violence; secondly, through positive complementarity, to attempt to make national courts responsible for prosecutions of those most responsible for human rights violations; and thirdly, to assume responsibility for prosecutions if positive complementarity failed. In the same way that the Inter-American Court of Human Rights became a focus for social movements and claim-making to effect local change in Latin America, so the ICC is becoming a focus for CSOs and human rights movements to promote the authority of international over national courts and give visibility to victims.[1184] In Kenya, the CSO lobbying for ICC prosecutions and their own role in outreach campaigns to educate the public about the importance of international prosecutions helped politicize the question of jurisdiction. The counter-narrative of the Jubilee Alliance's electoral campaign characterizing the ICC as neo-imperialist and interventionist succeeded in securing the indictees Kenyatta and Ruto government. The charge of neo-imperialism was reinforced at the regional level by recruiting the support of the African Union to denounce the ICC as anti-African on the grounds it was only prosecuting African leaders.[1185] In other words, the rescaling of justice resulted in the polarization of the Kenyan electorate around sovereignty and the regional mobilization of a number of African leaders against the Court.

The wider political significance of the Mau Mau claims for reparations in the UK High Court has been their role in the historical human rights revisionism

1182 K. Menkhaus, 'Local Security Systems in Somali East Africa' in L. Andersen, et al. (eds.), *Fragile States and Insecure People?: Violence, Security and Statehood in the Twenty-First Century*, Palgrave Macmillan, New York, NY 2007, p. 67, at p. 91.

1183 Zeleza 2014, o.c., p. 17.

1184 J.L. Cavallaro and S.E. Brewer, 'Re-evaluating Regional Human Rights Litigation in the Twenty-First Century: The Case of the Inter-American Court' (2008) 102 *American Journal of International Law* 768, at 770.

1185 L. García Iommi, 'Whose justice? The ICC 'Africa problem'' (2020) 34 *International Relations*, 105.

of political violence in both the colonial and postcolonial state.[1186] The Mau Mau claims reintroduced the memory of colonial state repression as an event around which Kenyans could once again be collectively mobilized against past colonial atrocities. The KHRC's human rights revisionist history of the Mau Mau and colonial state accountability brought into focus the human rights accountability for victims of the postcolonial state repression. The effect of the Mau Mau case against the Foreign Office in the UK High Court for reparations was to endorse the rehabilitation of the Mau Mau as heroes of independence and overturn their criminalized and stigmatized status as despised and distrusted terrorists by the colonial state and post-colonial elites. When President Mwai Kibaki, after his election in 2002, rescinded the ban against the Mau Mau as an illegal organization he opened the way for the KHRC to develop a human rights case against the British Government for reparations for the Mau Mau victims of colonial counterinsurgency policies. The KHRC Mau Mau Project introduced human rights as a counter discourse to the normalization of political violence as just part of ethnic competition in an electoral system in which the winner takes all. The human rights lens also drew attention to the chronic nature of elite impunity and the weakness of the legal system in holding those responsible accountable in the postcolonial state. The political impact of the UK High Court case was to allow the Mau Mau veterans to represent their victimhood as heroic and Kenyan independence as the achievement of 'national liberation' rather than 'consensual decolonization' which the presidencies of Kenyatta and Moi perpetuated to legitimate national unity around a strong centralized single-party state. The new decolonization narrative as a national struggle against colonialism whose victims had been left out of history was institutionalized in the Preamble to the new Constitution (2010). It led to the CSOs actively campaigning to prioritize ICC investigation because they had little confidence in the ICC positive complementarity strategy which relied on the integrity of the Kenyan justice system. The ICC intervention in Kenya premised on positive complementarity has revealed the processes of the politicization of multi-scalar justice. As Kendall notes: 'powers and interests are routed through court interventions: new categories of identity are generated through distinguishing between 'friends' and 'enemies' of the international community, and old colonial

[1186] The UK High Court awarded £19.9 million to 5,228 Kenyans who suffered torture and abuse during the Mau Mau uprising. There is little progress on this claim. See Statement to Parliament on settlement of Mau Mau claims Foreign & Commonwealth Office and the Rt Hon William Hague, June 6, 2013, https://www.gov.uk/government/news/statement-to-parliament-on-settlement-of-mau-mau-claims. However, the UK government has resisted a much larger claim for more than 40,000 Kenyans brought against the Foreign Office. See T. Odula, 'Kenyans' lawyer says UK not interested in settlement', *Daily News*, January 21, 2015, https://www.nydailynews.com/sdut-kenyans-lawyer-says-uk-not-interested-in-2015jan21-story.html\.

forms of identity are reinscribed through how conflict narratives are recounted in the terms of international criminal law'.[1187]

UN and regional international intervention to halt Kenya's escalating pattern of post-election violence brought the protagonists together in a National Accord to form a national unity government. The Kriegler and Waki Reports set out measures to regulate electoral disputes, to introduce constitutional reforms and to establish truth and justice mechanisms. International intervention secured the agreement of the political elite for these measures but not their commitment to them. The ICC intervention only happened because the Kenyan parliament failed to establish the Special Tribunal specific under positive complementarity. However, both key performative mechanisms enacting truth and justice were sabotaged. The ICC trials were undermined by domestic political manipulations and produced no verdicts – except the inverted ones where the indicted declared the non-outcomes were proof of their innocence. The Kenyan courts also failed to prosecute those charged with committing the post-election violence. The TJRC produced a comprehensive Report which included recommendations for reparations that are yet to be implemented more than a decade after its tabling. In 2015, President Kenyatta apologized on behalf of the government for the violations suffered by Kenyans in the past decades. He announced the establishment of a Restorative Justice Fund ($100 million) for victims, but no reparations have been paid because no reparations policy has been legislated.[1188] Even in the limited number of cases where national courts have awarded victims reparations, the government has not provided the funds.[1189] As performative transitional justice rituals they were incomplete, trapped in the liminal phase. They were hijacked by the elite turning them into performative gestures of compliance with transitional justice norms not as commitments to justice, truth, or reparations. They lacked performative efficacy because the political transition they were supposed to usher in was undermined by the interests of elites. They were not persuasive rituals, in Lynch's terms, because they could not generate a public consensus about the framing of the post-election violence – demonstrative act – or engender *communitas* – a unifying shared experience of transition which produced the feeling they were moving towards a better future. Elite pragmatism perpetuated the politicized ethnic divisions that had created the conditions for the violence in the first place, and turned the ICC trials into a new axis of political competition around which to forge alliances against

1187 Kendall 2014, o.c., p. 404.

1188 'Storm over Uhuru's Sh10 billion for victims reparations', *Journalist for Justice*, October 19, 2015, https://jfjustice.net/storm-over-uhurus-sh10-billion-for-victims-reparations/.

1189 A. Ndonga, 'Kenya: Still Grappling with a Stalled Transitional Justice Mandate', *ICTJ*, December 17, 2018, https://www.ictj.org/news/kenya-still-grappling-stalled-transitional-justice-mandate.

external intervention and shore up their impunity.[1190] As incomplete truth and justice rituals, they were unable to generate lasting effects because they failed to produce a narrative consensus about the past injustice, about who were the perpetrators and victims, and no unifying memorialization of it. Ironically, the UK High Court decisions about the Mau Mau veterans were able to generate a consensus in Kenyan society about the human rights violations committed by the colonial state but the ICC decisions were unable to generate the same consensus about the human rights violations committed by the post-colonial state and its agents.

1190 G. Lynch, *Performances of Injustice: The Politics of Truth, Justice and Reconciliation in Kenya*, Cambridge University Press, Cambridge 2018, p. 20.

CHAPTER 7
COLOMBIA
Peace, Justice and the State

7.1. INTRODUCTION

Little more than a year after the ratification of the Final Agreement (FA) between the Government of Colombia (GOC) and the Revolutionary Armed Forces of Colombia (*Fuerzas Armadas Revolucionarias de Colombia- Ejército del Pueblo* FARC-EP) by Congress, on November 28–29, 2016, rural social leaders and human rights defenders appeared in Bogotá wearing white masks to conceal their identities demanding protection from the threat of assassination. They had come to Bogotá to meet with the Minister of Defence, the Minister of the Interior and the Vice-President about their inclusion on a death list of 209 people.[1191] The public appearance of the death list alarmed them because of the growing number of social leaders that had been assassinated over the previous two years since the finalization of the FA.[1192] They were also haunted by the memory of an earlier peace agreement reached in the late 1980s which had resulted in the assassination of around 3,000 members of the Patriotic Union (*Unión Patriótica* (UP)), the leftist party established by FARC-EP and the Colombian Communist for them to participate in democratic elections.[1193] The Santos government had presented the peace accord as an important moment of transition – "Let's not

---

[1191] S. Palomino, 'Los líderes sociales en Colombia usan máscaras para que no los maten', *El Pais*, December 15, 2017, https://elpais.com/internacional/2017/12/15/billete_a_macondo/1513354118_012154.html.

[1192] The Public Defender found that based on information from the Early Warning System (*Sistema de Alertas Tempranas SAT*), 134 social leaders had been assassinated in 2016. *Informe Especial de Riesgo: 'Violencia y Amenazas Contra Los Líderes Sociales y Los Defensores de Derechos Humanos'*, Defensoría Delegada para la Prevención de Riesgos de Violaciones de los Derechos Humanos y el DIH. Sistema de Alertas Tempranas (SAT). Marzo 2017 Bogotá D.C., Colombia; J. A. Macías, '¿Por qué están asesinando a los líderes sociales en Colombia?', *C.elcolombiano*, December 14, 2017, https://www.elcolombiano.com/colombia/por-que-estan-asesinando-a-los-lideres-sociales-en-colombia-CI7857532. See also https://www.verdadabierta.com for current number of social leaders assassinated.

[1193] OHCHR registered 441 attacks, including 121 killings, against social leaders and human rights activists in 2017. Annual Report of the United Nations High Commissioner for Human Rights on the situation of human rights in Colombia, March 2, 2018, A/HRC/37/3/Add.3.

forget what we are doing today; we're trying to end more than 50 years of war" (Sergio Jaramillo government negotiator).[1194] For the United Nations High Commissioner for Human Rights (OHCHR), the plight of social leaders was a sign that the peace process was in crisis and the government needed to take seriously the question of accountability for the murders.[1195] In 2022, the new President Petro, with his policy of 'total peace', made the protection of social leaders a priority but the murder of social leaders continued.[1196] The current predicament of the social leaders raises questions about the future of the FA; the level of public support for it, its implementation, the peace imaginary behind it, and the ideas about justice underlying it. Does it represent a rupture with past cycles of peacemaking and political violence or not? Does the judicialization of politics through transitional justice initiatives provide a new basis for reaching a consensus about the past and achieving national reconciliation? Does the FA tackle the core recurrent conflicts that have plagued previous efforts to bring peace?

The death threats against social leaders highlight three major obstacles to implementation of the FA: firstly, the current limits of state territorial sovereignty; secondly, the lack of a national consensus in support of the FA; and thirdly, the question of ongoing impunity. Firstly, the geographical distribution of violence against social leaders and human rights activists largely maps the current limits of state sovereignty – the zones vacated by the FARC-EP now contested for control over by the state, leftist ELN guerrillas, paramilitaries and BACRIM – criminal organizations (*Bandas Criminales*). As the National Centre of Historical Memory (*Centro nacional de memoria histórica* – CNMH) Report, *BASTA YA! Colombia: Memories of War and Dignity*, observes, 'the continuing violence against these communities and organizations has its roots in their stigmatization and criminalization by powerful local interests who have simply equated militant left, human rights defender and subversive'.[1197] In the countryside, individuals continue to be victimized for claiming their rights for the restitution of land stolen during the war, for resisting new displacement driven by agribusiness and natural resource projects and for organizing politically.[1198] Their plight reveals

---

1194 H. Murphy, 'Colombian peace deal passed by Congress, ending 52-year war', *Reuters*, December 1, 2016, https://www.reuters.com/article/us-colombia-peace/colombian-peace-deal-passed-by-congress-ending-52-year-war-idUSKBN13P1D2.

1195 Annual Report of the United Nations High Commissioner for Human Rights on the situation of human rights in Colombia, March 2, 2018, A/HRC/37/3/Add.3.

1196 F.P. Cuartas and G. Sánchez-Garzoli, 'Q&A: Promises and Prospects for Human Rights in Colombia under Petro as ELN negotiations restart', *WOLA*, February 17, 2023, https://www.wola.org/analysis/qa-promises-prospects-for-human-rights-colombia-under-petro-as-eln-negotiations/.

1197 *BASTA YA! Colombia: Memories of War and Dignity*, General Report Historical Memory Group, National Centre for Historical Memory, 2016, p. 93.

1198 Ibid., p. 19.

the existence of historical 'shatter zones' of Colombia, frontiers where the state was either absent or its sovereignty had been franchised to local powerholders who competed for land, labour and resources with farmers displaced by conflict, private armies, bandits, smugglers and international corporations.[1199] Secondly, the failure of the national plebiscite held to ratify the FA revealed the strong public opposition to it but also the continuing ability of political elites to shape Colombian politics. Of the 40% who participated in the plebiscite, 50.2% rejected the peace accord and 49.8% percent approved it. Instead of overcoming political partisanship through direct democracy the plebiscite became an opportunity for the political elites to polarize the electorate and veto the FA.[1200] In other words, former President Uribe who headed the NO Campaign, acted as a political spoiler by denying the support of an important elite faction for the FA. Thirdly, the question of impunity remains historically embedded in the modes of governance exercised by a weak state through which violence becomes spatially and socially normalized. While the FA insisted on accountability and victims' rights, the amnesty provision has only served to polarize perspectives on the conflict, especially in respect to who are seen as perpetrators and who are seen as the deserving victims. While law and restorative justice framed the FA, it remains an open question as to whether the judicialization of the peace process will be able to help transform, or only serve to preserve, the political status quo and patterns of extreme inequality behind the conflict.

The focus of this chapter is how transitional justice norms were introduced into peacemaking in Colombia and how past Colombian models of peacemaking influenced the prioritization of transitional justice measures after large-scale violence and mass crimes. In Colombia, transitional justice was not a post-conflict project but became progressively integrated into peace negotiations. The traditional 'Colombian Way' of peacemaking had been determined by elite pactism and impunity.[1201] In the early 1980s, governments mobilized constituencies for peace by promising a 'democratic opening' of the political system which came to mean amnesty for political prisoners and armed insurgents, negotiations with armed opposition, dialogue among all key political actors (including representatives of the nations' guerrilla movements), and the establishment of ground rules for participation and democratic opposition'.[1202] The failure to

---

1199 J.C. Scott, *The Art of Not Being Governed: An Anarchist History of Upland Southeast Asia*, Yale University Press, New Haven, CT 2010.

1200 A.M. Matanock and M. García-Sánchez, 'The Colombian Paradox: Peace Processes, Elite Divisions, and Popular Plebiscite' (2017) 146 *Daedalus*, 152.

1201 This term is borrowed from the 'Chilean way', the practice of political reconciliation by the Chilean political elite who gradually rehabilitated their defeated opponents. See B. Loveman and E. Lira, *Las ardientes cenizas del olvido: vía chilena de reconciliación política 1932–1994*, Lom Ediciones, Santiago, Chile 2000.

1202 M.W. Chernick, 'Negotiated Settlement to Armed Conflict: Lessons from the Colombian Peace Process' (1988) 30 *Journal of Interamerican Studies and World Affairs* 53, at 54.

galvanize a national consensus around peacemaking by the late 1990s and the switch from political negotiations to prioritize a military solutions from 2000 under President Uribe brought the intensification of the judicialization of peacemaking with the introduction of transitional justice norms in the Justice and Peace Law (JPL) 975/2005; the Victims and Land Restitution Law (Victims Law) 1448/2011; and most recently in the FA (2016).[1203] The Colombian case highlights the interdependence between political agreements and transitional justice policy in peacemaking, something often concealed by the characterization of transitional justice measures as post-conflict. In Colombia, peace negotiations were progressively judicialized from the 1980s and from 2005 were increasingly shaped by transitional justice norms.

The Colombian case brings into sharp relief the tensions between criminal justice and political justice during political transitions. The chapter contextualizes the FA within the evolution of peacemaking in Colombia since 1958. It examines four different peace initiatives (1958, 1987, 2005, 2016) and their performative, demonstrative and representational dimensions in constructing historical violent events to mark moments of transition. Amnesty provisions have featured in all these peace initiatives. In fact, before 2005, amnesty had been taken for granted as a necessary condition to bring an end to armed conflict in Colombia.[1204] The chapter argues that the breakdown of elite political fixes or pacts has been the result of the re-emergence of recurrent unresolved historical conflicts behind these peace agreements: fragmented state sovereignty; the failure of the state to establish a monopoly over the use of violence; chronic elite impunity; and extreme inequality – especially the extreme concentration of land ownership. Historically, each elite pact was articulated and legitimated in the dominant global discourses of the day: anti-communism to prevent radicalization (1958); democratization and development to reduce poverty (1987); counterinsurgency against 'narco-terrorists' and neoliberalism to pacify the country in order to attract investment (2005); human rights, democracy and neoliberal development to expand rights and create economic opportunities to overcome social trauma (2011–2016). These peace agreements were expressed in the language of law – truces, amnesties, political rights, social reforms, and constitutional amendments. However, because of the chronic gap between legal form and substance in Colombia the 'symbolic powerfulness of law cohabits with its instrumental weakness'.[1205] Rather than a discourse of

1203 *Ley 1448 de 2011* (Unidad para las víctimas) Por la cual se dictan medidas de atención, asistencia y reparación integral a las víctimas del conflicto armado interno y se dictan otras disposiciones, March 3, 2011, https://www.unidadvictimas.gov.co/es/ley-1448-de-2011/13653.

1204 F. Gutiérrez-Sanín, F., 'La Constitución de 1991 como pacto de paz: discutiendo las anomalías' (2011) 13 *Estudios Socio-Jurídicos* 419, at 429.

1205 L. Eslava, 'Constitutionalization of Rights in Colombia: Establishing a ground for meaningful comparisons' (2009) 22 *Revisita Derecho del Estado* 183, at 195.

state authority, the law serves as a 'multiuse tool' for competing political elites 'who never enjoyed key monopolies: on the legitimate use of force, on taxation, and on customs revenues, for example'.[1206] In these peace agreements, law has operated as a macro institutional language for projecting state sovereignty in its absence, which taps into the popular hope in the efficacy of law where politics has failed.

We argue that contemporary Colombian transitional justice initiatives must be situated in the historical Colombian paradox – 'the production of law has allowed the shell of the State and its atomized ruling members to remain stable, while there is a general sense of society falling apart'.[1207] In this context, transitional justice discourse has been used as a symbolic and conservative strategy on the one hand, and as a 'democratic or emancipatory' one on the other.[1208] In the former, lip service is paid to victims' rights as a humanitarian gesture to help hide impunity; in the latter, transitional justice discourse is deployed to realize rights and challenge impunity. In the FA, the human rights lens of transitional justice simplifies the construction of the conflict around the subject positions of perpetrators and victims. Yet this binary construction is particularly problematic for the Colombian conflict because the temporal, spatial and political characteristics of more than 50 years of political violence prevent any easy narrative integration around the perpetrator/victim binary. The Colombian transitional justice solution to the problem of the narrative integration of diverse violence is to construct the category of 'victims of the Colombian conflict' which homogenizes victims and provides an historically inclusive national discourse through which the state can superficially represent itself as governing in the name of all victims. By contrast, the issue of perpetrators is managed selectively and unevenly shaped by prevailing ideological and political interests including the veto of legislation implementing the FA in Congress.

The state's deployment of transitional justice discourse and human rights language also taps into the distinctive character of the judicialization of politics in Colombia. Politics has been increasingly judicialized through different mechanisms since 1990. Firstly, the use of legalistic language has become the primary way in which the meaning of violence is expressed and demands for protection are made in public life.[1209] Secondly, 'the constitutionalization of daily life', encouraged by the progressive 1991 Constitution, has resulted in the expansion of a Colombian legal culture of rights consciousness and victim

---

1206 F. Gutiérrez-Sanín, 'The Courtroom and the Bivouac: Reflections on Law and Violence in Colombia' (2001) 28 *Latin American Perspectives* 56, at 64.

1207 Eslava 2009, o.c., p. 195.

1208 M.P. Saffon and R. Uprimny Yepes, 'Uses and Abuses of Transitional Justice in Colombia' in M. Bergsmo and P. Kalmanovitz (eds.), *Law in Peace Negotiations*, Torkel Opsahl Academic Publisher, Oslo 2010, p. 354, at p. 374.

1209 Gutiérrez-Sanín 2001, o.c., p. 59.

claim-making.[1210] As a result, there has been a massive expansion of individual rights claiming through the courts in response to the failure of politics.[1211] However, in this context law 'stands in for, often in a merely symbolic fashion, the incapacity of the State to respond to the social demands for security, social justice and participation'.[1212] Thirdly, the human rights lens of the Victims Law 1448/2011 reframed violence as the product of an internal political conflict in which there were perpetrators and victims challenging Uribe's construction of the conflict as a problem of criminality and narco-terrorism. Fourthly, human rights facilitated a legal-bureaucratic mode of governance based on the classification and registration of victims in a single National Register of Victims (*Registro Único de Víctimas* – RUV). The Register serves as a repository of memory, symbolic reparations for victims, and evidence for use in criminal trials.[1213] The Victims Agreement contained in the FA (2016) allowed the state to expand this legal-bureaucratic mode of governance by recoding and inverting the violence embodied in invisible victims from a sign of the state's weakness and territorial absence into a sign of the state's strength expressed through these legal 'institutional macroforms'.[1214] As a result, transitional justice in Colombia risks turning into the administration of hope – belief that rights will be realized – by producing long human rights victim queues waiting to be officially processed, but most likely destined to fail because of either the lack of state capacity, resources, or political will to process and compensate the more than 9.4 million registered victims. The human rights queues signify the hope the liberal promise of rights will be delivered while the waiting introduces the worrying doubt that they will not be – victims queues trapped in a state of permanent liminality.

7.2. JUDICIALIZATION OF POLITICS

7.2.1. LAW AND SPANISH COLONIZATION

In Latin America, the growing importance of law and courts in the arena of contemporary politics has been referred to as the 'judicialization of politics.[1215]

1210 E. Restrepo, 'Reforma Constitucional y Progreso Social: La "Constitucionalización de la Vida Cotidiana" en Colombia' (2002) *SELA (Seminario en Latinoamérica de Teoría Constitucional y Política) Papers*, Yale Law School, 1, https://hdl.handle.net/20.500.13051/17497.

1211 Eslava 2009, o.c., p. 183.

1212 Eslava 2009, o.c., pp. 196–7.

1213 J. Rivas, 'Official Victims' Registries: A Tool for the Recognition of Human Rights Violations' (2016) 8 *Journal of Human Rights Practice* 116, at 119.

1214 Gutiérrez-Sanín 2001, o.c., p. 59.

1215 A. Huneeus, et al., 'Cultures of Legality: Judicialization and Political Activism in Latin America' in J. A. Huneeus, et al. (eds.), *Cultures of Legality: Judicialization and Political Activism in Latin America*, Cambridge University Press, Cambridge 2010, p. 1.

On the one hand, it refers to the growing activism of the judiciary and the courts as defenders of constitutional rights while on the other, it refers to the use of the law, legal discourse and language by social movements and human rights defenders to advance political goals. The judicialization of politics is not new in Colombia and the salience of law and courts to politics dates back to the colonial era. Law was a key institution in the Spanish conquest of Latin America when it was used as a vehicle to legitimate colonial conquest and 'as a mechanism of political and cultural hegemony'.[1216] Papal bulls justified conquest, laws specified Spanish colonial privileges and indigenous litigants challenged these privileges throughout the colonial period. Law remained central to political authority after independence with the creation of constitutional republics throughout Latin America in the early 19th century. In the Latin American republics, political elites invested heavily in 'constitutional law as a means of imagining, constructing, and attempting to control the state'.[1217] Before the latest wave of constitutional reforms associated with democratization and human rights, Latin American states had enacted more than 200 constitutions.[1218] As foundational political acts, traditionally made between elites while excluding wider participation constitutions, were used as a mechanism to re-establish political legitimacy after political violence and disorder. In 19th century Latin America, the winning side in civil wars invariably claimed that their victory signified 'the restoration of constitutional rule'.[1219] Brian Loveman and Elizabeth Lira's coined term the 'Chilean way' to characterize the 19th century practice of political reconciliation between the victors and vanquished during civil wars.[1220] Peace was achieved through elite pacts in which the winners politically rehabilitated the losers on their terms through the constitutional provision of amnesty or pardon as an expression of national reconciliation. In the 20th century, the political elite have packaged promises and rights in new constitutions, alongside expanded executive power, appealing enough to gain popular support through plebiscites.[1221]

Since its independence in 1810, Colombia has had 10 national constitutions and each new constitution was evidence of the fragility of the transactional elite pacts that underpinned them. In the 19th century, competition for political power was reflected in a patchwork of constitutions at the national, regional

1216 Ibid.
1217 Ibid., p. 9.
1218 Ibid., p. 9.
1219 During the 19th century Chile experienced civils wars and internal rebellions in 1829–1830, 1851, 1859 and 1891. See B. Loveman and E. Lira, 'Truth, Justice, Reconciliation, and Impunity as Historical Themes: Chile, 1814–2006' (2007) 97 *Radical History Review* 43, at p. 49.
1220 Loveman and Lira 2007, o.c., p. 68.
1221 A. Breuer, 'The use of Government Initiated Referendums in Latin America. Towards a Theory of referendum causes' (2009) 29 *Revista de Ciencia Política*, 23.

and municipal levels producing a hyper-developed and fragmented legal order mediated by elites.[1222] From early after independence, the Colombian state used law as an instrument to create and maintain the façade of state authority whose weakness was exposed by civil wars initiated by regional caudillos.[1223] Elite pacts concluded civil wars but without resolving the fundamental political conflicts which dated back to the founding of the independent state. Law, and constitutionalism, played an instrumental role in the delegitimation of the predecessor government and the establishment of the legality and legitimacy of the new government. In the pactist tradition, 'every war generates agreements and each agreement generates wars'.[1224] Core recurrent political conflicts arose firstly, as a result of the state's incomplete consolidation of its territorial sovereignty, its failure to monopolize the use of violence and its inability to effectively tax peripheral regions; and secondly, from the chronic failure of the state to address extreme inequality in the distribution of land. The historical division between political elites of the centre, in the capital Bogotá, and those of the periphery was a major factor limiting state sovereignty and national integration. In the periphery, local elites were able to grow powerful and become large landholders often securing autonomous control over regions and, with the help of their own private armies, resist the expansion of central state power.[1225] The historical anxiety of the Colombian state over the threat of regional secession to form new republics was symptomatic of the chronic weakness of state territorial sovereignty.[1226] The central government's solution for the administration of the peripheral regions was shared governance through the two national political parties – the Conservatives and the Liberals – whose constituencies were attached by party loyalty and clientelism. Political affiliation extended across generations creating durable political subcultures and constituencies. Broadly speaking the Conservatives represented the landowning elite and the church while the Liberals represented the commercial elite and the secular state. During the 19th century, the Liberal and Conservative parties with their peasant militias fought a series of bloody civil wars to secure the spoils of government.[1227] The major

---

1222 M.A.A. Espinal, 'Ensamblajes institucionales y guerras civiles en la Colombia del siglo XIX' (2014) 11 *Co-herencia: Revista de Humanidades* 169, at 177.

1223 Ibid., p. 182.

1224 F. Gutiérrez-Sanín and A.M. Jaramillo, 'Paradoxical Pacts' in B. De Sousa Santos (ed.), *Reinventing Social Emancipation: Toward New Manifestos*, Verso, London 2005, p. 193.

1225 N. Richani, *Systems of Violence: The Political Economy of War and Peace in Colombia*, 2nd ed., SUNY Press, New York 2013, p. 114.

1226 R.A. Karl, *Forgotten Peace: Reform, Violence, and the Making of Contemporary Colombia*, University of California Press, Berkeley, CA 2017a, p. 184. For a discussion of the secession of Panama from Colombia and the role of the United States in supporting Panamanian elites see: S.J. Randall, *Colombia and the United States: Hegemony and Interdependence*, The University of Georgia Press, Athens and London 1992, pp. 71–99.

1227 There were nine major civil wars and tens of local wars in 19th century Colombia – *Guerra de los Supremos* (1839–42), 1851, 1854, 1859/62, 1876–7, 1884–5, 1895 and the *Guerra de los Mil*

tensions behind these civil wars are the key themes in Colombian state formation: competition between centralism versus federalism; between the executive and Congress; between provincial power and central order; between military power and civil power; and between a plebiscitary dictatorship and a patriotic civic republican state.[1228] These inter-elite wars included the violent repression, with the help of the army, of rural protest and rebellion over land. Elite dominance of politics was challenged only with the arrival on the national stage of the leading populist Liberal politician Gaitán who denounced state repression of workers and advocated for land reform for the rural poor. Gaitán's assassination in 1948 precipitated a bloody political struggle between rural Liberal and Conservative militias which became known as *La Violencia*. Between 1948–64 *La Violencia* resulted in around 200,000 (1.8% of the population) killed and more than 2 million (16% of the population) displaced.[1229]

7.2.2. COLOMBIAN CONSTITUTIONALISM

The new 1991 Constitution changed the judicialization of politics from an exercise in the political legitimation of government dominated by elites to an emphasis on the rights of citizens. The 1991 Constitution was drafted by a Constitutional Assembly and was conceived as a peace treaty promoting democratization and individual rights.[1230] The 1991 Constitution, strongly focused on human rights, emerged from efforts to promote peace and democratization by dismantling the elite monopoly of power which had been institutionalized in the power sharing agreement of the National Front Pact in 1958 to end *La Violencia*. The 1991 Constitution expanded individual rights and included judicial mechanisms to advance social reform in the form of the *tutela*, a writ that can be filed by anyone before a judge for immediate protection of their constitutional rights as a result of an action or omission by a public agency.[1231] The 1991 Constitution constrained the power of the

---

Días (1899–1902). They were generally linked to electoral questions. See E. Posada-Carbó, 'Elections and Civil Wars in Nineteenth-century Colombia: The 1875 Presidential Campaign' (1994) 26 *Journal of Latin American Studies* 621, at 649.

1228 Espinal 2014, o.c., p. 171.

1229 V.A. Guerrero Apráez, *Guerras civiles colombianas: Negociación, regulación y memoria*, Editorial Pontifica Universidad Javeriana, Bogotá 2016, p. 92.

1230 N.C. Sánchez León, 'Acceptance of International Criminal Justice: Country Study on Colombia' in S. Buckley-Zistel et al. (eds.), *After Nuremberg. Exploring Multiple Dimensions of the Acceptance of International Criminal Justice*, International Nuremberg Principles Academy, Nuremberg 2016, p. 1, at p. 3; Gutiérrez-Sanín 2011, o.c., p. 421.

1231 K. Merhof, 'Building a bridge between reality and the constitution: The establishment and development of the Colombian Constitutional Court' (2015) 13 *International Journal of Constitutional Law* 714, at 719; P. Delaney, 'Legislating for Equality in Colombia: Constitutional Jurisprudence, Tutelas, and Social Reform' (2008) 1 *The Equal Rights Review*, 50.

political elite by putting the 'state of siege provision' under the judicial review of the Constitutional Court rather than left in the hands of the president as it had been between 1949–1991. Governments had ruled under the 'state of siege' provisions for 35 years during this period.[1232] The Constitution 1991 also introduced the figure of 'political death' (*pérdida de investidura*), a political career ending sanction used against Congressman and local government councilors who violated the conflict-of-interest statute or other legal norms. The Court's activist role as a vehicle for social and political reform emerged from the vacuum created by the failure of political representation and the weakness of social movements long subjected to harsh state repression. Increasingly, international transitional justice norms have contributed to the judicialization of politics by shaping peace agreements which have been scrutinized by the international courts, the Inter-American Court of Human Rights and the ICC.[1233] The FA (2016) shows 'unparalleled reliance on international law to define terms and bolster its legitimacy; through construction of a process-heavy and lawyerly post-conflict mechanism; and by leaving resolution of particularly difficult accountability trade-offs to the future, so as to defer court review'.[1234] These Courts have played an important role in shaming Colombian leaders into action to investigate political crimes and officially recognize that there was a political conflict in the country and there were victims.[1235]

But, as Uprimny points out, 'judicialization has its merits, but it also comes with risks'.[1236] It can increase demands on the courts and overburden the legal system. The incapacity and/or inefficiency of the courts can cause long delays which only serves to undermine their legitimacy and help to perpetuate criminal impunity. Judicialization can also result in the manipulation of the courts 'to depoliticize some sensitive issues, to avoid being weighed down by the consequences of their decisions, or because they are faced with an institutional obstacle that prompts them to accept or even welcome the delegation of these matters to the judges'.[1237] Because courts are not designed to solve complex social and political problems, they can actually have the effect of demobilizing and undermining democracy. Judicialization can displace political reform as occurred with the 'Process 8000' campaign against political corruption and the infiltration of drug money in

1232 R. Uprimny Yepes, 'Judicialization of politics in Colombia: cases, merits and risks' (2007) 4 *Sur. International Journal of Human Rights* 48, at 51.

1233 X. Medellín-Urquiaga, 'The Normative Impact of the Inter-American Court of Human Rights on Latin-American National Prosecution of Mass Atrocities' (2013) 46 *Israel Law Review*, 405.

1234 C. Hillebrecht, et al., 'The Judicialization of Peace' (2018) 59 *Harvard International Law Journal* 279, at 318.

1235 M. Bocchese, '*El Coco* Does Not Frighten Anymore: ICC scrutiny and state cooperation in Colombia', Northwestern University, presented at 'The American Society of International Law Midyear Meeting', Los Angeles, CA November 8–10, 2018.

1236 Uprimny Yepes 2007, o.c., p. 63.

1237 Uprimny Yepes 2007, o.c., p. 57.

the 1994 presidential campaign.[1238] It can place too much confidence in the role of the Constitutional Court as an independent arbiter when it too is subject to political pressure and judicial conflicts and can become politicized. Justices face politically imposed constraints including 'restricting court jurisdictions, altering the composition of the court (by reducing the number of its members, by impeaching individual justices, and/or by packing the court with more friendly justices), passing laws or amendments aimed at reversing court decisions, or simply failing to implement court rulings'.[1239] The so called rights revolution through constitutional reform, especially through citizens' rights to access the Colombian Constitutional Court, has not ensured that the interests of the executive do not prevail over those of ordinary citizens.[1240]

7.3. CONFLICT, PEACE AGREEMENTS AND TRANSITION

7.3.1. THE JUDICIALIZATION OF PEACE INITIATIVES

The FA is but the latest in a long series of peace initiatives that have set out to bring an end to more than 50 years of armed conflict in Colombia. These peace initiatives have all been directed towards recovering state territorial control, the monopoly over the use of violence, legality, legitimacy, and the trust of its citizens. The dominant approach of Colombian governments to peace-making has been pactism – the management of political crises through agreements reached between political elites. The 'Colombian Way' of peace-making involved elite pacts based on amnesty, selective rehabilitation/reintegration of belligerents and social reforms.[1241] Historically, impunity has been the price paid – by the victims – to achieve a breakthrough to end bouts of political violence.[1242] On one count there have been 23 amnesties and 63 pardons over

---

1238 Uprimny Yepes 2007, o.c., p. 63.

1239 J.C. Rodríguez-Raga, 'Strategic Deference in the Colombian Constitutional Court, 1992–2006' in G. Helmke and J. Rios-Figueroa (eds.), *Courts in Latin America*, Cambridge University Press, Cambridge 2011, p. 84.

1240 Ibid., p. 81; See also B.M. Wilson, 'Institutional Reform and Rights Revolutions in Latin America: The Cases of Costa Rica and Colombia' (2009) 1 *Journal of Politics in Latin America* 59, at 75–6.

1241 The term 'Colombian Way' is borrowed from Loveman and Lira's term the 'Chilean Way'. See Loveman and Lira 2007, o.c., p. 68.

1242 See 'Table Amnesties and Pardons Granted Between 1981–1997' which provides details of crimes included and excluded under amnesties and pardons granted between 1981–1997 in H. Alviar García and K. Engle, 'The Distributive Politics of Impunity and Anti-Impunity: Lessons from Four Decades of Colombian Peace Negotiations' in K. Engle (ed.), *Anti-Impunity and the Human Rights Agenda*, Cambridge University Press, Cambridge 2017, p. 216, at p. 222.

two centuries of peace-making in Colombia.[1243] Since *La Violencia* (1948–1958), each peace agreement has established a commission to investigate the causes of the violence and published the findings in an official report, but usually without attempting to allocate responsibility.[1244] The fact that between 1958 and 2012 there were 15 commissions – 12 national and three local – to investigate the causes of violence is an index of the recurrent breakdown of peace agreements during this period.[1245] This section looks at three major peace initiatives in 1958, 1987 and 2005 to illustrate the practice of elite pactism as the basis for peace-making and how it was increasingly constrained by a popular desire for peace, democratic openings, the recognition of victims' rights, and judicialization of peace agreements. The three peace initiatives are amongst the most significant of the many peace initiatives dating from 1952.[1246] The 1958 peace initiative tried power sharing as a solution to end violence. The 1987 peace initiative managed to reach an agreement with a few guerrilla organizations and supported the creation of a constituent assembly to produce the 1991 Constitution. The 2005 Justice and Peace Law 975/2005 introduced transitional justice norms and recognized victims' rights but delivered greater benefits to the victimizers – the paramilitaries – than to the victims. What also distinguishes these peace initiatives is they each produced a major report from a commission of inquiry that addressed the conflict at a national level, not just an inquiry into a particular event or issue.[1247] These peace initiatives were premised on the need for amnesty – to different degrees – to bring all parties to the table; to secure

1243 J. Carrillo Lerma, 'Recognizing Conflict & Escaping Violence: Contemporary Colombian Migration' (2011) 1 *International Journal of Business, Humanities and Technology* 122, at 123.

1244 There are two periodizations of *La Violencia* one between 1948 and 1958 and the other between 1946 and 1964. The 1948–58 period begins with the assassination of Gaitan and ends with the arrival of the National Front FN in power. The period 1946–1964 begins with the coming to power of the Conservative President Ospina and the Conservative Party escalation of violence in the countryside to consolidate their power after 16 years out of office and ends with the FN government defeat of the last independent republics.

1245 See Anexo 3 Comisiones de investigación y comisiones extrajudiciales en Colombia (1991–2012) in J. Jaramillo Marín, *Pasados y Presentes de la Violencia en Colombia: Estudio sobre las comisiones de investigación (1958–2011)*, Editorial Pontifica Universidad Javeriana, Bogotá 2014, p. 240.

1246 Thornton identifies 20 peace accords over 20 years between 1984 and 2004. See C. Thornton and R. Gude, 'Towards Peace in Colombia: The economic obstacles to a Colombian Peace Process' (2011) 5 *The Peace and Conflict Review* 1, at 21. See also Chernick 1988, o.c., p. 53 and M.W. Chernick, *Acuerdo Posible: solución negociada al conflicto armado colombiano*, Ediciones Auora, Bogotá 2008.

1247 Some examples are: The Commission into the Events at the Palace of Justice (2005) investigating the M-19 guerrillas siege, the Commission established in 1994 to investigate the massacres in Trujillo between 1988 and 1991, the Commission established in 1991 that produced the report 'Pacify the Peace' as part of the Peace Accords between the Gaviria government and the Popular Liberation Army (EPL) and the Armed Movement Quintin Lame (MAQL), and, for example, the Commission for Ethics established in 2006 by the National Movement of the Victims of State Crimes (MOVICE). See J. Jaramillo Marín, 'Expertos y comisiones de estudio sobre la violencia en Colombia' (2011a) 39 *Estudios Políticos*, 231.

ceasefires from insurgent groups; to persuade insurgent groups to demobilize and embrace electoral politics; and to enable an inclusive national dialogue to address political and economic reform.[1248] Over time, these elite agreements were increasingly constrained by a society-wide demand for peace and democratic opening, the erosion of the traditional party duopoly, and the judicialization of peace negotiations increasingly shaped by transitional justice norms. The legal antecedents to the transitional justice measures set out in the FA (2016) can be traced back to these earlier peace agreements and the laws implementing them which progressively established a legal framework for peace, limited the scope of amnesty offered to members of armed groups, expanded criminal accountability balanced by restorative justice measures, and strengthened the rights of victims.

The cyclical pattern of peace initiatives, agreements and recurrence of political and criminal violence reveal certain characteristics of peace-making in Colombia. Firstly, the cycles of elite agreements producing temporary political fixes reflect their failure to resolve core issues underlying the 50-year conflict – a weak state lacking territorial sovereignty; lacking a monopoly over the use of violence; failure/inability to address chronic extreme inequality (especially in land); and a lack of political commitment to implement peace agreements. Secondly, the transience of peace agreements highlights the character of the conflict as a 'restless event' were framed and reframed by the dominant geopolitical discourses of the day. During the Cold War peace agreements were framed by anti-communism and counterinsurgency discourses, while in the immediate post-Cold War period they were framed by the discourses of democratisation and development as an antidote to violence.[1249] In the 2000s, the global securitization discourses of the 'War on Drugs' and the 'War on Terror' converged to criminalize all violence as a threat to the state under President Uribe's Democratic Security programme. The transitional justice discourse introduced the macro-political 'gospel of reconciliation' into the micropolitics of testimony in Colombia.[1250] Thirdly, from the 1980s, successive peace initiatives became progressively judicialized and internationalized with the development of legal frameworks for peace, the new 1991 Constitution which served as an inclusive peace agreement based on human rights, opening the way for the introduction of transitional justice measures in the JPL 975/2005, the Victims Law 1448/2011 and the FA 2016. Despite the interdependent judicialization and internationalization of peace processes, the transitional justice innovations around accountability – the JEPs alternate sanctions regime – reflect the importance of national ownership of peace processes for their legitimacy and prospect of engendering a long-term political commitment to their implementation and national reconciliation.

1248 Chernick 1988, o.c., p. 54.

1249 Jaramillo Marín 2014, o.c., p. 176.

1250 Jaramillo Marín 2014, o.c., p. 176.

7.3.2. THE INVESTIGATIVE COMMISSION 1958

Between 1958–1974 Colombia was governed by a political pact forged between the elites from the Conservative Party and Liberal Party in which they agreed to share power in a National Front (*Frente Nacional* – FN) government. The pact, set out in the Sitges and San Carlos agreements (1957), aimed to bring an end to *La Violencia* – the period of protracted internal conflict that had erupted in 1948, catalyzed by the assassination of the popular Liberal leader and presidential candidate, Jorge Eliécer Gaitán. President Gustavo Rojas Pinilla, the former commander-in-chief of the armed forces, had staged a coup d'état in 1953 with the support of sections of the Conservative Party, the military and the Liberal Party, to end *La Violencía* by granting a general amnesty to everyone involved in the violence but his initiative failed.[1251] The FN coalition between the Conservative and Liberal parties replaced the increasingly authoritarian Rojas government with the promise of ending the civil war and bringing about a democratic transition. The rationale underlying the FN elite power sharing pact was the construction of *La Violence* as the product of party-political rivalry between the Conservatives and the Liberals which could only be ended through a bi-party agreement. Power sharing between the Conservatives and Liberals as a solution to civil war and the threat of revolution had been first tried in 1905 to resolve the electoral political violence generated by the Conservative Party's monopolization of political power under the Regeneration (*La Regeneración* 1885–1900).[1252] The 'incomplete vote' model allocated seats on the ratio of 3:1 between the majority and minority party, irrespective of the actual proportion of electorates won. Characteristically, electoral violence took two main forms in Colombia. 'Shakedown violence', which occurred when the winners displaced the losers and their supporters – clients – from their positions in the outgoing administration, and 'retaliatory violence', which was unusual but with the notable exceptions of the 'Thousand Days War' (1899–1902) which left 100,000 dead and *La Violencia* (1946–1965) which resulted in 200,000 dead and two million displaced.[1253] The FN power sharing agreement was for a period of 16 years (1958–1974) and was endorsed by national plebiscite. It mandated the alternation of the presidency and party parity across all areas of government.

1251 J. Hartlyn, 'Military Governments and the Transition to Civilian Rule: The Colombian Experience of 1957–1958' (1984) 26 *Journal of Interamerican Studies and World Affairs* 245, at 248.

1252 The 'incomplete vote' powersharing system was adopted in Uruguay (1898), Colombia (1905) and Argentina (1912). The elite in Uruguay and Argentina introduced the 'incomplete vote' for fear of revolution by the opposition not electoral defeat. S. Mazzuca and J.A. Robinson, 'Political Conflict and Power Sharing in the Origins of Modern Colombia' (2009) 89 *Hispanic American Historical Review*, 285.

1253 J.C. Pollock, 'Violence, Politics and Elite Performance: the Political Sociology of *La Violencia* in Colombia's (1975) 10 *Studies in Comparative International Development* 22, at 28.

After the expiry of the FN in 1974, governments continued the power sharing arrangement based on Article 120 of the Constitution which obliged the new president to invite the runner-up to participate in government. This practice continued until 1986 when the Conservatives declined to participate in the Barco government.[1254]

The FN formula for peace was amnesty for the participants in the conflict, negotiations with individual armed groups, and the promise of development programmes for the areas worst affected by the conflict. Pacification involved the demobilization of militias and the punishment of those who did not, and the implementation of social reforms in the regions most affected by the violence. The FN saw its primary goal as re-establishing central government authority over a state territorially fragmented by the civil war and still controlled by different armed groups. Most were Liberal and Conservative militias but there were also communist guerrillas who had established 'independent republics' as autonomous landowning peasant enclaves on the rural frontier. In time, these 'independent republics' in Marquetalia, Riochiquito, Guyabero, Viotá and El Pato became the first strongholds of the FARC-EP.[1255] In the vision of the FN, national salvation would be managed by elites through the Office of National Rehabilitation (*Oficina Nacional de Rehabilitación*).[1256] This elite-led peace initiative supported parallel carrot and stick strategies to recover state political authority and territorial control. The FN negotiated 50 micro-pacts with different armed groups, including some of the Communists in the 'independent republics', offering them development funds to secure truces and their cooperation to implement peace.[1257] The micro-pacts were underpinned by a general pardon issued under Decree 0328 of November 28, 1958 for those who had committed crimes 'in connection with an attack or defence of the Government or the struggle between the political parties' before October 15, 1958 in the 'state of siege' departments.[1258] President Rojas had previously tried this strategy of micro-pactism and amnesty in 1953 but it failed when the state was unable to protect from assassination those guerrilla groups that had agreed to demobilize.[1259] The FN strategy rewarded those groups who agreed to demobilize but made those groups who did not the target of military pacification

1254 Chernick 1988, o.c., p. 83.

1255 T.E. Flores, 'Vertical Inequality, Land Reform, and Insurgency in Colombia' (2014) 20 *Peace Economics, Peace Science and Public Policy* 5, at 20–21.

1256 Ibid.

1257 Jaramillo Marín 2014, o.c., p. 68.

1258 Karl 2017a, o.c., p. 83.

1259 As a result of these assassinations in 1953, the Colombian left has remained very suspicious of any guarantees flowing from amnesty. M. Deas, 'The troubled course of Colombian peacemaking' (1986) 8 *Third World Quarterly* 639, at 650. Also L.J. Laplante, 'Transitional Justice in Times of Conflict: Colombia's *Ley de Justicia y Paz*' (2007) 28 *Michigan Journal of International Law* 49, at 59.

operations.[1260] With the ascendancy of anti-Communist Cold War geo-politics in the region, especially after the victory of the Cuban revolution in 1959, the FN increasingly criminalized the communists as outlaws/bandits and by 1964 military operations had overrun the independent republics.

As part of the FN agreement a commission of inquiry, The National Commission of Investigation into the Causes and Current Situation of Violence in the National Territory (*La Comisión Nacional Investigadora de las Causas y Situaciones Presentes de la Violencia en el Territorio Nacional*) which was abbreviated to The Investigative Commission (*La Comisión Investigadora* – CI)[1261] was established to audit the regions most affected by the civil war in order to make recommendations designed to alleviate the injustice these regions had suffered.[1262] The members of the CI were powerful establishment figures from the Liberal Party, Conservative Party, Catholic Church, and the military. The CI served as a vehicle to officially process the past and produce an account of why the civil war had happened and who was to blame. However, the CI Report, 'Violence in Colombia' (*La Violencia en Colombia*) (1962), obscured the origins of the conflict and collectivized responsibility for the violence, arguing everyone was to blame for *La Violencia* which arose from their 'actions, inaction, complacent silence or cowardice'.[1263] The investigators constructed violence as too diverse and complex to produce a linear narrative.

> '*La Violencia* is a process of processes, irregular in its manifestations and destabilizing in its rationales and actors; it is a problematic that cannot be confined, like a photograph, in time; it is a combination of stages and rationales with local, regional and national characteristics; it is an event that escapes a single linear and causal explanation; it is a phenomenon that has to be examined in its multiple discontinuities, scenarios and phases'.[1264]

Without a consensus about the origins or date of the conflict began, it was impossible to produce a unifying narrative about the past and therefore a consensus about the future. The CI discourse on violence as everyone's responsibility concealed the political economy of violence and very uneven distribution of casualties inflicted by *La Violencia*. The largest number of casualties were concentrated in the main coffee growing regions – for example, Tolima alone experienced around 40% of the casualties.[1265] In these regions the high levels of violence correlated with high levels of social mobilization associated with rising wages, literacy, urbanization, and economic growth. During the 1940s, the

1260 Jaramillo Marin 2014, o.c., p. 69.
1261 Established by Emergency Decree 0165, May 21, 1958.
1262 Karl 2017a, o.c., p. 44.
1263 Jaramillo Marín 2014, o.c., p. 85.
1264 Ibid., pp. 80–81. Translation by the authors.
1265 Pollock 1975, o.c., p. 25.

emergence of legal rights consciousness amongst rural and urban workers over the issues of land reform, land titles, and workers' conditions generated greater political support for the Liberal Party. When widespread violence erupted after the assassination of the Liberal leader Gaitán in 1948, many regional elites and landowners opportunistically evicted their tenants to expand coffee production and/or to replace them with cheaper labour. The impunity of the elite before the courts only exacerbated the civil violence.[1266]

The CI Report gained recognition as an historically authoritative piece of empirical research based on interviews with tens of thousands of the victims of the war but it had only limited political impact.[1267] While the FN government promoted 'living together and rehabilitation' – *convivencia y rehabilitación* – in practice it ushered in an authoritarian period governed under a 'state of emergency' marked by the expansion of executive power and the transfer of the prosecution of many crimes, including social protest and strikes, to military jurisdiction. The military's expanded legal powers increased their autonomy, which they justified as necessary for the preservation of order and stability.[1268] The recommendations of the CI Report were also implemented through decrees and emergency measures – 'to end political sectarianism they introduced unconditional and general amnesties; to counter the violence of gangs they supported rural vigilantes or the "guerrillas for peace"; to promote the capture of an outlaw they offered monetary rewards; to combat minor criminality they used social ostracism'.[1269] The pressing social problems of poverty, social decomposition, inter-party revenge, and proliferating criminal gangs demanded effective policy responses but instead were managed by emergency legal powers.[1270] The FN pact failed to democratize politics by preventing multiparty elections, by excluding from electoral politics those guerrillas who had established independent republics, and by pursuing the parallel policies of integration/rehabilitation of rebels on the one hand, and political cleansing on the other. As a result, the FN pact created the conditions which led to the further militarization of the guerrillas and expansion of state sanctioned self-defence militias which subsequently transformed themselves into right wing paramilitaries. For Colombians, '*la Violencia*' achieved the status of a national

---

1266 Pollock 1975, o.c., p. 25.

1267 Jaramillo Marin 2014, o.c., p. 74.

1268 J. Rios-Figueros, *Constitutional Courts as Mediators: Armed Conflict, Civil-Military Relations, and the Rule of Law in Latin America*, Cambridge University Press, Cambridge 2016, p. 52.

1269 Jaramillo Marín 2014, o.c., p. 86.

1270 Article 21 of the 1886 Constitution created the condition of a permanent judicial state of emergency allowing president to criminalize social sectors as 'internal enemies'. See R. M. García Villegas and R. Uprimny Yepes, ¿Controlando la excepcionalidad permanente en Colombia? Una defensa prudente del control judicial de los estados de excepción, (2005) 1 *Documentos de Discusión Dejusticia*, https://www.dejusticia.org/wp-content/uploads/2017/04/fi_name_recurso_198.pdf.

historical traumatic event but it never served as a 'positive unifying myth, as the Mexican Revolution did for much of Mexico's twentieth century'.[1271] Nevertheless, it did provide a national reference point as a single historical event for individuals to make sense of the period and integrate, at least momentarily, their diverse experiences as participants.

7.3.3. COMMISSION OF EXPERTS 1987 (*LAS VIOLENCIAS* 1985–1990)

The 1980s witnessed new peace initiatives by each successive government. The Colombian model of amnesty, negotiations with insurgent groups, and national dialogue was seen as the path to 'democratic opening'.[1272] President Turbay (1978–1982) introduced a 'security statute' which established a legal framework for peace negotiations based on amnesty and demobilization on the one hand, and exceptional powers given to the executive and military to counter insurgent armed groups and drugs cartels that did not co-operate. His successor, President Betancur (1982–1987), also tried to incentivize armed groups to demobilize and passed legislation (Law 35/1982) which recognized the possibility that the victims of insurgent violence could secure economic redress.[1273] The rights of these victims to compensation were enhanced by Law 49/1985 which allowed the executive to reprieve insurgents after they had been judged rather than receive automatic amnesty.[1274] The Law created the possibility for victims to seek truth and reparations from the victimizer because the offence was not legally ignored.[1275] However, the landowners and cattle ranchers who had been the target of guerrilla attacks resented the amnesties and pardons offered in Law 35/1982 and Law 49/1985 and in response established their own self-defence groups to fight extortion and kidnapping. President Betancur's optimistic peace negotiations based on amnesty, negotiations with insurgent

---

1271 Karl 2017a, o.c., p. 224.

1272 Chernick 1988, o.c., p. 54.

1273 M.A. Velásquez Ruiz, 'The emergence and consolidation of transitional justice within the realm of Colombia peacebuilding' in F.A.D. Pabón (ed.), *Truth, justice and reconciliation in Colombia: transitioning from violence*, Routledge, New York 2018, p. 50, at p. 52.

1274 Law 35/1982 offered amnesty to the authors of political crimes (rebellion, sedition and political violence) and authorized financing for rehabilitation and reinsertion programmes for fighters, including land rights and education. Law 49/1985 authorized the President to pardon people condemned of these crimes, with the possibility of extending the pardon to related crimes. See F. Sánchez and M. Chacón, 'Conflict, State and Decentralisation: From Social Progress to Armed Dispute for Local Control, 1974–2002' (2005) *Crisis States Programme*, Working paper no. 70, London, https://gsdrc.org/document-library/conflict-state-and-decentralisation-from-social-progress-to-an-armed-dispute-for-local-control-1974–2002/.

1275 Ibid., p. 53.

groups, and democratic opening failed because of opposition from the military, limited public support and the breakdown of the truce with the guerrillas in the context of growing levels of political and criminal violence. The response of President Virgilio Barco (1986–1990), his successor, was to launch a new peace agenda to reduce the violence.[1276] Under the Policy for Reconciliation, Normalization, and Rehabilitation (*Política de Reconciliación, Normalización y Rehabilitación*) President Barco sought to reactivate peace negotiations with the guerrillas, improve government relations with civil society and implement a National Plan for Rehabilitation (*Plan Nacional de Rehabilitación*). He departed from President Betancur's approach to peace by removing political reform from the agenda which presented the guerrilla organizations with the stark choice of negotiated surrender or face military escalation against them.[1277] In these previous negotiations the guerrilla organizations had rejected the offer of amnesty without a more comprehensive peace settlement.[1278] From their perspective the offer of amnesty constituted surrender and they had not been defeated militarily. Amnesty was a way for the government to deceive the public into believing total peace had been achieved.

In 1987, President Virgilio Barco established the Commission of Experts (*Comisión de Estudios sobre la Violencia* – CE) as a key element of his peace initiative. Its mandate was to investigate the causes of the evolving civil violence and to make recommendations about how to reduce it. Unlike the CI, the CE was not associated with a new formal political pact but the result of the failure of President Betancur's peace negotiations. During the FN (1958–1974) and post-FN periods (1974–1986), the military had set out to pacify the countryside by conducting counterinsurgency against the guerrillas and repressing popular movements with only limited success. In this unstable environment a 'dirty war' emerged in which guerrillas, narco-traffickers, paramilitaries, and organized crime used violence to control territory and coerce populations to secure their local political power. By the 1980s, the use of violence in everyday life had become so pervasive that criminal violence reached 10 times the level of political violence.[1279] The CE appointees were academic researchers and their investigation was funded by *Colciencias*, Colombia's national research grant body, as a social science research project. The commissioners became known as the '*Violentólogos*', the experts on violence, and they referred to themselves as

---

1276 *Acuerdos de la Uribe* (1984) between the Betancur government and the FARC-EP as preceded by Law 35/1982 which declared a general amnesty for political and politically related crimes. See Chapter III. Context: Origin and characteristic of the internal armed conflict in Colombia, Country Report: Colombia, IACHR (2004), https://www.cidh.org/countryrep/colombia04eng/chapter3.htm.

1277 M.W. Chernick 1988, o.c., p. 81.

1278 M.W. Chernick 1988, o.c., p. 61.

1279 Jaramillo Marín 2014, o.c., p. 113.

'intellectuals for democracy'.[1280] Their methodology classified the different kinds of violence based on an extensive review of published material. The research was conceived as a technocratic project whose findings and recommendations would provide the guidelines for more effective social engineering. It was not an ideological project to produce national unity but an instruction manual to recommend practical solutions to counter violence. The CE Report, 'Colombia, Violence and Democracy' (*Colombia: violencia y democracia*), identified five kinds of violence: political; urban; organized criminal violence; violence against minorities; and media violence.[1281] These different forms of violence were characterized as either 'negotiable' or 'non-negotiable' depending on whether violence was instrumentalized and whether a definite actor could be identified as responsible. The CE periodized violence as temporal: past, present, and future. In the past Colombia had experienced *La Violencia* produced by bi-party rivalry; in the present it was experiencing 'multiple violences' (1980s); and the future, it was expected, would bring the resolution of conflicts, a national pact, and the neutralization of violence. The CE argued there were continuities and discontinuities between these periods because some past battles were still being fought in the present. Social transformation was framed by the concepts of a 'culture of violence', 'democratic culture' and a 'new social pact'.[1282] Democratization as the recipe for post-Cold War transformation was, after all, the dominant liberal global discourse of the time. Democracy as the necessary condition for social and economic reform was endorsed by the World Bank which had made it a condition for development aid and loans, rather than the other way around.[1283] The CE argued that to bring about change, there had to be a new social pact in which the culture of peace and democracy had to substitute the culture of violence.[1284] Democratization was conceived as the only antidote to encompass the diversity of violence Colombia confronted. The plan outlined by the CE sought to progressively deactivate violence bit by bit, referred to as 'democratization by quotas'.[1285] By classifying most violence as non-negotiable they made all Colombians collectively responsible for it, thereby inverting the logic of criminal accountability which held individuals not society responsible. The CE made peace building, conceived as the reduction of violence by deepening democracy, not just the responsibility of the state but all citizens,

1280 Ibid., p. 125.

1281 G. Sánchez Gómez, *Colombia: Violencia y Democracia Comisión de estudios sobre la violencia (CVD)*, 5th ed., La Carreta Editores, Medellín 2009.

1282 J. Jaramillo Marín, 'Las comisiones de estudio sobre la violencia en Colombia: tramas narrativas y ofertas de sentido temporal para comprender la violencia' Tesis de Doctorado inédita, Doctorado en Ciencias Sociales, Flacso-México, 2011b, 228.

1283 B. De Sousa Santos, 'Colombia Between Neoliberal Peace and Democratic Peace' (2017) 11 *In Factis Pax* 41, at 42.

1284 Sánchez Gómez 2009, o.c., p. 22.

1285 Jaramillo Marín 2011b, o.c., p. 239.

especially the unions, businessmen, political parties, the media, and even the guerrillas.[1286] The CE called for a democratic pact to bring about the urgently needed political institutional reforms.[1287]

President Barco pursued separate peace negotiations with the different guerrilla organizations with only partial success while presiding over escalating violence emanating from left wing organizations, self-defence/paramilitaries and criminal organizations.[1288] The violence included car bombs and the assassination of politicians, party members, police, judges, journalists, human rights activists and ordinary citizens.[1289] The assassination of four presidential candidates led to mass demonstrations demanding a National Constituent Assembly to undertake democratic reforms to end the impunity and terror. The lasting legacy of President Barco's regime was his decision to issue martial Decree 927/1990 to ask Colombians in the 1990 presidential election if they supported the convocation of a Constituent Assembly. The Supreme Court upheld the Decree on the grounds that it offered the possibility of peace in a context where state institutions 'had lost all effectiveness' in managing the diverse forms of violence.[1290] The Constituent Assembly, which gained 88% support, became a mechanism to mobilize popular support through participatory democracy to create a broad-based momentum for peace. But as Lemaitre points out, rhetorically peace was an empty signifier that brought together protagonists around something they could agree on – it became incorporated in Article 22 of the 1991 Constitution as 'the right to peace'.[1291] The 1991 Constitution was a peace treaty in the form of a constitutional pact, a performative act of peacemaking between factions at war institutionalized in law. The liberal vision of peace advocating more democracy and more human rights prevailed in the Constitution over the 'social justice' vision of the Left or the 'law and order' vision of the Conservatives. This liberal vision of peace still constructed armed violence as the product of a political conflict which had been exacerbated by the FN bi-party pact monopolizing power. The remedy to protracted violent conflict offered in the 1991 Constitution was to make armed insurgency illegitimate through the process of amnesty, demobilization, democratic inclusion and the protection of their human rights.[1292] Yet the Constituent Assembly negotiations

---

1286 Sánchez Gómez 2009, o.c., p. 29.

1287 Sánchez Gómez 2009, o.c., p. 52.

1288 J. Lemaitre Ripoll, 'Constitution or barbarism? How to rethink law in "lawless" spaces' in C. Garavito (ed.), *Law and Society in Latin America*, Routledge, London 2014a, 55.

1289 J. Lemaitre Ripoll, 'The Peace at Hand: War and Peace in Colombia's 1991 Constituent Assembly' SELA Program 2012, Yale Law School, p. 6, https://law.yale.edu/sites/default/files/documents/pdf/sela/SELA12_Lemaitre_CV_Eng_20120511.pdf.

1290 W.C. Banks and E. Alvarez, 'The New Colombian Constitution: Democratic Victory or Popular Surrender?' (1991) 23 *University of Miami Inter-American Law Review* 39, at 56–57.

1291 Lemaitre Ripoll 2012, o.c., p. 5.

1292 President Gaviria had offered seats in the Constituent Assembly to different guerrilla groups, including the FARC-EP and ELN, to enter into negotiations. Lemaitre Ripoll 2012, o.c., p. 18.

were conducted against the backdrop of escalating criminal violence of the drug cartels using terrorist acts, kidnappings and assassination of the ruling elite to coerce the repeal of the extradition law, an important instrument of state collaboration with the US in the War on Drugs. Under the pressure of this cartel campaign of terror the Constituent Assembly adopted Article 35 which prohibited the extradition of native-born Colombians.[1293] The new Constitution made an important contribution towards social and political reform by strengthening individual rights protection against the abuse of state power, by outlawing organized violence, and by eroding the duopoly of political power held by the Liberals and Conservatives. But the enormous promise of the new Constitution could not be delivered by a weak state without the political will to address root causes of violence.[1294]

7.3.4. THE JUSTICE AND PEACE LAW 2005

In 2005 President Uribe introduced Law 975/2005, the Justice and Peace Law (*Ley de Justicia y Paz* – JPL), to advance the peace process through the Disarmament, Demobilization and Reinsertion (DDR) of his paramilitary allies. The impetus for the JPL initiative was the growing international concern over the largescale human rights abuses committed in Colombia under 'Plan Colombia', the state's 'War on Drugs' and 'War on Terror' conducted against the leftist guerrillas and drug cartels with the support of paramilitary forces. Between 1982 and 2002, violence in Colombia had evolved from generalized violence between criminal organizations to war between combatants – armies – and then to a war of massacres involving the use of terror against civilian populations as part of territorial cleansing operations. Between 2000 and 2009, President Uribe reverted from political negotiations to achieve peace to a military solution backed by significant US support. During this period Colombia's military and police forces doubled in size to 500,000 members and the defence budget tripled to nearly USD $12 billion.[1295] Uribe's war strategy sought to expand and then consolidate state control over national territory through the use of strategic partnerships with paramilitary forces, as well as agribusiness and mining companies. The intensified militarization of the Colombian conflict was Uribe's response to the earlier failed peace negotiations during the 1980's and 1990s in which the military had extracted concessions from civilian governments to criminalize the guerrillas

---

1293 Extradition was reinstated in 1997 by a constitutional amendment.

1294 D.T. Fox, et al., 'Lessons of the Colombian Constitutional Reform of 1991' in L.E. Miller (ed.), *Framing the State in Times of Transition: Case Studies in Constitution Making*, United States Institute of Peace, Washington, WA 2010, p. 467, at p. 481.

1295 A. Isacson and A. Poe, 'After Plan Colombia: Evaluating "Integrated Action", the Next Phase of U.S. Assistance' (2009) *International Policy Report*, p. 4.

and permit the recruitment of local self-defence militias which then evolved into the paramilitaries.[1296] By 2002, the paramilitaries wielded considerable political influence controlling more than a third of the seats in the national Congress and local municipalities.[1297] The extent of the formal pacts between politicians and paramilitaries during Uribe's government remained hidden until 2006 when investigations into what became known as the 'para-politics scandal' exposed them. One such secret agreement was the Ralito Pact signed in 2001 between 40 congressmen and leaders of the United Colombian Self-Defence units (*Autodefensas Unidas de Colombia* – AUC) with the declared purpose of refounding the nation; serving their mutual interests to control elections; and hold onto illegally acquired land.[1298] The war political economy, what Richani refers to as the 'war system', combined state partnerships with corporate investment to stimulate rural development and partnerships with paramilitaries to secure territory at the cost of largescale rural displacement and human rights abuses.[1299] The JPL 975/2005 was designed to formally dismantle Uribe's security partnership with the paramilitaries while at the same time consolidate their war gains, legalize their military role in the conduct of Plan Colombia, and minimize any legal penalties against them. Hence, the paramilitaries were allowed to hold onto laundered land titles of illegally acquired land; were subject to minimal or alternative punishments for their military activities; and paramilitary leaders were guaranteed non-extradition to the US.[1300] Through the JPL 975/2005, Uribe sought to politically normalize the status quo produced by the war system. In reality, the demobilization of paramilitaries under the JPL 975/2005 was not a peace process but an unsuccessful attempt by the state to establish a monopoly over the use of violence.[1301] Afterall, the paramilitaries were not the state's opponents with whom to make peace but allies in the counterinsurgency/war on terror.

1296 Colombian governments had legalized pro-establishment armed groups against communism under Decree 3398 in 1965. While the legality of these groups was revoked in 1989, Decree 356 of 1996 created a new legal framework for paramilitaries which led to the creation of self-defence called *Convivir*. While *Convivir* groups were legal the paramilitaries were not. The latter became organized under the United Self-Defence Forces of Colombia – AUC and were the subject of JPL (975/2005). See J. García-Godos and K.A.O. Lid, 'Transitional Justice and Victims' Rights before the End of a Conflict: The Unusual Case of Colombia' (2010) 42 *Journal of Latin American Studies* 487, at 492.

1297 Ibid., p. 493.

1298 'Breaking the Grip? Obstacles to Justice for Paramilitary Mafias in Colombia Report on Colombia', *Human Rights Watch*, New York, October 16, 2008, p. 90.

1299 Richani 2013, o.c., p. 193.

1300 C.J.L. Gómez, et al., 'Armed conflict, land grabs and primitive accumulation in Colombia: micro processes, macro trends and the puzzles in between' (2015) 42 *The Journal of Peasant Studies* 255, at 265.

1301 M.W. Chernick, 'Santos, the FARC and the Evolution of Peace Negotiations in Colombia' in B.M. Bagley and J.D. Rosen (eds.), *Colombia's political economy at the outset of the twenty-first century: from Uribe to Santos and beyond*, Lexington Books, Lanham, MD 2015, p. 141, at p. 143.

However, the legal significance of the JPL 975/2005 was that it introduced a transitional justice framework into the Colombian legal regime recognizing the right of victims to justice, truth and reparations. It built upon the legal antecedents of Law 418/1997 which provided a legal framework for the negotiation with insurgent groups and the recognition of victims' rights in conflict resolution.[1302] The first draft of the JPL 975/2005 was strongly criticized by national and international human rights organizations on the grounds it provided de facto amnesty for the paramilitaries and was rejected by the Congress.[1303] Controversially, paramilitaries were to be treated as combatants allowing them to benefit from recognition as legitimate political actors (counter-insurgents) rather than merely criminal ones. Paramilitary organizations had attempted to enter into negotiations with the government on the same terms as the guerrillas – i.e. to be treated as political actors – dating back to 1989.[1304] The redrafted JPL 975/2005 required perpetrators to confess to their crimes in the form of a voluntary unsworn testimony (*versión libre*) to become eligible for the benefits of an alternative punishment regime.[1305] They were not offered amnesty but massive plea-bargaining for generous sentences. Under the revised JPL 975/2005, the government established the National Commission for Reparation and Reconciliation (*La Comisión Nacional de Reparación y Reconciliación* – CNRR) with the mission to monitor the reintegration of demobilized paramilitaries and assess the reparations and restitution to victims. It created the first national registry of victims in which victims were required to register to become an accredited victim. Their role was to guarantee the participation of victims in the judicial processes and uphold their rights and to investigate and provide a public report on the reasons for the emergence and evolution of the illegal armed groups.[1306] The Group of Historical Memory (*Grupo de Memoria Histórica* – GMH) was established in 2007 as an autonomous sub-commission of the CNRR by the JPL (975/Art 50) with a mandate of eight years to investigate the origin and evolution of the illegal armed groups. Their aim was to produce a plural collective memory about what had happened during

1302 Velásquez Ruiz 2018, o.c., p. 56.

1303 García-Godos and Lid 2010, o.c., p. 496.

1304 Lemaitre Ripoll 2012, o.c., p. 23.

1305 The JPL required applicants for reduced sentences to provide a voluntary statement – 'free version' – to prosecutors without taking an oath to tell the truth. The courts subsequently determined whether the testimony was complete and truthful. In practice the process was seriously deficient because many applicants provided incomplete information about their identities, the registration of applicants' identities, because many paramilitaries avoided the investigation by lack of cooperation and by being able to ignore it because they had been granted pardons under earlier laws. Moreover, the Justice and Peace Unit responsible for taking testimonies was seriously under-resourced and individual prosecutors were regularly threatened. See *Breaking the Grip?* 2008, o.c., pp. 30–32.

1306 Jaramillo Marín 2014, o.c., p. 186.

the conflict by focusing on emblematic cases of victimization and resistance.[1307] These emblematic cases were used to provide a synthesis of structural factors and agency underlying the conflict. However, the approach was criticized for reducing the experience of suffering to representative cases distancing the real horror of events.

In practice, the JPL 975/2005 provided 'transitional justice lite'. From the outset, the JPL restricted the scope of accountability and victim recognition through its construction of the conflict. Firstly, the JPL dated the conflict from 1964 with the emergence of 'illegal armed groups' to 2005 with the establishment of the JPL, even though the conflict was ongoing. It framed the conflict as a 'war on terror' setting it apart from the historical experience of Colombian state formation concerned with establishing territorial sovereignty; competition between national and regional elites for power; and the extremely unequal distribution of land. The JPL 975/2005 displaced 'the locus of responsibility, literally scratching out *historical continuities* and *causalities* between political actors and economic interest groups not only within the temporal mandate of the Law but also beyond'.[1308] The construction of the conflict as a 'War on Terror' allowed President Uribe to justify selective negotiations with some illegal armed groups to the exclusion of others.[1309] Secondly, the top-down character of the transitional justice process allowed the state to represent itself as an arbiter above, rather than participant in, the conflict. Consequently, the Colombian military and police were excluded from any scrutiny or accountability.[1310] Thirdly, the JPL 975/2005 defined a victim as someone who had suffered damage as 'the consequence of illegal actions committed by an organized illegal armed group (*Ley de Justicia y Paz*, Article 5, amended Ley 1592, 2012)'.[1311] The victims of state violence received no recognition or legal rights to reparations. Fourthly, the CNRR never functioned as a truth commission to hear victims' testimonies. Its members were government appointees rather than respected independent high-profile public figures – the usual practice with truth commissions – and the confessions were made by paramilitaries about crimes they had committed as a condition for receiving amnesty. The absence of testimonies from other armed parties in the conflict – the leftist guerrillas and the Colombian security forces – provided a limited and uncontested view of the conflict. Fifthly, the formal legal and bureaucratic processes also served to restrict victim recognition. For official recognition, a victim needed to be identified in paramilitary confessions before the CNRR or through their registration in the RUV. However, victims

1307 Jaramillo Marín 2014, o.c., p. 201.

1308 A. Castillejo-Cuéllar, 'Historical Injuries, Temporality and the Law: Articulations of a Violent Past in Two Transitional Scenarios' (2014) 25 *Law and Critique* 47, at 54.

1309 Jaramillo Marín 2014, o.c., p. 174.

1310 Ibid., p. 174.

1311 Castillejo-Cuéllar 2014, o.c., p. 54.

were often disadvantaged by the partial confessions of the paramilitaries who were not required to reveal how they had benefited from their actions such as illicitly acquiring land.[1312] These deficiencies in the justice process significantly undermined the prospects for truth and reparations. Ultimately, only a limited number of paramilitaries confessed to crimes – only 3,200 of the 31,600 paramilitaries identified by the Disarmament, Demobilization and Reintegration (DDR) process were linked to crimes.[1313] Moreover, the JPL 975/2005 was open to abuse by allowing narcos – criminal actors – to be included on the official list of paramilitaries so they could benefit from the amnesty provisions. As Castillejo-Cuéllar observes, in some cases 'the law cleansed narcos of their illegal deeds'.[1314] However, the shortcomings in the transitional justice measures in the JPL 975/2005 were 'always secondary to the good faith of the parties … making the transition'.[1315]

While the DDR process favoured the interests of the paramilitaries, the GMH focused on the victims of the conflict and their memory of human rights abuse at the hands of different 'illegal armed groups'. The aim of the GMH was to recuperate the past through memory as an ethical act: 'it is necessary to reconstruct the past through apology and reparation with the intention of paying moral, social and legal debts to those affected'.[1316] The GMH's approach was to use emblematic case studies of violations in different geographical locations, at different times and by different perpetrators to illustrate the diversity and national impact of the violence. Following the earlier CE report, 'Colombia, Violence and Democracy', the GMH also emphasized the plurality of 'violences'. It published 15 monographs on different aspects of the conflict and a major Report, ¡*Basta Ya*! (It's Enough!).[1317] ¡*Basta Ya*! provided a comprehensive account of violence from 1964 but, unlike the previous commission reports, it did not provide a policy framework to address the problem of escalating violence. The Report did provide a counter-narrative to the 'war against the terrorists' violence narrative of the JPL and the CCNR which had eradicated the history of the conflict. However, the ¡*Basta Ya*! Report was not published until 2013, six years after the GMH had been established and three years after President Uribe had left office. The work of the GMH revealed the gap between the macro-politics of reconciliation based on elite pactism and the micro-politics of testimony which revealed the specificity of violence and the personal impact of the war. What the work of the GMH did was provide an important historical

1312 García and Engle 2017, o.c., p. 323.

1313 'Correcting Course: Victims and the Justice and Peace Law in Colombia', *Latin America Report*, No. 29, October 30, 2008, International Crisis Group, p. 2.

1314 Castillejo-Cuéllar 2014, o.c., p. 51.

1315 P. Burbidge, 'Justice and Peace? – The Role of Law in Resolving Colombia's Civil Conflict' (2008) 8 *International Criminal Law Review* 557, at 587.

1316 Jaramillo Marín 2014, o.c., p. 177.

1317 *¡BASTA YA!* 2016, o.c., p. 423.

and evidentiary resource for the evolving peace negotiations between the Santos government and the FARC-EP. The GMH also introduced *'las semanas por la memoria'* (weeks for memory) as spaces for socialization in which to present the findings of the reports to the affected communities. The GMH disseminated its work through reports, documentaries, multi-media material, audio, and photographic exhibitions in different public settings.[1318] Critics have argued *las semanas* displaced community engagement with the GMH findings for 'the institutional bureaucratization and ritualization of the suffering of victims'.[1319]

The transitional justice measures implemented through the JPL 975/2005 revealed the unequal distribution of power between perpetrators and victims. Moreover, this model of 'transitional justice lite' faced great difficulty gaining legitimacy because of its failure to address the needs of victims.[1320] It never solved the problem of how to reconcile 'the desire for justice by the victims and the desire for pardon by the perpetrators'.[1321] Afterall, the primary objective of the JPL 975/2005 was to demobilize, de-criminalize, and reintegrate the paramilitaries, Uribe's allies in the counterinsurgency war.[1322] Uribe's heavy-handed implementation of the Integrated Action Plan to re-establish state authority and territorial control in the countryside, alienated the rural population when the military carried out indiscriminate 'mass arrests of those suspected of being FARC-EP supporters'.[1323] The 'transitional justice lite' discourse of the JPL 975/2005 was used to manipulate the law to benefit the powerful rather than support its emancipatory democratic aims – 'to transform the asymmetrical power relations between victims and perpetrators and to help reconstruct the identity of victims as subjects with rights'.[1324] The para-politics scandal exposed the extent to which clientelism had corrupted Congressional politics engineered by the very paramilitary groups who were the primary beneficiaries of the JPL 975/2005. But the prosecution of politicians engaged in electoral fraud in partnership with regional paramilitaries did not solve the problem of macro-criminality as Senator Gina Parody complained in 2008: 'it's useless to convict Congressmen if in the regions the structures remain intact'.[1325] In practice, the JPL 975/2005 was a pact between allies in the counterinsurgency war that deployed transitional justice discourse as a symbolic strategy to legitimate and

---

1318 Jaramillo Marín 2014, o.c., p. 208.

1319 Ibid., p. 208.

1320 Ibid., p. 178.

1321 Ibid., p. 176.

1322 Laplante 2007, o.c., p. 62.

1323 Richani, N., 'The Politics of Negotiating Peace in Colombia' (2005) 38 *NACLA Report on the Americas* 17, at 37.

1324 M. García Villegas, et al., 'Impacto constitucional e institucional de la Ley de Justicia y Paz' in C. López-Hernandez (ed.), '*Y refundadaron la patria .... de cómo mafiosos y políticos reconfiguraron el Estado colombiano*', Dejusticia, Bogotá 2010, p. 318, at p. 319.

1325 *Breaking the Grip?* 2008, o.c., p. 102.

preserve the illegal gains from the counterinsurgency without punishment. The emphasis on peace/security over justice resulted in few prosecutions and limited compensation for victims. In particular, the provisions for land restitution for the displaced/dispossessed were ineffective. According to the Colombian Ministry of Agricultural and Rural Development around 6.5 million hectares of land was stolen, abandoned or forcibly changed hands as a result of conflict between 1995 and 2008.[1326] By 2009, 1.6% of the population held 20.5% of the country's most productive land. One of the most problematic legacies of the Uribe era was the erosion of public support for a negotiated peace, the approach taken by his predecessors from 1982, by historically compartmentalizing the conflict as a problem of terrorism.

To remedy the neglect of the victims in the JPL 975/2005, President Santos – President Uribe's successor – introduced the Victims Law 1448/2011 with a 10 year mandate.[1327] The Law was the state's response to the strong objections of civil society organizations to the benefits conferred by the JPL 975/2005 on the paramilitaries.[1328] The 'Victims Law' provided a legal mechanism for the displaced to reclaim their land and gain legal title to it through the Land Restitution Unit (*Unidad de Restitución de Tierras* – URT) which helped victims to document their case and submit it for judicial review. However, victims faced significant bureaucratic obstacles to making claims and threats of violence if successful.[1329] As Iván Cepedea, spokesperson for the Organization of Victims of State Crimes (MOVICE) pointed out, there could be no progress made with land restitution or victim compensation until, first, the para-politics and then the para-economy were controlled; and second, those who grabbed land were removed.[1330] Another serious shortcoming of the Victims' Law 1448/2011 was

---

1326 H. Alviar García and K. Engle, 'The Distributive Politics of Impunity and Anti-Impunity: Lessons from Four Decades of Colombian Peace Negotiations' in K. Engle (ed.), *Anti-Impunity and the Human Rights Agenda*, Cambridge University Press, Cambridge 2017, p. 216, at p. 239.

1327 Law 1448/2011 was passed as a transitional justice measure for the benefit of victims of the Colombian conflict since 1985 to ensure their 'rights to truth, justice and reparation with a guarantee of non-repetition, so that their status as victims is recognized and dignified through the materialization of their constitutional rights' (Article 1). Individuals are recognized as victims 'regardless of whether the perpetrator is individualized, apprehended, prosecuted or convicted of the punishable conduct and the family relationship that may exist between the perpetrator and the victim' (Article 3). Law 1448 of 2011 ('*Ley de Víctimas y Restitución de Tierras*' (Victims and Land Restitution Law)), Diario Oficial 48096, June 10, 2011.

1328 K.B. Sandvik and J. Lemaitre Ripoll, 'From IDPs to Victims in Colombia: A Bottom-Up Reading of Law in Post-Conflict Transitions' in M. Saul and J.A. Sweeney (eds.), *International Law and Post-Conflict Reconstruction Policy*, Routledge, London 2015, p. 251, at p. 252.

1329 'A land title is not enough: Ensuring sustainable land restitution in Colombia', *Amnesty International*, November 27, 2014, https://www.amnesty.org/en/documents/AMR23/031/2014/en/.

1330 D. Brown, 'The Challenges of Colombia's Victims Law', *Amnesty International*, June 15, 2011, https://www.amnestyusa.org/the-challenges-of-colombias-victims-law/.

its failure to address the state's responsibility to find and identify the more than 57,000 disappeared still unaccounted for. After three years of the Law's operation, only 1% of the more than six million displaced had received title to their land, but even more problematically, many had been prevented from actually returning. For them land restitution ended with the positive court decision.[1331] While 'land restitution' has been a key policy in the restorative justice repertoire, many IDPs now find it less attractive and would prefer compensation because of the legal obstacles to proving entitlement; ongoing security concerns over return; the problem of secondary displacement; poor economic prospects in many rural regions; and the reluctance of youth to return after growing up in cities.[1332] In Colombia, the implementation of transitional justice mechanisms during conflict through the JPL 975/2005 proved largely ineffective because the beneficiaries of the war were the beneficiaries of the Law, not its victims.

In 2012, President Santos introduced the Legal Framework for Peace (*El Marco Jurídico para la Paz* – MOJ) under Legislative Act 1/2012 in order to consolidate the numerous transitional justice initiatives.[1333] The MOJ established the criteria for the selection and prioritization of prosecutions focused on those most responsible and the conditional suspension of penal punishment. The Colombian Constitutional Court upheld the MOJ on the grounds that it aimed to achieve a stable and durable peace while addressing transitional justice obligations under IHL and IHRL. The Court drew on the jurisprudence of the IACtHR in the case of the *El Mozote* massacres in which Juez Diego García-Sayán balanced the right of the victim to justice with the right to peace – already enshrined in Article 22 of the 1991 Constitution.[1334] The Court's judgment did not challenge the transitional justice four pillars, just the balance of the right to justice with the right to guarantees of non-recurrence. The FA (2016) also cites the same IACtHR jurisprudence in highlighting the state's duty to attend equally to victims' rights and the right to peace.[1335] The MOJ prioritization and selection criteria for prosecutions was criticized by human rights organizations for denying the right to justice for most victims. The most inclusive transitional mechanism for victim recognition was their registration in the Victim Register (RUV) which entitled them to administrative justice through reparations.

1331 V. McKenzie, 'Colombia's land restitution law defrauding victims: Amnesty International', *Colombia Reports*, November 27, 2014, https://colombiareports.com/colombias-land-restitution-law-defrauding-victims-amnesty-international/.

1332 J. García-Godos and H. Wiig, 'Ideals and Realities of Restitution: the Colombian Land Restitution Programme' (2018) 10 *Journal of Human Rights Practice* 40, at 54.

1333 C.K. Lang, 'The Impact of Transitional Justice on Colombia's Rule of Law' (2019) 3 *Middle Atlantic Review of Latin American Studies* 15, at 20.

1334 L.J. Laplante, 'A Balancing Act: The Right to Peace and Justice' (2019) 59 *Harvard International Law Journal*, Comment.

1335 Ibid.

7.3.5. THE FINAL AGREEMENT 2016

The Final Agreement, signed on August 24, 2016 between the Government of Colombia and the FARC-EP, is the culmination of decades of failed peacemaking efforts and the development of a legal framework to negotiate peace. Between 1964 and 2017 the conflict had produced an estimated 200,000 dead, 100,000 disappeared, and 8.4 million internally displaced.[1336] The lack of political commitment of the Duque government (2018–2022) delayed the implementation of the FA but has since been revitalized under the Petro government that came to power in 2022. The FA consists of six areas of agreement – (1) Rural reform; (2) Political participation; (3) Ceasefire and ending conflict; (4) Solution for the problem of illicit drugs; (5) Victims; and (6) Implementation and Verification – and is by far the most comprehensive peace agreement attempted in Colombia.[1337] The FA is premised on the idea of 'territorial peace' which requires the establishment of the presence of the state throughout its territory.[1338] The centrepiece of the FA is the restorative justice programme set out in the 'Comprehensive System for Truth, Justice, Reparation and Non-repetition' (*Sistema Integral de Verdad, Justicia, Reparación y no Repetición* – SIVJRNR) which consists of four pillars – a special court; a truth commission; a special search unit for the disappeared; and a unit to dismantle ties between state officials and illegal armed groups – to guarantee the rights of victims.[1339] What distinguishes the FA from previous Colombian peace negotiations is its substantial transitional justice framework and its emphasis on victims' rights and restorative justice.[1340] Also new is the level of international

---

1336 The UV recorded a total of 9,472,019 victims of which 8,412,309 displaced persons at March 26, 2023, https://www.unidadvictimas.gov.co/es/registro-unico-de-victimas-ruv/37394.

1337 Acuerdo final para la terminación del conflicto y la construcción de una paz estable y duradera, El Gobierno Nacional y las FARC y EP, November 24, 2016, https://www.jep.gov.co/Normativa/Paginas/Acuerdo-Final.aspx.

1338 H. Cairo, et al., '"Territorial Peace": The Emergence of a Concept in Colombia's Peace Negotiations' (2018) 23 *Geopolitics*, 464.

1339 The Special Jurisdiction for Peace (*Jurisdicción Especial para la Paz* – JEP), September–December 2015. The JEP is organized into eight organs: the Commission for the Clarification of Truth, Social Harmony and Non Repetition (*Comisión para el Esclarecimiento de la Verdad, la Convivencia y la No Repetición* – CEV); The Unit Searching for the Disappeared (*Unidad de Búsqueda de personas dadas por desaparecidas* – UBPD); the Special Tribunal for Peace (*Tribunal Especial para la Paz*); Chamber for Recognition of Truth, Responsibility and Determination of Facts and Conduct (*Sala de reconocimiento de verdad, de responsabilidad y de determinación de los hechos y conductas*); Chamber for the Determination of Jurisdiction (*Sala de Definición de las Situaciones Jurídicas*); Chamber for Amnesty and Pardon (*Sala de Amnistía e Indulto*); Investigation and Prosecution Unit (*Unidad de Investigación y Acusación*); and the Executive Secretary (Secretaría Ejecutiva).

1340 On June 19, 2012, the Colombian Senate approved the Legal Framework for Peace (*Marco Legal para la Paz*), a bill establishing a transitional justice strategy that included the prioritization and selection of cases against those bearing the greatest responsibility for crimes against humanity and war crimes. See Sánchez León 2016, o.c., p. 7.

legal and diplomatic involvement in shaping the peace process. The FA was constituted as a Special Agreement under Article 3 of the Geneva Convention to strengthen compliance.[1341] Unlike any previous peace negotiations, the FA falls under the jurisdiction of two international courts: the Inter-American Court of Human Rights (IACtHR) and the International Criminal Court (ICC).[1342] The former, as a regional human rights instrument that has investigated criminal accountability in the context of internal conflict in the region for decades, and the latter, through a preliminary examination opened by the OTP in March 2005 to ensure state compliance with its international obligations to hold actors criminally accountable with respect to crimes against humanity committed in the context of the Colombian conflict. The response of the High Commissioner for Peace, Sergio Jaramillo, accorded with the Legal Framework for Peace (2012) which balanced the right to justice and the right to peace. Colombia would uphold international legal norms, but the priority was peace and the Colombian government, not an international court, would drive the peace process.[1343]

However, the FA has not escaped the influences of the political culture of the Colombian way in shaping impunity. These influences include as wide as possible amnesty as the basis for ending conflict; demobilization; elite consensus as a necessary condition for a viable peace agreement; and the rejection of external interference expressed in the idea that Colombians should work out their problems. While a general amnesty is an integral part of the FA, those most responsible for crimes against humanity and war crimes are to be held accountable but with reduced punishment.[1344] The emphasis of the FA on 'the rights of victims, the right to truth and on holistic reparations' puts restorative justice ahead of retribution.[1345] It reflects the trend in transitional justice which reduces punishment in exchange for the perpetrator's involvement in the investigation and reparations to repair the harm done to victims. Like previous Colombian peace initiatives, the FA addresses the recurrent core social and political conflicts: the weak state; exclusion; impunity; and persistent inequality – especially access to land. This latest transition employs the global discourses of neoliberal peace combined with restorative/reparative justice.

While the FA was meant to herald the transition to peace and reconciliation in Colombia, the failure to ratify the agreement by plebiscite in October 2016

[1341] L.B. Restrepo, 'The Legal Status of the Colombian Peace Agreement' (2016) 110 *AJIL Unbound*, 188.

[1342] S. Borda, et al., 'Colombia's constrained peace process: how courts alter peace-making' *openDemocracy*, July 26, 2016, https://www.opendemocracy.net/en/openglobalrights-openpage/colombia-s-constrained-peace-pr/.

[1343] Hillebrecht et al. 2018, o.c., p. 314. See also Borda et al. 2016, o.c.

[1344] Ley 1820, December 30, 2016 (por medio de la cual se dictan disposiciones sobre amnistía, indulto u tratamientos penales especiales y otras disposiciones) and Decree 277, February 17, 2017.

[1345] Hillebrecht et al. 2018, o.c., pp. 323–4.

revealed a highly polarized electorate. President Santos had used the Havana talks, which he had initiated in secret, to generate support for peace by inviting broad public participation in drafting the individual agreements. As Colombia's High Commissioner for Peace, Sergio Jaramillo observed, the peace process needed to put forward a vision for peace and convince people it would deliver a 'new social pact' in order to secure support.[1346] However, the narrow defeat of the plebiscite designed to provide popular legitimation for the peace process revealed the very different constructions of the conflict and peace imaginaries in Colombia and the distance between those who had participated directly in the talks and the public in Colombia polarized by conflicting political messaging about the talks.[1347] For the NO campaign, the conflict began in 1964 – with the emergence of the FARC-EP – and was a criminal problem with a military solution requiring the defeat and punishment of the FARC-EP 'terrorists'. For the YES campaign, the conflict began in the 1950s – with *La Violencia* – and was a political problem that could not be solved militarily and needed a political solution, especially major land redistribution. For the NO campaign, justice and reconciliation required the prosecution and punishment of the FARC-EP leaders and reparations for their victims. For the YES campaign, accountability needed to be balanced against the imperative of peace. For the supporters of the YES campaign, the victims included all the 'victims of the Colombian conflict' which had touched nearly everyone at some time over 50 years. The NO campaign's construction of the conflict as a problem of terrorism was the legacy of Uribe's democratic security policy which had polarized the electorate. The FA was subsequently approved by Congress but only after the inclusion of modifications demanded by the opposition.

Since 2016, the FA has faced significant obstacles to its implementation. Firstly, there is the problem of building a durable pro-peace constituency in a polarized electorate, and secondly, the problem of overcoming the architecture of impunity in Colombia. Even if these obstacles can be overcome, there remains the question of what kind of peace is imagined in the FA's design and its viability. Does the FA provide a solution for the chronic problems of fragmented territorial sovereignty, the state's lack of monopoly over the use of violence, the lack of state presence in peripheral regions, and the extreme inequality – especially concentration of land ownership – at the core of conflict in Colombia? What is on offer in the FA is a neoliberal peace – demobilization, political normalization, and symbolic forms of justice and reparations while leaving largely intact the

---

1346 'Jaramillo: "Peace is achievable"', *The City*, May 14, 2015, https://thecitypaperbogota.com/news/jaramillo-peace-is-achievable51413/8942.

1347 A. Idler, 'Colombia just voted no on its plebiscite for peace. Here's why and what it means', *The Washington Post*, October 3, 2016, https://www.washingtonpost.com/news/monkey-cage/wp/2016/10/03/colombia-just-voted-no-on-its-referendum-for-peace-heres-why-and-what-it-means/.

structural drivers of inequality shaped by the state's prioritization of economic development over social justice.[1348] The key to generating post-conflict political constituencies in support of the FA is through its successful implementation. While the plebiscite was supposed to mobilize broad public support in favour of the FA, it in fact provided the political opportunity for President Uribe to achieve the opposite. He used it to stage a political comeback by mobilizing the NO campaign around the old war constituency – cattle ranchers, paramilitaries, business conglomerates and the terrified urban middle class – he had originally forged to win presidential office in 2002. The success of the NO campaign provided Uribe's political allies with important political leverage in Congress to prevent the FA being fast-tracked as package through Congress and forced the close scrutiny of the FA, article by article, greatly delaying its implementation.[1349] Uribe's success as spoiler in the plebiscite turned the 2018 presidential election into a second plebiscite on the FA and boosted the chances of Iván Duque, the presidential candidate for the Democratic Centre Party – the party Uribe had established in 2014.[1350] When the Duque government (2018–2022) came to office he obstructed its implementation by trying to change articles in the agreement; by seeking to undermine and delegitimize the Special Jurisdiction for Peace (*Jurisdicción Especial para la Paz* – JEP) as leftist; and by cutting back on funding for the transitional justice process. The YES and NO plebiscite campaigns highlighted the division between elite factions – Santos v. Uribe – and the logic of veto which denied the FA essential political commitment for its implementation. It was only after Gustavo Petro became president in 2022 with a pro-FA mandate of 'total peace' that the momentum for its implementation changed.

7.4. ARCHITECTURE OF IMPUNITY

7.4.1. THE NORMALIZATION OF VIOLENCE

The most serious obstacle to the implementation of the FA is not only the 'impunity' institutionalized by the Amnesty Law and alternate sanctions regime denounced by the NO campaign – they wanted harsher punishments for the serious crimes committed by the FARC-EP leadership – but the broader 'architecture of impunity' in Colombia produced by the normalization of

1348 De Sousa Santos 2017, o.c., p. 44.

1349 R.A. Karl, 'The Politics of Peace in Colombia' (2017b) 49 *NACLA Report on the Americas* 405, at 406.

1350 F. Manetto, et al., 'La trampa de la polarización es atractiva en política y fatal para Colombia', *El País*, December 3, 2017, https://elpais.com/internacional/2017/12/03/colombia/1512266646_338897.html?rel=mas.

violence, invisibilization of victims and the spatial and social differentiation of rights. In other words, impunity produced by pervasive selective processes of social and political exclusion by which victims are made invisible through spatial, demographic, racial, and class stigmatization. In Colombia, the normalization of violence has produced a moral indifference to violent death and suffering of victims determined by place of residence, age, colour and poverty. Violent death is overwhelmingly the experience of the young poor – and usually black – males from the slums. In public opinion only the 'innocent' victim is the 'deserving' victim with the result that the criminalization and stigmatization of victims disqualifies them from having rights.[1351] Even the Victims Law 1448/2011, which confers rights to reparations from a special fund and official recognition by inclusion in the RUV, frames the victim category in terms of innocence – by which is meant not to be involved in an illegal armed group. The Victims' Law 1448/2011 conferred rights on victims but also helped create a hierarchy of victims by making eligibility dependent on the date the violations occurred. Hence, victims of forced displacement that occurred before 1985 are only entitled to symbolic reparations; those displaced between 1985–1991 are eligible for financial compensation but not land restitution; while only those victims whose land was grabbed after 1991 are eligible for land restitution.[1352] However, eligibility for land restitution requires that victims meet criteria for official recognition as forcibly displaced which can be difficult to establish – i.e. demonstrate ownership of land, prove you were forced off your land and dispossessed and did not just flee an increasingly violent region. Nevertheless, the Victims Law 1448/2011 focused on individual and collective reparations has been the most inclusive transitional justice measure based on the universalization of the suffering body as its meta-narrative.

The spatial normalization of violent death was reinforced by the 'war system'. Under his Democratic Security Policy, President Uribe declared 'two Zones of Rehabilitation and Consolidation in which constitutional rights were suspended and massive roundups of suspects were systematically conducted'.[1353] In these zones, the victims of military operations were rendered invisible by their official recording as a 'positive' (*positivo*), a legal homicide committed by state agents, when in fact many were 'false positives', cases of extrajudicial killings of non-combatants.[1354] The alleged 'false positive' involving the military concealment of extrajudicial killings was an extension of the widespread practice of the routine killing of insurgents and criminals with impunity. The patchwork character of

---

1351 J. Lemaitre Ripoll, 'Las zonas sin ley y la normalización de la violencia en México y Colombia' (2014b) *SELA (Seminario en Latinoamérica de Teoría Constitucional y Política)*, 8.

1352 'Colombia: The Victims and Land Restitution Law: An Amnesty International analysis', *Amnesty International*, April 17, 2012, p. 6.

1353 Richani 2013, o.c., p. 204.

1354 Lemaitre Ripoll 2014b, o.c., p. 8.

territorial sovereignty and the state's lack of a monopoly over the use of violence produced distinct spatial legal regimes. In zones under state control violent death was normalized by the stigmatization of life, in the zones outside state control violent death occurred in the absence of the law and where life had little value.[1355] In the late 1990s, the different political and criminal manifestations of violence became increasingly decentralized and diffused with the result that violent death became reified as an occurrence of war. Hence, the victims of state violence were made invisible by the way in which the state constructed itself as outside the conflict – it was fighting terrorists – and therefore not responsible for its victims. The objection by the NGO 'The Movement for Victims of State Crimes' (*el Movimiento de Víctimas de Crímenes de Estado* – MOVICE) that they were neither insurgents nor criminals highlights the process of invisibilization by criminalization. The victims of paramilitary violence were made invisible by being labelled undesirables and targets for social cleansing in the name of local security and community values.[1356] As Lemaitre points out, the creation of legal and moral spaces of exception only contributed to the increase in violence and the normalization of violent death amongst particular Colombians – the poor, racial minorities and the guerrillas.[1357]

The post-conflict challenge for transitional justice in Colombia has been to overcome the architecture of impunity by reversing the invisibilization of victims of violence through the prosecution of the perpetrators; providing reparations for victims; land restitution for the displaced and dispossessed; documenting the conflict; and the memorialization of victims. The first step was to re-establish political and legal jurisdiction over the spaces of exception produced by fragmented territorial sovereignty. Previous peace initiatives have always been encumbered by the paradoxical character of pacts.[1358] Between the stability of national macro-institutions and instability of local regimes there is an inertia to larger scale imaginaries, politics and identities because they are anchored in a multiplicity of competing local political economies and clientelist relations. These spaces of exception need to be reintegrated into the national territory, jurisdiction and community to overcome the inertia of pactism and clientelism. But the greater the complexity of local differentiation, the greater the difficulty of reconstituting the national level.[1359] The transitional justice initiatives promoting 'national unity and reconciliation' seek to reconstitute the nation as the 'promise of an imagined new future' for everyone.[1360] This requires the integration of all those who have been marginalized and persecuted through the normalization of

---

1355 Lemaitre Ripoll 2014b, o.c., p. 8.
1356 Lemaitre Ripoll 2014b, o.c., p. 17.
1357 Lemaitre Ripoll 2014b, o.c., p. 23.
1358 Gutiérrez-Sanín and Jaramillo 2005, o.c., p. 193.
1359 Ibid., p. 214.
1360 Castillejo-Cuéllar 2014, o.c., p. 48.

violence. However, the transitional justice mechanisms have different temporal registers to reconstitute the nation, firstly as an expression of state political and legal sovereignty, and secondly, as an expression of collective historical memory. The periodization of the conflict over 50 years tends to undermine the former in preference for the latter. The temporality of prosecutions and victim compensation address specific human rights violations and incidents, yet the regional and temporal diversity of violence prevents a simple unifying violence narrative around perpetrator and victim. Instead, the scale and diversity of violence results in national reterritorialization through the collectivization of victims of the Colombian conflict. The transitional justice project becomes the management of 'historical injuries' because violence exceeds the temporality of transitional justice technologies dealing with the legal management of the past.[1361] Instead of helping to make intelligible the structural causes of violence, the transitional justice reorientation towards historical injuries tends to diffuse responsibility and collectivize suffering. The collectivized victim is being deployed as a national symbol of inclusion.

7.4.2. MAKING VICTIMS VISIBLE

7.4.2.1. Generating Human Rights Queues

While the restorative justice approach of the Chapter 5 Victims Agreement of the FA (2016) represents an important advance in the recognition of victims' rights to achieve peace, it also taps into the particular Colombian pattern of judicialization Lemaitre refers to as 'magical legalism', the growing turn to law in response to the chronic failure of politics to provide solutions to endemic violence.[1362] The law has long been used as a legitimizing discourse by all sides in the Colombian conflict to advance the interests of elites and guard their impunity but it is only since the 1990s that the law has become a resource for victims.[1363] The human rights driven Constitutional Assembly and 1991 Constitution created the opportunity for individuals to take claims directly to the Constitutional Court. The most important provision was the 'act of public unconstitutionality' which allows a person to ask the Court to declare unconstitutional laws or decrees with legal effect and the 'act of *tutela*' used to protect fundamental rights against private individuals or organizations. These provisions contributed to what Esteban Restrepo calls 'the constitutionalization of everyday life': the practice of people – and social movements – turning to the Constitutional Court to solve

1361 Castillejo-Cuéllar 2014, o.c., p. 48.

1362 J. Lemaitre Ripoll, 'Legal fetishism: law and social movements in Colombia' (2008) 77 *Revista Jurídica de la Universidad de Puerto Rico*, 337.

1363 Gutiérrez-Sanín 2001, o.c., p. 59.

problems and promote progressive social change.[1364] In other words, in response to the ineffectiveness and illegitimacy of electoral politics and the weakness of political parties and civil society movements the legitimacy and the prestige of the Constitutional Court grew and individual claim-making increased. Julieta Lemaitre Ripoll, from a psychoanalytical perspective observes:

> If desire is awareness of a lack, then the lack of human dignity constitutes and gives force to the desire for law. It is an awareness of the blankness in the human stare where suffering has washed away all that we consider human. Law stands in that empty core and fills it by naming people victims, rights-holders, and citizens.[1365]

Lemaitre describes this judicialization process as the growth of 'magical legalism', public belief in the transformative capacity of law, just as 'magical realism' is the capacity of literature to transform reality.[1366] As a consequence, many Colombians have come to regard the Constitutional Court as so powerful that 'constitutional norms, by their mere invocation have the magical power to transform an oppressive reality'.[1367] But in practice, 'the symbolic powerfulness of law cohabits with its instrumental weakness'.[1368] The logic of the constitutionalization of everyday life has established judicialization as a political strategy for the socially marginalized and excluded. The transitional justice mechanisms for victim recognition through national registration and victim classification are in many ways an extension of the legal-bureaucratic mechanisms developed for *tutela* submissions and suffers from the same limitations. Transitional justice has extended the process of judicialization of politics by turning all the victims of the Colombian conflict into human rights claimants. The consequent explosion in the number of rights claimants, in total representing 19% of the population, has seriously overwhelmed the capacity of the judicial system as has already happened with the submission of *tutela*s, even though Colombia has the best ratio of judges and lawyers in Latin America.[1369] Between 1991–2013 the Constitutional Court received 4,200,357 *tutelas* but reviewed only 16,406 of them;[1370] between 1994 and 2004 the percentage of *tutelas* in ordinary justice grew from 2.65% to 13.57%; between 1994–2004 *tutelas* grew from 5% to 74%

1364 Restrepo 2002, o.c.

1365 Lemaitre Ripoll 2008, o.c., p. 337.

1366 Lemaitre Ripoll 2008, o.c., p. 331. The term 'magical legalism' resonates with the idea of Colombian Novel Prize writer Gabriel García Márquez 'magical reality': everything was possible in Latin America, furthermore, reality always superseded fantasy.

1367 Restrepo 2002, o.c., p. 8.

1368 Eslava 2009, o.c., p. 189.

1369 In 2004, Colombia had 10.4 judges and 304.5 lawyers per 100,000 inhabitants by contrast with Mexico which had 0.4 federal judges and 3.7 state judges and 208 lawyers per 100,000 inhabitants. See Rios-Figueros 2016, o.c., pp. 169–170.

1370 Rios-Figueros 2016, o.c., p. 66, note 37.

of total administrative justice cases.[1371] Now, victims of the conflict are not only seeking reparation under the transitional justice mechanisms but increasingly resorting to *tutela* submissions. In 2013, the highest number of *tutelas* (19.03% of all *tutelas*) were submitted by the Unit for the Comprehensive Care and Reparation of Victims (*Unidad para la Atención y Reparación Integral a las Víctimas* – UARIV) established by the Victims Law 1448/2011 to help victims to secure reparations. Popular resort to the *tutela* and Constitutional Court only highlights the larger problem of the lack of access to justice.[1372]

The transitional justice framing of the Colombian conflict has complemented the 'constitutionalization of everyday life' generating new human rights queues of victims waiting for legal remedies and satisfaction. These dual processes of judicialization have made victims visible by constituting them as subjects with human rights claims. Today human rights queues are constituted by the displaced waiting for land restitution; the families of the disappeared waiting for their missing member to be exhumed and identified; and the survivors of violence waiting for justice and reparations. By 2023, more than 9.4 million victims had been registered in the RUV making approximately one in every five Colombians a victim of the conflict.[1373] The official classification of victims has shaped victim rights, identities, claiming and mobilization. The experience of the 'displaced' illustrates how the judicialization process has transformed their status from humanitarian victims with needs, into victims of the conflict with human rights. The 'displaced' (*desplazamiento forzado*) are by far the largest category of victims, representing 89% of those registered in the RUV. Their political visibility and recognition as war victims evolved slowly over more than 30 years beginning with the groundbreaking Law 387/1997 which established their rights to humanitarian assistance and protection from displacement: the *Tutela* 025 (T-025) decision of the Constitutional Court (2004) which found there was 'an unconstitutional state of affairs' with respect to the situation of IDPs and established a special office to oversee compliance; the Justice and Peace

1371 M. Iturralde, 'Access to Constitutional Justice in Colombia: Opportunities and Challenges for Social and Political Change' in D.B. Maldonado (ed.), *Constitutionalism of the Global South: The Activist Tribunals of India, South Africa, and Colombia*, Cambridge University Press, Cambridge 2013, p. 376.

1372 Ibid., p. 380.

1373 On March 26, 2023 the number of officially registered victims on the national *Registro Único de Víctimas* (RUV) was 9,446,572. See https://www.unidadvictimas.gov.co/es/registro-unico-de-victimas-ruv/37394. The closure of the registration of victims for human rights abuses committed between 1985–2011 was contested by different NGOs because they argued many victims had not managed to register themselves. See '60 días para que 1 millón de víctimas pidan reparación', *El Tiempo*, April 10, 2015, https://www.eltiempo.com/archivo/documento/CMS-15550816. The RUV was originally established in 2005 under *Ley de Reparaciones* 28592 in response to the recommendations by the CVR to record the victims of political violence between May 1980 and November 2000. It was established as an administrative and not judicial mechanism. See S. Macher, 'El Registro Único de Víctimas', *Argumentos: Revista de Análisis y Crítica*, No. 4, September 2009.

Law 975/2005, which established their rights to reparations/land restitution; and Decree 1290/2008, which introduced administrative mechanisms to deliver individual reparations.[1374] In 2011, the Victims Law 1448/2011 established an official process for IDPs to gain legal recognition as victims of the conflict and become eligible for immediate humanitarian support and claim reparations for past harms. These included individual reparations indexed to the monthly national minimum wage – around USD $250 – which varied with the type of victimization – victims whose relatives had been murdered or forcibly disappeared received 40 times the minimum wage (around USD $10,000) and victims of forced displacement received 27 times the minimum wage (around USD $6,750).[1375] The Victims Law 1448/2011 also incorporated the 'differential approach' which prioritized the most vulnerable populations – women, indigenous communities, Afro-Colombian communities.[1376] The differential approach flowed from the Constitutional Court finding of Award 092 (2008) that the government had violated the Constitution and Colombia's international human rights obligations by failing to address the disparate impact of displacement on women which they needed to remedy through special programmes and protections for women.[1377] The recognition of the human rights of the displaced, and not just their humanitarian needs, changed women victims' self-presentation, mobilization and claim-making. Past experience of violations and suffering, not merely present destitution and economic need, became the basis for recognition as a deserving victim and eligible for reparations.[1378] But despite their legal entitlements, some women IDPs have had to struggle to be accepted as legitimate victims because of their stigmatization by other victim groups as – undeserving – leftist guerrilla sympathizers.[1379]

The long human rights queues in Colombia reflect the high expectations of victims that transitional justice laws will deliver their rights. The proportion of victims in the Colombian case at 19% of the population, stands out when compared to other transitional justice contexts where the proportion of recognized victims has usually not exceeded 1% of the population.[1380] What accounts for the

---

1374 K.B. Sandvik and J. Lemaitre Ripoll, 'Finding the Roads to Justice? Examining Trajectories of Transition for Internally Displaced Women in Colombia' (2017) 6 *Stability: International Journal of Security & Development* 1, at 3–5.

1375 A. Guarin, 'The Effects of Reparations: A Visual Interview with Arlen Guarin', *Matrix*, August 31, 2021, https://matrix.berkeley.edu/research-article/the-effects-of-reparations-a-visual-interview-with-arlen-guarin/.

1376 The 'differential approach' (*enfoque diferencial*), the idea that war impacted populations and territories differently, was a central theme in the peace negotiations. Cairo et al. 2018, o.c., p. 471.

1377 Cairo et al. 2018, o.c., p. 3.

1378 Cairo et al. 2018, o.c., p. 10.

1379 Sandvik and Lemaitre Ripoll 2015, o.c., p. 259.

1380 K. Sikkink et al., 'A Critical Assessment of Colombia's Reparations Policies in the Context of the Peace Process' in J. Bhabha et al. (eds.), *Time for Reparations*, University of Pennsylvania Press, Philadelphia, PA 2021, p. 119, at p. 125.

dramatic difference in the proportion of victims in the Colombian case is the length of the conflict over 50 years and the inclusion of the 'displaced' in the RUV who represent 89% of the total number of registered victims.[1381] Another factor in the growth of human rights queues has been the slow and incremental implementation of transitional justice measures since their recognition as victims of the conflict in the JPL 975/2005. Justice and reparations decisions under the JPL 975/2005 between 2005 and 2015 saw only 150 paramilitaries sanctioned in the Special Tribunals out the of 5,003 listed to be processed. Those sentenced accounted for only 5% of all victims.[1382] Of the 400,000 victims identified by the JPL 975/2005, only 3,136 had received reparations by 2015. The main reasons so few reparations were delivered under the JPL 975/2005 were because firstly, reparations were only determined at the end of the judicial process which can take up to seven years – and there have been few convictions; secondly, the primary responsibility for the payment of reparations fell on the perpetrators not the state; and thirdly, fear of retribution made victims reluctant to formally make claims.[1383] By 2008, of the 235,000 victims who had reported crimes, only 24 had received reparations payments.[1384] NGOs criticized JPL 975/2005 for 'the lack of a comprehensive reparations process, the privileging of amnesty over victims' rights, and the failure to effectively implement pro-human rights legislation'.[1385] The introduction of the Victims Law 1448/2011 by the Santos government made IDPs – displaced – officially visible as 'victims of the armed conflict' producing a form of 'humanitarian government' designed to regulate and depoliticize the huge number of victims of the conflict.[1386] Humanitarian government, articulated through the language of resilience, naturalizes the causes of violence and emphasizes the role of individual self-help in overcoming adversity.[1387] The inclusion of the displaced as victims of the conflict in the RUV massively increased the number of victims claiming reparations and immediately raised doubts about the capacity of the UARIV to meet the reparations expectations of all victims.[1388] The expectations raised by

---

1381 Victim reparations claims have on average have represented 1% of the population. In Colombia, the figure is 12.7% of the population. When the displaced/dispossessed are not included the claims are 2%.

1382 Lang 2019, o.c., p. 25.

1383 Lang 2019, o.c., p. 27. See also E. Pizarro Leongómez, *Victims and Reparation: The Colombian Experience*, President of the National Reparation and Reconciliation Commission Colombia, June 2010.

1384 N. Summers, 'Colombia's Victims' Law: Transitional Justice in a Time of Violent Conflict?' (2012) 25 *Harvard Human Rights Journal* 219, at 224.

1385 Ibid., pp. 224–5.

1386 D.I. Meza, 'Administrating Displaced People in Colombia through Humanitarian Government' (2022) 4 *Journal of Humanitarian Affairs* 4, at 5.

1387 Ibid., p. 11.

1388 The level of reparations paid to victims under the Victims Law 1448/2011 is much less than under JPL 975/2005. Reparations paid under the latter have been around USD $2,740 while under the former they have been USD $8,000. See Lang 2019, o.c., at p. 27.

the provision for land restitution by the Victims Law 1448/2011 are unlikely to be met. In 2016, halfway into the 10 year mandate of the Victims Law 1448/2011, only 10% of the more than six million victims have been repaired and only 5% of the more than six million hectares stolen had been restituted.[1389] By 2019, eight years into its mandate and after 'a large public investment in the visibility of the process, only 2% of the land in the country had changed ownership as a result of this restitution processes'.[1390] Despite the ambitious goals of the Victims Law 1448/2011, described as the largest reparations programme in history, the impressive numbers of cases handled only amount to a small proportion of the overall number of claims. Consequently, its restorative effect has been minimal beyond the symbolic performative exercise of the state bureaucracy being seen to be doing something by listening to victims' stories and officially registering and counting them. Buchely characterizes this process as an exercise in creating affective bureaucratic relations with victims who are then left waiting.[1391]

Getting registered on the RUV as a victim has also been difficult, particularly for the relatives of victims of 'enforced disappearance'. The 'disappeared' represent only 1% of all registered victims in the RUV but their actual number of over 100,000 makes them by far the largest number of disappeared in any country in Latin America. The disappeared in Colombia were only able to gain national visibility through their legal recognition as victims of 'enforced disappearance' after Colombia ratified the Inter-American Convention of Forced of Persons, which entered into force in Colombia on May 12, 2005, and the CED, which entered into force on August 10, 2012.[1392] Law 589/2000 (July 7) had made enforced disappearance a crime and placed responsibility on the state to locate victims of enforced disappeared through the Search Commission for Missing Persons (*Comisión de Búsqueda de Personas Desaparecidas* – CBPD) and officially document them in the National Registry of Missing Persons (*Registro Nacional de Desaparecidos* – RND).[1393] Yet, eight years after the Law 589/2000 had established the search mechanisms for the disappeared, hardly any cases had been investigated.[1394] The small size of the Prosecutor General's Unit made registration a drawn out, and for many, an empty process.[1395] Law 1408/2010, on

1389 Sandvik and Lemaitre Ripoll 2017, o.c., p. 12.

1390 L. Buchely, 'Peace, Land, and Bureaucracy in Colombia: An Analysis of the Implementation of the Victims and Land Restitution Law from a Multiscale Perspective of State Bureaucracies' (2020) 9 *Land* 181, at 176.

1391 Ibid., p. 203.

1392 See Report: Committee on Enforced Disappearances, Consideration of reports of States parties under art. 29, para. 1, of the Convention, Reports of States parties due in 2014 Colombia, received December 17, 2014, 21 CED/C/COL/1.

1393 C.M. Molina, et al., 'Forced disappearances and missing people in Colombia, South America' (2022) 6 *Forensic Science International: Reports* 1, at 2.

1394 Ibid., p. 12.

1395 T. Welsh, 'Mothers demand answers on fate of disappeared', *Colombia Reports*, November 30, 2010, https://colombiareports.com/mothers-demand-clarity-on-fate-disappeared-loved-ones/.

'Homage to Victims of Forced Disappearance' which established a unified DNA database to facilitate the identification of the missing, and Law 531 (2012), on people unaccounted for because of their enforced disappearance and other forms of involuntary disappearance, together established the criteria for recognition as disappeared. The establishment of the 'Search Unit for Missing Persons' (*Unidad de Búsqueda de Personas dadas por Desaparecidas* – UBPD) by Decree 589/2017 represented an important policy shift requiring the state to actively search for the 'disappeared'.[1396] Despite their recognition in the RND and the creation of the UBPD, the disappeared have remained largely politically invisible. As Paula Gaviria, the presidential adviser on human rights, declared in August 2017: "May the cause of the disappeared become a national cause", highlighting the fact that the disappeared never became a national emblematic political symbol of victimhood in Colombia as they did in Argentina.[1397]

With its emphasis on restorative justice, the FA made victim satisfaction of their rights to truth, justice, reparations and non-recurrence the main goal of transitional justice, thereby lengthening the human rights queues. Theses queues remain long because victims continue to register on the RUV as a result of ongoing violence, because of the delays in the implementation of the JEP resulting from a lack of political commitment by the Duque government, and because of a lack of the state capacity and resources to process so many victims within the period of the CEV and JEP mandates.[1398] In order to process so many victims and so many crimes while being as inclusive as possible, both the truth commission, The Commission for the Clarification of Truth, Social Harmony and Non-Repetition (*La Comisión para el Esclarecimiento de la Verdad, la Convivencia y la No Repetición* – CEV) and the JEP tribunals have categorized victims by the kind of violence they experienced. Both the CEV and the JEP recognized that because of the scale of the crimes and huge number of perpetrators and victims their activities would primarily have symbolic effects in their distinctive roles as discursive and judicial institutions.[1399] Individual cases were made emblematic to encapsulate the experience of tens and even hundreds of thousands of victims associated with particular crimes – i.e. enforced disappearance, extrajudicial killing, massacres, kidnapping, sexual violence, displacement, and dispossession

1396 'ICMP Welcomes the Establishment of the Search Unit for Missing Persons in Colombia', *International Commission of Missing Persons*, April 7, 2017, https://www.icmp.int/press-releases/icmp-welcomes-the-establishment-of-the-search-unit-for-missing-persons-in-colombia/.

1397 A. Moloney, 'Government: Colombia's 50,000 Disappeared Should Become 'National Cause'' *Reuters*, August 29, 2017, https://www.voanews.com/americas/government-colombias-50000-disappeared-should-become-national-cause. See also Humphrey 2018, o.c., p. 452.

1398 L. Haugaard and K. Nicholls, *Breaking the Silence: in search of Colombia's disappeared*, Latin America Working Group Education Fund and US Office on Colombia, Washington, WA 2010, p. 1.

1399 F.S. Hassellind, 'Integrating "storytelling" as a method in judicial processes? The case of the Justicia Especial para la Paz' (2022) 12 *Oñati Socio-Legal Series* 843, at 857.

of land. The following Section will briefly address the question of victim satisfaction arising from the efforts of the CEV and JEP to balance the right to justice and the right to peace.

7.4.2.2. The CEV and Victim Recognition

The CEV gave visibility to the victims of the conflict by inviting them to participate through individual testimonies, contributions to the collective submissions made by victim and human rights organizations, by officially recognizing them as victims of victimization, and by situating their victimization in the different phases of the conflict and diverse localities. The CEV started operating in November 2018 with a three year mandate to identify groups who had participated in the armed conflict and were responsible for serious human rights violations to lay the groundwork for non-recurrence.[1400] Its sources included: 1) reports by individuals and human rights organizations; 2) an analysis of reports published by previous ruth seeking bodies; and 3) the findings and insights into the conflict from participants and other CEV activities. The CEV also paid special attention to constitutionally protected groups identified by the 'differential focus' – indigenous and afro-Colombian communities, women and youth. Victim participation took place through more than 14,000 individual and collective testimonies, reports by community organizations, roundtables, community encounters and dialogues. Participation was organized around specific themes – sexual violence, the disappeared, youth, rural farmers and solidarity and dignity – in which victim working groups involving 4,476 individuals participated in 131 sessions referred to as tables.[1401] These tables sought to guarantee the participation of victims in the planning of four 'Encounters for Truth' (*Encuentros por la Verdad*) in which the experiences of victims were transmitted through individual testimonies, dramatic performances, academic fora, concerts, and art exhibitions in different communities and cities. The CEV organized additional 'Listening Spaces' (Espacios de Escucha) to broaden community participation located in 22 regionally distributed 'Truth Houses' (*Casas de la Verdad*). Six dialogues for non-repetition were organized at public round table meetings to examine the impact of the ongoing assassination of social leaders on the peace process in the regions most affected.

While a large number of victims participated in CEV truth seeking activities during the three years of its operation, they represent a very small fraction of the 9.4 million victims on the RUV. Consequently, the CEV truth seeking activities functioned mainly as symbolic and performative mini truth rituals

[1400] The CEV was established under Legislative Act 01/2017 and Decree 588/2017 structured its functioning.

[1401] 'A Review of How Colombia's Truth Commission is Advancing', *WOLA*, April 6, 2020, https://colombiapeace.org/advancing-truth-commission/.

which generated clusters of witnesses who, depending on their own experience of past violence, empathized and/or identified with emblematic victims. To a large degree these mini truth rituals were witnessed at the local, not national, level. A survey commissioned by the CEV in 2020, two years into its mandate, found that only 26% of Colombians even knew of its operations.[1402] Each local mini truth ritual contributed to the public documentation of human rights violations and to the overall CEV narrative about the diversity and changing faces of violence over time. Victims were recognized collectively as victims of particular human rights violations at different times and places. However, the most inclusive transitional justice measure was the reparations process established by the Victims Law 1448/2011. It made human suffering the basis for a unifying narrative of the conflict managed as an exercise in administrative justice – a bureaucratic exercise of victim evaluation and registration.

The main outcome of the CEV was the final Report of which the first two of the planned 10 volumes were published on June 28, 2022. The Report documented the already well-known history of the Colombian conflict researched by academics and framed as a history of serious human rights violations. It found that between 1985 and 2018, 450,664 people were killed, 80% of them were civilians, and 121,758 were disappeared. They were the victims of internal wars that had continued throughout the Cold War, the War on Drugs and the War on Terror. The Report did not seek to arrive at an 'official truth' but to serve as a document to hand over to 'the country as a milestone for reflection on the past'.[1403] In many ways, the Report provided an important counter-narrative to the dominant Uribista security discourse that Plan Colombia – the US supported counter-insurgency project – was justified because the nation had been threatened by terrorism. As José Alvear Restrepo from the Lawyers' Collective points out, this Uribista narrative does not correspond to the 'historical truth' because there were 'programmes … for extermination … from the Colombian state … to destroy organizations (in order) … to vacate regions that would later be invaded by transnational companies and megaprojects'.[1404] The Report apportioned blame for the violence to the paramilitaries responsible for 45% of the deaths; to the guerrillas responsible for 2% of the deaths; and to the military and police responsible for 12% of the deaths. It found that the conflict persisted for over 50 years because the numerous peace initiatives that had promoted democratic openings to integrate the guerrillas into the political mainstream

---

1402 A. Rudling, 'Who Is Afraid of a Truth Commission? The Narratives of the Opposition to the Final Report of the Colombian Truth Commission', *OpinioJuris*, November 2, 2022, https://opiniojuris.org/2022/11/02/who-is-afraid-of-a-truth-commission-the-narratives-of-the-opposition-to-the-final-report-of-the-colombian-truth-commission/.

1403 Ibid.

1404 R. Georgi, 'Peace that antagonizes: Reading Colombia's peace process as hegemonic crisis' (2023) 54 *Security Dialogue* 173, at 181.

were sabotaged by conservative political forces; because the model of violent accumulation in the periphery which included drug trafficking undermined it; because the US prohibitionist policy of the 'war on drugs' failed; because the democratic security model created internal enemies to be annihilated; because of the chronic impunity for violent crimes; and because of the colonial legacy of racism towards Afro-Colombians and indigenous peoples. The CEV Report did not manage to overcome the dilemma faced by all truth commissions that 'ideally, impossibly, they want to write a story based on interviews and facts that both sides can agree on'.[1405] In addition, in a world of 'post-truth politics', where there is no objective truth except what your side believes, the CEV had little prospect of generating a consensus about who were the victims and perpetrators. In a society polarized over the legitimacy of the transitional justice project, the institutionalization of the victims' right to the truth in the FA was unlikely to produce a unifying narrative. The reception of the Report reflected the polarized view of the conflict from the perspective of the left and right of politics – the former who accused the military of war crimes and the latter who blamed the leftist guerrillas for the trauma. The rightwing politicians and military dismissed the CEV as biased towards the FARC-EP and rejected the finding that the Cold War 'doctrine of internal enemy' which had resulted in extrajudicial killings – false positives – was state policy rather than the excesses of a few individuals. They argued that officializing a narrative of the conflict was antidemocratic because it erased the pluralism of views in Colombian society.[1406] The military response to the CEV was to submit an alternate account of the conflict – 'A Contribution to Truth: The Security Forces' Context Towards Historical Memory'.[1407]

7.4.2.3. *The JEP and Victim Satisfaction*

The JEP was established as the key transitional justice institution to guarantee victims' rights to justice. It was established by Article 5 of Legislative Act 01/2017 'to uphold the right of victims to justice; provide Colombian society with the truth; protect the rights of victims; contribute to achieving a stable and lasting peace; and adopt decisions that provide legal certainty to those who participated directly or indirectly in the internal armed conflict with regard to the acts referred to herein'.[1408] Its mandate was to investigate and prosecute FARC-EP

1405 R. Nolan, 'Sixty Years On: Rachel Nolan on Colombia's Truth Commission Report' (2022) 44 *London Review of Books*. See discussion below on the JEP and macrocase on the UP.

1406 Rudling 2022, o.c.

1407 A.B. Liévano, 'Colombia: New Challenges for the Military Who Don't Admit to their Crimes', *Justiceinfo.net*, September 1, 2022, https://www.justiceinfo.net/en/105798-colombia-new-challenges-military-dont-admit-crimes.html.

1408 *Acto Legislativo 01/2017 y el establecimiento del sistema integral de verdad, justicia, reparación y no repetición*, https://www.funcionpublica.gov.co/eva/gestornormativo/norma.php?i=80615.

members, the military and others – voluntarily submitting to its jurisdiction – who had participated in the Colombia armed conflict. Congress also restricted 'command responsibility' for the actions of insubordinate soldiers on the basis of not having effective control and knowledge of them.[1409] The JEP was constituted by judicial mechanisms to quickly assess eligibility for legal benefits of amnesty, pardon and the cessation of criminal proceedings; to prosecute those most responsible for IHL and IHRL crimes; to grant amnesty, pardon or early release from those who have stood trial or prosecuted for less serious crimes; and to impose a special sanctions regime on those who accepted responsibility for the crimes for which they had been indicted.[1410] Perpetrator acknowledgement of their crimes was the hinge on which the JEP's restorative justice goals turned. Julieta Lemaitre, the judge in charge of Case 01 on FARC-EP kidnapping summarized the three dimensions of acknowledgement as – 'a legal one, fulfilled by stating the exact charges and your willingness to accept them; a factual one, which involved talking about specific abductions and answering victims' questions; and a restorative one, in which you express your understanding of victims' suffering, the pain of their families in the absence of their loved ones and the long-term traces of your crimes'.[1411] The JEP had been the most difficult transitional justice measure to negotiate during the peace process because of the polarized views over amnesty. On the one hand, the FARC-EP did not want to demobilize without amnesty being granted to everyone; on the other hand, the rightwing parties wanted the FARC-EP prosecuted as terrorists. The outcome of the plebiscite campaign to secure popular endorsement of the FA largely turned on the NO campaign's demand to prosecute the FARC-EP as criminals. From its inception, the JEP was stigmatized as leftist and sympathetic to the

1409 K. Ambos and S. Aboueldahab, 'Command Responsibility and the Colombian Peace Process' in S. Ghanayim (ed.), *The Quest for Core Values in the Application of Legal Norms. Essays in Honor of Mordechai Kremnitzer*, Springer, Cham 2021, p. 259.

1410 The work of the Chamber of Recognition, Truth and the Determination of Facts and Actions (*Sala de Reconocimiento y Verdad y de Determinación de los Hechos y Conductas*), one of the JEP's eight organs, serves as a repository for reports and studies on the victims of violence and also reviews those documents, including case files from the criminal justice system, to establish whether the crimes fall under the jurisdiction of the JEP. When serious crimes are identified those most responsible (the military, guerrilla organizations and the paramilitary) mentioned are given the opportunity to present their side of the story. If the Chamber determines a case warrants further investigation it is referred to the Unit for Investigation and Analysis (*la Unidad de Investigación y Análisis*) for assessment to grant amnesty or pursue prosecution. The difficult task of reviewing the documentation of the conflict and its so many victims only highlights the enormity of the task. 'Habrá una sala de Reconocimiento y Verdad en la JEP', *La Opinion*, March 15, 2018, https://www.laopinion.com.co/colombia/habra-una-sala-de-reconocimiento-y-verdad-en-la-jep-150976#OP.

1411 A.B. Liévano, 'Colombia: The Day Farc Leaders Faced Victims of Kidnappings', *Justiceinfo.net*, July 1, 2022, https://www.justiceinfo.net/en/102992-colombia-day-farc-leaders-faced-victims-kidnappings.html.

FARC-EP by its rightwing opponents.[1412] The Duque government obstructed its establishment, jurisdiction, panel membership, and funding.[1413]

The JEP put victims at the centre of justice. However, with so many crimes and so many victims over more than 50 years of conflict, the challenge was how to uphold the victims' right of access to justice without engendering widespread disappointment and a sense of impunity amongst most victims. Official reports indicate that rebel armed groups, paramilitaries, state law enforcement agents, and non-combatants were responsible for: 4,210 documented massacres between 1958–2018; 24,447 deaths and 60,630 forced disappearances between 1970–2015; 37,165 kidnappings between 1958–2018; 15,738 victims of sexual violence between 1958–2018; and 7.7 million forced displacements between 1958–2018.[1414] The JEP strategy to manage the huge number of victims and crimes was to identify the main forms of victimization and classify the victims accordingly. Its methodology was firstly, to restrict prosecutions to those most responsible for crimes against humanity and war crimes; secondly, to organize investigations into macro-cases rather than adopt a case-by-case approach, centred on the most prevalent forms of victimization; and thirdly, establish criteria for prioritizing and selecting cases as emblematic/symbolic.

To restrict the number of potential prosecutions the JEP prioritized the prosecution of those most responsible for crimes against humanity and war crimes while providing as wide as possible general amnesty for those who took part in the armed conflict. A general amnesty was seen as a necessary concession to pacify a society polarized by the war, reintegrate combatants, and re-establish state territorial control. For the FARC-EP amnesty was politically and symbolically important because it recognized them as participants in a political struggle – not merely criminals/terrorists – and provided them legal guarantees against future prosecutions because of their guerrilla activities.[1415]

1412 R. Uprimny Yepes, 'Desprestigiar a la JEP', *Dejusticia*, April 19, 2017, https://www.dejusticia.org/?s=desprestigiar.

1413 In 2019, the Duque government cut the funding for transitional justice institutions – the JEP by 28%, the UBDP by 68% and the CEV by 40%. See R. Quintero, 'Colombia: The Special Jurisdiction for Peace, Analysis One Year and a Half After its Entry into Operation', *International Commission of Jurists*, Geneva, 2019, 27–28, https://www.icj.org/colombia-the-special-jurisdiction-for-peace-one-year-after-icj-analysis/. On the attempt to exclude human rights defenders from the Panel see G.I. Gómez 'Political Conflicts Over the JEP: A Sociolegal Perspective' in K. Ambos and S. Peters (eds.) *Transitional Justice in Colombia: The Special Jurisdiction for Peace*, Nomos, Baden-Baden 2022, p. 13.

1414 *Colombia en riesgo de impunidad: Puntos ciegos de la Justicia Transicional frente a crímenes internacionales de competencia de la CPI*, FIHD y CAJAR, May 2020 No 751e. (Report submitted to the ICC), 5, https://www.fidh.org/IMG/pdf/fidh-cajar_informe_colombia_en_riesgo_de_impunidad.pdf.

1415 N.C. Sánchez, 'Post-conflict in Colombia (18) Amnesty and pardon in the peace process', *openDemocracy*, September 22, 2016. https://www.opendemocracy.net/en/democraciaabierta/post-conflict-in-colombia-18-amnesty-and-pardon-in-peace-pro/.

The JEP's innovative approach to accountability emphasized restorative and reparative justice measures to benefit the victims over retributive justice to punish perpetrators. Its controversial special restorative sanctions (*sanciones propias*) regime allowed perpetrators to benefit from reduced sentences on the condition they told the whole truth about the serious violations they had committed and acknowledged their responsibility to the victims.[1416] The transitional justice policy of reduced punishment for truth had antecedents in the JPL 975/2005 which had also offered reduced punishments to paramilitaries in exchange for unsworn testimony (*versión libre*) about their crimes. The JEP restorative sanctions provided for sentences of between five and eight years served in 'restricted liberty' with the requirement that perpetrators provided reparations in the form of community service through activities such as rebuilding 'schools, roads, health centres and other facilities that were destroyed by them during armed attacks'.[1417] The prevailing ethos saw restorative sanctions as a way to repair the broken relationships between victims and perpetrators and consolidate peace. In practice, repairing relationships largely referred to the demobilization and reintegration of ex-guerrillas and the mandated community service perpetrators were required to provide as collective reparations to communities impacted by their violence. The victims were supposed to participate in determining the appropriate reparations measures referred to as 'TOARs' – 'work, activities and actions with reparative content'.[1418] Over time, the character of collective reparations changed from direct tangible community service in local development projects to more symbolic forms focused on satisfying moral harm which limited the linkages between local development projects and special sanctions.[1419] While there was initially strong national and international criticism of the amnesty provisions and alternate sanctions regime, the Constitutional Court endorsed the conditionality regime because it accepted there was a need to balance the prosecution of the most serious human rights violations – in agreement with the ICC – with the impossible task of fulfilling a maximalist position of the prosecution of all serious human rights violations.[1420] Lisa LaPlante also points out that prioritization is a normal feature of criminal

---

1416 C. Sandoval et al., 'The Challenges of Implementing Special Sanctions (*sanciones propias*) in Colombia and Providing Retribution, Reparation, Participation and Reincorporation' (2022) 14 *Journal of Human Rights Practice*, 478.

1417 M. Diaz Marquez, 'Opinion: Why Colombia is a pioneer in restorative justice', *Justice Rapid Response*, June 10, 2021, https://www.justicerapidresponse.org/opinion-why-colombia-is-a-pioneer-in-restorative-justice/.

1418 H. Martínez, 'TOAR anticipados y Sanciones Propias: reflexión informada para la Jurisdicción Especial para la Paz', *Dejusticia*, December 14, 2021, https://www.dejusticia.org/publication/toar-anticipados-y-sanciones-propias-reflexion-informada-para-la-jurisdiccion-especial-para-la-paz/.

1419 Sandoval et al. 2022, o.c., p. 494.

1420 Quintero 2019, o.c.

prosecutions because no transitional justice experience could ever possibly prosecute all the potential perpetrators and the prioritization of those cases most likely to succeed in court also preserved the basic rights of victims to truth and reparations.[1421] As Nestor Raul Correa, the JEP Tribunal Administrator noted, the policy of selective prosecution meant that trials would be largely symbolic. "If I were to give a random figure – of 200,000 crimes that have happened in these fifty years, we'll investigate 1,000".[1422]

To maximize the participation of the large number of victims in the prosecutions the JEP established macro-cases. The macro-case approach reflected the findings of the major reports on the history of violence during the Colombian conflict which emphasized its diversity. These include the Report: A Contribution to Understanding the Armed Conflict in Colombia (*Informe: Contribución al entendimiento del conflict armado en Colombia*), submitted to the Havana talks by the Commission on the History of the Conflict and Its Victims (*La Comisión Histórica del Conflicto y sus Víctimas* – CHCV) (2015) that emphasized the diversity of violence, and the earlier major reports on the Colombian conflict – *Colombia: violencia y democracia* (1987) and ¡*Basta Ya*! (2013).[1423] To address the diversity and scale of violence the JEP prosecutorial strategy identified seven macro-cases organized around the main forms of victimization – kidnappings; crimes against humanity; war crimes in particular departments; false positives; victimization by FARC-EP; the victimization of members of the UP;[1424] and the recruitment of child soldiers.[1425] The Constitutional Court supported the prosecutorial strategy of macro-cases arguing that a case-by-case approach to investigations risked producing a generalized sense of impunity.[1426] The macro-case

---

1421 Laplante 2019, o.c.

1422 J. S. Cobb, 'Colombia tribunal begins mammoth task of investigating, trying war crimes', *Reuters*, March 15, 2018, https://www.reuters.com/article/us-colombia-peace-court/colombia-tribunal-begins-mammoth-task-of-investigating-trying-war-crimes-idUSKCN1GR2P6.

1423 *Contribución al entendimiento del conflicto armado en Colombia*, La Comisión Histórica del Conflicto y sus Víctimas (CHCV), Bogotá, Febrero, 2015, http://www.altocomisionadoparalapaz.gov.co/mesadeconversaciones/PDF/Informe%20Comisi_n%20Hist_rica%20del%20Conflicto%20y%20sus%20V_ctimas.%20La%20Habana%2C%20Febrero%20de%202015.pdf. The CHCV Report pointed to complexity, discontinuity, regional diversity and prolonged character of the conflict and identified the main sources of victimization – forced displacement, land grabbing, kidnapping, extortion, military recruitment of minors, extrajudicial killings, targeted assassinations, sexual violence, forced disappearance and attacks against civilians. It also outlined the ongoing threat from illegal armed groups as they morphed into new criminal and security organizations with the changing political economy of violence and rural development.

1424 Demobilizing FARC-EP members remembered the experience of previous transition to mainstream party politics. By 1990 more than 2500 politicians, including two presidential candidates had been assassinated. See Nolan 2022, o.c.

1425 'What Macro-Cases has Colombia's Special Jurisdiction for Peace (JEP) Opened?', *WOLA*, March 13, 2020, https://colombiapeace.org/what-macro-cases-has-colombias-special-jurisdiction-for-peace-jep-opened/.

1426 The Legal Framework for Peace (Legislative Act 01/2012) introduced the strategy of macro-processes to overcome the serious limitation of the case-by-case approach to guarantee the

strategy sought to maximize the participation and recognition of victims through their collectivization. Under the JEP victims have 'the right to be fully informed, the right to appeal the decisions of the court's various chambers and sections, and the right to introduce or request evidence'.[1427] Yet because of the differences between macro-cases, the JEP has had to develop flexible modes of victim participation including the processes for victim accreditation, legal representation and participation in the court room, and victim protection.[1428] However, the limitations of victims' participation through collectivization has become more apparent with the progress of the macro-cases. Firstly, few victims have been able to participate as individuals in hearings to provide personal testimonies about the impact of crimes on their lives. For the most part, victims have participated collectively through the inclusion of their testimonies in victim reports, through legal representatives allocated to cases, and through victim accreditation.[1429] Many victims are dissatisfied with the experience of the collectivization of victim participation because the numbers make it a homogenizing and distancing process. The number of victims accredited to each macro-case ranges from more than 3,000 to 180,000.[1430] Using the earlier JPL 975/2005 process as a guide, the ratio of legal representatives to victims ranged from 1/425 to 1/976.[1431] What is more, the actual universe of victims associated with each macro-case is much larger than just those officially registered. In Case 01 on FARC-EP kidnapping only 2,528 were accredited out of a possible 21,396.[1432]

The JEP prosecution policy required the development of criteria for prioritizing and selecting the most emblematic cases – the most responsible for the worst crimes. Its mandate restricted prosecutions to political crimes

---

right to justice for victims of massive human rights violations. The macroprocesses strategy allowed the massive participation of victims in a structured way. See Alviar García and Engle 2017, o.c., p. 234.

1427 J.V. Trujillo, 'The Collectivization of Victim Participation: The Case of Colombia's Special Jurisdiction for Peace' in K. Ambos and J.S. Peters (eds.) *Transitional Justice in Colombia: The Special Jurisdiction for Peace*, Nomos, Baden-Baden 2022, p. 161, at p. 174.

1428 'COLOMBIA: Victim participation in transitional justice brings major challenges, panellists say', *Justice Rapid Response*, August 10, 2020, https://www.justicerapidresponse.org/colombia-victim-participation-in-transitional-justice-brings-major-challenges-panellists-say/.

1429 La acreditación de las víctimas ante la JEP, Boletín #60 del Observatorio sobre la JEP, August 2022, https://www.coljuristas.org/observatorio_jep/documentos/boletines/Boletin_60.pdf.

1430 For example, in Case 01 – Illegal Detentions of Individuals by the FARC-EP 21,396 kidnappings were identified, 3,410 victims accredited and 8 FARC leaders found guilty. In Case 05, Territorial Situation of the Northern Cauca and Southern Cauca Valley Regions has identified close to 400,000 victims, accredited 124,785 victims and a further 20,205 victims who are members of 47 Afro-descendant Community Councils. See JEP, https://www.jep.gov.co/macrocasos/.

1431 Trujillo 2022, o.c., p. 172.

1432 Sandoval et al. 2022, o.c., p. 489.

committed by the FARC-EP, the military, and others who voluntarily submitted to its jurisdiction. However, the issue of eligibility became increasingly politicized as a wide range of public officials, industrialists, military, paramilitary and ordinary civilians tried to attract the jurisdiction of the JEP to avoid prosecutions in the ordinary courts.[1433] Military and paramilitary leaders in particular were initially strongly opposed to the JEP but they increasingly came to favour its jurisdiction either to avoid the criminal courts or to have the JEP review their criminal court convictions and sentences in order to benefit from the alternate sanctions. In 2017, the Supreme Court rejected the applications of ex-Congressional deputies convicted for their role in the infamous para-politics scandal to have their convictions reviewed by the JEP under the Amnesty Law (2016). The Court decided their actions did not constitute political crimes.[1434] However, in July 2022, the Appeals Chamber of the JEP found that paramilitary commanders who were 'functionally and materially incorporated into the armed forces' fell under its jurisdiction.[1435] In doing so it gave Rodrigo Tovar Pupo – alias 'Jorge 40', a notorious paramilitary leader in the AUC – the opportunity to appear before the JEP rather than serve his 40 year prison sentence.[1436] Paramilitaries had been excluded from the JEP jurisdiction because they were not rebels, had not signed the FA, and still remained subject to the provisions of the JPL 975/2005.[1437] The Appeals Chamber argued the state had promoted a counterinsurgency strategy which facilitated the outsourcing of security roles to paramilitaries. The decision contradicted the fact that since the early 1980s the state had adopted legislation to curb paramilitary expansion and criminalize them, not recognize them as performing legitimate state functions.[1438] The

1433 An accused once accepted under the JEP's jurisdiction cannot be prosecuted in the ordinary criminal courts. C. Oqueno, 'Civiles implicados en el conflict armado en Colombia piden acogerse al tribunal de paz', *El País*, September 1, 2019, https://elpais.com/internacional/2019/09/05/colombia/1567715953_212442.html.

1434 'Parapolíticos no pueden acceder a beneficios de la Ley de Amnistía: Corte Suprema', *El Espectador*, July 14, 2017, https://www.elespectador.com/noticias/judicial/parapoliticos-no-pueden-acceder-la-jep-corte-suprema-articulo-703126.

1435 Appeals Chamber (JEP) Decision TP-SA 1187 of July 21, 2022. See S. Vargas Niño, 'Colombia's Special Jurisdiction for Peace Bends the Law to Dub Paramilitaries as State Officials: The Time For Critique is Now', *OpinioJuris*, September 16, 2022, https://opiniojuris.org/2022/09/16/colombias-special-jurisdiction-for-peace-bends-the-law-to-dub-paramilitaries-as-state-officials-the-time-for-critique-is-now/.

1436 'Colombia: ex paramilitar "Jorge 40" aspira a tribunal de paz', *Los Angeles Times*, January 26, 2023, https://www.latimes.com/espanol/internacional/articulo/2023-01-27/colombia-ex-paramilitar-jorge-40-aspira-a-tribunal-de-paz. The notorious AUC paramilitary leader, Salvatore Mancuso, currently serving a sentence for drug trafficking in the US after being extradited, is also trying to attract JEP jurisdiction to benefit from the special sanctions regime. 'Los hornos del horror en Colombia', *El País*, May 15, 2023, https://elpais.com/opinion/2023-05-15/los-hornos-del-horro-en-colombia.html.

1437 Ibid.

1438 Ibid.

Appeals Chamber decision failed to acknowledge that if they were indeed part of the military the state was accountable for their actions.

The JEP macro-case approach came under scrutiny by the ICC and the IACtHR because it limited the potential number of prosecutions and denied many victims their individual right of access to justice.[1439] Thus, the ICC paid close attention to the JEP's handling of Case 03, 'Illegitimately Perpetrated Deaths Presented as Combat Casualties by Agents of the State', in which 29 generals and colonels were investigated over 1,228 'false positives', the extrajudicial killings allegedly committed by the Colombian military.[1440] The JEP prioritized Case 03 because new evidence revealed that extrajudicial killing was more widespread and systematic than first thought; because the number of victims (6,402) was double the original figure; because the alleged perpetrators remained active members of the military; because the level of collaboration between the military and paramilitary units was significant; and because the victims systematically targeted were the most vulnerable in society.[1441] The shadow of the IACtHR was an important factor in the prioritization of Case 06 'Victimization of Patriotic Union (UP) Members by the Armed Forces'. Families and victim organizations first petitioned the IACHR in December 1993 over the escalating assassination of UP members. On June 13, 2018, more than 24 years later, the IACHR finally presented the case *'Members and Militants of the UP' v. the Republic of Colombia* to the IACtHR, alleging the state had failed to protect the lives of the members and families of the UP and uphold their right to democratic participation in politics.[1442] In its judgment the IACtHR expressed concern about the impact of the JEP policy of selective prosecution and reduced punishment on the victims' right of access to justice.[1443] However, after the indictments of 25 senior military leaders in Case 03 and 8, and FARC-EP leaders in Case 01, the OTP Karim Khan validated the JEP alternate sanctions regime by announcing on October 28, 2021 the closure of the ICC's preliminary examination of Colombia it had opened 17 years before. In response, Sergio Jaramillo, the former peace commissioner, observed: "This is a triumph for the peace deal and the JEP: for the first time the ICC recognizes the transitional system of a country as being in line with the

1439 R. Urueña, 'Prosecutorial Politics: The ICC's Influence in Colombian Peace Processes, 2003–2017' (2017) 111 *American Journal of International Law*, 104.

1440 '29 generales y coroneles, en la mira de la CPI por ejecuciones extrajudiciales', *El Espectador*, July 9, 2017, https://www.elespectador.com/colombia-20/jep-y-desaparecidos/29-generales-y-coroneles-en-la-mira-de-la-cpi-por-ejecuciones-extrajudiciales-article/.

1441 E.M. Restrepo, 'Perverse Incentives: Extrajudicial Killings in Colombia' (2021) 22 *Georgetown Journal of International Affairs* 219, at 223.

1442 Inter-American Court of Human Rights, Case of *'Members and Militants of the Patriotic Union' vs. Colombia*, Judgment of July 27, 2022, 9.

1443 Ibid. The IACtHR noted that 'the collective dimension of the right to truth transcends the victims of the specific case, making society as a whole an injured party'. The authorities showed an 'indifference to events that attacked the very foundations of a democratic society'.

Rome Statute."[1444] The Duque government signed an agreement with the OTP they would continue to support the JEP process and fund it.

Given the scale of the crimes, perpetrators and victims produced by the Colombian conflict, retributive justice measured by the number of convictions handed down could never be an adequate index of the JEP's success. Only restorative justice through reconciliation generated by public recognition of the truth and victim satisfaction could be a persuasive measure of its success. Victim satisfaction hinged on the victim's experience of participation of a specific macro-case which functioned as a discrete transitional justice ritual able to generate a shared experience (*communitas*) of justice for the accredited victims. The macro-cases prioritized emblematic cases around which a ritual community – constituted by the accused and the accredited victims and those collectively classified as victims – was forged through their overall experience of the judicial processes which included the investigation; indictments; perpetrator acceptance or rejection of the charges; victim testimonies and witnessing; and perpetrator acknowledgement of the impact of their crimes on individuals, families and communities. However, the limitations of this prosecutorial strategy for victim satisfaction have become evident over time with the slow progress of prosecutions, the limited opportunities for direct victim participation in the trial process, and the dissatisfaction of other victim groups over their feeling of exclusion because of the prioritization of particular macro-cases. Progress has been slow because of the lack of political commitment of the Duque government to support the JEP and because of the complexity of the cases and the size of the task.[1445] The most advanced macro-cases – Case 01 on FARC-EP kidnapping and Case 03 on military extrajudicial killing – in which FARC-EP and military leaders admitted their responsibility have taken almost five years. The fifth indictment (Case 05) against 10 FARC-EP regional commanders for war crimes and crimes against humanity targeting two ethnic groups with more than 180,000 accredited victims was only issued on March 8, 2023.[1446] Defending this indictment Julieta Lemaitre, the judge in charge of the FARC-EP kidnapping case, regretted the slow progress of the JEP which she pointed out had limited resources and only 10 years to bring charges. She observed, 'It is clear that there will be no further final results before 10 years have passed, since five years have already passed and the only product is the indictment of two of six FARC-EP structures that operated in the zone, and not even for all the crimes committed'.[1447] Victims have also been

[1444] A.B. Liévano, 'The ICC Backs Colombia's Transitional Justice Model', *Justiceinfo.net*, November 9, 2021, https://www.justiceinfo.net/en/84121-icc-backs-colombia-transitional-justice-model.html.

[1445] A. Isacson, 'A Long Way to Go: Implementing Colombia's peace accord after five years', *WOLA*, November 23, 2021, https://www.wola.org/analysis/a-long-way-to-go-implementing-colombias-peace-accord-after-five-years/.

[1446] Liévano 2021, o.c.

[1447] Liévano 2021, o.c.

dissatisfied with their experience of macro-case collectivization. They have had limited opportunities to participate in the Tribunal hearings and when they do it has often been remotely through video links. Many victims expected they would get the opportunity to confront their victimizers in Court; to question them about the details of specific incidents and the fate of their family members; or to be asked for forgiveness. Collective representation through the appointment of legal representatives has not greatly improved the experience of participation. In an attempt to address the limitations of the experience of collective participation the JEP organized outreach activities holding symbolic commemorative events and extrajudicial encounters.[1448]

Many victims were dissatisfied with the JEP's announcement in February 2022 that it was establishing three new macro-cases focused on: 1) other crimes committed by the FARC-EP – kidnapping, recruitment of child soldiers, land mines, town sieges; 2) crimes carried out by Army officials, policemen and other state agents, with an emphasis on sexual violence, torture, land dispossession and massacres, including those in collusion with right-wing paramilitary groups; and 3) the suffering of indigenous persons and Afro-Colombians, who jointly account for 10% of Colombia's population and 18% of its registered victims.[1449] The JEP decided to establish the new macro-cases based on its analysis of 458 reports submitted by victims' groups and state agencies that had identified 258,000 criminal offences.[1450] Many victims groups felt excluded from the decision-making process to prioritize these new macro-cases especially because they believed they were likely to be the last ones. Victims' groups representing victims of massacres and disappearances in *Comuna* 13 in Medellín, sexual violence, and landmines were particularly active in lobbying the JEP to prioritize these violations by creating more macro-cases. Victims' groups also criticized the move away from the victim-centred focus on emblematic crimes and worst affected regions to the behaviour of specific actors.[1451]

7.4.3. NEOLIBERAL PEACE

Another limitation of the FA is the peace imaginary underlying it. To what extent will the sociological design of the FA be able to resolve the recurrent core issues of the recovery of state territorial sovereignty, succeed in securing a monopoly over the use of violence, and address the major issue of land

1448 Trujillo 2022, o.c., p. 174.
1449 A.B. Liévano, 'First Rift Between Colombia's Peace Tribunal and the Victims', *Justiceinfo.net*, March 14, 2022, https://www.justiceinfo.net/en/88737-first-rift-between-colombia-peace-tribunal-victims.html.
1450 Ibid.
1451 Ibid.

concentration? While there is an emphasis on restorative justice in the Victims Agreement, the Rural Development Agreement puts economic interests before victims' rights. The government's non-negotiable commitment to neoliberal development is also a commitment to neoliberal peace in which priority is given to attracting international corporate investment for agricultural and mining development as the engine of national development.[1452] Neoliberal peace is about state reterritorialization through corporate and security partnerships. The sidelining of land redistribution in the peace agenda, historically a key item in the FARC-EP's political platform, represented a major concession by them.[1453] The issue of land restitution embodies the conflict between restorative justice for the displaced and the priority of supporting agribusiness development in the FA. Land grabbing was integral to the war system. It merged counterinsurgency with social cleansing to seize land and consolidate state presence through alliances with local business and security providers – the paramilitaries. The neoliberal peace model perpetuates this strategy of the war system in which sovereignty was parceled out to local conglomerates or corporate groups to support counterinsurgency and state reterritorialization through development. The franchising of rural governance through agribusiness projects and the co-option of the political system by local powerholders raises questions about the effectiveness of the strategy.[1454] Afterall, amongst the opponents of the FA – Uribe's war constituency of ranchers, landholders, paras, business groups – were the beneficiaries of mass displacement, land grabs, and land title laundering. The new concentration of landholdings in the hands of international corporations arising out of the war political economy makes them stakeholders in the peace process with interests opposed to land redistribution.[1455] The slow progress in land restitution provided for under the Victims Law 1448/2011 suggests there are considerable barriers to the realization of these rights. Amnesty International reported that by August 2014 only about 64,000 claims had been lodged for land restitution under the law.[1456] Of these, only about 650 had been ruled on with restitution judges and magistrates finding in favour of the land claimants in 96% of cases but the area of land restituted – 30,000 hectares – represented approximately 0.005% of all the land grabbed.

1452 J. Glennie, 'Colombia's unethical development', *The Guardian*, June 6, 2011, https://www.theguardian.com/global-development/poverty-matters/2011/jun/06/colombia-amoral-development-uribe.

1453 Alviar García and Engle 2017, o.c., p. 238.

1454 C. López-Hernandez, '"La refundación de la patria", de la teoría a la evidencia' in C. López-Hernandez (ed.), *y refundadaron la patria .... de cómo mafiosos y políticos reconfiguraron el Estado colombiano*, Debate, Bogotá 2010, p. 29.

1455 A. Gómez-Suárez et al., 'Foreign Investors and the Colombian Peace Process' (2016) 18 *International Community Law Review* 223, at 247.

1456 'Colombia: A Land Title is Not Enough: Ensuring Sustainable Land Restitution in Colombia', *Amnesty International*, November 27, 2014, p. 29.

The continuing crisis over the political assassination of social leaders is not just a failure of protection but the failure to recognize the way the war political economy and development model were intertwined and remain so under neoliberal peace. Take the example of the 'mining locomotive', one of the key sectors of resource development, in which by 2012 over one third of Colombia was subject to mining leases or designated 'strategic mining areas'.[1457] In order to regulate corporate mining projects in these post-conflict zones, the Santos government introduced Corporate Social Responsibility (CSR) agreements as a human rights protection mechanism. CSR promotes economic regulation through 'incentives' instead of 'institutional regulation' to produce co-regulation through public-private cooperation under a regime of 'global coherence', compliance with international standards, policies, and practices. The emergence of the international CSR regime is explained as 'an effort to bridge the gap between the State's abilities (and objectives) and the market forces unleashed by globalization'.[1458] In post-conflict Colombia, CSR became part of the state's strategy for the recovery of sovereignty over areas previously not directly under its control. Yet the policy, by delegating 'responsibility for the social mediation of mining development' to corporations, represents a 'strategy of selective absence'.[1459] In other words, the state franchises control over zones designated for development – ZIDRES Areas of Interest for Rural, Economic and Social Development[1460] – to global corporations, thereby prioritizing economic development over the claims of IDPs for social justice and land restitution. Moreover, the main thrust of land restitution is to provide access to undeveloped land rather than the recovery of the land from which IDPs were displaced which has often already been integrated into agribusiness investment and production. From the perspective of the state, the international investor regime takes priority over social justice for the displaced in peace consolidation under the principle of proportionality.[1461]

The logic of CSR seeks to identify the common interest of the corporations and civil society couched in the language of making peace. However, rather than producing an alignment with the interests of 'civil society', mining corporations are more often aligned with the interests of neo/paramilitary groups and security forces by choice or coercion. In some instances mining companies have gained

1457 E. R. Grégoire and L. M. Monzón, (2017) 38 *Canadian Journal of Development Studies / Revue canadienne d'études du développement* 253, at 257.

1458 Ibid., p. 254.

1459 Ibid., p. 257.

1460 Law 1776 on January 29, 2016, established 'The Areas of Interest for Rural, Economic and Social Development' (*Zonas de Interés de Desarrollo Rural, Económico y Social* – ZIDRES) to promote competitive economic development in rural farming areas in Colombia in more than seven million hectares of land. ZIDRES: Areas of Interest for Rural, Economic and Social Development. https://www.abcolombia.org.uk/zidres-background/.

1461 Gómez-Suárez et al. 2016, o.c., p. 240.

access to territory by getting the help of paramilitaries to pacify and control local communities through terror and displacement, suppressing protests over mining and workers' demands.[1462] Mining also creates new opportunities for neo-paramilitaries including 'extortion of companies, accessing royalties paid to local governments through corruption and electoral manipulation, providing "protection", controlling subcontractors and using the sector's structure for money laundering'.[1463] The institutionalization of CSR for the co-regulation of the international mining sector reveals how the Colombian corporate state is evolving under neoliberal peace. A new 'public-private sovereignty' is emerging shaped by partners with multilateral organizations and corporations on the one hand, and the older partners under Plan Colombia – counterinsurgency – who opportunistically extort rents from the new political economy. Human rights become subordinated to a definition of 'common good' in which corporate interests take priority over the interest of local communities in their attempts to recover their land and their resistance to new projects threatening to precipitate new cycles of disappearance and displacement. The negative effects of neo-extractivism are 'forcible land seizure, the eviction of peasants, indigenous and Afro-descendant populations from their ancestral lands, the physical elimination of resistance leaders, the contamination of water and land, and an alarming increase in cancer rates among rural populations'.[1464] Moreover, the continued absence of the state in large parts of the countryside stalls the implementation of the peace agreement. Illegal economies (drugs) thrive and impunity reigns amongst the drug gangs as well as private and public security forces.[1465]

7.5. CONCLUSION

In August 2019, the FARC-EP leader and negotiator Luciano Marín (*alias* Iván Márquez) announced he was breaking with the 2016 Peace Accords and taking up arms. He denounced the government's failure to keep its promises: "The state has not fulfilled its most important obligations, which is to guarantee the life of its citizens and especially avoid assassinations for political reasons".[1466] The ongoing crisis over the failure to protect demobilized guerrillas, social leaders, and human rights defenders from assassination or prosecute those responsible

1462 Gómez-Suárez et al. 2016, o.c., pp. 261–2.
1463 Ibid., p. 261.
1464 De Sousa Santos 2017, o.c., at p. 55.
1465 A. Isacson, A Long Way to Go: Implementing Colombia's peace accord after five years', *WOLA*, November 23, 2021, https://www.wola.org/wp-content/uploads/2021/11/pdf_211123_web_colombia_5_years.pages.pdf.
1466 D. Baddour and A. Falola, 'As Colombia peace accord unravels, ex-FARC leaders take up arms, announce return to conflict', *The Washington Post*, August 29, 2019.

raises questions about the role of law in the peace process in Colombia. Do the JEP mechanisms have the capacity and resources to implement the FA and is the neoliberal peace imaginary fit for purpose, especially to help address the fundamental structural question of extreme inequality in Colombia? The assassinations point to the limits of the state's judicial sovereignty outside the cities and the tensions between the rights of victims and the priorities of the neoliberal development model in which the claims of the displaced for land restitution clash with government support for agribusiness and mining interests. The law is proving to be an 'unreliable ally' in advancing the peace process because its opponents have been able to challenge the articles of the FA in Congress and in the Constitutional Court and to obstruct its implementation through legal tactics and corruption.[1467] Since the 1990s, the progressive judicialization of peace initiatives has occurred through the constitutionalization of everyday life in Colombia in response to the chronic failure of politics and through the imposition of the international accountability agenda on the terms of political transitions and peacemaking. Judicialization has proceeded through the creation of legal frameworks for peace negotiations; the shift from amnesty to pardons acknowledging crimes thereby establishing the rights of victims to reparations; the introduction of alternate forms of punishment to incarceration; the shift of responsibility for reparations from just the perpetrators to the state; and the recognition of victims' rights to truth, justice, reparations, and non-recurrence. Judicialization expanded in the 1990s after the 1980s peace initiatives based on amnesty, negotiations, demobilization, and democratic openings repeatedly broke down. Transitional justice measures were gradually introduced through key laws – JPL 975/2005, the Victims Law 1448/20, and the FA 2016. But what is becoming apparent in Colombia is that 'more judicialization does not necessarily mean more accountability' in the peace processes.[1468] Firstly, by endorsing the JEP's selective prosecutorial regime the ICC has removed any credible threat of its future intervention if the JEP does not perform to its satisfaction, and secondly, the very ambitious scope of the transitional justice measures for restorative justice and victim reparations may not be deliverable. Transitional justice measures have enhanced legal equality through the recognition of victims as rights bearers but if they are not experienced as having tangible effects on individual lives they risk engendering mass disillusionment.[1469] The performative impact of the JEP prosecution strategy hinges on the efficacy of the emblematic cases engendering *communitas* in victims accredited to the particular macro-case. Each macro-case encompasses a different cohort of victims who constitute the primary

---

1467 Karl 2017b, o.c., p. 406.

1468 Borda et al. 2016, o.c.

1469 M. Somers and C.N. Roberts, 'Towards a New Sociology of Rights: A Genealogy of "Buried Bodies" of Citizenship and Human Rights' (2008) 4 *Annual Review of Law and Social Science*, 385.

witnesses. The JEP emphasis on victim satisfaction means the perception of the outcome ultimately lies with victim experience of participation, perpetrator acknowledgement and the alternate sanctions regime prioritizing restorative goals over punishment. The other dimension is whether the emblematic cases are seen to be balanced in such a polarized community and able to contribute to reconciliation – i.e. both the right and the left of politics believe the truth about the conduct of the war by their 'enemy' has been exposed and condemned. The positive public reception of Case 01 on FARC-EP kidnapping policy and Case 03 on the military practice of 'false positives' was encouraging.[1470] The JEP's avoidance of any official narrative/truth on the grounds of the plurality of violences – a stance previous commissions have taken – has turned the victims into the only vehicle for shared national identification and unity – everyone has been touched by such a long conflict – and the empirical reference for the narrative of collective suffering or trauma. This only emphasizes the lack of national consensus about the peace process and its expected outcomes.

The risk is the implementation process will become increasingly politicized and resisted as the contradictions of the neoliberal peace, the veto of certain elites against the FA, and the competition between victim groups for prioritization of particular macro-cases by the JEP are played out. The failure of the plebiscite to ratify the FA revealed the fact that elite pacts still underpinned stability in Colombian politics. The plebiscite, which was supposed to serve as an act of direct democracy to overcome partisan divisions in Colombia, in fact provided an opportunity for the elites opposed to the FA to polarize the electorate and veto the peace process. In other words, the plebiscite amplified elite division 'rather than provide additional legitimacy to and strengthening of the peace process'.[1471] The electoral victory of President Duque in the 2018 presidential election placed those who had long opposed the FA in charge of implementing it with the result that the President performed a balancing act 'claiming full support for the settlement abroad while criticizing it domestically'.[1472] Across the different areas of the peace agreement conflicting interests circumscribe who is identified as a perpetrator, who is seen as most responsible and who is recognized as a victim. The victims' experience of the transitional justice measures is increasingly differentiated according to their classification and macro-case. There are conflicts over the priority of rights, in particular government support for investment in agribusiness to promote agricultural development versus victims' rights to land restitution for small holders. Moreover, the legacy

1470 A.B. Liévano, 'How Colombia's JEP Earns the Respect of Sceptical Victims', *Justiceinfo.net*, January 13, 2023, https://www.justiceinfo.net/en/111069-how-colombia-jep-earns-respect-sceptical-victims.html.

1471 Matanock and García-Sánchez 2017, o.c., p. 160.

1472 F. Serrano, 'Colombia's Uneasy Peace', *Foreign Policy*, July 16, 2019, https://foreignpolicy.com/2019/07/16/colombias-uneasy-peace.

of the war system which previously merged counterinsurgency, displacement and development has been perpetuated in the peace and development project using business and security partnerships as vehicles to help recover territorial sovereignty. The 'demobilized' paramilitaries continue to exploit local politics and even benefit from the provisions of the FA meant to redress the disadvantage of victims. In March 2022, Jorge Rodrigo Tovar, the son of 'Jorge 40' the notorious AUC paramilitary leader, ran as a candidate for one of the 16 seats in Congress reserved for victims of guerrilla violence and won.[1473] The legacy of the war system continues with increased killing of social leaders and in ongoing displacement.[1474] Between 2016–2020 more than 1000 social leaders were killed.[1475] They are in part the victims of the extractivist development model which sees Colombian campesinos, Afro-Colombians and indigenous populations as obstacles to progress in regions where the state still has little presence.[1476]

The electoral victory of the first leftist President Petro in 2022 brought a renewed commitment to implement the FA and monitor its progress.[1477] In his election campaign Petro was very critical of President Duque's over reliance on the military to establish security and made implementation of the FA a key election promise.[1478] In office, the Petro government has focused on the implementation of the Ethnic Chapter concerned with the rights of Afro-Colombians and Indigenous people whose communities are concentrated in the regions most impacted by the highest levels of violence.[1479] On October 26, 2022,

---

[1473] J.D. Quesada, 'Son of notorious paramilitary leader wins seat reserved for victims of Colombia's armed conflict', *El País*, March 22, 2022, https://english.elpais.com/international/2022-03-22/son-of-notorious-paramilitary-leader-wins-seat-reserved-for-victims-of-colombias-armed-conflict.html.

[1474] The UN Office for the Coordination of Humanitarian Affairs (OCHA) said that the number of direct attacks against civilians in 2021 rose 37% to more than 2,400. Forced Displacement in Colombia more than double in 2021: Report, *Al Jazeera*, February 16, 2022, https://www.aljazeera.com/news/2022/2/16/forced-displacement-in-colombia-more-than-doubled-in-2021-report.

[1475] Colombia: World Report 2023, Human Rights Watch, https://www.hrw.org/world-report/2023/country-chapters/colombia.

[1476] R.C. Doughman, 'Might the Keys to Peace Open the Doors to Extractivism? Reflections on Colombia's Post-conflict Extractive Economy' in F. Cante and H. Quehi (eds.), *Handbook of Research on Transitional Justice and Peace Building in Turbulent Regions*, IGI Global, Hershey, PA 2015, p. 444, at p. 465.

[1477] The process will be monitored nationally and internationally by the Committee to Monitor, Promote, and Verify the Implementation (CSIVI), the UN Verification Mission in Colombia, the Mission to Support the Peace Process in Colombia (OEA/MAPP), the Ombudsman's Office and the Catholic Church. See 'Colombia: 'Renewed hope' for consolidating peace says Guterres', *UN News*, January 2, 2023, https://news.un.org/en/story/2023/01/1132122.

[1478] 'Protecting Colombia's Most Vulnerable on the Road to "Total Peace"', *Latin America Report*, No. 98, February 24, 2023, International Crisis Group, p. 3.

[1479] National Police statistics for 2019–2020 reveal the national homicide rate was 25/100,000 with the highest rates of homicide in the Departments of Cauca (53.71/100,00), Chocó

Congress passed Petro's 'Total Peace Law' to promote a new social justice and security agenda.[1480] The Total Peace Law authorizes the government to undertake negotiations with illegal armed groups of guerrillas and criminal organizations responsible for ongoing violence, massacres and narcotrafficking.[1481] The 'Total Peace' strategy has created five Strategic Zones for Comprehensive Intervention in which a strong State presence will be established to help prevent violence and expand human rights guarantees. The Law puts the community at the heart of the negotiations and proposes a fund for peace to guarantee social investments in the zones worst affected by violence. It views human security as the product of guarantees to the right to life, socio-economic wellbeing, and protection of the natural environment. Total Peace prioritizes humanitarian concerns for victims over the criminal accountability of the illegal armed groups. The focus on alleviating suffering and safeguarding lives gives visibility to victims but does not eliminate the causes of ongoing displacement and poverty. Petro's strategy to end the ongoing violence is to enter into local mini agreements with different illegal armed groups rather than attempt to negotiate national level agreements like the FA.[1482] This strategy of peacemaking through mini agreements has historical antecedents in the National Front's use of micro-pacts to negotiate the end to *La Violencia* in the late 1950s.[1483] The micro-pact strategy seeks to negotiate with all groups simultaneously to avoid the dynamic in which the demobilization of one group allows a new group to occupy a zone just vacated.[1484] However, Petro is facing obstacles to negotiate with and demobilize criminal groups because the Attorney General has refused to lift arrest warrants for their detention and insists they be prosecuted in the criminal courts.[1485]

The Colombian experience of transitional justice intervention as the exception – transitional justice measures introduced during conflict instead of after it – only highlights that all transitions have both political justice and criminal justice dimensions. When transitional justice measures are introduced post-conflict, they are shaped by the political agreement that precedes them. When transitional justice measures are introduced during a conflict, they are more likely to be able to shape the terms of the political agreement. In fact, the

(54.31/100,000), Putumayo (42.8/100,000) and Valle de Cauca (45.17/100,000). Situation of human rights in Colombia – Report of the United Nations High Commissioner for Human Rights (A/HRC/46/76), 22 February–19 March 2021.

1480 *Proyecto de Ley No. 181 de 2022* 'Por medio del cual se define la política de paz de Estado, y se dictan otras disposiciones', El Senado de Colombia, October 24, 2022.

1481 These include the Army of National Liberation (*Ejército de Liberación Nacional* – ELN), dissident FARC-EP groups and the criminal group *Clan del Golfo*.

1482 E. Dickenson, 'Colombia's Last Guerrillas Make First Step toward "Total Peace"', *International Crisis Group*, November 23, 2022, https://www.crisisgroup.org/latin-america-caribbean/andes/colombia/colombias-last-guerrillas-make-first-step-toward-total-peace.

1483 Karl 2017a, o.c., p. 83. See Section 6.3.1 for a discussion of these mini-agreements.

1484 Dickenson 2022, o.c.

1485 'Protecting Colombia's Most Vulnerable', o.c.

transitional justice post-conflict formulation of historical violence as a question of criminal justice and not political justice is a key strategy of depoliticization. In Colombia, the restless peace agreements reveal a recurrent set of foundational conflicts about fragmented territorial sovereignty, elite pactism, impunity, and extreme inequality, especially land concentration. Because the FA has not brought about any real political transition, the emancipatory potential of justice is circumscribed by elite interests opposed to the FA and more concerned with perpetuating the war system in peace time to facilitate agribusiness investments. The very basis of neoliberal peace built on new partnerships with corporations and security providers reinforces a regional pattern of state rescaling and decentralization. When a state adopts neoliberal peace but does not control its national territory, hold a monopoly over the use of violence, or hold the unique power of taxation, it is likely to produce new forms of fragmentation without integration while conjuring up the appearance of stronger national governance and territorial sovereignty. The continued focus on criminal justice and impunity/amnesty instead of political justice has ironically distorted peace processes. As Alviar and Engle point out 'if in the twentieth century a permissive approach to amnesties and pardons was often used as a means to avoid consideration of the wider political and reform agenda, a very different approach in the twenty-first century has led to many of the same results'.[1486] The focus on impunity has diverted attention from the causes of conflict – land concentration, development policy, and the war system – which are obscured by the concentration on criminal responsibility which transitional justice can only ever address selectively and symbolically.

[1486] Alviar García and Engle 2017, o.c., p. 241.

CHAPTER 8
CONCLUSION

8.1. TRANSITIONAL JUSTICE AS CONFLICT MANAGEMENT

This book has been a study about transitional justice and impunity in an era in which criminal accountability after atrocity is seen as mandatory for the successful transition to peace. The UN endorsed four pillars insists that states uphold international human rights and humanitarian standards to meet victims' rights to justice, truth, reparations and guarantees of non-repetition after mass violence. Criminal accountability is also seen as a judicial necessity to (re)establish democratic state sovereignty based on the rule of law and to secure a monopoly over the use of force. The insistence on accountability reflects the historical normative shift in the international legal order prioritizing human security over state security with the expansion of global norms of individual human rights' protection, what Teitel refers to as the emergence of 'humanity's law'.[1487] After WWII, the Nuremberg trials signalled the internationalization of the legal protection of the individual and restrictions on state sovereignty. However, during the Cold War, sovereignty reasserted itself over the international legal protection of the individual because the US and USSR superpowers supported authoritarian governments as clients to consolidate their spheres of influence and because the UN Charter gave concessions to recently decolonized states to limit their international obligations and duties and expand their sovereignty rights to support their development.[1488] The emergence of the transitional justice project coincided with the post-Cold War expansion of global human rights and a new regime of international intervention to enforce them when a state's repressive actions were condemned by the international community.[1489] Nevertheless, states have resisted the imposition of global human rights norms and accountability by asserting their sovereignty through amnesty laws or undermined transitional justice measures states agreed to in political agreements made at transition.

1487 R.G. Teitel, *Humanity's Law*, Oxford University Press Oxford, 2011.

1488 J. N. Maogoto, 'Sovereignty in Transition: Human Rights and International Justice' (2005) 7 *University of Notre Dame Australia Law Review* 83, at 89.

1489 Ibid., p. 95.

For the victims denied justice in the courts by amnesty laws, their repeal is seen as the urgent solution to allow investigations to proceed; for mass graves to be exhumed; and for prosecutions to be launched. This book has argued that overcoming impunity at transition is not just a matter of repealing amnesty laws but challenging the political agreements and political cultures that underpin them. The political agreements reached at transition strongly shape the design of transitional justice measures and the extent to which they are adopted and implemented. Moreover, as the case studies have shown, political agreements reached during transitions are not just epiphenomenal but expressions of a much longer genealogy of conflict and history of political fixes. Seen in the context of the genealogy of conflict, contemporary transitional justice mechanisms are just the latest approach to conflict management. The conflicts they intervene in are invariably recurrent ones, reflecting a particular history of state formation – the consolidation of sovereignty, legality, legitimacy and citizen identity. Amnesty laws are one way to avoid accountability; the manipulation of the design and implementation of transitional justice processes is another.

Transitional justice has expanded its focus from prosecuting atrocity to preventing atrocity. The UN's four pillars of transitional justice – victims' rights to justice, truth, reparations, and guarantees of non-repetition – reflect this expansion of human rights protection from civil and political rights to include the social and economic rights in order to address the root causes of conflict and prevent its recurrence.[1490] Transitional justice has evolved into a multifaceted and ambitious conflict management approach concerned with solving conflicts, building peace and reconstructing societies through justice. It has promoted human security for peace-making 'with a strongly built-in normative dimension which defines – at least implicitly – the desired end state of political change and transition'.[1491] International development aid has been directed towards transitional justice initiatives in support of the development-security-governance nexus. Human rights protection is supported to strengthen the legitimacy of state institutions, promote democratic governance, and implement preferred neoliberal economic policy. The evolution of the transitional justice project into an increasingly multifaceted approach to human rights protection raises questions about its current aims, priorities, and outcomes. Colleen Murphy argues transitional justice is a 'special kind of justice' which during transition confronts 1) pervasive structural inequality; 2) normalized collective

---

1490 N. Roht-Arriaza, 'Measures of Non-Repetition in Transitional Justice: The Missing Link?', in P. Gready and S. Robins (eds.), *From Transitional to Transformative Justice*, Cambridge University Press, Cambridge 2019, p. 123.

1491 S. K. Hellsten, 'Transitional justice as a philosophical and practical challenge: critical notes on Colleen Murphy's new theory of the 'conceptual foundations of transitional justice" (2018) 14 *Journal of Global Ethics*, 169.

and political wrongdoing; 3) serious existential uncertainty; and 4) fundamental uncertainty about authority.[1492] But transitional justice is less a 'special kind of justice' than a justice project which simultaneously seeks to establish the rule of law and create the necessary social and political conditions to normalize the force of law by criminalizing the violence on which the predecessor regime was founded. If, as Tony Judt argues, war creates the conditions for atrocity then, in the imaginary of transitional justice, the rule of law creates the conditions for peace.[1493] The often-observed dilemma of transitional justice balancing peace and justice arises from the fact that the force of law is highly dependent on its social normalization and on criminality becoming the exception.

The emphasis on accountability in international law is premised on the not well articulated theories about the transformative effects of retributive justice for victims and society at large. Criminal justice is thought to play a foundational role in transition to support liberalizing political change and demonstrate the justice and legitimacy of the successor regime. 'Trials offer a transitional mechanism for normative transformation to express public condemnation of aspects of the past, as well as public legitimation of the new role of law'.[1494] Legal rules and procedures provide an objective basis for producing legal facts/objective truth to change public knowledge and understanding about the past. Trials seek to produce an authoritative account about the past to bring closure by drawing a thick line between the past and present and to create the conditions for social peace through reconciliation. The liberal vision of democratic transition imagines conflict resolution as a product of the 'ecumenical goal of reconciliation between adversaries, the inclusion of excluded elements, and of making opposites compatible'.[1495] By removing the memory of political violence from the arena of democratic contest between opposed positions, the liberal vision is elevated to 'a higher meta-political sphere of foundational values' to diffuse its antagonistic politicization.[1496] While transitional justice has been promoted as a non-partisan normative legal technology for managing conflict it readily becomes politicized firstly, by compromises forced on it by the dynamics of the internal conflicts in which it intervenes; and secondly, through its close association with the politically normative project of democracy, economic liberalization and human rights. Transitional justice compartmentalizes the management of conflict through its narrow focus on human rights and individual responsibility. However, the political violence it addresses is

1492 C. Muprhy, *The Conceptual Foundations of Transitional Justice,* Cambridge University Press, Cambridge 2017.

1493 Judt 2008, o.c.

1494 Teitel 1997, o.c., p. 2036.

1495 A. Gómez López-Quiñones, 'A Secret Agreement: The Historical Memory Debate and the Limits of Recognition' (2012) 11 *Hispanic Issues On Line* 87, at 97.

1496 Ibid., p. 98.

symptomatic of enduring political conflicts with their distinctive genealogies, characteristics, and history of political fixes. Transitional justice measures also become politicized when the successor regime uses trials to delegitimize the predecessor regime by deploying criminal law 'primarily for its normative rather than punitive purposes'.[1497] Writing on the role of transitional justice in the Colombian peace process, Saffon and Uprimny observe that 'the question still remains of whether transitional justice legal standards actually work as effective normative limits to the political options available for bringing about a transition'.[1498]

This concluding chapter outlines how transitional justice as a conflict management model is limited by the characteristics of internal conflicts it intervenes in, the political agreements that underpin transition, and the restlessness of memory which renders all justice measures incomplete. Firstly, the judicialization of internal conflict as a conflict management strategy to produce closure is resisted by the political impetus to season justice by limiting prosecutions and/or reducing punishment. Secondly, the consolidation of transitional justice as soft law and hard law has increasingly transformed human rights protection into a top-down administrative project rather than a bottom-up generative and emancipatory one. In the process, the rehabilitation of the state as legitimate, territorially sovereign and trustworthy becomes a priority for UN human rights bodies and human rights courts, to ensure states meet their obligations under international law; to generate public consensus in support of transitional justice measures; and to establish its reputation as a reliable partner to secure external international donor financial support for reconstruction and development to consolidate peace. Thirdly, the international priority to rehabilitate the state often masks the way states in transition implement their transitional justice obligations as performative and symbolic measures to enact closure on the past. States can adopt the grammar of transitional justice and use trials and truth commissions as performative rituals without real commitment to the implementation of their decisions, findings, or recommendations. Transitional justice becomes an exercise in compliance and political legitimation and only secondarily about individual and collective healing. Fourthly, a gap persists between the individual traumatic memory of victims and official institutionalized historical memory. Because memory plays an important role in justice, the contestation over memory can disrupt state sponsored history/memory and political fixes. Moreover, the social depth of the obligations in which the living feel towards the dead usually exceeds any state sponsored project to achieve memory closure. Transitional justice mechanisms of retribution, truth, and amnesty as strategies to bring closure to the past are all incomplete.

1497 Teitel 1997, o.c., p. 2037.

1498 Saffon and Uprimny 2010, o.c., p. 354.

8.2. TRANSITIONAL JUSTICE INTERVENTION IN POST-CONFLICT SOCIETIES

The emergence of Phase II transitional justice (Teitel's periodization) coincided with third wave democratization and the end of the Cold War. Its focus was on victims of Cold War repression by authoritarian governments whose internal politics was shaped by the geo-political rivalries between the superpowers for regional control. In postcolonial states, transitional justice addressed the victims of internal struggles for power in newly independent states which became articulated with Cold War politics and the interests of former colonial/mandate rulers. The transitional justice initiatives explored in this book addressed the victims of Cold War state counterinsurgency policy in Uruguay and Colombia and the Francoist dictatorship in Spain. US National Security Doctrine supported the anti-Communist dictatorship against leftist armed insurgency in Uruguay and a largescale counterinsurgency war in Colombia to defeat leftist guerrillas and to destroy the large illegal drug economy in that country. In the case of Spain, US strategic backing for Franco's dictatorship as an anti-communist ally in the 1950s saw Spain rehabilitated as part of the Western alliance and accepted as a member of the UN (1955) and NATO (1982). The case studies of transitional justice intervention in the post-colonial states of Lebanon (2005) and Kenya (2008) addressed the victims of elite pactism and ethnic/sectarian clientelist politics shaped by Cold War regional geo-politics. The rescaling of justice and international judicial intervention in these states reflected the political contingencies of sovereignty in clientelist post-colonial states in the post-Cold War period. Transitional justice intervention in these cases was shaped by its international reach at the time of the precipitating political crisis, by the genealogy of conflict, and by the legacy of social polarization.

The reach of transitional justice has been limited by the ability of elites to dictate the terms of transition. The more elites have dominated transition, the less transitional justice has been applied.[1499] Elites sought to either prevent the introduction of transitional justice measures or minimize their scope and implementation where they could not be avoided. In the case studies explored, the date at which political transition/political crisis occurred was an important factor determining the reach of transitional justice. Uruguay and Colombia represent contrasting examples of early Phase II and mature Phase IV transitional justice interventions, respectively. In Uruguay, a US client state in Latin America during the Cold War, political transition was managed by military and political elites early in Phase II transitional justice at a time when international judicial processes for human rights protection were limited – the IACtHR was a nascent

[1499] Posner and Vermeule 2004, o.c., p. 770.

court, international tribunalization had not occurred, and the ICC did not exist. The Naval Club pact (1984) embraced amnesty and amnesia to bring closure on the dictatorship and restore democracy. Uruguayans overwhelmingly supported the return to democracy, demonstrated in their rejection of the 1980 military initiated referendum, but were divided over retributive justice for the victims of military repression. In the absence of justice measures, elections became the key transitional ritual and source of legitimacy for the successor regime. The transition exceptionalism narrative reinforced democracy as the pivotal source of political legitimacy by bracketing off the dictatorship as an historical aberration in the Uruguayan democratic tradition. When human rights lawyers and victim organizations tried to pursue justice in the courts for the victims of military repression in 1986, President Sanguinetti passed the Expiry Law closing off any legal redress in the courts. Civil society campaigns twice tried to repeal the Expiry law by plebiscite in 1989 and 2009 but failed thereby reinforcing the authority of the democratic majority as sacred. The public's collective experience of transition (*communitas)* was their participation in the elections which remained the key legitimating transition ritual. Democratic normalization, especially the electoral success of the leftist Broad Front governments (2010–2020) guerrillas and the election of a former MLN-*Tupamaro*, José Mujica, as president (2010–2015), only reinforced the exceptionalism narrative. Its widespread public acceptance has been behind the contemporary questioning of the radical Left (*Tupamaros*) about their decision in the 1960s to choose the path of armed revolutionary struggle when their post-dictatorship electoral success demonstrated the path of reform had been an option. Even after the Expiry Law was repealed in 2011, the leftist *Frente Amplio* government never initiated comprehensive transitional justice measures. Instead, the prosecution of senior military and political figures of the dictatorship era proceeded on a case-by-case basis through presidential exemptions permitted under the Expiry Law and through the judicial activism of judges.

By contrast, the case study on Colombia represents an example of (Sharp's) Phase IV transitional justice, when the UN had institutionalized the four pillars in transitional justice soft law and hard law, international human rights courts intervened to require states to meet their obligations under international law, and restorative justice and distributive justice measures were introduced in the peace agreement to guarantee non-recurrence of human rights violations. In Colombia, transitional justice norms were introduced during an ongoing conflict; integrated into the peace negotiations and agreement; supported by civil society and human rights advocates; instituted in the shadow of two international courts; reinforced by neo-constitutionalism; and institutionalized in the peace agreement with strong monitoring provisions to ensure implementation. However, the comprehensive transitional justice agenda introduced through the FA was the result of a long struggle to challenge the Colombian way of conflict management – elite pactism, amnesty and political fixes – arising from the chronic problems of a weak state – uneven territorial presence, lack of a monopoly over the use of violence, control over economic resources and effective taxation. At different times, the reach of the state was circumscribed by the power of regional political elites; left-wing and right-wing political movements with their own militias; and armed criminal gangs. In most cases these serial Colombian peace negotiations and agreements amounted to a state discursive strategy to conjure sovereignty at a time it was limited. The incremental judicialization of peace negotiations opened the way for transitional justice to emerge as the dominant normative framework employed in peace negotiations. Between 2005 and 2016 transitional justice norms and measures were progressively incorporated in the peace negotiations to meet the expectations of victims for rights to truth, justice, and reparations. A key problem in these successive peace negotiations was the absence of any real political transition and the persistence of the asymmetrical power relationship between perpetrator and victim sectors of society. This was apparent in the political contingency of government support for the implementation of the FA. Thus the ambivalence of the Duque government (2018–2022) towards the Final Agreement (2016) saw him promote the Colombian state as a reliable peace partner internationally while criticizing and white anting the implementation of the peace agreement at home.[1500] The incorporation of comprehensive transitional justice measures in the FA (2016) distinguished it from earlier peace agreements; its implementation remains contingent on the support of political elites. The fate of the FA (2016) depends on whether it can effectively address the foundational questions about state sovereignty, identity, inequality and citizenship that previous agreement have either put off or failed to resolve. The Colombia case study highlights the fact that transitional justice measures intervene in a genealogy of conflict historically managed by elite pactism and political fixes. For the protagonists, conflicts can never be quarantined by judicial processes from the historical memory of earlier crises, political fixes, and transitions. In their experience, political fixes do not produce closure but only temporary peace. Moreover, transitional justice measures are readily seen as politicized if they can be represented as supporting the interests of one side.

Characteristically post-conflict societies are divided societies. The approach of transitional justice is to compartmentalize and depoliticize political conflict by individualizing responsibility for political violence as a crime.[1501] Truth, justice and reparations are supposed to generate a consensus about who was responsible and an inclusive narrative that create the conditions for reconciliation. This idealized vision of the social effects of truth and justice are contradicted by the politicization of transitional justice measures at many stages.

1500 The expression 'white anting' is an Australian term meaning to subvert or undermine from within.

1501 Hillebrecht et al. 2018, o.c., p. 296.

The capacity of trials to serve as a non-partisan method for conflict management and produce closure is limited firstly by the political compromises necessary to initiate negotiations, and secondly, by the polarizing impact of verdicts. Political justice demands both sides must be included in any political settlement. They need to be decriminalized and legitimized as political actors to persuade them to participate in negotiations to end conflict and continue to live together.[1502] Criminal justice mitigates against political reconciliation because verdicts tend to polarize the already divided society into the guilty and innocent sides. Internal conflict leaves the legacy of the subject positions of perpetrator, bystander and victim which are not easily reconciled in post-conflict society.

Human rights discourse constructs the victim as part of the perpetrator-victim binary. The victim – of human rights violations – constitutes a legal status which confers rights. However, the category of victim refers to multiple political subject positions. It is a political identity of victimhood constituted by the shared traumatic experience of specific acts of violence – families of the disappeared, victims of rape in war, political prisoners. The category of victim is an empowering political identity which has become one of the most effective subject positions 'from which to express political demands in liberal-capitalist societies'.[1503] The language of rights confers legitimacy on the victim and demands a response by the state to meet its obligations under international law to avoid international shaming. Moreover, the historical shift in the late 20th century to state commemoration of victims has reinforced the contemporary political significance of victims. State commemorative practices focused on victims, Tony Judt argues, encourages citizens to understand the past through the vector of the historical victimhood of their ancestors, which fragments the past into competing victimhoods.[1504] As Mamdani points out, post-conflict societies need new inclusive political subjectivities which transcend past subjectivities to be able to reconcile. Writing on post-apartheid South Africa, Mamdani argues that a new more inclusive post-apartheid subject position of 'survivors' was needed to replace the apartheid subject positions of yesterday's perpetrators, beneficiaries and victims to make reconciliation possible.[1505] In post-apartheid South Africa, the 'survivor' category was inclusive on the basis of shared suffering for a better society.[1506] Meister extends the analysis of post-apartheid re-subjectification by arguing that transition required a new consensus achieved by distinguishing

1502 M. Mamdani 2015, o.c., p. 67.

1503 Gómez López-Quiñones 2012, p. 95.

1504 T. Judt, 'The Past Is Another Country: Myth and Memory in Postwar Europe' in I. Deák, et al. (eds.), *The Politics of Retribution in Europe: World War II and Its Aftermath*, Princeton University Press, Princeton, NJ 2000, p. 293.

1505 Mamdani 2015, o.c., p. 80.

1506 M. Humphrey, 'From Terror to Trauma: Commissioning Truth for National Reconciliation' (2000) 6 *Social Identities* 7, at 18.

between perpetrators and beneficiaries – including bystanders – and persuading the latter to acknowledge that apartheid was wrong, that the victims of apartheid had suffered unjustly, and they should change sides – i.e. identify with the victim's position. In the reconciliation narrative, the 'good' victims were those who were persuaded to abandon any desire for criminal retribution and accept moral victory and recognition as enough. The 'bad' victims were those who rejected the subject position of survivor and insisted on criminal accountability as the terms for reconciliation.[1507]

Another response to the demand for accountability in a divided postcolonial society has been to neutralize responsibility by blaming both sides. In Uruguay, the theory of the two demons – extremists on both sides were to blame – was used to justify the policy of amnesty and amnesia. The victim, at the centre of transitional justice, has also been neutralized by foregrounding the humanitarian focus on suffering instead of rights to justice. The 'Pact of Forgetting' in Spain was underpinned by a humanitarian framing of suffering as the experience of both sides. In Colombia, the rights of the victims of the conflict were recognized only slowly in the history of the judicialization of peace initiatives. At first, the state only recognized as victims those harmed by the insurgents, not the victims of the state led counterinsurgency and its paramilitary allies. The recognition of the victim's right to reparation in the Victims Law 1448/2011 included both sides and resulted in the registration of around 20% of the population as victims. In the FA (2016) the idea that everyone was touched by the 50 years of conflict made the suffering victim the most inclusive post-conflict identity.

8.3. TRANSITIONAL JUSTICE AS TOP-DOWN OR BOTTOM-UP

Transitional justice as the judicialization of conflict initially focused on criminal punishment of perpetrators of violence but it expanded to include prevention. The UN four pillars of transitional justice normalization of the victims' right to justice, truth, reparations, and guarantees of non-repetition – duty of prevention – reflect its expansion from the protection of civil and political rights, to broader economic and social rights in an effort to address the underlying social and economic conditions of conflict and violence.[1508] Yet despite the increasing victim-centred focus of transitional justice and the growth in the role of victim organizations and human rights CSOs in the promotion of

1507 Meister 2002, o.c., p. 91.

1508 Guidance Note of the Secretary-General: United Nations Approach to Transitional Justice, March 3, 2010, https://peacemaker.un.org/documents/guidance-note-secretary-general-un-approach-transitional-justice.

transitional justice soft law, the more the state is seen as an essential partner in fulfilling the expanded transitional justice agenda, the more top-down it has become. International human rights organizations, international prosecutors, and transitional justice handbooks insist on the imperative of justice for victims but prioritize the rehabilitation of the state so it is able to fulfill its obligations under international law, deliver impartial justice, and act as a trusted conduit for international development aid and loans. However, the prioritization of state rehabilitation also positions the political elite/class as gatekeepers of transitional justice processes which they can choose to support or subvert. This is especially true where there has been no regime transition and no transformation. The Colombian case illustrates how transitional justice processes can be co-opted to perpetuate the same pattern of elite competition and legitimation in a post-conflict society. Thus, the defeat of the Santos government's plebiscite (2016) to endorse the Final Agreement by the NO campaign led by former President Uribe reset the peace agenda for the forthcoming Presidential election (May 2018). The NO Campaign rejected the FA restorative justice provisions for conditional amnesty and reduced punishment for FARC leaders who they denounced as criminals and narco-terrorists. However, Uribe's stance on criminal accountability was not a principled position but one intended to marginalize the FARC-EP by denying them political legitimacy as a partner in the peace agreement and prevent their political reintegration as a legitimate political party able to contest elections. Historically, amnesty had been the norm in every peace agreement over 50 years in Colombia. Uribe's own controversial Peace and Justice Law 975/2005 had proposed amnesty for the paramilitaries to protect them from prosecution for their role in human rights abuses committed as allies in the counterinsurgency campaign. It was only after the Colombian Constitutional Court ruled against amnesty for crimes against humanity in 2006 that its application was restricted. In Colombia, conservative political elites were able to obstruct the transitional justice mechanisms to advance peace to contest political power in the post-conflict state.

A major driver of judicialization in the post-conflict state has been the international legal insistence on accountability for crimes against humanity and war crimes. What is new about this demand for legal accountability after political transition is the application of international human rights standards as the basis for post-conflict justice. Now accountability is supposed to deliver victims' justice, not victors' justice. The case study on transitional justice in Spain showed how victors' justice was an historical feature of political transitions used by successor regimes to consolidate their legitimacy and criminalize their political opponents. During the 1920s and 1930s, the nationalists/monarchists and the republicans/revolutionaries in succession each sought to prosecute their opponents to criminalize and delegitimize them. In the 1920s, the opposition progressive and revolutionary parties made demands for 'political responsibilities' – demands for 'retribution for past political offences and for a purge of the state administration'– to delegitimize the ruling conservative (pro-nationalist and pro-monarchist) politicians and military leaders.[1509] One of the first initiatives of the Second Republic (1931–39) was to establish a Responsibilities Commission to investigate the actions of the previous dictatorship to criminalize it; to mobilize public opinion against the monarchy; and to demonstrate the revolutionary credentials of the Provisional government.[1510] When the Spanish Civil War ended with the military defeat of the Republicans by the Nationalists, Franco promulgated the 'Law of Political Responsibilities' (1939) establishing the legal basis for his 40 year persecution of anyone who, through acts of omission or commission, had supported the 'Reds'. Under Franco, accountability as victors' justice resulted in the criminalization of the Second Republic and its supporters and their ongoing persecution, stigmatization, and demonization under Franco's authoritarian rule. Pointedly, it was the failure of the post-Franco democratic government to administer victims' justice for those persecuted during the Civil War and dictatorship that permitted the institutionalization of public amnesia about the past by inverting justice. Victors' justice enables one side to absolve itself of responsibility for past crimes. At the end of WWII, the Nuremberg trials, as victors' justice, judged the Nazis to be solely responsible for the war. As a consequence, the Nuremberg verdicts allowed France, along with the other Nazi occupied countries in Europe, to represent themselves as the Nazis' victims whose citizens were innocent resisters thereby allowing the post-war governments to conceal the extent of collaboration in Vichy France. President de Gaulle portrayed the Vichy government as an historical aberration foisted upon an 'unwilling country by the treasonable activities of a minority' during the Nazi occupation.[1511] He could then claim to govern in the name of the French as 'innocent victims' – the post-Vichy category of Mamdani's 'survivors' – facilitated by official public amnesia about the collective responsibility of the French under occupation.[1512] Interestingly victims' justice and victors' justice are two sides of the same coin; both seek to use accountability to criminalize their opponents and exclude them from the post-transition political order through convictions and/or political ostracization. Moreover, even 'victims' justice needs a victor who can establish the rule of law under which victims may obtain justice'.[1513] The proximity of victims' justice and victors' justice has made international legal intervention in divided societies problematic. Those opposed to international trials accuse the international courts of administering victors' justice, while those supporting the trials regard them as delivering victims' justice.

[1509] Boyd 1984, o.c., p. 152.
[1510] Boyd 1984, o.c., p. 155.
[1511] Judt 2000, o.c., p. 304.
[1512] Mamdani 2015, o.c., p. 80.
[1513] Mamdani 2015, o.c., p. 81.

State rehabilitation through strengthening the rule of law has become a priority in transitional justice policy so the state can assume responsibility for meeting its obligations under international law. In our case studies, international legal intervention to ensure the states meet their obligations has taken different paths. In the case of Uruguay, effective international legal intervention occurred only after the IACtHR decision on the Gelman case obligating Uruguay to investigate her forced disappearance thereby rendering ineffective the Expiry Law (1986) 26 years after the return to democracy.[1514] Even when President Mujica's *Frente Amplio* government finally acted to repeal the Expiry Law to avoid the international opprobrium from the IACtHR decision, the parliamentary vote came up against strong resistance on the grounds that the proposal to repeal of the Expiry Law had already been twice rejected by democratic referendum.[1515] In the case of Lebanon, international legal intervention was the result of the extraordinary UN Security Council decision to investigate the Hariri assassination and then establish the hybrid Special Tribunal for Lebanon under Chapter VII, after the Lebanese government failed to endorse the proposal they had originally agreed to. Once the STL had been established, the March 8 alliance opposition campaigned against it, eroding its legitimacy amongst its constituencies, withdrawing cooperation with the STL, and forcing the STL to hold trials in absentia in The Hague. In the case of Kenya, the ICC intervened after the refusal of the Kenya parliament to cooperate, under positive complementarity, to establish a special national tribunal, as required by the Waki Report, to investigate and prosecute those responsible for the 2007 post-election violence. In Kenya, civil society movements pushed for ICC intervention because they did not trust state institutions while the Jubilee Alliance, formed by the indicted political elite, closed ranks against the ICC and denounced it as a 'neo-colonialist' institution. In the case of Colombia, the peace negotiations and transitional justice policy were designed and implemented in the shadow of IACtHR and the ICC because they had jurisdiction over crimes against humanity and war crimes committed during the conflict. Colombia was subject to the jurisdiction of the IACtHR as a member of the Organization of American States and a signatory to the American Convention on Human Rights (1978) and to the jurisdiction of the ICC as a signatory to the Treaty of Rome (2002). In accord with the principle of positive complementarity the Colombian state cooperated with the ICC to establish transitional justice institutions. The ICC had initiated a preliminary examination of the conflict because of the provisions for amnesty in the Peace and Justice Law 975/2005. The Colombian transitional justice measures evolved in the shadow of these two international courts with

[1514] *Gelman v. Uruguay*, Inter-American Court of Human Rights, Judgment of February 24, 2011 (Merits and Reparations), Costa Rica.

[1515] L. Roniger, 'Transitional Justice and Protracted Accountability in Re-democratised Uruguay, 1985–2011' (2011) 43 *Journal of Latin American Studies* 693, at 721.

the Victims Law 1448/2011 and the FA 2016. In these examples the perceived legitimacy of international legal intervention hinged on whether it was seen as enhancing or undermining state sovereignty. In the cases of Kenya and Lebanon, international legal intervention was sabotaged by elites who characterized international justice as neo-imperialist. This critique was politically potent because of the foundational value of sovereignty/independence for these post-colonial states. In the Colombian case, transitional justice measures were introduced by the state in the shadow of the IACtHR and ICC and reflected its priorities and preferences. In Uruguay, sovereignty defined as democratic consensus limited the way the state assumed responsibility to pursue justice and truth. In Spain, historical justice for human rights violations committed during the Civil War and dictatorship has been restricted by a mutual amnesty and amnesia pact and remains dependent on the political contingency of which party holds government.

The expansion of the scope of transitional justice measures to address social and economic rights has also reinforced its top-down character and the role of political elites as partners and gatekeepers. Increasingly, international development aid has been channeled through transitional justice processes and integrated into policies designed to address issues such as inequality and poverty as the structural causes of conflict. Transitional justice has come to be administered as part of a development-security-governance nexus concerned with multiple forms of justice. As the transitional justice agenda has expanded it has been integrated with the politically normative agenda of democratization, economic liberalization and individual human rights protection raising doubts about its impartiality as a justice project. Moreover, if the end point of transition is the establishment of neoliberal democracy, as Hellsten argues, it raises the question as to whether the expanded model of transitional justice is really viable.[1516] She notes that while internationally democratic and authoritarian states have embraced the market economy, it has not necessarily led to democratization. Given the current destabilization of liberal democratic governments in the context of the economic distortions of globalization and the emergence of nationalist and populist politics in response of those who feel left out, the transitional justice end project looks less clear. The tensions between different forms of justice and the priorities of economic development over restoration of victims' rights are clearly apparent in the Colombian peace process. A major goal of the Colombian transitional justice process has been the national registration of the more than 9.4 million victims over 50 years of political violence. Of these victims around 89% had experienced internal displacement/dispossession and many have sought the restitution of their land as reparations. However, while the government has legislated to support land restitution as a reparation measure,

1516 Hellsten 2018, o.c., p. 171.

it has at the same time subordinated individual victims' rights to the economic priorities of agribusiness monocultural investment megaprojects. Instead of recovering possession of their original land, displaced individuals have been allocated land conditional on their participation in large-scale agricultural development projects such oil palm plantations. In summary, the expansion of human rights protection in transitional justice processes has reinforced its top-down character because of its reliance on the state as the vehicle to administer criminal justice, democratization, reconstruction, and development. The top-down emphasis has also helped politicize transitional justice in divided societies firstly, because victims' justice, like victors' justice, seeks to delegitimize and exclude its opponents; and secondly, because it has become integrated with a politically normative model of neoliberal peace.

8.4. TRANSITIONAL JUSTICE IMPLEMENTATION

Transitional justice, with its ever-expanding toolkit, is now seen as international best practice for the post-conflict management of the legacies of political violence. However, the priority given to state rehabilitation in partnership with political elites puts these elites in the position of gatekeepers able to increasingly co-opt and manipulate transitional justice measures. The ritual and symbolic structure of transitional justice allows its performative acts – the verdicts of trials, the hearings and reports of truth commissions, the official registration of victims entitled to reparation – to be misrepresented or misconstrued as the fulfilment rather than the first steps – the decisions, findings or recommendations – that still need to be implemented and consolidated. The effectiveness of transitional justice measures is contingent on the political commitment of political elites to implement and institutionalize the outcomes of trials, truth commissions and reparations. Two examples illustrate how successor governments have embraced transitional justice measures as performative acts to enhance their legitimacy as a gesture of compliance while not delivering very much. The first example is the Peace and Justice Law 975/2005 introduced by President Uribe to promote peace and preserve impunity in Colombia and the second example is the Law of Historical Memory (2007) introduced by PM Zapatero to recognize the Republican victims of the Spanish Civil War and challenge impunity.

The key to the design of the transitional justice measures is how past violence is constructed – in the language of political semiosis how the demonstrative act of framing a 'historical violent event' orients the community to view and understand the violent event. In any conflict there is an epistemic struggle over the meaning of violence; the definition of the perpetrator and victim; who can participate in the process; and what reconciliation means. How past violence is constructed is one of the key issues in political negotiations at transition and what transitional justice policy is pursued. The construction of past violence sets out the parameters and scope of transitional justice measures addressing victims' rights to justice, truth, reparation, and non-repetition, while at the same time pursuing the political aim of successor regime legitimation conferred by compliance with international human rights standards. But, in the name of best practice, transitional justice can be co-opted to serve the latter goals rather than realize the former. As a discourse, transitional justice functions as a 'ambiguous consensus' which allows the inclusion of very different if not contradictory interpretations.[1517] Moreover, its very abstract goals – justice, truth, reparations, non-recurrence – allow for a big gap between the promise of performative mechanisms and what is eventually implemented. In Colombia, transitional justice measures have progressively framed conflict management and the peace process since 2005. From the perspective of the judicialization of peace initiatives, the process dates from the early 1980s. Through the Peace and Justice Law 975/2005, President Uribe co-opted the grammar of transitional justice to frame and manage the demilitarization and demobilization of the paramilitaries – his allies in the state counterinsurgency war. A contested issue in this process was who were the perpetrators and who are the victims. The Peace and Justice Law 975/2005 institutionalized the political agreement between pro-Uribe political elites and paramilitary organizations to officially remove the paramilitaries from the field to repair the state's poor human rights reputation through its partnership with them. Victims' rights were first outlined in the Peace and Justice Law 975/2005 but not legislated for until the Victims' Law 1448/2011. The principle of non-discrimination applied to the victims of the conflict generated a dispute over who should be recognized as victims. In Uribe's 'Democratic Security' narrative, the patriotic security forces had sacrificed their lives for democracy in a war against narco-terrorists. The army and the state were the victims, not victimizers, and the guerrillas were criminals who did not deserve political recognition as partners in peace – President Duque (2018–2022) embraced the same view. Uribe's supporters in the Senate blocked the Victims Law 1448/2011 on the grounds that the proposed reparations were too expensive and they equalized entitlements for both 'terrorists' and 'state agents'.[1518] The National Reparation and Reconciliation Commission (CNRR) established by Uribe was biased towards interests of the paramilitaries not their victims. Its truth-seeking focused on the 'open testimonies' (*versiones libres*) of the paramilitaries, excluding the experiences of their victims. A more comprehensive truth project was initiated by the CNRR in 2008 undertaken by The Historical Memory Group (GMH), with a mandate to investigate the 'reasons for the emergence and

1517 D. Lecombe, 'A Conflicted Peace: Epistemic Struggles around the Definition of Transitional Justice in Colombia' in A. Lyons (ed.), *Contested Transitions: Dilemmas of Transitional Justice in Colombia and Comparative Experience*, CEP – Banco de la República Luis Ángel Arango, Bogotá 2010, p. 168.

1518 Ibid., p. 167.

evolution of illegal armed groups'.[1519] To guarantee its independence, the GMH sought funding from international sources and expanded the scope of historical memory conducting interviews with a wide range of victims. The 24 reports it published between 2009 and 2013 revealed the plurality of experiences of the war but its major Report, *¡Basta Ya!*, was only published in 2013, three years after President had left office.[1520] This Report did not attempt to produce an official truth or collective memory; only to illustrate and bring to the public attention the pervasive impact of the war throughout the country and its range of victims. The Victims Law 1448/2011 recognized the rights of victims to reparations but broke the nexus between perpetrator and victim in criminal justice. The rights of victims for compensation became an exercise in administrative justice in the form of welfare payments collapsing the distinction between needs and rights of victims.[1521] The reconciliation process was problematic because with no transition, no post-conflict context, and no change in the asymmetrical subject positions of perpetrator and victim there was no inclusive post-conflict category of survivor. Under the JPL 975/2005 process victims were obliged to accept formal acts of repentance from paramilitaries with no change in the political status quo and 'with a new public legitimacy for the dispossession of the political and legal attributes of the victims.[1522] Guarantees of non-repetition were equated with the Disarmament, Demobilization and Reintegration (DDR) process which was subsequently exposed in many cases as fraudulent because former paramilitaries entered new careers in criminal economies. The post-peace agreement killing of social leaders continues to reveal that for the most vulnerable populations the transitional justice guarantees of non-repetition have failed.[1523]

In Spain, limited transitional justice measures were introduced to challenge the terms of democratic transition in 1977 which had adopted amnesty and amnesia as the way to bring closure on the past. In 2007, the Zapatero Socialist government promulgated the Law of Historical Memory to promote the democratization of memory of the Civil War as part of his government's broader agenda to expand citizens' rights. The LHM supported Republican families in

---

1519 P.R. Alcalá and M.V. Uribe, 'Constructing Memory amidst War: The Historical Memory Group of Colombia' (2016) 10 *The International Journal of Transitional Justice* 6, at 12.

1520 M.C. Herrera, et al., 'Memory Institutions and Policies in Colombia: The Historical Memory Group and the Historical Commission on the Conflict and Its Victims' in B. Bevernage and N. Wouters (eds.), *The Palgrave Handbook of State-Sponsored History After 1945*, Palgrave Macmillan, London 2018, p. 727, at p. 728.

1521 I. Cepeda-Castro, 'A Model of Democracy for Justice' in A. Lyons (ed.), *Contested Transitions: Dilemmas of Transitional Justice in Colombia and Comparative Experience*, CEP – Banco de la República Luis Ángel Arango, Bogotá 2010, p. 179, at p. 183.

1522 Ibid., p. 182.

1523 I. Santaeulalia, 'Petro, el presidente de la paz al que se le descontroló la guerra', *El País*, July 5, 2023, https://elpais.com/america-colombia/2023-07-05/petro-el-presidente-de-la-paz-al-que-se-le-descontrolo-la-guerra.html.

their search for relatives buried in clandestine mass graves, providing national grants to support civil society organizations in the exhumation of mass graves (2006); National Protocols for Exhumations (2011); and a law opening Civil War archives to facilitate civil society organization in their search for mass graves and the identity of remains (2011). It embraced human rights as a constitutive discourse to bring into existence a more inclusive and comprehensive history of the Spanish Civil War by exhuming its missing victims. In practice, the PSOE entered into a partnership with civil society exhumation groups to implement the LHM's human rights agenda. While the LHM did raise public awareness about the fate of the disappeared by facilitating the exhumation of mass graves, it also polarized society over the wisdom of reviving the past. Instead of generating a more inclusive national narrative about the Spanish Civil War the exhumations resulted in the pluralization and fragmentation of memory. Moreover, the LHM turned out to be a politically contingent transitional justice measure. As soon as the conservative government (Popular Party) returned to power in 2011 they immediately withdrew support for the national grants for CSO exhumations and stopped new prosecutions under universal jurisdiction in Spanish courts signalling their intention to distance themselves from international justice. The democratization of memory promoted as the protection of human rights – right to know the fate of family members – in the LHM did not produce a more inclusive national memory of the Civil War. It rather fragmented memory resulting from the multiplicity of groups signifying exhumed remains – according to their own social and political agendas – or from its atomization with the individualization and privatization of memory.

Once amnesty and amnesia have been adopted as a strategy of closure at transition it has been difficult to reverse them. The case studies on Uruguay and Spain illustrate the political contingency of attempts to subsequently introduce effective truth and justice measures. Even when progressive governments cautiously and selectively try to introduce transitional justice measures, they are quickly undermined when conservative governments opposed to them return to power. The post-transition experience of Brazil after the dictatorship (1964–1985) highlights the political contingency of attempts to reverse amnesty and amnesia. In Brazil, the Amnesty Law remains despite several IACtHR rulings against Brazil on the grounds of the doctrine of 'conventionality control'.[1524] At transition there was a widespread expectation in Brazilian civil society that democratic elections; a new human rights constitution (1988); judicial reform; and the arrival of

---

1524 In the 2006 case of *Almonacid Arellano v. Chile*, the IACtHR argued that when a state has ratified an international treaty such as the American Convention on Human Rights, the courts are bound by that Convention. See A. Gurmendi, 'At Long Last, Brazil's Amnesty Law Is Declared Anti-Conventional', *OpinioJuris*, August 16, 2019, https://opiniojuris.org/2019/08/16/at-long-last-brazils-amnesty-law-is-declared-anti-conventional/.

progressive pro-poor governments would expand and consolidate human rights protection.[1525] As it turned out, civil society organizations emerged as the main drivers of transitional justice initiatives, not the state.[1526] Even when the progressive left wing Workers Party (PT) governments under the presidencies of Luiz Inácio Lula da Silva (2003–2011) and Dilma Rousseff (2011–2016) pursued a strong social justice agenda in partnership with diverse human rights NGOs – on justice, environmental protection, sexual identity, women, and urban citizenship – they introduced only limited transitional justice measures.[1527] In 2011, after IACtHR decision on the failure to investigate crimes against humanity, the PT government established the National Truth Commission (*Comissão Nacional da Verdade* – CNV) but because of its restricted mandate and limited resources, the CNV was forced form partnerships with civil society organizations, unique amongst truth commissions, to create around 100 local truth commissions.[1528] The recommendations of the CNV Report were largely ignored.[1529] As with most truth commissions, their recommendations have been only selectively implemented usually avoiding justice measures altogether.[1530] Brazil illustrates the inertia of the amnesty and amnesia policy once installed and the difficulty of generating a post-transition consensus for justice even when progressive governments championing human rights come to power. The election of the right-wing government of President Jair Bolsonaro saw the systematic stripping away of the PT's progressive human rights protections – LGBTQ rights, indigenous land rights, environmental protections – won over several decades. President Bolsonaro labelled anyone who resisted his anti-human rights, pro-dictatorship, and pro-market policies the enemy. The return of Luiz Inácio Lula da Silva to the presidency in 2022 renewed hope that he would reactivate a strong human rights agenda on public security, criminal accountability, the

---

1525 N. Schneider and G. Iecker de Aleida, 'The Brazilian National Truth Commission (2012–2014) as a State-Commissioned History Project' in B. Bevernage and N. Wouters (eds.), *The Palgrave Handbook of State-Sponsored History After 1945*, Palgrave Macmillan, London 2018, p. 637.

1526 The Catholic Church produced the Brazil Never Again (*Brasil Nunca Mais*), by Editora Vozes Ltda., Petropolis, 1985. The English edition: J. Dassin, *Torture in Brazil: A Shocking Report on the Pervasive Use of Torture by Brazilian Military Governments, 1964–1979*, University of Texas Press, Institute of Latin American Studies, Austin, TX 1998.

1527 Ibid., o.c., at 638–9. The first official government report by the Special Secretariat of Human Rights *(Secretaria Especial dos Direitos Humanos)* (2007) was based largely on investigations conducted by the families of the victims themselves.

1528 Schneider and Iecker de Aleida 2018, o.c., p. 649.

1529 H.C. Martín, et al., 'Explaining the timeliness of implementation of truth commission recommendations' (2022) 59 *Journal of Peace Research* 710, at 717; F. Ghelfi, et al., 'Brazil's National Truth Commission: Recommendations for a Pending Democratic Agenda' in E. Skaar, et al. (eds.), *Latin American Experiences with Truth Commission Recommendations: Beyond Words, Vol. II*, Intersentia, Cambridge 2022, p. 197, at p. 226.

1530 Martín, et al. 2002, o.c., p. 717.

environment, women's rights, LBQT rights, and indigenous rights. But in such a highly polarized electorate there is little prospect of generating a new justice consensus to repeal the Amnesty law.

8.5. MEMORY, JUSTICE AND LAW'S LIMITS

During democratic transitions the competing 'claims of the past, and their clash with those of the present and future' shape political and legal outcomes.[1531] Because justice is partly a form of remembrance to keep the victims, crimes, and perpetrators from being forgotten 'memory occupies a vital place at the heart of justice'.[1532] What Booth refers to as 'memory-justice' is situated at the centre of judicial practices but goes well beyond them leaving judicial closure incomplete.[1533] The three judicial approaches to the management of memory are trials and punishment (indictments); truth and acknowledgement (truth commissions); and forgetting (amnesty) to allow a divided society to share a future. These memory-justice approaches to political transition all seek to produce closure through different strategies: through the institutionalization of memory in trials, through the socially diffuse remembrance in truth commissions, and through restorative forgetting in amnesty laws. They are driven by different imperatives: 'to fulfill a debt to the dead by punishing the perpetrators; to preserve justice; to save victims from the second death of forgetting; to put our present and future goods over our ties to the past'.[1534] But memory-justice demands more than these different legal strategies designed to produce closure can deliver.

Justice as retribution is supposed to produce closure by drawing a thick line on the past. Trials fulfil memory-justice by bringing truth to light; by institutionalizing the facts of crime as a form of official memory; by punishing perpetrators as justice demands; by helping to reintegrate the victims of crime into society; and by upholding the duty of the living to remember the dead. The expected political effects of trials after mass violence are that guilty verdicts will delegitimize the actions of the predecessor regime/government; will serve as a deterrence to political crimes in the future; and will help restore the political community and the legal order. Trials seek to transform the 'lived world of justice' into a settled historic event and thereby finalize the debt to the victims. They also contribute to reaffirmation and restoration of the political community after atrocity and trauma. But retributive justice remains incomplete

1531 W.J. Booth, 'The Unforgotten: Memories of Justice' (2001) 95 *The American Political Science Review* 777, at 778.
1532 Ibid., p. 777.
1533 Ibid.
1534 Ibid., p. 788.

for memory-justice, not just because victims feel too many perpetrators escaped accountability, but because trials can be used to quit the debt to the victims and unburden society too quickly. From the perspective of memory-justice the weight of responsibility extends beyond the narrow guilt of the relatively few individuals convicted to the co-responsibility of the political community. It corresponds to a sense of shame arising from membership in that community that went along with repression as supporters or bystanders. While trials and punishment of the guilty bring legal closure, shame endures.[1535]

Justice as truth pursues closure through unity based on remembrance as a defence against forgetting. It seeks to keep faith with the victims by not colluding with the perpetrators' project of the effacement of their crimes. Thus, the focus of truth commissions on the 'disappeared' is motivated by the imperative to expose hidden crimes and to preserve the memory of the victims to avoid their second death by being forgotten. For the families of the disappeared the truth commission report is a 'sepulchre', a revised historical narrative in which to insert their recovered dead from oblivion. Even though the 'right to know' the truth about the fate of the disappeared may provide the legal basis for human rights claiming, it is the moral and humanitarian aspects which often carry greater cultural legitimacy for the public. Firstly, there is the obligation of the living towards the dead; secondly, the humanitarian appeals for the alleviation of the surviving family's suffering; and thirdly, empathetic witnessing of the suffering of the victims. As victim-centred institutions, truth commissions respond to the post-conflict persistence of traumatic memory for individuals and also to the historical importance of remembrance for society: the debt owed to the dead. The memory-truth is less about an historical account or legal determination of responsibility than the restoration of a community through reintegration of the forgotten.[1536] However, the narration of the traumatic memory of victims as collective memory is not straightforward. The experience of those living in 'trauma time' resists easy translation into linear narrative time. The creation of an inclusive collective memory necessarily involves selective forgetting. In divided post-conflict societies there needs to be a new unifying post-conflict identity. In the case of South Africa, the post-apartheid state needed to govern in the name of the 'survivors' – yesterday's perpetrators, beneficiaries, victims.[1537] The role of the collective memory is to prevent forgetting as a precondition for the post-transition community. The incompleteness of truth as justice can be found in the dissonance between private traumatic memory and the collective reconciliation narrative, and whether victims are willing to accept the gap as necessary for closure or want to challenge the collective narrative. The exhumation movement in Spain sought to do just that.

1535 Ibid., p. 787.
1536 Booth 2001, o.c., p. 787.
1537 Mamdani 2015, o.c., p. 87.

Memory-justice as forgetting seeks to achieve closure by quarantining memory to prevent the past disrupting the future. Instead of keeping memory of the crimes and victims alive, it seeks to release society from the negative consequences of their feelings of grievance, resentment or revenge. Amnesty is used to draw a thick line on the past and officially close accountability and any investigation of the past by focusing on the future. While amnesty usually goes hand-in-hand with official amnesia, in practice it means installing a default memory and expunging another. While amnesty may seek to overturn the moral imperative of memory-justice to past injustice and orient society towards the present and future, it cannot completely erase the need of the living to fulfil their 'debt to the victims or to the carrying out of the demands of justice for its own sake'.[1538] The political logic of amnesty is the avoidance of past division and desire for revenge for a shared future premised on the erasure of memory. In Uruguay, amnesty was justified as a moral decision 'to give priority to the possibility of a future of agreement over a past of division (Senator Manuel Flores Silva)'.[1539] However, amnesty as a path to produce closure remains vulnerable to disruption by the silenced but never forgotten claims of victims demanding memory-justice. The moral obligation of the living to the dead not to forget them means it is not in their power to forgive in the victims' name. 'The irreversibility of time means that past injustices cannot be undone and cannot be made to disappear entirely'.[1540]

8.6. CONCLUSION: WHERE TO?

Today the judicialization of the management of conflict to uphold international standards of justice normalized in the four pillars is considered best practice. Moreover, transitional justice has merged with peacemaking insisting on criminal accountability for gross human rights violations (IHL and IHRL) and putting victims' rights at the centre of justice. From an historical and comparative perspective, transitional justice interventions represent the expansion of international law through human rights protection into internal conflicts. Even though transitional justice discourse constructs this intervention as legal and based on universal law (IHRL and IHL), in practice it seeks to transform historical practices of elite conflict management which have evolved with respect to particular genealogies of conflict. Transitional justice is an expression of the globalization of international law standards to guide post-conflict justice which contests elite cooption of the law to assert the prerogative of sovereignty and regime legitimation. The capacity of transitional justice to assert international

1538 Booth 2001, o.c., p. 785.
1539 Weschler 1998, o.c., p. 184.
1540 Booth 2001, o.c., p. 785.

legal norms in conflict management has grown as its capacity to influence political negotiations during transition with a shift from post-conflict to ongoing conflict situations. What are the likely long-term outcomes of transitional justice interventions in post-conflict, post-Cold War, (often postcolonial states) internal conflicts? Two issues will shape the course of transitional justice interventions: First, the historical trajectory of the relationship between the international protection of individual rights and the prerogative of state sovereignty; and second, the way contemporary transitional justice outcomes will pre-figure the future iterations of political conflict anchored in unresolved conflicts in the process of state formation.

From our case studies it is apparent that states will continue to push back against international legal intervention in the name of sovereignty. Resistance is likely to take the form of amnesty laws or, more likely, the selective adoption of transitional justice measures and half-hearted implementation. International tribunals have been denounced as neo-imperialist or neo-colonialist to undermine their legitimacy, and transitional justice processes are manipulated by elites to defend their self-interest. International legal intervention in internal conflict is politically fraught because of the legacy of polarized political subjectivities produced during internal conflict and the difficulty of forging a unifying post-conflict identity. While international courts claim to act in the name of victims' justice, their opponents denounce them as administering victors' justice. Victims' and victors' justice nevertheless are only possible if one side prevails in the post-conflict context. Often the successor state's adoption of the grammar of transitional justice is only an expression of a shift in the balance of power between perpetrators and victims. The successor state manoeuvres between an epistemic human rights community – international and national coalition of lawyers, human rights activists – and a political and military elite seeking to resolve conflict along traditional lines through pactism, amnesty and amnesia.

At the same time that transitional justice mechanisms have expanded the scope of rights protection, the rehabilitated state has been prioritized and the role of civil society has been diminished in shaping transitional justice processes. The politically normative goals of transitional justice and neoliberal development agenda have tended to empower political elites as gatekeepers. The pioneering role of the families of victims in human rights forensics – the partnership between families, human rights advocates and forensics anthropologists – in strengthening human rights protection has been usurped by more bureaucratically centralized and hi-tech forensic technologies depoliticizing the search for the disappeared.[1541] Memory politics around victimhood has also been

[1541] L.A. Smith, 'The missing, the martyred and the disappeared: Global networks, technical intensification and the end of human rights genetics' (2017) 47 *Social Studies of Science* 398, at 400.

eroded by the political demobilization of memory through its individualization and privatization as grief or by the proliferation of victimhood as identity politics on both sides of the conflict. The former is depoliticizing because it removes individual traumatic memory from wider social memory, and the latter, because it fragments identity and limits the possibility of a broader collective memory and reconciliation project.

The reassertion of sovereignty over international protection of individual rights is being felt in another way through populism. Democratic transition and the expansion and consolidation of human rights protection has been closely linked to the arrival of progressive governments into power to support them. Constitutional reforms which have expanded rights – indigenous rights, gender, sexuality, education, health, housing, education – as social justice have recently faced significant challenges with the democratic election of authoritarian leaders. Our case studies, especially on Spain and Colombia, revealed just how politically contingent the protection of human rights are on progressive governments continuing to hold office. Interestingly, the appeal of populism reflects deep anxieties about sovereignty – in the sense of the state's ability to protect its citizens and deliver on its promises – and dramatized by the state's preoccupation with security and citizens' experience of physical and economic insecurity daily life. What the victims, or those that fear they will become victims want, is ironically more state.

BIBLIOGRAPHY

BOOKS, CHAPTERS, ARTICLES

'A land title is not enough: ensuring sustainable land restitution in Colombia', *Amnesty International*, November 27, 2014, www.amnesty.org/en/documents/AMR23/031/2014/en/.

'A Review of How Colombia's Truth Commission is Advancing', *WOLA*, April 6, 2020, https://colombiapeace.org/advancing-truth-commission/.

'Argentina: Events of 2021', *World Report*, 2022, *Human Rights Watch*, https://www.hrw.org/world-report/2022/country-chapters/argentina.

'ARGENTINA: Legal Memorandum, The Full Stop and Due Obedience Laws, Submitted by Amnesty International and the International Commission of Jurists', *Amnesty International* December 2003, AMR 13/018/2003.

'Breaking the Grip? Obstacles to Justice for Paramilitary Mafias in Colombia Report on Colombia', *Human Rights Watch*, October 16, 2008, New York.

'Colombia: The Victims and Land Restitution Law: An Amnesty International analysis', *Amnesty International*, April 17, 2012.

'Colombia: Victim participation in transitional justice brings major challenges, panellists say', *Justice Rapid Response*, August 10, 2020, https://www.justicerapidresponse.org/colombia-victim-participation-in-transitional-justice-brings-major-challenges-panellists-say/.

'Constitutions and Peace Processes: A Primer', Berghof Foundation and the UN Department of Political and Peacebuilding Affairs, Berlin, 2020. https://peacemaker.un.org/sites/peacemaker.un.org/files/2021_ConstitutionsPeaceProcessesPrimer_EN.pdf.

'Correcting Course: Victims and the Justice and Peace Law in Colombia', *Latin America Report*, No. 29, October 30, 2008, International Crisis Group.

'ICMP Welcomes the Establishment of the Search Unit for Missing Persons in Colombia', *International Commission of Missing Persons*, April 7, 2017, https://www.icmp.int/press-releases/icmp-welcomes-the-establishment-of-the-search-unit-for-missing-persons-in-colombia/.

'Kenya's Rift Valley: Old Wounds, Devolution's New Anxieties', *Africa Report*, No. 248, May 30, 2017, International Crisis Group, Brussels.

'Lebanon: Only an international investigation can ensure Beirut explosion victims' rights to truth, justice and remedy', *Amnesty International*, September 7, 2020, https://www.amnesty.org/en/documents/mde18/2997/2020/en/.

'Lebanon's Self-Defeating Survival Strategies', *Middle East Report*, No. 160, July 20, 2015, International Crisis Group.

'Protecting Colombia's Most Vulnerable on the Road to "Total Peace"', *Latin America Report*, No. 98, February 24, 2023, International Crisis Group.

'Storm over Uhuru's Sh10 billion for victims reparations', *Journalist for Justice*, October 19, 2015. https://jfjustice.net/storm-over-uhurus-sh10-billion-for-victims-reparations/.

'The Lebanese High Judicial Council in Light of International Standards', A Briefing paper, February 2017, International Commission of Jurists, Geneva.

'The Special Tribunal for Lebanon. Selective Justice?', *Amnesty International*, February 25, 2009, London, https://www.amnesty.org/download/Documents/48000/mde180012009en.pdf.

'"They Killed Us from the Inside": An Investigation into the August 4 Beirut Blast', *Human Rights Watch*, August 3, 2021, https://www.hrw.org/sites/default/files/media_2021/08/lebanon0821_web.pdf.

'Trial by Fire: The Politics of the Special Tribunal for Lebanon' *Middle East Report*, No. 100, December 2, 2010, International Crisis Group.

'Truth and Reconciliation Commission of South Africa Report', Macmillan Reference, London, 1999.

'What Macro-Cases has Colombia's Special Jurisdiction for Peace (JEP) Opened?', *WOLA*, March 13, 2020. https://colombiapeace.org/what-macro-cases-has-colombias-special-jurisdiction-for-peace-jep-opened/.

Abdi, A., 'Kenya, Again, Represses Civil Society: Government Board Targets Groups Critical of Elections Process' *Human Rights Watch*, November 7, 2017, https://www.hrw.org/news/2017/11/07/kenya-again-represses-civil-society.

Achugar, M., et al., 'Re/constructing the past: How young people remember the Uruguayan dictatorship' (2013) 24 *Discourse & Society*, 265.

Achugar, M., *What we Remember: The Construction of Memory in Military Discourse*, John Benjamins, Philadelphia, PA 2008.

Ackerman, B. 'Brazil's Constitutional Dilemma in Comparative Perspective: Do Chile and Spain Cast Light on the Bolsonaro Crisis' (2020) *Blog of the International Journal of Constitutional Law*, July 17, 2020. https://macmillan.yale.edu/news/brazils-constitutional-dilemma-comparative-perspective-do-chile-and-spain-cast-light-bolsonaro.

Acunha, F.J.G., et al., 'The Brazilian Constitution of 1988 and its ancient ghosts: comparison, history and the ever-present need to fight authoritarianism' (2018) 5 *Revista de Investigações Constitucionais*, 17.

Aguilar Fernández, P., *Memory and amnesia: the role of the Spanish Civil War in the transition to democracy*, Berghahn Books, New York/Oxford 2002.

Ajulu, R., *Post-Colonial Kenya: The Rise of an Authoritarian and Predatory State*, Taylor & Francis, Milton 2021.

Akhavan, P., 'Reconciling Crimes Against Humanity with the Laws of War: Human Rights, Armed Conflict, and the Limits of Progressive Jurisprudence' (2008) 6 *Journal of International Criminal Justice*, 21.

Al-Khazen, F., 'The Communal Pact of National Identities: The Making and Politics of the 1943 National Pact', Papers on Lebanon 12, Centre for Lebanese Studies, Oxford, 1991.

Alamuddin, A. and Bonini, A., 'The UN Investigation of the Hariri Assassination' in A. Alamuddin et al. (eds.), *The Special Tribunal for Lebanon*, Oxford University Press, Oxford 2014, p. 50.

Alcalá, P.R., and Uribe, M.V., 'Constructing Memory amidst War: The Historical Memory Group of Colombia' (2016) 10 *The International Journal of Transitional Justice*, 6.

Aldana-Pindell, R., 'An Emerging Universality of Justiciable Victims' Rights in the Criminal Process to Curtail Impunity for State-Sponsored Crimes' (2004) 26 *Human Rights Quarterly*, 605.

Allier-montaño, E. and Ovalle, C.V., '"As an Unhealed Wound": Memory and Justice in Post-Dictatorship Uruguay' in E. Allier-Montaño and E. Crenzel (eds.), *The Struggle for Memory in Latin America: Recent History and Political Violence*, Palgrave Macmillan, New York 2015, p. 35.

Allier, E., 'The Peace Commission: A Consensus on the Recent in Uruguay?' (2006) 81 *European Review of Latin American and Caribbean Studies*, 87.

Altman, D., 'Popular initiatives in Uruguay: confidence votes on government or political loyalties' (2002) 21 *Electoral Studies*, 617.

Alvarez, J.E., 'Promoting the "rule of law" in Latin America: Problems and Prospects' (1991) 25 *The George Washington Journal of International Law and Economics*, 281.

Alviar García, H., and K. Engle, 'The Distributive Politics of Impunity and Anti-Impunity: Lessons from Four Decades of Colombian Peace Negotiations' in K. Engle (ed.), *Anti-Impunity and the Human Rights Agenda*, Cambridge University Press, Cambridge 2017, p. 216.

Ambos, K. and Aboueldahab, S., 'Command Responsibility and the Colombian Peace Process' in S. Ghanayim (ed.) *The Quest for Core Values in the Application of Legal Norms. Essays in Honor of Mordechai Kremnitzer*, Springer, Cham 2021, p. 259.

Ambos, K., 'Judicial Creativity at the Special Tribunal for Lebanon: Is There a Crime of Terrorism under International Law?' (2011) 24 *Leiden Journal of International Law*, 655.

Analytical Guide to the Work of the International Law Commission, International Law Commission, updated June 9, 2022, https://legal.un.org/ilc/guide/7_7.shtml.

Anderson, D.M. and McKnight, J., 'Kenya at War: Al-Shabaab and its Enemies in Eastern Africa' (2014) 114 *African Affairs*, 1.

Anderson, D.M., '"Yours in Struggle for Majimbo'. Nationalism and the Party Politics of Decolonization in Kenya, 1955–64' (2005b) 40 *Journal of Contemporary History*, 547.

Anderson, D.M., 'Vigilantes, violence and the politics of public order in Kenya' (2002) 101 *African Affairs*, 531.

Anderson, D., *Histories of the Hanged: Britain's Dirty War in Kenya and the End of Empire*, Weidenfeld & Nicholson, London 2005a.

Anderson, J.H., 'Special Tribunal for Lebanon's "Second Best Justice"', *Justiceinfo.net*, March 22, 2022. https://www.justiceinfo.net/en/88918-special-tribunal-for-lebanons-second-best-justice.html.

Anghie, A., *Imperialism, Sovereignty and the Making of International Law*, Cambridge University Press, Cambridge 2005.

Aragoneses, A., 'Legal Silences and the Memory of Francoism in Spain' in A. Gliszczyńska-Grabias and U. Belavusau (eds.), *Law and Memory: Towards Legal Governance of History*, Cambridge University Press, Cambridge 2017, p. 175.

Aretxaga, B., 'Madness and the Politically Real: Reflections on Violence in Postdictatorial Spain' in M.-J.D. Good, et al. (eds.), *Postcolonial Disorders: Reflections on Subjectivity in the Contemporary World*, University of California Press, Berkeley and Los Angeles, CA 2008, p. 43.

Arguelhes, D.W., 'Transformative Constitutionalism in Latin America: The Emergence of a New *Ius Commune*' (2019) 17 *International Journal of Constitutional Law*, 368.

Bahout, J., 'The Unraveling of Lebanon's Taif Agreement: Limits of Sect-Based Power Sharing' (2016) May Carnegie Endowment for International Peace, https://carnegieendowment.org/files/CP_271_Bahout_Taif_Final.pdf.

Bakiner, O., 'Conclusion' in E. Skaar, et al. (eds.), *Latin American Experiences with Truth Commission Recommendations: Beyond Words, Vol. II*, Intersentia, Cambridge 2022, p. 485.

Balint, J.L., 'The Place of Law in Addressing Internal Regime Conflicts' (1996) 59 *Law and Contemporary Problems*, 103.

Balint, J.L., 'The "Mau Mau" Legal Hearings and Recognizing the Crimes of the British Colonial State: A Limited Constitutive Moment' (2016) 3 *Critical Analysis of Law*, 261.

Banks, W.C. and E. Alvarez, E. 'The New Colombian Constitution: Democratic Victory or Popular Surrender?' (1991) 23 *University of Miami Inter-American Law Review*, 39.

Barahona De Brito, A., 'Truth, Justice, Memory, and Democratisation in the Southern Cone' in A. Barahona De Brito, et al. (eds.), *The Politics of Memory: Transitional Justice in Democratizing Societies*, Oxford University Press, Oxford 2001, 119.

Barahona De Brito, A., *Human Rights and Democratization in Latin America*, Oxford University Press, Oxford 1997.

Barros, R., *Constitutionalism and Dictatorship: Pinochet, the Junta, and the 1980 Constitution*, Cambridge University Press, Cambridge 2002.

Bassiouni, M.C., 'Searching for Peace and Achieving Justice: The Need for Accountability' (1996) 59 *Law and Contemporary Problems*, 9.

Baumann, H., 'Citizen Hariri and neoliberal politics in postwar Lebanon', PhD Thesis, SOAS, University of London, 2012, http://eprints.soas.ac.uk/14240.

Baxi, U., 'Constitutionalism as a site of state formative practices' (2000) 21 *Cardozo Law Review*, 1183.

Beevor, A., *The Battle for Spain; The Spanish Civil War 1936–1939*, Weidenfeld & Nicolson, London 2006.

Bell, C., 'Peace Agreements: Their Nature and Legal Status' (2006) 100 *American Journal of International Law*, 373.

Bell, C., *On the law of peace agreements and the lex pacificatoria*, Oxford University Press, Oxford 2008.

Bell, C., 'The "New Law" of Transitional Justice' in K. Ambos, et al. (eds.), *Building a Future on Peace and Justice: Studies on Transitional Justice, Peace and Development*, Springer, Berlin, Heidelberg 2009, p. 105.

Bell, C., 'Power-sharing and human rights law' (2013) 17 *The International Journal of Human Rights*, 204.

Bell, C., 'Contending with the Past: Transitional Justice and Political Settlement Processes' in R. Duthie and P. Seils (eds.), *Justice Mosaics: How Context Shapes Transitional Justice in Fractured Societies*, International Center for Transitional Justice, New York 2017, p. 85.

Benjamin, W. et al., *Toward the Critique of Violence: A Critical Edition*, Stanford University Press, Redwood City, CA 2021.

Bentancur, V.P. et al., 'The Case of Uruguay's *Frente Amplio*' in F. Rosenblatt, et al. (eds.), *Diminished Parties: Democratic Representation in Contemporary Latin America*, Cambridge University Press, Cambridge 2021, p. 29.

Berat, L. and Shain, Y., 'Retribution or Truth-Telling in South Africa? Legacies of the Transitional Phase' (1995) 20 *Law and Social Inquiry*, 163.

Bermeo, N.G., *Ordinary People in Extraordinary Times: The Citizenry and the Breakdown of Democracy*, Princeton University Press, Princeton, NJ 2020.

Berti, B. and Lee, D., 'Lebanon and the United Nations Special Tribunal: Between (Un) Accountability and (In)stability' (2014) 17 *Strategic Assessment*, 95.

Berti, B., 'Balancing Justice, Stability and Legitimacy: Lebanon and the UN Special Tribunal – Understanding the Domestic Impact of International Criminal Justice' (2014a) 19 *Mediterranean Politics* 117.

Besson, S., 'The Law in Human Rights Theory' (2013) 7 *Zeitschrift für Menschenrechte – Journal for Human Rights*, 120.

Biesca, S.G., 'El proceso de la recuperación de la 'memoria histórica' en España: Una aproximación a los movimientos sociales por la memoria' (2006) 19 *International Journal of Iberian Studies* 25.

Bikundo, E., *International Criminal Law: Using or Abusing Legality?* Routledge, London, 2016.

Binder, C., 'The Prohibition of Amnesties by the Inter-American Court of Human Rights' (2011) 12 *German Law Journal*, 1203.

Bjork, C. and Goebertus, J., 'Complementarity in Action: The Role of Civil Society and the ICC in the Rule of Law Strengthening in Kenya' (2011) 14 *Yale Human Rights and Development Law Journal*, 205.

Blick, A., 'The Special Tribunal for Lebanon: How did it survive for so long?' *EJIL: Talk!*, September 20, 2021, https://www.ejiltalk.org/the-special-tribunal-for-lebanon-how-did-it-survive-for-so-long/.

Bocchese, M., '*El Coco* Does Not Frighten Anymore: ICC scrutiny and state cooperation in Colombia' Northwestern University, presented at 'The American Society of International Law Midyear Meeting', Los Angeles, CA November 8–10, 2018.

Booth, W.J., 'The Unforgotten: Memories of Justice' (2001) 95 *The American Political Science Review*, 777.

Borda, S. et al., 'Colombia's Constrained Peace Process: How Courts Alter Peace-Making' *openDemocracy*, July 26, 2016, https://www.opendemocracy.net/en/openglobalrights-openpage/colombia-s-constrained-peace-pr/.

Bourdieu, P., *Outline of a Theory of Practice*, Cambridge University Press, Cambridge 1977.

Bouvard, M.G., *Revolutionizing Motherhood: The Mothers of the Plaza de Mayo*, Rowman & Littlefield Publishers, Wilmington, DE 2002.

Bowcott, O., 'International criminal court abandons case against William Ruto', *The Guardian*, April 5, 2016, https://www.theguardian.com/world/2016/apr/05/international-criminal-court-william-ruto-kenya-deputy-president-election-violence.

Boyd, C.P., ''Responsibilities' and the Spanish Republic 1931–6' (1984) 14 *European History Quarterly* 151.

Branch, D. and Cheeseman, N., 'The politics of control in Kenya: Understanding the bureaucratic-executive state, 1952–78' (2006) 33 *Review of African Political Economy*, 11.

Branch, D. and Cheeseman, N., 'Democratization, sequencing, and state failure in Africa: Lessons from Kenya' (2008) 108 *African Affairs*, 1.

Branch, D., *Defeating Mau Mau, Creating Kenya: Counterinsurgency, Civil War, and Decolonization*, Cambridge University Press, Cambridge 2009.

Branch, D., *Kenya Between Hope and Despair, 1963–2011*, Yale University Press, New Haven and London 2011.

Branch, D., 'Violence, decolonisation and the Cold War in Kenya's north-eastern province, 1963–1978' (2014) 8 *Journal of Eastern African Studies*, 642.

Breuer, A., 'The use of Government Initiated Referendums in Latin America. Towards a Theory of referendum causes' (2009) 29 *Revista de Ciencia Política*, 23.

Brody, R. and González, F., '*Nunca Más*: An Analysis of International Instruments on "Disappearances", (1997) 19 *Human Rights Quarterly*, 365.

Brown, D., 'The Challenges of Colombia's Victims Law', *Amnesty International*, June 15, 2011, https://www.amnestyusa.org/the-challenges-of-colombias-victims-law/.

Brown, S. and Sriram, C.L., 'The Big Fish Won't Fry Themselves: Criminal Accountability for Post-Election Violence in Kenya' (2012) 111 *African Affairs*, 244.

Brown, S., 'Authoritarian leaders and multiparty elections in Africa: How foreign donors help to keep Kenya's Daniel arap Moi in power' (2001) 22 *Third World Quarterly*, 725.

Buchan, R., *International Law and the Construction of the Liberal Peace*, Hart Publishing, Oxford 2013.

Buchely, L., 'Peace, Land, and Bureaucracy in Colombia: An Analysis of the Implementation of the Victims and Land Restitution Law from a Multiscale Perspective of State Bureaucracies' (2020) 9 *Land*, 181.

Burbidge, P., 'Justice and Peace? – The Role of Law in Resolving Colombia's Civil Conflict' (2008) 8 *International Criminal Law Review*, 557.

Burchianti, M.E., 'Building Bridges of Memory: The Mothers of the Plaza de Mayo and the Cultural Politics of Maternal Memories' (2004) 15 *History and Anthropology*, 133.

Burgis-Kasthala, M., 'Defining Justice during Transition? International and Domestic Contestations over the Special Tribunal for Lebanon' (2013) 7 *International Journal of Transitional Justice*, 497.

Burgis-Kasthala, M. and A. Saouli, 'The Politics of Normative Intervention and the Special Tribunal for Lebanon' (2022) 16 *Journal of Intervention and Statebuilding*, 79.

Buriano, A., 'A 30 años de la ley de caducidad uruguaya ¿qué y cómo debemos conmemorar?' (2017) 10 *Antíteses*, 351.

Buriano, A., 'Ley de Caducidad en Uruguay y esencia ético-política de la izquierda' (2011) 19 *Perfiles latinoamericanos*, 173.

Burt, J.-M., et al., 'Civil Society and the Resurgent Struggle against Impunity in Uruguay (1986–2012)' (2013a) 7 *International Journal of Transitional Justice*, 306.

Burt, J.-M., 'Judge's Removal Causes Concerns over Human Rights Investigations in Uruguay', *WOLA*, February 20, 2013, https://www.wola.org/analysis/judges-removal-causes-concerns-over-human-rights-investigations-in-uruguay/.

Caetano, G., et al., 'La partidocracia uruguaya. Historia y teoría de la centralidad de los partidos políticos' (1987) 44 *Cuadernos del CLAEH*, 37.

Caetano, G., 'La partidocracia uruguaya: tradicíon y agenda reciente' (1995) 32 *Secuencia: Revvisita de historia y ciencias sociales*, 103.

Cairo, H., et al., '"Territorial Peace": The Emergence of a Concept in Colombia's Peace Negotiations' (2018) 23 *Geopolitics*, 464.

CAMINS, E.L., 'Needs or Rights? Exploring the Limitations of Individual Reparations for Violations of International Humanitarian Law' (2016) 10 *International Journal of Transitional Justice*, 126.

Canel, E., 'Municipal Decentralization and Participatory Democracy: Building a New Mode of Urban Politics in Montevideo City?' (2001) 71 *European Review of Latin American and Caribbean Studies*, 25.

Caraballo, F.L., and Corradi, M.F., 'De la "Ley de Caducidad" al "voto verde": Nuevas formas de resistencia en marcos de legalidad. El caso de la Comisión Nacional Pro Referéndum' (2019) 17 *EU-topías: Revista de interculturalidad, comunicación y estudios europeos*, 101.

Carlson, K.B., 'ICC case against Kenyan lawyer Gicheru: it matters, but not for victims of the violence', *The Conversation*, March 15, 2022, https://theconversation.com/icc-case-against-kenyan-lawyer-gicheru-it-matters-but-not-for-victims-of-the-violence-178938.

Carina, R., 'The Empire's Ghosts Return' (2009) 487 *New African* 18.

Carrillo Lerma, J., 'Recognizing Conflict & Escaping Violence: Contemporary Colombian Migration' (2011) 1 *International Journal of Business, Humanities and Technology*, 122.

Cassel, D., 'Lessons from the Americas: Guidelines for International Responses to Amnesties for Atrocities' (1996) 59 *Law and Contemporary Social Problems*, 197.

Cassel, D., 'The expanding scope and impact of reparations awarded by the Inter-American Court of Human Rights' (2004) 27 *Hastings International and Comparative Law Review*, 91.

Cassese, A., 'The Legitimacy of International Criminal Tribunals and the Current Prospects of International Criminal Justice' (2012) 25 *Leiden Journal of International Law*, 491.

Castillejo-Cuéllar, A., 'Historical Injuries, Temporality and the Law: Articulations of a Violent Past in Two Transitional Scenarios' (2014) 26 *Law and Critique*, 47.

Cavallaro, J.L. and Brewer, S.E., 'Re-evaluating Regional Human Rights Litigation in the Twenty-First Century: The Case of the Inter-American Court' (2008) 102 *American Journal of International Law*, 768.

Cenarro, A., 'Memory beyond the Public Sphere: The Francoist Repression Remembered in Aragon' (2002) 14 *History and Memory*, 165.

Cepeda Espinosa, M.J., 'Responsive Constitutionalism' (2019) 15 *Annual Review of Law and Social Change,* 21.

Cepeda-Castro, I., 'A Model of Democracy for Justice' in A. Lyons (ed.), *Contested Transitions: Dilemmas of Transitional Justice in Colombia and Comparative Experience*, CEP – Banco de la República Luis Ángel Arango, Bogotá 2010, p. 179.

Champagne, P., et al. (eds.), *Pierre Bourdieu: On the State: Lectures at the Collège de France, 1989–1992*, Polity, Cambridge 2014.

Chernick, 'Negotiated Settlement to Armed Conflict: Lessons from the Colombian Peace Process' (1988) 30 *Journal of Interamerican Studies and World Affairs*, 53.

CHERNICK, M.W., *Acuerdo Posible: solución negociada al conflicto armado colombiano*, Ediciones Auora, Bogotá 2008.

CHERNICK, M.W., 'Santos, the FARC and the Evolution of Peace Negotiations in Colombia' in B.M. BAGLEY and J.D. ROSEN (eds.), *Colombia's political economy at the outset of the twenty-first century: from Uribe to Santos and beyond*, Lexington Books, Lanham, MD 2015, p. 141.

CISNEROS DE ALENCAR, A.M., 'Cooperation Between the Universal and Inter-American Human Rights Systems in the Framework of the Universal Periodic Review Mechanism' (2010) 7 *SUR International Journal on Human Rights*, 171.

CLEMENS, E.S., 'Toward a Historicized Sociology: Theorizing Events, Processes, and Emergence' (2007) 33 *Annual Review of Sociology*, 527.

CLOUGH, M.S., 'Mau Mau and the Contest for Memory', in E. S. A. ODHIAMBO, and J. LONSDALE (eds.) *Mau Mau & Nationhood: Arms, Authority & Narration*, James Currey, Oxford 2003, 251.

CLUA-LOSADA and O. RIBERA-ALMANDOZ, 'Authoritarian Neoliberalism and the Disciplining of Labour' in C. B. TANSEL (ed.) *States of Discipline: Authoritarian Neoliberalism and the Contested Reproduction of Capitalist Order (Transforming Capitalism)*, Rowman & Littlefield Publishers, London/New York 2017, 33.

COBB, S., 'The Domestication of Violence in Mediation' (1997) 31 *Law & Society Review*, 397.

COHEN-ALMAGOR R. and HALEVA-AMIR S., 'The Israel-Hezbollah War and the Winograd Committee' (2008) II *Journal of Parliamentary and Political Law*, 113.

Colombia: World Report 2023, Human Rights Watch, https://www.hrw.org/world-report/2023/country-chapters/colombia.

COPPEDGE, M., 'The Evolution of Latin American Party Systems' in S. MAINWARING and A. VALENZUELA (eds.), *Politics, Society and Democracy*, Routledge, Oxford 1998, p. 171.

COSSE, I. and MARKARIAN, V., *1975: año de la orientalidad: identidad, memoria e historia en una dictadura*, Ediciones Trice, Montevideo, 1996.

COUSO, J., 'The Possibilities and Limits of a Constitution-Making Transnational Legal Order: The Case of Chile' in G. SHAFFER et al. (eds.), *Constitution-Making and Transnational Legal Order*, Cambridge University Press, Cambridge 2019, p. 265.

CRAWFORD, J., 'Is Syria giving universal jurisdiction new life?', *Justiceinfo.net*, March, 4, 2019, https://www.justiceinfo.net/en/tribunals/national-tribunals/40483-is-syria-giving-universal-jurisdiction-new-life.html.

CRENZEL, 'Genesis, Uses, and Significations of the Nunca Más Report in Argentina' (2015) 42 *Latin American Perspectives*, 20.

CROSSLEY, N., 'A Model Case of R2P Prevention? Mediation in the Aftermath of Kenya's 2007 Presidential Elections', (2013) 5 *Global Responsibility to Protect*, 192.

CUARTAS, F.P. and SÁNCHEZ-GARZOLI, G., 'Q&A: Promises and Prospects for Human Rights in Colombia under Petro as ELN negotiations restart', *WOLA*, February 17, 2023, https://www.wola.org/analysis/qa-promises-prospects-for-human-rights-colombia-under-petro-as-eln-negotiations/.

D'ORSI, L., 'Trauma and the Politics of Memory of the Uruguayan Dictatorship' (2015) 42 *Latin American Perspectives*, 162.

DAMGAARD, C., *Individual Criminal Responsibility for Core International Crimes: Selected Pertinent Issues*, Springer Berlin, Heidelberg 2008.

Dassin, J., *Torture in Brazil: A Shocking Report on the Pervasive Use of Torture by Brazilian Military Governments, 1964–1979*, University of Texas Press, Institute of Latin American Studies, Austin, TX 1998.

David, L., 'Against Standardization of Memory' (2017) 39 *Human Rights Quarterly*, 296.

Davidovic, M., "The Law of 'Never Again': Transitional Justice and the Transformation of the Norm of Non-Recurrence', (2021) 15 *International Journal of Transitional Justice*, 386.

De Certeau, M., *The Writing of History*, Columbia University Press, New York, NY 1988.

De Greiff, P., 'Justice and Reparations' in P. de Greiff (ed.), *The Handbook of Reparations*, Oxford University Press, Oxford 2006, p. 1.

De Greiff, P. 'Theorizing Transitional Justice' in M.S. williams, et al. (eds.), *Transitional Justice: Nomos Li*, New York University Press, NY 2012, p. 31.

De Greiff, P., '"Truth without Facts". On the Erosion of the Fact-Finding Function of Truth Commissions' in P. Alston and S. Knuckey (eds.), *The Transformation of Human Rights Fact-Finding*, Oxford University Press, New York, NY 2016, p. 281.

De Greiff, P., 'The Future of the Past: Reflections on the Present State and Prospects of Transitional Justice' (2020) 14 *International Journal of Transitional Justice*, 251.

De León, W., 'Former President Juan Maria Bordaberry is condemned to thirty years of prison and 15 years of precautionary detention for the offenses of "crimes against the constitution," two "political homicides" and the "forced disappearance" of nine citizens', *The National Security Archive*, March 30, 2010, http://nsarchive.gwu.edu/NSAEBB/NSAEBB309/Summary.pdf.

De Sousa Santos, B., 'Colombia Between Neoliberal Peace and Democratic Peace' (2017) 11 *In Factis Pax*, 41.

Deas, M., 'The troubled course of Colombian peacemaking' (1986) 8 *Third World Quarterly*, 639.

Delaney, P., 'Legislating for Equality in Colombia: Constitutional Jurisprudence, Tutelas, and Social Reform' (2008) 1 *The Equal Rights Review*, 50.

Delgado, M.M. et al., *"So the People Can Decide": the experience of the plebiscite against the impunity law in Uruguay: (1986–1989)*, International Human Rights Internship Program, Institute of International Education, Washington, 2001.

Demasi, C., 'Un repaso a la teoría de los dos demonios' in A. Marchesi, et al. (eds.), *El presente de la dictadura: Estudios y reflexiones a 30 años del golpe de Estado en Uruguay*, Ediciones Trilce, Montevideo 2004, p. 67.

Demasi, C., 'La partidocracia uruguaya: aportes para la discusión de una hipótesis' (2013) 3 *Contemporánea: Historia y problemas del siglo XX*, 267.

Derrida, J., 'Force of Law: The "Mystical Foundations" of Authority' in G. Anidjar (ed.), *Acts of Religion*, Routledge, New York, NY 2002, p. 358.

Diaz Marquez, M., 'Opinion: Why Colombia is a pioneer in restorative justice' *Justice Rapid Response*, June 10, 2021, https://www.justicerapidresponse.org/opinion-why-colombia-is-a-pioneer-in-restorative-justice/.

Dickenson, E., 'Colombia's Last Guerrillas Make First Step toward "Total Peace"', *International Crisis Group*, November 23, 2022, https://www.crisisgroup.org/latin-america-caribbean/andes/colombia/colombias-last-guerrillas-make-first-step-toward-total-peace.

Doughman, R.C., 'Might the Keys to Peace Open the Doors to Extractivism? Reflections on Colombia's Post-conflict Extractive Economy' in F. Cante and H. Quehi (eds.), *Handbook of Research on Transitional Justice and Peace Building in Turbulent Regions*, IGI Global, Hershey, PA 2015, p. 444.

Duarte, Á., 'The Republic, or Spain Freed from Itself' in J. Moreno-Luzón and X.M. Nuñez (eds.), *Metaphors of Spain: Representations of Spanish National Identity in the Twentieth Century*, Berghahn Books, London 2017, p. 63.

Dworkin, A., 'Protracted, neglected, and ineffective: Lessons from the Lebanon tribunal' *European Council on Foreign Relations*, September 4, 2020 https://ecfr.eu/article/commentary_protracted_neglected_and_ineffective_lessons_from_the_lebanon_tr/.

Dykmann, K., 'Impunity and the Right to Truth in the Inter-American System of Human Rights' (2007) 7 *Iberoamericana*, 45.

Eaton, K., *Politics Beyond the Capital: The Design of Subnational Institutions in South America*, Stanford University Press, Stanford, CA, 2020.

Ebrahim, H. and Miller, L.E., 'Creating the Birth Certificate of a New South Africa' in L.E. Miller and L. Aucoin (eds.), *Framing the State in Times of Transition: Case Studies in Constitution Making*, United States Institute of Peace, 2010, p. 111.

Edgerton, R., *Mau Mau: An African Crucible*, Collier MacMillan Publishers, London 1989.

Edkins, J., *Trauma and the Memory of Politics*, Cambridge University Press, Cambridge/New York 2003.

El-Husseini, R., *Pax Syriana: Elite Politics in Postwar Lebanon*, Syracuse University Press, Syracuse, NY 2012.

Elberling, B., 'The Next Step in History-Writing through Criminal Law: Exactly How Tailor-Made Is the Special Tribunal for Lebanon?' (2008) 21 *Leiden Journal of International Law*, 529.

Elias, J., 'Beirut Blast: International Investigation?' *Lebanon Law Review*, April 2, 2021.

Elkins, C., 'Alchemy of Evidence: Mau Mau, the British Empire, and the High Court of Justice' (2011) 39 *The Journal of Imperial and Commonwealth History*, 731.

Elkins, C., *Imperial Reckoning: The Untold Story of Britain's Gulag in Kenya*, Henry Holt and Company, New York 2005, p. 244.

Elster, J., *Closing the Books: Transitional Justice in Historical Perspective*, Cambridge University Press, Cambridge 2004.

Encarnación, O.G., 'Reconciliation after Democratization: Coping with the Past in Spain' (2008) 123 *Political Science Quarterly*, 435.

Encarnación, O.G., 'Justice in Times of Transition: Lessons from the Iberian Experience' (2012) 56 *International Studies Quarterly*, 179.

Engle, K., 'Self-Critique, (Anti) Politics and Criminalization: Reflections on the History and Trajectory of the Human Rights Movement' in J.M. Beneyto and D. Kennedy (eds.), *New Approaches to International Law: The European and the American Experiences*, T.M.C. Asser Press, The Hague 2013, p. 41.

Errandonea, J., 'Justicia transicional en Uruguay' (2008) 47 *Revista IIDH (Instituto Interamericano de Derechos Humanos)*, 13.

Eslava, L., 'Constitutionalization of Rights in Colombia: Establishing a ground for meaningful comparisons' (2009) 22 *Revisita Derecho del Estado*, 183.

Espinal, M.A.A. 'Ensamblajes institucionales y guerras civiles en la Colombia del siglo XIX' (2014) 11 *Co-herencia: Revista de Humanidades*, 169.

Espinosa-Maestre, F., *Shoot the Messenger? Spanish Democracy and the Crimes of Francoism*, Sussex Academic Press, Brighton/Portland/Toronto 2013.

Etxeberria, G.F., 'Exhumaciones Contemporáneas en España: Las Fosas Comunes de la Guerra Civil' (2012) 18 *Boletín Galego de Medicina Legal e Forense*, 13.

Faber, S., *Exhuming Franco: Spain's Second Transition*, Vanderbilt University Press, Nashville, TN 2021.

Fawaz, L., 'The changing Balance of forces between Beirut and Damascus in the nineteenth and twentieth centuries' (1990) 55–6 *Revue des mondes musulmans et de la Méditerranée*, 208.

Fawaz, L.T., *An Occasion for War: Civil Conflict in Lebanon and Damascus in 1860*, University of California Press, Berkeley CA 1994.

Feitlowitz, M., *A Lexicon of Terror: Argentina and the Legacies of Torture*, Oxford University Press, New York, NY 1998.

Feres Júnior, J., 'The Semantics of Asymmetric Counter-concepts: The Case of "Latin America" In the US' (2005) 7/8 *Anales: Iberoamerikanska Institutet*, 83.

Fernández De Mata, I., 'The "Logics" of Violence and Franco's Mass Graves: An Ethnohistorical Approach' (2004) 2 *International Journal of the Humanities*, 2527.

Fernandez-Torne, C. and Ouziel, P., 'Democratising and Decolonising Spain: The Limits of The New Law on Memory', *Justiceinfo.net*, December 5, 2022, https://www.justiceinfo.net/en/109817-democratising-decolonising-spain-limits-new-law-memory.html.

Ferrándiz, F., and Robben, C.G.M., 'Introduction: the Ethnography of Exhumations' in F. Ferrándiz and C.G.M. Robben (eds.), *Necropolitics: Mass Graves and Exhumations in the Age of Human Rights*, University of Pennsylvania Press, Philadelphia, PA 2015, p. 1.

Ferrándiz, F., 'De las fosas comunes a los derechos humanos: El descubrimiento de las *desapariciones forzadas* en la España contemporánea' (2010) 19 *Revisita de Antropología Social*, 161.

Ferrándiz, F., 'Exhuming the defeated: civil war mass graves in 21st-century Spain' (2013) 40 *American Ethnologist* 38.

Ferrándiz, F., 'Subterranean Autopsies: Exhumations of Mass Graves in Contemporary Spain' in E. Schindel and P. Colombo (eds.), *Space and the Memories of Violence: Landscapes of Erasure, Disappearance and Exception*, Springer, 2014, p. 61.

Ferrándiz, F., 'Mass Graves, Landscapes of Terror: A Spanish Tale' in F. Ferrándiz (ed.), *Necropolitics: Mass Graves and Exhumations in the Age of Human Rights*, University of Pennsylvania Press, Philadelphia, PA 2015, p. 92.

Ferrándiz, F., 'Unburials, Generals, and Phantom Militarism: Engaging with the Spanish Civil War Legacy', (2019) 60 *Current anthropology*, S62.

Ferrándiz. F. and Baer, A. 'Digital Memory: The Visual Recording of Mass Grave Exhumations in Contemporary Spain' (2008) 9 *Forum Qualitative Social Research*, Art. 35, https://www.qualitative-research.net/index.php/fqs/article/view/1152.

Ferrer, E.F., 'The Right to the Truth as an Autonomous Right Under the Inter-American Human Rights System', (2016) 9 *Mexican Law Review*, 121.

FINCH, M., *A Political Economy of Uruguay since 1870*, Palgrave Macmillan, London 1981.

FINCH, H., 'Democratisation in Uruguay' (1985) 7 *Third World Quarterly*, 594.

FLETCHER, L.E. and WEINSTEIN, H.M., 'Violence and Social Repair: Rethinking the Contribution of Justice to Reconciliation' (2002) 24 *Human Rights Quarterly*, 573.

FLETCHER, L.E. and WEINSTEIN, H.M., 'Writing Transitional Justice: An Empirical Evaluation of Transitional Justice Scholarship in Academic Journals' (2015) 7 *Journal of Human Rights Practice*, 177.

FLORES, T.E., 'Vertical Inequality, Land Reform, and Insurgency in Colombia' (2014) 20 *Peace Economics, Peace Science and Public Policy*, 5.

FOUAD, L., Criminal responsibility and legal proceedings in the aftermath of the Beirut blast: throwing (more) dust in the eyes of the Lebanese?, *Revue des Juristes de Sciences Po*, February 25, 2021. https://www.revuedesjuristesdesciencespo.com/index.php/2021/02/25/criminal-responsibility-and-legal-proceedings-in-the-aftermath-of-the-beirut-blast-throwing-more-dust-in-the-eyes-of-the-lebanese/.

FOX, D.T., et al., 'Lessons of the Colombian Constitutional Reform of 1991' in L.E. MILLER (ed.), *Framing the State in Times of Transition: Case Studies in Constitution Making*, United States Institute of Peace, Washington, WA 2010, p. 467.

FOX, M., 'Hope and Disappointment in Uruguay's Elections' *Upside Down World*, November 2, 2009, http://upsidedownworld.org/main/content/view/2193/1/.

FREEMAN, M., 'Anthropology and the Democratisation of Human Rights' (2002a) 6 *The International Journal of Human Rights*, 37.

FREEMAN, M., 'Transitional Justice: Fundamental Goals and Unavoidable Complications' (2002b) 28 *Manitoba Law Journal*, 113.

FREGONESE, S., 'Beyond the 'Weak State': Hybrid Sovereignties in Beirut' (2012) 30 *Environment and Planning D: Society and Space*, 655.

GALVÁN PUENTE, S., 'Legislative measures as guarantees of non-repetition: a reality in the Inter-American Court, and a possible solution for the European Court' (2009) 49 *Revista IIDH (Instituto Interamericano de derechos humanos)*, 69.

GAMARRA, Y., 'National Responses in Latin America to International Events Propelling the Justice Cascade: The *Gelman* Case' in J.M. BENEYTO and D. KENNEDY (eds.), *New Approaches to International Law: The European and the American Experiences*, T.M.C. Asser Press, The Hague 2013, p. 75.

GARCÍA IOMMI, L., 'Whose justice? The ICC 'Africa problem'' (2020) 34 *International Relations*, 105.

GARCÍA LORCA, F., *Obras completas*. Edición a cargo de Arturo del Hoyo, 2 vols, Aguilar, Madrid, 1974.

GARCÍA VILLEGAS, M., et al., 'Impacto constitucional e institucional de la Ley de Justicia y Paz', in C. LÓPEZ-HERNANDEZ (ed.), '*Y refundadaron la patria .... de cómo mafiosos y políticos reconfiguraron el Estado colombiano*', Dejusticia, Bogotá 2010, 318.

GARCÍA-GODOS, J. and LID, K.A.O., 'Transitional Justice and Victims' Rights before the End of a Conflict: The Unusual Case of Colombia' (2010) 42 *Journal of Latin American Studies*, 487.

GARCÍA-GODOS, J. and WIIG, H., 'Ideals and Realities of Restitution: the Colombian Land Restitution Programme' (2018) 10 *Journal of Human Rights Practice*, 40.

García-Villegas, M., *The Powers of Law: A Comparative Analysis of Sociopolitical Legal Studies*, Cambridge University Press, Cambridge 2018.

Georgi, R., 'Peace that antagonizes: Reading Colombia's peace process as hegemonic crisis' (2023) 54 *Security Dialogue*, 173.

Geukjian, O., *Lebanon After the Syrian Withdrawal: External Intervention, Power-Sharing and Political Instability,* Routledge, London 2016.

Ghai, Y.P., 'Constitutions and constitutionalism: the fate of the 2010 constitution' in G.R. Murunga, et al. (eds.), *Kenya: the struggle for a new constitutional order*, Zed, London 2014, p. 119.

Ghelfi, F., et al., 'Brazil's National Truth Commission: Recommendations for a Pending Democratic Agenda' in E. Skaar, et al. (eds.), *Latin American Experiences with Truth Commission Recommendations: Beyond Words Vol. II*, Intersentia, Cambridge 2022, p. 197.

Gil, A.G., 'Spain as an Example of Total Oblivion with Partial Rehabilitation' in J. Almqvist and C. Esposito (eds.), *The Role of Courts in Transitional Justice: Voices from Latin America and Spain*, Routledge, London 2013, p. 108.

Gillespie, C.G., 'Uruguay's Return to Democracy' (1985) 4 *Bulletin of Latin American Research*, 99.

Gillespie, C.G., *Negotiating Democracy: Politicians and Generals in Uruguay*, Cambridge University Press, Cambridge 2006.

Girard, R., *Violence and the Sacred*, John Hopkins University Press, Baltimore, MD 1977.

Gissel, L., 'Contemporary Transitional Justice: Normalising a Politics of Exception' (2016) 31 *Global Society*, 353.

Glinz, C., 'Kenya's New Constitution: a Transforming Document or Less than Meets the Eye?' (2011) 44 *Verfassung und Recht in Übersee/Law and Politics in Africa, Asia and Latin America*, 60.

Golob, S.R., 'Volver: The Return Of/To Transitional Justice Politics in Spain' (2008) 9 *Journal of Spanish Cultural Studies*, 127.

Gómez López-Quiñones, A., 'A Secret Agreement: The Historical Memory Debate and the Limits of Recognition' (2012) 11 *Hispanic Issues On Line*, 87.

Gómez-Suárez, A. et al., 'Foreign Investors and the Colombian Peace Process' (2016) 18 *International Community Law Review*, 223.

Gómez, C.J.L. et al., 'Armed conflict, land grabs and primitive accumulation in Colombia: micro processes, macro trends and the puzzles in between' (2015) 42 *The Journal of Peasant Studies*, 255.

Gómez, G.I., 'Political Conflicts Over the JEP: A Sociolegal Perspective' in K. Ambos and S. Peters (eds.) *Transitional Justice in Colombia: The Special Jurisdiction for Peace*, Nomos, Baden-Baden 2022, p. 13.

Goransky, M.D., 'Dictatorship Trials and Reconciliation in Argentina' (2018) *FICHL Policy Brief Series*, 1.

Goti, J.M., 'Dignity, Vengeance, and Fostering Democracy' (1998) 29 *The University of Miami Inter-American Law Review*, 417.

Graham, T. and Hodges, E., '"Red Lines" in Beirut Blast Investigation: How Exactly Lebanese Politicians Escape Accountability' *Just Security*, March 6, 2021, https://www.justsecurity.org/75252/red-lines-in-beirut-blast-investigation-how-exactly-lebanese-politicians-escape-accountability/.

Grandin, G., *Empire's Workshop: Latin America, the United States, and the Rise of the New Imperialism*, Henry Holt and Company, New York, NY 2006.

Gray, J., *Enlightenment's wake: politics and culture at the close of the modern age*, Routledge, Oxford 2007.

Gready, P. and Robins, S., 'Transitional Justice and Theories of Change: Towards evaluation as understanding', (2020) 14 *International Journal of Transitional Justice*, 280.

Gready, P., 'Culture, Testimony, and the Toolbox of Transitional Justice' (2008) 20 *Peace Review*, 41.

Grégoire, E.R. and Monzón, L. M., 'Institutionalising CSR in Colombia's extractive sector: disciplining society, destabilising enforcement?' (2017) 38 *Canadian Journal of Development Studies / Revue canadienne d'études du développement*, 253.

Griffin, L. J., 'Narrative, event-structure, and causal interpretation in historical sociology' (1993) 98 *American Journal of Sociology*, 1094.

Grover, L., 'Transitional Justice, International Law and the United Nations' (2019) 88 *Nordic Journal of International Law*, 359.

Guarin, A., 'The Effects of Reparations: A Visual Interview with Arlen Guarin', *Matrix*, August 31, 2021, https://matrix.berkeley.edu/research-article/the-effects-of-reparations-a-visual-interview-with-arlen-guarin/.

Guerrero Apráez, V. A., *Guerras civiles colombianas: Negociación, regulación y memoria*, Editorial Pontifica Universidad Javeriana, Bogotá 2016.

Gurmendi, A., 'At Long Last, Brazil's Amnesty Law Is Declared Anti-Conventional', *OpinioJuris*, August 16, 2019, http://opiniojuris.org/2019/08/16/at-long-last-brazils-amnesty-law-is-declared-anti-conventional/.

Gusfield, J.R., 'Moral Passage: The Symbolic Process in Public Designations of Deviance' (1967) 15 *Social Problems*, 175.

Gutiérrez-Sanín, F. and Jaramillo Marín, A., 'Paradoxical Pacts' in B. De Sousa Santos (ed.), *Reinventing Social Emancipation: Toward New Manifestos*, Verso, London 2005, p. 193.

Gutiérrez-Sanín, F., 'The Courtroom and the Bivouac: Reflections on Law and Violence in Colombia' (2001) 28 *Latin American Perspectives*, 56.

Gutiérrez-Sanín, F., 'La Constitución de 1991 como pacto de paz: discutiendo las anomalías' (2011) 13 *Estudios Socio-Jurídicos*, 419.

Hall, J., 'Displacing Evil: The 1991 Lebanese Amnesty, the City and the Possibility of Justice' in S. Dam and J. Hall (eds.), *Inside and Outside the Law: Perspectives on Evil, Law and the State*, Inter-Disciplinary Press, Oxford, 2009, p. 61.

Hall, J., 'Tragedy of State: The 1991 Lebanese Amnesty Law and the Possibility of Justice' (2010), Balamand University, Beirut (unpublished) 1.

Hanafi, S., et al., 'Trial of the Status Quo: the politics of mediated justice in the Special Tribunal for Lebanon' (2016) 24 *Arab Studies Journal*, 68.

Hansen, T.B. and Stepputat, F., 'Sovereignty Revisited' (2006) 35 *Annual Review of Anthropology*, 295.

Hansen, T.O., 'The vertical and horizontal expansion of transitional justice: Explanations and implications for a contested field' in S. Buckley-Zistel, et al. (eds.), *Transitional Justice Theories*, Routledge, Oxford 2014, p. 105.

Harris, W., 'Investigating Lebanon's Political Murders: International Idealism in the Realist Middle East?' (2013) 67 *Middle East Journal*, 9.

Hartlyn, J., 'Military Governments and the Transition to Civilian Rule: The Colombian Experience of 1957–1958' (1984) 26 *Journal of Interamerican Studies and World Affairs*, 245.

Harwood, C., 'The UN International Independent Investigation Commission in Lebanon' in J. Meierhenrich (ed.), *The Law and Practice of International Commissions of Inquiry*, Oxford University Press, Oxford 2017, p. 20.

Hassellind, F.S., 'Integrating "storytelling" as a method in judicial processes? The case of the Justicia Especial para la Paz' (2022) 12 *Oñati Socio-Legal Series*, 843.

Haugaard, L. and Nicholls, K., *Breaking the Silence: in search of Colombia's disappeared*, Latin America Working Group Education Fund and US Office on Colombia, Washington, WA 2010.

Haugbolle, S. and Hastrap, A., 'Introduction: Outlines of a New Politics of Memory in the Middle East' (2008) 13 *Mediterranean Politics*, 133.

Haugbolle, S., *War and Memory in Lebanon*, Cambridge University Press, Cambridge 2010.

Haugbolle, S., 'The historiography and the memory of the Lebanese civil war', *SciencesPo*, October 25, 2011, https://www.sciencespo.fr/mass-violence-war-massacre-resistance/fr/document/historiography-and-memory-lebanese-civil-war.

Hay, E., 'International(ized) Constitutions and Peacebuilding' (2014) 27 *Leiden Journal of International Law*, 141.

Hazbun, W., 'Assembling security in a 'weak state:' the contentious politics of plural governance in Lebanon since 2005' (2016) 37 *Third World Quarterly*, 1053.

Heath-Kelly, C. and Fernández de Mosteyrín, L., 'The political use of victimhood: Spanish collective memory of ETA through the war on terror paradigm' (2021) 47 *Review of International Studies*, 1.

Hellsten, S.K., 'Transitional justice as a philosophical and practical challenge: critical notes on Colleen Murphy's new theory of the 'conceptual foundations of transitional justice" (2018) 14 *Journal of Global Ethics*, 169.

Hepworth, A., 'Site of memory and dismemory: the Valley of the Fallen in Spain' (2014) 16 *Journal of Genocide Research*, 463.

Hermez, S., *War Is Coming: Between Past and Future Violence in Lebanon*, Ethnography of Political Violence, University of Pennsylvania Press, Philadelphia, PA 2017.

Herrera, M.C., et al., 'Memory Institutions and Policies in Colombia: The Historical Memory Group and the Historical Commission on the Conflict and Its Victims' in B. Bevernage and N. Wouters (eds.), *The Palgrave Handbook of State-Sponsored History After 1945*, Palgrave Macmillan, London 2018, p. 727.

Hill-Cawthorne, L., 'Rights under International Humanitarian Law' (2018) 28 *European Journal of International Law*, 1187.

Hillebrecht, C., et al., 'The judicialization of peace' (2018) 59 *Harvard International Law Journal*, 279.

Hinnebusch, R., *The international politics of the Middle East*, Manchester University Press, Manchester 2018.

Hirschl, R., 'The New Constitutionalism and the Judicialization of Pure Politics Worldwide' (2006) 75 *Fordham Law Review*, 721.

HITE, K. and MORLINO, L., 'Problematizing the Links between Authoritarian Legacies and "Good" Democracy' in K. HITE and P. CESARINI (eds.), *Authoritarian Legacies and Democracy in Latin America and Southern Europe*, University of Notre Dame Press, Notre Dame, IL 2004, p. 25.

HOBBS, H., 'Hybrid Tribunals and the Composition of the Court: In Search of Sociological Legitimacy' (2016) 16 *Chicago Journal of International Law*, 482.

HOFFMAN, D. and LUBKEMANN, S.C., 'Warscape Ethnography in West Africa and the Anthropology of "Events"' (2005) 78 *Anthropological Quarterly*, 315.

HOLLANDER, N.C., *Love in a Time of Hate: Liberation Psychology in Latin America*, Rutgers University Press, New Brunswick, NJ 1997.

HOLLANDER, N.C., 'Psychoanalysis and the Problem of the Bystander in Times of Terror' in L. Layton, et al. (eds.), *Psychoanalysis, Class and Politics: Encounters in the Clinical Setting*, Routledge, Oxford 2006, p. 154.

HOLLANDER, N.C., *Uprooted Minds: Surviving the Politics of Terror in the Americas*, Routledge, New York 2014.

HOURANI, A., 'Ideologies of the Mountain and City' in R. OWEN (ed.), *Essays on the Crisis in Lebanon*, Ithaca Press, London 1976, p. 35.

HUMPHREY, C., 'Remembering an "Enemy": The Bogd Khaan in Twentieth Century Mongolia' in R.S. WATSON (ed.), *Memory, History and Opposition: Under State Socialism*, School of American Research Press, Santa Fe, NM 1994, p. 21.

HUMPHREY, M. and VALVERDE, E., 'Peace and Justice Service of Uruguay / El Servicio Paz y Justicia' in L. STAN and N. NEDELSKY (eds.), *Encyclopedia on Transitional Justice*, Cambridge University Press, Cambridge 2013, p. 3.

HUMPHREY, M. and VALVERDE, E., 'From private memory to public memory: transitional justice and the revision of official memory of the Dirty War in Argentina' in C. ANDREWS and M. MCGUIRE (eds.), *Post-Conflict Literature: Human Rights, Peace, Justice*, Routledge, Abingdon 2016, p. 130.

HUMPHREY, M., 'From Terror to Trauma: Commissioning Truth for National Reconciliation' (2000) 6 *Social Identities*, 7.

HUMPHREY, M., 'The Politics of Trauma' (2010) 32 *Arts: The Journal of the Sydney University Arts Association*, 37.

HUMPHREY, M., 'The Special Tribunal for Lebanon: emergency law, trauma and justice' (2011) 33 *Arab Studies Quarterly*, 4.

HUMPHREY, M., 'Law, Memory and Amnesty in Spain' (2014) 13 *The Macquarie Law Journal*, 25.

HUMPHREY, M., 'The political lives of the 'disappeared' in the transition from conflict to peace in Colombia' (2018) 19 *Politics, Religion & Ideology*, 452.

HUNEEUS, A., et al., 'Cultures of Legality: Judicialization and Political Activism in Latin America' in J. A. HUNEEUS, et al. (eds.), *Cultures of Legality: Judicialization and Political Activism in Latin America*, Cambridge University Press, Cambridge 2010, p. 1.

ISACSON, A. and POE, A., 'After Plan Colombia: Evaluating "Integrated Action", the Next Phase of U.S. Assistance' (2009) *International Policy Report*.

ISACSON, A., 'A Long Way to Go: Implementing Colombia's peace accord after five years' *WOLA*, November 23, 2021, https://www.wola.org/analysis/a-long-way-to-go-implementing-colombias-peace-accord-after-five-years/.

ITURRALDE, M., 'Access to Constitutional Justice in Colombia: Opportunities and Challenges for Social and Political Change' in D.B. MALDONADO (ed.), *Constitutionalism of the Global South: The Activist Tribunals of India, South Africa, and Colombia*, Cambridge University Press, Cambridge 2013, p. 376.

JARAMILLO MARÍN, J., 'Expertos y comisiones de estudio sobre la violencia en Colombia' (2011a) 39 *Estudios Políticos*, 231.

JARAMILLO MARÍN, J., 'Las comisiones de estudio sobre la violencia en Colombia: tramas narrativas y ofertas de sentido temporal para comprender la violencia', Tesis de Doctorado inédita. Doctorado en Ciencias Sociales, Flacso-México, 2011b, 228.

JARAMILLO MARÍN, J., *Pasados y Presentes de la Violencia en Colombia: Estudio sobre las comisiones de investigación (1958–2011)*, Editorial Pontifica Universidad Javeriana, Bogotá 2014.

JENSEN, D.L., 'The Ottoman Turks in Sixteenth Century French Diplomacy' (1985) 16 *The Sixteenth Century Journal*, 451.

JIMENO, R., *Amnesties, Pardons and Transitional Justice: Spain's Pact of Forgetting*, Routledge, London 2017.

JOHNSON, M., 'Factional Politics in Lebanon: The Case of the 'Islamic Society of Benevolent Intentions' (Al-Maqāṣid) in Beirut' (1978) 14 *Middle Eastern Studies*, 56.

JOHNSON, M., *All Honourable Men: The Social Origins of War in Lebanon*, IB Tauris, London and New York 2001.

JOUANNET, E., 'Universalism and Imperialism: The True-False Paradox of International Law?' (2007) 18 *European Journal of International Law*, 379.

JUDT, T., 'The Past Is Another Country: Myth and Memory in Postwar Europe' in I. DEÁK, et al. (eds.), *The Politics of Retribution in Europe: World War II and Its Aftermath*, Princeton University Press, Princeton, NJ 2000, p. 293.

JUDT, T., 'What Have We Learned, If Anything?', *New York Review of Books*, May 1, 2008, https://www.nybooks.com/articles/2008/05/01/what-have-we-learned-if-anything/.

JURDI, N.N., 'The Crime of Terrorism in Lebanese and International Law' in A. ALAMUDDIN, et al. (eds.), *The Special Tribunal for Lebanon: Law and Practice*, Oxford University Press, Oxford 2014, p. 73.

KABEBERI, N., 'The role of the state in shrinking political spaces for CSOs in Kenya' (2016) 3 *Perspectives Africa: Political Analysis and Commentary*, 28.

KAMUNGI, P.M., 'The politics of displacement in multiparty Kenya' (2009) 27 *Journal of Contemporary African Studies*, 345.

KARL, R.A., *Forgotten Peace: Reform, Violence, and the Making of Contemporary Colombia*, University of California Press, Berkeley, CA 2017a.

KARL, R.A., 'The Politics of Peace in Colombia' (2017b) 49 *NACLA Report on the Americas*, 405.

KAUFMAN, E., *Uruguay in Transition: From Civilian to Military Rule*, Transaction Inc., New Brunswick, NJ 1979.

KAVRAN, O., 'The Special Tribunal for Lebanon and its Outreach Programme' (2022) 20 *Journal of International Criminal Justice*, 81.

KECK, M.E. and SIKKINK, K., *Activists beyond Borders: Advocacy Networks in International Politics*, Cornell University Press, New York, NY 1998.

KEES VAN, K. and VERBEEK, B., 'The Politics of International Norms: Subsidiarity and the Imperfect Competence Regime of the European Union' (2007) 13 *European Journal of International Relations*, 217.

KENDALL, S. '"UhuRuto" and Other Leviathans: The International Criminal Court and the Kenyan Political Order' (2014) 7 *African Journal of Legal Studies*, 399.

KENDALL, S. and NOUWEN, S., 'Representational Practices at the International Criminal Court: The Gap Between Juridified and Abstract Victimhood' (2014) 76 *Law and Contemporary Problems*, 235.

KHADIAGALA, G.M., 'Forty Days and Nights of Peacemaking in Kenya' (2008) 7 *Journal of African Elections*, 17.

KHALAF, S., *Persistence and Change in 19th Century Lebanon: A Sociological Essay*, American University of Beirut, Beirut 1979.

KHALAF, S., *Civil and Uncivil Violence in Lebanon: A History of the Internationalization of Communal Conflict*, Columbia University Press, New York, NY 2002.

KIRCHHEIMER, O., *Political justice: the use of legal procedure for political ends*, Princeton University Press, Princeton, NJ 2015.

KLARIN, M., 'The Impact of the ICTY Trials on Public Opinion in the Former Yugoslavia' (2009) 7 *Journal of International Criminal Justice*, 89.

KLINKNER, M. and DAVIS, H., *The Right to the Truth in International Law: Victims' Rights in Human Rights and International Criminal Law*, Routledge, London 2020.

KLOPP, J.M., '"Ethnic clashes" and Winning Elections: The Case of Kenya's Electoral Despotism' (2001) 35 *Canadian Journal of African Studies*, 473.

KNARR, J.C., 'The New Left and the Nation' (2010) 38 *Latin American Perspectives*, 110.

KNUDSEN, A. and HANAFI, S., 'Special Tribunal for Lebanon (STL): Impartial or Imposed International Justice?' (2013) 31 *Nordic Journal of Human Rights*, 176.

KNUDSEN, A., 'Acquiescence to Assassinations in Post-Civil War Lebanon?' (2010) 15 *Mediterranean Politics*, 1.

KOSELLECK, R., *Futures Past: On the Semantics of Historical Time*, MIT Press, Cambridge MA 1985.

KOSELLECK, R., 'War Memorials: Identity Formations of the Survivors' in R. KOSELLECK (ed.), *The Practice of Conceptual History. Timing History, Spacing Concepts*, Stanford University Press, Stanford CA 2002, p. 285.

KOSKENNIEMI, M., 'Between Impunity and Show Trials' (2002) 6 *Max Planck Yearbook of United Nations Law Online*, 1.

KOSKENNIEMI, M., *The Politics of International Law*, Hart Publishing, Oxford 2011.

KOSKENNIEMI, M., 'Hegemonic Regimes' in M.A. YOUNG (ed.), *Regime Interaction in International Law: Facing Fragmentation*, Cambridge University Press, Cambridge 2012, p. 305.

KOSKENNIEMI, M., 'International Law as "Global Governance"' in C. TOMLINS and J. DESAUTELS-STEIN (eds.), *Searching for Contemporary Legal Thought*, Cambridge University Press, Cambridge 2017, p. 199.

KOVRAS, I., 'Institutionalized Silences for the Missing in Lebanon' in I. KOVRAS (ed.), *Grassroots Activism and the Evolution of Transitional Justice: The Families of the Disappeared*, Cambridge University Press, Cambridge 2017, p. 129.

KRAMER, D. and WEISSBRODT, D., 'The 1980 U.N. Commission on Human Rights and the Disappeared' (1980) 3 *Human Rights Quarterly*, 18.

KRITZ, N., *Transitional Justice: How Emerging Democracies Reckon with Former Regimes*, United States Institute of Peace, Washington, WA 1995.

KROTOSZYŃSKI, M., 'The Transitional Justice Models and the Justifications of Means of Dealing with the Past' (2016) 6 *Oñati Socio-Legal Series*, 584.

KUNZ, R., 'Judging International Judgments Anew? The Human Rights Courts before Domestic Courts' (2020) 30 *European Journal of International Law*, 1129.

KURZE, A., et al., 'Contested spaces of transitional justice: legal empowerment in global post-conflict contexts revisited' (2015) 19 *The International Journal of Human Rights*, 260.

LABELLE, M.M., 'A New Age of Empire? Arab 'Anti-Americanism', US Intervention, and the Lebanese Civil War of 1958' (2013) 35 *The International History Review*, 42.

LAGOS, R., '"To Never Again Live It, To Never Again Deny It": The Valech Report on Torture' in E.Q. HUTCHISON, et al. (eds.), *The Chile Reader: History, Culture, Politics*, Duke University Press, Durham, NC 2013, p. 588.

LAMBOURNE, W., 'Transformative justice, reconciliation and peacebuilding' in S. BUCKLEY-ZISTEL (ed.), *Transitional Justice Theories*, Routledge, New York 2014, p. 19.

LANG, C.K., 'The Impact of Transitional Justice on Colombia's Rule of Law' (2019) 3 *Middle Atlantic Review of Latin American Studies*, 15.

LANGE, M., *Comparative-Historical Methods*, SAGE Publications, London 2013.

LANGGUTH, A.J., *Hidden Terrors*, Pantheon Books, New York, NY 1978.

LAPLANTE, L.J., 'Transitional Justice in Times of Conflict: Colombia's Ley de Justicia y Paz' (2007) 28 *Michigan Journal of International Law*, 49.

LAPLANTE, L.J., 'A Balancing Act: The Right to Peace and Justice' (2019) 59 *Harvard International Law Journal*, Comment.

LECOMBE, D., 'A Conflicted Peace: Epistemic Struggles around the Definition of Transitional Justice in Colombia' in A. LYONS (ed.), *Contested Transitions: Dilemmas of Transitional Justice in Colombia and Comparative Experience*, CEP – Banco de la República Luis Ángel Arango, Bogotá 2010, p. 168.

LEMAITRE RIPOLL, J., 'Legal fetishism: law and social movements in Colombia' (2008) 77 *Revista Jurídica de la Universidad de Puerto Rico*, 337.

LEMAITRE RIPOLL, J., 'The Peace at Hand: War and Peace in Colombia's 1991 Constituent Assembly', SELA Program 2012, Yale Law School, https://law.yale.edu/sites/default/files/documents/pdf/sela/SELA12_Lemaitre_CV_Eng_20120511.pdf.

LEMAITRE RIPOLL, J., 'Constitution or barbarism? How to rethink law in "lawless" spaces' in C. GARAVITO (ed.), *Law and Society in Latin America*, Routledge, London 2014a, p. 55.

LEMAITRE RIPOLL, J., 'Las zonas sin ley y la normalización de la violencia en México y Colombia' (2014b) *SELA (Seminario en Latinoamérica de Teoría Constitucional y Política)*, 8.

LENOIR, G., 'In Lebanon, the Lokman Slim Foundation Will Keep the Memory of Political Assassinations', *Justiceinfo.net*, February 3, 2022, https://www.justiceinfo.net/en/87214-lebanon-lokman-slim-foundation-keep-memory-political-assassinations.html.

LESSA, F., et al., 'New Ruling by Uruguay's Supreme Court of Justice once again Jeopardizes the Search for Truth and Justice for Dictatorship-Era Crimes', *WOLA*, November, 7 2017, https://www.wola.org/analysis/new-ruling-uruguays-supreme-court-justice-jeopardizes-search-truth-justice-dictatorship-era-crimes/.

Lessa, F., 'Barriers to Justice: The *Ley de Cauducidad* and Impunity in Uruguay' in F. Lessa and L.A. Payne (eds.), *Amnesty in the Age of Human Rights Accountability: Comparative and International Perspectives*, Cambridge University Press, Cambridge 2012, p. 123.

Lessa, F., *Memory and Transitional Justice in Argentina and Uruguay: Against Impunity*, Palgrave Macmillan, New York 2013.

Lessard, G., 'Preventive reparations at a crossroads: the Inter-American Court of Human Rights and Colombia's search for peace' (2017) 22 *The International Journal of Human Rights*, 1209.

Levy, D. and Sznaider, N., 'Sovereignty transformed: a sociology of human rights' (2006) 57 *The British Journal of Sociology*, 657.

Levy, D. and Sznaider, N., *Human Rights and Memory*, Penn State University Press, University Park, PA 2021.

Liévano, A.B., 'The ICC Backs Colombia's Transitional Justice Model', *Justiceinfo.net*, November 9, 2021, https://www.justiceinfo.net/en/84121-icc-backs-colombia-transitional-justice-model.html.

Liévano, A.B., 'Colombia: The Day Farc Leaders Faced Victims of Kidnappings', *Justiceinfo.net*, July 1, 2022, https://www.justiceinfo.net/en/102992-colombia-day-farc-leaders-faced-victims-kidnappings.html.

Liévano, A.B., 'First Rift Between Colombia's Peace Tribunal and the Victims', *Justiceinfo.net*, March 14, 2022, https://www.justiceinfo.net/en/88737-first-rift-between-colombia-peace-tribunal-victims.html.

Liévano, A.B., 'Colombia: New Challenges for the Military Who Don't Admit to their Crimes', *Justiceinfo.net*, September 1, 2022, https://www.justiceinfo.net/en/105798-colombia-new-challenges-military-dont-admit-crimes.html.

Liévano, A.B., 'How Colombia's JEP Earns the Respect of Sceptical Victims', *Justiceinfo.net*, January 13, 2023, https://www.justiceinfo.net/en/111069-how-colombia-jep-earns-respect-sceptical-victims.html.

Liscano, C. and Díaz, M. C., *La impunidad y su relato. El caso Mariana Mota*, Planeta, Montevideo, 2022.

López Lerma, M., 'What Judicial Memory for the Amnesty Law of 1977?' in D. Gozdecka and M. Kmak (eds.), *Europe at the Edge of Pluralism*, Intersentia, Brussels 2015, p. 191.

López-Hernandez, C., '"La refundación de la patria", de la teoría a la evidencia' in C. López-Hernandez (ed.), *y refundadaron la patria …. de cómo mafiosos y políticos reconfiguraron el Estado colombiano*, Debate, Bogotá 2010, p. 29.

Loveman, B. and Lira, E., *Las ardientes cenizas del olvido: vía chilena de reconciliación política 1932–1994*, Lom Ediciones, Santiago, Chile 2000.

Loveman, B. and Lira, E., 'Truth, Justice, Reconciliation, and Impunity as Historical Themes: Chile, 1814–2006' (2007) 97 *Radical History Review*, 43.

Loveman, B. *For la Patria: Politics and the Armed Forces in Latin America*, Rowman & Littlefield Publishers, Lanham, MD 2004.

Luna, J.P., '*Frente Amplio* and the Crafting of a Social Democratic Alternative in Uruguay' (2007) 49 *Latin American Politics and Society*, 1.

Luna, J.P., Segmented Representation: Political Party Strategies in Unequal Democracies, Oxford University Press, Oxford 2014.

LUTZ, C. and SIKKINK, K., 'The justice cascade: The evolution and impact of foreign human rights trials in Latin America', (2001) 2 *Chicago Journal of International Law*, 1.

LYNCH, G. 'Electing the 'alliance of the accused': the success of the Jubilee Alliance in Kenya's Rift Valley', (2014) 8 *Journal of Eastern African Studies*, 93.

LYNCH, G., *Performances of Injustice: The Politics of Truth, Justice and Reconciliation in Kenya*, Cambridge University Press, Cambridge 2018.

MACARTHUR, J., 'How the West was Won: Regional Politics and Prophetic Promises in the 2007 Kenya Elections' (2008) 2 *Journal of Eastern African Studies*, 227.

MACBRIDE, S., et al., *Israel in Lebanon: Report of International Commission to enquire into reported violations of International Law by Israel during its invasion of the Lebanon*, Ithaca Press, London 1983.

MACEY, J., et al., 'A War Crimes "Wiki": The Need for an Open Database to Ensure Syrian Accountability', *Yale Journal of International Law*, December 4, 2017, http://www.yjil.yale.edu/a-war-crimes-wiki-the-need-for-an-open-database-to-ensure-syrian-accountability/.

MACHER, S., 'El Registro Único de Víctimas', *Argumentos: Revista de Análisis y Crítica*, No. 4, September 2009.

MAKDISI, U., *The Culture of Sectarianism: Community, History, and Violence in Nineteenth-Century Ottoman Lebanon*, University of California Press, Berkeley CA 2000.

MAKTABI, R., 'The Lebanese census of 1932 revisited. Who are the Lebanese?' (1999) 26 *British Journal of Middle East Studies*, 219.

MALITI, T., 'ICC Prosecutor Asks Court to Admit as Evidence Statements of Witnesses Who Recanted', *International Justice Monitor*, June 4, 2015, https://www.ijmonitor.org/2015/06/icc-prosecutor-asks-court-to-admit-as-evidence-statements-of-witnesses-who-recanted/.

MALITI, T., 'Senior Prosecutor Says Kenya Unwilling to Prosecute Two Kenyans Wanted by ICC', *International Justice Monitor*, July 28, 2017, https://www.ijmonitor.org/2017/07/senior-prosecutor-says-kenya-unwilling-to-prosecute-two-kenyans-wanted-by-icc/.

MALLAT, C., 'Special Dossier on the "Sabra and Shatila" case in Belgium' (2002–3) XII, *The Palestinian Yearbook of International Law*, 183.

MALLINDER, L. 'Uruguay's Evolving Experience of Amnesty and Civil Society's Response' (March 16, 2009), Working Paper No. 4 From Beyond Legalism: Amnesties, Transition and Conflict Transformation, Institute of Criminology and Justice, Queen's University, Belfast, 19, http://ssrn.com/abstract=1387362.

MALOMBE, D., *Justice Delayed: A Status Report on Historical Injustices in Kenya*, Kenya Human Rights Commission, Nairobi 2011.

MALONE, L. A., 'The Kahan Report, Ariel Sharon and the Sabra-Shatila Massacres in Lebanon: Responsibility under International Law for Massacres of Civilian Populations' (1985) 2 *Utah Law Review*, 373.

MAMDANI, M., 'Mau Mau: Understanding Counter-Insurgency' (2006) 2 *Africa Review of Books*, 7.

MAMDANI, M., 'Kenya: you cannot solve political problems through the courts' (2013) 51 *The Africa Report*, 25.

MAMDANI, M., 'Beyond Nuremberg: The Historical Significance of the Post-apartheid Transition in South Africa' (2015) 43 *Politics & Society*, 61.

Manby, B., *Citizenship in Africa: The Law of Belonging*, Bloomsbury Publishing, London 2018.
Maogoto, J.N., 'Sovereignty in Transition: Human Rights and International Justice' (2005) 7 *University of Notre Dame Australia Law Review*, 83.
Marchesi, A., *Latin America's Radical Left: Rebellion and Cold War in the Global 1960s*, Cambridge University Press, Cambridge 2018.
Mareček, L., 'Terrorism as a Crime Under International Customary Law Introduced by Special Tribunal for Lebanon' (2017) 7 *The Lawyer Quarterly: International Journal for Legal Research*, 73.
Martín, H.C., et al., 'Explaining the timeliness of implementation of truth commission recommendations' (2022) 59 *Journal of Peace Research*, 710.
Martínez, H., 'TOAR anticipados y Sanciones Propias: reflexión informada para la Jurisdicción Especial para la Paz', *Dejusticia*, December 14, 2021, https://www.dejusticia.org/publication/toar-anticipados-y-sanciones-propias-reflexion-informada-para-la-jurisdiccion-especial-para-la-paz/.
Matanock, A.M. and García-Sánchez, M., 'The Colombian Paradox: Peace Processes, Elite Divisions, and Popular Plebiscite' (2017) 146 *Daedalus*, 152.
Mati, J. M., 'Antinomies in the struggle for the transformation of the Kenyan constitution (1990–2010)' (2013) 31 *Journal of Contemporary African Studies*, 235.
Maupeu, H., 'Revisiting Post-Election Violence' (2008) 38 *Les Cahiers d'Afrique de l'Est/The East African Review*, 193.
Maxon, R.M., *Kenya's Independence Constitution: Constitution-making and End of Empire*, Fairleigh Dickinson University Press, Plymouth 2011.
Mazrui, A., 'On Heroes and Uhuru-Worship' (1963) 11 *Transition*, 24.
Mazzuca, S. and Robinson, J.A., 'Political Conflict and Power Sharing in the Origins of Modern Colombia' (2009) 89 *Hispanic American Historical Review*, 285.
Mbembé, A., 'Necropolitics' (2003) 15 *Public Culture*, 11.
McAuliffe, P., *Transitional Justice and Rule of Law Reconstruction: A Contentious Relationship*, Routledge, London 2014.
McAuliffe, P., 'Transitional Justice, Institutions and Temporality: Towards a Dynamic Understanding' (2021) 21 *International Criminal Law Review*, 817.
McKenzie, V., 'Colombia's land restitution law defrauding victims: Amnesty International', *Colombia Reports*, November 27, 2014, https://colombiareports.com/colombias-land-restitution-law-defrauding-victims-amnesty-international/.
McSherry, J.P., 'Strategic Alliance: Menem and the Military-Security Forces in Argentina' (1997) 24 *Latin American Perspectives*, 63.
McSherry, J.P., 'Operation Condor: Clandestine Inter-American System' (1999) 26 *Social Justice*, 144.
Medellín-Urquiaga, X., 'The Normative Impact of the Inter-American Court of Human Rights on Latin-American National Prosecution of Mass Atrocities' (2013) 46 *Israel Law Review*, 405.
Meister, R., 'Human Rights and the Politics of Victimhood' (2002) 16 *Ethics and International Affairs*, 91.
Meister, R., *After Evil: A Politics of Human Rights*, Columbia University Press, New York, NY 2011.

Méndez, J.E., 'Constitutionalism and Transitional Justice' in M. Rosenfeld and A.S. Sajó (eds.), *The Oxford Handbook of Comparative Constitutional Law*, Oxford University Press, Oxford 2012, p. 1270.

Méndez, J.E., 'Victims as Protagonists in Transitional Justice' (2016) 10 *International Journal of Transitional Justice*, 1.

Menkhaus, K., 'Local Security Systems in Somali East Africa' in L. Andersen, et al. (eds.), *Fragile States and Insecure People?: Violence, Security and Statehood in the Twenty-First Century*, Palgrave Macmillan, New York, NY 2007, p. 67.

Merhof, K., 'Building a bridge between reality and the constitution: The establishment and development of the Colombian Constitutional Court' (2015) 13 *International Journal of Constitutional Law*, 714.

Meza, D.I., 'Administrating Displaced People in Colombia through Humanitarian Government' (2022) 4 *Journal of Humanitarian Affairs*, 4.

Michel, V. and Sikkink, K., 'Human Rights Prosecutions and the Participation Rights of Victims in Latin America' (2013) 47 *Law & Society Review*, 873.

Michelini, F., 'Reflections on Uruguayan Law No. 18831 a Year After Its Enactment' (2013) 20 *Human Rights Brief*, 2.

Molina, C.M. et al., 'Forced disappearances and missing people in Colombia, South America' (2022) 6 *Forensic Science International: Reports*, 1.

Moreno, L., 'Europeanisation and Catalonia's in(ter)dependence' (2017) 6 *Global Constitutionalism* 218.

Moreno, L., 'Federalization in multinational Spain' in M. Burgess and J. Pinder (eds.), *Multinational Federations*, Routledge, London 2007, p. 86.

Moyn, S., *The Last Utopia: Human Rights in History*, Belknap Press, Cambridge, MA 2012.

Moyn, S., 'Anti-Impunity as Deflection of Argument' in D.M. Davis, et al. (eds.), *Anti-Impunity and the Human Rights Agenda*, Cambridge University Press, Cambridge 2016, p. 68.

Mugraby, M., 'The Syndrome of One-Time Exceptions and the Drive to Establish the Proposed Hariri Court' (2008) 13 *Mediterranean Politics*, 171.

Muhula, R. and Ndegwa, S.N., 'Instrumentalism and constitution-making in Kenya: triumphs, challenges and opportunities beyond the 2013 elections' in G.R. Murunga, et al. (eds.), *Kenya: The Struggle for a New Constitutional Order*, Zed Books, London 2014, p. 79.

Muprhy, C., *The Conceptual Foundations of Transitional Justice*, Cambridge University Press, Cambridge 2017.

Musila, G.M., 'Options for Transitional Justice in Kenya: Autonomy and the Challenge of External Prescriptions' (2009) 3 *International Journal of Transitional Justice*, 445.

Mutua, M., 'Justice under Siege: The Rule of Law and Judicial Subservience in Kenya' (2001) 23 *Human Rights Quarterly*, 96.

Mutuma, K., 'Kenya's annulled presidential election: A step in the right direction?' (2021) 35 *Speculum Juris*, 92.

Naftali, P., 'The 'Right to Truth' in International Law: The 'Last Utopia'?' in A. Gliszczyńska-Grabias and U. Belavusau (eds.), *Law and Memory: Towards Legal Governance of History*, Cambridge University Press, Cambridge 2017, p. 70.

NAGLE, J. and CLANCY, M-A., 'Power-sharing after Civil War: Thirty Years since Lebanon's Taif Agreement' (2019) 25 *Nationalism and Ethnic Politics*, 1.
NAQVI, Y., 'The right to truth in international law: fact or fiction?' (2006) 88 *International Review of the Red Cross*, 245.
NAROTZKY, S. and SMITH, G., '"Being politico" in Spain: An Ethnographic Account of Memories, Silences and Public Politics', (2002) *History & Memory: Studies in Representation of the Past*, 189.
NASONG'O, W.S., 'Revisiting 'the two faces of civil society' in constitutional reform in Kenya' in G.R. MURUNGA, et al. (eds.), *Kenya: The Struggle for a New Constitutional Order*, Zed Books, London 2014, p. 97.
NAVIA, P., 'Do Plebiscites and Referenda Hinder or Foster Democratic Institutions and Accountability? Evidence from Latin America' (Annual Meeting of the American Political Science Association 2006).
NDEGWA, S.N., 'Citizenship and Ethnicity: An Examination of the Two Transition Moments in Kenyan Politics' (1997) 91 *The American Political Science Review*, 599.
NDONGA, A., 'Kenya: Still Grappling with a Stalled Transitional Justice Mandate', *ICTJ*, December 17, 2018, https://www.ictj.org/news/kenya-still-grappling-stalled-transitional-justice-mandate.
NEAL, M.W. and TANSEY, R., 'The dynamics of effective corrupt leadership: Lessons from Rafik Hariri's political career in Lebanon' (2010) 21 *The Leadership Quarterly*, 33.
NESIAH, V., 'The ambitions and traumas of transitional governance: Expelling and replicating colonialism' in E.H.D. DE GROOF and M. WIEBUSCH (eds.), *International Law and Transitional Governance: Critical Perspectives*, Taylor & Francis, London 2020, p. 139.
NÍ AOLÁIN, F., 'After Things Fall Apart: Challenges for Transitional Justice Futures' (2017) 11 *Human Rights and International Law Discourses*, 23.
NICHOLS, L., *The International Criminal Court and the End of Impunity in Kenya*, Springer, Heidelberg 2015.
NIELSEN, E., 'Hybrid International Criminal Tribunals: Political Interference and Judicial Independence' (2010) 15 *UCLA Journal of International Law and Foreign Affairs*, 289.
NINO, C.S., *Radical Evil on Trial*, Yale University Press, New Haven and London 1996.
NOAR, D., 'The Arena of the Zu'ama – Reviewing Hizballah's Role in Lebanon' (2014) 18 *Middle East Review of International Affairs*, 8.
NOLAN, R., 'Sixty Years On: Rachel Nolan on Colombia's Truth Commission Report' (2022) 44 *London Review of Books*.
O'DONNELL, M., 'New Dirty War Judgments in Argentina: National Courts and Domestic Prosecutions of the International Human Rights Violations' (2009) 84 *New York Law Review*, 333.
OCHIENG, W.R. and ATIENO-ODHIAMBO, E. S., 'Prologue: On Decolonization' in B.A. OGOT and W.R. OCHIENG' (eds.), *Decolonization and Independence in Kenya 1940–93*, James Currey, London 1995, p. xi.
OLÁSOLO, H., *International Criminal Law: Transitional Criminal Organizations and Transitional Justice*, Brill Nijhoff, Leiden 2018.
ORENTLICHER, D.F., 'Settling Accounts: The Duty to Prosecute Human Rights Violations of a Previous Regime' (1991) 100 *Yale Law Review*, 2537.

OSIEL, M.J., 'Why Prosecute – Critics of Punishment for Mass Atrocity' (2000) 22 *Human Rights Quarterly*, 118.

OTTERMAN, M., *American Torture: From the Cold War to Abu Ghraib and Beyond*, Melbourne University Press, Melbourne 2007.

PAGNUCCO R. and MCCARTHY, J.D., 'Advocating Nonviolent Direct Action in Latin America: The Antecedents and Emergence of SERPAJ' in S. ZUNES, et al. (eds.), *Nonviolent Social Movements: A Geographical Perspective*, Wiley-Blackwell, Oxford 1999, p. 235.

PAIGE, A., 'How "Transitions" Reshaped Human Rights: A Conceptual History of Transitional Justice' (2009) 31 *Human Rights Quarterly*, 321.

PAOLANTONIO, M.D., 'A Memory of Justice as a Democratic Pedagogical Force' (2006) 28 *Review of Education, Pedagogy, and Cultural Studies*, 141.

PARMENTIER, S., 'Global Justice in the Aftermath of Mass Violence. The Role of the International Criminal Court in Dealing with Political Crimes' (2003) 41 *International Annals of Criminology*, 203.

PATIÑO, M.C.G., 'Rights Related to Enforced Disappearance: New Rights in the International Convention for the Protection of All Persons from Enforced Disappearance' in A. VON ARNAULD, et al. (eds.), *The Cambridge Handbook of New Human Rights*, Cambridge University Press, Cambridge 2020, p. 415.

PAYNE, S.G., 'Spanish Conservatism 1834–1923' (1978) 13 *Journal of Contemporary History*, 765.

PERELLI, C., 'Putting conservatism to good use: women and unorthodox politics in Uruguay, from breakdown to transition' in J.S. JAQUETTE (ed.), *The Women's Movement in Latin America: Feminism and the Transition to Democracy*, Routledge, Oxford 1989, p. 95.

PICARD, E., 'Post-war Lebanese communities in search of reconciliation' in V. MAKRIDES and J. RÜPKE (eds.), *Religionen im Konflikt*, Aschendorff Verlag, Münster 2005, p. 127.

PICARD, E., *The Demobilization of the Lebanese Militias*, Centre for Lebanese Studies, Oxford 1999.

POLLOCK, J.C., 'Violence, Politics and Elite Performance: the Political Sociology of *La Violencia* in Colombia' (1975) 10 *Studies in Comparative International Development*, 22.

POSADA-CARBÓ, E., 'Elections and Civil Wars in Nineteenth-century Colombia: The 1875 Presidential Campaign' (1994) 26 *Journal of Latin American Studies*, 621.

POSNER, E.A. and VERMEULE, A., 'Transitional Justice as Ordinary Justice' (2004) 117 *Harvard Law Review*, 761.

POSNER, E.A., 'Do States Have a Moral Obligation to Obey International Law?' (2003) 55 *Stanford Law Review*, 1901.

POWELL, C. 'Revisiting Spain's Transition to Democracy' in S. FLORENSA (ed.), *The Arab Transition in a Changing World. Building Democracies in the Light of International Experiences: A Critical and Demanding Challenge for the Arab World*, iMED, Barcelona 2016, p. 38.

POWELL, C., 'The Long Road to Europe: Spain and the European Community 1957–86' in J. BAQUERO CRUZ and C. CLOSA MONTETRO (eds.), *European Integration from Rome to Berlin 1957–2007*, PIE Peter Lang, Brussels 2009, p. 39.

PRESTON, P., *Franco: A Biography*, Harper Collins, London 1993.

PRESTON, P., *The Spanish Civil War: Reaction, Revolution and Revenge*, Harper Perennial, London 2007.

PRESTON, P., *The Spanish Holocaust: Inquisition and Extermination in Twentieth-Century Spain*, Harper Press, London 2012.

PRIORELLI, G., 'The fight against the 'anti-nation' as a historical mission: the delegitimization of the enemy in Italian Fascism and Spanish Fascism' (2018) 18 *Revista História: Debates e Tendências*, 449.

PRUNIER, G., 'Kenya: histories of hidden war', *Democracy Now*, February, 29, 2008, https://www.opendemocracy.net/en/kenya_behind_the_crisis/.

QUINTERO, R., 'Colombia: The Special Jurisdiction for Peace, Analysis One Year and a Half After its Entry into Operation', *International Commission of Jurists*, Geneva, 2019, 27–28, https://www.icj.org/colombia-the-special-jurisdiction-for-peace-one-year-after-icj-analysis/.

RANDALL, S.J., *Colombia and the United States: Hegemony and Interdependence*, The University of Georgia Press, Athens and London 1992.

RANKIN, A., 'Reflections on the non-revolution in Uruguay' (1995) 211 *New Left Review*, 131.

RENSHAW, L., *Exhuming Loss: Memory, Materiality and Mass Graves of the Spanish Civil War*, Left Coast Press, Walnut Creek, CA 2011.

RESTREPO, E., 'Reforma Constitucional y Progreso Social: La "Constitucionalización de la Vida Cotidiana" en Colombia' (2002) 14 *SELA (Seminario en Latinoamérica de Teoría Constitucional y Política) Papers*, Yale Law School, 1, http://hdl.handle.net/20.500.13051/17497.

RESTREPO, E.M., 'Perverse Incentives: Extrajudicial Killings in Colombia' (2021) 22 *Georgetown Journal of International Affairs*, 219.

RESTREPO, L.B., 'The Legal Status of the Colombian Peace Agreement' (2016) 110 *AJIL Unbound*, 188.

RIAL, J., 'The Social Imaginary: Utopian Political Myths in Uruguay (Change and Permanence during and after the Dictatorship)' in S. SOSNOWSKI and L. B. POPKIN (eds.), *Repression, Exile and Democracy: Uruguayan Culture*, Durham, NC 1993, p. 59.

RIBEIRO DE MENEZES, A., *Embodying Memory in Contemporary Spain*, Palgrave MacMillan, New York 2014.

RICHANI, N., 'The Politics of Negotiating Peace in Colombia' (2005) 38 *NACLA Report on the Americas*, 17.

RICHANI, N., Systems of Violence: The Political Economy of War and Peace in Colombia, 2nd ed., SUNY Press, New York 2013.

RICHARDS, M., 'From War Culture to Civil Society: Francoism, Social Change and Memories of the Spanish Civil War' (2002) 14 *History & Memory*, 93.

RICHARDS, M., *After the Civil War: Making Memory and Re-Making Spain since 1936*, Cambridge University Press, Cambridge 2013.

RICO, A., *Cómo nos domina la clase gobernante. Orden político y obediencia social en la democracia posdictadura: Uruguay 1985–2005*, Ediciones Trilce, Montevideo, 2005.

RICOEUR, P., *Time and Narrative*, University of Chicago Press, Chicago, IL 1984.

RICOEUR, P., *Memory, History, Forgetting*, University of Chicago Press, Chicago, IL 2004.

RILLA, J., 'Uruguay 1980: transición y democracia plebiscitaria' (2011) 150 *Nueva Sociedad*, 1.

RIOS-FIGUEROS, J., *Constitutional Courts as Mediators: Armed Conflict, Civil-Military Relations, and the Rule of Law in Latin America*, Cambridge University Press, Cambridge 2016.

RIVAS, J., 'Official Victims' Registries: A Tool for the Recognition of Human Rights Violations' (2016) 8 *Journal of Human Rights Practice*, 116.

RODD, R., 'Democratic Citizenship as Uruguayan Cultural Heritage' (2019) 6 *Democratic Theory*, 27.

RODRÍGUEZ-GARAVITO, C., 'Toward a Sociology of the Global Rule of Law Field: Neoliberalism, Neo-constitutionalism, and the Contest over Judicial Reform in Latin America' in Y. DEZALAY and B.G. GARTH (eds.), *Lawyers and the Rule of Law in an Era of Globalization*, Routledge, London/New York 2011, p. 156.

RODRÍGUEZ-RAGA, J.C., 'Strategic Deference in the Colombian Constitutional Court, 1992–2006', in G. HELMKE and J. RIOS-FIGUEROA (eds.), *Courts in Latin America*, Cambridge University Press, Cambridge 2011, p. 84.

ROEDER, P.G. and ROTHCHILD, D.S., 'Conclusion: Nation-State Stewardship and the Alternatives to Power Sharing' in P.G. ROEDER and D.S. ROTHCHILD (eds.), *Sustainable Peace: Power and Democracy After Civil Wars*, Cornell University Press, Ithaca London, 2005, p. 319.

ROHT-ARRIAZA, N. and POPKIN, M., 'Truth as Justice Investigatory Commissions in Latin America' (1995) 20 *Law & Social Inquiry*, 79.

ROHT-ARRIAZA, N., 'State Responsibility to Investigate and Prosecute Grave Human Rights Violations in International Law' (1990) 78 *California Law Review*, 449.

ROHT-ARRIAZA, N., 'Reparations Decisions and Dilemmas' (2004) 27 *Hastings International and Comparative Law Review*, 157.

ROHT-ARRIAZA, N., 'The new landscape of transitional justice' in N. ROHT-ARRIAZA and J. MARIECURRENA (eds.), *Transitional Justice in the Twenty-First Century: Beyond Truth and Justice*, Cambridge University Press, Cambridge and New York 2012, p. 1.

ROHT-ARRIAZA, N., 'After Amnesties are Gone: Latin American National Courts and the new Contours of the Fight Against Impunity' (2015) 37 *Human Rights Quarterly*, 341.

ROHT-ARRIAZA, N., 'Measures of Non-Repetition in Transitional Justice: The Missing Link?' in P. GREADY and S. ROBINS (eds.), *From Transitional to Transformative Justice*, Cambridge University Press, Cambridge, 2019, p. 123.

ROJAS, H. and SHAFTOE, M., 'Reparations for the Victims' in H. ROJAS and M. SHAFTOE (eds.), *Human Rights and Transitional Justice in Chile. Memory Politics and Transitional Justice*, Springer International Publishing, Cham 2021, p. 91.

ROMANIN, E.A., 'Decir la verdad, hacer justicia: Los Juicios por la Verdad en Argentina' (2013) 94 *European Review of Latin American and Caribbean Studies / Revista Europea de Estudios Latinoamericanos y del Caribe*, 5.

RONIGER, L. and SZNAJDER, M., *The Legacy of Human-Rights Violations in the Southern Cone: Argentina, Chile, and Uruguay*, Oxford University Press, Oxford 1999.

RONIGER, L., 'How a Shattered Civil Religion is Rebuilt Through Contestation: Uruguay and the Legacy of Authoritarianism' (2006) 36 *Revista de Ciencia Política (Santiago)*, 411.

RONIGER, L., 'Transitional Justice and Protracted Accountability in Re-democratised Uruguay, 1985-2011', (2011) 43 *Journal of Latin American Studies*, 693.

Rosenn, K. S., 'Brazil's New Constitution: An Exercise in Transient Constitutionalism for a Transitional Society' (1990) 38 *The American Journal of Comparative Law*, 773.

Rosiny, S., 'A Quarter Century of 'Transitory Power-Sharing'. Lebanon's Unfulfilled Ta'if Agreement of 1989 Revisited' (2015) 17 *Civil Wars*, 485.

Roth, R., 'Tribunal spécial sur le Liban: retour sur une expérience' (2017) XLX :1 *Revue belge de droit international*, 290, https://archive-ouverte.unige.ch/unige:104034.

Rudling, A., 'Who Is Afraid of a Truth Commission? The Narratives of the Opposition to the Final Report of the Colombian Truth Commission', *OpinioJuris*, November 2, 2022, https://opiniojuris.org/2022/11/02/who-is-afraid-of-a-truth-commission-the-narratives-of-the-opposition-to-the-final-report-of-the-colombian-truth-commission/.

Ruffinelli, J., *Para verte mejor: el nuevo cine uruguayo y todo lo anterior*, Ediciones Trilce, Montevideo 2015, p. 172.

Ryan, J.J., 'Turning on their Masters: State Terrorism and Unlearning Democracy in Uruguay' in C. Menjívar and N. Rodríguez (eds.), *When States Kill: Latin America, the U.S. and Technologies of Terror*, University of Texas, Austin, TX 2005, p. 278.

Saadeh, R., 'On Justice Denied: Interrogating Amnesty and Amnesia in Post-conflict Lebanon' *Yale Journal of International Affairs*, November 23, 2021, https://www.yalejournal.org/publications/on-justice-denied-interrogating-amnesty-and-amnesia-in-post-conflict-lebanon.

Saffon, M.P. and Uprimny, R., 'Uses and Abuses of Transitional Justice in Colombia' in M. Bergsmo and P. Kalmanovitz (eds.), *Law in Peace Negotiations*, Torkel Opsahl Academic Publisher, Oslo 2010, p. 354.

Saghieh, N., 'Lebanon's General Amnesty in the Age of Corona: The Right to Health as a Tool for Political Ends', *The Legal Agenda*, January 29, 2021, https://english.legal-agenda.com/lebanons-general-amnesty-in-the-age-of-corona-the-right-to-health-as-a-tool-for-political-ends/.

Sala, G., 'Federalism without Adjectives in Spain' (2013) 44 *Publius: The Journal of Federalism*, 109.

Salgueiro, E., 'Uruguay: a law to benefit perpetrators of crimes against humanity?', *Justiceinfo.net*, November 30, 2021, https://www.justiceinfo.net/en/84967-uruguay-law-benefit-perpetrators-crimes-against-humanity.html.

Salloukh, B., 'Syria and Lebanon: A Brotherhood Transformed' (2005) 236 *MERIP*, http://www.merip.org/mer/mer236/syria-lebanon-brotherhood-transformed.

Salloukh, B. et al., *The Politics of Sectarianism in Postwar Lebanon*, Pluto Press, London 2015.

Sánchez León, N.C., 'Acceptance of International Criminal Justice: Country Study on Colombia' in S. Buckley-Zistel et al. (eds.), *After Nuremberg. Exploring Multiple Dimensions of the Acceptance of International Criminal Justice*, International Nuremberg Principles Academy, Nuremberg 2016, p. 1.

Sánchez, F. and Chacón, M., 'Conflict, State and Decentralisation: From Social Progress to Armed Dispute for Local Control, 1974–2002' (2005) *Crisis States Programme*, Working paper no. 70, London, https://gsdrc.org/document-library/conflict-state-and-decentralisation-from-social-progress-to-an-armed-dispute-for-local-control-1974-2002/.

Sánchez, N.C., 'Post-conflict in Colombia (18) Amnesty and pardon in the peace process', *openDemocracy*, September 22, 2016, https://www.opendemocracy.net/en/democraciaabierta/post-conflict-in-colombia-18-amnesty-and-pardon-in-peace-pro/.

Sandoval, C. et al., 'The Challenges of Implementing Special Sanctions (*Sanciones Propias*) in Colombia and Providing Retribution, Reparation, Participation and Reincorporation' (2022) 14 *Journal of Human Rights Practice*, 478.

Sandoval, C.A.V. and Veçoso, F.F.C., 'A Human Rights' Tale of Competing Narratives' (2017) 8 *Revista Direito e Práxis*, 1603.

Sandvik, K.B. and Lemaitre, J., 'From IDPs to Victims in Colombia: A Bottom-Up Reading of Law in Post-Conflict Transitions' in M. Saul and J.A. Sweeney (eds.), *International Law and Post-Conflict Reconstruction Policy*, Routledge, London 2015, p. 251.

Sandvik, K.B. and Lemaitre, J. 'Finding the Roads to Justice? Examining Trajectories of Transition for Internally Displaced Women in Colombia' (2017) 6 *Stability: International Journal of Security & Development*, 1.

Santos Juliá, J.C., et al., *Victimas de la guerra civil,* Ediciones Temas de Hoy, Madrid 1999.

Sarkin, J., 'Why the Theory and Practice of Transitional Justice Needs to be Better Integrated in all Places around the World' (2021) 4 *Al Muntaqa*, 39.

Saul, B., 'Compensation for unlawful death in international law: a focus on the Inter-American Court of Human Rights' (2004) 19 *American University International Law Review*, 523.

Saul, B., *Defining Terrorism in International Law*, Oxford University Press, Oxford 2006.

Saul, B., 'Legislating from a Radical Hague: The United Nations Special Tribunal for Lebanon Invents an International Crime of Transnational Terrorism' (2011) 24 *Leiden Journal of International Law*, 677.

Scarry, E., *The Body in Pain: The Making and Unmaking of the World*, Oxford University Press, Oxford 1985.

Scharrer, T., '"Ambiguous citizens": Kenyan Somalis and the question of belonging' (2018) 12 *Journal of Eastern African Studies*, 494.

Schneider, N. and Iecker de Aleida, G., 'The Brazilian National Truth Commission (2012–2014) as a State-Commissioned History Project' in B. Bevernage and N. Wouters (eds.), *The Palgrave Handbook of State-Sponsored History After 1945*, Palgrave Macmillan, London 2018, p. 637.

Schröder, P., 'Natural Law, Sovereignty and International Law: A Comparative Perspective' in I. Hunter and D. Saunders (eds.), *Natural Law and Civil Sovereignty: Moral Right and State Authority in Early Modern Political Thought*, Palgrave Macmillan Limited, London 2002, p. 204.

Scott, D., *Omens of Adversity: Tragedy, Time, Memory, Justice*, Duke University Press, Durham, NC 2013.

Scott, J.C., *The Art of Not Being Governed: An Anarchist History of Upland Southeast Asia*, Yale University Press, New Haven, CT 2010.

Scovazzi, T. and Citroni, G., *The Struggle Against Enforced Disappearance and the 2007 United Nations Convention*, Martinus Nijhoff Publishers, Leiden 2007.

Sebaali, G., 'Lebanon and Israel: Agreements, Resolutions, and Local Laws' (2020) *Lebanon Law Review*.

Serrano, F., 'Colombia's Uneasy Peace', *Foreign Policy*, July 16, 2019, https://foreignpolicy.com/2019/07/16/colombias-uneasy-peace.

Sharnak, D., 'Uruguay's long transitional decade and a new era of gendered activism' (2017) 23 *Journal of Iberian and Latin American Studies*, 383.

Sharp, D.N., 'Interrogating the Peripheries: The Preoccupations of Fourth Generation Transitional Justice' (2013a) 26 *Harvard Human Rights Journal*, 149.

Sharp, D.N., 'Beyond the Post-Conflict Checklist: Linking Peacebuilding and Transitional Justice through the Lens of Critique' (2013b) 14 *Chicago Journal of International Law*, 165.

Sharp, D.N., 'Addressing Dilemmas of the Global and the Local in Transitional Justice' (2014) 29 *Emory International Law Review*, 71.

Sharp, D.N., *Rethinking Transitional Justice for the Twenty-First Century: Beyond the End of History*, Cambridge University Press, Cambridge 2018.

Shehadi, N.,'The Special Tribunal for Lebanon: The UN on Trial?', (2007) MEP/IL BP 07/01, Chatham House, *Middle East/International Law Briefing Paper*, 3.

Shelton, D.L., 'Soft Law' in D. Armstrong (ed.), *Handbook of International Law*, Routledge, London 2008, p. 68.

Shilaho, W.K., *Political Power and Tribalism in Kenya*, Palgrave MacMillan, London 2018.

Shorrock, W.I., 'The Origin of the French Mandate in Syria and Lebanon: The Railroad Question, 1901–1914' (1970) 1 *International Journal of Middle East Studies*, 133.

Sikkink, K. and Kim, H.J., 'The Justice Cascade: The Origins and Effectiveness of Prosecutions of Human Rights Violations' (2013) 9 *Annual Review of Law and Social Science*, 269.

Sikkink, K. et al., 'A Critical Assessment of Colombia's Reparations Policies in the Context of the Peace Process' in S. Bhabha, et al. (eds.), *Time for Reparations*, University of Pennsylvania Press, Philadelphia, PA 2021, p. 119.

Sikkink, K., *Mixed Signals: U.S. Human Rights Policy and Latin America*, Cornell University Press, Ithaca, NY 2004.

Sikkink, K., *The Justice Cascade: how human rights trials are changing the world*, W.W. Norton & Co, New York, NY 2011.

Skaar, E., 'Legal Development and Human Rights in Uruguay: 1985–2002' (2007) 8 *Human Rights Review*, 52.

Skaar, E. 'Uruguay: reconstructing peace and democracy through transitional justice' in E. Skaar, et al. (eds.), *After Violence: Transitional Justice, Peace, and Democracy*, Routledge, London 2015, p. 67.

Slim, R., 'Hezbollah's campaign against the Special Tribunal for Lebanon' (2010) *Foreign Policy*, August 13, 2010.

Slomich, J., 'The Ta'if Accord: legalizing the Syrian occupation of Lebanon' (1999) 22 *Suffolk Transnational Law Review*, 619.

Smith, L.A., 'The missing, the martyred and the disappeared: Global networks, technical intensification and the end of human rights genetics' (2017) 47 *Social Studies of Science*, 398.

Smulovitz, C., 'Petitioning and Creating Rights: Judicialization in Argentina' in R. Sieder, et al. (eds.), *The Judicialization of Politics in Latin America*, Palgrave, London 2005, p. 161.

Solé i Barjau, Q., 'Inhumados en el Valle de los Caídos. Los primeros traslados desde la provincia de Madrid' (2009) *Hispania Nova: Revista de Historia Contemporánea*, 9, https://www.researchgate.net/publication/41207683_Inhumados_en_el_Valle_de_los_Caidos_Los_primeros_traslados_desde_la_provincia_de_Madrid.

SOLTMAN, D., 'Applauding Uruguay's Quest for Justice: Dictatorship, Amnesty, and Repeal of Uruguay Law No. 15.848' (2014) 12 *Washington University Global Studies Law Review*, 829.
SOMERS, M. and ROBERTS, C.N., 'Towards a New Sociology of Rights: A Genealogy of "Buried Bodies" of Citizenship and Human Rights' (2008) 4 *Annual Review of Law and Social Science*, 385.
SONDROL, P.C., '1984 Revisited? A Re-Examination of Uruguay's Military Dictatorship' (1992) 11 *Bulletin of Latin American Research*, 187.
SORBY, K.R., 'Lebanon: The Crisis of 1958' (2000) 9 *Asian and African Studies*, 76.
SØRENSEN, G., 'War and State-Making' (2016) 32 *Security Dialogue*, 341.
SRIRAM, C.L., 'The Special Tribunal for Lebanon, Promoting Justice or Prolonging Conflict?' (2012) 24 *Reconciliation, Reform and Resilience: Positive Peace for Lebanon, Reconciliation Resources*, 49, https://www.c-r.org/accord-article/special-tribunal-lebanon.
SRIRAM, C.L., and BROWN, S., 'Kenya in the Shadow of the ICC: Complementarity, Gravity and Impact' (2012) 12 *International Criminal Law Review*, 219.
STRAIGHT, B., 'Making Sense of Violence in the "Badlands" of Kenya' (2009) 34 *Anthropology and Humanism*, 21.
STRAUSS, A., 'The 1992 Referendum in South Africa' (2008) 31 *The Journal of Modern African Studies*, 339.
SUBOTIĆ, J., 'The Transformation of International Transitional Justice Advocacy' (2012) 6 *International Journal of Transitional Justice*, 106.
SULLIVAN, S., 'Changing the Premise of International Legal Remedies: the Unfounded Adoption of Assurances and Guarantees of Non-Repetition' (2002) 7 *UCLA Journal of International Law & Foreign Affairs*, 265.
SUMALLA, J.M.T., *Historical Memory and Criminal Justice in Spain: A Case of Late Transitional Justice*, Intersentia, Brussels 2013.
SUMMERS, N., 'Colombia's Victims' Law: Transitional Justice in a Time of Violent Conflict?', (2012) 25 *Harvard Human Rights Journal*, 219.
SUNDAR, N., 'Toward and anthropology of culpability' (2004) 31 *American Ethnologist*, 145.
SWEENEY, J.A., 'The Elusive Right to Truth in Transitional Human Rights Jurisprudence' (2018) 67 *International and Comparative Law Quarterly*, 353.
SZPALA, M., 'The acquittal of Croatian generals is challenging the reconciliation process in the region', *Analyses*, Center for Eastern Studies, November 11, 2012, https://www.osw.waw.pl/en/publikacje/analyses/2012-11-21/acquittal-croatian-generals-challenging-reconciliation-process.
TABBARAH, B., 'The Legal Nature of the Special Tribunal for Lebanon' in A. ALAMUDDIN, et al. (eds.), *The Special Tribunal for Lebanon: Law and Practice*, Oxford University Press, Oxford 2014, p. 32.
TARROW, S., 'From comparative historical analysis to "local theory": The Italian city-state route to the modern state' (2004) 33 *Theory and Society*, 443.
TASIOULAS, J., 'Saving Human Rights from Human Rights Law' (2019) 52 *Vanderbilt Journal of Transnational Law*, 1167.
TAYLOR, P.B., 'The Uruguayan Coup D'état of 1933' (1952) 32 *The Hispanic American Historical Review*, 301.

Teitel, R.G., 'Transitional Jurisprudence: The Role of Law in Political Transformation' (1997) 106 *Yale Law Journal*, 2009.

Teitel, R.G. *Transitional Justice*, Oxford University Press, Oxford 2000.

Teitel, R.G., 'Humanity's Law: Rule of Law for the New Global Politics' (2002) 35 *Cornell International Law Journal*, 355.

Teitel, R.G., 'Transitional Justice Genealogy' (2003) 16 *Harvard Human Rights Journal*, 69.

Teitel, R.G., *Humanity's Law*, Oxford University Press, Oxford 2011.

Teitel, R.G., 'Global Transitions, New Perspectives on Legality, and Judicial Review' in A. Sarat (ed.), *Transitions: Legal Change, Legal Meanings*, The University of Alabama Press, Tuscaloosa, Alabama 2012, p. 213.

Teitel, R.G., *Globalising Transitional Justice*, Oxford University Press, Oxford 2014.

Teitel, R.G., 'Transitional Justice and Judicial Activism – A Right to Accountability?' (2015) 48 *Cornell International Law Review*, 385.

Thomassen, B., 'Thinking with Liminality: To the Boundaries of an Anthropological Concept' in A. Horvath, et al. (eds.), *Breaking Boundaries: Varieties of Liminality*, Berghahn Books 2015, p. 39.

Thornton, C., and Gude, R., 'Towards Peace in Colombia: The economic obstacles to a Colombian Peace Process' (2011) 5 *The Peace and Conflict Review*, 1.

Tilly, C., 'Coercion, Capital, and European States, A.D. 990–1990' in E. Castañeda and C.L. Schneider (eds.), *Collective Violence, Contentious Politics, and Social Change: A Charles Tilly Reader*, Routledge, London 2017, p. 140.

Trigo, A., 'Contracultura del insilio en Uruguay (1973–1985)' (1990) 43 *Revista Hispánica Moderna*, 228.

Trujillo, J.V., 'The Collectivization of Victim Participation: The Case of Colombia's Special Jurisdiction for Peace' in K. Ambos and J.S. Peters (eds.) *Transitional Justice in Colombia: The Special Jurisdiction for Peace*, Nomos, Baden-Baden 2022, p. 161.

Tueni, G., *Une guerre pour les autres*, J.C. Lattes, Paris, 1985.

Turner, C., 'Human Rights and the Empire of (International) Law' (2011) 29 *Minnesota Journal of Law & Inequality*, 313.

Turner, C., *Violence, Law and the Impossibility of Transitional Justice*, Routledge, Oxford 2016.

Turner, V., *The Ritual Process: Structure and Anti-Structure*, Aldine Publishing, Chicago 1969.

Uprimny Yepes, R., 'Desprestigiar a la JEP', Dejusticia, April 19, 2017, https://www.dejusticia.org/?s=desprestigiar.

Uprimny Yepes, R., 'Judicialization of politics in Colombia: cases, merits and risks' (2007) 4 *Sur. International Journal of Human Rights*, 48.

Urueña, R., 'Prosecutorial Politics: The ICC's Influence in Colombian Peace Processes, 2003–2017' (2017) 111 *American Journal of International Law*, 104.

Valverde, E. 'The experience of *Exilio* and Insilio in Reshaping Uruguayan Identity' (2001) III/2 *Bulletin of the Royal Institute for Inter-Faith Studies*, 177.

Valverde, E., 'Constructing victimhood in post-Franco's Spain: the recovery of memory by the grandchildren of victims of the Civil War and dictatorship' ('Konstruisanje žrtve u Španiji nakon Franka:obnovljeno sećanje unuka žrtava građanskog rata i diktature'), (2012) 15 *Temida. The Journal of Victimization, Human Rights and Gender*, 77.

Valverde, E., 'What's happening in Spain? Can the Indignados resurrect the Spanish left?', *Australian OPTIONS* (South Australia), 2013.

Valverde, E. and Hanley, J., 'Tolerancia y derechos humanos en Uruguay', (2017) 27 *Tabula Rasa*, 459.

Van Arkadie, B., 'Reflections on land policy and the independence settlement in Kenya' (2016) 43 *Review of African Political Economy*, 60.

Van Damme, R., 'The Presumption of Innocence: an Antidote for Sacrificial Venom? Patterns of Girard's 'Primitive' Sacred in Late Medieval and Early Modern Criminal Law' (2016) 45 *Netherlands Journal of Legal Philosophy*, 10.

Van Den Herik, P. L. and Harwood, C., 'Commissions of Inquiry and the Charm of International Criminal Law: Between Transactional and Authoritative Approaches' in P. Alston and S. Knuckey (eds.), *The Transformation of Human Rights Fact-Finding*, Oxford University Press, New York, NY 2016, p. 233.

Van Der Wilt, H., 'The Legacy of the Special Tribunal for Lebanon' in A. Alamuddin, et al. (eds.), *The Special Tribunal for Lebanon: Law and Practice*, Oxford University Press, Oxford 2014, p. 268.

Van Klink, B., 'Symbolic Legislation: An Essentially Political Concept' in B. Van Klink and B. Van Beers (ed.), *Symbolic Legislation Theory and Developments in Biolaw*, Springer, Cham 2016, p. 19.

Van Sliedregt, E. and Van Den Herik, P.L., 'Introduction: The STL Interlocutory Decision on the Definition of Terrorism – Judicial Ingenuity or Radicalism?' (2011) 24 *Leiden Journal of International Law*, 651.

Vargas Niño, S., 'Colombia's Special Jurisdiction for Peace Bends the Law to Dub Paramilitaries as State Officials: The Time For Critique is Now', *OpinioJuris*, September 16, 2022, https://opiniojuris.org/2022/09/16/colombias-special-jurisdiction-for-peace-bends-the-law-to-dub-paramilitaries-as-state-officials-the-time-for-critique-is-now/.

Velásquez Ruiz, M.A., 'The emergence and consolidation of transitional justice within the realm of Colombia peacebuilding' in F.A.D. Pabón (ed.), *Truth, justice and reconciliation in Colombia: transitioning from violence*, Routledge, New York 2018, p. 50.

Verbitsky, H., *The Flight: Confessions of an Argentine Dirty Warrior*, The New Press, New York, NY 1996.

Verdery, K., *The Political Lives of Dead Bodies: Reburial and Postsocialist Change*, Columbia University Press, New York, NY 1999.

Vicente, L. and Melón, M., 'A European Court of Human Rights' Decision Devoid of Justice', *IJ Central*, December, 14 2012, https://www.foroporlamemoria.info/2012/12/a-european-court-of-human-rights-decision-devoid-of-justice/.

Viñar, M. and M., *Fracturas de Memoria Crónicas para una memoria por venir*, Ediciones Trilce, Montevideo 1993.

Vinjamuri, L. and Snyder, J., 'Law and Politics in Transitional Justice' (2015) 18 *Annual Review of Political Science*, 303.

Vinyes, R., 'La memoria del estado' in R. Vinyes (ed.), *El estado y la memoria: gobiernos y ciudadanos frente a los traumas de la historia*, RBA Libros, Barcelona 2009, p. 23.

von Bernstorff, J., 'The Decay of the International Rule of Law Project (1990–2015)' in H. Krieger, et al. (eds.), *The International Rule of Law: Rise or Decline?*, Oxford University Press, Oxford 2019, p. 33.

von Bogdandy, A. and Urueña, A., 'International transformative constitutionalism in Latin America' (2020) 114 *American Journal of International Law*, 403.

Wagner-Pacifici, R. and Hall, M., 'Resolution of Social Conflict' (2012) 38 *Annual Review of Sociology*, 181.

Wagner-Pacifici, R., 'Theorizing the Restlessness of Events' (2010) 115 *American Journal of Sociology*, 1351.

Wagner-Pacifici, R., *What is an event*, University of Chicago, Chicago 2017.

Wählisch, M., 'Legitimacy Defects and Legal Flaws of the Special Tribunal for Lebanon: Dilemmas of the 'Peace Through Justice Theorem'' in N. Hayashi and C.M. Bailliet (eds.), *The Legitimacy of International Criminal Tribunals*, Cambridge University Press, Cambridge 2017, p. 297.

Wasserman, G., *Politics of Decolonization: Kenya Europeans and the Land Issue 1960-65*, Cambridge University Press, Cambridge 1976.

Weiner, A.S., 'Constitutions as Peace Treaties: A Cautionary Tale for the Arab Spring' (2011) 64 *Stanford Law Review (Online)*, 1.

Weinstein, M., 'The Decline and Fall of Democracy in Uruguay: Lessons for the Future' in S. Sosnowski and L.B. Popkin (eds.), *Repression, Exile, and Democracy: Uruguayan Culture*, Duke University, London, Durham 1993, p. 83.

Welsh, T., 'Mothers demand answers on fate of disappeared' *Colombia Reports*, 30 November, 2010, https://colombiareports.com/mothers-demand-clarity-on-fate-disappeared-loved-ones/.

Wenger, M., 'Primer: Lebanon's 15-Year Civil War 1975-1990' (1990) 162 *MERIP*, https://merip.org/1990/01/primer-lebanons-15-year-war-1975-1990/.

Weschler, L., *A Miracle, A Universe: Settling Accounts with Torturers*, University of Chicago Press, Chicago, IL 1998.

Whittaker, H., 'Legacies of Empire: State Violence and Collective Punishment in Kenya's North Eastern Province, *c.* 1963–Present' (2015) 43 *The Journal of Imperial and Commonwealth History*, 641.

Wieland, C., 'Syrian-Lebanese relations. The impossible dissociation between Lebanon and Syria' in M. Felsch and M. Wählisch (eds.), *Lebanon and the Arab Uprisings: In the Eye of the Hurricane*, Routledge, Oxford 2016.

Wierda, M., et al., 'Early Reflections on Local Perceptions, Legitimacy and Legacy of the Special Tribunal for Lebanon' (2007) 5 *Journal of International Criminal Justice*, 1065.

Wilson, B.M., 'Institutional Reform and Rights Revolutions in Latin America: The Cases of Costa Rica and Colombia' (2009) 1 *Journal of Latin American Politics*, 59.

Witten, S.M., 'Velásquez Rodríguez Case' (1989) 83 *American Journal of International Law*, 361.

Worboys, K.J., 'The Traumatic Journey from Dictatorship to Democracy: Peacekeeping Operations and Civil-Military Relations in Argentina, 1989-1999' (2007) 33 *Armed Forces and Society*, 149.

Wouters, J., 'International Law, Informal Law-Making, and Global Governance in Times of Anti-Globalism and Populism' in H. Krieger, et al. (eds.), *The International Rule of Law: Rise or Decline?* Oxford University Press, Oxford 2019, p. 243.

Wrong, M., *It's Our Turn to Eat: The Story of a Kenyan Whistleblower*, Harper Perennial, London 2009.

Yaffé, J., 'La dictadura uruguaya (1973–1985): nuevas perspectivas de investigación e interpretación historiográfica' (2012) 38 *Estudos Ibero-Americanos*, 13.

Zalaquett, J., 'Confronting Human Rights Violations Committed by Former Governments: Applicable Principles and Political Constraints' (1990) 13 *Hamline Law Review*, 623.

Zeleza, P.T., 'The protracted transition to the Second Republic in Kenya' in G.R. Murunga, et al. (eds.), *Kenya: The Struggle for a New Constitutional Order*, Zed Books, London 2014, p. 17.

Zoglin, K., 'Paraguay's Archive of Terror: International Cooperation and Operation Condor' (2001) 32 *The University of Miami Inter-American Law Review*, 57.

LAWS, DOCUMENTS, REPORTS

M. A. Badreddine – 'Order Terminating Proceedings Against Mustafa Amine Badreddine Without Prejudice and Ordering the Filing of an Amended Consolidated Indictment', Trial Chamber, STL-11-01, July 7, 2016, http://www.legal-tools.org/doc/0b7008/.

'National Visiting Professional programme', Special Tribunal Lebanon, https://www.facebook.com/STLebanon/posts/the-stls-national-visiting-professional-programme-provides-lebanese-legal-practi/358121117635385/.

'Statement of the Prosecutor of the International Criminal Court, Fatou Bensouda, on the alleged crimes committed by ISIS', *ICC*, April 5, 2015, https://www.icc-cpi.int/news/statement-prosecutor-international-criminal-court-fatou-bensouda-alleged-crimes-committed-isis.

'Statement of the Prosecutor of the International Criminal Court, Fatou Bensouda, on the status of the Government of Kenya's cooperation with the Prosecution's investigations in the Kenyatta case', *ICC*, December 4, 2014, https://www.icc-cpi.int/Pages/item.aspx?name=otp-stat-04-12-2014.

'The Act of Killing', Director: Joshua Oppenheimer, Final Cut for Real, (film) 2012.

'UN experts: Uruguay must step up search for disappeared persons and fight impunity', UN Working Group on Enforced or Involuntary Disappearances, *OHCHR*, July 15, 2022, https://www.ohchr.org/en/press-releases/2022/07/un-experts-uruguay-must-step-search-disappeared-persons-and-fight-impunity.

'UN rights experts call for accountability following Beirut's 'unprecedented' lethal explosion', UN News, *OHCHR*, August 13, 2020, https://www.ohchr.org/en/press-releases/2022/08/un-experts-call-international-investigation-2020-beirut-explosion.

'Uruguay must annul law that protects police and military torture suspect', *Amnesty International* https://www.amnesty.org/en/latest/news/2009/10/uruguay-debe-anular-legislacion-protege-autores-tortura-policial-militar-20091020/.

'Victims of sexual torture seek justice in Uruguay', *UN OHCHR*, October 28, 2021 https://www.ohchr.org/en/stories/2021/10/victims-sexual-torture-seek-justice-uruguay.

'Who are the missing? (Spain)', *ICMP*, https://www.icmp.int/the-missing/where-are-the-missing/spain/.

122/000157 Proposición de Ley para la reforma de la Ley 52/2007, de 26 de diciembre, por la que se reconocen y amplían derechos y se establecen medidas en favor de quienes padecieron persecución o violencia durante la guerra civil y la dictadura, Congreso de los Diputados, December 22, 2017, Nos. 190-1, http://ctxt.es/es/20180620/Politica/20301/documentos-ctxt-memoria-historica-psoe-propuesta-de-ley-politica-espa%C3%B1a-guerra-civil-dictadura.htm.

Acto Legislativo 01/2017 y el establecimiento del sistema integral de verdad, justicia, reparación y no repetición, https://ihl-databases.icrc.org/en/national-practice/legislative-act-n1-2017-constitutional-reform-establishing-system-truth-justice.

Acuerdo final para la terminación del conflicto y la construcción de una paz estable y duradera, El Gobierno Nacional y las FARC y EP, 24 noviembre 2016, https://www.jep.gov.co/Normativa/Paginas/Acuerdo-Final.aspx.

Almonacid Arellano et al. v. Chile, IACtHR, Judgment of September 26, 2006, https://www.corteidh.or.cr/docs/casos/articulos/seriec_154_ing.pdf.

Annan, K., The Secretary-General, Statement of the Secretary-General on the Situation in the Middle East, 5, delivered to the Security Council, UN Doc. S/PRST/2005/4, February 15, 2005.

Annex 'Letter dated 15 May 2007 from the President of Lebanon addressed to the Secretary-General' (from President Lahoud), UN Doc S/2007/286.

Annual Report of the United Nations High Commissioner for Human Rights on the situation of human rights in Colombia, March 2, 2018, A/HRC/37/3/Add.3.

Annual Report Uruguay 2010, *Amnesty International*, May 28, 2010, http://www.amnestyusa.org/research/reports/annual-report-uruguay-2010.

Appeals Chamber (JEP), Decision TP-SA 1187 of July 21, 2022, En asunto de Rodrigo Tovar Pupo, JEP, República de Colombia, https://www.scribd.com/document/590353649/Auto-de-Apelacion#.

Application for the disqualification and withdrawal of Judge Afif Chamseddine, Case No. OTP/AC/2010/01, Filed Before: The President, Mr Antonio Cassese by General Jamil El Sayed, October 20, 2010, Special Tribunal for Lebanon.

Artigas, S., 'Todos le hicieron el juego a Manini Ríos', *Laizquiarda Diario*, miércoles, 13 de marzo 2019, https://www.laizquierdadiario.com.uy/Todos-le-hicieron-el-juego-a-Manini-Rios.

Basic Pinciples and Guidelines on the Right to a Remedy and Reparation for Victims of Gross Violations of International Human Rights Law and Serious Violations of International Humanitarian Law, December 16, 2005, General Assembly Resolution 60/147, https://www.ohchr.org/en/instruments-mechanisms/instruments/basic-principles-and-guidelines-right-remedy-and-reparation.

Brincat Report, Need for international condemnation of the Franco regime, Doc.10737, 4 November 2005, Political Affairs Committee, Parliamentary Assembly of the Council of Europe, http://assembly.coe.int/nw/xml/XRef/X2H-Xref-ViewHTML.asp?FileID=11217&lang=en.

Case of *'Members and Militants of the Patriotic Union' vs. Colombia*, Inter-American Court of Human Rights, Judgment of July 27, 2022, 9.

Case STL-11-01/1, *Interlocutory Decision on the Applicable Law: Terrorism, Conspiracy, Homicide, Perpetration, Cumulative Charging, STL (Appeals Chamber)*, February 16, 2011, para. 85.

Causa General, Decreto de 26 abril de 1940 concediendo amplias facultades al Fiscal del Tribunal Supremo para proceder a instruir <<Causa general>> en la que se reúnan las pruebas de los hechos delictivos cometidos en todo el territorio nacional durante la dominación roja, ((BOE) Núm. 125, 4 mayo 1940.)

Civil Society Coalition on Kenya's second universal periodic review (ASCK_UPR) June 14, 2014, KHRC, Nairobi.

Colombia – Report of the United Nations High Commissioner for Human Rights (A/HRC/46/76), 22 February – 19 March 2021.

Colombia en riesgo de impunidad: Puntos ciegos de la Justicia Transicional frente a crímenes internacionales de competencia de la CPI, FIHD y CAJAR, Mayo 2020 No 751e, (Report submitted to the ICC), 5, https://www.fidh.org/IMG/pdf/fidh-cajar_informe_colombia_en_riesgo_de_impunidad.pdf.

Colombia, Country Report: Colombia, IACHR (2004), http://www.cidh.org/countryrep/colombia04eng/chapter3.htm.

Commission of Inquiry into Post-Election Violence (CIPEV) (Waki Report), The Government of Kenya, Nairobi, (2008), 1, http://www.kenyalaw.org/Downloads/Reports/Commission_of_Inquiry_into_Post_Election_Violence.pdf.

Contribución al entendimiento del conflicto armado en Colombia, La Comisión Histórica del Conflicto y sus Víctimas (CHCV), Bogotá, Febrero, 2015, http://www.altocomisionadoparalapaz.gov.co/mesadeconversaciones/PDF/Informe%20Comisi_n%20Hist_rica%20del%20Conflicto%20y%20sus%20V_ctimas.%20La%20Habana%2C%20Febrero%20de%202015.pdf.

de Greiff, P., Report of the Special Rapporteur on the promotion of truth, justice, reparation and guarantees of non-recurrence: Mission to Spain, A/HRC/27/56/Add.1, July 22, 2014.

Decile a Mario que no vuelva (Tell Mario not to Return), Director M. Handler, Uruguay, Spain, Twelve Cats SL, 2007.

Decree-Law September 23, 1939, (*Ley de 23 septiembre 1939 considerando no delictivos determinados hechos actuación político-social cometidos por personas desde el catorce de abril de mil novecientos treinta y uno hasta el dieciocho de julio de mil novecientos treinta y seis*, (BOE) No. 273, September 23, 1939).

Doha Agreement, 'On the Results of the Lebanese National Dialogue Conference', May 21, 2008, https://peacemaker.un.org/sites/peacemaker.un.org/files/Lebanon_DohaAgreement2008_Engl.pdf.

Draft Articles on Responsibility of States for Internationally Wrongful Acts, in Report of the International Law Commission on the Work of Its Fifty-third Session, UN GAOR, 56th Sess., Supp.10, art. 30, UN Doc. A/56/10 (2001) https://legal.un.org/ilc/texts/instruments/english/commentaries/9_6_2001.pdf.

Final report submitted by Theo van Boven, Special Rapporteur, 'Study concerning the right to restitution, compensation and rehabilitation for victims of gross violations of human right and fundamental freedoms' (E/CN.4/Sub.2/1993/8, July 2, 1993).

Fitzgerald, P. and Annan, K., *Report on the Mission of Inquiry into the Circumstances, Causes and Consequences of the 14 February Beirut Bombing*, 9–10, delivered within a Letter from the Secretary-General to the Security Council, U.N. Doc. S/2005/203 (March 24, 2005).

García, M. Villegas and Uprimny, R., ¿Controlando la excepcionalidad permanente en colombia? Una defensa prudente del control judicial de los estados de excepción, 1 *Document de Discusión Dejusticia*, November 1, 2015, https://www.dejusticia.org/wp-content/uploads/2017/04/fi_name_recurso_198.pdf.

Gelman v. Uruguay, Inter-American Court of Human Rights, Judgment of February 24, 2011 (Merits and Reparations), Costa Rica.

Godínez-Cruz v. Honduras, Case 8097, Ser. C, No. 5, Inter-American Court of Human Rights, OAS Doc, OEA/Ser.L/V/III.21/Doc.14 (1989) (judgment of January 20, 1989).

Guatemala Nunca Más, Proyecto Interdiocesano de Recuperación de la Memoria Historica. Guatemala City: Oficina de Derechos Humanos del Arzobispado de Guatemala, 1998.

Guidance Note of the Secretary-General: United Nations Approach to Transitional Justice, March 2010, https://peacemaker.un.org/documents/guidance-note-secretary-general-un-approach-transitional-justice.

Hay futuro, si hay verdad, informe final de la Comisión de la Verdad sobre el conflicto armado, Comisión de la Verdad, Bogotá, 2022, https://www.comisiondelaverdad.co/hay-futuro-si-hay-verdad.

Human Rights Council Resolution S-2/1, 'The grave situation of human rights in Lebanon caused by Israeli military operations', August 11, 2006, www2.ohchr.org/english/bodies/hrcouncil/specialsession/2/.

Informe Especial de Riesgo: 'Violencia y Amenazas Contra Los Líderes Sociales y Los Defensores de Derechos Humanos', Defensoría Delegada para la Prevención de Riesgos de Violaciones de los Derechos Humanos y el DIH, Sistema de Alertas Tempranas (SAT), Marzo 2017 Bogotá D.C., Colombia.

Informe: Comisión de Expertos para el Futuro del Valle de los Caídos, Entrega al Ministro de la Presidencia En Madrid, el 29 de noviembre de 2011.

International Convention for the Protection of All Persons from Enforced Disappearance, A/RES/61/177, December 20, 2006.

International Covenant on Civil and Political Rights, article 2; ICPPED, article 24/2; Report of the independent expert to update the Set of principles to combat impunity, UNCHR E/CN.4/2005/102/Add.1, principles 2–5; Guidance Note, UNSG, March 2010, 1.

Joinet, L., 'Question of the impunity of perpetrators of human rights violations (civil and political). Final report prepared by Mr. Joinet pursuant to Sub-Commission decision 1996/119', in (ESC, UNCHR, Sub-Commission on Prevention of Discrimination and Protection of Minorities, 1996).

Kenyan National Dialogue and Reconciliation, 'Annotated Agenda and Timetable', February 1, 2008.

La acreditación de las víctimas ante la JEP, Boletín #60 del Observatorio sobre la JEP, agosto, 2022, https://www.coljuristas.org/observatorio_jep/documentos/boletines/Boletin_60.pdf.

Law 1448 of 2011 ('*Ley de Víctimas y Restitución de Tierras*' (Victims and Land Restitution Law)), Diario Oficial No. 48096, June 10, 2011.

Law 1776 of January 29, 2016 (Crea y desarrolla las Zonas de Interés de desarrollo rural, económico y social (The Areas of Interest for Rural, Economic and Social Development' (*Zonas de Interés de Desarrollo Rural, Económico y Social* – ZIDRES). Diario Oficial No. 49.770.

Law No. 84 of August 26, 1991, Granting General Amnesty to Crimes Committed before March 28, 1991 (Beirut: Dar al-Manshourat al-Houquouquiya-Matbaat Sader, Vol. 3), 3532.

Law of Democratic Memory (*Ley 20/2022, de 19 de octubre, de Memoria Democrática*, (BOE) A-2022-17099).

Law of Historical Memory (*Ley 52/2007, de 26 de diciembre, por la que se reconocen y amplían derechos y se establecen medidas en favor de quienes padecieron persecución o violencia durante la guerra civil y la dictadura.* (BOE) A-2007-22296), https://www.boe.es/eli/es/l/2007/12/26/52/con.

Law of National Pacification (*Ley 15.737 de 22/03/1985. Ley de Amnistía. Aprobación de la Convención Americana sobre Derechos Humanos llamada Pacto de San José de Costa Rica. Creación de la Comisión Nacional de Repatriación. República Oriental del Uruguay)*, http://www.impo.com.uy/bases/leyes/15737-1985%20).

Law of National Pacification (*Ley de Pacificación Nacional*), No. 22.924, 22 de septiembre de1983, República Argentina, BO 27 de septiembre de 1983.

Law of Political Responsibilities, (*Ley de 9 de febrero de 1939 de Responsabilidades Políticas*, (BOE) Núm. 44, de 13 de febrero de 1939).

Law of Public Order (*Ley 45/1959, de 30 de julio de Orden Público*, (BOE) Núm. 182, 31 julio 1959).

Law of State Security (*Ley de 4 de enero de 1941 para le seguridad del Estado*, (BOE) Núm. 101, April 11, 1941).

Law of the New Revised Edition of the Penal Code (*Ley de 19 julio de 1944 para una nueva edición refundida del Código Penal vigente*, (BOE) Núm. 204, 22 julio 1944).

Law of the Repression of Freemasonry and Communism (*Ley de 1 de marzo 1940 sobre de represión de la masonería y del comunismo*, (BOE) Núm. 204, 22 julio 1944).

Law to create a memorial to Our Glorious Crusade at Cuelga-muros. (*Decreto de 1 de abril de 1940 disponiendo se alcen Basílica, Monasterio, Cuartel de Juventudes, en la finca situada en* las *vertientes de la Sierra del Guadarrama (El Escorial), conocida por Cuelga-muros, para perpetuar la memoria de los caídos en nuestra Gloriosa Cruzada.* (BOE) Núm. 93, de 2 de abril de 1940, p. 2240–1).

Lest We Forget: The Faces of Impunity in Kenya, Kenyan Human Rights Commission, Nairobi, 2011.

Letter dated 22 May 2008 from the Permanent Observer of the League of Arab States to the United Nations addressed to the President of the Security Council, S/2008/392, 10.

Ley 1820, 30 dic 2016, (por medio de la cual se dictan disposiciones sobre amnistía, indulto u tratamientos penales especiales y otras disposiciones), and Decree 277, 17 feb 2017.

Maidanik y Otros vs. Uruguay, Corte Interamericana de Derechos Humanos, Caso Sentencia de 15 de noviembre de 2021 *(Fondo y Reparaciones)*. https://www.corteidh.or.cr/docs/casos/articulos/resumen_444_esp.pdf?prm=ep-app.

Ministerio de Defensa Nacional, Expediente No. 2016.01433-0, Tema 226 Tribunales de Honor, https://www.docdroid.net/Ds2ekUz/expediente-completo-del-tribunal-de-honor.pdf.

Mundialito (The Little World Cup), Director Sebastián Bednarik, Spanish, Uruguay, Coral Films, 2010.

'Never Forgotten: Lebanon's Missing People', *Amnesty International*, MDE 18/001/2011, April 14, 2011, https://reliefweb.int/report/israel/never-forgotten-lebanon's-missing-people.

Nunca Más en Chile: Síntesis Corregida y Actualizada del Informe Rettig, Comisión Chilena de Derechos Humanos, LOM, 1999.

Nunca Más, informe de la Comisión sobre la Desaparición de Personas (CONADEP) (Never Again: Report of the Commission about the Disappeared), Universitaria De Buenos Aires, Buenos Aires, 1984.

Orentlicher, D.F., 'Impunity: Report of the independent expert to update the Set of principles to combat impunity. Addendum: Updated Set of principles for the protection and promotion of human rights through action to combat impunity', UN Doc. E/CN.4/2005/102/Add.1.

Pizarro Leongómez, E., *Victims and Reparation: The Colombian Experience*, President of the National Reparation and Reconciliation Commission Colombia, June 2010.

Prosecutor v. Salim Jamil Ayyash, Hassan Habib Merhi, Hussein Hassan Oneissi, Assad Hassan Sabra, STL-11-01/TC, August 18, 2020.

Proyecto de Ley No. 181 de 2022 'Por medio del cual se define la política de paz de Estado, y se dictan otras disposiciones', El Senado de Colombia, 24 octubre 2022.

Reglamento De Los Tribunales De Honor De Las Fuerzas Armadas, Decreto No. 55/985 de 08/02/1985 artículo 1, https://www.impo.com.uy/bases/decretos-reglamento/55-1985.

Report from OHCHR Fact-Finding Mission to Kenya between 6–28 February 2008, OHCHR 28 February 2008, https://www.ohchr.org/sites/default/files/Documents/Press/OHCHRKenyareport.pdf.

Report of the Commission of Inquiry on Lebanon Pursuant to Human Rights Council Resolution S-2/1, November 23, 2006, http://www.refworld.org/docid/45c30b6e0.html.

Report of the DOD Commission on Beirut International Airport Terrorist Act, October 23, 1983, https://fas.org/irp/threat/beirut-1983.pdf.

Report of the Independent Expert to Update the Set of Principles to Combat Impunity,' UN Doc. E/CN.4/2005/102, February 18, 2005, 76.

Report of the International Independent Investigation Commission established pursuant to UNSCR 1595 (2005), S/2005/662, October 19, 2005, 3.

Report of the Judicial Commission Appointed to Inquire into Tribal Clashes in Kenya (Akiwumi Report), 4 volumes, Nairobi, 1999.

Report of the Secretary-General on the Establishment of a Special Tribunal for Lebanon Doc S/2006/893.

Report of the Special Rapporteur in the Field of Cultural Rights. Shaheed Farida: Memorialisation Processes UN GAOR, Human Rights Council, 25th Session Agenda Item 3, UN Doc A/HRC/25/49, January 23, 2014.

Report of the Special Rapporteur on the promotion of truth, justice, reparation and guarantees of non-recurrence, Pablo de Greiff, Human Rights Council August 9, 2012, A/HRC/21/46, 4.

Report on CODESA Agreements, The Nelson Mandela Foundation, https://omalley.nelsonmandela.org/omalley/index.php/site/q/03lv02039/04lv02046/05lv02047/06lv02049/07lv02059.htm.

Report: Committee on Enforced Disappearances, Consideration of reports of States parties under article 29, paragraph 1, of the Convention, Reports of States parties due in 2014 Colombia, received December 17, 2014, 21, CED/C/COL/1.

Revised Kriegler and Waki Commission Reports, Dialogue Africa Foundation 2009, https://www.kas.de/c/document_library/get_file?uuid=d8aa1729-8a9e-7226-acee-8193fd67a21a&groupId=252038.

Rome Statute of the International Criminal Court, Done at Rome on July 17, 1998, in force on July 1, 2002, United Nations, Treaty Series, vol. 2187, No. 38544, Depositary: Secretary-General of the United Nations, http://treaties.un.org.

Securing Justice – Establishing a domestic mechanism for the 2007/8 post-election violence in Kenya, Kenyans for Peace with Truth and Justice, https://kptj.africog.org/securing-justice-establishing-a-domestic-mechanism-for-the-2007-8-post-election-violence-in-kenya/.

Smaira, D., and Cassehgari, R., 'Failing to Deal with the Past What Cost to Lebanon?', Report, International Center for Transitional Justice, New York, 2014.

Special Rapporteur on the promotion of truth, justice, reparation and guarantees of non-repetition, A/HRC/RES/ 18/7, October 13, 2011.

Special Tribunal for Lebanon, Third Annual Report (2011–2012), https://www.legal-tools.org/doc/272706/pdf/.

Special Tribunal for Lebanon, Fifth Annual Report, 2013–2014, https://www.legal-tools.org/doc/7cdb46/.

Statement attributable to the Spokesperson for the Secretary-General – on the Special Tribunal for Lebanon, UNSG, January 12, 2023, https://www.un.org/sg/en/content/sg/statement/2023-01-12/statement-attributable-the-spokesperson-for-the-secretary-general---the-special-tribunal-for-lebanon.

Statement of Judge Antonio Cassese, President of the Special Tribunal for Lebanon August 11, 2011, News, Special Tribunal for Lebanon, https://www.stl-tsl.org/en/media/press-releases/670-statement-of-judge-antonio-cassese-president-of-the-special-tribunal-for-lebanon.

Statement to Parliament on settlement of Mau Mau claims Foreign & Commonwealth Office and the Rt Hon William Hague, June 6, 2013, https://www.gov.uk/government/news/statement-to-parliament-on-settlement-of-mau-mau-claims.

Statute of the Special Tribunal for Lebanon, Documents, Special Tribunal for Lebanon, https://www.legal-tools.org/doc/da0bbb/.

STL Close-Up https://www.stl-tsl.org/images/stories/About/STL_Close-up_EN.pdf.

STL proceedings, Live Coverage – Day 2, January 17, 2014, https://now.mmedia.me/lb/en/NewsReports/530848-live-coverage-stl-proceedings.

Study on the right to truth: Report of the Office of the United Nations High Commissioner for Human Rights, Geneva: UN, February 8, 2006, E/CN.4/2006/91, 6.

Syria Accountability and Lebanese Sovereignty Restoration Act of 2003, Public Law 108–175-(108th Congress) December 12, 2003.

The Chilean Commission on Truth and Reconciliation (Rettig Commission) Report.

The National Commission on Political Imprisonment and Torture Report (Valech Report).

The Prosecutor v. Paul Gicheru ICC-01/09-01/20, Decision Terminating the Proceedings against Paul Gicheru, 14 October 2022, https://www.icc-cpi.int/court-record/icc-01/09-01/20-337.

The Report by the Parliamentary Select Committee to Investigate Ethnic Clashes in Western and other parts of Kenya, National Assembly, Kenya, 1992.

The Right to Truth in the Americas, Inter-American Commission on Human Rights, OEA/Ser.L/V/II.152 Doc. 213, August 2014.

Truth, Justice and Reconciliation Report, Volume IIA, TJRC, Nairobi 2013, for selected amendments between 1963-1969, 1982-91, 21.

UN OHCHR 'Rule of Law Tools for Post-Conflict States: Reparations Programmes' (Geneva OHCHR 2008).

UN OHCHR, 'Rule of Law Tools for Post-Conflict States: National Consultations on Transitional Justice', (2009) United Nations, New York and Geneva.

UN Special Tribunal for Lebanon (Appeals Chamber), Interlocutory Decision on the Appliable Law: Terrorism, Conspiracy, Homicide, Perpetration, Cumulative Charging, STL-11-01, February 16, 2011.

UN Treaty Collection, Chapter IV, Human Rights, 16 International Convention for the Protection of All Persons from Enforced Disappearance, https://treaties.un.org/pages/ViewDetails.aspx?src=TREATY&mtdsg_no=IV-16&chapter=4.

UNGA Res/60/288, adopted on 8 September 2006, Global Counter-Terrorism Strategy.

UNGA Res/68/119, adopted on16 December 2013, Measures to eliminate international terrorism.

UNHCR Lebanon: Fact Sheet, September 2021, Relief Web, November 26, 2021, https://reliefweb.int/report/lebanon/unhcr-lebanon-fact-sheet-september-2021.

UNSC Resolution 1377 of November 12, 2001, Declaration on the Global effort to Combat Terrorism. https://digitallibrary.un.org/record/452238?ln=en.

UNSC Resolution 1664 (2006, 29 March 2006) S/RES/1664, (on negotiation of an agreement with the Government of Lebanon aimed at establishing a tribunal of international character), https://digitallibrary.un.org/record/571640?ln=en.

UNSC Resolution 1595 (2005), adopted on April 7, 2005, (on establishment of an international independent commission to assist in investigation of the terrorist bombing in Lebanon), https://digitallibrary.un.org/record/545254?ln=en.

UNSC, 'Letter dated 7 May 1996 from the Secretary-General addressed to the President of the Security Council', https://digitallibrary.un.org/record/212595?ln=en.

Updated Set of principles for the protection and promotion of human rights through action to combat impunity, UN Doc, E/CN.4/2005/102/Add.1, 8 February, https://www.ohchr.org/en/special-procedures/sr-truth-justice-reparation-and-non-recurrence/international-standards.

Uruguay Nunca Más: Informe Sobre Violación a los Derechos Humanos (*Uruguay Never Again: Report on Human Rights Violations*) Servicio Paz y Justicia, Montevideo, 1989.

US Department of State, 'State Sponsors of Terrorism', https://web.archive.org/web/20090610080648/http://www.state.gov/s/ct/c14151.htm.

US State Department list of State Sponsors of Terrorism, https://www.state.gov/state-sponsors-of-terrorism/.

van Boven, T., Special Rapporteur, 'Study concerning the right to restitution, compensation and rehabilitation for victims of gross violations of human rights and fundamental freedoms' (E/CN.4/Sub.2/1993/8, July 2, 1993).

van Boven, T., The United Nations Basic Principles and Guidelines on the Right To A Remedy and Reparation for Victims of Gross Violations of International Human Rights Law and Serious Violations of International Humanitarian Law, United Nations Audiovisual Library of International Law, 2010 https://legal.un.org/avl/pdf/ha/ga_60-147/ga_60-147_e.pdf, p. 2.

Velásquez Rodríguez v. Honduras, Case 7920, Ser. C, No. 4, Inter-Am. Ct. H.R. 35, OAS OEA/Ser.L/V/III.19/Doc.13 (1988) (judgment of July 29, 1988).

Victims' case in the *Ayyash et al.* trial, *STL Bulletin*, August 28–September 8, 2019. https://www.stl-tsl.org/en/media/press-releases/5922-victims-case-in-the-ayyash-et-al-trial-begins.

NEWSPAPERS

'29 generales y coroneles, en la mira de la CPI por ejecuciones extrajudiciales', *El Espectador*, July 9, 2017, https://www.elespectador.com/colombia-20/jep-y-desaparecidos/29-generales-y-coroneles-en-la-mira-de-la-cpi-por-ejecuciones-extrajudiciales-article/.

'60 días para que 1 millón de víctimas pidan reparación', April 10, 2015, *El Tiempo*, https://www.eltiempo.com/archivo/documento/CMS-15550816.

'A diez años, ¿nunca más el Día del Nunca Más?', *El País* (Uruguay), June 19, 2017, https://www.elpais.com.uy/informacion/a-diez-anos-nunca-mas-el-dia-del-nunca-mas.

'Colombia: 'Renewed hope' for consolidating peace says Guterres', *UN News*, January 2, 2023, https://news.un.org/en/story/2023/01/1132122.

'Colombia: ex paramilitar "Jorge 40" aspira a tribunal de paz', *Los Angeles Times*, January 26, 2023, https://www.latimes.com/espanol/internacional/articulo/2023-01-27/colombia-ex-paramilitar-jorge-40-aspira-a-tribunal-de-paz.

'Comienzan los trabajos de exhumación de la fosa 112 de Paterna', *El País*, August 21, 2018, https://www.lavanguardia.com/local/valencia/20180821/451398864197/exhumacion-fosa-112-paterna-valencia-fusilados-franquismo.html.

'El secretario de Justicia del PSOE pide que se trate la memoria histórica sin tapujos', *El País*, August 6, 2017, https://elpais.com/ccaa/2017/08/06/valencia/1502011110_876636.htmlhttps://elpais.com/ccaa/2017/08/06/valencia/1502011110_876636.html.

'Forced Displacement in Colombia more than double in 2021: Report', *Al Jazeera*, February 16, 2022, https://www.aljazeera.com/news/2022/2/16/forced-displacement-in-colombia-more-than-doubled-in-2021-report.

'Generalitat denuncia "agresiones fascistas" a independentistas', *HISPANTV*, August 4, 2018, https://www.hispantv.com/noticias/espana/384415/torra-catalunya-agresion-fascistas-independentistas.

'Hammdeh, Hawi and El-Murr STL-11-02' in L.E. Jreissati, UPDATE: Researching the Special Tribunal for Lebanon (STL), (2022) *GlobaLex*, March/April, https://www.nyulawglobal.org/globalex/Special_Tribunal_Lebanon1.html#cases-hamadeh-hawi-and-el-murr-2011.

'Jaramillo: "Peace is achievable"', *The City*, May 14, 2015, https://thecitypaperbogota.com/news/jaramillo-peace-is-achievable51413/8942.

'Lebanon to form body to probe civil war disappearances', *Arab News*, November 12, 2018, http://www.arabnews.com/node/1403736/middle-east.

'Los hornos del horror en Colombia', *El País*, May 15, 2023, https://elpais.com/opinion/2023-05-15/los-hornos-del-horro-en-colombia.html.

'Parapolíticos no pueden acceder a beneficios de la Ley de Amnistía: Corte Suprema', *El Espectador*, July 14, 2017, https://www.elespectador.com/noticias/judicial/parapoliticos-no-pueden-acceder-la-jep-corte-suprema-articulo-703126.

'Universal Jurisdiction in Sweden: Victims of Syria's Chemical Weapons Attacks Demand Justice', *Civil Rights Defenders*, April 2021, https://www.justiceinitiative.org/uploads/c3cda961-388f-4d50-b8b7-e28e5598d1e2/faq_chemical-weapons-criminal-complaints-in-sweden_04192021.pdf.

'Uruguay Open to Rights Cases of Dictator Era', *New York Times*, July 1, 2011, https://www.nytimes.com/2011/07/01/world/americas/01uruguay.html.

'Uruguayan president caught on the wrong foot forced to sack six generals and minister of Defense', *Mercopress*, April 2, 2019, https://en.mercopress.com/2019/04/02/uruguayan-president-caught-on-the-wrong-foot-forced-to-sack-six-generals-and-minister-of-defense.

'Who's Afraid of a False Witness?' posted by Qifa Nabki, https://qifanabki.com/2010/10/06/lebanon-false-witness/comment-page-1/.

Baddour, D. and Falola, A., 'As Colombia peace accord unravels, ex-FARC leaders take up arms, announce return to conflict', *The Washington Post*, August 29, 2019.

Barcala, D. and Calvo, L., 'El Estado no asumirá las exhumaciones de las fosas franquistas', *publico.es*, March 11, 2009, https://www.publico.es/actualidad/no-asumira-exhumaciones-fosas-franquistas.html.

Beard, D., 'Ex-Leaders on Trial Defended for 'Trying to Save' Argentine', *Chicago Tribune*, May 26, 1985. https://www.chicagotribune.com/news/ct-xpm-1985-05-26-8502020506-story.html.

Bluhm, M., 'Cassese hopes tribunal's work will instil 'culture of accountability' in Lebanon', *The Daily Star*, May 17, 2010, http://www.dailystar.com.lb/article.asp?edition_id=1&categ_id=16&article_id=114937#axzz14lygGKJw.

Blum, C., 'No Details on the Indictment for Months: Registrar', *The Daily Star*, December 7, 2010.

Brookes, P., 'The Siege of Lebanon', *The New York Post*, June 18, 2007, http://nypost.com/2007/06/18/the-siege-of-lebanon/.

Campanella, G.D., 'Uruguay reconoce crímenes de la dictadura en un acto oficial sin la presencia del presidente', *El País*, June 16, 2023, https://elpais.com/internacional/2023-06-16/uruguay-reconoce-crimenes-de-la-dictadura-en-un-acto-oficial-sin-la-presencia-del-presidente.html.

Castaldi, M., 'Uruguay's Supreme Court rules against dictatorship trials', *Reuters*, February 13, 2013. https://www.reuters.com/article/us-uruguay-rights-idUSBRE91L0ZL20130223.

Cerna, C.M., 'Honor Tribunals in Uruguay today', *Global Military Justice Reform*, February 2, 2019, http://globalmjreform.blogspot.com/2019/02/honor-tribunals-in-uruguay-today.html.

Christian, S., 'Uruguay Votes to Retain Amnesty for the Military', *New York Times*, April 17, 1989, https://www.nytimes.com/1989/04/17/world/uruguay-votes-to-retain-amnesty-for-the-military.html.

Chulov, M., 'Lebanese government quits following Beirut port explosion', *The Guardian*, August 11, 2020.

Chulov, M., 'Lebanon's mass revolt against corruption and poverty continues', *The Guardian*, October 23, 2019.

Cobb, J. S., 'Colombia tribunal begins mammoth task of investigating, trying war crimes', March 16, 2018, https://www.reuters.com/article/us-colombia-peace-court/colombia-tribunal-begins-mammoth-task-of-investigating-trying-war-crimes-idUSKCN1GR2P6.

Colprensa, 'Habrá una sala de Reconocimiento y Verdad en la JEP', *La Opinion*, March 15, 2018, https://www.laopinion.com.co/colombia/habra-una-sala-de-reconocimiento-y-verdad-en-la-jep-150976#OP.

Cué, C.E. 'Government to use decree to give legal coverage to plans to exhume Franco's body', *El País*, August, 21 2018, https://english.elpais.com/elpais/2018/08/21/inenglish/1534840526_621180.html.

Evans, D., 'Syria seeks arrest of Lebanese former PM Hariri', *Reuters*, December 12, 2012, http://uk.reuters.com/article/uk-syria-crisis-lebanon-idUKBRE8BB1EV20121212.

Fisk, R., 'Lebanon is a sectarian nation, yet it has avoided civil war while the Middle East burns – here's why', *The Independent*, October 20, 2016, http://www.independent.co.uk/voices/lebanon-civil-war-avoided-peaceful-nation-middle-east-syria-turkey-israel-conflict-robert-fisk-a7371326.html.

Ford, P., 'Despite Bitterness, Uruguayans Uphold Army Amnesty', *The Christian Science Monitor*, April 19, 1989, https://www.csmonitor.com/1989/0419/ouru.html.

Glennie, J., 'Colombia's unethical development', June 6, 2011, *The Guardian*, https://www.theguardian.com/global-development/poverty-matters/2011/jun/06/colombia-amoral-development-uribe.

Guede, A., 'Críticas a Zapatero por crear la comisión del Valle de los Caídos poco antes del 20N', *El País*, February 1, 2012, https://elpais.com/politica/2012/02/01/actualidad/1328106053_049636.html.

Haberkorn, L., 'Gavazzo admitió que arrojó el cuerpo de Roberto Gomensoro al Río Negro', *El Observador*, March 30, 2019.

Hadchiti, M., 'Judicial Disputes Over Appointing Alternative Judge In The Beirut Blast Case', *The 961*, September 22, 2022, https://www.the961.com/judicial-disputes-over-alternative-judge-beirut-blast-case/.

Hedgecoe, G., 'Spain's controversial attempt to confront its painful past', *Politico*, July 14, 2022, https://www.politico.eu/article/francisco-franco-eta-pedro-sanchez-spain-controversial-attempt-to-confront-its-painful-past/.

Houssari, N., 'Lebanese MPs fail to reach agreement on draft amnesty law', *Arab News*, May 29, 2020, https://www.arabnews.com/node/1681471/middle-east.

Houssari, N., 'Lebanon faces judicial paralysis as judges refuse to work', *Arab News*, August 23, 2022, https://www.arabnews.com/node/2148881/middle-east.

Hubbard, B. and Saad, H., 'Lebanon's Vanishing Prime Minister Is Back at Work. Now What?', *New York Times*, November 25, 2017, https://www.nytimes.com/2017/11/25/world/middleeast/lebanon-saad-hariri-iran-saudi-arabia.html?searchResultPosition=4.

Hubbardaug, B., 'Iran Out to Remake Mideast With Arab Enforcer: Hezbollah', *New York Times*, August 27, 2017, https://www.nytimes.com/2017/08/27/world/middleeast/hezbollah-iran-syria-israel-lebanon.html.

Hunt, W. 'The Ghost in The Ballot Box: Catalonia's Crisis in Context', *Dissent*, October 10, 2017. https://www.dissentmagazine.org/online_articles/catalonia-independence-referendum-crisis-history-franco.

Idler, A., 'Colombia just voted no on its plebiscite for peace. Here's why and what it means', *The Washington Post*, October 3, 2016, https://www.washingtonpost.com/news/monkey-cage/wp/2016/10/03/colombia-just-voted-no-on-its-referendum-for-peace-heres-why-and-what-it-means/.

Jones, S., 'Exhumation of civil war dead from Spain's Valley of Cuelgamuros begins', *The Guardian*, June 2, 2023, https://www.theguardian.com/world/2023/jun/12/exhumation-of-civil-war-dead-from-spain-valley-of-cuelgamuros-begins.

Jones, S., 'Far right breakthrough in Andalucía send shockwave through Spanish politics', *The Guardian*, December 9, 2018, https://www.theguardian.com/world/2018/dec/09/far-right-andalucia-seville-vox-party-shockwave-spanish-politics.

Jones, S., 'Remains of anti-Franco activist who died in 1973 recovered in Catalonia', *The Guardian*, February 22, 2023, https://www.theguardian.com/world/2023/feb/22/remains-cipriano-martos-anti-franco-activist-who-died-in-1973-recovered-catalonia.

Jones, S., 'Spain passes law to bring 'justice' to Franco-era victims', *The Guardian*, October 6, 2022, https://www.theguardian.com/world/2022/oct/05/spain-passes-law-to-bring-dignity-to-franco-era-victims.

Kersten, M., 'Trials and Tribulations at the Special Tribunal for Lebanon', *Justice in Conflict*, January 28, 2014, https://justiceinconflict.org/2014/01/28/trials-and-tribulations-at-the-special-tribunal-for-lebanon/.

Krauss, C., 'Britain Arrests Pinochet to Face Charges by Spain', *New York Times*, October 18, 1998, https://www.nytimes.com/1998/10/18/world/britain-arrests-pinochet-to-face-charges-by-spain.html.

L. Elliott, 'White daisies bloom in Uruguay's streets, in memory of dictatorship missing', *Reuters*, May 21, 2023, https://www.reuters.com/world/americas/white-daisies-bloom-uruguays-streets-memory-dictatorship-missing-2023-05-20/.

Le Goff, P. and Lessa, F., 'Uruguay's Supreme Court of Injustice', *The Argentina Independent*, March 21, 2013, http://www.argentinaindependent.com/socialissues/humanrights/uruguays-supreme-court-of-injustice/.

Legrand, C., 'Uruguay split over ending of amnesty for rights violations under dictatorship', *The Guardian*, April 26, 2011, https://www.theguardian.com/world/2011/apr/26/uruguay-human-rights-amnesty-legrand.

Lessa, F. and Le Goff, P.-L., 'A silent anniversary in Uruguay?', *Al Jazeera*, June 27, 2013, https://www.aljazeera.com/opinions/2013/6/27/a-silent-anniversary-in-uruguay.

Lessa, F. and Le Goff, P.-F., 'Elusive Justice in Uruguay', *Al Jazeera*, February 13, 2014. https://www.aljazeera.com/opinions/2014/2/13/elusive-justice-in-uruguay.

Macías, J.A., '¿Por qué están asesinando a los líderes sociales en Colombia?', *C.elcolombiano*, December 14, 2017, https://www.elcolombiano.com/colombia/por-que-estan-asesinando-a-los-lideres-sociales-en-colombia-CI7857532.

Madowo, L., 'Kenya is sliding into a dictatorship', *The Washington Post*, February 7, 2018, https://www.washingtonpost.com/news/global-opinions/wp/2018/02/07/kenya-is-sliding-into-a-dictatorship/?noredirect=on.

Mamdani, M., 'How land issues, the ICC played out in the election', *Daily Nation*, March 17, 2013, https://www.nation.co.ke/oped/opinion/How-land-issues-the-ICC-played-out-in-the-election-/440808-1722824-vfg49n/index.html.

Manetto, F. et al., 'La trampa de la polarización es atractiva en política y fatal para Colombia', *El País*, December 3, 2017, https://elpais.com/internacional/2017/12/03/colombia/1512266646_338897.html?rel=mas.

Minder, R., 'In Spain's 'Stolen-Babies' Scandal, Doctor Escapes Punishment', *New York Times* October 8, 2018. https://www.nytimes.com/2018/10/08/world/europe/spain-stolen-babies-ines-madrigal.html.

Moloney, A., 'Government: Colombia's 50,000 Disappeared Should Become 'National Cause'', *Reuters*, August 29, 2017, https://www.reuters.com/article/us-colombia-rights-missing-idUSKCN1B92XA.

Mujica, J., 'En la perspectiva de un gobierno progresista', in J.A. Louis (ed.), *Y si gana el Frente Amplio? Uruguay decide su future*, Capital Intelectual, *Le Monde Diplomatique*, edición Cono Sur, Buenos Aires, 2004, 29.

Murphy, H., 'Colombian peace deal passed by Congress, ending 52-year war', *Reuters*, December 1, 2016, https://www.reuters.com/article/us-colombia-peace/colombian-peace-deal-passed-by-congress-ending-52-year-war-idUSKBN13P1D2.

Mutiga. M., 'Fumbling for Justice for Kenya', *New York Times*, December 26, 2014, https://www.nytimes.com/2014/12/27/opinion/mutiga-fumbling-justice-for-kenya.html?_r=0.

Ndunda, J., 'Kenya will not withdraw from ICC, says Githu Muigai', *The Star*, February 27, 2018, https://www.the-star.co.ke/news/2018-02-27-kenya-will-not-withdraw-from-icc-says-githu-muigai/.

Nicas, J., 'Chile Says 'No' to Left-Leaning Constitution After 3 Years Debate', *New York Times*, September 4, 2022.

Odula, T., 'Kenyans' lawyer says UK not interested in settlement', *Daily News*, January 21, 2015, https://www.nydailynews.com/sdut-kenyans-lawyer-says-uk-not-interested-in-2015jan21-story.html\.

Oqueno, C., 'Civiles implicados en el conflict armado en Colombia piden acogerse al tribunal de paz', *El País*, September 1, 2019, https://www.elespectador.com/noticias/judicial/parapoliticos-no-pueden-acceder-la-jep-corte-suprema-articulo-703126.

Palomino, S., 'Los líderes sociales en Colombia usan máscaras para que no los maten', *El Pais*, December 15, 2017, https://elpais.com/internacional/2017/12/15/billete_a_macondo/1513354118_012154.html.

Pizarro, M.J. 'After 50 years, could Colombia finally have awoken from its nightmare?', *The Guardian*, August 20, 2022.

Quesada, J.D., 'Son of notorious paramilitary leader wins seat reserved for victims of Colombia's armed conflict', *El País*, March 22, 2022, https://english.elpais.com/international/2022-03-22/son-of-notorious-paramilitary-leader-wins-seat-reserved-for-victims-of-colombias-armed-conflict.html.

Rohter, L., 'Uruguay: Compensation for Dictatorship', *New York Times*, April 22, 2003, https://www.nytimes.com/2003/04/22/world/world-briefing-americas-uruguay-compensation-for-dictatorship.html.

Saiz, E., 'La fosa común de Pico Reja se cierra tras ser recuperados los cuerpos de 1.800 víctimas del franquismo', *El País*, February 21, 2023, https://elpais.com/espana/2023-02-21/la-fosa-de-pico-reja-el-mayor-osario-de-las-victimas-del-franquismo-pendiente-del-adn.html.

Santaeulalia, I., 'Petro, el presidente de la paz al que se le descontroló la guerra', *El País*, July 5, 2023, https://elpais.com/america-colombia/2023-07-05/petro-el-presidente-de-la-paz-al-que-se-le-descontrolo-la-guerra.html.

Schaer, C., 'Prosecuting Syrian War-Crimes Suspects from Berlin', *The Atlantic*, July 31, 2021, https://www.theatlantic.com/international/archive/2019/07/can-germany-convict-syrian-war-criminals/595054/.

Servant, J.-C., 'No Safe Haven in Kenya', *Le Monde Diplomatique*, February 2008, http://mondediplo.com/2008/02/06kenya.

Shadid, A., 'Ousted Lebanese Leader Swallows Rivals' Bitter Pill', *New York Times*, January 25, 2011. www.nytimes.com/2011/01/26/world/middleeast/26lebanon.html.

Shehadi, N., 'Shutting down Hariri tribunal a reckless move', *Arab News*, June 25, 2022. https://www.arabnews.com/node/2110686.

Silva, N., 'Frente Amplio acordó eliminar los Tribunales de Honor militar', *La Republica*, April 27, 2019.

Smith, L., 'Hariri's Moderate Awakening', *The Weekly Standard*, January 17, 2014.

Turkewitz, J. and Glatsky, G., 'Colombia Panel's Report Is a Step Toward Mending a Civil War's Scars', *New York Times*, June 28, 2022.

'UN human rights experts call for justice and accountability in response to Beirut explosion', *UN News*, August 13, 2020, https://www.ohchr.org/en/press-releases/2020/08/un-human-rights-experts-call-justice-and-accountability-response-beirut?LangID=E&NewsID=26163.

Yoldi, J., 'El fiscal acusa a Garzón de abrir una "causa general" por el franquismo', *El País*, October 20, 2008, https://elpais.com/diario/2008/10/21/espana/1224540007_850215.html.

Young, M., 'Hariri verdict: Is the UN capable of delivering justice?', *The National News*, August 25, 2020, https://www.thenationalnews.com/opinion/comment/hariri-verdict-is-the-un-capable-of-delivering-justice-1.1068280.

SERIES ON TRANSITIONAL JUSTICE

The *Series on Transitional Justice* offers a platform for high-quality research within the rapidly growing field of transitional justice. The research is, of necessity inter-disciplinary in nature, drawing from disciplines such as law, political science, history, sociology, criminology, anthropology and psychology, as well as from various specialised fields of study such as human rights, victimology and peace studies. Furthermore, the research is international in outlook, drawing on the knowledge and experience of academics and other specialists in many different regions of the world.

Established in 2007 as the first of its kind, this series is aimed at a variety of audiences who are either working or interested in fields such as crime and justice; human rights; humanitarian law and human security; conflict resolution and peace building. These audiences include academics, researchers, students, policy makers, practitioners, non-governmental organisations and the media.

All books published within the series are subject to a double-blind peer review by recognised authorities in the field.

The General Editors of the Series are:
- Prof. Stephan Parmentier (KU Leuven, Belgium)
- Prof. Jeremy Sarkin (NOVA University of Lisbon, Portugal)
- Dr. Mina Rauschenbach (KU Leuven, Belgium)

The general editors receive support from an Advisory Board, consisting of internationally renowned academics and practitioners.

Published titles within this Series:

12. Anne-Marie de Brouwer, Charlotte Ku, Renée Römkens and Larissa van den Herik (eds.), *Sexual Violence as an International Crime: Interdisciplinary Approaches* (2012), 978-1-78068-002-6
13. Estelle Zinsstag and Martha Albertson Fineman (eds.), *Feminist Perspectives on Transitional Justice: From International and Criminal to Alternative Forms of Justice* (2013), 978-1-78068-142-9
14. Josep M. Tamarit Sumalla, *Historical Memory and Criminal Justice in Spain: A Case of Late Transitional Justice* (2013), 978-1-78068-143-6
15. Catherine Jenkins and Max du Plessis (eds.), *Law, Nation-Building & Transformation: The South African Experience in Perspective* (2014), 978-1-78068-184-9
16. Susanne Buckley-Zistel and Stefanie Schäfer (eds.), *Memorials in Times of Transition* (2014), 978-1-78068-211-2
17. Nico Wouters (ed.), *Transitional Justice and Memory in Europe (1945–2013)* (2014), 978-1-78068-214-3
18. Agata Fijalkowski and Raluca Grosescu (eds.), *Transitional Criminal Justice in Post-Dictatorial and Post-Conflict Societies* (2015), 978-1-78068-260-0
19. S. Elizabeth Bird and Fraser M. Ottanelli (eds.), *The Performance of Memory as Transitional Justice* (2014), 978-1-78068-262-4
20. Bo Viktor Nylund, *Child Soldiers and Transitional Justice* (2016), 978-1-78068-394-2
21. Peter Malcontent (ed.), *Facing the Past: Amending Historical Injustices through Instruments of Transitional Justice* (2016), 978-1-78068-403-1
22. Francesca Capone, *Reparations for Child Victims of Armed Conflict: State of the Field and Current Challenges* (2017), 978-1-78068-438-3
23. Cheryl S. White, *Bridging Divides in Transitional Justice: The Extraordinary Chambers in the Courts of Cambodia* (2017), 978-1-78068-440-6
24. Jeremy Sarkin (ed.), *The Global Impact and Legacy of Truth Commissions* (2019), 978-1-78068-794-0
25. Camila de Gamboa Tapias and Bert van Roermund (eds.), *Just Memories: Remembrance and Restoration in the Aftermath of Political Violence* (2020), 978-1-78068-908-1
26. Grazyna Baranowska, *Rights of Families of Disappeared Persons* (2021), 978-1-83970-137-5

27. Elin Skaar, Eric Wiebelhaus-Brahm and Jemima García-Godos, *Exploring Truth Commission Recommendations in a Comparative Perspective: Beyond Words Vol. I* (2022), 978-1-83970-178-8
28. Elin Skaar, Eric Wiebelhaus-Brahm and Jemima García-Godos (eds.), *Latin American Experiences with Truth Commission Recommendations: Beyond Words Vol. II* (2022), 978-1-83970-179-5
29. Lucia Elena Arantes Ferreira Bastos, *Transitional Justice in Brazil: Walking the Tightrope* (2023), 978-1-83970-327-0

For previous volumes in the series, please visit https://www.larcier-intersentia.com/en/series/series-transitional-justice.html

Series on Transitional Justice, Volume 30

www.ingramcontent.com/pod-product-compliance
Ingram Content Group UK Ltd.
Pitfield, Milton Keynes, MK11 3LW, UK
UKHW051913100926
8556IPUK00006B/866

9 781839 705533